WESTMAR COLLEGE LIBRARY

W9-BUT-429

WESTMAR COLLEGE LIBRARY

THE REVOLUTIONARY CORPORATIONS:

Engines of plenty, engines of growth, engines of change

JOHN DESMOND GLOVER
Chairman, Cambridge Research Institute
Lovett-Learned Professor of Business Administration, *emeritus*
Harvard University Graduate School of Business Administration

106291

DOW JONES-IRWIN
Homewood, Illinois 60430

© John Desmond Glover, 1980

All rights reserved. No part of this publication may be reproduced, stored in a retrieval system, or transmitted, in any form or by any means, electronic, mechanical, photocopying, recording, or otherwise, without the prior written permission of the copyright holder.

This publication is designed to provide accurate and authoritative information in regard to the subject matter covered. It is sold with the understanding that the publisher is not engaged in rendering legal, accounting, or other professional service. If legal advice or other expert assistance is required, the services of a competent professional person should be sought.

From a Declaration of Principles jointly adopted by a Committee of the American Bar Association and a Committee of Publishers.

ISBN 0-87094-217-4
Library of Congress Catalog Card No. 80-66021
Printed in the United States of America

1 2 3 4 5 6 7 8 9 0 K 7 6 5 4 3 2 1 0

R

Preface

This book is about our modern industrial order, its emergence and present state. It is about the very large business corporations that have come to characterize our industrial structure, that are among the most distinguishing institutions of our whole American System. It is about their central role in our continuing, all-impacting Industrial Revolution.

Scores, if not hundreds, of books and more than hundreds of articles have been written on "Big Business" already. Why should there now be another?

Much of the literature has been written out of ignorance and prejudice; much has been plain argumentative; much has expressed ideological advocacy; much is polemical—sometimes downright vitriolic. Much is far more hypothetical than descriptive and analytical. Much is apologetic or just plain glossy. Much has been of ephemeral interest.

Few items have assembled and presented heavy statistical documentation needed to *describe,* with reasonable accuracy and in quantitative terms, and then to *explain* the emergence over the past 100 years of very large corporations as *characteristic,* indeed, literally *essential* elements in the dynamic structure of American industry, our economy, and of our System as a whole.

I was moved to undertake this work by a sense, increasing over the years, of the stunning disparity between the importance of The Large Corporations to America, so manifest all around us, and the scantiness of searching, penetrating inquiry into their emergence and place in our evolving scheme of things.

This work is addressed primarily to a professional audience—mostly to economists, teachers, and researchers in fields of economics and business administration, and to managers of corporations. I hope that it may come to the attention of members of Congress and their staff experts; jurists and their law clerks; members of faculties of law; and editors of our newspapers and journals. Also, I hope that other professionals may look into it—some historians, perhaps, and maybe some demographers, and people with interests in general systems theory, for instance.

I hope that this work may help them in their own efforts toward a better understanding of the extraordinary evolution through which we have been—and *are*—passing, and the roles in that national development played by our large corporations.

Obviously, this book is not for light summer reading. It's long and heavy-laden with pages and pages of supporting and, I hope, illuminating statistics. In my judgment, the extensive and detailed documentation offered here is a major aspect of the whole effort. No one reader will want to, nor need, give attention to each and every exhibit and table. Much can properly, and will surely, be skipped over by the general reader. But readers with special interests may well choose to pause and linger here and there in the forest of data presented.

The work is not addressed to a large, popular audience. But any and all readers are warmly welcome.

If this work reaches and interests even a small but significant group of earnest professionals—scholars, commentators, people of action—and contributes to serious discussion of what I believe are topics of enormous importance, I shall be content.

I am, I know, fortunate that Earle Birdzell, for many years with the General Electric Company, was willing to write an Introduction and Executive Summary for this work. Mr. Birdzell is not only widely experienced in business himself, but has had a long-standing personal as well as professional interest in the American corporation and its place in the American economic, social, and political system. He is also, by avocation as well as by vocation, a voracious wide- and free-ranging reader in many fields. In the course of writing this Introduction and Executive Summary, Birdzell came up with, I think, some interesting formulations of his own.

Writing for a business audience, as Earle Birdzell has done many times before, he succeeds in setting down, in relatively few words, matters that I wish many more high-level executives of our "Revolutionary Corporations" understood about the origins, evolution, and growth of these large corporations, and about the emergent agenda confronting the distinctive institutions over whose affairs they preside. His Introduction and Summary may intrigue a number of these busy people sufficiently that they may be inclined at least to browse here and there in this rather voluminous text, so heavily set about by massive and telling statistical documentation.

I have a number of acknowledgments I am proud to record.

As researcher, teacher, consultant, board member, over many years, I have had an unusual privilege of spending hours and days with literally hundreds of business executives and leaders of scores of industries, at home and abroad, in clinical studies in the field, in classrooms, in conferences, in offices, in boardrooms—observing, listening, questioning, recording, trying to understand, and participating in policy formulation and strategic decision making. Those opportunities, exposures, and experiences are reflected in what the reader finds here.

Among people who have helped me greatly, in one way or another, I think of Alison Jennings McCance, Daniel F. Borge, Anne Mundo, Claire M. Tebo, Melissa A. Maxwell, Helen B. Vandkjaer, and Nancy M. Fleming.

The editors of Dow Jones-Irwin did a splendid job of preparing a long and complex manuscript for printing; I thank them.

The Harvard Business School gave me some of the time and some of the incidental funds I have needed for research and writing.

The Business Roundtable made a contribution to the research funds of the Harvard Business School to defray a portion of the clerical, secretarial, and similar costs.

I acknowledge my intellectual debt to the late Professor Joseph A. Schumpeter, of Harvard, in whose courses, seminars, and office, a generation ago I spent many stimulating hours; my lasting gratitude to another mentor, the late Professor W. Leonard Crum, also of Harvard and later of the University of California, who tried hard to instill in me some of his own passion for statistical rigor and verbal precision; my continuing appreciation of my friend and colleague of many years, Professor Edmund P. Learned, of the Harvard Business School. My obligation to my dear friends and companions of the Harvard Business School is no doubt obvious. From them and with them, over a span of more than 40 years, I learned much of what I think I have come to know about the worlds of ideas and of action in business and affairs.

Since 1967, I have been Chairman of the Cambridge Research Institute, a business and economics consulting firm. In recent years, this firm has been the focus of my principal activity. Here, stimulated by my colleagues, I have continued to learn about the problems and processes of running complex undertakings, not only in the profit making, but the nonprofit and public sectors as well.

It may be appropriate to make note of the fact that, since 1976, I have been a member of the Board of Allied Chemical Corporation.

It surely goes without saying that only I am responsible for what appears in this volume.

Especially, am I grateful to my loving and ever-charming wife, Ruth Adams, who encouraged me, helped me in many ways, and who countenanced my deep and extended involvement with this undertaking, as she has in other instances.

John Desmond Glover

Contents

List of tables and exhibits

Summary and commentary
on *The Revolutionary Corporations*

by L. E. BIRDZELL, JR.

PRELIMINARY OVERVIEW

The Revolutionary Corporations concerns the far-reaching changes that took place in American life during the successive periods 1880-1929 and 1929-71 (with the Great Depression ending the first and starting the second), the concurrent development of large corporations, and the causal links between changes and corporations. It is a theory of large corporations and their place in American life.

Over the whole 1880-1971 period, the most pervasive contributing cause to changes in American life, whether cultural, moral, social, political, or economic, was a historically unprecedented movement of population from farms and other rural areas to cities. This shift was made both possible and necessary by a precipitous rise in agricultural productivity. Much of this rise is traceable in its turn to the introduction of mechanical power and mechanically powered farm implements, supplied by the subjects of Dr. Glover's book—large corporations.

Cities live by trading the products of urban labor for raw materials, fuel, food, and the products of urban labor in other cities; and a historically unprecedented degree of urbanization required a historically unprecedented development of the national transportation network. Again, large corporations manufactured the locomotives, the cars, the steel rails, then built the railroad lines, and finally operated the railroad system.

The exponential increase in the exchange of goods within and between cities required a corresponding increase in communications.

The need was met in substantial part by telegraph and telephone networks, supplied by large corporations.

Urbanization ran in parallel with a fourfold increase in population, a further fourfold increase in per capita output of goods and services, and a reduction in the work week from 60 hours to 40 hours. This multiplies out to approximately a sixfold increase in the productivity of an hour worked. The increase in productivity can be traced to a more skilled work force, a better organized work force, and most of all to an increase in the amount of mechanical energy and energy-using tools employed by each worker. The shift to energy-intensive production required new systems for generating power and new systems for supplying fuel. Here, also, large corporations played a major part in developing both systems.

The demands of rising industrial production required creation of one more major system in the infrastructure of the urbanized economy—a raw materials supply and processing system. Once again, the large corporation provided the institutional framework for the raw materials system.

More than 80 percent of the assets of large corporations are part of the five systems for providing power, communications, transportation, fuel, and raw materials.

What Dr. Glover calls, not unreasonably, the corporate revolution produced in the United States and Western Europe the most urbanized, and the most economically productive, societies in human history. They are also societies self-conscious of what are probably also history's most complex agendas of problems and putative solutions—cultural, social, political, economic. The history of large corporations has been obscured by controversy; and Dr. Glover's effort to rescue that history from the realm of legend is aimed at clarifying the agendas, both of problems and of solutions.

Dr. Glover devised 54 "industry categories" as a framework for describing the distribution of large corporations through the American economy. Within this framework, one can measure the part played by large corporations in each industry category by, first, their "occurrence," by which Dr. Glover means simply the number of large corporations in a given industry category, and second, by their "presence"—absolute, the dollar amount of their assets, and relative, the share of large corporations in the dollar value of all assets in the industry category.

Within industry, the primary feature of the corporate revolution was an unprecedented expansion in the output of the supply system. The change in the pattern of demand was equally drastic, but it was a derivative change, made possible by the increased efficiency of the supply system. Dr. Glover's industry categories are to be viewed as supply systems that include in the same industry categories both final product manufacturers and the producers of parts, components, and key specialized services upon whom the final product manufacturers depend for major inputs.

Raw materials production and processing and retail distribution are classified separately from the product industry categories, partly because of problems of data availability and partly because the separation helps to locate more precisely the areas where large corporations operate. An investigator interested only in the motor vehicle supply system and the number of corporations and amount invested in it (for example) might very well wish to include in Dr. Glover's motor vehicle industry category additional businesses and investment drawn from materials supply and the distribution function.

Finally, there is the preliminary question of defining "large corporation." For this purpose Dr. Glover goes back to The 200 Largest Corporations of 1929, the smallest of which had assets of approximately $250 million in 1971 dollars.[1] Measured by asset size of $250 million (1971 dollars), The Largest 200 of 1929 were succeeded by a Largest 559 of 1971. The advantage of the $250 million figure is that most of the statistical data we have on the asset size of large corporations comes from the Internal Revenue Service, and their largest asset size begins with $250 million. The choice of asset size for a "large" corporation being admittedly arbitrary, the selection of a group for which we have statistical information is slightly less arbitrary than other possible choices.

Table A lists Dr. Glover's 54 industry categories and the changes in "occurrence" of large corporations in each of the categories between 1929 and 1971. In 51 industry categories, the number of large corporations increased by 390. In three industry categories, occurrence of large corporations declined by a total of 31. The net change of 359 understates the rate of development of new large corporations, since it does not take account of the disappearance of many of the 1929 Largest 200 and their replacement by newcomers. (Table A is located in an Appendix at the end of this Summary and Commentary.)

There have been two contradictory views, both with Harvard antecedents, of the role of large corporations in the urbanization and expansion of the American economy. Joseph A. Schumpeter viewed large corporations as powerful engines of change and growth, transforming the economy by a process of "creative destruction" based on innovation. The alternative tradition, associated with Edward H. Chamberlin, viewed large corporations as monopolistic in character, damping out growth by their effort to conserve their positions, exclude competitors, and exploit "market power." This second tradition fits nicely with populist ideology and has supplied much of the economic rationalization of antitrust. Dr. Glover studied under both Schumpeter and Chamberlin.

Dr. Glover's approach, as outlined in Table A, makes *The Revolutionary Corporations* a powerful answer to the Chamberlin tradition. The first characteristic of monopoly is the power to exclude competitors. Yet the largest corporations of 1929, whose power so concerned Berle and Means, were wholly unable to preserve the private hunting grounds of large corporations from being overrun by poachers. The 200 corporations of 1929 with assets over $250 million (1971 dollars) became 559 by 1971. In industry after industry, the entrenched power attributed to large corporations in the Chamberlin tradition proved insufficient to exclude post-1929 newcomers. The old-line steel companies had to share their markets with 8 new large corporations; in nonferrous metals, the 10 newcomers outnumbered 8 first families of 1929; petroleum had to accommodate a 50 percent increase in numbers of corporations sharing their allegedly "obscene" profits; the 4 giants of the 1929 food industry lacked the elementary monopoly power needed to keep out no less than 15 newcomers—and so on down the list.

The period 1929-71 included the Great Depression, but basically it was a period of economic expansion for the United States. Yet the large corporations of 1929 proved far from immortal. The prototype of the large American corporation was the railroad; and of 43 railroads listed among The 200 Largest of 1929, only 13 persist as large corporations in 1971. Of the 21 large corporations in railroad transportation in 1971, 8 were not among the large corporations of 1929.

The large electrical utilities of 1929—39 of them—went through the reorganization process of the Public Utility Holding Company Act of 1935. How many of the original 39 have to be written off to political risks is far from clear; but at any rate some of the largest certainly perished in PUHC proceedings.

In 1929, there were 110 large corporations outside the railroad and utility categories. Eight of these were in the transit category; they sank into municipal ownership and thus disappeared from the Berle-Means category of all-powerful corporations. Dr. Glover is unable to find another 22 of them among The Largest Corporations of 1971. The death rate, among these 110 menacing citadels of corporate power, was 27 percent. Table A thus understates the number of new entrants among The 559 Largest Corporations of 1971; it should be somewhat more than 30 plus 390, or 420.

Table B consolidates the categories of Table A into the transportation-power-communications-fuel-materials complex for 1929 and 1971. In these five major systems were 90.6 percent of large corporation assets in 1929 and 81.5 percent in 1971. The "presence" (in Dr. Glover's terminology) of large corporations was where it had to be to support the urbanization of American society and the accompanying expansion in productivity. In each industry where large corporations were strongly present, the physical production processes required very large asset systems. In addition, in some industries (e.g., petroleum, iron and steel) there were substantial economies in organizing highly integrated production, from raw materials to usable products, for the better control of throughputs. Given the technology available, no rational designer of an economic system would have organized the production processes in these industries otherwise than through large corporations or equally large-scale institutional alternatives. (Table B is also located in the Appendix at the end of this Summary and Commentary, as are Tables C through G.)

The Revolutionary Corporations calls attention to many of the cases where the assets held by large corporations are generically different from the assets held by smaller corporations operating in the same industry categories. In most categories, numerous corporations much smaller than the over-$250 million asset size operate successfully. But often it is evident that they are doing different things from the large corporations. A small steel company, for instance, cannot be operating a blast furnace complex; any company that does would be in the large corporation class. Nor can a "small" petroleum corporation be operating a modern refinery; the price of a modern refinery is now around $500 million, or even more.

In instances of this kind, the populist view of large corporations as concentrations or consolidations of smaller corporations is misleading. Historically, some "consolidations" took place; but the successful ones—the survivors—were those in which the facilities acquired from the smaller predecessor companies were soon scrapped and replaced with larger scale production equipment suited to the requirements of the growing American economy. The consolidations served the useful purposes of providing continuity of employment and preventing loss to investors in the obsolete constituent enterprises, and they speeded the adoption of the emerging large-scale technologies. The explanation of the survival and prosperity of some of the consolidations was the transformation of their underlying production systems. Without the transformation, very few survived and even fewer prospered. Add the fact that many large corporations were not formed by merger, and consolidation is left as neither a sufficient nor a necessary condition of the development of any given large corporation.

A preliminary overview would be incomplete without recognition of Dr. Glover's use of the systems approach and the ecosystem analogy in the interpretation of the growth of the American economy.

Systems analysis emphasizes the interdependence of the constituent elements of the system and the way the elements work together to produce a unified, systematic whole. Growth in one element is likely to lead to growth in another, which may lead in turn to further growth in the first . . . , just as the growth of the American economy has brought about, and been brought about by, the growth of large corporations. Often these reciprocal causes are themselves set in motion by some outside factor, exemplified by the technological explosion of the past century. The new technologies stimulated the development of large corporations, and the efforts of large corporations stimulated the further development of the new technologies. In systems where every element depends on every other, a complete account of change and growth would have to include the active and passive contributions of every element.

Urbanization, the technological explosion, the rise in population, advances in material welfare, qualitative improvements in the human condition, and the growth of large corporations were interrelated features of the American ecosystem. No one of these features of the system was a necessary and sufficient cause of another; all were contributing partners to a revolution in American life. The large corporation in particular was the institution that supplied the transportation, power, fuel, communications, and materials systems essential to the urban-corporate revolution. It was also the institution that translated the emerging technologies into urbanization and growth in the quantity and variety of goods and services available to Americans. Overall, large corporations marched to a creatively destructive pace of change that Schumpeter would have found entirely satisfying.

THE CORPORATE REVOLUTION: THE ARGUMENT IN SUMMARY

The corporate-urban revolution of 1880-1971 changed all aspects of American life

Historically, periods of rapid change have often been destructive, characterized by collapse of an existing high culture and a general retrogression in human welfare, followed by a centuries-long period of rebuilding. The urban population chiefly affected by changes for better and for worse was never more than a small percentage of the whole, and rural populations survived at marginal subsistence levels equally deplorable before and after the upheavals that overturned the urban cultures.

The changes in Western culture in the 19th and 20th centuries were unprecedented in two respects. First, they shifted the great majority of the population from farm to city. Second, they greatly advanced the economic, social, and political welfare of very large numbers of people, not merely of a small urban minority.

In the United States of 1880, 21,793,000 people lived on farms— 43.8 percent of a population of just over 50 million. In 1970, 9,712,000 lived on farms—4.8 percent of a population of 203 million. The number of farms declined from 4 million to less than 3 million, but total acreage cultivated (by less than half the former farm population) went from 536 million to 1,102 million acres.

Per capita gross national product (1958 dollars) rose from $774 in 1880 to $1,671 in 1929 and $3,555 in 1970. Life expectancy at birth rose from 47.3 years in 1900 to 71.1 years in 1971, while the annual death rate fell from 17.2 per thousand in 1900 to 9.5 in 1970. Massachusetts has data on infant mortality from 1851, and for the period 1880 to 1970, infant mortality in the first year of life declined by a factor of 10: from 161.3 per thousand live births to 16.8 per thousand live births.

In 1880, we had 563 institutions of higher education, with a total faculty of 5,553. The corresponding figures for 1930 are 1,409 and 82,386; and by 1970 we had 2,525 higher education institutions with a total faculty estimated at 729,000.

The average work week in manufacturing declined from 60.0 hours in 1890 to 39.8 hours in 1970. Average hourly earnings in manufacturing were 19.9 cents in 1890 and $3.36 in 1970. The Consumer Price Index rose from 27 in 1890 to 116.3 in 1970 (1967=100), but the 1,768 percent increase in wage rates more than offset the 431 percent rise in prices.

Any finite set of figures on the advancement in the general welfare during the years since 1880 is necessarily merely illustrative—a reminder that for the overwhelming majority the benefits conferred by the changes of the past century begin with life itself and go on to a quality of life and length of life and general well-being beyond anything open to more than a tiny minority in 1880.

Urbanization and growth rested on the development of power, mechanically powered machinery, transportation, fuel, communications, and materials.

Powered machinery. The farms of 1880 got 11.6 million horsepower from work animals and only 668,000 horsepower from steam tractors and other mechanical sources. By 1929, work animals supplied 18 million horsepower, but by now mechanical horsepower was up to 27.3 million. By 1970, horsepower from work animals was down to 1.5 million and mechanical horsepower exceeded 288 million.

Power does not of itself increase productivity; it has to be applied by machines. For agriculture, the farm machinery manufacturers and inventors of the 19th and 20th centuries tooled the mechanization of the farm to the point where a fraction of the former agricultural work force is now feeding four times the former population. Farm mechanization, incidentally, is still going on; the farm workers of 1970 were only half as numerous as the farm workers of 1952.

The American farm population, unlike farmers in many other countries, was receptive to change and innovation. At the same time that agricultural production was mechanized, agricultural colleges, agricultural experiment stations, seed and chemical companies, and the farmers themselves were upgrading the biology of the farm, from breed lines to seeds and fertilizers.

Mechanization was not the only cause of rising farm productivity per farm worker, and it was so intertwined with the changes in the methods and materials of farming that little purpose would be served by trying to estimate the relative contributions in numbers.

For present needs it is enough to note that the agricultural revolution was in part a mechanical revolution, and that the innovation required for the revolution was carried out by large corporations in the farm machinery industry. Even within the biological sources of improved productivity, large corporations in the chemical industry are the main sources of supply of fertilizers and agricultural chemicals used against plant disease and pests, and both fertilizers and chemicals have been major contibutors to improvement in farm productivity.

Transportation. Cities live by a continuous inflow of goods, supplies, and people and by a continuous outflow of goods, supplies, people, and services. They have to be built, repaired, heated, fed, and clothed. The urban community lives by exchange, with the countryside, with other urban communities, within itself. If the release of people from food production was the first requirement of urbanization, a transportation network was a concurrent second.

Providing a transportation network fell to the railroads, which were virtually the prototype of the large corporation. In the 50 years from 1830 to 1880, railroad mileage in the United States had increased from a beginning 23 miles to 93,300 miles. During the years 1880-1930, America added another 209,900 miles to the railroad system, bringing the network to 303,200 miles. An even more striking evidence of the expansion of transportation was the rise in the horsepower of railroad prime movers from 8,592,000 to 109,743,000—a growth of 1,177 percent on a not insubstantial base.

This was also the period of introduction of the automobile and the construction of the highway network. The horsepower of automobile and truck prime movers went from 32,000 in 1899 to 1.4 billion in 1930. It kept multiplying to 19.3 billion by 1970. State and federal governments funded and constructed the highway system, largely by taxes on motor vehicles; but the construction of the rolling stock for the automotive transportation system added $2,742 million in assets to manufacturing industry by 1929.

Electric power. Electric power was a great convenience in the development of cities. Early 19th century factories powered their machinery by drive shafts, pulleys, and belts turned by stationary steam engines puffing and smoking in the factory itself. All the advantages lay with the new system of delivering power through copper wires from a central generating station to individual motors located at each machine: safety, cleanliness, efficiency.

On urban transit lines, the wires were an even more welcome substitute for horse-drawn street cars and for the steam locomotives of the first elevated trains. They also made the subways feasible.

From the central station, one distribution network could take care of the street cars, the street lighting system, the "L," factories, and commercial and household users. The cities and the new electrical generating and distribution systems were made to order for each other.

The statistics begin with 1902; and from a central station generating capacity of 1,212,000 kilowatts in 1902, America went to 29,839,000 kilowatts in 1929—a 2,362 percent growth. Not all of this energy went to transportation and industry; much of it was applied in individual households to better lighting, doing household chores, and, in the 1929-71 period, to air conditioning and heating.

Just as railroads do not come in small packages, so the corporate asset systems needed for producing and distributing electricity for an urban community added up to large corporations.

Communications. The volume of business transacted within and between the new cities required a new communications system. We had the Morse telegraph by the time of the Civil War, and by the last years of the 19th century the Bell companies were building telephone networks in the major cities and linking both their own and other networks with long-distance lines. As with transportation and the power networks, the asset systems implied in a local, regional, or national telephone network were enough to make the owner a large corporation.

From 1880 to 1929, the bellwether of communications growth was the telephone system. We had 54,000 telephones in 1880 and 20,068,000 by 1929. As measured by miles of wire, the size of the network grew from 34,000 miles to 74,542,000 miles. The increase was a meaningless 219,141 percent of the starting figure.

Fuel. The energy and electric power systems required coal and petroleum. Coal deposits were not commonly found in $250 million fields, efficient mining did not require a large asset system, and, once extracted, coal is usable as fuel with far less processing than petroleum. Thus petroleum, but not coal, became a major center of operation of large corporations. Capital invested in petroleum refining increased from $37 million in 1880 to $6,092 million in 1929—an increase of 16,365 percent, where growth might be thought to have been retarded by the operations of the most notorious trust of the era.

Materials: Iron and steel. The 19th century industrial revolution was built of steel. It ran on steel wheels pulled by steel locomotives on steel rails. It farmed with steel implements pulled by steel tractors. It built its factories and offices on steel frames. The electrically powered cities drew their energy from steel turbines and generators. It traded internationally in steel ships, and it fought its wars with steel weapons and steel projectiles. And as Mao Tse-tung found out, you do not make steel in backyard ovens. A business organization with the equipment to make steel at competitive costs will be a corporation with a large asset system and many investors.

Between 1880 and 1929, capital invested in the iron and steel industries increased by $6.2 billion.

Materials: Chemicals. Before World War I, Germany was the center of the world's chemical industry. After 1914, a combination of the British blockade and American entry into World War I cut American customers off from their German suppliers. The United States undertook development of its own chemical industry.

The new chemical companies were a different breed of large corporation. What determines the asset size of a chemical company is not a simple question of the price tag on an efficient plant for producing some chemical or other. The performance of its development laboratory is the primary factor determinative of its size. Manufacturing assets are whatever it takes to satisfy the markets for the family of products developed in its laboratory.

The investment in the chemical industry, in large corporations, grew by a little more than $4 billion between 1880 and 1929. Between 1929 and 1971, investment in chemicals exploded. In 1929, large corporations centered in iron and steel had three times the assets of large corporations centered in chemicals; by 1971, the chemical companies had passed the steel companies, by $30.4 billion to $23.4 billion.

Large corporations center in industry categories that require large physical asset systems or integrated production organizations

A main point of *The Revolutionary Corporations* is that large corporations are distributed through the economic ecosystem where they are able to perform a useful economic function. If size itself conferred inherent competitive advantages or enabled investors to earn larger profits, large corporations would be distributed through the economy more or less at random. But the patterned distribution of large corporations indicates that size is advantageous, or even viable, only under the special circumstances of particular industries.

Large corporations occur in 50 of Dr. Glover's 54 industry categories. But as Tables C to F (see the Appendix) show, the distribution of large corporations is very uneven. In Table C, the 50 industry categories that include large corporations are arranged in order of large corporation presence—that is, amount of assets held. In Table D, the same 50 categories are rearranged in order of occurrence (i.e., number) of large corporations. In Table E, the 50 categories are arranged in order of average size of the large corporations in each category. Finally, in Table F, the 50 categories are arranged in order of relative presence of large corporations—i.e., the percentage of industry assets held by large corporations.

As we shall see a little later, it is a mistake to assume that all corporations in a given industry category have similar assets, with the "presence" or "relative presence" of large corporations indicating the share of this homogeneous asset corpus held by large corporations. Typically, large corporations and small corporations, even in the same industry category, have physically different asset systems. The more useful working assumption is that in the ecosystem that constitutes an "industry category," "presence" is a measure of the category assets that come packaged in large units and that thereby make their holder a large corporation.

Arranged in order of presence, the Top 20 industry categories account for 86.6 percent of the large corporation assets of 1971. In order of occurrence, the Top 20 industry categories account for 84.7 percent of assets. In order of average large corporation size, the Top 20 industry categories account for 84 percent of large corporation assets. And in order of relative presence, the Top 20 account for 78.9 percent of total assets of large corporations.

The following 11 industry categories are in all four Top 20's—by occurrence, presence, average size, and relative presence:

Electricity, gas, and sanitary services.
Petroleum.
Telephone and telegraph services.
Motor vehicles.
Rail transportation.
Chemicals.
General merchandise.
Iron and steel.
Office and computing equipment.
Radio communication equipment and electronic supplies.
Air transportation.

The following six industry categories are in three Top 20's:

Nonferrous metals.
Lumber and paper products.
Aircraft.
Pharmaceuticals.
Rubber and tires.
Tobacco.

Electrical machinery, Photographic equipment, and Food categories each occurred on two lists of Top 20's. The following industry categories occurred on only one of the four lists:

Farm, construction and mining machinery (presence).
Nonmetallic minerals (occurrence).
Services (occurrence).
Fabricated metal products (occurrence).
Food stores (occurrence).
Scientific, control, and measuring devices (firm size).

Meat (firm size).
Metal cans (relative occurrence).
Household appliances (relative occurrence).
Dairy products (relative occurrence).
Soaps, cleaners (relative occurrence).
Glass (relative occurrence).

The 11 industries that are in all four Top 20 lists account for 71.4 percent of large corporation assets, and another 10.7 percent of assets are in the 6 industry categories on three Top 20 lists.

With 17 of the 54 industry categories accounting for 82.1 percent of the assets of large corporations, there is virtually no possibility that the distribution of large corporations over industry categories is merely random. In each of the 11 industry categories on all four Top 20 lists, there were ten or more large corporations, average size of the large corporations varied upward from $1 billion of assets, and large corporations owned a minimum of 63% of total assets in the industry—with an average of 79.6 percent.

The figures confirm what is evident from an inspection of the list of industry categories in which large corporations are centered. Some aspects of the production process in each of these industry systems require, for compelling reasons of technology or economics, a large asset system; and the business organizations that do what requires a large asset system are, willy-nilly, large corporations. It is equally true that each of these industry categories contains many smaller corporations doing things that do not require large asset systems.

With industry categories varying from those in which most of the assets are of kinds that make a large asset system to those in which large asset systems are nonexistent, one would expect to find an intermediate group of industries where neither large corporations, with their large asset systems, nor smaller corporations are clearly the prevailing form of business life. In such industry systems, differences in degree of vertical integration, research and development effort, use of advertising and other consumer mass marketing methods, product line range and variety, and differences in size or other characteristics of products have led to differences in size of firms, but without conferring an overwhelming advantage or an overwhelming disadvantage. One would expect also to find the claim that size confers some intrinsic competitive advantage of its own advanced most often in industries where large and small corporations are competing directly, say, with an asset division between large and small corporations of 60 percent to 40 percent or narrower:

Lumber and paper products.
Farm, construction, and mining machinery.
Nonmetallic minerals.
Aircraft.
Food.

Foodstores.

Scientific, control, and measuring devices.

Soft drinks.

Much of the controversy over large corporation economic advantages and "power" has in fact related to food products and food stores. The relative absence of controversy in other "60-40" categories suggests that in these other categories the functions performed by large corporations are different enough that they are not seen as a threat to smaller corporations on grounds of pure size. The likely interpretation is that in these industry categories, the technology and economics of production systems require large asset systems sometimes, but not predominantly. The possession of a large asset system does not appear to confer power to prevent smaller corporations from doing the things that do not require a large asset system.

Overall, large corporations, as measured by asset size, are overwhelmingly concentrated in industry categories where a very large asset system is physically necessary to some production processes; or where there are obvious advantages to integrating vertically; or where there are technological or economic advantages in producing a broad line of related products; or where there are advantages in multiplant operations; or where several of these factors are present.

At the level of generality of the 54 industry categories, large corporations and smaller corporations coexist in most of them, with large corporations holding a majority of asset dollars in 24 categories and smaller corporations in 30. Over the period 1929 to 1971, large corporations expanded in a number of categories where, formerly, they had a minority presence, and their assets became somewhat less heavily concentrated in categories where they formerly had had a majority presence. But this apparent statistical dispersion of large corporation presence is partly a consequence of the decline of the railroad industry, where large corporations were heavily concentrated indeed in 1929.

Integration was an important contributing factor in the growth of large corporations

Dr. Glover attributes the size of large corporations (1) to asset systems physically different from the asset systems of smaller corporations and (2) to integrative business strategies and goals qualitatively different from the stategies and goals of smaller corporations.

Among critics of large corporations, the second source of corporate size is more suspect than the first. Historically, the production process has been divided among firms engaged in mining, processing, parts fabrication, assembly, wholesaling, and retailing. The planning and coordination of the flows of materials—"throughputs"—through these several levels of production can sometimes be simplified, with substantial economies, by putting the process under a single management. Also, in some supply systems, new investment can be more consistently planned for the overall production process, with an eye to overall needs and overall returns, than for the separate steps. New investment planning was of special importance to the growing economy of the corporate revolution. And in some basic processing industries, processing facilities are so costly that their construction would be improvident without some way of hedging against changes in the price and availability of the ore or other raw material—and the only way to hedge on the scale, and for the time period, required is to buy the ore, petroleum, or whatever in the ground.

The economic historian Alfred Chandler shares Dr. Glover's view of the importance of integration in explaining the growth of large corporations, and it may not be amiss to draw on the Chandler account of the formation of the Standard Oil Trust to illustrate the application of integrative business strategies with real cost advantages.[2]

The trust was formed by the consolidation of 40 refining companies, previously associated in a cartel held together by a common interest in low bulk freight rates. The reason for the formation of the trust was a shift to pipeline transportation, initiated by Tidewater, a competing oil company formed by crude oil producers to reduce their dependence on the Standard cartel of refiners. The need to relocate and consolidate refining capacity, including closing down existing refineries, consequent upon the shift to movement by pipeline, forced the change from a cartel of independent refiners to a single consolidated organization, set up in the form of a trust because of the difficulty of getting a corporate charter with holding company powers. (Chandler, *The Visible Hand*, pp. 321-23.)

The physical changes to pipeline transportation and consolidation of refining capacity in larger and more efficient facilities, which required the organizational change from cartel to trust, had real cost advantages. "The economies permitted by the greatly expanded volume and carefully scheduled throughput cut the average cost of producing a gallon of refined oil from 1.5 cents to 0.5 cent, and the costs in the great new refineries were still lower." (Chandler, *The Visible Hand*, p. 324.) From 1870 to 1895 the price of refined kerosene dropped from 26 cents to 8 cents per gallon; and from 1880 to 1897, the price of refined oil fell from 9.125 cents a gallon to 5.91 cents.[3]

According to Professor Chandler, of the many consolidations by trust and merger between 1870 and 1910, virtually none proved financially viable except those that managed Standard's feat of integrating operations and moving to a product-cost curve more favorable than that attainable by the constituent companies.[4]

The antitrust laws are sometimes characterized as a "charade" because they permit the continued survival of corporations formed by mergers that would, if they occurred today, be held illegal. This argument is evidently an oversimplification. Trusts may cause short-term welfare losses. In the case of trusts that, because of a failure to achieve greater efficiency, did not survive, any short-term welfare losses were not offset by long-term gains. In the case of trusts that did make the transition to more efficient production and hence survived, the strong probability is that the long-term welfare gains offset the earlier losses.[5] In any case, once the American system had made its investment in finding out which potential trusts would, and which would not, produce long-term efficiency gains, it would be merely wasteful to dissolve the sources of the gains, whether or not they were adequate to offset the original losses.

Dr. Glover's view that the present place of large corporations in the American economic system has little or nothing to do with earlier trust and merger movements rests partly on the statistical distribution of large corporations, concentrated as they are in industries where the need for large-scale organization is difficult to dispute, and partly on the causal discontinuity introduced by the change in the nature of their asset systems and the adoption of integrative business strategies. The existence of a trust in the corporate ancestry is neither a necessary nor a sufficient condition of present existence as a large business organization. It has seemed a worthwhile collateral journey to notice that Chandler's recent study of the history of the trusts invites the same conclusion.

There is one other important aspect of integration. In several industries, corporation size arises from research and development centered on a family of products marketable through similar channels. This technological integration has been a conspicuous feature in the development of large electrical equipment companies, farm implement manufacturers, chemical companies, and pharmaceutical companies. Common technology is an integrative factor of somewhat less apparent importance—though still important enough to mention —in a number of other industries: Wood products, Iron and steel, Petroleum, Rubber, Automobiles.

Dr. Glover maintains that large corporations are, in general, different species of business organizations from smaller corporations. They differ in the physical characteristics of their asset systems, in their organization of goals and strategies, and in the purposes they serve in the American economic system. Table E makes the point in a summary way. The average size of large corporations in 35 of the 50 industry categories where they occur is more than 500 times the average size of the smaller corporations in the same industry category. In several cases the multiple exceeds 2,000. In only 2 of the remaining 15 categories (aircraft and alcoholic beverages) is the size ratio less than 100:1.

Except in the world of *Gulliver's Travels,* the taxonomic probability of finding adult specimens of the same species with a 10:1 size difference is low. The improbability applies as between large corporations and small corporations; and it applies to large corporations among themselves. The largest corporations are more than 100 times the size of the large corporations near the $250 million (1971 dollars) breaking point we have used to define "large" corporations. Even when we narrow the difference by using average sizes within industry categories (instead of extreme sizes), Table E shows a gradual transition in average size, across industry categories, over a 19.7:1 ratio, beginning at the top with a category with $6,274 million average asset size of large corporations and ending with a one-large-corporation category with an asset size of $318 million.

In short, of all the differences one might enumerate between different corporations—say, between a telephone company and a motion picture company or between a large retail merchandising chain and a Madison Avenue shop—size may well be the least important.

Smaller corporations prospered during the urban revolution

Dr. Glover's ecosystem analogy prepares us for the discovery that the growth of large corporations during the period 1880-1971 went along with a substantial growth of smaller corporations. On the most savage of the populist analogies, the ecologist would expect to find growth in the numbers of lions associated with growth in the numbers of antelopes, zebras, impalas, and other species included in the carnivores' diets.

In the more pedestrian reality, we find that the successful operation of almost any kind of production facility requires a multitude of supporting services: access to raw materials, supplies, parts; repair services; lawyers, accountants, and engineers; unskilled labor; skilled labor; bankers and brokers; distributors; direct accounts; freight forwarders, exporters, truck lines, railroads, airports; power, fuel—even management consultants. Large corporations can provide these supporting services for themselves; but the urban community, by making supporting services readily available to small corporations, becomes an environment particularly well-suited to the growth and multiplication of businesses built around small asset systems and not highly integrated. Often, too, the supporting services themselves are supplied by relatively small, specialized businesses.

It is not surprising, therefore, that with urbanization came a large increase in the numbers of smaller corporations and a reduction in their average size. Table G gives the numbers for the period 1929-71.[6] The numbers of small corporations grew by a factor of 4.085; the numbers of large corporations grew by a factor of 2.789. The average size of large corporations did not increase substantially; for both 1929 and 1971, it lay in the $1,200-1,300 million (1971 dollars) range. The average size of smaller corporations declined markedly, from $1.1 million to $465 thousand—a decline in asset size that may not necessarily be matched by declines in size measured by sales, profits, employees, or value added.

There are cases where the association between growth of large corporations and growth of smaller corporations is so close as to amount to symbiosis. Dr. Glover cites the fact that in 1971 there were 43,946 firms engaged in the wholesale and retail distribution of motor vehicles and equipment, with total assets of more than $21 billion. The automobile manufacturing system includes also some 25,000 parts manufacturers with annual sales approximating $50 billion—among them, 13 out of 17 large corporations in the motor vehicle category. Production schedules and marketing are simplified for these suppliers, wholesalers, and retailers by the consolidation of motor vehicle assembly in four large purchasing and marketing organizations.

A third not unlikely reason for growth in numbers of small corporations is a rise in the number of people with the necessary qualifications to operate them. A fourth is that they have tax advantages (both statutory and informal) over large corporations. And a fifth is that the growth of technology has created many new opportunities for the repair, maintenance and installation specialists who fill column after column in today's Yellow Pages.

Small corporations have obviously been part of the surge of the corporate-urban revolution. By definition, they have not occupied the niches in the transportation-power-communications-fuel-materials systems where the minimum asset commitment exceeded $250 million (1971 dollars). But in the myriad niches of these and other areas of the economic ecosystem that did not require large asset systems or a high degree of integration, smaller corporations made their own contributions to the corporate revolution. In services, in distribution, in specialty manufacturing, in agriculture, they fleshed out the skeleton of the transportation-power-communications-fuel-materials infrastructure. The importance of their contribution, either absolutely or by comparison to the contribution of large corporations, is difficult to measure statistically, but it certainly exceeded anything to be inferred from comparing aggregate assets of corporations whose niches in the production ecosystem do not require large asset systems to the aggregate assets of corporations in niches that do require such systems.

Large corporations, innovation, and the urban revolution were systematically interdependent

Many items of industrial and transportation equipment developed in the Industrial Revolution (both in the United States and in Europe) were too costly for practical commercial use so long as proprietorships and partnerships were the only available business entities. Their use required more capital than any one investor could prudently venture. The problem was not new, and the solution—the joint stock corporation—had been used long since to raise capital for turnpikes, canals, the early railroads, banks, and, for that matter, for the early colonization of North America.

The revolution could not have occurred in the way it did without forms of private business organization capable of assembling the funds necessary to buy large and complex asset systems. Without them, it might not have occurred at all, because the revolution was flatly contrary to much of the system of received values and philosophy given voice in American politics, and government was probably not available as an alternative vehicle for assembling the required asset systems. The revolution was the action of people taking advantage of an opportunity offered by private corporations to vote with their purses and with their feet, acting more wisely than they talked—or at least differently.

But this is only the beginning of the part played by large corporations in the revolution. They did far more than assemble capital and count the people's votes.

Large corporations themselves contributed by far the greater part of the size and complexity that eventually came to characterize many asset systems. The common scenario was for the genius of an individual inventor to produce a major discovery, and for a corporation (or several of them) then to be formed to develop and market it. But the limits of the human mind are such that, no matter how talented and foresighted the inventor, within a few years the thousands or millions of people who are producing, redesigning, selling, and using his invention will change and reshape it almost beyond recognition. Usually, the changes will be in the direction of greater size and greater complexity—like the contrast between the Wright brothers' airplane and the 747 or the Concorde, or the contrast between the "General" of Civil War fame and the last of the great steam locomotives built for the Union Pacific. This does not happen out of corporate vanity. America built 747s instead of replicas of the Wright brothers' plane because more people will pay more money for 747s, and they pay more because 747s fly more people farther faster cheaper.

As a rule, a great invention becomes a research agenda for a new field of innovation. Predominantly, the selection among the available research agendas (few inventions are "great" except in retrospect, after their development) and the carrying out of the developmental research has been part of the role of the large corporation. It is from manufacturing and selling and using a product that useful ways surface to expand its utility and marketability, to modify it so that it can be made more easily, to reshape the underlying concept and apply it to different uses.

There were no large corporations building airplanes when Wilbur and Orville Wright made their first successful flight at Kitty Hawk. Yet a handful of large airframe manufacturers are responsible for the multitude of differences between the Wrights' flying machine and the modern jet transport plane. Similarly, our leading computer manufacturers did not "invent" the computer, but only a museum director would today buy the devices built by those who claim that honor. It was decades after Duryea and Daimler had shown the feasibility of gasoline-powered buggies that the automobile came to be cheap enough, reliable enough, and convenient enough to have a major effect on American society. The drug companies did not invent the first antibiotic; but the invention caused no revolution in medicine until the drug companies figured out how to produce antibiotics in quantity.

The large corporation was not a passive consequence of an age of technological movement in directions that required the formation of large asset systems. The corporations contributed entirely too much to the technological movement for their role to be called "passive."

In some cases, the technological link to change was more devious than the scenario just considered. A set of transportation and communication links can change the geographic size of a market from the dimensions of a township to worldwide. Such a change in market matrix entails a change in production matrix from blacksmith shop to steel mill. If all the automobiles built in Detroit had to be sold in Wayne County, Detroit would not be the automobile capital of the world—nor would anyplace else without a cheap transportation system see the mass production of automobiles.

Over these decades of urbanization, less and less of what Americans eat, wear, inhabit, and use for their leisure time is made at or near the place where they live. The transportation network made possible substantial efficiency gains from specializing production of each product to the region, and to the scale of manufacturing, that is most advantageous for that product. And in its turn the specialization of production generated the freight that fed the further growth of the transportation network.

In the end, of course, one has to face one pervasive reason that large corporations became large: people spend a lot of money on their products and services. In retrospect, it seems by no means inevitable that American consumers should have financed the growth of the large corporations that, intentionally or not, were carrying through the urban-social-corporate revolution. No such revolution was ever adopted as a political goal, and it seems highly improbable that it could have been so adopted. The prevalent verbalizations of American traditions sounded against big cities, big business, big banks, big unions, big universities, big hospitals, big churches, big armies, big navies, big government, big anything. That is what some of our sounding furies say, but it is not the way the verbally inarticulate mass of us acted in the years surveyed by *The Revolutionary Corporations*. Otherwise, the book could not have been written.

IMPLICATIONS: POLICY, ECONOMIC, MANAGERIAL

American public policy toward large corporations has reflected both a recognition of the part they have played in *The Revolutionary*

Corporations and a rural tradition of distrust of size and power. It is not surprising that the policy outcomes are sometimes muddled. Dr. Glover's list of confusions would include:

1. In antitrust, it is uncertain whether a large corporation that overshadows others by achieving product, cost, and price advantages is, or is not, subject to legal attack. In some instances, competitive moves that would be proper for small companies are said to be improper for large, even though the advantage to buyers would be similar in both cases: more value for the money. Antimerger legislation and its interpretation additionally reflect an economically costly bias against large corporations.

2. The corporation income tax is biased against large corporations, and it is also biased against successful corporations. In Dr. Glover's view, a value-added tax, which would apply equally to efficient and inefficient producers, large and small, would be preferable.

3. Although Dr. Glover would have us take a more objective and pragmatic view of the race of corporate Titans, he does not favor the partnership between business and government summed up in the phrase, "military-industrial complex," or in the modern planning practice of Japan or France. He views the separation of the centers of gravity of economic and political power as important to the preservation of both political freedom and economic freedom.

4. Dr. Glover views the large corporation as too important to the public interest to be operated wholly by reference to the private interests of its stockholders. People and institutions alike cannot make themselves indispensable without picking up some responsibilities in the process. But Dr. Glover still wants to separate economic from political power; and he would achieve separation by encouraging management decision-making, on matters in which the public may be politically interested, according to norms defensible in public.

5. Dr. Glover's view of large corporations as the true radicals in bringing about social change presents a challenge to corporate directors and officers. (It presents a far more drastic challenge to competing revolutionists who thought they had preempted the role for themselves.) The appealing simplicity of a single-minded focus on the interests of stockholders or the running of a product business carries an internal contradiction. It leaves the corporation and its stockholders vulnerable to changes in its business environment that have, in far too many cases, been perceived fatally late (if at all). Successful management requires a probing consciousness of what the large corporation can do for American aspirations, an active search for understanding of those aspirations (people who already know what they are, are usually wrong), and a willingness to advance them with the practical efficiency Americans expect of large business corporations.

6. This need for the corporation to undertake the management of

change requires direction and planning to transcend a concept of the corporation as a producer and seller of some limited type of goods or services. The right management model is not supplied by the steam locomotive company, which disappeared from view with the steam locomotive, but by the steamship line that transformed itself into a leading chemical company, or the cigarette producer that took the surgeon general's warnings seriously enough to metamorphose into a leading producer and seller of beer.

This emphasis on the management of change, the redeployment of assets into new and more efficient uses and structures, makes Dr. Glover one of the more forceful proponents of the role played by the new conglomerate corporations in that process.

7. The field of corporate governance is thickly sown with mines, and Dr. Glover does little more than voice the belief that changes are needed. Surely, the modern corporation could better perform its purely economic role if it did not project politically the public image of a self-perpetuating autocracy. There remains ample public support for operating business corporations at a high level of efficiency and with a sure hand at the helm, but few any longer believe that autocratic management methods and one-man rule are particularly efficient, either administratively or for strategic decision-making. And it is worth remembering that the last people in the world who want corporations to succeed in structuring into public visibility the popular constraints to which they move, are the anticorporate militants.

8. Dr. Glover is a Harvard-trained economist, but he is not kind to prevailing traditions in economics. He adds only a few strokes to the autopsy now under way on the corpus of Keynesian macroeconomics. The main thrust is against a different area of intellectual disaster. An empirically defensible microeconomics must predict that the growth of large corporations will go along with

Rising employment.

Rising real wages.

Rising per capita GNP.

Rising productivity.

Major innovations in consumers' goods.

Major innovations in methods of production.

Major innovations in business organization.

Extensive turnover in the membership of the leading corporations.

At least, that is the empirical record, 1880-1929 and 1929-70. The last economics to score a passing grade on this test was that of Joseph A. Schumpeter, a respected teacher of Dr. Glover's. An economics that fails to predict the corporate/urban revolution might be written off as merely so much time lost in the ongoing scientific enterprise. But the economics developed in the tradition stemming from Edward Chamberlin has to be read as predicting that the growth of large corporations would have virtually the opposite of the consequences that in fact accompanied it. What made the failure scandalous was that the followers of this mistaken economics palmed it off wholesale on Congress, courts, regulatory agencies, and the antitrust bar.

The accurate assessment of strengths and weaknesses is the first step in formulating an American strategy for the future; and certainly large corporations belong on the list of our national strengths. The weaknesses include the constellation of beliefs that prevents American society from making full use of the potentials of the corporate institution. Corporations and their managements can help by examining and correcting the ways they themselves feed and fortify such beliefs, but that alone will not be enough unless the rest of us extend our David Harum tradition of skepticism to antibigness mythology. *The Revolutionary Corporations* will advance the cause of realism substantially.

L. E. Birdzell, Jr.

═ NOTES ═

1. The subject of Adolph A. Berle and Gardiner C. Means, *The Modern Corporation and Private Property* (New York: The Macmillan Company, 1932). The corporations used are "nonfinancial." See Appendix Note C on some of the statistical problems.

2. *The Visible Hand* (Cambridge: Harvard University Press, 1977), chaps. 10 and 11, esp. chap. 10. Dr. Glover cities also the more extended accounts in John G. McLean and Robert W. Haigh, *The Growth of Integrated Oil Companies* (Boston: Harvard Business School, 1953), and Ralph W. Hidy and Muriel E. Hidy, *History of Standard Oil Company (New Jersey): Pioneering in Big Business, 1892-1911* (New York: Harper & Brothers, 1955). These sources make it clear that John D. Rockefeller and his associates foresaw and deliberately pursued the economies achievable by integration and large scale.

3. Ida M. Tarbell, *The History of the Standard Oil Company* (Gloucester: Peter Smith [reprint] 1950), pp. 381-85, 240-41.

4. Chandler, *The Visible Hand*, p. 316, note 2: "American manufacturers began in the 1870s to . . . set up nationwide associations to control price and production. They did so primarily as a response to the continuing price decline, which became increasingly oppressive after the panic of 1873 ushered in a prolonged economic depression." Ibid., p. 336, referring to the later trusts and mergers as well: ". . . (S)uccessful mergers met two conditions. They consolidated production, and built their own marketing and purchasing organizations. And they operated in industries where technology and markets permitted such integration to increase the speed and lower the cost of materials through the processes of production and distribution. For these reasons the long-lived mergers came to cluster in the same industries in which the first large integrated enterprise appeared in the 1880s." And finally (ibid., p. 338): "Those (trusts) formed to control competition or to profit from the process of merger itself often brought short-term gains. But they rarely assured long-term profits. Unless the newly formed combination used the resources under its control more efficiently than had the constituent companies before they joined the merger, the consolidation had little staying power."

5. The arithmetic of such comparisons heavily favors the long term, because an "investment" in short-term welfare losses is justified by long-term annual returns equal to an interest rate appropriate to the "investment," together with some allowance for amortization over the long term. Similarly, economic expansion favors the long term.

6. The 1929-71 growth in numbers of smaller corporations may be partly attributable to the popularity of incorporating to save or postpone income taxes. However, the number of unincorporated proprietorships also rose during the same period. The increase in number of small firms is real.

APPENDIX TO SUMMARY AND COMMENTARY

Notes

A. *The Revolutionary Corporations* is a manual of statistics on the growth of the large corporations and their role in American society. Perhaps a summary for the general reader should have dispensed with the statistics altogether. But a summary of an argument for the proposition that large corporations have functioned as engines of growth and change in the United States of the past 90 years would be hopelessly incomplete without drawing on Dr. Glover's evidence. On the other hand, compressing the spirit of a statistical argument extended over nine chapters into half a dozen tables cannot possibly do full justice to the original. But a summary never does.

B. The most a summary can hope to do is to offer a sufficiently challenging case for Dr. Glover's basic proposition to encourage those interested in the full story to go back to the original. The summary argument occasionally adds information and observations from other sources that seemed likely to add clarity or force to the brief statement, even though the references had not been thought useful to the fuller statement in the original. A few pertinent figures are drawn from *Historical Statistics of the United States* (Bureau of the Census, 1975); otherwise, the basic data are Dr. Glover's.

C. The following observations on statistical points may be of interest to some readers:
    1. The domain of the study is "nonfinancial corporations." Statistics relating to financial corporations are excluded. Their assets are intangible counterparts of the tangible assets of nonfinancial corporations, and hence are substantially duplicative.
    2. Assets are used as a measure of size because of the accident of data availability. This measure exaggerates the importance of capital-intensive industries in the United States economy and underemphasizes the importance of labor-intensive industries. However, for purposes of studying a revolution characterized by the substitution of machine power for man power and woman power, the capital-intensive bias may be more useful than harmful.
    3. The formulation of meaningful industry categories is a difficult undertaking, with numerous pitfalls that emerge only when one tries it. Dr. Glover's 54 industry categories are subdivisions of American economic geography, not types of corporation. Because each corporation must be assigned to one category on the basis of its principal business,
        i.   The asset numbers for all categories are overstated by inclusion of assets actually used in other categories, and
        ii. The assets of all categories are understated by exclusion of assets owned by corporations in other categories, but actually used in the given category.

The two kinds of error are fortunately not cumulative, but neither can they be expected to cancel out exactly. They lead to such anomalies as the omission from assets in "Household appliances" of those of General Electric and Westinghouse used in producing household appliances, and the inclusion of the steel companies' coal mines in "Iron and steel" rather than "Coal." All this results from the fact that conventional microeconomics has not yet worked out the changes in the theory of the firm, the theory of markets, and the related statistical classifications needed to accommodate the invention of firms that are simply "in business" as entrepreneurs, not in any particular business.

TABLE A
Occurrence of Large Corporations—1929 and 1971

		Occurrence		Increase (decrease)
	Industry Category	1929	1971	
1.	Agriculture, fisheries	0	0	0
2.	Iron and steel	11	19	8
3.	Nonferrous metals	8	18	10
4.	Coal	4	3	(1)
5.	Petroleum	20	30	10
6.	Construction	0	3	3
7.	Food and kindred products	4	19	15
8.	Meat and meat products	3	5	2
9.	Dairy and dairy products	2	6	4
10.	Alcoholic beverages	0	5	5
11.	Soft drinks and flavorings	1	2	1
12.	Tobacco manufacturing	4	5	1
13.	Textile mill products	1	9	8
14.	Apparel and other finished fabric products	0	5	5
15.	Lumber and paper	4	17	13
16.	Furniture and fixtures	0	0	0
17.	Printing and publishing	0	7	7
18.	Chemicals and allied products	4	26	22
19.	Pharmaceuticals and medical equipment and supplies	0	21	21
20.	Soaps, cleaners, toiletries	1	5	4
21.	Rubber and tires	4	5	1
22.	Leather and leather products	1	2	1
23.	Nonmetallic mineral mining: stone, clay, concrete and products	0	13	13
24.	Glass and glass products	1	4	3
25.	Fabricated metal products*	2	10	8
26.	Metal cans	2	4	2
27.	Machinery*	2	9	7
28.	Farm, construction, and mining machinery	2	7	5
29.	Office, computing, and accounting machines	0	11	11
30.	Electrical machinery*	2	8	6
31.	Household appliances	0	7	6
32.	Radio, TV, communication equipment, electronic components	1	14	13
33.	Scientific, measuring, and control devices; watches and clocks	0	2	2
34.	Photographic equipment, supplies	1	2	1
35.	Motor vehicles and equipment	4	17	13
36.	Aircraft, guided missiles, and parts	0	10	10
37.	Ship and boat building and repair	0	0	0
38.	Railroad and transportation equipment	3	4	1
39.	Other and miscellaneous manufacturing	0	5	5
40.	Rail transportation, terminals, etc.	43	21	(22)
41.	Transit	8	0	(8)
42.	Motor transportation	0	5	5
43.	Water transportation	1	3	2
44.	Air transportation	0	12	12
45.	Electric, gas, sanitary services	39	106	67
46.	Telephone, telegraph and other communication services, except broadcasting	4	11	7
47.	Radio and TV broadcasting	0	2	2
48.	Wholesale trade, except petroleum	0	1	1
49.	Retail trade, except general merchandise, food stores, gas stations	2	7	6
50.	General merchandise and mail order	6	20	14
51.	Food stores	1	10	9
52.	Motion pictures	4	5	1

TABLE A *(continued)*

	Industry Category	Occurrence 1929	Occurrence 1971	Increase (decrease)
53.	Services, except motion pictures	0	12	12
54.	Real estate	1	6	5
	Total increases in occurrence: 390			
	Total decreases in occurrence: 31			

*Excluding concerns classified in more specifically defined categories.

TABLE B
Basic systems: Largest Corporation presence, 1929 and 1971

	Largest Corporations' assets (millions of 1971 dollars)	
	1971	1929
Power system		
Electric, gas, and sanitary services	$120,891.8	$ 56,547.2
Electrical machinery	12,711.6	2,360.7
Information handling system		
Telephone and telegraph	69,014.0	15,882.6
Office and computing equipment	21,463.1	-0-
Radio and communication equipment	19,967.1	858.9
Printing and publishing	2,702.1	-0-
Broadcasting	1,326.2	-0-
Transportation system		
Motor vehicle products	44,561.3	7,683.8
Railroad transportation	32,347.5	77,507.7
Air transportation	12,199.2	-0-
Aircraft and missiles manufacture	12,783.2	-0-
Rubber and tires	9,149.0	2,687.7
Railroad equipment	2,133.0	995.4
Water transportation	1,110.1	306.8
Urban transit	-0-	4,291.4
Motor transportation	3,580.6	-0-
Fuel system		
Petroleum	105,846.3	24,496.7
Coal	1,413.6	2,130.4
Materials system		
Chemicals	30,416.4	4,083.1
Iron and steel	23,407.7	11,975.5
Nonferrous metals	17,760.1	6,001.3
Wood and paper products	17,385.7	3,100.0
Nonmetallic minerals	6,089.6	-0-
Glass	3,742.1	311.7
Textiles	4,579.7	349.4
Power system	133,603.4	58,907.9
Information handling system	114,472.5	16,741.5
Transportation system	117,863.9	93,472.8
Fuel system	107,259.9	26,627.1
Materials system	103,381.3	25,821.0
Totals	$576,581.0	$221,570.3
All assets, Large Corporations	$707,197.0	$244,485.3
LC assets in basic systems as percentage of all LC assets	81.5%	90.6%

TABLE C
Industry Categories in order of presence: 1971

	(1) Category	(2) Presence (millions of 1971 dollars)	(3) Relative presence	(4) Cumulative assets (percent)	(5) Occurrence	(6) Cumulative occurrence (percent)
1.	Electricity	$120,892	88.1	17.1%	106	18.9%
2.	Petroleum	105,846	91.4	32.1	30	24.3
3.	Telephone	69,014	86.2	41.8	11	26.3
4.	Motor vehicles	44,561	76.9	48.1	17	29.3
5.	Rail transport	32,348	74.5	52.7	21	33.0
6.	Chemicals	30,416	76.5	57.0	26	37.7
7.	General merchandise	24,491	63.0	60.5	20	41.3
8.	Iron and steel	23,408	82.4	63.8	19	44.6
9.	Office . . . computing	21,463	86.5	66.8	11	46.6
10.	Radio, communication	19,967	77.1	69.6	14	49.1
11.	Nonferrous metals	17,760	55.4	72.1	18	52.3
12.	Wood . . . products	17,386	49.8	74.6	17	55.4
13.	Aircraft	12,783	52.8	76.4	10	57.1
14.	Electric machinery	12,712	61.6	78.2	8	58.6
15.	Food	12,322	45.6	79.9	19	62.0
16.	Air transport	12,199	73.5	81.7	12	64.1
17.	Pharmaceuticals	12,058	87.8	83.4	21	67.9
18.	Rubber and tires	9,149	70.0	84.7	5	68.6
19.	Tobacco	7,046	88.6	85.7	5	69.6
20.	Farm . . . machinery	6,670	44.2	86.6	7	70.9
21.	Nonmetallic minerals	6,090	40.5	87.5	13	73.2
22.	Fabricated metal products	5,892	25.0	88.3	10	75.0
23.	Meat	5,325	61.3	89.1	5	75.9
24.	Food stores	5,194	40.0	89.8	10	77.7
25.	Dairy	5,065	86.1	90.5	6	78.8
26.	Services	4,952	8.9	91.2	12	80.1
27.	Textiles	4,580	30.1	91.9	9	82.5
28.	Soaps and cleaners	4,370	79.6	92.5	5	83.4
29.	Household appliances	4,360	86.3	93.1	7	84.6
30.	Photo equipment	3,915	94.5	94.2	2	85.0
31.	Metal cans	3,743	94.4	94.2	4	85.7
32.	Glass	3,742	77.3	94.7	4	86.4
33.	Motor transport	3,581	26.7	95.2	5	87.3
34.	Retail trade	3,550	5.2	95.7	7	88.6
35.	Alcoholic beverages	3,355	36.8	96.2	6	89.6
36.	Machinery	3,301	14.7	96.7	9	91.3
37.	Printing and publishing	2,702	12.9	97.0	7	92.5
38.	Apparel	2,471	21.7	97.4	5	93.4
39.	Scientific equipment	2,454	47.2	97.7	2	93.8
40.	Railroad equipment	2,138	33.8	98.0	4	94.5
41.	Real estate	2,031	2.2	98.3	6	95.5
42.	Miscellaneous manufacture	1,951	20.1	98.6	4	96.3
43.	Motion pictures	1,947	30.3	99.1	5	97.1
44.	Soft drinks	1,936	41.6	99.3	2	97.5
45.	Coal	1,414	37.0	99.4	3	98.0
46.	Broadcasting	1,326	25.1	99.5	2	98.4
47.	Construction	1,201	2.5	99.7	3	98.9
48.	Water transport	1,110	17.1	99.9	3	99.5
49.	Leather	697	18.3	99.95	2	99.8
50.	Wholesale trade	318	0.4	100.0	1	100.0

TABLE D
Industry Categories in order of occurrence: 1971

	(1) Category	(2) Occurrence	(3) Cumulative occurrence	(4) Cumulative occurrence (percent)	(5) Presence (millions of 1971 dollars)	(6) Cumulative presence (percent)
1.	Electricity, gas...	106	106	19.0%	$120,892	17.1%
2.	Petroleum	30	136	24.3	105,846	32.1
3.	Chemicals	26	162	29.0	30,416	36.4
4.	Pharmaceuticals	21	183	32.7	12,058	38.1
5.	Rail transport	21	204	36.5	32,348	42.6
6.	General merchandise	20	224	40.1	24,491	46.1
7.	Iron and steel	19	243	43.5	23,408	49.4
8.	Food	19	262	46.9	12,322	51.2
9.	Nonferrous metals	18	280	50.1	17,760	53.7
10.	Motor vehicles	17	297	53.1	44,561	60.0
11.	Wood . . . products	17	314	56.2	17,386	62.4
12.	Radio, communication	14*	326*	58.7	19,967	65.3
13.	Nonmetallic minerals	13	339	61.0	6,090	66.1
14.	Air transport	12	351	63.1	12,199	67.8
15.	Services	12	363	65.3	4,952	68.5
16.	Telephone	11	374	67.3	69,014	78.3
17.	Office . . . computing	11	385	69.2	21,463	81.3
18.	Aircraft	10	395	71.0	12,783	83.1
19.	Fabricated metal products	10	405	72.8	5,892	84.0
20.	Food stores	10	415	74.6	5,194	84.7
21.	Textiles	9	424	76.2	4,580	85.4
22.	Machinery	9	433	77.8	3,301	85.8
23.	Electrical machinery	8	441	79.2	12,712	87.6
24.	Farm . . . machinery	7	448	80.5	6,670	88.6
25.	Household appliances	7	455	81.8	4,360	89.2
26.	Retail trade	7	462	83.0	3,550	89.7
27.	Printing and publishing	7	469	84.3	2,702	90.1
28.	Dairy	6	475	85.3	5,065	90.8
29.	Alcoholic beverages	6	481	86.4	3,355	91.3
30.	Real estate	6	487	87.5	2,031	91.5
31.	Rubber and tires	5	492	88.4	9,149	92.8
32.	Tobacco	5	497	89.3	7,046	93.8
33.	Meat	5	502	90.2	5,325	94.6
34.	Soaps, cleaners	5	507	91.1	4,370	95.2
35.	Motor transport	5	512	91.9	3,581	95.7
36.	Apparel	5	517	92.8	2,471	96.1
37.	Motion pictures	5	522	93.7	1,947	96.3
38.	Metal cans	4	526	94.5	3,743	96.9
39.	Glass	4	530	95.2	3,742	97.4
40.	Railroad equipment	4	534	95.9	2,133	97.7
41.	Miscellaneous manufacture	5	539	96.6	1,951	98.0
42.	Coal	3	542	97.1	1,414	98.2
43.	Construction	3	545	97.7	1,201	98.4
44.	Water transport	3	548	98.2	1,110	98.5
45.	Photo equipment	2	550	98.6	3,915	99.0
46.	Scientific equipment	2	552	98.9	2,454	99.4
47.	Soft drinks	2	554	99.3	1,936	99.7
48.	Broadcasting	2	556	99.6	1,326	99.9
49.	Leather	2	558	100.0	697	99.95
50.	Wholesale trade	1	559*	100.0	318	100.0

*Includes Western Electric and the electronics manufacturing operations of General Telephone & Electronics counted as one company. These companies are not included in the total number of The 559. See Notes to Exhibit 1, Notes 53 and 54.

TABLE E
Industry Categories in order of average size of Largest Corporations: 1971

		(2)	(3)	(4)	(5)	(6)
	(1)	Average size (millions of 1971 dollars)			Presence (millions of 1971 dollars)	Cumulative presence (percent)
	Category	Largest Corporations	All other corporations	(2) ÷ (3)		
1.	Telephone	$6,274	$3.205	1,958	$ 69,014	9.8%
2.	Petroleum	3,528	1.288	2,746	105,846	24.8
3.	Motor vehicles	2,621	5.622	466	44,561	31.1
4.	Photo equipment	1,958	0.365	5,364	3,915	31.7
5.	Office . . . computing	1,951	6.134	318	21,463	34.7
6.	Rubber and tires	1,830	0.630	2,905	9,149	36.0
7.	Electrical machinery	1,589	1.705	932	12,712	37.8
8.	Rail transport	1,540	0.611	2,520	32,348	42.4
9.	Radio, communication	1,426	1.038	1,374	19,967	45.2
10.	Tobacco	1,409	12.583	112	7,046	46.2
11.	Aircraft	1,278	14.189	90	12,783	48.0
12.	Iron and steel	1,232	2.263	544	23,408	51.3
13.	Scientific equipment	1,227	1.705	720	2,454	51.7
14.	General merchandise	1,225	0.629	1,948	24,491	55.1
15.	Chemicals	1,170	1.405	833	30,416	59.4
16.	Electricity	1,140	2.002	569	120,892	76.5
17.	Meat	1,065	1.325	804	5,325	77.3
18.	Wood . . . products	1,023	1.241	824	17,386	79.7
19.	Air transportation	1,017	1.287	790	12,199	81.5
20.	Nonferrous metals	987	4.710	210	17,760	84.0
21.	Soft drinks	968	1.226	790	1,936	84.3
22.	Farm . . . machinery	953	2.888	330	6,670	85.2
23.	Metal cans	936	1.672	560	3,743	85.7
24.	Glass	936	1.169	800	3,742	86.3
25.	Soaps, cleaners	874	0.519	1,684	4,370	86.9
26.	Dairy	844	0.385	2,192	5,065	87.6
27.	Motor transportation	716	0.359	1,994	3,581	88.1
28.	Broadcasting	663	1.008	658	1,326	88.3
29.	Food	649	1.640	396	12,322	90.0
30.	Household appliances	623	1.533	406	4,360	90.6
31.	Fabricated metal products	589	0.778	757	5,892	91.5
32.	Pharmaceuticals	574	0.409	1,403	12,058	93.2
33.	Alcoholic beverages	559	13.717	41	3,355	93.6
34.	Railroad equipment	533	3.121	177	2,138	93.8
35.	Miscellaneous manufacturing	533	0.663	804	1,951	94.1
36.	Food stores	519	0.288	1,802	5,194	94.9
37.	Textiles	509	1.820	280	4,580	95.5
38.	Retail trade	507	0.201	2,522	3,550	96.0
39.	Apparel	494	0.525	941	2,471	96.4
40.	Coal	471	1.365	345	1,414	96.6
41.	Nonmetallic minerals	468	0.809	578	6,090	97.4
42.	Services	413	0.183	2,257	4,952	98.1
43.	Construction	400	0.329	1,216	1,201	98.3
44.	Motion pictures	389	0.445	874	1,947	98.6
45.	Printing and publishing	386	0.686	563	2,702	98.9
46.	Water transportation	370	0.842	439	1,110	99.1
47.	Machinery	367	0.867	423	3,301	99.6
48.	Leather	349	1.373	254	697	99.7
49.	Real estate	339	0.337	1,006	2,031	99.95
50.	Wholesale trade	318	0.539	590	318	100.0

TABLE F
Industry Categories in order of relative presence of Largest Corporations: 1971

	Category	Relative presence	Presence (millions of 1971 dollars)	Cumulative presence (percent)
1.	Photo equipment	94.5	$ 3,915	0.6%
2.	Metal cans	94.4	3,743	1.1
3.	Petroleum	91.4	105,846	16.0
4.	Tobacco	88.6	7,046	17.0
5.	Electricity	88.1	120,892	34.1
6.	Pharmaceuticals	87.8	12,058	35.8
7.	Office . . . computing	86.5	21,463	38.9
8.	Household appliances	86.3	4,360	39.5
9.	Telephone	86.2	69,014	49.3
10.	Dairy	86.1	5,065	50.0
11.	Iron and steel	82.4	23,408	53.5
12.	Soaps, cleaners	79.6	4,370	53.9
13.	Glass	77.3	3,742	54.4
14.	Radio, communication	77.1	19,967	57.3
15.	Motor vehicles	76.9	44,561	63.6
16.	Chemicals	76.5	30,416	67.9
17.	Rail transportation	74.5	32,348	72.4
18.	Air transportation	73.5	12,199	74.2
19.	Rubber and tires	70.0	9,149	75.4
20.	General merchandise	63.0	24,491	78.9
21.	Electrical machinery	61.6	12,712	80.7
22.	Meat	61.3	5,325	81.5
23.	Nonferrous metals	55.4	17,760	84.0
24.	Aircraft	52.8	12,783	85.8
25.	Wood . . . products	49.8	17,386	88.2
26.	Scientific equipment	47.2	2,454	88.6
27.	Food	45.6	12,322	90.3
28.	Farm . . . machinery	44.2	6,670	91.3
29.	Soft drinks	41.6	1,936	91.5
30.	Nonmetallic minerals	40.5	6,090	92.4
31.	Food stores	40.0	5,194	93.1
32.	Coal	37.0	1,414	93.3
33.	Alcoholic beverages	36.8	3,355	93.8
34.	Railroad equipment	33.8	2,133	94.1
35.	Motion pictures	30.3	1,947	94.4
36.	Textiles	30.1	4,580	95.0
37.	Motor transportation	26.7	3,581	95.5
38.	Broadcasting	25.1	1,326	95.7
39.	Fabricated metal products	25.0	5,892	96.6
40.	Apparel	21.7	2,471	96.9
41.	Miscellaneous manufacturing	20.1	1,951	97.2
42.	Leather	18.3	697	97.3
43.	Water transportation	17.1	1,110	97.4
44.	Machinery	14.7	3,301	97.9
45.	Printing and publishing	12.9	2,702	98.3
46.	Services	8.9	4,952	99.0
47.	Retail trade	5.2	3,550	99.5
48.	Construction	2.5	1,201	99.7
49.	Real estate	2.2	2,031	99.96
50.	Wholesale trade	0.4	318	100.0

TABLE G
The small corporation in revolution

(1)	(2)	(3)	(4)	(5)	(6)	(7)	(8)
	Number of small corporations		Growth multiple	Assets of small corporations (millions of 1971 dollars)		Growth multiple	Asset growth rate per year (percent)
Industry	1929	1971	(3) ÷ (2)	1929	1971	(5) ÷ (6)	
Agriculture, forestry, and fisheries	9,430	39,932	4.235	$ 6,564.5	$ 11,800.0	1.798	1.41%
Mining and quarrying . . .	12,498	12,610	1.008	34,164.3	24,628.4	0.721	—
Construction	18,358	143,089	7.794	9,493.9	47,041.8	4.955	3.89
Manufacturing	92,143	200,639	2.177	135,218.5	225,019.8	1.664	1.22
Transportation and other public utilities	21,513	70,944	3.298	84,091.2	69,432.6	0.826	—
Wholesale and retail trade	129,080	538,626	4.173	61,554.9	177,330.9	2.881	2.55
Services	35,967	287,763	8.001	21,263.9	55,326.9	2.602	2.30
Miscellaneous	2,900	21,438	7.392	773.0	847.0	1.096	0.218
Totals	321,889	1,315,051	4.085	$353,124.2	$611,427.4	1.731	1.31%

Note: For purposes of comparison, the overall compound growth rate of assets of corporations larger than $250 million (1971 dollars) was 2.56 percent.

1

Engines of plenty; engines of growth; engines of change

SUMMARY: THE CORPORATE REVOLUTION

The past hundred years have been an era of extraordinary growth, development, *change* in America. No aspect of life and living, of thought and thinking, of being and doing, has been untouched. Over the past 50 years, over the past generation, the pace of change has risen and risen again. It is no exaggeration to label the whole experience a *revolution,* so total and engulfing has been our transformation of the nation we were to the nation we now are.

All sorts of agents have taken part in the continuing, pervasive processes of change and have helped drive them. Individuals and families, of course; universities and schools, also; and units of government and unions and foundations. Most of the drive and certainly the lion's share of the actual concrete, visible implementation of changes have come from the business sector. And within that sector, our large, our *largest* corporations have been the principal instrumentalities of development. Artifacts of their workings are now around us, everywhere. So preeminent have been their roles in the development of our economy and our society, in our entire *System,* that it is no exaggeration to label this unprecedented transformation the *Corporate* Revolution.

The large, the *very* large business corporation is one of the distinguishing institutions of the American community, of American life. The large business corporation is *the* distinguishing feature of the structure of American industry and the American economy. It is also one of the least understood of our institutions, and one of the most controversial.

In the aggregate, the American economy is the most bounteous of the world. In per capita terms, none is more plentiful. Much of that opulence flows directly from the workings of large-scale, vertically integrated, multiplant, multiproduct, capital-intensive, massive-overhead, technology-intensive corporations. The whole American System now utterly depends upon the workings of a small number of very large corporations that produce infrasupport, such as energy in its several forms, transportation, communication, steel, nonferrous metals, chemicals; to say nothing of pharmaceuticals, motor vehicles, computers, aircraft, and electrical equipment.

Over the last hundred years, and especially since the turn of the century, the American community and economy have achieved growth extraordinary in the world's entire history. From 1870 to 1920, our population grew by a factor of 2.7, from 40 million to 106 million; from 1920 to 1970, we grew by a factor of almost 2, from those 106 million to 203 million; over the 100 years, we grew by more than 500 percent. Today, we are about 220 million—persons to be cherished; bodies to be sustained.

More. That growing population produced, and was supported by, a tide of goods and services that rose so much more rapidly that, over the period, we achieved a level of well-being that had never been seen before: In nutrition; housing; health and life expectancy; education and consequent scope for self-realization of the individual. A major share of the extraordinary surge of production that supported this expansion and material and human advance flowed out of the workings of large corporations.

The increases in production and consumption, of course, were not merely a matter of *more* of the same. On the contrary, what was *added* were goods and services of many *different* sorts—goods and services that were undreamed of in 1870, or in 1900, or in 1930, or, even in 1945. Besides, what was "added" was not merely *added;* much of what was added, in fact, *displaced* that which had been. In terms of specifics, almost nothing of what was produced and consumed in the past, by way of goods and services, has persisted up to the 1970s from 1870, or from 1900, or 1930. Even among generic raw materials such as wheat, coal, and steel, specifications have greatly changed. Since 1945, the composition of our production and consumption has been transformed by the introduction of pharmaceuticals; new chemicals; a whole constellation of products of electronics, aviation and air transportation; new foods; mass distribution.

In concrete detail, our national product, our very way of life has been utterly transformed, not merely once, but several times over.

This plenty, this growth, this change would not have been possible, would not, could not have happened without the ongoing evolution—indeed, the continuing *Revolution*—so characteristic of our industrial structure. Over the past 100 years, the past 70 years, the past quarter-century, the Industrial Revolution in America entered a new era, brought about a new industrial order; increased its pace, spread its reach, and penetrated ever more deeply into our economy, our daily living.

For better or worse—there are those who look wistfully and romantically back to earlier times—the principal engines creating that plenty, pushing that growth, driving and leading that change, were the growing numbers of increasingly large business corporations. The extraordinary present-day levels of American production and consumption would simply not be possible without an industrial organization of the sort represented by these few hundred very large corporations. This bald fact is not widely recognized. It stands in contradiction to our traditional way of thinking.

Beyond its *economic* significance, the corporation has become a major institution in the American political system. But there is no provision for that fact in our traditional ideology.

As a nation, we have before us a lot of "unfinished business" by way of thinking through the implications of those uneasy facts.

That is what this book is about.

* * * * *

The rest of Chapter 1 is a running summary of the work.

THE MODERN CORPORATION AND PRIVATE PROPERTY

In 1932, a book appeared that was a landmark in the literature about business and about large corporations in particular: this was *The Modern Corporation and Private Property,* by A. A. Berle, Jr., and Gardiner C. Means.[1] It listed the then 200 largest *nonfinancial* corporations, and gave the dollar values of their assets as of about December 31, 1929.[2,3] In 1929 dollars, these largest corporations reported about $80 billion of assets. In terms of 1971 dollars, these assets came to about $244.5 billion; in 1977 dollars, something like $360 billion.[4] Altogether, these 200 companies held about 41 percent of the total assets of the then 322,000 nonfinancial corporations.

The Berle and Means roster of The 200 Largest Corporations of 1929 is given in Exhibit 1, at the end of this chapter. In this exhibit, these corporations are grouped according to a number of "Industry Categories," several of which are conceived and defined as industry *systems* composed of both similar and dissimilar, but interactive, interrelated corporate entities, large and small, each and all mutually affecting the others through webs of symbiotic, supportive, and competitive relationships.[5]

Those authors were struck by the fact that the managers of large corporations owned mere fractions of the equity of the companies they ran. This "separation" of management and ownership in large corporations, they believed, led to irresponsibility, in contrast to small businesses, whose owners were managers and whose managers were owners.

Berle and Means were struck also by how "ubiquitous" was the presence of large corporations. It seemed to them that large corporations and their workings and artifacts were everywhere.

They were dismayed by the thought that the business community had been, and was being "concentrated," by means of combinations and mergers, into fewer and fewer, larger and larger entities that were taking over the industrial structure of the country.

They feared that among the consequences of the rise of very large corporations were the growth of autocracy and corresponding depersonalization, even dehumanization of modern industry; the diminution of initiative and enterprise; the growth of monopoly powers; the emergence of a new *political* institution with, perhaps, the potential of superseding the State "as the dominant form of social organization."

In much of what they said, they were merely harking back to Adam Smith, whose misgivings as to the inadequacies of large corporations, as he knew them in the 18th century—with their supposed bureaucratic rigidity and lack of initiative and responsiveness—were at least as strong as his devotion to free enterprise of *small* businesses.

Berle and Means were also picking up, almost literally, ideas expressed 35 years earlier by Mr. Justice Rufus Peckham in the case of the *Trans-Missouri Freight Association* [166 U.S. 290 (1897)]. In an often quoted dictum in that decision, the Supreme Court, through the words of Mr. Justice Peckham, extolled the human, ethical, social, and political, as well as the economic values and merits that it perceived to inhere in *small* businesses. The Justices endowed with a sort of legitimacy some notions that were, and still are, almost an article of faith in American thought.

The work of Berle and Means was a powerful articulation and rationalization of Populist ideology long present in America. This ideology was a rallying point for the urban-rural Democratic coalition that supported Franklin Roosevelt and his New Deal. Ideas embedded and latent in *The Modern Corporation and Private Property* found expression in the Securities and Exchange legislation of 1933 and 1934; in a milestone amendment to the Bankruptcy Act, which gave the Interstate Commerce Commission control over the thoroughgoing financial reorganization of the nation's railroads; and the Public Utility Holding Company Act of 1935, under which the electric and gas utilities were restructured. Largely inspired by the work of Berle and Means, proponents tried to get Congress to require corporations engaged in interstate commerce to be chartered under federal, not state, authority. They failed; but that idea still lingers on.

The 200 Largest Nonfinancial Corporations of 1929 had emerged in an industry structure composed of 322,000 nonfinancial corporations; 134,000 corporations in finance, insurance, and real estate; about 2 million unincorporated, mostly family-owned and operated businesses, largely in retailing and "services"; 6.5 million family farms; and some hundreds of thousands of self-employed artisans and professionals, producers of goodness knows how many different kinds of goods and services. All these many different kinds and sizes of productive entities coexisted in an extraordinary *system* of symbiotic supplier-producer-customer relationships.

The 200 Largest Corporations of 1929, highly visible as they were, were not really all that "ubiquitous," to use the word of Berle and Means. In fact, their occurrence (in terms of numbers) and presence (in terms of relative asset "masses") throughout the business community were highly selective and localized in a limited number of particular industry groups and "Industry Categories." More than three-quarters (169 of them) were in four major "Industry Groups" (as then defined by the Census): "Food and kindred products, beverages and tobacco" (13); "Chemicals and allied products" (25); "Metal and metal products" (36); and "Transportation and public utilities" (95).

In the more revealing and meaningful terms of "Industry Categories," 139 of the companies holding 82.5 percent of the total assets of The 200, were in eight Industry Categories:* "Iron and steel" (11); "Nonferrous metals" (8); "Petroleum" (20); "Rail transportation" (43); "Transit" (8); "Electric, gas, and sanitary services" (39); "Telephone, telegraph . . . " (4); "General merchandise" (6).

The other 61 largest corporations were scattered among 26 Industry Categories. Significantly, none of the Largest Corporations of 1929 showed up in 20 Industry Categories. (See Exhibits 2 and 3.)

THE ADVANCING INDUSTRIAL REVOLUTION IN AMERICA, 1880-1930

The emergence of large corporations in the half-century prior to 1930 was part and parcel of the continuing Industrial Revolution in America. Large companies were, and had been, active sources of our national development.

Large corporations provided key inputs and indispensable elements of infrastructure to the whole expanding and evolving economy. In reciprocal fashion, the development of the whole provided support and opportunities for them as it did for smaller businesses

---

*The concept and definition of "Industry Categories" are discussed below.

and for the individual. The "System" and its individual components grew and evolved hand in hand.

It is absolutely necessary that the root causes—the *etiology*—of the rise of large corporations be understood: in fact, the rise of large corporations both stemmed from, and actively energized, the advance of the continuing Industrial Revolution in America. Their emergence, growth, and very nature were, and continue to be, integrally related to the very essence of our industrial and economic development.

As it has happened, however, the rise of large corporations has more often than not been attributed to determinants that, actually, were scarcely more than incidental to our national development: self-seeking adventures of individual "Robber Barons" and other "Malefactors of Great Wealth"; building of "trusts," "combinations," mergers, and systems of multilayered holding companies and other devices whereby smaller companies were "concentrated" into larger and larger corporate entities; sustained predation by particular canny, less-than-scrupulous corporations bent on monopoly through monopolizing strategems and practices in particular "lines of commerce" and "relevant markets."

This sort of perception of history, so emotionally troublesome, yet so lacking in basic explanation, has been, and continues to be, a major source of simplistic, fruitless and, worse, dysfunctional administrative and legislative actions and proposals, and judicial decisions, aimed at large corporations, as such, to the neglect of the root causes, deep in our economic and industrial system, that occasioned and made possible their emergence and growth.

To be sure, early trusts were constructs of financiers, bankers, lawyers, and entrepreneurs: the Standard Oil Trust, the Tobacco and Sugar trusts, for instance. Large railroads and utility holding companies of the 1920s had also been put together from preexisting corporations, although individual railroads and utilities had been *relatively* large from their very beginnings early in the 19th century. And it was true that a few of the large manufacturing companies of 1929-30 were assemblages of smaller companies: United States Steel, General Motors, and General Foods, for instance. Some of the then largest companies, as a matter of fact, were pieces of dissolved "trusts," including some of the largest petroleum and tobacco companies.

More generally, however, the Largest Companies of those times were those whose particular sets of strengths—clarity and effectiveness of policy, business acumen, technological and managerial skills, and—who knows?—perhaps a bit of luck—had enabled them to capitalize upon emerging opportunities and to grow and develop faster than, and ahead of, the expanding and advancing industrial structure as a whole.

"Combination," "consolidation," or "concentration" of that

which formerly had been diffuse and separate, although undeniably present in the business community, did not, and does not, amount to a valid general explanation of the growth of large-scale enterprise and big companies up to 1929 and since.

If the factors that gave rise, and still give rise, to very large corporations had been, and were still, merely adventitious or fortuitous (such as monopolistic predation, the workings of promoters of "combinations," and the like) rather than factors intrinsic to our national evolution, then we might expect that these Largest Companies would have been spread rather evenly, or would have occurred something like randomly throughout the whole industrial structure. But such was not, and is not, the case. Even the trusts, whose purposes, explicitly or implicitly, generally did envision the erection of *large* enterprises, did not occur randomly throughout the business community.

In fact, the "occurrence" (numbers) and "presence" (asset masses) of large corporations here and there in the industrial structure were strongly ordered. That ordered occurrence and presence of the largest corporations of 1929 (and today), here and there in our vast industrial *ecosystem,* was no mere happenstance. It was a manifestation of the existence and workings of underlying trends and developments—technological, demographic, political, legislative, economic, "cultural"—that emerged and advanced in the decades after the Civil War and the decade after World War I, ready to be exploited and turned to practical account by organizing entrepreneurs who saw, and made much of, developing opportunities. Here were opportunities for economies of scale in production and distribution; vertical integration; multiproduct, multiplant operations; of mechanization and consequent capital-intensivity; of technology-intensivity; of new concepts and techniques of organization and management. (See Chapters 3 and 4.)

Granted that "Robber Barons," "Wolves of Wall Street," "Plungers," "Malefactors of Great Wealth," and such really did engage in rough-tough manipulation and infighting, in the perspective of history it is clear that these were incidents on the surface of deep-running forces, not fundamental causes of the rise of very large corporations. Had not the forces making for growth been very real, all the finaglings and frenzied finance in the world could not have erected institutions of any significant viability and dynamism.

The emergence and clusterings of The Largest Corporations of 1929 in railroads, utilities, communications, iron and steel and their products, nonferrous metals, petroleum and chemicals and allied products, rubber products, electrical machinery, and motor vehicles were consequences of systemic growth associated with our continuing national development, back to the turn of the century and before. (See Tables 3, 4, 5, and 6; Exhibits 11, 12, 13, and 14.) These were, to underline the point, industries that tended to be characterized by imperatives and opportunities of large scale, capital-intensivity, integration, multiplant operations, and the other attributes of large corporations.

These industries, so much the bailiwicks of very large corporations, had grown far more rapidly than other industries from which large corporations were totally absent or tended to be of far less importance. In the infrastructure—the railroads, the electric and gas utilities, and the communications companies—and in manufacturing, the most spectacular growths of invested capital and of production, from 1880 to 1930, took place precisely in industries especially characterized by the emergence of *large* corporations. Contrariwise, growths tended to be far less in industries that were, and continued to be, characterized by larger numbers of smaller companies.

Far from inhibiting economic and industrial growth and development, or being incapable of dynamism, it was precisely the dynamism of large corporations that accounted for the notable growths of the particular industries in which they emerged, and that did so much to energize our whole development.

All this would have astonished Adam Smith and might well have captured the objective attention of economists, legislators, and jurists.

In sum, The Largest Corporations of 1929 occurred pretty much where pragmatic analysis and the logics of evolving technologies and opportunities would indicate.

To repeat, because the contrary is so embedded in popular thought, these large corporations were prime *engines* of *growth* and *change* in the chapter of the history of our continuing Industrial Revolution that ran through the first decades of the 20th century.

The year 1929 was, perhaps, the apogee of an era that had begun 50 to 60 years earlier. The roster of The 200 Largest Nonfinancial Corporations of 1929 provides a benchmark for the study of the evolution of American industry in the preceding half-century and for the evolution of our industrial and economic structure that continues to this very time.

THE LARGEST NONFINANCIAL CORPORATIONS OF 1971

In Chapters 5 and 6, we begin to observe and ponder the occurrence and presence of very large corporations in American industry in the year 1971, four decades later on.[6]

By 1971, the American community had increased in size, diversity, and complexity far beyond anything even a visionary might have foreseen in 1929: 65 million households; close to 11 million business proprietorships and partnerships; 1.7 million business corporations, 1.6 million of them nonfinancial, the rest in finance and insurance.

Exhibit 1, in addition to The 200 Largest Nonfinancial Corporations of 1929, as given by Berle and Means, also displays The 200 Largest and The Next 359 Largest Nonfinancial Corporations of 1971.* Of course, there is no magic to the number 200, any more than there is to 500. That happened to be the "largest" as Berle and Means defined the group for their own purposes. The Top 200 of 1971 are shown for purposes of comparison—and contrast!—with the roster of 1929.

But, in 1971, as measured by reported values of assets, there were at least 559 publicly held corporations as large as any on the list of 1929. That larger figure, in itself, was a rough index of economic growth.

As we shall see, not only was the number of largest corporations of 1971 much greater than that of 1929, but the aggregate mass of their assets was much greater, and the composition of the roster was greatly and significantly different. Those changes were manifestations of *transformation,* not only of our industrial structure, but of the whole modern American "Way of Life."

The 1.6 million nonfinancial corporations of 1971, up from 322,000 in 1929, held assets reported at $1,410.5 billion in 1971 dollars. (In 1977 dollars, something like $2,100 billion.[7] Of this asset mass, in 1971 dollars, The 559 Largest Corporations of 1971 held $707.2 billion, which is to say something more than 50 percent. The 200 Largest Corporations of 1971, alone, held $538 billion of assets, up by almost $300 billion from the $244.5 billion of 1929 (in 1971 dollars). (See Exhibit 15.)

As in 1929, few, if any, of The Largest Corporations of 1971 were to be found in Agriculture, Construction, and Services—Industry Groups characterized by *large numbers* of *small firms.* They were clustered in two Major Industry Groups. Of The 559 of 1971, 494 of them were to be found in Manufacturing and Transportation and other utilities; 334 in the former and 160 in the latter Group. The 494 Largest Corporations in these two Industry Groups held about 94 percent of the total assets of The 559.

By way of a first rough indication of the relative masses of these Largest Corporations of 1971, it can be noted that the 334 Largest Corporations in Manufacturing held almost two-thirds of the total assets of *all* corporations in the Group. The 160 largest in Transportation and other utilities held over three-quarters of *all* the assets in that Group. (See Exhibit 15.)

The 200 Largest Companies of 1929 had held a bit over 40 percent of all corporate nonfinancial assets. The 200 Largest of 1971 held a bit less, 38.4 percent. But the 559 Largest of 1971, the largest of

*This roster was compiled by the author with the assistance of Alison Jennings McCance and Daniel F. Borge. See Appendix A.

which was much larger than any of The 200 of 1929 and the smallest of which was at least as large as the smallest of The 200 of 1929, held just about 50 percent of all nonfinancial corporate assets. (See Exhibit 15.)

Did this mean that "concentration" had been taking place in American industry over those 40-some years? No. What had notably happened within the community of largest corporations was the emergence of *numbers,* large numbers of large corporations in Industry Categories that, in 1929, had existed, if at all, only in "proto" form. Relatively more of the assets of American industry were of *kinds held by large,* not by small, corporations. More of that in a moment.

Two principal factors had been at work. A *net* increase had occurred in the "presence" of some companies already existing in 1929 (numbers of The Largest of 1929 had shrunk or even disappeared). More significantly, companies in *new* fields, economically negligible in 1929, had forged ahead, leading American industry in a new chapter in the history of our continuing Industrial Revolution and our development.

As in 1929, The Largest Companies of 1971 tended to cluster in certain Industry Categories, again pretty much where one might expect. In the seven "regulated" industries (sometimes thought to be "natural monopolies" because of large minimum scale, capital-intensivity, and small directly variable costs), which now included industries that had been of no great economic consequence in 1929, Air transportation, Motor transportation, and Radio and TV broadcasting, there was a total of 160 very large corporations. Together, these 160 corporations held $240.5 billion of assets—over one-third of all the assets of The 559, and over one-sixth of *all* the assets of *all* nonfinancial corporations. (See Exhibit 26.)

Another 84 of The Largest of 1971 were in the characteristically "integrated" industries: Iron and steel; Nonferrous metals; Petroleum; Lumber . . . wood . . . paper. Together, these companies held $164.4 billion of assets.

These 244 companies in 12 Industry Categories, where one would readily expect to find big companies, held well over half of all the assets of The 559, and about 30 percent of *all* the assets of *all* nonfinancial corporations.

Another 237 of The 559 of 1971 now appeared in those 19 Industry Categories that had 7 or more of The Largest firms. These were industries in which, by the definition of seven or more "specimens," the occurrence of very large corporations was fairly common. For instance, 26 of the companies were in "Chemicals and allied products"; 21 were in Pharmaceuticals. The occurrence of *numbers* of companies in these industries, not just one or two happenstance creations of promoters, suggests the presence of numerous *significant* opportunities for corporate growth to considerable size, as through economies of scale; multiplant, multiproduct, and multidivisional operations; technological development, and the like.

Altogether, the 487 corporations in these three broad classes of industries, comprising 30 of 54 Industry Categories, held about $642 billion of assets, that is, about 91 percent of all the assets of The 559 and 46 percent of all the assets of all nonfinancial corporations. (See Exhibit 29.)

These data for 1971 give strong corroboration to the observation concerning the occurrence of The Largest Corporations of 1929: they emerged and grew most often and to large proportions in particular Industry Categories where the basics of economics and technology combined to present notable opportunities for corporate growth.

Especially suggestive as to the conditions encouraging to the appearance and growth of large corporations was the occurrence of 70 of The Largest Corporations of 1971 in Industries where *none* of the Largest had been in 1929. Of these companies, 41 appeared among The Next 359, 29 among The 200. These 70 companies had appeared and grown in Industries that, although there were some precursor companies as early as 1929, had flowered only after, and partly in consequence of, World War II: Pharmaceuticals; Office . . . computing . . . machines; Aircraft, and Air transportation; Household appliances; Scientific devices; Radio and TV broadcasting; and Motor transportation. In each of these, it was the larger companies, not the smallest, that really led the pack in the development and, especially, in successful application of technological innovations and the introduction of new products, new services, and new methods of production, management, and marketing.

In the 40-some years, from 1929 through 1971, as in the 50 years before 1929, large corporations were prime engines of growth, prime engines of change.

INDUSTRY SYSTEMS, "CONCENTRATION," AND "PRESENCE" OF LARGE CORPORATIONS

Chapters 5 and 6 are concerned with concepts that may either obscure or elucidate structures of industries, the nature of industry performance, and industrial and economic development.

For about 40 years, economists, jurists, lawyers, and businessmen, themselves, have been wrestling with concepts like "concentration," "market power," "dominant market share," "monopoly power in a relevant market," lessening of competition in a "line of commerce." Each of these concepts, in its own way, necessarily presupposes a reasonably well-defined "industry" composed of identifiable producers who make an identifiable and definable "product"; and/or an identifiable "market," which presumably is an identifiable *system* composed of (*a*) identifiable *buyers* and (*b*) identifiable *sellers* of (*c*) an identifiable *"product"*—all presumably in some identifiable *"place,"* and presumably, still further, at some identifiable *time*.

Such concepts and definitions, in sum, presuppose the existence of "industries," clusters of sellers and buyers, and "products," each surrounded by reasonably clear, identifiable boundaries setting each apart from all others. Unfortunately—or fortunately—the real world is not nearly so simple.

Often, especially for advocacy purposes of litigation or administration, attempts are made, sometimes successfully from a complainant's point of view, to define "industries," "markets," and even "sections of the country" in such narrow fashion that a particular company can be shown to be "dominant" therein, with monopoly power to gain more than "competitive profits"; or if not a single company, then a "Big Three," "Big Four," "Big Eight" or what have you, who, it is alleged, enjoy a "shared monopoly."

The results of "concentration," "monopolistic competition," and the like, are widely supposed to include such undesirable phenomena as unnecessarily high prices, inferior quality, idle capacity, lack of innovation, antisocial excess profits, and such antisocial behavior as "product proliferation" and "excessive" advertising and promotion. All this leads, some suppose, to, among other things, (*a*) a Gross National Product smaller than might be; (*b*) a National Income whose distribution is badly distorted; (*c*) frustrated would-be competitors who are damaged; and (*d*) consumers who get less for their money of goods and services that are inferior—all as compared to what would obtain if only sellers and buyers were many and small and products being sold and bought were essentially fungible, and if there were no such "concentration" or "dominance."

This is a big and controversial topic, indeed. The point, here, is that such concepts, notions, and hypotheses have special significance for *large* corporations. Being *large,* they are, ipso facto, "few." Being *few,* they are open to suspicion of explicit or tacit restraint of competition, and to outright attacks as "monopolists" and the like.

This is no place to try to bring order out of prevailing theoretical and legal chaos. But, here, the basic verity can and must be insisted upon that, in fact, the most dynamic sectors of industry and of the private sector of the Gross National Product, for a hundred years, and especially in the past forty, have been precisely those most characterized by the occurrence and presence of very large corporations.

One avenue for trying to escape from prevalent unsatisfying, and palpably misleading, hypothetical and legalistic analyses is to understand the business community of the United States as being an "ecosystem," made up of a number of "subsystems"—"Industry Categories," important ones of which are composed of varying, but "large" numbers of highly *interrelated* firms of many different kinds and sizes.[5] Within these industry subsystems, say, Iron and steel, Petroleum, Chemicals and allied products, Motor vehicles and equipment, and Lumber . . . wood . . . products . . . paper, for instance, component companies of many different specific kinds and sizes exist and function. They interreact among themselves in many different ways: as buyers, sellers, and competitors, actual and *potential,* as to some or all of their particular outputs. In fact, depending upon circumstances, particular companies may be, at one and the same time, each others' suppliers, customers, and competitors.

Over time, in organic fashion, mostly by relatively minor incremental changes, but occasionally through major discontinuities, individual corporations can, and do, change their natures, as determined by the inputs and production processes they use, the outputs they produce, the way they are organized, the way they finance themselves. They may become more or less integrated, upstream and downstream. Some grow; some decline. Relationships among corporations can and do change. In consequence, whole Industry Categories can and do change and evolve. Such has been the case, for instance, in Food and kindred products and in Nonmetallic mineral mining, stone, clay, concrete, and their products. In the process, whole "lines of commerce" appear or disappear; "markets" come and go or are restructured. Some firms pass through a whole life-cycle from birth to maturity to extinction. Others abort early. A few persist, perhaps for decades, through adaptive transformation.

Surrounding all producers of whatever goods or services, at all times, are changing rosters of actual or potential customers downstream and suppliers upstream, with whom they interact in any or all of several ways, such as through term supply-contracts or simple "spot" purchases and sales. Firms, themselves, always have at least a few "make-or-buy" and "sell-or-process" options to expand "vertically" upstream or downstream. They have options to extend or contract their product lines. As they expand or shrink their product offerings, patterns of actual and potential competition are altered. They have options to substitute among inputs and outputs.

Producers in some industries, who compete in some instances may, or do, also buy and sell outputs and inputs among themselves. This occurs, for example, in Petroleum; Iron and steel; Lumber . . . wood . . . paper; Chemicals; Food; Pharmaceuticals; Radio . . . communication equipment. And such relationships change as sellers and buyers find and develop better alternatives.

The encompassing total system is interactive throughout: within, across, and among Industry Categories. Each Industry Category has its own dynamics. Whole Industry Categories interact among themselves. Thousands, tens of thousands, hundreds of thousands—millions!—of interactions take place everyday among companies in different Industry Categories: Electric utilities, for instance, supply energy to chemical companies. Chemical companies provide inputs for companies in Textile mill products, Petroleum, Motor vehicles and equipment. Petroleum provides major inputs for Electric utilities and for Chemicals and allied products; Fabricated metal products for Chemicals and allied products.*

Over time, patterns of interactions change quantitatively and qualitatively, as whole Industry Categories grow, shrink, and evolve. The whole system evolves in ways analogous to ecosystems of nature.†

Industries, lines of commerce, markets, and such, as defined in terms of the intrinsic natures and objective technical specifications of particular *outputs* of firms and "establishments" (e.g., plants), are arbitrary, indeed. They do not correspond well with roles and functions of firms and clusters of firms as, in fact, they are organized and behave individually in operating and strategic decisions, and interact among themselves in buying and selling. In general, such arbitrary constructs of the mind bear little enough relationship to the dynamic, real structures of industry systems, as defined by behavior, and markets composed of sentient and dynamic buyers and sellers. Derived concepts such as "concentration," "market dominance," or even "market share" are equally arbitrary and time-bound, and have equal power to obscure significant dynamic behavioral realities that cannot be so easily and neatly labeled and measured. Even the broad Industry Categories employed here need to be used with caution, for they, also, are necessarily and always in conditions of flux and development.

As one views corporations as components of industry systems, and observes them in those contexts, as is attempted in this work, their places in the encompassing scheme of things can be better understood as the elements they really are of an ordered, but organic and evolving whole, not just fortuitous entities existing in narrowly circumscribed static settings.

There is rhyme and reason as to where, and why, large corporations have appeared—or have not.

OCCURRENCE AND PRESENCE OF SMALL AND LARGE CORPORATIONS

Chapters 7 and 8 continue to search out, and firm up, greater understanding of where and why, in the whole structure of industry, large corporations have appeared.

---

*Such systemic interrelationships and interdependencies are recognized in "input-output tables" that have become common tools of econometric analysis.

†The coefficients of the input-output relationships of each "cell" in the input-output matrix change over time in consequence of technological change, change in relative values, constraints of public policy, changes in opportunity costs, etc., etc.

In sum, the data show how *different* large corporations are from small. Because of that difference, large corporations and small occupy very different niches and perform very different functions in our industrial structure and economy. Anyone who would better understand our contemporary industrial economy must grasp firmly those essential, well-nigh self-evident facts.

The emergence of large corporations is no mere matter of any process of concentration, especially of something that in some previous epoch had been unconcentrated. The emergence of large corporations has been an essential part of the processes of *innovation, transformation,* and *development* that have taken place in our industry as it has grown in magnitude and scale.

In earlier chapters, attention is given primarily to the *occurrence,* that is to say, the *numbers* of large corporations appearing in various Industry Groups and Industry Categories. The occurrence of large corporations among Industry Groups, Categories, and sectors was, and is, not a random phenomenon. Study of the relative *presence,* that is to say, the relative *asset masses* of large corporations here and there in industry, throws considerable additional light on the natures of the structures of industries and upon the evolution of the business community as a whole.

In thinking about "very small," "small," "large," and "very large" corporations, one must keep in mind from the outset that the entities involved differ in *kind* as well as in size or scale. Indeed, to emphasize, their differences as to *kind* are far more meaningful than their differences as to size. "Small" and "smaller" companies, in whatever Industry Group or Category or sector one may have in mind, are not merely "large" or "very large" corporations scaled down, or *vice versa.*

For example, in 1971, there were about 320,000 corporations in the asset-size bracket $100,000 to $250,000. These companies held $51 billion of assets, that is, 3.6 percent of all corporate assets. Their average size was $160,000. There were 4,000 corporations in the size bracket $10 million to $25 million; they held $61 billion of assets, that is, 4.3 percent of all corporate assets. Their average size was $15 million. These companies were, on the average, about 100 times the average size of the smaller corporations.

As reported by the IRS, there were 615 corporations holding assets of more than $250 million; in total, they held $770 billion of assets, representing well over 50 percent of all corporate assets. Their average size was $1.3 billion; which is to say that, on the average, they were about 100 times the size of the companies in the $10 million-$25 million range and about *10,000* times the size of the average companies in the $100,000 to $250,000 bracket.

Mid-size companies in the range of $10 million to $25 million are not mere magnified replicas of smaller companies, in which everything is multiplied by 100. Nor are the very largest companies mere scaled-up models of mid-size companies, in which all aspects are reproduced 100-fold, let alone being scaled-up replicas of the "small" companies, in which everything is merely multiplied by 10,000! They hold very *different kinds* of assets. They are not mere "concentrations" of the equivalents of hundreds or thousands of smallish firms.

The adjectives "big" and "small," useful as they may be, even as attached to corporations, necessarily suggest differences in *size*. But differences in dollar measures of assets (or of sales!), that appear to reflect differences in *sizes* of corporations in given industries, are closer to being surrogates for indications of differences as to *kinds*. Those are the differences that count in our contemporary industrial structure!

In sum, the masses of data that are presented in Chapters 7 and 8 reveal three general relationships:

1. Differences in "relative presence" of corporations of various sizes in the several Industry Categories reflect differences in the *kinds* of assets that are held by companies of those Categories. In Industry Categories where the relative presence of large companies is high—say, over 60 percent—the asset masses are more characteristic of *kinds* of assets held by large corporations. (See Exhibit 43.) Where the relative presence of *smaller* and *small* corporations is greater, say between 100 percent and 80 percent, the asset masses of those Industry Categories tend to be characterized more by *kinds* of assets held by smaller and small companies. (See Exhibit 52.)

2. Relative *occurrence* and relative *presence* of large corporations show strong association. Large corporations tend to occur relatively more often in Industry Categories whose asset masses are characterized by kinds of assets held by large companies. The inverse is true of Industry Categories characterized by the presence of small and smaller firms. There are clear functional relationships between relative occurrence and relative presence for both larger and large firms and for smaller and small firms.

3. A further association is that large corporations tend to occur, and their relative presence tends to be greater, in Industry Categories where their own average size *and* the average sizes of *other* firms, also, tend to be higher. The inverse is true of smaller and small companies: their occurrence and presence tend, both, to be greater in those Industry Categories where the *average size* of companies, exclusive of The 559, tends to be smaller.

These several relationships indicate that assets in Industry Categories characterized by (*a*) the occurrence and (*b*) the presence of large corporations and (*c*) larger average corporate size tend to be of very different kinds from those of Industries characterized by the occurrence and presence of smaller and small companies, as well as smaller average size.

These multiple associations are not mere statistical curiosities. They reflect *qualitative* as well as quantitative *differences* among firms of greatly different masses. That point, to repeat, is of the essence in understanding the very special roles played in our economy by the Largest Corporations. These roles are vastly different from those of smaller and small firms.

The assembled data indicate that particular underlying, basic conditions in several of the Industry systems have tended, in varying degrees, to encourage or permit the emergence of numbers of larger companies, their attainment of relative importance in those industry systems, and their growth to large and very large size. Conditions in other Industry Categories have been such that they are characterized to varying degrees by large numbers of smallish firms.

The "profiles" of the several Industry Categories, as given in terms of *occurrences* in them of numbers of corporations of various sizes, the *presence* of firms of various sizes, and *average size* of corporations, are set forth in a number of summary and detailed statistical tabulations in Chapter 8.

Explanations of the very different shapes of these profiles described by the patternings of hundreds and of thousands of firms in over 50 Industry Categories are not to be found in the idiosyncratic or adventitious behaviors of a handful of business adventurers and entrepreneurs. Explanations are to be sought—and found—in such "objective" factors as natures of inputs, conversion systems, outputs, and of input and output markets; potential economies of scale in access to critical inputs, in production, in marketing, and in financing; potential economies of vertical integration and of multiplant and multiproduct operations; state of the development of technology and managerial skills in the particular Industries. Social and political factors, no doubt, have also been at work in varying ways and to varying degrees that have had impacts on those profiles: public policy, provisions of taxation, subsidies, quotas, and tariffs, for instance.

The stronger the factors making for size in particular Industry systems, the greater have been the occurrence and presence of large firms and the larger the average size of both large and other firms. And the inverse has also held.

The development and patterning of large corporations in the business community has been an ordered process, no mere aberration to be explained in simplistic terms, or easily redirected or changed by simple legislative measures or judicial decrees. The growth and distribution of large corporations throughout the structure of American industry have been of the very essence of the nation's development over the past century.

THE LARGEST CORPORATIONS AND AMERICAN DEVELOPMENT, 1929-1971; THE DEMOGRAPHICS OF CORPORATIONS

In Chapters 9 and 10, the continuing development of large (and small) corporations is placed in context. First, in Chapter 9, attention is given to the "dynamic demographics" of corporations in the four decades 1921-71—the growth in numbers and the change in industry distribution of corporations of all sizes, especially very large corporations. Second, in Chapter 10, the development of corporations is placed in the context of the dynamic demographics of the American people and of the growing and transforming streams of production and patterns of consumption.

Among the outstanding features in the demographics of corporations in the years between 1929 and 1971 were these: (1) a corporate community growing in numbers and mass (faster than the human population) and changing markedly as to the "profiles" of "Major Industry Groups," as measured by numbers of firms and asset masses therein; (2) especially great growth of small incorporated business enterprises in industry sectors where data presented earlier strongly suggest that small scale is a positive advantage or, at least, that there are not strong advantages in large scale; (3) notable growth in numbers and total asset mass of very large corporations in Industries previously characterized by them, as well as in "new" Industries made possible by the several factors associated with *large* corporations.

Between 1929 and 1971, the nonfinancial corporate population increased by 1,270,000, from 322,000 to 1,592,000. In 1971 dollars, their total reported assets grew by $812 billion, from $598 billion to $1,411 billion. Of this total asset growth, $463 billion, or about 57 percent, was accounted for by The Largest Corporations (those that held assets in excess of $250 million in 1971 dollars), of which there were 200 in 1929 and 559 in 1971.

The greatest growth in numbers of corporations—*small* corporations—took place in Construction, Wholesale and retail trade, Services, and Transportation (no doubt, mostly independent truckers), and in Agriculture, forestry, and fisheries. The increase in numbers of corporations in these four Major Industry Groups accounted for about 70 percent of the total increase in numbers of companies.

The American corporate community had also grown tremendously in rich diversity. Its composition as to all the various kinds of enterprise now to be found had changed greatly, much of the change being occasioned by the emergence and growth of many kinds of enterprise scarcely known, or even nonexistent, in 1929.

A major feature in these corporate demographics was the growth in number, asset mass, and diversity of The Largest Corporations. Far from supplanting or "concentrating" small enterprise, the burgeoning community of large companies lived, grew, and evolved in symbiotic mutual relationships with the increasing hundreds of thousands of smaller and small corporations. (See Exhibits 54 and 55.)

In terms of Industry Categories, the largest increases in *numbers* of The Largest Corporations took place in industries particularly characteristic of "modern" and modernizing industries, e.g., Electric and gas utilities; Chemicals; Pharmaceuticals; Food processing; Radio . . . communication equipment . . . ; Motor vehicles and equipment; Air transportation; Office . . . computing . . . machines; Petroleum; Aircraft . . . . In 1929, none of The Largest Corporations had been identified with industries that became of major importance in the years after World War II: Pharmaceuticals; Office . . . computing machines; Household appliances; Radio . . . communication equipment . . . ; Aircraft . . . ; and Air transportation.* (See Exhibits 57 and 58.)

Correspondingly, occurrence and presence of Large Corporations being strongly associated, the greatest increases in *asset mass* took place in very much the same industries. (See Exhibit 59.)

Of particular significance are the growths in numbers and asset masses of Largest Corporations in Industries particularly associated with technological and sociological "revolutions" of the post-World War II era. Aside from the electric and gas utilities and telecommunications, notable increases in numbers of very large firms had come about, for instance, in Chemicals (the tremendous advance in petrochemicals); Pharmaceuticals (a giant leap forward in applied life sciences, molecular biology, and such); Food processing (largely associated with social and cultural changes associated with changing lifestyles and occupational patterns); Radio . . . communication . . . equipment (a "fallout" from wartime advances in sciences and application of radiation phenomena); Aircraft and Air transportation; and Office . . . computing . . . machines (largely associated with developments in computational technology combined with advances in electronics).

Large Corporations were in the vanguard of agents that were leading America into a far different era. They were, so obviously, prime engines of change. This historical fact would surely have amazed and tickled the fancy of the inquiring Adam Smith. It should give pause, and occasion for further thought, to inveterate, programmed critics of "Big Business."

One rather melancholy note: the number of railroads among The Largest Corporations decreased by 22; the reported value of railroad assets among the asset masses of The Largest companies had shrunk

---

*Some of The Largest Corporations had had positions in certain industries that acquired later importance; e.g., General Electric and Westinghouse in "Home appliances."

by almost $50 billion. Part of the decline and shrinkage was perhaps nominal rather than real—the consequence, in likelihood, of waves of bankruptcies and reorganizations in the 1930s, 1960s, and 1970s. But much of the shrinkage of value was surely all too real, reflecting disinvestment and consumption of capital in consequence of a near-lethal mixture of politicized and bungling regulation, poor management, and the growth of alternative modes of transport.

Another note of mixed emotional impact: transit companies had disappeared from the roster of Largest companies. This disappearance was primarily a consequence of takeovers by public authorities, sometimes in "bailout" operations.

Particular mention should also be made of the growth of the Electric and gas utilities and of the Telephone, telegraph . . . services. The former had passed through traumatic reorganization in consequence of the Public Utility Holding Company Act of 1935. When the dust cleared, the utility industry was scarcely recognizable, so complete had been the reshuffling of ownership and other relationships among the utilities. Because of both reorganization and real growth in the industry, the number of utilities among The Largest Corporations rose from 39, in 1929, to 106 in 1971. The value of their assets, in 1971 dollars, despite all the financial reorganization, more than doubled from $57 billion to $121 billion, accounting for almost 14 percent of the total increase in the assets of all of The Largest Corporations.

There is real question whether, from rational points of view, the present highly fragmented structure of the electric and gas utilities is preferable to a more consolidated, regionalized structure. But that is a whole other story. In any event, it seemed that America's thirst for electrified energy could never be slaked.

Telephone and telegraph companies among The Largest Corporations increased from 4 to 11; assets increased more than fourfold, from $16 billion to $69 billion. It would seem that there was no end to the need of Americans to communicate, be it in words, numbers, or images.

The increases in the assets of The Largest companies in these two Industry Categories, totaling about $118 billion, accounted for something like one-seventh of the entire increase in all corporate assets between 1929 and 1971!

The increases in the uses of electric power and communication were both indexes of and energizing forces in the growth and transformation of the American economy. These were no mere consequences of concentration, but real, honest-to-goodness surges of development.

In sum, the growth of the Largest Corporations of the many different kinds had gone hand in hand with the growth and changing composition of American industry. Indeed, the growth of these companies was a major, if not *the* major driving force behind the expansion and transformation of our industrial structure, in our continuing Industrial *Revolution.*

THE LARGEST CORPORATIONS AND AMERICAN DEVELOPMENT, 1929-1971; THE EVOLVING ENVIRONMENT

The development of the roster of The Largest Corporations took place in the immediate context of the development of the corporate community as a whole. This community is made up of all corporations of all sizes and all kinds, great and small. As actual and potential suppliers, customers, and agents; as suppliers' suppliers; as customers' customers; as actual and potential competitors, each is related to all, directly and indirectly.

This business community, as is shown, has grown and evolved in extraordinary fashion. Even now, it continues, still, to grow and evolve.

This business community exists and develops in the larger context of the encompassing environment which is the entire American System. This system includes, besides the business community, the human population of individuals and households in their millions; the many units of government; and the flowing and changing stream of goods and services they all produce, exchange, and consume.

In Chapter 10, the development of Large Corporations is related to the growth and change in the ambient System.

The kind of people we are is related to the kinds of goods and services we produce and have available for consumption. The kinds of goods and services we are able to generate are related to the kinds of businesses we have. The kinds of businesses we have are related to the "externalities" round about them, including the changing kinds of inputs that are available to them—goods and services from other businesses, and human resources from the human population. The kinds of goods and services that businesses are able to sell depend upon the kinds of buyers standing ready to buy—individuals, households, other businesses, and units of government.

As various elements in this system grow and evolve, that development makes possible and induces development in still other elements.

This is no mere hypothetical speculation. The reality of the economic community, including producing, consuming, and investing industry sectors; including sectors of "final demand," is measured, as was said, by "input/output" tables that represent in quantified fashion the interdependencies among the several producing sectors as well as the sources of the goods and services that are finally consumed.

All this has particular relevance for understanding the place of our Largest Corporations in the total scheme of things—in the American System. The growth and development of these productive entities has proceeded in systemic fashion with the system as a whole. Their growth and development, of course, has been made possible by the development of the whole. Most especially, the growth and development of these Largest Corporations has been basic to the material plenty that characterizes the system, to the growth of that system, and, most especially, to the distinctive qualitative changes that have transformed that system from what it used to be.

Consider our human demographics.

Between 1929 and 1971, we Americans not only grew in numbers; more spectacularly and significantly, as a people we were transformed in many ways. Previously living in rural and small communities, we became one of the most urban peoples in the world. Historically an agrarian people, we were now strongly industrial. Once a young people, like many Third World countries today (almost half of us in 1929 were under the age of 20), we are now much older (in 1971, over 30 percent of us were over 45). Our life expectancy increased by 14 years. In occupation, we had become a nation of white-collar and skilled blue-collar workers. The educational level of Americans had increased dramatically as the years and level of schooling and training advanced.

This transformation from rural-agrarian to urban-industrial; from agricultural and blue-collar workers to white-collar and skilled workers (with an increase of 20 million in women employed); from a youthful to a mature age distribution; from educational attainments typically stopping with grammar school to an annual flow of more than a million young people with collegiate and graduate degrees— all this went hand in hand with the increasing plenty, generated by our increasingly sophisticated industrial apparatus. This transformation of our population was made possible by our industrial development. The industrial development was supported by these transforming demographic changes. (See Exhibits 60-64.)

Direct connection between the development of the community of The Largest Corporations and the rest of the system, in terms of *growth* and *change*, is documented by data measuring both origination of Gross National Product in the several industry sectors and allocation of the flow of that wealth into consumption and investment expenditures for the outputs of industries. Sectors strongly characterized by the presence of The Largest Corporations were energizing sources—"leading" is not too strong a word—for both growth and for change in what we Americans produce and what we consume.

Briefly, between 1947 and 1971, when the Gross National Product rose by something like $614 billion (in 1971 dollars), an increase by a factor of 2.37, "Gross Product Originating" in some ten industry sectors strongly characterized by the presence of The Largest Corporations increased even more rapidly: Petroleum; Chemicals; Rubber and miscellaneous plastic products; Electrical machinery; Motor vehicles and equipment; Air transportation; Electric, gas . . . services; Telephone and telegraph; for instance.* Two large-company sectors failed to increase, the Railroads and Local and highway transportation (reflecting the decline of mass transit). Among certain industry sectors marked by small companies, Gross Product Originating in Motor freight transportation; Wholesale trade; and Services did increase more rapidly than the GNP as a whole. On the other hand, the Gross Product Originating in several small-company industries declined significantly: Coal mining; Leather and leather products; Water transportation. Agriculture, forestry, and fisheries, a sector deeply characterized by small business, although increasing absolutely, lagged notably behind in relative terms. (See Exhibits 66 and 67.)

On the allocation side, total expenditures, in 1971 dollars, rose from $302 billion in 1929 to $450 billion in 1945, to $1,063 billion in 1971, an increase of about 359 percent.† (See Exhibits 68 and 69.)

"Government purchases of goods and services" at federal and state and local levels (these do not include "transfer payments" like welfare and Social Security), rose from $38 billion in 1929, to $71 billion in 1947, to $234 billion in 1971; an increase of over 600 percent over the 42 years.

"Personal consumption expenditures" rose from $208 billion in 1929, to $296 billion in 1947, to $668 billion in 1971, an increase over the span of time of about 320 percent.

The *mix* of those allocations changed dramatically in the direction of purchases of outputs of goods and services produced by industries strongly characterized by presence of The Largest Corporations. A few examples make the point:

Expenditures	Percent increase 1929-71
Total personal consumption expenditures	321.2%
Motor vehicles and parts	461.9
Kitchen and other household appliances	700.0
Radio and television receivers	900.0
Gasoline and oil	766.7
Drug preparations and sundries	700.0
Electricity and gas	1,700.0
Telephone and telegraph	1,100.0

---

*Data as to "Gross Product Originating" by industry sectors, unfortunately, do not extend back to 1929.

†Reasonably reliable detailed data of this sort do go back to 1929.

The data come to this: the growth of The Largest Corporations in numbers and in asset mass—"occurrence" and "presence"—has been an integral element in the quantitative growth and the qualitative change, the *development,* of the entire American System—its economy, its society. For over 100 years, and more obviously over the past half-century, in networks and complexes of systemic, symbiotic relationships, the community of The Largest Corporations has grown and evolved in mutually dependent, supportive and interactive fashion with the rest of the total American human environmental system.

There is no way the American System could have developed into anything like it now is by means of an industrial structure characterized by small-scale, local enterprise, indispensable though small business is in many spheres where large scale is inappropriate and not viable. Suggestions that the American economy would be more productive at lower levels of cost and price if only large corporations were broken up into many pieces, or if American industry were organized on the basis of very, very large numbers of very small entities, must be dismissed as mere fanciful, dreamlike, fine-spun hypotheses, contary to ascertainable fact and reasonable analysis.

Our Large Corporations have, indeed, been indispensable engines of plenty, engines of growth, engines of change.

This fact clashes with another fact, just as clear: a very American ideological predisposition inclines us toward "smallness," against bigness; against any sizable mass of power.

Some implications of that clash are the subject of Chapter 13.

CORPORATE STRATEGIES, 1929-1971; PERSISTENCE, FALL, AND RISE OF VERY LARGE CORPORATIONS

Before getting on to that challenging collision between fact and feeling, we consider one further set of data and one further piece of analysis that round out the examination of the patterned occurrence and presence of very large corporations and industries, their place in the structure of the American System, and their roles in the rise of a new industrial order and in the development of that system. We look at persistence, decline, disappearance, emergence, and growth of individual Large Corporations over the period 1929-71. This is the subject of Chapter 11.

The varied fortunes of particular companies, taken together, tell us a great deal about the dynamics of our industrial system. In the many life histories of our Largest Corporations over the past 40 years and more lie important morals and lessons for corporate managements and implications for public policies.

The composition of the roster of The Largest Corporations in 1971 was very different from that of 1929. Moreover, there were now at least 559 companies as large as those on the earlier list.

Of The 200 of 1929, only 100 were identifiably still around in 1971. Of these, 75 were no longer among The Top 200; they had declined in relative ranking down among The Next 359. In fact, a few had actually shrunk in size over the 40-odd years! An even 100—half!—had disappeared from sight.

Mere size was no guarantee of vitality or longevity; not even of survival. Not even in an era of surging growth and forward movement.

On the brighter side, over the four decades, hundreds of corporations—459 of The 559 Largest of 1971—did grow to the point where they entered into, and swelled the ranks of The Largest. Many of these had been obscure little companies in 1929, if they had existed at all. Many of the newcomers had arisen in "newer" industries that had grown on the basis of new technologies, of applied science, or of innovation in business policy and basic strategy, and successful development and application of newer management techniques.

Of The Top 200 of 1971, no fewer than 125 had come to the fore as they prospered while older companies subsided or disappeared from view.

This turnover among The Largest Corporations—turbulence is not too strong a word—came about in various ways. (See Exhibits 70 and 71 and Appendix A.)

As to disappearance, first: two industries that had contained 82 of The 200 of 1929, the railroads (43) and the utilities (39), were utterly restructured. Through a combination of hard times, tenuous financial practices, and government policy, 64 of these companies disappeared, as such, in processes of reorganization and/or bankruptcy. New and fewer entities survived.

The four largest motion picture companies of 1929 were broken up by court-ordered divestiture in consequence of successful antitrust prosecution.

Each and every one of the eight Transit companies on the list of 1929 "disappeared" through combinations of bankruptcies and bailouts and takeovers by public authorities. Hard times, the automobile, and politicization of decision-making, especially as to fares and wages and employment, removed these and other mass-transit operations from the private sector, if not from the scene entirely.

The four largest coal companies of 1929 all disappeared. Depression, rising labor costs, and, especially, lethal competition from oil and gas, which continues to this day, were responsible in varying degrees. Maybe, someday, coal may make a comeback—given constructive government policy, technological advance, and, especially, massive allocations of capital, large-scale organization and large-scale managerial know-how.

Aside from such wholesale disappearances, a number of the Largest of 1929 were merged into larger, often much healthier companies, sometimes "conglomerates" that picked them up as "bargains," in part for their cash flow, which provided capital for redeployment into more promising uses, in part for their excess working capital, and even for "valuable" accumulated losses. Other corporate lions of 1929 simply disappeared, leaving scarcely a trace. Some of their names, once upon a time, had been household words; some were regarded as fit vehicles for prudent investments: Baldwin Locomotive Works, International Mercantile Marine, American Woolen, Studebaker, for instance—now gone with Ninevah and Tyre.

Now there were new household words in both newer and older industries—like Pepsico, International Business Machines, Xerox, Pfizer, General Mills, Avon Products, Whirlpool, Kaiser, Texas Instruments, Polaroid, Boeing, United Airlines, Columbia Broadcasting, Sperry and Hutchinson, Holiday Inns, and McDonald's—just for instance. All told, 350 corporations (not counting reorganized railroads and refurbished and expanded utilities) had come onto the roster of Largest Corporations. (See Exhibit 70, Part 2, and Exhibit 72.)

Some economists and political commentators have particular concern as to whether smaller companies can flourish and grow in the shade, so to speak, of established, much larger corporations. Evidence says "Yes." They ponder whether the preexistence, as it were, of large companies acts as a "barrier to entry" of smaller and small firms. Broad-brush evidence, spanning many industries and long spans of time, says "No."

In 11 Industry Categories where there were 64 of The 200 Largest of 1929, a total of 139 companies not on that list emerged among The 559 Largest of 1971, while 47 of the 64 of 1929 disappeared in one way or another from view. Altogether, 125 companies among The 200 Largest of 1971 had not been among The 200 of 1929. Of The 559 Largest of 1971, 448 had not been among The 200 of 1929. (See Exhibit 70, Parts 1 and 2, and Exhibits 71 and 72.)

Turnover, turbulence was even more a consequence of corporate growth than of decline. And not only of growth; even more, of innovation and change. Growth and change in our industry and economy were no mere abstractions brought on by abstract, unembodied, impersonal "forces." These developments were concrete results of specific actions of particular entities—among them, these 125 of the newer Largest Corporations of 1971: engines of growth, engines of change.

Behind the statistics of turnover among large corporations, their rise and fall, lies many a drama of doings, of complacence in executive suites and boardrooms; cautionary tales of managerial ineptitude; melancholy thoughts of what might have been; legends of imagination, decisiveness, perseverance, and daring. Models of what not to do; of what to do and how. Lots of "cases" for use in business schools committed to the training of entrepreneurial, responsible managers.

The ephemeral, fugitive nature of corporate vitality and success often escapes the consciousness of onlookers—critics and students— and practitioners alike.

Large size is no assurance of persistence. Newness is no barrier to growth.

LARGE CORPORATIONS: DEVELOPMENTS IN THE 1970s

Chapter 12 examines data that relate to the development and fortunes of our Largest Corporations since 1971, a benchmark year.

One purpose of this review of data of the 70s was to see whether patterns of occurrence and presence of very large corporations among the several Industry Categories, so clearly to be seen in the data of 1929 and 1971, still appeared in data that became available while this work was in progress. Another was to see whether the historic phenomena of growth, regression, and turnover in the membership of The Largest Corporations still went on.

In brief, the answer in both matters is "Yes." And this was fully to be expected.

The very Largest Corporations still accounted for about half of the assets of all nonfinancial corporations. They still occurred, and their presence was great in certain industrial sectors, far less or not at all in others.

Half of all the assets of nonfinancial corporations, in 1975, was still of sorts held by very large companies. The very Largest Corporations still occurred and their presence was greatest in Industry Categories where one would expect; for example, Telecommunications; Electric and gas utilities; Petroleum; Office and computing machines; Motor vehicles; Pharmaceuticals; Ferrous metal industries; Chemicals and allied products. In other Industry Categories, as was true in the past, their presence was relatively low, or nonexistent; for instance in Agriculture, forestry and fisheries; Furniture and fixtures; Retail trade; Construction; Wholesale trade; Services; Apparel. (See Exhibit 76, Parts 1 and 2.)

One trend, which was especially gratifying in light of widespread fears to the contrary, was the growth in *numbers* of corporations, especially small corporations. The total number of nonfinancial corporations, between 1971 and 1975, increased by a net of 275,000, from 1,596,200 to 1,867,400. Of this increase, 225,000, or 82 percent, had assets in 1975 of less than $1 million (in 1975 dollars). Small business was—it really should not be surprising—alive and well in America.

Size, alone, as in earlier periods, was no assurance of prosperity or even continuity. This is clear from what happened between 1971 and 1977 among The Largest Corporations in a sample of six important, large-corporation Industries: Petroleum; Chemical and allied products; Iron and steel; Food processing; Office, computing, and accounting machines; and Lumber . . . wood . . . paper and allied products. The growth rates among these companies were very uneven and, in a word, disappointing. Relative positions of many of the largest firms in all these industries changed dramatically. While some of the firms prospered and grew in "real" terms, a number of the Largest Corporations in these Industry Categories seem actually to have regressed.

In those six years of the 70s, numbers of firms not large enough to be on the roster of Largest Corporations in 1971 came on to the roster of The Largest in 1977 because of asset growth. Between 1971 and 1977, 19 companies in the Petroleum Industry Category grew to a size that would have put them on the roster had they then been that large in 1971. Six companies in Chemicals and allied products and in Food processing were added to the list. Four were added in Lumber . . . wood . . . paper and allied products. One was added in Office, computing, and accounting machines, in consequence of spectacularly successful growth over those six years.

Only in Iron and steel was there no addition to the roster; indeed, the smallest of the Largest steel companies of 1971 had disappeared through merger into a larger steel company.

In point of fact, the balance sheet values of the Largest Corporations of 1977 in these six important Industry Categories, as compared to those of 1971, strongly suggest that, although the figures do indicate some growth, in total, much of the seeming growth of the group of companies as a whole was a product of inflation. It is sure that *real* growth was notably less than the raw dollar figures would suggest. In *real* terms, it is likely that as many as half—perhaps more— of this sample of the Largest Corporations of 1971 barely kept up, if, indeed, they did, over the six following years, with the nominal growth of Gross National Product including the magnifying effects of inflation.

In recent years, numbers of key companies in key industries, perhaps whole industries, have failed to generate *real* additions to capital. This is concealed by the effects of inflation upon corporate income statements and balance sheets. In some, perhaps many, instances, we are actually *consuming* capital. There is a real question whether we are currently generating enough new industrial capital to provide *modern* jobs at internationally competitive levels so as even to maintain *current* per capita levels of Gross National Product, let alone to increase the level of national production, and to further our national economic and social development.

Congress is going to be called upon to give increasingly sophisticated, constructive thought to goals and objectives of national development and policies and means for their achievement.

THE LARGE CORPORATIONS: PUBLIC AND CORPORATE POLICY

Chapter 13 explores issues now before America and the managements of our large corporations that stem from the unresolved, even unrecognized dissonance between our absolute material need for very large-scale enterprise and our abiding unease in the presence of size and power of whatever sorts.

The occurrence and presence of very large corporations, here and there in American industry, are resultants of deep-rooted factors having to do with imperatives and comparative advantages of large-scale, massive-overhead, low-marginal cost activity; vertical integration; capital-intensivity; technology-intensivity; multiplant operation; multiproduct production and distribution; and such. In their respective spheres, very large corporations have been truly engines of plenty, of growth, and of change.

Until and unless the American people opt for a very different kind of life, large enterprises having those attributes will remain with us.

Until and unless the American people opt for taking over these enterprises and turning them into arms of government, they will remain in the private sector as privately owned corporations.

Nevertheless, essential though they may be, in the sense of providing the material base for the support of the American System, large corporations do appear in our midst as masses of *power,* looming far above the individual, seemingly beyond his control or even comprehension, apparently going their own ways for their own purposes.

The "image" of the large corporation, as perceived by most Americans, is inherently ambiguous. Are they necessary? Perhaps. But very disquieting.

There is an abiding tension between material facts and ideological predilection.

It is no wonder that public policy toward large corporations is uncertain, even inadvertent.

In the persistent tension between the economic necessity of large, institutional corporate enterprise and Americans' ideological preference for human-scale, "personal" business lie a number of implications and unresolved issues, some quite new.

Acceptance of bigness in business

This tension is manifested by the fact that the United States has no explicit, clear policy as regards large corporations. It might seem that bigness, as such, is not a violation of the Sherman Antitrust Act. But even that backhanded policy, enunciated long ago by the Supreme Court, not by Congress, is now less than altogether certain. Bills are continually being introduced in Congress and in state legislatures aimed in one way or another at bigness. In regulatory actions and in consequence of public and private litigation, clouds of uncertainty have arisen as to how far, and/or whether large corporations, or, at any rate, corporations with relatively large "shares" in "markets" or "lines of commerce," defined particular ways, are free to engage in *competitive* acts and behavior that, presumably, are completely open to smaller corporations, or, at any rate, companies with smaller "shares."[8]

It does sometimes seem that We-the-People would trade off economic efficiency for smallness, and that we would set different standards of behavior and performance for large and small corporations. But, then again, sometimes it does not.

Need for new ways of thinking about the American System

One implication of the abiding tension between economic necessity and ideological inclination is that, eventually, we shall have to accept the large corporation for what it is, an essential institution and instrument of the American System. When we pass that point of acceptance in principle, we can then deal pragmatically in a constructive mode with such matters as how the large corporation may best contribute to the common wealth, and how it may best be governed in its outward behavior and inner workings.

It is unlikely that we shall make any such resolve any time in the near future.

Another implication of the contradiction between the facts of big enterprise and our thoughts about it is that we stand in need of more sophisticated ways of thinking about the structure, the workings, and, especially, the dynamics of the American System.

We are beginning to understand the nature and workings of complex ecological systems of nature. We are now aware that an action taken here or there within such a system will surely have repercussions elsewhere in the system, and that some of these may be highly undesirable. We have not yet come to a comparable level of awareness as regards our own economic-industrial system.

Over time, it is probable that we shall be less inclined, as we often are now, to approach economic and social questions in a simplistic, mechanistic, often normative, even moralistic fashion. It is probable, and sorely needed, that we shall come increasingly to approach public economic issues in a more pragmatic, "systems" mode of thought; to think through what the real objectives are of national policies and their *total*, not just "first-strike" consequences.

That time, unfortunately, is also not likely to arrive in a rush, soon.

More particularly, we stand in need of a received economics that reasonably accurately describes and then explains how our industry and economy works, and how it is we have come to where we are from where we were.

Widely accepted hypotheses of the "micro-" economics of "monopolistic" and "imperfect" competition, which purport to describe the outcomes of competition among sellers who are "few" (and, ipso facto, large corporations are "few"!), lead to conclusions, in "macro-" terms, that bear little or no relationship to observable and measured historical facts. If these hypotheses, formulated over 40 years ago, had been valid, we would now, presumably, behold an economy in which prices and profits were endemically at monopoly levels; in which there had been no growth, no innovation, no development; in which the standard of life was pretty static as to content, and, at best, static as to level as well.

Clearly, this branch of economics has served us badly. Not only has it not been constructive in helping us to understand the structure, workings, and development of American industry, it has seriously confused and misled us.

This same failure of the economics of "monopolistic" and "imperfect" competition to explain dynamic realities was pointed out a generation ago by the late, great Professor Joseph A. Schumpeter of Harvard:

> ... If we list the items that enter the modern workman's budget and from 1899 on observe the course of their prices not in terms of money but in terms of the hours of labor that will buy them—i.e., each year's money prices divided by each year's hourly wage rates—we cannot fail to be struck by the rate of the advance which, considering the spectacular improvement in qualities, seems to have been greater and not smaller than it ever was before. If we economists were given less to wishful thinking and more to the observation of facts, doubts would immediately arise as to the realistic virtues of a theory that would have led us to expect a very different result. Nor is this all. As soon as we go into details and inquire into the individual items in which progress was most conspicuous, the trail leads

not to the doors of those firms that work under conditions of comparatively free competition but precisely to the doors of the large concerns—which, as in the case of agricultural machinery, also account for much of the progress in the competitive sector—and a shocking suspicion dawns upon us that big business may have had more to do with creating that standard of life than with keeping it down.[9]

Schumpeter went on to sketch a *dynamic systems* way of thinking that would do, and has done, a far better job of describing and explaining the System that we live in and that is dealt with in this work. It is a great pity of our time that more economists did not look where he was pointing.

Much thought has been directed by economists these past 40 years, especially under the leadership of John Maynard Keynes, toward trying to understand the nature and causes of cyclical or, in any case, short-run oscillations in such variables as employment, production, investment, interest, and money. A myriad of ideas have come forth from this branch of economics as to how, if at all, public fiscal and monetary policies might attenuate or offset such fluctuations. But little of all this has had anything to do with helping us to understand *growth, change,* and *development* of the American System. As Lord Keynes, himself, said, his tremendously influential work, *The General Theory of Employment, Interest and Money,* was ". . . primarily a study of the forces which determine *changes in the scale of output and employment as a whole.* . . ."[10] (Italics added.) *The General Theory* was not a treatise on the *development* of industrial, urban nations.

Some of our economists have been greatly interested in the *development* of Third World countries. Some of that interest, it seems, has cooled, in part because of the magnitude of the problems faced, and their seeming inherent intractability, magnified by frequent lack of competence and the more than occasional corruptibility of the leaders of many of those countries. In any event, not many of those earnest economists became greatly interested in our own developmental processes and problems, at home.

Altogether, mainstream economics in the United States has not been greatly preoccupied with the development—the growth and change—of our industrial structure and economy and of the encompassing System of which they are parts.

One particular implication of the state of tension, confusion, and irresolution in which America now finds itself is that we economists need to begin again to construct an economics that, as objectively and as rigorously as possible, will describe, explain, and help our policy-makers, our Executive Branch, and our Judiciary understand the American System—what it is, how it works, how it develops over time, how we got to where we are, and what the total impacts may be, throughout that System, of various policy alternatives.

Future development needs of the American System

Interest in our national development over the last 100 years, and especially over the last 40 or 50, and of the distinctive roles played by large corporations in that development, leads quickly to thoughts as to our national development in years ahead.

Over the next couple of decades, we shall have to provide jobs and sustenance for a population increasing each year by about a million and a half to two million souls. Even if we were to have no growth in real Gross National Product per capita, we would still have to raise the level of annual GNP by something like $300 billion, from something like $1,900 billion in 1977 to a hypothetical figure of $2,200 billion (in 1977 dollars) in the year 2000. This would represent an average annual rate of increase of a mere $66/100$ of 1 percent. Even that modest, scarcely perceptible, increase in the flow of wealth would require substantial increases in annual *net* capital formation.

If, for many different reasons, we wish to expand our Gross National Product faster than that, say at a rate of 3.2 percent, for the rest of the century—a rate that we have achieved in the past, and that was not generally judged to be excessive—we would have to approximately double annual GNP to something like $3,900 billion in 2000 (in 1977 dollars). Such an increase would make it possible not only to increase GNP per capita, but to improve significantly the well-being of our less fortunate fellow citizens and neighbors, to provide many needed and desired private, communal, and public amenities, and to contribute a share to the development of the Third and, especially, Fourth worlds.

Lower goals and lesser priorities would, of course, call for lower levels of production and capital formation.

Were we to adopt a national objective of, say, 3.2 percent average annual growth in Gross National Product, our annual Gross Private Domestic Investment would have to rise from a flow of something less than $300 billion, in 1977, to something over $600 billion (in 1977 dollars) in the year 2000. Of that flow of investment, based on recent experience, about 60 percent would have to be made by non-financial corporations of all kinds, large and small. In turn, about 60 percent of that would have to be made by the then Largest Corporations, of sizes comparable with the Largest of 1971. Those may number something like 1,500 to 2,000, by then. In any case, we are talking about an annual flow, by 2000, of *gross* investment amounting to around $220 billion into the kinds of assets that are, and will be, held by the Largest Corporations, if we are to generate the needed increases in volumes and levels of metals, energy, pharmaceuticals, computers and the like, rail and air transport, communications, appliances, electrical machinery, electronics, motor vehicles, and so on.

In terms of *net* annual investment, which runs at something like 60 percent of gross, we are looking at a figure, for the year 2000, of the order of $130 billion a year being committed by the then Largest Corporations, alone. And it is to *net* investment that we must look primarily for expansion of jobs and production.

In a political atmosphere little preoccupied by expansion and development, as compared to regulation and distribution, however desirable such policies may be, it is not clear when, or if, we shall cast up constructive public policies for that kind and that magnitude of economic growth and development.

This is a pity. For, unless we do generate such system *growth* and produce such system *development,* we shall find it politically and materially difficult or impossible to provide significant social and economic progress for our less fortunate citizens, for unmet communal needs, for measurable assistance to backward and lagging parts of the world.

Populist jeremiads from political leaders and aspirants will provide no more jobs, put no more bread on the table for anyone. Constructive public policies, in contrast, are called for.

By the year 2000, the assets (in 1977 dollars) of our existing Largest Corporations, and/or their successors or counterparts, will have to do more than double the value of their assets as compared to those of 1971, in *real* constant dollar terms. This means an average annual compound growth rate well over 3 percent. We have no clear indication that that will happen or that Congress has any concern over the matter.

Not only that. In many instances, large corporations upon which we depend for critical elements of our national support will have to conserve and redeploy capital from applications of diminishing comparative advantage into new, different uses, compatible with contemporary changes in comparative advantages around the world that affect the viability and competitive strength of American industry.

The entire American community, including individuals and households, smaller corporations and family businesses, and government has a lively interest in the vitality and development, over the decades to come, of these engines of growth and change.

Capital formation and taxation

Our Largest Corporations account for a large fraction of the whole flow of capital formation and its allocation; they are especially prominent in Industry Categories closely associated with infrastructure support of our urban industrial economy and society, and with industries, generally, that characterize "modernity." They have particular significance in the whole picture of capital formation and allocation and, accordingly, of our continuing development.

So do they, also, in the matter of taxation. Our Largest Corporations currently pay almost *two-thirds* of the *total* corporate income tax (net of credits, refunds, etc.). To an extent probably not generally recognized, whatever effects the corporate income tax may have in, and upon, our economy generally, they originate in, and are transmitted through, a few hundred of the very largest nonfinancial corporations. (See Exhibits 78 and 79.) Any measure that gives rise to tax liability, or is directed at increasing, decreasing, or changing the taxation of corporations has particular significance for the profitability and workings of those few Largest and their role in the processes of capital formation and allocation.

Moreover, our Largest Corporations, also to an extent perhaps not generally recognized, are a principal medium whereby the existence and operations of taxes on *individual* income and capital gains have impacts upon *corporate* capital formation, patterns of allocation of capital, and upon the growth of corporations.

First, the existence and workings of these taxes favor retention of corporate earnings over payment of dividends. They foster allocation and reallocation of capital by corporations as compared to either consumption or to allocation of capital by dividend recipients. This retention, so strongly encouraged by taxes upon individuals and other dividend recipients, is a prime source of *growth of corporations.*

This consequence of taxes upon individuals may well be a very good thing, altogether. But it was almost surely no part of explicit congressional intent.

Second, because these taxes favor corporate financial policies and operations that defer tax liability of dividend recipients and that put capital gains rather than dividends in the hands of stockholders, they provide strong motivation for mergers and acquisitions, among other financial measures. Tax considerations, along with presently depressed corporate values, are a major factor making for mergers and acquisitions in comparison to other motivation, such as possible real operating economies attributable to economies of greater scale, of vertical integration, and the like. Operating, "business" economies from merger are vulnerable to antitrust attack.

Indeed, *the combination* of tax considerations, that foster mergers and acquisitions, together with possible interpretations of the Clayton Act that discourage mergers and acquisitions where there would be real significant economies of scale, integration and such, goes a long way to explain the rise of "conglomerates," that is to say, assemblages of unlike companies with little or no possibility for operating economies or useful exchange among them of products or services. Never an intention of Congress, de facto national policy fosters the growth of "conglomerates"!

Although conglomerates and the very nature of conglomeracy are viewed with jaundiced eye by critics and by many in politics and government, and by some in business, they do, or may, actually serve socially useful functions by way of conserving capital and reallocating it from less profitable to more advantageous and more profitable uses within the corporate structure, beyond the reach of income taxes that would cycle accumulated capital into current public expenditures.

Tax reform and Large Corporations

Because The Largest Corporations pay the lion's share of all corporate income taxes, any serious reform of the way we tax corporations—in fact, any significant changes of any kind—necessarily would have major effect on and, especially, through these few hundred companies.

The burden of the corporate net income tax now falls most capriciously upon corporations of different sizes; of different structures of revenues and of costs and of capitalization; of different Industries. Under the tax upon net corporate income, the burdens of the costs of government fall upon corporations in ways that bear no significant relationship, direct or indirect, to the benefits they derive from those outlays nor to the social costs generated by their respective operations. Not by Congressional deliberate intent, but in fact, inefficient corporations, even large ones, are subsidized by the more efficient, even small ones, and by all other taxpayers including individuals and partnerships.

The corporate net income tax hangs as a disincentive over, and a drag upon, efforts to improve productivity and efficiency of corporations. It imposes a heavy penalty on precisely those corporations most able, and most needed, to contribute the capital formation we shall need so urgently.

The corporate net income tax places American corporations at a comparative disadvantage in competition with corporations of nations, such as Common Market countries, that impose a value-added tax on all corporations, profitable and unprofitable, alike. Moreover, that tax is generally remitted upon goods and services sold in export markets, which gives those foreign companies a considerable advantage in world trade, and even in the United States.

It could be that, with hard work and good fortune, we may come to see, and prefer, the practical advantages and the greater economic justice of the value-added tax over some of the dysfunctional characteristics of the corporate net income tax we now use.

In any case, removal of the double taxation of corporate earnings, once in the hands of the corporation and again in the hands of dividend recipients, would go a long way to ameliorate drag on capital formation, pressures in the direction of acquisitions and mergers, and pressures that distort processes of allocation of capital.

Large Corporations in Antitrust

As mentioned, the status of "bigness," as such, under antitrust law is far from clear. The murkiness traces back to the ambivalent American attitude toward bigness: we like and want the benefits of large-scale enterprise; of the economies of vertical integration, of multiplant and multiproduct production, of massive applications of new technologies; and the rest. But we are edgy about the presence of power. We hanker after the ideal of *small*, proprietary business.

The Supreme Court, it would seem, has said that bigness, per se, is not a "conspiracy" nor a restraint of trade. But certain important judicial interpretations of Section 2 of the Sherman Act, in cases involving allegations of attempts to "monopolize" and alleged acts of "monopolizing," do, in fact, seem to run in discriminating fashion against bigness, in both a relative, as well as an absolute, sense. *Big* competitors engage at their peril in competitive acts that, apparently, are completely open to small competitors.[8]

Section 7 of the Clayton Act, as regards acquisition by one company of the assets or the stock of another, implicitly discriminates against bigness. Acquisitions of assets or stock by large corporations, and not necessarily the largest, in a "line of commerce," have been struck down. On the other hand, some acquisitions have been let stand by administrative action and judicial decision that are very hard to distinguish from some that were not.

Briefs, findings and awards of juries, opinions and decisions of judges in continuing public and private litigation, add to the confusion, uncertainty, and tension.

Congress seems always to have bills before it that would go after bigness in one way or another. Only rarely are any of these adopted. Bills are currently around that would prohibit absolutely large corporations from making absolutely large acquisitions, but not relatively small corporations from making relatively large acquisitions. On the other hand, Congress itself has neither endorsed nor repudiated the idea, expressed in the *Steel* decision, that bigness is not an offense. Neither has it endorsed nor repudiated ideas expressed in the *Alcoa* decision (and since that decision, in other cases), that bigness *is* bad, that smallness is *good,* and that larger corporations should be, and are, prevented by law from acting like enterprising competitors and should be, and—under possible heavy penalty of treble damages—are, required to stand impassive before activities of smaller competitors designed to take business away from them.

From time to time, various proposals are put forth for breaking up large corporations. Congress holds hearings that seldom go far beyond declarative expressions of ideological preferences of the individuals testifying. But the fact is, technical and engineering problems aside, there is simply no way that our Largest Corporations can be fragmented into *large numbers* of really *small* operations. The nature of their assets and the magnitude of their scale stand in contradiction to such notions. Nor, when it comes down to practicalities, does it emerge that consumers and the nation as a whole would benefit. So, repeated hearings are about as far as Congress appears willing to go— for now.

It looks as though this ambiguous state of affairs will continue into the future. Juries and district and appellate judges, and Justices of the United States will continue to read their various and contradictory interpretations and predilections into law. Congress, no doubt accurately reflecting feelings of constituents, will continue unable and unwilling to take a clear stand. In time, if and when we become more understanding of the new industrial order in which we now live, we may well come to a resolve in favor of economic and technological imperatives.

As an alternative, we may, indeed, opt for an entirely different and "simpler" economic order, more like our own of the early 19th century, and similar to those of less developed economies and nations in our own day.

Resolution of the issue is probably not close at hand.

The Large Corporation, a modern institution

Large corporations, in law and for practical purposes, have become *institutions*. No longer are they, nor can they be, managed as mere *private* enterprises, run by their own private lights for their own private ends. They are too essential to the general and particular welfare of the entire community, too affected with, and too affecting of public interests of all sorts.

That is a technical and economic fact. It is also a political fact.

Many implications flow from that fact.

For one, it seems clear enough that public and peer opinion, to say nothing of law, now requires corporate decisions and actions to abide by values and norms expected of good citizens in a benevolent and upward-looking nation. Knavery on the part of directors, officers, or managers, even at junior levels, whether on small or large scale, whether unlawful or only unseemly and unbecoming, is incompatible with the status of corporations as important institutions in the community, and with expectations people have of important institutions, and of people, upon which and upon whom they rely.

For another, because large corporations *are* institutions, their governance, formerly regarded as their own internal, private affair, has now become a matter of public interest. Official, quasi-official, and private pressures now bear on corporations in such matters as the election of officers and directors; structure and workings of corporate boards and their committees; accounting policies, procedures, and practices; disclosures and representations to stockholders and the public at large; *rights* of employees, former employees—even of would-be employees—in conditions of employment, compensation and benefits, assignment to jobs, promotion, discharge, and the many other aspects of work and working in organizations.

As organizations of moment in the community, corporations have the capacity to become—in a real sense, they already are—institutions of political significance, akin to church, press, universities, unions, and other voluntary associations that individuals and groups have formed for their various purposes. In particular, they have the potential of standing alongside the individual and other institutions as counterpoise in our system of checks and balances that protect each from all, especially from the potential oppression inherent in the political powers of massive, growing, and often unresponsive government.

Such a role requires that the corporation maintain its credibility as an institution worthy of regard and respect. That independence also requires that the corporation keep itself at arm's length from government and other big institutions of our socio-politico-economic system.[11]

Viability and vitality

The *raison d'être* of the corporation is to *produce*. In a free economy, this requires that the corporation be able to compete effectively in input markets for human resources, capital, materials, space; in output markets, for sale of its goods and services; be able to convert inputs into outputs efficiently; to evolve appropriately in response to changing exigencies and opportunities in the surrounding environment; and to relate itself effectively to other significant entities: to other corporations; to government agencies; to labor unions, and to private organizations and groups of many sorts.

Stockholders, creditors, employees, suppliers, distributors, customers, local taxing authorities, indeed the community at large, all, have a lively interest in the corporation's continued healthy operations.

In fact, the vitality of too many corporations, as measured by commonly used financial and statistical life signs, has left much to be desired over the past decade and more. Their so-so earnings records represent capital formation considerably below levels the economy requires for adequate development. In a goodly number of instances, because of high and seemingly increasing inflation, *real* earnings, based on tough, objective accounting, were almost surely less than those reported on the basis of "generally accepted accounting principles," which include capital consumption allowances related to historical costs, and amortization and depreciation at rates slower than realities of obsolescence and "replacement" would indicate. In many instances, *real* losses are concealed by apparent profits arising out of inflation.

Some managements, probably, have been complacent or simply unequal to the task of leading their companies in a changing world. The problems of some industries, the utilities for example, have been exacerbated by unresponsive, often doctrinaire, or politically influenced regulatory commissions. Our tax structure, as mentioned, is something of a drag in its own right.

Not only do directors, managers, stockholders of corporations have grounds for concern, We-the-People, also, have a genuine interest in the health and good management of our corporations, just as we do in the health of other key institutions including our universities, our hospitals, our labor unions.

Management's mandate

Directors and executives of The Largest Corporations rarely own more than a very small fraction of the equity of the company they manage. The sanction under which they operate is ability to produce *results,* not mere ownership, as is the case with small businesses. To maintain that sanction, they have to *continue* to produce results. It is, in principle, a pragmatic rather than a philosophical sanction.

Producing "results" is now far more than simply getting good rates of return on assets employed, one year at a time. Indispensable as it is, efficient management within present and established lines of business, with present product facilities, management structures and the rest, for many companies will not suffice to produce acceptable results. In a rapidly changing world, getting *results* is increasingly a matter of "asset-management" through such measures as mergers and acquisitions, setting up of joint ventures and redeployment of assets out of older uses into new, even into different, industries, and taking measures to minimize taxes.

More and more, the directors and executives of our Largest Corporations are faced with the necessity of *transforming* their companies, even as they operate from year to year. Old comparative advantages and sources of competitive strength are disappearing into history. New sources of supply are needed; new manufacturing processes are needed; new products, even whole new product lines—whole new categories of goods and services; new channels of distribution; new financial structures; new management capabilities and organization structures; new management information systems.

Directors and managers now find themselves judged by stockholders, the financial community, employees, unions, and the public at large, not only by their ability to produce goods and services and utilize given and available resources at a profit, but also to meet new and evolving societal expectations, and to deal with a host of new issues raised by changing and emerging circumstances of a dynamic and complex world. The leaderships of many of our Largest Corporations are increasingly aware of, and responsive to, these new, more complex norms. That awareness and that point of view are getting passed down through the organization in a number of leading corporations.

If the mandate to manage is to be retained, the results called for will increasingly include successful adaptation and evolution, successful redeployment of assets, successful transformation of strategy and policy, all, beyond current, year-by-year profits.

Directors and managers of our Largest Corporations will find it helpful, in maintaining their mandate to lead their companies, to bear in mind that these engines of plenty, of growth, of change are, indeed, to the rest of the community, awesome institutions. Continued recognition of political fact should help them keep useful perspective; to maintain a sense of responsibility, constraint, and accountability; and to preserve a sense—not too strong, please—of justifiable pride at being chosen for important positions of leadership in our economy and community of institutions.

NOTES

1. Adolf A. Means, Jr., and Gardiner C. Means, *The Modern Corporation and Private Property* (New York: The Macmillan Company, 1932).

2. This book, like that of Berle and Means and other studies of business corporations, is primarily concerned with *nonfinancial* corporations, rather to the exclusion of those in finance and, say, insurance. This focus is somewhat arbitrary, but it does reduce the bulk of the work, documentation, and consequent text—and that is a blessing for reader as well as writer.

   There are other reasons. Financial institutions, indispensable though they may be, are intermediaries, facilitators. The services they produce are largely means to ends. Although they figure importantly in the network of transactions and the system of relationships of ownership and credit, their contributions to the Gross National Product and National Income are relatively small.

   A companion study of the rise and systemic functions of financial institutions in the American System that would place the evolution of those institutions in the context of the evolution of the whole, would be a fascinating enterprise—for some other occasion.

3. *Corporate size* in this work, as in that of Berle and Means, is measured by value of *assets*. The Internal Revenue Service, in its massive compilation of corporate financial data, also uses *assets* when classifying corporations by size. In an ideal sense, for measuring corporate size, I would prefer "value added," which, in principle, is the difference between the value of the corporation's sales and the total cost of inputs of goods and services purchased from vendors. In general concept, value added is a measure of the contribution by the corporation to the Gross National Product. Accordingly, it is a measure of the *impact* of the individual corporation upon the economy

through its generation of wealth. However, such data are difficult or impossible to come by from data published by corporations.

Value of *sales* is another yardstick for measuring size. In its determination, it is probably a less ambiguous figure than value of assets. However, value of sales is also probably somewhat less reliable than value of assets as a surrogate for measuring and comparing relative contributions to, or relative impacts upon, the economy as among very capital-intensive industries, such as utilities, and less capital-intensive industries, such as retailing.

As a practical and significant consideration, use of value of assets makes it possible to place and measure industries in the context of the comprehensive compilations published by the Internal Revenue Service.

4. The 1929 figures are "inflated" to express values in approximate terms of 1971 and 1977 dollars of less purchasing power. In no sense do they represent "current" or "replacement" costs of those particular assets.

The smallest corporation on the 1929 list held assets reported as $82 million. Between 1929 and 1971, the general price level, as measured by several key indexes used for reporting National Income Account data in "constant dollars," rose by a factor somewhat greater than 3. (See *Economic Report of the President . . . January 1979*, Tables B-3 and B-4, pp. 186-88.) Multiplying the $82 million figure by something more than three–specifically 3.0675–gives a round figure of $250 million, in terms of 1971 dollars. By happy chance, the figure of $250 million was also the lower limit of the largest size class for which corporation income statement, balance sheet, and tax data are given by the IRS *Source Book* for 1971. This was convenient for making broad, not too precise observations and comparisons relating to The Largest Corporations of 1929 and 1971 and their place in the corporate community.

See also Appendix A, General Note 7.

5. These Industry Categories are described and defined in Appendix B, Note 3, in terms of Standard Enterprise Classification Codes and Standard Industry Classification Codes.

6. The year 1971 was used in this study because, when it was begun, that was the latest year for which the extensive, detailed financial data of corporations published by the Internal Revenue Service were available. This massive publication is entitled *Source Book, Statistics of Income . . . Corporations Income Tax Returns*. There is a lag of several years in the publication of these data, in part because corporation returns are "open" for three years for purposes of amendment. Actual compilation and publication require additional time. In Chapter 12, we consider the corporate population of 1975, and a large sample of The Largest Corporations of 1977.

7. Between 1971 and 1977, because of inflation, the "deflators" rose by a factor of about 1.5 (*Economic Report . . . 1979*).

8. See Chapter 13, Notes 6, 7, and 8.

9. Joseph A. Schumpeter, *Capitalism, Socialism, and Democracy*, 3d ed. (New York: Harper & Brothers, 1950), pp. 81-82.

10. John Maynard Keynes, *The General Theory of Employment, Interest and Money* (New York: Harcourt, Brace & Co., 1936), p. iii.

11. See Chapter 13, Note 10.

EXHIBIT 1
The 200 Largest Nonfinancial Corporations, 1929 and 1971, and the 559 Largest in 1971, as measured by assets; by Industry Category*

Industry Category†	Reported values of assets ($ millions)		
	1929	1929 (in 1971 dollars)	1971
1. Agriculture and fisheries			
Among The 200 Largest			
Total, 200 Largest, 1929	$ 0.0	$ 0.0	
Total, 200 Largest, 1971			$ 0.0
Among The Next 359 Largest, 1971			
Total, 359 Next Largest, 1971			$ 0.0
Total, 559 Largest, 1971			$ 0.0
2. Iron and steel			
Among The 200 Largest			
United States Steel Corporation	$ 2,286.1	$ 7,012.6	$ 6,408.6
Bethlehem Steel Corporation	801.6	2,458.9	3,452.3
Republic Steel Corporation	331.7	1,017.5	1,755.3
Lykes-Youngstown Corp.[1]*†	235.7	723.0	1,439.1
Jones & Laughlin Steel Corporation[2]	222.0	681.0	
Wheeling-Pittsburg Steel Corp.[3]	128.3	393.6	
Crucible Steel Company of America[4]	124.3	381.3	
National Steel Corporation	120.8	370.6	1,842.9
Armco Steel Corporation[5]	104.3	319.9	2,044.4
Inland Steel Corporation	103.2	316.6	1,376.6
Cliffs Corporation[6]	98.0	300.6	
Total, 200 Largest, 1929	$ 4,556.0	$ 13,975.5	
Total, 200 Largest, 1971			$ 18,319.2
Among The Next 359 Largest, 1971			
Kaiser Steel Corporation			$ 727.3
Wheeling-Pittsburgh Steel Corp.[3]	[$ 128.3	$ 393.6]	610.8
Ogden Corporation.			557.5
Colt Industries Incorporated[4]	[124.3	381.3]	537.6
Allegheny Ludlum Industries Incorporated			441.9
Chromalloy American Corporation			351.3
Interlake Incorporated			349.0
Hanna Mining Company			315.5
Granite City Steel Company			312.7
McLouth Steel Corporation			309.9
Cyclops Corporation			304.5
NVF Company			270.5
Total, 359 Next Largest, 1971			$ 5,088.5
Total, 559 Largest, 1971			$ 23,407.7
3. Nonferrous metals			
Among The 200 Largest			
Anaconda Company	$ 680.6	$ 2,087.7	$ 1,454.1
Kennecott Copper Corporation	337.8	1,036.2	1,843.2
Aluminum Company of America	300.0	920.3	2,664.6
American Smelting & Refining Company	241.0	739.3	905.9
Phelps Dodge Corporation	124.7	382.5	988.7
NL Industries[7]	108.4	332.5	
American Metal Climax, Inc.[8]	82.4	252.7	1,253.3
United States Smelting, Refining & Mining Co.[9]	81.5	250.0	
Reynolds Metals Company			1,928.0
Kaiser Aluminum & Chemical Corporation			1,670.1
Total, 200 Largest, 1929	$ 1,956.4	$ 6,001.3	
Total, 200 Largest, 1971			$ 12,707.9

*See Appendix B, "Industry Categories and Their Composition."
†For explanatory footnotes and comments on individual corporations, see Appendix A, "Notes to Exhibit 1."

EXHIBIT 1 *(continued)*

Industry Category	Reported values of assets ($ millions)		
	1929	1929 (in 1971 dollars)	1971
3. Nonferrous metals *(continued)*			
Among The Next 359 Largest			
NL Industries[7]	[$ 108.4	$ 332.5]	$ 782.4
Newmont Mining Corporation			744.6
Englehard Minerals & Chemicals Corporation			696.5
Cerro Corporation			551.3
Revere Copper & Brass Incorporated			479.1
Essex International Incorporated			407.9
Howmet Corporation			386.4
Cyprus Mines Corporation			367.5
General Cable Corporation			332.8
Scovill Manufacturing Company			303.7
Total, 359 Next Largest, 1971			$ 5,052.2
Total, 559 Largest, 1971			$ 17,760.1
4. Coal			
Among The 200 Largest			
Glen Alden Coal Company[10]	$ 300.0	$ 920.3	
Pittsburgh Coal Company[11]	171.5	526.1	
Philadelphia & Reading Coal Corporation[12]	129.0	395.7	
Consolidation Coal Company[11]	94.0	288.3	
Total, 200 Largest, 1929	$ 694.5	$ 2,130.4	
Total, 200 Largest, 1971			$ 0.0
Among The Next 359 Largest			
Utah International Incorporated			$ 528.8
Pittston Company			446.6
Eastern Gas and Fuel Associates			438.2
Total, 359 Next Largest, 1971			$ 1,413.6
Total, 559 Largest, 1971			$ 1,413.6
5. Petroleum			
Among The 200 Largest			
Standard Oil Company (New Jersey)	$ 1,767.3	$ 5,421.2	$ 20,315.2
Standard Oil Company (Indiana)	850.0	2,607.4	5,650.7
Mobil Oil Corporation [13, 19]	708.4	2,173.0	8,552.3
Texaco Incorporated[14]	609.8	1,870.6	10,933.3
Standard Oil Company of California	604.7	1,854.9	7,513.2
Shell Oil Company[15]	486.4	1,492.0	4,646.3
Gulf Oil Corporation	430.9	1,321.8	9,466.0
Sinclair Oil Corporation[16]	400.6	1,228.8	
The Prairie Oil & Gas Company[17]	209.8	643.6	
Prairie Pipe Line Company[17]	140.5	431.0	
Phillips Petroleum Company	145.3	445.7	3,166.7
Union Oil of California[18]			2,564.8
Union Oil Associates, Incorporated[18]	240.0	736.2	
The Pure Oil Company[18]	215.4	660.7	
Vacuum Oil Company[19]	205.7	631.0	
Continental Oil Company[11]	198.0	607.4	3,048.7
Atlantic Richfield Company[20]	167.2	512.9	4,704.1
Richfield Oil Company of California[20]	131.9	404.6	
Tide Water Associated Oil Company[21]	251.4	771.2	
Sinclair Crude Oil Purchasing Company[16]	111.9	343.3	
Marathon Oil Company[22]	110.6	339.3	1,391.4
Tenneco Corporation			4,565.2
Sun Oil Company			2,813.3
Occidental Petroleum Corporation			2,580.0
Cities Service Company[23]	[989.6	3,035.6]	2,325.3
Getty Oil Company[21]			2,015.3
Standard Oil Company (Ohio)			1,815.2
Amerada Hess Corporation			1,328.2
Ashland Oil Incorporated			1,030.2
Total, 200 Largest, 1929	$ 7,985.9	$ 24,496.7	
Total, 200 Largest, 1971			$100,425.4

EXHIBIT 1 *(continued)*

	Reported values of assets ($ millions)		
Industry Category	1929	1929 (in 1971 dollars)	1971
5. Petroleum *(continued)*			
Among The Next 359 Largest			
Schlumberger Ltd.			$ 861.2
Kerr-McGee Corporation			762.5
Williams Company			722.3
Halliburton Company			685.2
Superior Oil Company			540.8
Murphy Oil Corporation			492.1
Zapata Corporation			464.1
Commonwealth Oil Refining Company Incorporated			357.8
McCulloch Oil Corporation			276.5
Fluor Corporation			258.4
Total, 359 Next Largest, 1971			$ 5,420.9
Total, 559 Largest, 1971			$105,846.3
6. Construction			
Among The 200 Largest			
Total, 200 Largest, 1929	$ 0.0	$ 0.0	
Total, 200 Largest, 1971			$ 0.0
Among The Next 359 Largest			
Dillingham Corporation			$ 528.6
J. Ray McDermott & Company Incorporated			373.8
Kaiser Industries Corporation			298.8
Total, 359 Next Largest, 1971			$ 1,201.2
Total, 559 Largest, 1971			$ 1,201.2
7. Food and kindred products, except: Meat; Dairy; Alcoholic beverages			
Among The 200 Largest			
United Brands Co.[24]	$ 226.0	$ 693.3	
Amstar Corp.[25]	157.1	481.9	
Nabisco Inc.[26]	133.2	408.6	
CPC International Inc.[27]	126.7	388.7	$ 1,042.7
General Foods Corporation[27]			1,596.8
Ralston Purina Company			897.9
Total, 200 Largest, 1929	$ 643.0	$ 1,972.4	
Total, 200 Largest, 1971			$ 3,537.4
Among The Next 359 Largest			
General Mills Incorporated			$ 817.8
H. J. Heinz Company			808.2
Norton Simon Incorporated			791.4
Consolidated Foods Corporation			782.0
Standard Brands Incorporated			697.3
Campbell Soup Company			677.5
Nabisco Inc.	[$ 133.2	$ 408.6]	633.4
Delmonte Corporation			584.2
Castle & Cooke Incorporated			537.7
Quaker Oats Company			423.7
Pillsbury Company			407.1
Kellogg Company			378.3
Amstar Corp.	[$ 157.1	$ 481.9]	335.0
Anderson Clayton & Company			329.1
Great Western United Corporation			313.3
Libby McNeil & Libby			268.5
Total, 359 Next Largest, 1971			$ 8,784.5
Total, 559 Largest, 1971			$ 12,321.9

EXHIBIT 1 *(continued)*

Industry Category	1929	1929 (in 1971 dollars)	1971
8. Meat and meat products			
Among The 200 Largest			
Greyhound Corporation[28]			$ 1,143.2
Armour & Company[28]	$ 452.3	$ 1,387.4	
Swift & Company	351.2	1,077.3	
Ling-Temco-Vought Incorporated[2, 29]			1,961.5
Wilson & Company, Incorporated[29]	98.0	300.6	
United Brands Company[24]	[226.0	693.3]	1,069.2
Total, 200 Largest, 1929	$ 901.5	$ 2,765.4	
Total, 200 Largest, 1971			$ 4,173.9
Among The Next 359 Largest			
Swift & Company	[$ 351.2	$ 1,077.3]	$ 869.3
General Host Corporation			281.9
Total, 359 Next Largest, 1971			$ 1,151.2
Total, 559 Largest, 1971			$ 5,325.1
9. Dairy and dairy products			
Among The 200 Largest			
Kraftco Company[30]	$ 224.5	$ 688.7	$ 1,163.8
The Borden Company	174.0	533.7	1,258.0
Beatrice Foods Company			934.2
Total, 200 Largest, 1929	$ 398.5	$ 1,222.4	
Total, 200 Largest, 1971			$ 3,356.0
Among The Next 359 Largest			
Foremost-McKesson Incorporated			713.0
Carnation Company			594.6
Pet Incorporated			401.4
Total, 359 Next Largest, 1971			$ 1,709.0
Total, 559 Largest, 1971			$ 5,065.0
10. Alcoholic beverages			
Among The 200 Largest			
National Distillers & Chemical Corporation			$ 932.2
Total, 200 Largest, 1929	$ 0.0	$ 0.0	
Total, 200 Largest, 1971			$ 932.2
Among The Next 359 Largest			
Joseph E. Seagram & Sons Incorporated			$ 874.2
Anheuser-Busch Incorporated			653.9
Joseph Schlitz Brewing Company			369.7
Heublein Incorporated			267.4
Pabst Brewing Company			257.7
Total, 359 Next Largest, 1971			$ 2,422.9
Total, 559 Largest, 1971			$ 3,355.1
11. Bottled and canned soft drinks and flavorings			
Among The 200 Largest			
Coca Cola Company			$ 1,107.9
Total, 200 Largest, 1929	$ 0.0	$ 0.0	
Total, 200 Largest, 1971			$ 1,107.9
Among The Next 359 Largest			
Pepsico Incorporated			$ 827.7
Total, 359 Next Largest, 1971			$ 827.7
Total, 559 Largest, 1971			$ 1,935.6
12. Tobacco manufacturing			
Among The 200 Largest			
American Brands[31]	$ 265.4	$ 814.1	$ 1,929.0
R. J. Reynolds Industries[32]	163.1	500.3	1,972.7
Liggett & Myers Inc.[33]	150.3	461.0	
Loews Corporation[34]			1,153.9

Reported values of assets ($ millions)

EXHIBIT 1 *(continued)*

	Reported values of assets ($ millions)		
Industry Category	1929	1929 (in 1971 dollars)	1971
12. Tobacco manufacturing *(continued)*			
P. Lorillard Company[34]	$ 110.0	$ 337.4	
Philip Morris Incorporated			$ 1,392.0
Total, 200 Largest, 1929	$ 688.8	$ 2,112.9	
Total, 200 Largest, 1971			$ 6,447.6
Among The Next 359 Largest			
Liggett & Myers Inc.	[$ 150.3	$ 461.0]	$ 597.9
Total, 359 Next Largest, 1971			$ 597.9
Total, 559 Largest, 1971			$ 7,045.5
13. Textile mill products			
Among The 200 Largest			
American Woolen Company[35]	$ 113.9	$ 349.4	
Burlington Industries Incorporated			$ 1,390.2
Total, 200 Largest, 1929	$ 113.9	$ 349.4	
Total, 200 Largest, 1971			$ 1,390.2
Among The Next 359 Largest			
United Merchants & Manufacturers Incorporated			$ 815.3
J. P. Stevens & Company Incorporated			617.7
Springs Mills Incorporated			347.3
M. Lowenstein & Sons Incorporated			312.0
Indian Head Incorporated			294.3
Dan River Incorporated			280.5
Cannon Mills Company			266.2
West Point–Pepperell Incorporated			256.2
Total, 359 Next Largest, 1971			$ 3,189.5
Total, 559 Largest, 1971			$ 4,579.7
14. Apparel and other finished fabric products			
Among The 200 Largest			
U.S. Industries Incorporated			$ 933.5
Total, 200 Largest, 1929	$ 0.0	$ 0.0	
Total, 200 Largest, 1971			$ 933.5
Among The Next 359 Largest			
Genesco Incorporated			$ 616.4
Kayser-Roth Corporation			362.8
Cluett Peabody & Company Incorporated			307.7
Hart Schaffner & Marx			250.1
Total, 359 Next Largest, 1971			$ 1,537.0
Total, 559 Largest, 1971			$ 2,470.5
15. Lumber and wood products and paper and allied products, except: Furniture			
Among The 200 Largest			
International Paper Company[36, 37]	$ 686.5	$ 2,105.8	$ 2,037.9
Crown Zellerbach Corporation	117.7	361.0	1,030.7
Long-Bell Corporation[37]	116.1	356.1	
Minnesota & Ontario Paper Company[38]	90.3	277.0	
Boise Cascade Corporation[38]			2,194.1
Weyerhaeuser Company			2,077.8
Georgia Pacific Corporation			1,872.7
Champion International			1,398.0
St. Regis Paper Company			957.2
Kimberly Clark Company			938.5
Total, 200 Largest, 1929	$ 1,010.6	$ 3,100.0	
Total, 200 Largest, 1971			$ 12,506.9
Among The Next 359 Largest			
Mead Corporation			$ 868.9
Scott Paper Company			858.6
Union Camp Corporation			573.4
Westvaco Corporation			529.7

EXHIBIT 1 *(continued)*

Industry Category	Reported values of assets ($ millions)		
	1929	1929 (in 1971 dollars)	1971
15. Lumber . . . wood . . . paper . . . products *(continued)*			
Evans Products Company			$ 516.6
Great Northern Nekoosa Corporation			441.1
Diamond International Corporation			404.0
Hammermill Paper Company			358.2
Potlatch Forests Incorporated			328.3
Total, 359 Next Largest, 1971			$ 4,878.8
Total, 559 Largest, 1971			$ 17,385.7
16. Furniture and fixtures			
Among The 200 Largest			
Total, 200 Largest, 1929	$ 0.0	$ 0.0	
Total, 200 Largest, 1971			$ 0.0
Among The Next 359 Largest, 1971			
Total, 359 Next Largest, 1971			$ 0.0
Total, 559 Largest, 1971			$ 0.0
17. Printing and publishing and allied industries			
Total, 200 Largest, 1929	$ 0.0	$ 0.0	
Total, 200 Largest, 1971			$ 0.0
Among The Next 359 Largest			
Time Incorporated			$ 544.1
Times-Mirror Company			441.1
Macmillan Incorporated			410.0
Grolier Incorporated			399.1
McGraw-Hill Incorporated			352.3
R. R. Donnelley & Sons Company			303.3
Gannett Company Incorporated			252.2
Total, 359 Next Largest, 1971			$ 2,702.1
Total, 559 Largest, 1971			$ 2,702.1
18. Chemicals and allied products, except: Pharmaceuticals; Soaps, cleaners, and toiletries			
Among The 200 Largest			
E. I. Du Pont de Nemours and Company	$ 497.3	$ 1,525.5	$ 3,998.5
Union Carbide Corporation	306.6	940.5	3,554.7
Allied Chemical Corporation[39]	277.2	850.3	1,636.7
Koppers Company Inc.[40]	250.0	766.9	
Dow Chemical Company			3,078.8
Monsanto Company			2,153.5
Minnesota Mining & Manufacturing Company			1,745.2
Celanese Corporation			1,660.0
W. R. Grace & Company			1,647.7
Olin Corporation			1,190.9
FMC Corporation			1,095.5
Total, 200 Largest, 1929	$ 1,331.1	$ 4,083.1	
Total, 200 Largest, 1971			$ 21,761.5
Among The Next 359 Largest			
Dart Industries Incorporated			$ 833.6
Hercules Incorporated			781.8
Diamond Shamrock Corporation			702.9
Ethyl Corporation			639.8
Rohm & Haas Company			634.3
GAF Corporation			588.3
Airco Incorporated			583.3
Armstrong Cork Company			560.4
Stauffer Chemical Company			504.9
Akzona Incorporated			491.2
Air Products and Chemicals Incorporated			452.8
Koppers Company Inc.[40]	[$ 250.0	$ 766.9]	430.7
Pennwalt Corporation			390.6

EXHIBIT 1 *(continued)*

Industry Category	1929	1929 (in 1971 dollars)	1971
18. Chemicals . . . *(continued)*			
The Sherwin Williams Company			$ 390.5
Cabot Corporation			372.9
Chemetron Corporation			296.9
Total, 359 Next Largest, 1971			$ 8,654.9
Total, 559 Largest, 1971			$ 30,416.4
19. Pharmaceuticals and medical equipment and supplies			
Among The 200 Largest			
American Cyanamid Company			$ 1,281.2
Warner-Lambert Company			1,085.7
Pfizer Incorporated			1,036.6
American Home Products Corporation			925.5
Total, 200 Largest, 1929	$ 0.0	$ 0.0	
Total, 200 Largest, 1971			$ 4,329.0
Among The Next 359 Largest			
Johnson & Johnson			$ 830.0
Eli Lilly & Company			787.3
Squibb Corporation			780.7
Merck & Company Incorporated			709.2
Abbott Laboratories			464.6
Sterling Drug Incorporated			457.8
Upjohn Company			421.2
American Hospital Supply Corporation			394.7
Schering-Plough Corporation			378.4
Richardson-Merrell Incorporated			374.3
Baxter Laboratories Incorporated			368.6
Morton-Norwich Products Incorporated			366.4
Sybron Corporation			302.2
Smith Kline & French Laboratories			297.3
Miles Laboratories Incorporated			275.1
Becton Dickinson & Company			267.4
G. D. Searle & Company			253.8
Total, 359 Next Largest, 1971			$ 7,729.0
Total, 559 Largest, 1971			$ 12,058.0
20. Soaps, cleaners, and toiletries			
Among The 200 Largest			
Procter & Gamble Company	$ 109.4	$ 335.6	$ 2,013.0
Total, 200 Largest, 1929	$ 109.4	$ 335.6	
Total, 200 Largest, 1971			$ 2,013.0
Among The Next 359 Largest			
Bristol-Myers Company			$ 796.4
Colgate-Palmolive Company			652.9
Avon Products Incorporated			506.6
Revlon Incorporated			401.5
Total, 359 Next Largest, 1971			$ 2,357.4
Total, 559 Largest, 1971			$ 4,370.4
21. Rubber and tires			
Among The 200 Largest			
Uniroyal, Incorporated[41]	$ 307.8	$ 944.2	$ 1,365.4
Goodyear Tire & Rubber Company	243.2	746.0	3,183.5
The H. F. Goodrich Company	163.6	501.8	1,342.3
The Firestone Tire & Rubber Company	161.6	495.7	2,344.3
General Tire & Rubber Company			913.5
Total, 200 Largest, 1929	$ 876.2	$ 2,687.7	
Total, 200 Largest, 1971			$ 9,149.0
Among The Next 359 Largest			
Total, 359 Next Largest, 1971			$ 0.0
Total, 559 Largest, 1971			$ 9,149.0

Reported values of assets ($ millions)

EXHIBIT 1 *(continued)*

Industry Category	Reported values of assets ($ millions)		
	1929	1929 (in 1971 dollars)	1971
22. Leather and leather products			
Among The 200 Largest			
International Shoe Company[42]	$ 113.3	$ 347.5	
Total, 200 Largest, 1929	$ 113.3	$ 347.5	
Total, 200 Largest, 1971			$ 0.0
Among The Next 359 Largest			
Interco Incorporated[42]	[$ 113.3	$ 347.5]	$ 437.9
Brown Group Incorporated			258.8
Total, 359 Next Largest, 1971			$ 696.7
Total, 559 Largest, 1971			$ 696.7
23. Nonmetallic mineral mining; Stone, clay, concrete and their products			
Among The 200 Largest			
Total, 200 Largest, 1929	$ 0.0	$ 0.0	
Total, 200 Largest, 1971			$ 0.0
Among The Next 359 Largest			
Jim Walter Corporation			$ 809.0
Texas Gulf Sulphur Company			670.0
Johns-Manville Corporation			653.7
United States Gypsum Company			589.0
International Minerals & Chemical Corporation			556.5
Owens-Corning Fiberglas Corporation			474.7
National Gypsum Company			442.9
Lone Star Industries Incorporated			384.6
Flintkote Company			346.5
Norton Company			325.5
Carborundum Company			298.6
Freeport Minerals Company			283.7
Ideal Basic Industries Incorporated			254.9
Total, 359 Next Largest, 1971			$ 6,089.6
Total, 559 Largest, 1971			$ 6,089.6
24. Glass and glass products			
Among The 200 Largest			
PPG Industries Inc.[43]	$ 101.6	$ 311.7	$ 1,320.7
Owens-Illinois Incorporated			1,387.7
Total, 200 Largest, 1929	$ 101.6	$ 311.7	
Total, 200 Largest, 1971			$ 2,708.4
Among The Next 359 Largest			
Corning Glass Works			$ 599.1
Libby-Owens Ford Company			434.6
Total, 359 Next Largest, 1971			$ 1,033.7
Total, 559 Largest, 1971			$ 3,742.1
25. Fabricated metal products, except: Machinery; Transportation equipment; Metal cans			
Among The 200 Largest			
American Standard Incorporated[44]	$ 199.4	$ 611.7	$ 1,183.2
Crane Company[45]	115.9	355.5	
Total, 200 Largest, 1929	$ 315.3	$ 967.2	
Total, 200 Largest, 1971			$ 1,183.2
Among The Next 359 Largest			
Combustion Engineering Incorporated			$ 721.5
Babcock & Wilcox Company			659.0
Crane Company[45]	[$ 115.9	$ 355.5]	589.2
Walter Kidde & Company Incorporated[46]			556.2
Gillette Company			555.5
Whittaker Corporation			536.5
Timken Company			420.6

EXHIBIT 1 *(continued)*

Industry Category	1929	1929 (in 1971 dollars)	1971
25. Fabricated metal products *(continued)*			
Universal Oil Products Company			$ 381.8
Chicago Bridge & Iron Company			288.8
Total, 359 Next Largest, 1971			$ 4,709.1
Total, 559 Largest, 1971			$ 5,892.3
26. Metal cans			
Among The 200 Largest			
American Can Company	$ 191.3	$ 586.8	$ 1,491.4
Continental Can Company Incorporated	83.2	255.2	1,571.1
Total, 200 Largest, 1929	$ 274.5	$ 842.0	
Total, 200 Largest, 1971			$ 3,062.5
Among The Next 359 Largest			
Crown Cork & Seal Company Incorporated			$ 398.1
National Can Corporation			282.2
Total, 359 Next Largest, 1971			$ 680.3
Total, 559 Largest, 1971			$ 3,742.8
27. Machinery, except: Electrical; Farm, construction, and mining; Office, computing and accounting			
Among The 200 Largest			
The Singer Company[47]	$ 210.0	$ 644.2	
USM Corp.[48]	94.1	288.7	
Total, 200 Largest, 1929	$ 304.1	$ 932.9	
Total, 200 Largest, 1971			$ 0.0
Among The Next 359 Largest			
Studebaker-Worthington Incorporated[49, 56]	[$ 134.2	$ 411.7]	$ 674.0
USM Corp.[48]	[94.1	288.7]	484.6
Sundstrand Corporation			359.8
Cummins Engine Corporation Incorporated			354.5
Harris-Intertype Corporation			331.8
Federal-Mogul Corporation			301.2
Ex-Cell-o Corporation			282.8
Curtis-Wright Corporation			258.9
Cincinnati Milacron Incorporated			252.9
Total, 359 Next Largest, 1971			$ 3,300.5
Total, 559 Largest, 1971			$ 3,300.5
28. Farm, construction, and mining machinery			
Among The 200 Largest			
International Harvester Company[50]	$ 384.0	$ 1,177.9	
Deere & Company	94.6	290.2	$ 1,458.6
Caterpillar Tractor Company			1,811.1
Total, 200 Largest, 1929	$ 478.6	$ 1,468.1	
Total, 200 Largest, 1971			$ 3,269.7
Among The Next 359 Largest			
Allis-Chalmers Corporation			$ 781.9
Ingersoll-Rand Company			768.0
Dresser Industries Incorporated			710.2
Clark Equipment Company			585.6
Otis Elevator Company			554.9
Total, 359 Next Largest, 1971			$ 3,400.6
Total, 559 Largest, 1971			$ 6,670.3
29. Office, computing, and accounting machines			
Among The 200 Largest			
International Business Machines Corporation			$ 9,576.2
Xerox Corporation			2,156.1
Litton Industries Incorporated			1,976.0
National Cash Register Company			1,689.3
Sperry Rand Corporation			1,653.8

The table header spans "Reported values of assets ($ millions)".

EXHIBIT 1 *(continued)*

Industry Category	1929	Reported values of assets ($ millions) 1929 (in 1971 dollars)	1971
29. Office, computing, and accounting machines *(continued)*			
Burroughs Corporation			$ 1,487.8
Control Data Corporation			1,430.8
Total, 200 Largest, 1929	$ 0.0	$ 0.0	
Total, 200 Largest, 1971			$ 19,970.0
Among The Next 359 Largest			
SCM Corporation			$ 542.9
Addressograph Multigraph Corporation			370.3
Pitney-Bowes Incorporated			324.5
Memorex Corporation			255.4
Total, 359 Next Largest, 1971			$ 1,493.1
Total, 559 Largest, 1971			$ 21,463.1
30. Electrical machinery, equipment, and supplies, except: Radio, TV, and communication equipment; Electronic components and accessories; Household appliances			
Among The 200 Largest			
General Electric Company	$ 515.7	$ 1,581.9	$ 6,887.8
Westinghouse Electric Corporation[51]	253.9	778.8	3,537.9
Total, 200 Largest, 1929	$ 769.6	$ 2,360.7	
Total, 200 Largest, 1971			$ 10,425.7
Among The Next 359 Largest			
Emerson Electric Company			$ 457.7
McGraw-Edison Company			435.9
North American Philips Corporation			414.3
UV Industries Incorporated[9]			365.0
Gould Incorporated	[$ 81.5	$ 250.0]	359.9
I-T-E Imperial Corporation			253.1
Total, 359 Next Largest, 1971			$ 2,285.9
Total, 559 Largest, 1971			$ 12,711.6
31. Household appliances			
Among The 200 Largest			
Singer Company[47]	[$ 210.0	$ 644.2]	$ 1,669.7
Total, 200 Largest, 1929	$ 0.0	$ 0.0	
Total, 200 Largest, 1971			$ 1,669.7
Among The Next 359 Largest			
Whirlpool Corporation			$ 623.9
White Consolidated Industries Incorporated			580.6
Carrier Corporation			515.5
Sunbeam Corporation			361.6
Hoover Company			309.1
Fedders Corporation			299.1
Total, 359 Next Largest, 1971			$ 2,689.8
Total, 559 Largest, 1971			$ 4,359.5
32. Radio, TV, and communication equipment; Electronic components and accessories			
Among The 200 Largest			
RCA Corp.	$ 280.0	$ 858.9	$ 3,022.2
International Telephone & Telegraph Corporation[52]	[521.2	1,598.8]	7,630.3
Western Electric Company Incorporated[53]			4,012.2
Total, 200 Largest, 1929	$ 280.0	$ 858.9	
Total, 200 Largest, 1971			$ 14,664.7
Among The Next 359 Largest			
GTE Automatic Electric Company, and GTE Sylvania Co.[54]			$ 1,100.0*
Motorola Incorporated			646.7

*See footnote (*) on Industry Category 46 (Telephone, telegraph, etc.).

EXHIBIT 1 *(continued)*

Industry Category	Reported values of assets ($ millions)		
	1929	1929 (in 1971 dollars)	1971
32. Radio . . . communication equipment *(continued)*			
Raytheon Company			$ 612.5
Texas Instruments Incorporated			579.9
Lear Siegler Incorporated			382.7
Zenith Radio Corporation			374.6
Ampex Corporation			364.0
Collins Radio Company			339.0
Magnavox Company			311.2
General Instrument Corporation			297.3
Hewlett-Packard Company			294.5
Total, 359 Next Largest, 1971			$ 5,302.4
Total, 559 Largest, 1971			$ 19,967.1
33. Scientific, measuring, and control devices; Watches and clocks			
Among The 200 Largest			
Honeywell Incorporated			$ 2,183.1
Total, 200 Largest, 1929	$ 0.0	$ 0.0	
Total, 200 Largest, 1971			$ 2,183.1
Among The Next 359 Largest			
Cenco Incorporated			$ 270.9
Total, 359 Next Largest, 1971			$ 270.9
Total, 559 Largest, 1971			$ 2,454.0
34. Photographic equipment and supplies			
Among The 200 Largest			
Eastman Kodak Company	$ 163.4	$ 501.2	$ 3,298.0
Total, 200 Largest, 1929	$ 163.4	$ 501.2	
Total, 200 Largest, 1971			$ 3,298.0
Among The Next 359 Largest			
Polaroid Corporation			$ 617.1
Total, 359 Next Largest, 1971			$ 617.1
Total, 559 Largest, 1971			$ 3,915.1
35. Motor vehicles and equipment			
Among The 200 Largest			
General Motors Corporation	$ 1,400.0	$ 4,294.5	$ 18,241.9
Ford Motor Company	761.0	2,334.4	10,509.8
Chrysler Corporation	209.7	643.3	4,999.7
Studebaker-Worthington[49, 56]	134.2	411.7	
International Harvester Company[50]	[384.0	1,177.9]	2,026.2
Signal Companies Incorporated			1,273.4
Bendix Corporation			1,199.3
TRW Incorporated			1,115.9
Borg-Warner Corporation			963.0
Total, 200 Largest, 1929	$ 2,504.9	$ 7,683.8	
Total, 200 Largest, 1971			$ 40,329.2
Among The Next 359 Largest			
Eaton Corporation			$ 836.7
White Motor Corporation			564.6
Fruehauf Corporation			539.9
American Motors Corporation			525.4
Dana Corporation			493.2
Budd Company			407.9
Eltra Corporation			307.0
A. O. Smith Corporation			283.0
Champion Spark Plug Company			274.4
Total, 359 Next Largest, 1971			$ 4,232.1
Total, 559 Largest, 1971			$ 44,561.3

EXHIBIT 1 *(continued)*

Industry Category	Reported values of assets ($ millions)		
	1929	1929 (in 1971 dollars)	1971
36. Aircraft, guided missiles, and parts			
Among The 200 Largest			
The Boeing Company			$ 2,464.4
McDonnell Douglas Corporation			2,119.6
Lockheed Aircraft Corporation			1,471.2
United Aircraft Corporation			1,397.4
North American Rockwell Corporation			1,381.2
General Dynamics Corporation			1,171.4
Martin Marietta Corporation			1,030.1
Textron Incorporated[35]			973.4
Total, 200 Largest, 1929	$ 0.0	$ 0.0	
Total, 200 Largest, 1971			$ 12,008.7
Among The Next 359 Largest			
Northrop Corporation			$ 409.9
Grumman Corporation			364.6
Total, 359 Next Largest, 1971			$ 774.5
Total, 559 Largest, 1971			$ 12,783.2
37. Ship and boat building and repair			
Among The 200 Largest			
Total, 200 Largest, 1929	$ 0.0	$ 0.0	
Total, 200 Largest, 1971			$ 0.0
Among The Next 359 Largest, 1971			
Total, 359 Next Largest, 1971			$ 0.0
Total, 559 Largest, 1971			$ 0.0
38. Railroad equipment and street cars and other transportation equipment			
Among The 200 Largest			
ACF Industries Inc.[55]	$ 119.5	$ 366.6	
American Locomotive Company[56]	106.2	325.8	
The Baldwin Locomotive Works[28]	98.8	303.1	
Total, 200 Largest, 1929	$ 324.5	$ 995.4	
Total, 200 Largest, 1971			$ 0.0
Among The Next 359 Largest			
General American Transportation Corporation			$ 847.7
ACF Industries Inc.[55]	[$ 119.5	$ 366.6]	497.4
Pullman Incorporated[57]	[315.5	967.8]	460.6
North American Car Corporation			327.3
Total, 359 Next Largest, 1971			$ 2,133.0
Total, 559 Largest, 1971			$ 2,133.0
39. Other and miscellaneous manufacturing			
Among The 200 Largest			
Total, 200 Largest, 1929	$ 0.0	$ 0.0	
Total, 200 Largest, 1971			$ 0.0
Among The Next 359 Largest			
AMF Incorporated			$ 590.2
Brunswick Corporation			431.4
Bangor Punta Corporation			332.9
Fuqua Industries Incorporated			308.2
Insilco Corporation			288.2
Total, 359 Next Largest, 1971			$ 1,950.9
Total, 559 Largest, 1971			$ 1,950.9
40. Rail transportation, terminals, and related services[58]			
Among The 200 Largest			
Penn Central Company[59]			$ 4,488.7
The Pennsylvania Railroad Company[59]	$ 2,600.0	$ 7,975.5	
The New York Central Railroad Company[59]	2,250.0	6,901.9	
New York, New Haven and Hartford Railroad Co.[59]	560.8	1,720.3	

EXHIBIT 1 *(continued)*

Industry Category	Reported values of assets ($ millions)		
	1929	1929 (in 1971 dollars)	1971
40. Rail transportation *(continued)*			
Southern Pacific Company	$ 2,156.7	$ 6,616.7	$ 3,175.8
Alleghany Corporation[60]	1,600.0	4,908.0	
Santa Fe Industries Inc.[61]	1,135.4	3,482.8	2,281.7
Union Pacific Corporation[62]	1,121.1	3,439.0	2,765.0
Seaboard Coast Line Ind. Inc.[63]			2,195.9
Atlantic Coast Line Railroad Company[63]	840.0	2,576.7	
Seaboard Air Line Railroad Company[63]	283.1	868.4	
Burlington Northern Incorporated[64]			2,925.1
Northern Pacific Railway Company[64]	813.9	2,496.6	
Great Northern Railway Company[64]	812.4	2,492.0	
Chicago, Burlington & Quincy Railroad Company[64]	645.4	1,979.8	
Spokane, Portland and Seattle Railroad Company[64]	140.2	430.1	
Chicago, Milwaukee, St. Paul & Pacific Railroad & Co.[65]	776.1	2,380.7	
Illinois Central Industries, Incorporated[66]	680.9	2,088.7	1,252.7
Southern Railway Company[67]	655.5	2,010.7	1,642.8
Northwest Industries, Inc.[12]	641.0	1,966.3	
Reading Company[68]	565.0	1,733.1	
Norfolk and Western Railway Company[69, 81]	497.0	1,524.5	2,789.7
The Wheeling and Lake Erie Railway Company[60, 69]	104.1	319.3	
New York, Chicago and St. Louis Railroad Co.[60, 69]	350.0	1,073.6	
The Delaware and Hudson Company[69]	269.4	826.4	
Wabash Railway Company[69]	334.6	1,026.4	
Erie Railroad Company[60, 69]	560.9	1,720.6	
The Delaware Lackawanna & Western Railroad Co.[69]	189.3	580.7	
The Chesapeake and Ohio Railway Corp.[60, 70]			2,614.3
Baltimore and Ohio Railroad Company[70]	1,040.8	3,192.7	
Western Maryland Railway Company[70]	168.2	516.0	
Chicago, Rock Island & Pacific Railway Co.[71]	477.4	1,464.4	
St. Louis-San Francisco Railway Company[72]	439.9	1,349.4	
Pullman Railroad Company[57]	315.5	967.8	
Missouri-Kansas-Texas Railroad Company[73]	314.0	963.2	
Boston and Maine Railroad[74]	256.4	786.5	
Chicago & Alton Railroad Company[75]	161.8	496.3	
The Western Pacific Railroad Corporation[76]	156.0	478.5	
Chicago Great Western Railroad Company[77]	149.2	457.7	
Kansas City Southern Industries, Inc.[60, 78]	146.1	448.2	
St. Louis Southwestern Railway Company	139.4	427.6	
Florida East Coast Railway Company	123.6	379.1	
Chicago & Eastern Illinois Railway Company	97.4	298.8	
Chicago Union Station Company	96.8	296.9	
Lehigh Valley Railroad Company[79]	226.0	693.3	
Rio Grande Industries Inc.[80]	223.4	685.3	
The Virginian Railway Company[81]	152.7	468.4	
Mississippi River Corporation			1,528.9
Total, 200 Largest, 1929	$25,267.4	$ 77,507.7	
Total, 200 Largest, 1971			$ 27,660.6
Among The Next 359 Largest			
Northwest Industries Inc.[12]	[$ 641.0	$ 1,966.3]	$ 817.4
Trailer Train Company			744.6
Chicago, Milwaukee, St. Paul & Pacific Railroad Co.[65]	[776.1	2,380.7]	675.3
St. Louis-San Francisco Railway Company[72]	[439.9	1,349.4]	508.9
Chicago, Rock Island & Pacific Railway Co.[71]	[477.4	1,464.4]	446.8
Rio Grande Industries Inc.[80]	[223.4	685.3]	332.9
Reading Company[68]	[565.0	1,733.1]	316.1
Gulf Mobile & Ohio Railroad Company[75]			297.6
Kansas City Southern Industries Inc.[60, 78]	[146.1	448.2]	282.9
Soo Line Railroad Company			264.4
Total, 359 Next Largest, 1971			$ 4,686.9
Total, 559 Largest, 1971			$ 32,347.5

EXHIBIT 1 *(continued)*

Industry Category	Reported values of assets ($ millions)		
	1929	1929 (in 1971 dollars)	1971
41. Transit			
Among The 200 Largest			
Interborough Rapid Transit Company[82]	$ 458.6	$ 1,406.8	
Brooklyn-Manhattan Transit Corporation[83]	288.5	885.0	
Hudson & Manhattan Railroad Company[84]	131.7	404.0	
Third Avenue Railway Company[85]	110.0	337.4	
Boston Elevated Railway Company[86]	109.7	336.5	
Chicago Railways Company[87]	108.2	331.9	
The United Railways and Electric Company of Baltimore[88]	96.7	296.6	
Philadelphia Rapid Transit Company[89]	95.6	293.6	
Total, 200 Largest, 1929	$ 1,399.0	$ 4,291.4	
Total, 200 Largest, 1971			$ 0.0
Among The Next 359 Largest, 1971			
Total, 359 Next Largest, 1971			$ 0.0
Total, 559 Largest, 1971			$ 0.0
42. Motor transportation			
Among The 200 Largest			
IU International Corporation			$ 1,406.8
Tank Lines Incorporated			1,258.3
Total, 200 Largest, 1929	$ 0.0	$ 0.0	
Total, 200 Largest, 1971			$ 2,665.1
Among The Next 359 Largest			
Ryder Systems Incorporated			$ 368.4
Consolidated Freightways Incorporated			279.0
Leaseway Transportation Corporation			268.1
Total, 359 Next Largest, 1971			$ 915.5
Total, 559 Largest, 1971			$ 3,580.6
43. Water transportation			
Among The 200 Largest			
International Mercantile Marine Company[46]	$ 100.0	$ 306.8	
Total, 200 Largest, 1929	$ 100.0	$ 306.8	
Total, 200 Largest, 1971			$ 0.0
Among The Next 359 Largest			
American Export Industries Incorporated			$ 408.0
Seatrain Lines Incorporated			389.6
American President Lines			312.5
Total, 359 Next Largest, 1971			$ 1,110.1
Total, 559 Largest, 1971			$ 1,110.1
44. Air transportation			
Among The 200 Largest			
United Air Lines Incorporated			$ 2,232.7
Pan American World Airways Incorporated			1,829.0
American Airlines Incorporated			1,662.6
Trans World Airlines Incorporated			1,413.0
Eastern Air Lines Incorporated			1,072.7
Northwest Airlines Incorporated			944.3
Total, 200 Largest, 1929	$ 0.0	$ 0.0	
Total, 200 Largest, 1971			$ 9,154.3
Among The Next 359 Largest			
Delta Air Lines Incorporated			$ 780.7
Flying Tiger Corporation			658.1
Continental Air Lines Incorporated			508.8
National Airlines Incorporated			409.9
Braniff Airways Incorporated			347.0
Western Air Lines Incorporated			340.4
Total, 359 Next Largest, 1971			$ 3,044.9
Total, 559 Largest, 1971			$ 12,199.2

EXHIBIT 1 *(continued)*

Industry Category	Reported values of assets ($ millions)		
	1929	1929 (in 1971 dollars)	1971
45. Electric, gas, and sanitary services[90]			
Among The 200 Largest			
American Commonwealth Power Corporation	$ 184.4	$ 565.6	
American Water Works and Electric Company	378.5	1,161.0	
Associated Gas & Electric Company	900.4	2,762.0	
New England Gas and Electric Association	108.7	333.4	
Railway and Bus Associates	112.2	344.2	
Central Public Service Company	199.5	612.0	
Cities Service Company[23]	989.6	3,035.6	
Consolidated Gas Company of New York	1,171.5	3,593.6	
Consolidated Gas, Elec. Light and Power Co. Baltimore	135.9	416.9	
Detroit Edison Company	296.1	908.3	
Duke Power Company	212.1	650.6	
Edison Electric Illuminating Company of Boston	156.3	479.5	
American Gas and Light Company[91]	431.0	1,322.1	
American Power and Light Company[91]	754.1	2,313.2	
Electric Power and Light Corporation[91]	560.0	1,717.8	
National Power and Light Company[91]	500.0	1,533.8	
Commonwealth Edison Company	440.0	1,349.7	
Middle West Utilities Company	1,120.0	3,435.6	
Midland United Company	298.1	914.4	
North American Light and Power Company	308.4	946.0	
Peoples Gas, Light and Coke Company	192.1	589.3	
Public Service Company of Northern Illinois	190.0	582.8	
Brooklyn Union Gas Company	123.7	379.4	
Eastern Gas and Fuel Associates	158.7	486.8	
Lone Star Gas Corporation	109.0	334.4	
North American Company	810.3	2,485.6	
Pacific Gas and Electric Company	428.2	1,313.5	
Pacific Lighting Corporation	203.4	623.9	
Southern California Edison Company, Ltd.	340.6	1,044.8	
Stone and Webster, Incorporated	400.0	1,227.0	
Tri-Utilities Corporation	346.0	1,061.4	
Columbia Gas and Electric Corporation	529.2	1,623.3	
Commonwealth and Southern Corporation	1,133.7	3,477.6	
Niagara Hudson Power Corporation	756.9	2,321.8	
Public Service Corporation of New Jersey	634.6	1,946.6	
United States Improvement Company	802.0	2,460.1	
United Light and Power Company	520.1	1,595.4	
United States Electric Power Corporation	1,125.8	3,453.3	
Utilities Power and Light Corporation	373.1	1,144.5	
Consolidated Edison Company of New York Incorporated			$ 4,888.2
Pacific Gas & Electric Company			4,633.8
Tennessee Valley Authority			3,993.8
Commonwealth Edison Company			3,915.9
American Electric Power Company Incorporated			3,809.0
Southern Company			3,709.1
Southern California Edison Company			3,499.0
Public Service Electric & Gas Company			3,013.9
Philadelphia Electric Company			2,402.3
General Public Utilities Corporation			2,395.8
Detroit Edison Company			2,394.1
Columbia Gas Systems Incorporated			2,313.8
Consumers Power Company			2,215.6
Virginia Electric & Power Company			2,137.8
Duke Power Company			2,102.3
Middle South Utilities Incorporated			2,006.6
El Paso Natural Gas Company			1,975.8
Texas Utilities Company			1,884.3
Texas Eastern Transmission Corporation			1,881.7
American Natural Gas Company			1,785.4

EXHIBIT 1 *(continued)*

Industry Category	Reported values of assets ($ millions)		
	1929	1929 (in 1971 dollars)	1971
45. Electric, gas, and sanitary services *(continued)*			
Niagara Mohawk Power Corporation			$ 1,774.2
Florida Power & Light Company			1,761.1
Northeast Utilities			1,718.7
Pennzoil United Incorporated			1,545.1
Union Electric Company			1,505.0
Northern Natural Gas Company			1,493.2
Baltimore Gas & Electric Company			1,458.3
Northern States Power Company (Minnesota)			1,433.6
Peoples Gas Company			1,407.7
Allegheny Power System Incorporated			1,366.1
Transcontinental Gas Pipe Line Corporation			1,362.6
Consolidated Natural Gas Company			1,337.3
Central & South West Corporation			1,291.5
Pennsylvania Power & Light Company			1,283.0
Pacific Lighting Corporation			1,279.1
New England Electric System			1,210.5
Long Island Lighting Company			1,158.5
Ohio Edison Company			1,146.7
Panhandle Eastern Pipe Line Company			1,116.3
Carolina Power & Light Company			1,114.1
Potomac Electric Power Company			1,113.0
Houston Lighting & Power Company			1,085.5
Wisconsin Electric Power Company			1,056.0
Pacific Power & Light Company			1,035.1
Gulf States Utilities Company			978.9
Duquesne Light Company			914.2
Cleveland Electric Illuminating Company			895.6
Total, 200 Largest, 1929	$18,434.3	$ 56,547.2	
Total, 200 Largest, 1971			$ 91,799.1
Among The Next 359 Largest			
Illinois Power Company			$ 889.6
Boston Edison Company			882.5
Cincinnati Gas & Electric Company			877.7
Public Service Company of Colorado			873.5
Northern Indiana Public Service Company			859.1
Florida Power Corporation			817.3
Public Service Company of Indiana Incorporated			763.8
Northern Illinois Gas Company			762.0
New York State Electric & Gas Corporation			760.4
American Water Works Company Incorporated			720.3
Southern Natural Gas Company			716.1
Texas Gas Transmission Corporation			715.5
Coastal States Gas Producing Company			661.7
South Carolina Electric & Gas Company			635.7
Arizona Public Service Company			623.2
Dayton Power & Light Company			612.9
San Diego Gas & Electric Company			596.7
Lone Star Gas Company			560.6
Oklahoma Gas & Electric Company			557.8
Delmarva Power & Light Company			538.7
Kansas City Power & Light Company			521.8
Utah Power & Light Company			520.4
Rochester Gas & Electric Corporation			502.9
Arkansas Louisiana Gas Company			497.4
Central Illinois Public Service Company			477.7
Houston Natural Gas Corporation			467.9
Portland General Electric Company			464.2
Puget Sound Power & Light Company			461.3
Idaho Power Company			448.2
Tampa Electric Company			439.5

EXHIBIT 1 *(continued)*

		Reported values of assets ($ millions)	
Industry Category	1929	1929 (in 1971 dollars)	1971
45. Electric, gas, and sanitary services *(continued)*			
Indianapolis Power & Light Company			$ 408.4
Atlantic City Electric Company			398.2
Louisville Gas & Electric Company			396.8
Southwestern Public Service Company			382.0
National Fuel Gas Company			370.9
Florida Gas Company			370.1
Colorado Interstate Corporation			366.6
Central Illinois Light Company			365.3
Kentucky Utilities Company			360.8
Washington Water Power Company			360.4
Brooklyn Union Gas Company			360.1
Washington Gas Light Company			358.4
Toledo Edison Company			355.5
Wisconsin Power & Light Company			355.1
Wisconsin Public Service Corporation			346.4
Hawaiian Electric Company Incorporated			346.2
Iowa Illinois Gas & Electric Company			341.9
Montana Power Company			339.9
Great Lakes Gas Transmission Company			335.8
Central Maine Power Company			331.2
New England Gas & Electric Association			326.2
Orange & Rockland Utilities Incorporated			316.3
Kansas Power & Light Company			302.5
Public Service Company of New Hampshire			300.0
Central Hudson Gas & Electric Corporation			284.1
Iowa Electric Light & Power Company			281.6
Kansas Gas & Electric Company			280.1
Iowa Power & Light Company			264.0
United Illuminating Company			261.5
Total, 359 Next Largest, 1971			$ 29,092.7
Total, 559 Largest, 1971			$120,891.8
46. Telephone, telegraph, and other communication services, except: Radio and TV broadcasting			
Among The 200 Largest			
American Telephone & Telegraph Company[53]	$ 4,228.4	$ 12,970.6	$ 54,547.9
International Telephone & Telegraph Corporation[52]	521.2	1,598.8	
Western Union Corp.	332.2	1,019.0	1,139.9
Associated Telephone Utilities Company[92]	95.9	294.2	
General Telephone & Electronics Corporation[54, 92]			7,519.9*
United Utilities Incorporated			1,556.1
Continental Telephone Corporation			1,407.4
Total, 200 Largest, 1929	$ 5,177.7	$ 15,882.6	
Total, 200 Largest, 1971			$ 66,171.2
Among The Next 359 Largest			
Southern New England Telephone Company			$ 865.0
Central Telephone & Utilities Corporation			743.6
Communications Satellite Corporation			329.2
Cincinnati Bell Incorporated			327.5
Mid Continent Telephone Corporation			314.6
Rochester Telephone Corporation			262.9
Total, 359 Next Largest, 1971			$ 2,842.8
Total, 559 Largest, 1971			$ 69,014.0

---

*The assets reported by General Telephone & Electronics Corporation in 1971 were placed at $8,619.9 million. The lesser figure given here excludes $1,100.0 million, the estimated value of the assets of the company's manufacturing subsidiaries. See Appendix A, "Notes to Exhibit 1": Company note 54.

EXHIBIT 1 *(continued)*

Industry Category	Reported values of assets ($ millions)		
	1929	1929 (in 1971 dollars)	1971
47. Radio and TV broadcasting			
Among The 200 Largest			
Total, 200 Largest, 1929	$ 0.0	$ 0.0	
Total, 200 Largest, 1971			$ 0.0
Among The Next 359 Largest			
Columbia Broadcasting System Incorporated			$ 830.1
American Broadcasting Companies Incorporated			496.1
Total, 359 Next Largest, 1971			$ 1,326.2
Total, 559 Largest, 1971			$ 1,326.2
48. Wholesale trade, except: Petroleum and petroleum products			
Among The 200 Largest			
Total, 200 Largest, 1929	$ 0.0	$ 0.0	
Total, 200 Largest, 1971			$ 0.0
Among The Next 359 Largest			
Alco Standard Corporation			$ 318.3
Total, 359 Next Largest, 1971			$ 318.3
Total, 559 Largest, 1971			$ 318.3
49. Retail trade, except: General merchandise; Food stores; Gas stations			
Among The 200 Largest			
United Stores Corporation (Union Cigars Store)[93]	$ 161.5	$ 495.4	
Drug, Incorporated	158.0	484.7	
Rapid American Corporation[10, 93]			$ 1,571.8
Total, 200 Largest, 1929	$ 319.5	$ 980.1	
Total, 200 Largest, 1971			$ 1,571.8
Among The Next 359 Largest			
AMFAC Incorporated			$ 451.9
Farmland Industries, Incorporated			345.3
Zale Corporation			329.6
Wickes Corporation			294.4
Agway Incorporated			293.4
National Industries Incorporated			263.9
Total, 359 Next Largest, 1971			$ 1,978.5
Total, 559 Largest, 1971			$ 3,550.3
50. General merchandise and mail order			
Among The 200 Largest			
Sears Roebuck & Company	$ 251.8	$ 772.4	$ 8,312.4
Marcor Incorporated[94]			2,370.8
Montgomery Ward & Company[94]	187.5	575.2	
F. W. Woolworth Company	165.4	507.4	1,580.2
Marshall Field & Company[95]	137.2	420.9	
S. S. Kresge Company	109.5	335.9	1,095.9
R. H. Macy & Company, Incorporated[96]	97.0	297.5	
J. C. Penney Company Incorporated			1,923.9
Federated Department Stores Incorporated			1,279.8
May Department Stores Company			951.9
Allied Stores Corporation			951.7
W. T. Grant Company			944.7
Total, 200 Largest, 1929	$ 948.4	$ 2,909.2	
Total, 200 Largest, 1971			$ 19,411.3
Among The Next 359 Largest			
Dayton-Hudson Corporation			$ 748.2
R. H. Macy & Company, Incorporated[96]	[$ 97.0	$ 297.5]	615.7
Gamble-Skogmo Incorporated			565.0
Associated Dry Goods Corporation			539.1
Gimbel Brothers Incorporated			497.9
Broadway Hale Stores Incorporated			485.2
Arlen Realty and Development Corporation			400.2

EXHIBIT 1 *(continued)*

		Reported values of assets ($ millions)		
Industry Category		1929	1929 (in 1971 dollars)	1971
50. General merchandise and mail order *(continued)*				
Vornado Incorporated				$ 333.9
Zayre Corporation				317.2
Marshall Field & Company[95]	[$ 137.2		$ 420.9]	291.0
Interstate Stores Incorporated				286.2
Total, 359 Next Largest, 1971				$ 5,079.6
Total, 559 Largest, 1971				$ 24,490.9
51. Food stores				
Among The 200 Largest				
Great Atlantic & Pacific Tea Company, Inc.	$ 147.3		$ 451.8	$ 978.9
Safeway Stores Incorporated				964.5
Total, 200 Largest, 1929	$ 147.3		$ 451.8	
Total, 200 Largest, 1971				$ 1,943.4
Among The Next 359 Largest				
Kroger Company				$ 756.4
Jewel Companies Incorporated				518.0
Food Fair Stores Incorporated				405.0
Lucky Stores Incorporated				364.8
Acme Markets Incorporated				354.6
Southland Corporation				326.5
National Tea Company				275.1
Grand Union Company				249.8
Total, 359 Next Largest, 1971				$ 3,250.2
Total, 559 Largest, 1971				$ 5,193.6
52. Motion pictures				
Among The 200 Largest				
General Theatres Equipment Incorporated	$ 360.0		$ 1,104.3	
Paramount Publix Corporation[97]	236.7		726.1	
Warner Brothers Pictures Inc.[98]	167.1		512.6	
Loews Incorporated[34]	124.2		381.0	
Total, 200 Largest, 1929	$ 888.0		$ 2,723.9	
Total, 200 Largest, 1971				$ 0.0
Among The Next 359 Largest				
Kinney Services Incorporated[98]	[$ 167.1		$ 512.6]	$ 578.9
Walt Disney Productions				497.3
MCA Incorporated				351.7
Columbia Pictures Industries Incorporated				269.2
Metro Goldwyn Mayer Incorporated				249.7
Total, 359 Next Largest, 1971				$ 1,946.8
Total, 559 Largest, 1971				$ 1,946.8
53. Services, except: Motion pictures				
Among The 200 Largest				
Total, 200 Largest, 1929	$ 0.0		$ 0.0	
Total, 200 Largest, 1971				$ 0.0
Among The Next 359 Largest				
Holiday Inns Incorporated				$ 764.2
Trans Union Corporation				694.9
Sperry & Hutchinson Company				589.2
Hilton Hotels Corporation				468.0
Marriot Corporation				369.9
University Computing Company				345.1
ARA Services Incorporated				330.9
McDonalds Corporation				319.3
American Medicorp Incorporated				283.8
Ramada Inns Incorporated				271.7
Del E. Webb Corporation				261.6
Dun & Bradstreet Incorporated				253.7
Total, 359 Next Largest, 1971				$ 4,952.3
Total, 559 Largest, 1971				$ 4,952.3

EXHIBIT 1 *(concluded)*

Industry Category	Reported values of assets ($ millions)		
	1929	1929 (in 1971 dollars)	1971
54. Real estate			
Among The 200 Largest			
U.S. Realty & Improvement Company	$ 124.6	$ 382.2	
Total, 200 Largest, 1929	$ 124.6	$ 382.2	
Total, 200 Largest, 1971			$ 0.0
Among The Next 359 Largest			
Uris Building Corporation			$ 467.3
General Development Corporation			342.2
Tishman Realty & Construction Company Incorporated . . .			330.9
U.S. Financial			310.7
Deltona Corporation			303.3
Madison Square Garden Corporation			276.8
Total, 359 Next Largest, 1971			$ 2,031.2
Total, 559 Largest, 1971			$ 2,031.2
* * * * *			
Total, 200 Largest, all industries, 1929	$79,701.8	$244,485.3	
Total, 200 Largest, all industries, 1971			$538,240.3
Total, Next 359 Largest, all industries			$168,954.5
Total, 559 Largest, all industries, 1971			$707,194.8

2

The Modern Corporation and Private Property

A half-century ago, by the mid-to-late 1920s, when the curtain goes up for the purposes of this study of the place of Big Business in America, the large corporation had become the usual—and in some instances, the only—means of organizing productive activities in a number of important lines of business in America. American business no longer resembled the economy of small enterprise known to and approved by Alexander Hamilton and Thomas Jefferson and, a generation later, Andrew Jackson. More than an oddity or aberration, more, indeed, than a commonplace, the large corporation, even then,—40 to 50 years ago—was becoming *characteristic* of American business. To the extent that the material base of American life and the workings of the American economy had, by then, become different from those of other countries and other times—and they were markedly different, in fact—it was in consequence of the rise of large business corporations.

This had been long suspected and widely feared. And in 1932, a book appeared that described the community of Big Business as had not been done before. This was *The Modern Corporation and Private Property,* by Adolf A. Berle, Jr., and Gardiner C. Means.[1] Appearing in that depression and election, turning-point year, this book, as noted in the previous Chapter, gave new expression to deep-seated, old Populist misgivings about Big Business. It provided data, intellectual groundwork, and rationale for government intervention in important matters relating to the corporation, and it exerted major influence upon the objectives evolved, and measures taken, by the New Deal.

Writing shortly after the Great Crash of 1929, and in the depths of The Depression, of the presence and workings of big corporations, Berle and Means stated flatly, but accurately enough, that "these

great companies form the very framework of American industry."
They put their point:

> These great companies form the very framework of American industry.
> The individual must come in contact with them almost constantly. He may
> own an interest in one or more of them; he may be employed by one of
> them, but above all he is continually accepting their service. If he travels
> any distance he is almost certain to ride on one of the great railroad sys-
> tems. The engine which draws him has probably been constructed by the
> American Locomotive Company or the Baldwin Locomotive Works; the
> car in which he rides is likely to have been made by the American Car and
> Foundry Company.... His electric refrigerator may be the product of
> General Motors Co., or one of the two great electric companies, General
> Electric and Westinghouse Electric.... He probably buys at least some of
> his groceries from the Great Atlantic and Pacific Tea Co.,... some of his
> drugs, directly or indirectly from the Union Drug Company ... although
> his suit may not be made of American Woolen Company cloth, it has
> doubtless been stitched on a Singer sewing machine.... When he steps out
> to the movies he will probably see a Paramount, Fox or Warner Brothers
> picture (taken on Eastman Kodak film) at a theatre controlled by one of
> these producing groups. No matter which of the alluring cigarette adver-
> tisements he succumbs to, he is almost sure to find himself smoking one
> of the many brands put out by the "big four" tobacco companies, and he
> probably stops to buy them at the United Cigar Store on the corner.
> Even where the individual does not come in direct contact, he cannot
> escape indirect contact with these companies, so ubiquitous have they
> become....[2]

Some of these company names linger on—General Motors and
General Electric, for instance. Others of these names, which have disappeared from the business community and are now scarcely more
meaningful than those of vanished kings and tribes of the Old Testa-
ment, may evoke twinges of nostalgia in those who yearn for the
good old days: Baldwin Locomotive Works, American Woolen Company, United Cigar Stores. But more of that later on.

Berle and Means were persuaded that this community of large corporations had, and would have, deleterious impacts of three distinct
kinds upon the American system: economic, social, and political.

These harmful consequences, in turn, they believed, were inherent
in two essential characteristics of these big companies. First, their
very size, and the complexity that went along with that size. Second,
the separateness—or what they called "separation"—of ownership
and control that was all but universal among them.

This second point deserves a bit of amplification; the point was
central to the major thrust of that book and to the great influence it
came to have on public policy. In summary, the point was this: those
who ran these large corporations—the *managers*—had comparatively
little financial stake in their prosperity over the longer run. The
stockholders, who were the lawful *owners* of these large corporations, for practical purposes exercised no control over them. More—
and worse—the interests of the two groups, owners and managers,

could not be assumed to be congruent. Indeed, it is clear that Berle and Means were of the view that the respective interests of these two groups were inherently in conflict. Whereas the stockholders were interested in profits and dividends, the managers were interested in what *they* could get—even at the expense of the corporation and its owners; they were not necessarily interested in corporate profits, as such, and certainly not greatly interested in distributing the corporation's assets—which they controlled—to its owners. Managers, according to this line of thought, were interested in exercising control over the *power* residing in the great wealth organized under the aegis of the corporation. They were interested in gains to be gotten by insiders.

Berle and Means, as were others before them and since, were concerned with what they perceived to be economic implications of the rise of the big corporation. They were concerned about the institutionalizing and "concentration" of large masses of wealth and the resultant depersonalization of that wealth. Institutionalization and depersonalization of large aggregations of wealth, they thought, followed upon the separateness of ownership and control and the wresting of that control from owners by managers through various legal and practical devices that, themselves, became institutionalized. Wealth not owned by those who controlled it was "depersonalized." Control, wrung from the hands of owners in such fashion that it could not easily be regained, was "institutionalized." In earlier times, said Berle and Means, wealth was controlled by those who owned it, and *vice versa;* it was, therefore, a *personal* phenomenon; so, also, was control. Control of wealth was guided and conditioned—these authors said—by *personal* initiative and *personal* responsibility.

The institutionalization and depersonalization of ownership, and the control of important aggregations of productive wealth by non-owning managers severed the use of that wealth from *personal* initiative and quest for gain, and from the constraints and discipline of *personal* financial responsibility. These developments, according to Berle and Means, were undermining the vitalism of an economy based upon the self-interest and responsiveness of individualistic enterprise. It was that individualistic enterprise, held in check by competition and the "conditions of supply and demand," that, in the theory and liberal ideology of the 18th and 19th centuries, was supposed to act, and was widely believed to have in fact acted, as the "best guarantee of economic efficiency."[3]

Berle and Means were perhaps equally preoccupied, as had been Senator John Sherman of Ohio (the father of the Anti-Trust Act that carries his name) and his largely Republican colleagues in Congress in an earlier generation, with the *social* and *political* consequences of the rise of "bigness." These good men, in the closing years of the 19th Century, foresaw even in their time, 40 years ahead of Berle and Means, the possible eventual prominence of the large corporation in the productive sector of the American community.

As to *social* consequences, Berle and Means, in a way reminiscent of Alexis de Tocqueville, Karl Marx, and other 19th century commentators before and after, saw large-scale, capitalistic enterprise—the large business corporation—as inherently hostile to human dignity and to self-realization of the individual. They said:

> As private enterprise disappears with increasing size, so also does individual initiative. . . . Group activity, the coordinating of the different steps in production, the extreme division of labor in large-scale enterprise necessarily imply not individualism but cooperation and acceptance of authority almost to the point of autocracy. . . . At the very pinnacle of this hierarchy or organization in a great corporation, there alone, can individual initiative have a measure of free play. Yet even there a limit is set by the willingness and ability of subordinates to carry out the will of their superiors. In modern industry, individual liberty is necessarily curbed.[4]

Berle and Means saw the rise of the large corporation as nothing less than a "revolution" in the structure, distribution, and locus of *power*. They saw in the large business corporation not only a means for production, but a new kind of *political* organism. To this effect, they quoted Walther Rathenau, a German industrialist and politician of the preceding generation:

> The depersonalization of ownership, the objectification of enterprise, the detachment of property from the possessor, lead to a point where the enterprise becomes transformed into an institution which resembles the state in character.[5]

In Berle's and Means's own words, the modern corporation was not to be regarded merely as one form of organization among others, "but potentially (if not yet actually) . . . the dominant institution of the modern world." And they concluded their tremendously influential work with this paragraph:

> The rise of the modern corporation has brought a concentration of economic power which can compete on equal terms with the modern state—economic power versus political power, each strong in its own field. The state seeks in some aspects to regulate the corporation, while the corporation, steadily becoming more powerful, makes every effort to avoid such regulation. Where its own interests are concerned, it even attempts to dominate the state. The future may see the economic organism, now typified by the corporation, not only on an equal plane with the state, but possibly even superseding it as the dominant form of social organization. The law of corporations, accordingly, might well be considered as a potential constitutional law for the new economic state, while business practice is increasingly assuming the aspect of economic statesmanship.[6]

Adolf Berle and Gardiner Means were by no means the first to question the efficiency of large business organizations. Nor were they the first to observe the separateness of the ownership and the control of big companies, and to see in that separateness cause for deep concerns. Adam Smith had preceded them in all of this in 1776, in its own way another turning-point year.

In his *Inquiry into the Nature and Causes of the Wealth of Nations,* written in the early glimmerings of the Industrial Revolution, Adam Smith gave only passing attention to corporate enterprise, but what he did say was vastly influential. He gave voice to a mixture of disparagement and apprehension that many scholars, politicians, and individualistic businessmen, for instance, were to feel for decades to come, even to this day, when they looked at or thought about the corporation. He expressed the idea that large "joint-stock" companies, the big corporations of his time, all of which were established and could only be established by royal charter or by act of Parliament, would necessarily take on qualities of large bureaucracies (to use a modern word with derogatory overtones Smith surely would have found to his liking). In Smith's mind, sizable joint-stock companies could not manage business affairs with effectiveness and efficiency.

Listen, while the sometime Professor of Moral Philosophy describes the separateness between ownership and "controul" in the large corporation of 200 years ago:

> The trade of a joint stock company is always managed by a court of directors. This court, indeed, is frequently subject in many respects, to the controuls of a general court of proprietors. But the greater part of those proprietors seldom pretend to understand anything of the business of the company; and when the spirit of faction happens not to prevail among them, give themselves no trouble about it, but receive contently such half yearly or yearly dividend, as the directors think proper to make to them. This total exemption from trouble and from risk, beyond a limited sum, encourages many people to become adventurers in joint stock companies, who would, upon no account, hazard their fortunes in any private co-partnery . . . .[7]

And listen, further, as he draws out this splenetic sketch of the management of the large joint-stock companies of his day:

> . . . the directors of such companies, however, being the managers rather of other people's money than of their own, it cannot well be expected that they should watch over it with the same anxious vigilance with which partners in a private copartnery watch over their own. Like the stewards of a rich man, they are apt to consider attention to small matters as not for their master's honour, and very easily give themselves a dispensation from having it. Negligence and profusion, therefore, must always prevail, more or less, in the management of such a company. . . .[7]

In the thinking of Adam Smith, the defects of large corporations stemmed from two root causes: size combined with complexity, and the separateness of ownership and control. The very size of those companies implied the necessity of employing numerous hired managers to run them. This *size,* in turn, with exceptions only, implied *complexity.* Their very size, moreover, implied the need for far larger aggregations of capital than could be put up by single proprietors or even groups of partners. In joint-stock corporations, the presence of many managers and the absence of personal financial responsibility would lead to bumbling, sloth, and negligence. The only instances in which large corporations could function effectively,

Smith thought, were in undertakings where operating problems would be sufficiently simple and repetitive that even inherently inept and unzealous corporate officials could be entrusted to run them tolerably well. He said:

> The only trades which it seems possible for a joint stock company to carry on successfully, without exclusive privilege, are those, of which all the operations are capable of being reduced to what is called a routine, or to such a uniformity of method as admits of little or no variation.[7]

Not much of a role for the corporation. Such misgivings are linked, part and parcel, with the opposing traditional affection held by Populism and received economic theory for an industrial structure of *large numbers* of *small*, "competitive" enterprises: such a business community, according to this thinking, gives rise to lower costs and greater outputs than a business community made up of a few, large-scale "oligopolists." Smith continues in a way that even many of his admirers have little noted, perhaps, nor long remembered:

> Of this kind [of trade] is, first, the banking trade; secondly, the trade of insurance from fire, and from sea risk and capture in time of war; thirdly, the trade of making and maintaining a navigable cut or canal; and, fourthly, the similar trade of bringing water for the supply of a great city.[7]

The good Doctor goes on: a joint-stock company, in contrast to a proprietorship or partnership—a "copartnery"—can look forward to success (in the absence of a monopoly granted by the State, and by no means always then), and therefore should be established only if the management of it were quite simple and easy and reducible to strict rule and method. But, more than just that, he said, there are two additional constraining conditions:

> First, it ought to appear with the clearest evidence, that the undertaking is of greater and more general utility than the greater part of common trades; and secondly, that it requires a greater capital than can easily be collected into a private copartnery. If a moderate capital were sufficient, the greater utility of the undertaking would not be sufficient reason for establishing a joint stock company; because, in this case, the demand for what it was to produce, would readily and easily be supplied by private adventurers.[7]

In short, investors should be chary about putting money into large companies and the State should exercise its sovereign powers to charter them only in very special circumstances.

For the rest, Smith much preferred, and looked to, organizations *owned* as well as *operated* by those who ran and managed them: proprietorships and copartneries of active partners. It was the self-interest of financially responsible managers, he argued—not the uninspired, trudging work of hired hands—that would assure the motivation necessary to competitive striving for effectiveness and efficiency and for meeting the needs of customers and others. Such businesses, inevitably, would be *small*.

Aside from intrinsic, well-nigh genetic inefficiency, Adam Smith attributed also inherent defects of monopoly to large business enterprises. They stood apart, in his mind, from the *many small* privately owned enterprises whose pluralistic competition for inputs and for sales of outputs—that's a modern concept grafted on to Smith's thinking—would, "as if guided by an unseen hand," lead to an optimal allocation of resources, minimum prices, and just rewards for the factors of production.

With such views, Berle and Means were in general agreement. They expressed misgivings as to the size and complexity of the "modern corporation." They were troubled by the lack of union between direct, personal economic incentive, on the one side, and entrepreneurial and energetic, financially responsible management behavior on the other—the identity of interest and role, the very connection. In the large corporation, they missed the congruence of incentive and control that were assumed to lead to something like optimal economic results. But Berle and Means were ready to go farther: they sensed that there were more than just *economic* implications in corporate size and in the separateness of the ownership and control of large corporations. They pondered the possibility that the effectiveness of profits and other income as incentives for management was subject to diminishing return as the scale of corporate size increased far, far beyond anything that had been envisaged by early protagonists of private, capitalistic enterprise in a laissez-faire economic system. They speculated:

> Just what motives are effective today, insofar as control is concerned, must be a matter of conjecture. But it is probable that more could be learned regarding them by studying the motives of an Alexander the Great, seeking new worlds to conquer, than by considering the motives of a petty tradesman of the days of Adam Smith.[8]

So: Berle and Means were by no means the first to question the productive efficiency of the large corporation and the effectiveness of an economic system that included significant numbers of such corporations. And, as we see, it was really no unique discovery that ownership and control were separate in the large corporation. But yet, *The Modern Corporation and Private Property* had great and immediate influence on the thinking of many. There were good reasons.

First of all, in the days of Adam Smith, large corporations were rare. Any problems they might have had could be only slight creakings in the body economic. By the 1930s, however, the community of large corporations had become the "very framework of American industry." Any serious malady among them must necessarily constitute an economic epidemic of frightening dimensions. So Berle and Means, and then many others, came to think.

Second, Berle and Means gave rigorous, detailed, and extensive documentation of the separateness of ownership and control that was characteristic of the very largest of America's industrial corporations. They showed, in case after case, just how this was accomplished. To begin with, stock ownership was generally widely diffused among large numbers of broadly scattered holders. The proxy mechanism through which any group of them could possibly hope to exercise any degree of control was, in fact, fully under the control of the managements. Understandably, the managers used that mechanism to vote themselves into power and to take other measures that would weaken the grasp of ownership and strengthen their own. By the 1930s, this situation had become so general as to be hardly newsworthy.

But Berle and Means went on to show how new devices had been developed that enabled nonowner managements to *institutionalize* their de facto control and, more, to cast intricate, apparently entirely legal networks of control over enormous corporate structures. Especially among railroads and public electric and gas utilities, had managements and in-groups built up pyramids of holding-company structures. They had piled corporation upon corporation. They interconnected corporation with corporation through strands of intercorporate debt and equity holdings. They employed voting trusts and nonvoting stock that, whatever their financial purposes, worked in fact to disenfranchise ownership and to place and institutionalize control in their own hands, beyond the reach of anyone. The documentation offered by Berle and Means was not only impressive. In the bottom of a Depression, whose basic nature and causes—its *etiology,* as distinct from its symptomatology—are still not fully understood, the documentation was shocking.

The legitimized separateness of ownership and control of the country's largest businesses meant that these corporations—so ubiquitous, such pervasive and looming features on the American scene—had become *institutions* with identities and lives of their own. They now had a selfhood quite apart not only from owners, but from managers as well. Managers could die or pass from the scene, but the institutions they had created could go on and on, always and forever beyond control by ownership, and subject to control by managers only of the moment. And in this, Berle and Means saw portentous *political* consequences. These were the corporations, and these were the devices that would make possible the emergence of institutions that were now rising to an "equal plane with the state." The large corporation would possibly even supersede the state as "the dominant form of social organization," was now boding to come forward as "potentially the dominant institution of the modern world."

For their thoughts and findings, Berle and Means put together an impressive mass of supporting facts. It was this array of evidence that spoke for itself that, as much as anything, distinguished their work from the accumulation of polemical literature that attacked "Big Business." The principal factual base of Berle's and Means's work was a roster of the names of the 200 largest nonfinancial corporations as of December 31, 1929, together with the dollar values of their assets. This roster is included in Exhibit 1, placed at the end of Chapter 1. The authors also presented data that suggested, if they did not prove, that, going back to 1909, and especially since 1920, The 200 Largest Corporations had been growing faster than all other corporations. More important, Berle and Means put together extensive detailed data that clearly and surely showed how these corporations were controlled by management and in-groups who, themselves, had little or no financial stake. In case after case, they revealed the independence of the controlling group from the ownership. Given this evidence, which was beyond doubt or argument, it is not to be wondered at that many people were convinced that the managements of large corporations had, indeed, become self-perpetuating and responsible to no one, working their will beyond the reach of ownership, able to engage with impunity in many kinds of self-serving actions and practices at the expense of those owners and, in all likelihood, to the detriment of the community at large.

The Modern Corporation and Private Property made more than just a splash. Its effect was not merely philosophical and intellectual, confined to a professional few. The work and its ideas were rapidly picked up—one could say embraced—by the "Brain Trust" of the New Deal and their Congressional colleagues. Within months of the inauguration of Franklin Roosevelt, the work of Berle and Means played an important part in inspiring and guiding the new Administration to draft and introduce, and to get passed, the bill that became the Securities Act of 1933. This act required, among other things, corporations to disclose material facts about themselves: their business, financial arrangements between managers and the corporation, all details concerning issues of securities and about their issuers; it required disclosure of insider transactions in corporate securities and corporate assets.

About a year later, strongly influenced by Berle and Means, the administration proposed, and Congress passed, the Securities Exchange Act of 1934. This legislation provided for the regulation, by the Securities and Exchange Commission, of securities markets, including major exchanges.

Other legislative measures were strongly influenced by that book. One such was the amendment of the federal Bankruptcy Act, through Chapter X, which brought bankruptcies of corporations having assets of more than $3 million under the control of the Securities and Exchange Commission (the "SEC"). The Bankruptcy Act was also amended by "Section 77," which was designed to encourage and facilitate formal bankruptcies and financial reorganizations of interstate railroads. The roads, by then, were hopelessly unable to meet their many and varied obligations. The new legislation placed control over those bankruptcy proceedings under the Interstate Commerce Commission. Under this legislation, the railroad industry of America was utterly restructured. In a later chapter, we shall see how extensive that restructuring was.

A still further measure much beholden to *The Modern Corporation and Private Property* was the Public Utility Holding Company Act of 1935. This measure empowered and directed the SEC to require simplification of systems of public utility holding companies. The measure was intended to eliminate from these structures of corporations, which were piled one upon another and interlinked in tangled intrasystem, intercompany networks of debts and equities, all sorts of property interests, contracts, and practices detrimental and burdensome to bona fide financial interests, or that obstructed regulation of operating subsidiaries by the several states. In the next few years, no doubt somewhat slowed down by World War II, large and intricate holding company systems were dismantled, and the entire public utility industry was restructured, even more completely than the railroads—another point to which we shall return.

Beyond legislation actually passed, *The Modern Corporation and Private Property* also served as inspiration for a number of proposals, some of which got so far in Congress as being drafted into bills that would have required corporations engaged in interstate commerce to obtain federal—not state—charters to create them, to legitimize their existence, and to provide for their governance. None of these measures was passed. But the matter has often been raised again. Even now, the idea is far from dead. In the spring of 1976, Ralph Nader and his associates issued a new study of the corporation, in which they came out in favor of federal chartering and licensing of corporations.[9]

The Modern Corporation and Private Property is still something of a classic. The deeply rooted Populist ideas and anxieties to which it gave extensive and sophisticated documentation have not altogether disappeared. Revelations in the last couple of years of illegal, immoral, corrupt, and corrupting actions of a number of managements of large American corporations in this country and abroad have surely revived, probably in magnified fashion, old fears and suspicions, and given rise to new ones.

When Berle and Means were writing their book, now more than 40 years ago, they were troubled by concerns about the future economic, social, and political orders of an America in which the large corporation might even supersede the State as the dominant form of social organization. They judged, correctly enough, that the "great companies" of that time already formed "the very framework of American industry." But they could not know, then, that the large corporation in America was still in its very early stages of development, that it was far from reaching its apogee in size, complexity, or significance. The large corporations of our day are very different from theirs. They could not know that the American economy had not yet gotten even halfway to the level it would reach four decades further along in its evolution. Socially and politically, as we know, America has moved a long, long way.

Without taking anything away from Berle and Means, nor from the good Doctor Smith, we ought now, from this later perspective, to be able to reach some additional, perhaps different, understandings of the large corporation and its place as an institution. Looking at the large corporations of then and now—seeing them in the contexts of their own times, looking at how they have changed and seeing these changes in the dynamic context of a changing America—we ought now to be able to evaluate the validity of some of their speculations and concerns. We may see new problems in the community of our largest corporations. We may come to discern the outlines of some new thinking about these institutions and how we may want them to fit in the scheme of things.

THE ATTACK ON BIG BUSINESS

Noteworthy as they are, the forebodings and strictures of Adam Smith and of Berle and Means are but a sampling of the misgivings and polemics directed at the large corporation and the community of Big Business. These eminent, influential gents had, and still have, lots of company in their concerns. The critics have been legion; their charges, profuse. This is not the place, and there is no need to rehearse, all that has been said. I have already done that, over 20 years ago, in an analytical compendium I put together of those criticisms, entitled *The Attack on Big Business.*[10] For anyone interested, that volume can still serve as a *catalogue raisonné* of that attack; although the flow of criticism has hardly ever slackened, few new themes have been added over the passing years.

Most of these many misgivings, and the issues they raise, are just as lively now as they were years, even decades, ago. And we shall want to speak to some of these issues in later chapters. For that reason, a few points can be usefully made right here.

The criticisms of large corporations and of Big Business as a generality are basically of three sorts: economic, social, and political. Large corporations and Big Business as a generality have been said to be inefficient instrumentalities of economic life; to be incompatible with an individually responsible, enterprising, innovative, dynamic populace; to be antithetical to, and corruptive of, popular democracy.

By and large, it is fair to say, the economic counts among the charges have probably been the least persuasive. Despite the weight of criticism stemming from economics, the counts have seemed at odds with facts observable in everyday life. The effectiveness and efficiency of American business are not easily to be seen in daily life and practical affairs as inferior to those of industry in, say, Guatemala, Iceland, or the Soviet Union, or other countries where production is organized differently. Be that as it may, we shall have occasion to consider what some economists have had to say.

The major misgivings and doubts about bigness in business, in the popular mind as well as in intellectual thought, seem pretty clearly to lie in the social and political planes. Anxieties and preoccupations of these sorts have often been voiced by, among many others, eminent jurists as they have tried to help clarify where, if at all, in the American System, and under law, these large private-sector institutions of public import may properly fit. A quick look at a few such expressions will help lay some groundwork for discussion later on.

For many critics—sociologists, theologians, poets, artists, and novelists, among others—the growth of the large-scale-enterprise economy has been a thing to deplore for what they fear it does to the social and political structures and qualities of life in America: individuals *within* large corporations and individuals *outside*—competitors, suppliers, customers, even bystanders—are all harmed by the rise and presence of these large entities. For the critics, public policy calls for public action to protect the community at large from the inferior way of life associated with bigness in commerce and industry.

Such is the chain of reasoning, as I read it, in the often quoted dictum of the Supreme Court in the *Trans-Missouri* decision, one of the early cases under the Sherman Antitrust Act:

> ... ["trusts" or "combinations"] may even temporarily, or perhaps permanently, reduce the price of the article traded in or manufactured, by reducing the expense inseparable from the running of many different companies for the same purpose. Trade or commerce under those circumstances may nevertheless be badly and unfortunately restrained by driving out of business the small dealers and worthy men whose lives have been spent therein, and who might be unable to readjust themselves to their altered surroundings. Mere reduction in the price of the commodity dealt in might be dearly paid for by the ruin of such a class and the absorption of control over one commodity by an all-powerful combination of capital ....
> ... the result in any event is unfortunate for the country, by depriving it of the services of a large number of small but independent dealers, who were familiar with the business, and who had spent their lives in it, and who supported themselves and their families from the small profits realized therein. Whether they be able to find other avenues to earn their livelihood is not so material, because it is not for the real prosperity of any country that such changes should occur which result in transferring an independent business man, the head of his establishment, small though it might be, into a mere servant or agent of a corporation for selling the commodities which he once manufactured or dealt in; having no voice in shaping the business policy of the company, and bound to obey orders issued by others....[11]

Almost a quarter of a century later, in a landmark case that had been in litigation for years, the Supreme Court held that the Sherman Act "did not make mere size an offense." Even a minority opinion agreed that a large corporation "is entitled to maintain its size and the power that legitimately goes with it, *provided no law has been transgressed in obtaining it.*"[12]

Such appears still to stand as the law of the land: despite misgivings of critics, despite even the dictum of *Trans-Missouri,* bigness *per se* is not unlawful—maybe.

But the matter of the place of the large corporation has not been let to rest. In the notable case of *United States* v. *Aluminum Company of America,* Judge Learned Hand, a generation later, speaking for the Second Circuit Court of Appeals, harked back to ideas like those expressed in the *Trans-Missouri* decision long before the *Steel* case. Congress, he wrote,

> ...did not condone "good trusts" and condemn "bad ones"; it forbade all. Moreover, in so doing it was not necessarily actuated by economic motives alone. It is possible, because of its indirect social or moral effect, to prefer a system of small producers, each dependent for his success upon his own skill and character, to one in which the great mass of those engaged must accept the direction of a few. These considerations, which we have suggested only as possible purposes of the Act, we think the [relevant] decisions prove to have been in fact its purposes.[13]

A few paragraphs further on, Judge Hand again emphasized the court's belief that Congress has had other than just "economic reasons" in passing the Antitrust Acts. There are, he said, other reasons

> ...based upon the belief that great industrial consolidations are inherently undesirable, regardless of their economic results .... Throughout the history of [the Antitrust Acts] it has been constantly assumed that one of their purposes was to perpetuate and preserve, for its own sake and in spite of possible cost, an organization of industry in small units which can effectively compete with each other ....[14]

Judge Hand went on, much farther, as many critics were happy to see, almost to the point of a direct attack on the *Steel* doctrine: bigness, he suggests, *can* be unlawful even if achieved by means that are not, of themselves, unlawful, such as the diligent, zealous, and foresighted exploitation of opportunities. Such behavior, the circuit court held, although not illegal per se, led to an unlawful *result:* undoubted preeminence in an industry. Alcoa, by its actions, had foreclosed opportunities in the aluminum industry to "newcomers." He said:

> ...It was not inevitable that it [the company] should always anticipate increases in the demand for ingot and be prepared to supply them. Nothing compelled it to keep doubling and redoubling its capacity before others entered the field. It insists that it never excluded competitors; but we can think of no more effective exclusion than progressively to embrace each new opportunity as it opened, and to face every newcomer with new capacity already geared into a great organization, having the advantage of experience, trade connections and the élite of personnel.[15]

That came pretty close to expressing a reversal of the idea that bigness, of itself, is not unlawful.

A few years later, Mr. Justice William O. Douglas, dissenting in the *Standard Oil of California* case, voiced the continuing and deep concern of critics over bigness in itself. As I read Mr. Justice Douglas in his dissent, he did not, along with the majority, really want Standard Oil of California to enter exclusive supply contracts with independent gasoline dealers. With the court, he believed that such contracts would impair the genuine independence of the dealers and injure competition. However—and here he differed with his colleagues—he seems to have feared that

> the lessons [Mr. Justice Louis D.] Brandeis taught on the curse of bigness have largely been forgotten in high places. Size is allowed to become a menace to existing and putative competitors. Price control is allowed to escape the influences of the competitive market and to gravitate into the hands of the few. But beyond all that there is the effect on the community when independents are swallowed up by the trusts and entrepreneurs become employees of absentee owners. Then there is a serious loss in citizenship. Local leadership is diluted. He who was a leader in the village becomes dependent on outsiders for his action and policy. Clerks responsible to a superior in a distant place take the place of resident proprietors beholden to no one. These are the prices which the nation pays for the almost ceaseless growth in bigness on the part of industry.[16]

Withal that these long, long-standing kinds of *social* preoccupations have remained a minority view, not only in our body of law, but also, apparently, in popular thought as well, they have not gone away in all these years. Not at all. They seem as alive as ever.

Forceful and widespread protest over bribery of high officials and mischievous machinations of certain large American corporations abroad, and over potentially corrupting contributions to politicians by some at home, would seem to show that concerns about bigness in business of a *political* nature are perhaps more with us now than they have been for a long time—since, say, the grubby administration of Warren Harding.

The fact is that large corporations have never fitted comfortably into the generally accepted vision of the American scheme of things. Pragmatically, they have been accepted. Ideologically, they are still an anomaly. The position of large-scale private enterprise in America (of all places!) is an ambivalent one—and uneasily evolving. That uncomfortable fact is of major interest to this work.

THE LARGEST CORPORATIONS OF 1929

We turn now to consideration of the very largest corporations in the United States at the close of 1929—or, if one rather, at the opening of its third decade in the 20th century. Which companies were the largest? What *was* the American business community? Where and how did these largest corporations fit in the encompassing community of American business? That's our starting point. That was the context in which Berle and Means constructed their roster of The 200 Largest Nonfinancial Corporations of their day. Seeing these particular corporations—as best we can—in a context of a time of long ago and far away, works wonders in developing a sense of the historical sweep of our evolution and transformation as a nation over the past four decades.

The 200 Largest Nonfinancial Corporations of 1929 held assets whose aggregate book value was then reported to be about $79.7 billion. In more modern money, we may take it that this figure translates into something like $245 billion in 1971 dollars, and something like $370 billion in 1977 dollars.

These corporations occurred very unevenly throughout the industrial structure of the time. As may be seen in Exhibit 1 and, more easily, in Exhibit 2, 43 of these 200 Largest Corporations occurred in the one Industry Category Rail transportation. These 43 companies held 31.7 percent of the aggregate reported assets of the 200 Largest Nonfinancial Corporations of 1929. The next most numerous and largest clustering of companies was the 39 corporations in the Industry Category Electric, gas, and sanitary services; they held 23.1 percent of the aggregate assets of The 200. Together, these 82 companies in the two industries, rails and utilities, held almost 65 percent of the total assets of The 200 Largest Nonfinancial Corporations.

At the other end of the scale, none of the Largest Corporations occurred in 20 other Industry Categories, ranging from Agriculture and fisheries to Services. And in each of ten other Industry Categories only a single one of The 200 occurred, and their presence, measured in dollar terms, was not great.

The notably uneven occurrence and presence of the largest corporations among the several Industry Categories was not particularly noted, let alone considered in any depth, by Berle and Means. But this unevenness was not happenstance. There was reason underlying these facts. The patterning of the occurrence and presence of The 200 Largest Nonfinancial Corporations throughout the industrial structure of 1929 was a major indicator of the status and advance of the continuing Industrial Revolution in America.

As Berle and Means said, many of the names of these largest corporations were—and still are—commonplace: General Motors, General Electric, the Great Atlantic and Pacific Tea Company, Eastman Kodak. They could have mentioned, also, United States Steel, Aluminum Company of America, DuPont, just to name a few more that were and still are luminaries of the corporate world. But what of the others, besides American Woolen and Baldwin Locomotive, once tall on the American business scene, that have been rather lost from clear view or, somehow, somewhere, disappeared: Koppers Company and Pullman, or Studebaker, Alleghany Corporation, Middle West Utilities, and International Mercantile Marine?

Berle and Means said that "these great companies form the very framework of American industry." But the two major industries in their time most notably characterized by Big Business—the rails and the utilities—were soon to be reorganized almost beyond recognition. Of the 43 largest railroad corporations, only six were still on the list of 200 Largest Nonfinancials in 1971; of the 29 utilities, perhaps

EXHIBIT 2
Industry distribution of the numbers and assets of The 200 Largest Nonfinancial Corporations, 1929
(values in 1929 dollars)

Industry Category	Number of firms	Assets held ($ millions)	Number of firms as percentage of The 200	Assets as percentage of total assets held by The 200
1. Agriculture	0	$ 0.0	0.0%	0.0%
2. Iron and steel	11	4,556.0	5.5	5.7
3. Nonferrous metals	8	1,956.4	4.0	2.5
4. Coal	4	694.5	2.0	0.9
5. Petroleum	20	7,985.9	10.0	10.0
6. Construction	0	0.0	0.0	0.0
7. Food	4	643.0	2.0	0.8
8. Meat	3	901.5	1.5	1.1
9. Dairy	2	398.5	1.0	0.5
10. Alcoholic beverages	0	0.0	0.0	0.0
11. ... Soft drinks	0	0.0	0.0	0.0
12. Tobacco	4	688.8	2.0	0.9
13. Textiles	1	113.9	0.5	0.1
14. Apparel	0	0.0	0.0	0.0
15. Lumber ... wood ... paper ... products	4	1,010.6	2.0	1.3
16. Furniture and fixtures	0	0.0	0.0	0.0
17. Printing and publishing	0	0.0	0.0	0.0
18. Chemicals	4	1,331.1	2.0	1.7
19. Pharmaceuticals	0	0.0	0.0	0.0
20. Soaps, cleaners	1	109.4	0.5	0.1
21. Rubber and tires	4	876.2	2.0	1.1
22. Leather	1	113.3	0.5	0.1
23. Nonmetallic mineral products	0	0.0	0.0	0.0
24. Glass	1	101.6	0.5	0.1
25. Fabricated metal products	2	315.3	1.0	0.4
26. Metal cans	2	274.5	1.0	0.3
27. Machinery	2	304.1	1.0	0.4
28. Farm, construction ... machinery	2	478.6	1.0	0.6
29. Office ... computing ... machines	0	0.0	0.0	0.0
30. Electrical machinery	2	769.6	1.0	1.0
31. Household appliances	0	0.0	0.0	0.0
32. Radio ... communication equipment	1	280.0	0.5	0.4
33. Scientific ... control ... devices ... measuring	0	0.0	0.0	0.0
34. Photographic equipment	1	163.4	0.5	0.2
35. Motor vehicles	4	2,504.9	2.0	3.1
36. Aircraft	0	0.0	0.0	0.0
37. Ship ... building	0	0.0	0.0	0.0
38. Railroad equipment	3	324.5	1.5	0.4
39. Other and miscellaneous manufacturing	0	0.0	0.0	0.0
40. Rail transportation	43	25,267.4	21.5	31.7
41. Transit	8	1,399.0	4.0	1.8
42. Motor transportation	0	0.0	0.0	0.0
43. Water transportation	1	100.0	0.5	0.1
44. Air transportation	0	0.0	0.0	0.0
45. Electric, gas ... sanitary	39	18,434.3	19.5	23.1
46. Telephone, telegraph : ... services	4	5,177.7	2.0	6.5
47. Radio and TV broadcasting	0	0.0	0.0	0.0
48. Wholesale trade	0	0.0	0.0	0.0
49. Retail trade	2	319.5	1.0	0.4
50. General merchandise	6	948.4	3.0	1.2
51. Food stores	1	147.3	0.5	0.2
52. Motion pictures	4	888.0	2.0	1.1
53. Services	0	0.0	0.0	0.0
54. Real estate	1	124.6	0.5	0.2
Total	200	$79,701.8	100.0%	100.0%

Note: Data are derived from Exhibit 1.

only half a dozen. In addition, another 50 corporations in a number of other industries had dropped from sight. Clearly, mere size and sometime prominent membership in the "very framework of American industry" were not enough to assure survival.

On the other hand, nowhere on the roster of Largest Corporations of 1929 were General Foods, Pfizer, International Business Machines, Boeing, United Airlines, nor more than 100 others of the largest and best-known corporations that were among The 200 Largest of 1971. Equally clearly, in the structures of American industry in 1929, there were elements of dynamism, capacity for change, for upheaval, even, that passed unnoticed at the time.

We'll get back to that matter later on.

Now, for a look at the Largest Corporations of 1929 and the structure of American industry of which they were a part.

NOTES

1. Adolf A. Berle and Gardiner C. Means, *The Modern Corporation and Private Property* (New York: The Macmillan Co., 1932).

2. Ibid., pp. 24-25.

3. Ibid., p. 8.

4. Ibid., p. 349.

5. Ibid., p. 352.

6. Ibid., p. 357.

7. Adam Smith, *An Inquiry into the Nature and Causes of the Wealth of Nations* (New York: The Modern Library, 1937), p. 713. Members of the banking and fire, casualty, and marine insurance fraternities may feel put down, under Smith's depreciatory stare. But he explains it all:

   > Though the principles of the banking trade may appear somewhat abstruse, the practice is capable of being reduced to strict rules. To depart upon any occasion from those rules, in consequence of some flattering speculation of extraordinary gain, is almost always extremely dangerous, and frequently fatal to the banking company which attempts it . . . . The value of the risk, either from fire, or from loss by sea, or by capture, though it cannot, perhaps, be calculated very exactly, admits, however, of such gross estimation as renders it, in some degree, reducible to strict rule and method . . .

8. Berle and Means, *The Modern Corporation*, p. 350.

9. Ralph Nader et al., *Constitutionalizing the Corporation: The Case for the Federal Chartering of Giant Corporations* (Washington, D.C.: The Corporate Accountability Research Group, 1976).

10. J. D. Glover, *The Attack on Big Business* (Boston: Harvard University School of Business Administration, Division of Research, 1954).

11. *United States v. Trans-Missouri Freight Association*, 116 U.S. 290 (1897); quoted by Glover, *Attack on Big Business*, pp. 171-72.

12. *United States v. United States Steel Corporation*, 251 U.S. 417 (1920), pp. 451 and 460. (Italics added.)

13. *United States v. Aluminum Company of America et al.*, 148 F.2d. (1945), p. 427. This interpretation of the Sherman Act and its intent is rejected by Robert H. Bork, *The*

Antitrust Paradox, A Policy at War with Itself (New York: Basic Books, Inc., 1978), pp. 51-53, 165-70.

14. *U.S.* v. *Aluminum Co.,* pp. 428 and 429.

15. Ibid., p. 431. This case never reached the Supreme Court; these ideas of the Second Circuit have never been directly passed upon.

16. *Standard Oil Company of California and Standard Stations, Inc.* v. *United States,* 337 U.S. 293 (1949), pp. 318 and 319.

Glover: THE REVOLUTIONARY CORPORATIONS
page proofs of camera copy for chaps. 3-6 (pp. 111-225)
covers msp. 128-312
July 16, 1980

3

The Largest Nonfinancial Corporations of 1929-1930; pattern and order in their occurrence and presence

When our nation's 15th census was taken in the early months of 1930, we numbered about 120 million souls. In the preceding year of 1929, America's Gross National Product came to $103 billion; this figure translates into something like $300 billion of 1971 dollars and $450 billion of 1977 dollars. After subtracting from the Gross National Product, depreciation and other similar allowances, indirect business taxes and other deductions, the National Income—expendable and investable incomes from wages, salaries, dividends, and interest other than on government securities—came to $87 billion, say, roughly $260 billion in 1971 dollars and $390 billion in 1977 dollars.[1]

The total productive apparatus of the United States that generated that product and income was made up of workers, corporations, proprietorships, partnerships, family farms, self-employed artisans and professionals, households and institutions, and government agencies of many kinds at the several levels. A few facts will sketch this encompassing context in which The 200 Largest Corporations and the community of Big Business had their existence and operated.

Seeing these corporations in their milieu, one can much better grasp what it was that they were, in a *functional* sense, and where they fitted in the scheme of things: in the "American System," an *ecological* system. A useful analogy, here, is the richer, more informative picture one gets of a creature of nature, say a beaver or a bumblebee or even an earthworm, when one sees it as an entity in its surrounding context, than one gets when looking at it in a laboratory, detached from its real functioning, living environment. In real life, a living creature takes in "inputs" of animal or vegetable matter; its excretions—"outputs"—are recycled and, sooner or later, turn up as inputs for other forms of plant or animal life. The individual is positioned in various "chains" and flows of nitrogen, of complex chemicals that are nutrients, of parasites to which it is host at some point in *their* life cycles. It competes for mates and breeds with members of its own species. It competes for space and food—more or less amiably—with its own kind and to the death with other species. Its health improves and its numbers increase when its world is genial. When conditions are harsh, the creature weakens and its numbers dwindle. Over time, in response to systemic changes, the prototype of the species evolves—or devolves, or even disappears, like the dinosaurs—into a form of life better adapted to the new circumstances.

Seeing the Largest Corporations in *their* context, one can better appreciate where they came from, how it was they arose, and what their destinies were likely to be. They, like all other entities of the American community, are located at various points in the scheme of things and fill their respective niches in the total system.

In 1929-30, business corporations of all kinds and all sizes numbered 456,000, and they produced about 53 percent of the National Income. Almost all of America's agriculture was carried on by means of 6.5 million farms—family enterprises, mostly, whose land and buildings, alone, were valued at about $48 billion—averaging a bit over $7,000 each. Most products reached ultimate buyers through 1.7 million retail outlets, more than 90 percent of them proprietorships or partnerships; then, more than now, "Mom-and-Pop's" family business. Altogether, they sold about $50 billion of merchandise of all kinds. Another 300,000 small, unincorporated businesses provided "services"; again, more than 90 percent of them were partnerships or proprietorships and, again, mostly family affairs.

Some hundreds of thousands of persons were self-employed: doctors, lawyers, accountants, artists, piano-tuners. Some indeterminate number of households—scores of thousands, anyway—were also economically productive units on a modest scale in the "cash economy": dressmaking, music lessons; room and board for paying guests; jams, jellies, and baked goods. Some thousands of institutions were active in education, religion, and health care. Some thousands of units of local, state, and federal government rounded out the lists of productive agents, including public irrigation, fire, school, and sewage districts.[2]

A labor force of almost 50 million—counting all of the "economically active population" *ten* (!) years old and over—worked in all these places of employment, provided the brains, the skills, and some of the physical energy that guided and impelled the whole flow of production. Our people led their domestic lives in almost 30 million households.

These were the entities that produced the consumable and capital wealth and the welfare of the nation. These millions of entities were interlinked among themselves in a vast network of all sorts of relationships—employees and employers, buyers and sellers, consignors and consignees, borrowers and lenders, creditors and debtors, landlords and tenants, lessors and lessees, principals and agents, suppliers of components and makers of products—in such a way as to constitute a productive *community*. Flowing along the lines of this network of relationships were the goods and services that were being produced, bought and sold, and—in the opposite direction—the streams of payments of moneys in exchange for goods and services rendered and for financing, that brought all of these millions of elements together, each interconnected, directly or indirectly, with all the others: a productive *system*.[3]

Of the National Income produced and consumed and invested, in 1929, more than 90 percent came out of the business sector (which excludes households and institutions and instrumentalities of government). Of the 90 percent that was produced by the business sector, about 5 percent, in turn, related to financial activities of all sorts—corporate and noncorporate—that created, negotiated, transferred, and realized upon property rights of all sorts. About 95 percent of the 90 percent of the National Income that came out of the business sector, which is to say about 85 percent of the total National Income, came from nonfinancial, business-sector entities. Of the 85 percent, in turn, about 53 percent, which is to say something over 45 percent of the whole National Income, was generated by nonfinancial business *corporations,* as distinct from self-employment, proprietorships of business, partnerships, family farms, and other forms of private business. Somewhere near one-half, overall, of the literal support and sustenance of the American people came out of business corporations other than those in finance.[4]

In those winter days, as 1929 came to an end and 1930 began, the American people were beginning to realize they had some problems. The shocks in the stock market that fall had registered, shall we say, seven or eight on a "Richter scale" of economic quakes. We know now that worse was to come. Few, if any realized that in the next three years the Gross National Product would decline (in constant dollar terms) by 30 percent and that six million—12 percent of the work force—would be unemployed. They could not have known that, in a couple of years, millions of mortgages on farms and homes would be in default and that the financial structure, whose workings helped the nation's free-enterprise productive apparatus to operate, would be in such a state of disarray that it would grind to a stop. But that is another story, of long ago and far away. Those people had their problems. We have ours.

In any event, taken as a functioning, dynamic whole, the encompassing productive *system* just sketched out was the setting of the corporate population profiled in Exhibit 3. The 456,000 corporations had no existence separate from the *system* of which they were a part; the system had no meaning and could not have functioned apart from them.

Of the 456,000 corporations, about one-third—134,000—were engaged in all kinds of financial activities and with real estate. The other 332,000 were engaged in producing those goods and services that comprised about half of the National Income of that year.

It is the *nonfinancial corporations* of the productive system that are the particular focus of this study.[5] These are the productive engines that, as mentioned, generated half, overall, of the wherewithal needed and desired to sustain our people and institutions; that produced practically *all* of those goods and services that come from large-scale production, and that—unlike the outputs of family farms, proprietorships, and partnerships—were peculiarly associated with "Industrialism." At the close of 1929 and the outset of 1930, these 322,000 nonfinancial corporations held assets of all sorts—land and buildings, machinery, inventories, cash and receivables and other current assets, and various other useful properties, tangible and intangible—carried on their books to the value of $195 billion. (In 1971 dollars, that would amount to something like $600 billion; in 1977 dollars, $850-$900 billion.)

It is hard to say with any precision, but it is a fair guess that, excluding public productive assets (schools, highways, canals, harbor works for instance) these corporate assets represented as much as three-quarters of the American people's net accumulation, over time, of productive capital values from the days when the first settlers started to earn their livings on the banks of the James River and the shores of Cape Cod Bay.

And of these productive assets held by all nonfinancial corporations, something like 40 percent was held by The 200 Largest.

* * * * *

Exhibit 1, at the end of Chapter 1, lists The 200 Largest Nonfinancial Corporations of 1929, together with their reported assets in both 1929 and something like 1971 dollars. (It also shows The 200 Largest of 1971, along with their assets; these data will be dealt with in a later chapter.) Exhibit 2, in Chapter 2, summarizes by Industry Categories the 1929 data shown in Exhibit 1.

Exhibit 3, herewith, sets forth in summary form the numbers and assets of all the corporations of 1929, as reported and classified by the then Bureau of Internal Revenue according to Major Industry Groups.

A bit later on in this Chapter, Exhibits 4-10, inclusive, analyze the data as to the numbers and assets of The 200 Largest Nonfinancial Corporations of 1929 with the purpose of discerning pattern and order, where they exist, and of trying to determine what the pattern

EXHIBIT 3
The 200 Largest Nonfinancial Corporations of 1929 compared to All Other U.S. Nonfinancial Corporations, by Major Industry Groups; numbers of firms and values of assets

	All corporations[a]		The 200 Largest Corporations[b]		
Major Industry Groups[c]	Number of firms	Value of assets ($ millions)	Number of firms	Value of assets ($ millions)	Assets held by The 200 as percentage of assets of all corporations, by Major Industry Groups
Agriculture, forestry and fisheries	9,430	$ 2,140	0	$ 0.0	0.0%
Mining and quarrying[d]	12,502	11,832	4	694.5	5.9[d]
Construction	18,358	3,095	0	0.0	0.0
Manufacturing:					
Food and kindred products, beverages and tobacco	14,845	9,800	13	2,631.8	26.9
Textiles and textile products	14,340	6,623	1	113.9	1.7
Lumber and wood products and paper and allied products	9,568	6,245	4	1,010.6	16.2
Printing, publishing, and allied products	11,170	2,838	0	0.0	0.0
Chemicals and allied substances	7,071	14,031	25[e]	9,426.4	67.2[e]
Rubber and tires	614	1,422	4	876.2	61.6
Leather and leather products	2,433	1,198	1	113.3	9.5
Stone, clay, and glass products	4,561	2,393	1	101.6	4.2
Metal and metal products	20,156	23,079	36[f]	11,483.9	49.8
Other and miscellaneous manufacturing	7,472	2,654	2	443.4	16.7
Manufacturing (subtotal)	92,230	$ 70,282	87	$26,201.1	37.3%
Transportation and other public utilities	21,608	77,792	95	50,378.4	64.6
Wholesale and retail trade	129,089	21,842	9	1,415.2	6.4
Services	35,967	7,820	4	888.0	11.4
Nature of business not allocable	2,900	252	0	0	0.0
Total, nonfinancial corporations[g]	322,084	$195,054	199	$79,577.2	40.8%
Finance, insurance, and real estate	133,937	140,724	1[g]	124.6[g]	
Total, all industries	456,021	$335,778	200	$79,701.8	

Note: Data are rounded.

[a] Source: U.S. Treasury Department, Bureau of Internal Revenue; *Statistics of Income 1929;* Table 19, p. 332.

[b] Data derived from Exhibit 1.

[c] These Major Industry Groups are categories used by the Bureau of Internal Revenue in *Statistics of Income, 1929.* These categories are of limited usefulness. They did not relate to categories used by other government agencies. Some categories are too broad to be meaningful, for example, Metal and metal products. They implicitly relate to an earlier industrial structure. They show separately, for instance, Leather and leather products, a cluster of industries that had played a prominent part in the 19th century surge of the Industrial Revolution in America. But these Major Industry Groups fail, for instance, to show separately petroleum and automobiles, which, in terms of economic and industrial significance, had already overtaken and surpassed by a wide margin Leather and leather products. The failure to segregate the railroads from the rapidly growing and, in total, already almost as large, electric and telephone utilities is, perhaps, a similar example of "cultural lag."

Then, as now, the industry categories used by government agencies, including IRS, also do not easily accommodate characteristically integrated industries, e.g., Iron and steel; Nonferrous metals; and Forestry, lumber and wood products including paper; and Petroleum. These characteristically integrated industries reach across numbers of "industries" as traditionally conceived, bringing together under one corporate "roof," and often in continuously flowing processes, a number of identifiable steps: extraction, transportation, processing, manufacturing, and even distribution.

[d] As used here, mining and quarrying excludes petroleum production, which is included in Chemicals and allied products. Accordingly, total investments in Mining and quarrying are understated to that extent. Also understated is the presence of large corporations in those industries. This is but one example of problems confronted in studying the presence or absence of large corporations in various industries. See Footnote e.

[e] Includes 20 integrated oil companies and five chemical and soap companies. The percentage figure of total assets in this industry group held by the largest companies is somewhat overstated because the assets of those companies include assets employed in other industries, e.g., extractive and transportation (pipelines).

[f] The data for The 200 Largest Corporations in Metal and metal products includes companies and assets in the following Industry Categories, as shown in Exhibit 2: Iron and steel; Nonferrous metals; Fabricated metal products; Metal cans; Machinery; Farm, construction . . . machinery; Electrical machinery; Motor vehicles; Railroad equipment. Other and miscellaneous manufacturing includes Radio . . . communication equipment and one company in Photographic equipment.

[g] There was one real estate company with assets of 124.6 million dollars on Berle's and Means's List of The 200 Largest Nonfinancial Corporations for 1929. In that year the Internal Revenue Service combined finance and real estate in the same Major Industrial Group, so that it was not possible to separate real estate from the finance industries.

and order thus revealed may indicate concerning the structure of American industry in those times.

The data in Exhibit 3, so far as our purposes are concerned, leave much to be desired. The breakdown of the data by Major Industry Groups conceals almost as much as it reveals. But these are the data we have, so we must make the best of them. And the data suggest some important things about the structure of American industry that are confirmed by later information.

First, as to the picture overall of business corporations in the total structure of industry; the 322,000 nonfinancial corporations were distributed very unevenly throughout the industrial structure of the times. They occurred in very different numbers among the Major Industry Groups. And their presence in these Industry Groups, as measured by the mass of their assets, varied even more widely. The patterning and order revealed by the occurrence of those corporations among industries and in their relative presence in those industries as measured by assets, give hints as to the nature of the industrial structure that had so far emerged and that was to continue to evolve over the next decades. That development would have astounded people of the day, could they have known what was to come.

The largest *occurrence* of business corporations, 129,000 of them—being 40 percent of the total number—were in wholesale and retail distribution. But, numerous as they were, the *presence* (their *mass,* as measured by the value of their assets) of these corporations in these industries was relatively small. The corporations in wholesale and retail trade held only 11 percent of all nonfinancial corporate assets: $22 billion. They represented only 8 percent of the total number of entities—1.7 million of them—that were engaged in trade, the rest being proprietorships and partnerships. Within wholesale and retail trade, corporate assets (as contrasted to noncorporate) were probably less than 15 percent of the total.

The noncorporate form of business, typically *small, private* business clearly dominated in these lines of commerce.

The corporations engaged in services and construction also counted for relatively little, when it comes to numbers (and as to values of assets) in comparison to both (*a*) the unincorporated businesses in those industries and (*b*) corporations in other industries. Services and construction were also sectors where the family firm and partnership —*small* businesses—predominated.

The *occurrence* and *presence*—number and mass—of corporations were even lower in agriculture, whether measured in relation to all nonfinancial corporations or in relation to all entities of whatever forms of organization that were active in all the various forms of agriculture. Most farming and other agricultural activities were carried on by individuals and partnerships—mostly by families. As mentioned earlier, there were 6 million farms; the value of their land and buildings, not counting equipment and inventories, was about $50 billion. In comparison, there were only 9,000 corporations in agriculture and their assets came to only $2 billion. These corporations represented only 3 percent of the whole number of nonfinancial corporations, and their assets only 1 percent of the total of nonfinancial corporate assets.

In contrast, the *presence* of corporations stood large in other sectors, and in these, the corporation was the predominant form of organization. This was notably true in Transportation and other public utilities. And it was surely true in manufacturing generally, certainly more so in some industries than others. It was probably true of Chemicals and allied substances (which included the petroleum, as well as the chemical companies, a number of which, as we shall see, were among the very largest). The Major Industry Group called by the Bureau of Internal Revenue Metal and metal products no doubt included the large steel and nonferrous metals companies, along with the makers of automobiles, farm equipment, and electrical products, and others. In this aggregation of industries, the corporation was surely predominant.

There are strong indications, although available data are not complete or detailed enough to nail the point down, that family and partnership enterprise predominated in small-scale, less-capital-intensive operations and older, traditional industries and lines of business. Examples would be agriculture, retailing and wholesaling, for instance. On the other side, the *corporate* form was predominant in large-scale, "newer" industries, that is, newer since their rise just before, and especially after the Civil War: railroads, electric and gas utilities, telephone systems; automobiles; farm equipment; and typically integrated industries such as the metals; lumber and the products of wood, including paper; chemicals and petroleum. The small business—family farms and "copartneries"—favored by Adam Smith, Thomas Jefferson, and Andrew Jackson, although still the norm in several sectors, was not associated with "industry" of the sort that was coming increasingly to characterize the American system.

We pass, now, from the matter of the *form* of business organizations to matters having to do with the *size* of *corporations.*

Exhibit 3 also sets forth an effort to compare the occurrence and relative presence of The 200 Largest Nonfinancial Corporations of 1929 among the Major Industry Groups for which the then Bureau of Internal Revenue reported data. Only a few direct comparisons are possible. But, together with a few inferences, they throw further light on the occurrence and presence of the corporation, as a form of organization. More particularly, they shed a light on the relative occurrence and presence among *all* corporations, in several industry sectors, of The 200 Largest Companies.

As Exhibit 3 indicates, and as other exhibits will show more clearly, The 200 Largest Nonfinancial Corporations and their assets were distributed very unevenly throughout the American industrial structure—far less evenly, indeed, than were corporations generally.

Not one of The 200 Largest showed up in either Agriculture or Construction among the Major Industry Groups, nor in Printing, publishing, and allied products.

In contrast, 95 of The Largest had arisen among the railroads and other utilities. These 95 firms held almost two-thirds of all corporate assets in those industries; and this must be close to saying two-thirds of *all* assets. In Chemicals and allied substances—and this includes petroleum, chemicals, and soaps—25 of the largest firms held over two-thirds of all corporate assets. In the broad cluster of industries called Metals and metal products, 36 large firms, including those in Iron and steel, Nonferrous metals, Motor vehicles and equipment (as well as other metal products and machinery) held almost 50 percent of all corporate assets of the Group. Of The 200 Largest Nonfinancial Corporations, these 156 held $71 billion of assets. These $71 billion represented 62 percent of all corporate assets in those particular industries. These holdings accounted for 37 percent of all *corporate* assets in *all* nonfinancial industries. These 156 particular corporations held over 89 percent of all the assets of The 200. Their relative presence was massive.

The others of The 200 Largest, 44 in number, were spread among all the other industries and Groups. These 44 held $8.6 billion of assets, being about 4 percent of all corporate assets. Although not outstandingly prominent on the industrial scene as a whole, holding only 4 percent of all corporate assets, a number of these 44 other corporations stood out prominently in their respective industries. The four large tire and rubber companies, for instance, held $876 million of assets—less than ½ of 1 percent of all nonfinancial corporate assets, and only 1 percent of the assets of The 200 Largest. But they were clearly prominent in Rubber and tires, holding among them over 60 percent of the corporate assets in that industry.

The 13 largest companies in Food and kindred products, beverages and tobacco held 27 percent of all corporate assets in those industries. The four largest in Lumber and wood products and paper and allied products, with their assets of $1 billion, accounted for 16 percent of the corporate assets in those industries. The nine largest in Wholesale and retail trade—and these were mostly the large mail-order houses and certain retail chains—held about 6 percent of the assets in distribution.

Four motion picture companies held 11 percent of all corporate assets in Services, but their presence in the production and distribution of motion pictures was well over 90 percent. So dominant were they, in fact, that in later years they were subject to a successful antitrust dissolution suit.

The four largest companies shown in Exhibit 3 to be in Mining and quarrying were, in fact, in *coal* mining. Their presence in that industry was doubtless several times larger than their 5.8 percent of *all* mining and quarrying.

Then there were six of The Largest Companies scattered among Textiles and textile products, Leather and leather products, Stone, clay, and glass products, and Other and miscellaneous manufacturing and Real estate. None of these was clearly dominant in its particular industry; altogether they held less than ½ of 1 percent of all corporate assets.

Another set of measurements is readily at hand for getting a deeper sense of what these largest companies were and how and where in the system they fitted, along with other members of the corporate community. And those measurements concern the size of these Largest firms relative to other corporations. The data in Exhibit 4 compare the sizes of the Largest firms to the sizes of all others. These data strongly suggest that the *natures* of the very largest firms were very different from those of the others, and that the Largest firms and smaller firms fitted into very different "niches" in the American "ecological *system.*"

EXHIBIT 4
The 200 Largest Nonfinancial Corporations of 1929 compared to All Other U.S. Nonfinancial Corporations; average and relative sizes, by Major Industry Groups

Major Industry Groups	(1) Average size of corporations, exclusive of The 200 Largest ($000)	(2) Average size of The 200 Largest ($000)	(3) (2) ÷ (1)
Agriculture, forestry, and fisheries	$ 227	–	–
Mining and quarrying	891	$173,625	195
Construction	169	–	–
Manufacturing			
Food and kindred products, beverages, and tobacco	483	202,446	419
Textiles and textile products	454	113,900	251
Lumber and wood products and paper and allied products	547	252,650	462
Printing, publishing, and allied products	254	–	–
Chemicals and allied substances	654	377,056	577
Rubber and tires	895	219,050	245
Leather and leather products	446	113,300	254
Stone, clay, and glass products	503	101,600	202
Metal and metal products	576	318,998	554
Other and miscellaneous manufacturing	296	221,700	749
Manufacturing (subtotal)	$ 478	$301,162	630
Transportation and other public utilities	1,274	530,299	416
Wholesale and retail trade	158	157,244	995
Services	193	222,000	1,152
Nature of business not allocable	87	–	–
Total nonfinancial corporations*	$ 359	$399,885	1,114

*Excludes Real estate.

In the industrial and Major Industry Groups in which they occurred, the average sizes of The 200 Largest Corporations ranged from $101.6 million (in 1929 dollars), in Stone, clay, and glass products, to $530 million in Transportation and other public utilities. The average size of The 200 Largest that were in Manufacturing (87 of them) was $301 million. Overall, the average size of The 200 Largest was just about $400 million.

The contrast between these average sizes and the average sizes of all other corporations, including the next largest just below The 200, is stunning. Overall, the average assets of all nonfinancial corporations other than The 200 Largest was $359 *thousand*, in contrast to the overall average of $400 *million* for The 200. The average size of corporations in Construction was $159 thousand (none of The 200 was in Construction). At the other end of the size spectrum, the average size of corporations, *exclusive* of members of The 200, in Transportation and other public utilities was about $1.3 million.

Overall, the average sizes of The 200 Largest Nonfinancial Corporations tended to be *hundreds of times* larger than the averages of the other companies. And that includes, say, the next 200 (or whatever number) largest corporations just down the size scale from the Largest group.

An inference of major purport comes quickly to mind: these Largest Corporations were surely not simply *bigger* than the others. Far more important, they must have been *different*. Those 9 of The 200 Largest Companies, for example, which were in Wholesale and retail trade were, on the average, almost a *thousand* times as large as the average of all others in that Major Industry Group. This relationship between average sizes cannot be taken merely as quantitative. These data cannot be taken to mean, for instance, that the larger ones were *qualitatively* the same, only they had a *thousand* times as much of the same inventories, and of the same kinds of receivables and physical facilities; a thousand times the purchases of the same kinds of inputs, and a thousand times the sales of the same kinds of outputs.

A big, brown bear is, indeed, 20 times larger than a badger. But the difference does not stop there. And they fit into very different *niches* in the ecological system of which they are parts. They occupy very different "spaces," even in the same terrain. They fit in very different positions in the cycles of liquids, nutrient proteins, carbohydrates, hydrocarbons, organic mineral salts, and parasites.

The average size of the 87 largest corporations in Manufacturing was $301 million, *630 times* the size of the average of the other firms in this broad class of industries. Industry by industry, this difference ranged from 202 times in Stone, clay, and glass products to 577 times in Chemicals and allied substances. Again, one inference pushes forward that the Largest Companies were generating outputs that were *different* from those of smaller firms. Another inference presents itself to the effect that the equipment and other assets used by the largest firms in production were *different* from those of smaller firms, not that they simply had some hundreds of times the same *kinds* of plants, machines, and other assets and means of conversion.

These differences in average sizes are not primarily quantitative measures; they are, I think, far more accurately, surrogates for indicating differences in kind. More of this point later on.

These inferences cause others to arise. If the outputs of the largest firms were qualitatively *different* from the averages of the others, as were the means of conversion, were not the inputs also different? Firms, like living things in nature, do not take in merely generally undifferentiated, *generic* kinds of inputs—say, like "land," "labor," and "capital." Like living things in nature, they take in *specific* kinds, as well as *amounts,* of inputs, appropriate to their specific natures.

In short, although for statistical and other conceptual purposes there may be a "genus" of corporations called Stone, clay, and glass or Chemicals and allied substances, or whatever, those at the smallest end of the size spectrum must be *qualitatively* different from those at the largest end. In the community of corporations, as in communities in nature, there are, within "genera," very different kinds of "species," distinct in their places and functionings in the "system" and distinct in many attributes, including size. We shall return to this topic in a few moments when we discuss the data in Exhibits 9 and 10, below.

The 200 Largest Nonfinancial Corporations of 1929-30, with their almost $80 billion of assets, held 41 percent of all nonfinancial corporate assets. Large they certainly were, and visible; and dominant in several important industries. But, spread among the several industries as unevenly as they were, they were not really so "ubiquitous" as they may have seemed. They fitted into the system in highly specific ways. And that is a very revealing datum, as we shall see.

Unfortunately, that is about as far as one can go, for 1929-30, in making direct comparisons between the Largest Corporations and the rest of the corporate community, and the more comprehensive business community. In later years, the statistics of the Internal Revenue Service are much more detailed. However, analysis of the data relating to the 200 Largest Corporations of 1929-30 do, of themselves, as we shall now go on to see, throw additional light on the industrial structure of America as it had evolved up to just before the Great Depression.

Exhibits 5-10, inclusive, analyze the data relating to The 200 Largest Nonfinancial Corporations in several different ways. Basic to this analysis is the classification of the companies according to 54 "Industry Categories." These Industry Categories were specially designed in the course of this project to accommodate and reveal the structures of industry as they had been evolved in practice. They are defined in terms of the "Standard Enterprise Classification" and the "Standard Industry Classification" established by the federal government for assembling and classifying industry data in uniform fashion for statistical and study purposes. These Industry Categories are described in Appendix B.

What these exhibits show is summarized in the following paragraphs.

First of all, as suggested a few paragraphs back, and as shown in Exhibits 1 and 2, The 200 Largest Nonfinancial Corporations occurred primarily in a few industries, and for every good reasons. They occurred relatively infrequently or not at all in the majority of industries—also for good reasons. The pattern and order of that distribution tell a lot about the structure of American industry and the American economy.

The Largest Corporations of 1929, as was true in 1971, occurred in particular sectors of the industrial structure where opportunities existed and could be designed that were particularly conducive to the emergence of very large companies: economies of scale in production and distribution; of vertical integration; of multiplant, multiproduct operations; of mechanization and capital-intensivity; of technology-intensivity. Where these circumstances were weak or nonexistent, large corporations emerged less often or not at all.

Of these 200 companies, 138 occurred in 9 out of the 54 Industry Categories. (See Exhibit 5.) As mentioned, 95 of these companies,

EXHIBIT 5

Regulated and integrated industries and industries with seven or more of The 200 Largest Nonfinancial Corporations: 1929*

Industry Category†	Number of companies	Percentage of The 200 Companies	Assets held (billions of 1929 dollars)	Average value of assets per company (millions of 1929 dollars)	Percentage of the total assets held by The 200 Companies
Utilities, regulated industries					
Railroad transportation	43	21.5%	$25.3	$ 588.4	31.7%
Electric, gas, and sanitary	39	19.5	18.4	471.8	23.1
Transit	8	4.0	1.4	175.0	1.8
Telephone, telegraph	4	2.0	5.2	1,300.0	6.5
Water transportation	1	0.5	0.1	100.0	‡
Subtotals, regulated industries	95	47.5%	$50.4	$ 530.3	63.2%
Integrated industries					
Petroleum	20	10.0%	$ 8.0	$ 400.0	10.0%
Iron and steel	11	5.5	4.6	418.2	5.7
Nonferrous metals	8	4.0	2.0	250.0	2.5
Lumber . . . wood . . . paper	4	2.0	1.0	252.7	1.3
Subtotals, integrated industries	43	21.5%	$15.6	$ 362.8	19.6%
Totals, regulated and integrated industries	138	69.0%	$66.0	$ 478.3	82.8%
Other industries					
None	—	—	—	—	—

*Data are derived from Exhibit 1.

†These Industry Categories are not to be confused with the Treasury's Major Industry Groups of 1929, as cited in Exhibit 3. For details as to the structure of the Industry Categories designed for this study, see Appendix B, "Industry Categories and Their Composition."

‡Less than $1/_{10}$ of 1 percent.

which held 63 percent of the aggregate assets of The 200, occurred in 5 industries characterized by "natural monopoly" and public regulation—the "utilities": Railroad transportation; Electric and gas, and sanitary services; Transit; Telephone and telegraph. (Water transportation was included in this Major Industry Group for comparative purposes. The major impacts of federal government programs on the American merchant marine place this industry very much in the position of being regulated.) The technologies and physical facilities of these industries were, and still are, inherently associated with relatively large corporate size and large scale of operating units within their own systems. These are industries of great opportunities for economies of systems-integration and multiplant operations. They are also extraordinarily capital-intensive in terms of capital investment per employee and capital investment per dollar of sales.

Another 43 companies, holding almost 20 percent of the assets of The 200, occurred in 4 Industry Categories characterized by opportunities for economies of both scale and integration of vertically contiguous processes, together with other advantages associated with bringing together under one corporate entity and one management a series of steps reaching from extraction through reduction and refining, through manufacture, and at least to early stages of distribution. These industries were Petroleum; Iron and steel; Nonferrous metals; and Lumber and wood products and paper and allied products.

Following these 138 companies in the five Utilities and regulated industry *categories* and the four Integrated industries were 34 companies in eight industries in which the occurrence of very large companies was "fairly frequent"—that is to say, where there were 4 to 6 of The 200. (See Exhibit 6.) These 34 held about 11 percent of the assets of the 200 Largest. Not only were very large corporations fairly frequent in these Industry Categories, their *presence* in several of

EXHIBIT 6
Industries with four to six of The 200 Largest Nonfinancial Corporations: 1929*

Industry Category	Number of companies	Assets held (millions of 1929 dollars)	Average value of assets per company (millions of 1929 dollars)	Percentage of the total assets held by The 200 Largest Companies
Coal	4	$ 694.5	$173.6	†
Food and kindred products (except meat, etc.)	4	643.0	160.8	†
Tobacco	4	688.8	172.2	†
Chemicals and allied products	4	1,331.1	332.8	1.7%
Rubber and tires	4	876.2	219.1	1.1
Motor vehicles and equipment	4	2,504.9	626.2	3.1
General merchandise and mail order	6	948.4	158.1	1.2
Motion pictures	4	888.0	222.0	1.1
Totals	34	$8,574.9	$252.2	10.8%

*Data derived from Exhibit 1.
†Less than 1 percent.

them (in terms of asset values) was dominant, as already suggested or shown by the data in Exhibit 3. This dominance is directly apparent, in some instances, and reasonably inferred in others.

These explanations of the important occurrence and presence of a number of the largest companies in these eight industries—as different as they are—are probably more complex than in the cases of the five Utilities and regulated industries and the four Integrated industries. In each of the eight, there were no doubt economies of scale either in production (as in Rubber and tires), or in distribution (as in General merchandise and mail order), or in both. In Motor vehicles and equipment, there were surely economies of vertical integration as well.

Beyond such inherent and necessary considerations, it is probable that factors of innovative but "monopolistic" or restrictive practices were also often present and significant. These would include patents and trademarks, generally regarded as legitimate ways of encouraging and protecting entrepreneurship. In a number of instances, successful antitrust actions were brought against certain practices, such as "block booking" in motion picture distribution, and allegedly discriminatory discounts and rebates in food distribution.

In other cases, patents (Chemicals and allied products) and strong consumer preferences (Food and tobacco) were probably also partially explanatory of the rise of particular large corporations to prominence in those industries. In these and several other industries growth was probably encouraged by opportunities for economies of multiproduct lines, based on similar technologies and use of common production and distribution apparatus and facilities.

Beyond the "objective" reasons that "explain" the rise of 172 of The 200 Largest Companies in the 17 industries tabulated in Exhibits 4 and 5, "human" factors were also at work. It is sure that in the rise of each one of these companies, the conceptual, entrepreneurial, and organizing genius of individual founders and managers played decisive roles. Granted the inherent logic and objective economies implicit in various technologies and other "objective" factors and developments operating in the American environment generally, these were not enough to explain the rise of particular companies. Understanding of the basic technologies and economies, perception of the opportunities, assembling necessary finances and human talents, the organization of technical and managerial linkages among component parts, and ingenious controls over complex interrelated operations also were present in the particular instances. Of such were the contributions of people like Carnegie, Rockefeller, Vail (the organizing genius in the rise of the Bell System of American Telephone and Telegraph), Guggenheim, Firestone, Ford, Sears, and Goldwyn.

In the rise of some large corporations, socially useful contributions were supplemented by equal or even greater genius for sharp, even predatory practices and outright rascality. The putting together of some of the railroad and utility complexes might be good examples.

But that sorry fact should not obscure the existence and workings of powerful underlying forces ready to be exploited and turned to practical account.

The remaining 28 companies of the 200 Largest arose in 17 other industries. These were the industries in which one, two, or at the most three of the Largest Corporations arose. (See Exhibit 7.) In nine of these industries, only one of the largest occurred. In six industries, there were two. In two industries, there were three. Altogether, these 28 companies held less than 7 percent of the total assets of The 200. The somewhat smaller size and the scattering of these 28 companies among 17 Industry categories stand in contrast to the occurrence and presence of the 138 firms in the four utilities industries. In these 17 latter industries the representative Largest companies were spread very thin.

Although the numbers and, especially, the mass of these 28 companies was minor compared to the others of The 200, in certain industries their presence, relative to other companies in the same industries, was commanding. This was true, or probably true, in Meat packing; Metal cans; Electrical machinery; Photographic equipment. It was not the case, however, in Textiles; Leather; Stone, clay, and glass products. It is hard to say, from these data, as to other industries.

EXHIBIT 7
Industries with one to three of The 200 Largest Nonfinancial Corporations: 1929*

Industry Category	Number of companies	Assets held (millions of 1929 dollars)	Average value of assets per company (millions of 1929 dollars)	Percentage of the assets held by The 200 Largest Companies
Meat and meat products	3	$ 901.5	$300.5	1.1%
Dairy and dairy products	2	398.5	199.3	†
Textile mill products	1	113.9	113.9	†
Soaps, perfumes, toiletries	1	109.4	109.4	†
Leather and leather products	1	113.3	113.3	†
Glass and glass products	1	101.6	101.6	†
Fabricated metal products (except cans, machinery and transportation equipment)	2	315.3	157.7	†
Metal cans	2	274.5	137.3	†
Machinery	1	304.1	152.1	†
Farm, construction, mining... equipment	2	478.6	239.3	†
Electrical machinery	2	769.6	384.8	1.0
Radio...communication equipment	1	280.0	280.0	†
Railroad equipment and streetcars	3	324.5	108.2	†
Photographic equipment	1	163.4	163.4	†
Retail trade	2	319.5	159.8	†
Food stores	1	147.3	147.3	†
Real estate	1	124.6	124.6	†
Total	28	$5,239.6	$187.1	6.6%

*Data derived from Exhibit 1.
†Less than 1 percent.

The reasons for the emergence of large companies in these industries were far more diverse than in the other industries in which the occurrence of large companies was far more common and their presence more massive.

No doubt production economies of scale and integration play a part in the rise of very large companies in Meat packing. Technical excellence, as well, probably played an important part in the rise of the two large companies in Electrical machinery, in Radio and communication equipment, and the three in Railroad equipment and streetcars. Commercial, merchandising, and financial skills of founders and managers probably played major roles in the use of the particular companies in Dairy and dairy products; Soaps; Metal cans; Photographic equipment; Retail trade; and Food stores. Some companies developed great skill in realizing production and marketing economies from broad product lines. In some instances, managements of these companies have found ways of institutionalizing such skills up to this very day.

Finally and tellingly, none of The 200 Largest Nonfinancial Corporations arose in 20 other industries. Twelve of these industries were "older industries." Their basic technologies, ways of doing business, and structures were well formed prior to 1929. Some, such as Printing and publishing, dated back to the dawn of the Industrial Revolution in the 18th century or even earlier.[6]

No singular economies of scale or integration had arisen in these industries. Nor had really unique and great possibilities for distinguishing technological excellence yet appeared. No great opportunities had yet been developed for product differentiation or decisively innovative commercial, financial, or organizational skills. There were no tough "barriers to entry" in the form of massive minimum scale, highly specialized proprietary knowledge, or staunch consumer commitments to particular brands. "Entry" by newcomers, in contrast to, say, the regulated industries and integrated industries, or into

TABLE 1
Twenty industries in which none of the Largest Nonfinancial Corporations was primarily engaged: 1929

"Older" industries	"Newer" industries
Agriculture and fisheries	Pharmaceuticals
Alcoholic beverages	Household appliances
Apparel	Radio and television broadcasting
Printing and publishing	Motor transportation
Ship and boat building	Office, computing, and accounting machines
Wholesale trade	Scientific, measuring, and control devices
Construction	Aircraft and parts
Bottled and canned soft drinks	Air transportation
Furniture and fixtures	
Nonmetallic mineral products	
Other and miscellaneous manufacturing	
Services other than motion pictures	

Note: See Note 8 at the end of this chapter.

chemicals and automobiles, was relatively easy.[7] The conditions for the emergence of very large corporations in these industries were a long way off.

Eight of the industries in which none of the largest companies had arisen were "newer" ones. These were industries which, as we know them, developed after 1929, indeed, mostly after World War II. Their time had not yet come.

Pattern and order underlay the occurrence and presence of The 200 Largest Corporations among the several industries. Part of the pattern and order shows up in the summary Table 2.

In the industries in which these companies tended to occur, they tended to do so in substantial numbers. They manifested a strong tendency to appear in clusters. And where they tended to appear in numbers, their presence, as measured by the value, or "mass," of their assets was also great. Although one cannot tell with as much certainty and precision as one would like, the available data do suggest, as does reason, that their relative presence in those industries was also significant, if not dominant.

Further: in those industries where the largest firms tended to arise in substantial numbers, and in considerable absolute and relative mass, the average size of those firms was substantially larger than that of the largest firms that occurred in industries where the population of big firms was sparser.

Where the big companies tended to be numerous, they tended also to be larger. Where they tended to be less numerous, they tended also to be smaller.

In sum, Table 2 suggests pattern and order in the existence and positioning of large corporations in the business community. Pattern and order are sketched by the association of occurrence, presence,

TABLE 2
Summary: Occurrence and presence of The 200 Largest Nonfinancial Corporations (assets held, average values of assets per company, percentages of the total assets held by The 200 Companies): 1929

	Number of Industry Categories	Number of companies	Assets held ($ billions)	Average value of assets per company ($ millions)	Percentage of the total assets held by The 200 Companies
Utilities, regulated industries	5	95	$50.4	$530.3	63.2%
Integrated industries	4	43	15.6	362.8	19.6
Industries with four to six of the Largest Companies	8	34	8.6	252.2	10.8
Industries with one to three of the Largest Companies . . .	17	28	5.2	187.1	6.6
Totals	34	200	$79.7	$399.0	100.0%
Industries with none of the Largest Companies	20	0	—	—	—
	54	—	—	—	—

Note: Numbers may not check out exactly because of rounding.

and scale of the largest companies in various identifiable kinds of industries. The data show covariation among (*a*) the *number* of companies occurring in certain kinds of industries (e.g., 95 in the five utilities and regulated industries versus 28 in 17 industries where occurrence was infrequent); (*b*) aggregate assets held by the largest companies ($50.4 billion in the utilities and regulated industries versus $5.2 billion in the latter 17 industries); and (*c*) the average size of company (e.g., $530 million for the 95 utilities corporations versus $187 million for the 28 companies in the 17 industries where the occurrence of the largest companies was infrequent and their presence relatively less.)[9]

In 20 industries, none of the Largest Corporations occurred. (See Exhibit 8.) Several of these were "older" industries in which large numbers of small corporations occurred, and even larger numbers of unincorporated enterprises: Agriculture, Construction, Apparel, Printing and publishing, and Services.

Several of the industries in which none of the largest firms had yet arisen were still in their infancy. Their technology and their economic relevance were not yet ready to sustain very large-scale organization: Pharmaceuticals; Office, computing, and accounting machines; Household appliances; Scientific, measuring, and control devices; Radio and television broadcasting; Aircraft; Motor freight; and Air transportation.

EXHIBIT 8
Industry distribution of The 200 Largest Nonfinancial Corporations, 1929; summary

	Number of industries	Number of companies	Value of assets held by companies among The 200 (billions of 1929 dollars)	Percentage of the assets of The 200 Companies held
Industries with none of The 200 . .	20			
"Older" industries*	(12)	0	–	–
"Newer" industries†	(8)	0	–	–
Utilities and other regulated industries	5	95	$50.4	63.2%
Integrated industries	4	43	15.6	19.6
Other industries with 4 to 6 companies	8	34	8.6	10.8
Other industries with 1 to 3 companies	17	28	5.2	6.6
Totals	54	200	$79.7	100.0%

Note: Figures are rounded.

*"Older" industries, as defined and used here, are those industries which, although well established prior to 1929 and even, with two exceptions, long before the Industrial Revolution, contained none of the largest companies in 1929: Agriculture and fisheries; Construction; Alcoholic beverages; Bottled and canned soft drinks; Apparel; Furniture and fixtures; Printing and publishing; Nonmetallic mineral products; Ship and boat building; Other and miscellaneous manufacturing; Wholesale trade; Services other than motion pictures.

†"Newer" industries, as defined and used here, are those industries which "came of age" after 1929, as during World War II, or even later, although there were companies established in some of those industries as early as World War I: Pharmaceuticals; Office, computing and accounting machines; Household appliances; Scientific, measuring, and control devices; Radio and TV broadcasting; Aircraft and parts; Motor freight; Air transportation.

A few more of the available data for 1929, shown in Exhibits 9 and 10, give further indication that the Largest Corporations did, indeed, tend to occur where better opportunities for larger-scale, more capital-intensive organizations presented themselves. The data also suggest the obverse: The Largest Companies did not tend to occur where smaller-scale, less capital-intensive organizations were the norm. These data are not as powerful and definitive as one would like, statistically speaking, but, taken together with other data, they do show the tendency that has been described.

Exhibits 9 and 10, taken together and with the data in Exhibit 4 and Table 1, suggest: (*a*) larger numbers of the Largest Companies tended to occur and their presence was important in industries where the average sizes, both of *all* corporations in the industry (exclusive of the largest) and of the *Largest* Companies, were larger; and (*b*) they did not tend to occur and their presence was relatively unimportant in industries where the average sizes, both of *all* corporations in the industry (exclusive of the largest) and of the *Largest* Companies, were smaller.

For example, in Chemicals and allied substances, the 25 Largest Companies held 67.1 percent of the total Major Industry Groups assets. The average size of the Largest firms was $377 *million;* the average size of all firms in the group, *excluding* the Largest, was $654 *thousand.* In contrast, the nine Largest firms in Wholesale and retail trade held only 6.4 percent of the total assets of that "Major Indus-

EXHIBIT 9

Illustrations of the occurrence and relative presence of The 200 Largest Nonfinancial Corporations in large-scale, generally capital-intensive Major Industry Groups: 1929 (values in 1929 dollars)

Major Industry Groups*	Number of companies	Industry assets total ($ billions)	Number of companies among The 200	Assets of the Largest Companies ($ billions)	Assets of the Largest Companies as percentage of assets of all companies in industry group	Average assets per company excluding The 200 ($ thousands)	Average assets of the companies among The 200 ($ millions)
Transportation and other public utilities	21,608	$ 77.8	95†	$50.4	64.6%	$1,274	$530
Rubber and related products	614	1.4	4	0.9	61.6	895	219
Chemicals and allied substances	7,071	14.0	25‡	9.4	67.2	654	377
Metal and metal products	20,156	23.1	36	11.5	49.8	576	319
Lumber ... wood ... paper	9,568	6.2	4	1.0	16.2	547	253
Totals and averages§	59,017	$122.5	154	$73.2	59.8%	$ 838	$475
Totals and averages excluding Transportation	37,409	$ 44.6	59	$22.8	51.1%	$ 584	$386

Note: Percentages and averages are based on Exhibit 3.

* See Exhibit 3, Footnote c for comments on the Major Industry Groups used by the Bureau of Internal Revenue in 1929.

† Includes one company in Water transportation.

‡ Includes 20 Petroleum companies.

§ The averages are substantially affected by the occurrence and presence of large companies in Transportation and ... public utilities. Accordingly separate totals and averages are computed omitting the data for that Major Industry Group.

try Group." The average size of those Largest companies was $156 million—less than half the size of the average of the Largest firms in Chemicals. The average size of all firms in the Wholesale and retail group, excluding the largest, was $157 thousand—less than one-quarter the average size of the companies (excluding the Largest) in Chemicals and allied substances.

In those Major Industry Groups where the Largest Companies held more than half of the assets, the average assets per company, excluding The 200, was $838,000 and the average assets for the Largest companies was $386 million. Setting aside the rails and other utilities, the average size of companies excluding The 200 was $584,000 and the average assets of the Largest Corporations was $386 million. Both sets of data indicate that in those industry groups where the presence of the Largest companies was great, the average sizes of all companies was substantially greater than in those where the presence of the Largest companies was relatively minor. The average

EXHIBIT 10

Illustrations of the relative absence of The 200 Largest Nonfinancial Corporations from smaller-scale, generally less capital-intensive Major Industry Groups: 1929 (values in 1929 dollars)

Major Industry Groups	Number of companies	Industry assets total ($ billions)	Number of companies among The 200	Assets of the Largest Companies ($ billions)	Assets of the Largest Companies as percentage of assets of all companies in industry group	Average assets per company excluding The 200 ($ thousands)	Average assets of the companies among The 200 ($ millions)
Wholesale and retail trade	129,089	$21.8	9	$1.4	6.4%	$158	$157
Services*	35,967	7.8	4*	0.9*	11.4	193	222
Construction	18,358	3.1	0	0.0	0.0	169	—
Agriculture, forestry and fisheries	9,430	2.1	0	0.0	0.0	227	—
Printing, publishing, and allied products	11,170	2.8	0	0.0	0.0	254	—
Other . . . manufacturing	7,472	2.7	2	0.4	16.7	296	222
Textiles	14,340	6.6	1	0.1	1.7	454	114
Leather	2,433	1.2	1	0.1	9.5	446	113
Food†	14,845	9.8	13	2.6	26.9	483	202
Stone, clay, and glass products . .	4,561	2.4	1	0.1	4.2	503	102
Mining and quarrying	12,502	11.8	4	0.7	5.9	891‡	174
Totals and averages	260,167	$72.1	30	$6.3	9.2%	$253	$210

Note: Percentages and averages are based on Exhibit 3.

*Including four motion picture companies and their assets, presumably included in this Major Industry Group by the Bureau of Internal Revenue in 1929.

†The Major Industry Group called Food includes six separate Industry Categories: Food and kindred products; Meat and meat products; Dairy and dairy products; Alcoholic beverages; Bottled and soft drinks; Tobacco manufacturing. A breakdown of the Group data for those Industry Categories is as follows:

	Number of companies among The 200	Assets of the Largest Companies ($ billions)	Average assets of the companies among The 200 ($ millions)
Food	4	$0.4	$161
Meat	3	0.9	301
Dairy	2	0.4	199
Alcoholic beverages	—	—	—
Bottled . . . soft drinks	—	—	—
Tobacco	4	0.7	172

‡This figure probably reflects a heavy influence of the presence of sizable nonferrous metals companies just below The 200 in size.

assets of companies in those industries, excluding The 200, came to $253,000—considerably less than half the figure for those industries in which The 200 loomed large; the average size of the Largest Companies in the industries in which their presence was minor was also very much less.

What this adds up to is this: forces operating to foster the emergence and growth of the very largest companies in industries of large scale and relative capital-intensivity operated also to produce other companies that, although smaller, were still sizable. Both the Largest Companies and the not-so-large in those industries were larger than companies in other industries in which such forces were operating with less effect—in some industries with very little effect, indeed.

In earlier pages, the Largest Companies of 1929-30 were shown, as they are again shown in Exhibits 9 and 10, to have been hundreds of times larger than even the averages of the other firms in their respective industries.

Overall, the conclusion again pushes itself forward that the very largest companies were not only *larger* than other companies; but, far more significant, that they were *different in kind*. Perhaps Sears, Roebuck and the A&P were of the same "genus" as the local neighborhood or country general store and the local corner Mom-and-Pop. Maybe not. But, surely, they were not of the same "species." DuPont and Texaco were surely not of the same species as some small firm that made, say, shoe polish, also categorized under Chemicals and allied products.

These biggest companies were not qualitatively the same as smaller ones, just scaled up and magnified. They were different "animals" altogether.

These largest firms fitted into "niches" in the American productive "ecosystem" far different from those of the "typical" smaller firms. They were far, far larger. They were responses to opportunities and requirements for economies of scale and integration. In fact, they manifested—they were—forms of economic "life" that had developed and evolved over the preceding decades. They were utterly unlike anything known to Adam Smith, Alexander Hamilton, Thomas Jefferson, or Andrew Jackson. Many had almost exploded—such was the rapidity of their appearance and growth—after the trust-busting days of Teddy Roosevelt, during World War I, and in the 1920s.

They were *new* phenomena, not to be understood, explained, or dealt with in terms of earlier paradigms, ideals, concepts, hypotheses, or theories.

In the span of a single lifetime prior to 1929, one of the world's greatest revolutions had been unfolding. And hardly anybody understood—or could then have understood—what was happening. The United States had been—it has continued to be—one of the most rapidly and profoundly *developing* countries of all. Its development is still far from done.

NOTES

1. For data, see U.S. Department of Commerce, Office of Business Economics, *The National Income and Product Accounts of the United States, 1929-1965* (Washington, D.C.: U.S. Government Printing Office, 1966). For relevant Gross National Product deflators, see, e.g., *Economic Report of the President . . . 1979* (Washington, D.C.: U.S. Government Printing Office, 1979), Table B-3.

2. United States Department of Commerce, Bureau of the Census, *Historical Statistics of the United States, Colonial Times to 1957* (Washington, D.C.: U.S. Government Printing Office, 1960), pp. 520, 524, 526.

3. A *system* is a collectivity of interrelated, interacting parts. There are many different kinds of systems, natural and man-made: mechanical systems, such as the solar system; organic systems, such as a fresh water pond. See John D. Glover, "Environment: 'Community,' 'Culture,' 'Habitat,' and 'Product,'" a technical note prepared for use in instruction at the Harvard Business School, Boston, Mass. File no. 4-367-018. This document sets forth concepts for visualizing the United States as an *ecosystem,* and is related to special compilations of data useful in measuring its composition, its size, its internal relationships, and its dynamics. See Appendix B.

4. See United States Department of Commerce, *The National Income and Product Accounts, 1929-1965.*

5. See Chapter 1, Note 2.

6. There was a purpose to the groupings of Industry Categories in Exhibits 5, 6, and 7. These groupings, as the reader can note, were as follows:

    Exhibit 5: Regulated and integrated industries and industries with seven or more of the 200 Largest Nonfinancial Corporations . . .
    Exhibit 6: Other Industries with four to six of the 200 Largest . . .
    Exhibit 7: Other Industries with one to three of the 200 Largest . . .

    The purpose was to reveal pattern and order, if such there were, in the occurrence (numbers) and presence (asset values) of the largest corporations among the several Industry Categories. The reasoning runs like this: if occurrence, for example, were simply a random or chance matter, the probability would be that occurrences would be distributed rather evenly or, at least, "randomly"—that is, having no apparent relation to "logic" or "reason"—among the 54 industries. Such might also be the case, were the founding and rise of large corporations simply the contingent or idiosyncratic consequences of the actions of individual entrepreneurs. If such were the case, large corporations would be as likely, or unlikely, to arise in any one industry as in any other.

    If, on the other hand, notable clusters of large corporations occurred in some industries and not at all in others, the explanation would run to "order" rather than happenstance.

    Another possible explanation of the occurrence of large corporations in certain industries might run in terms of conspiracy—an often popular sort of theory of history. According to such a theory, certain groups of individuals and their colleagues would, or did, conspire to aid, abet, and mutually support each other in fostering the growth of their own particular companies at the expense of others not party to the conspiracy.

    The best support for a theory of conspiracy, of course, is direct evidence. But circumstantial evidence, such as "common parallel action," has sometimes, in certain cases, sufficed to incline, or even persuade, jurists toward or even persuade such a theory.

    In the absence of direct evidence of conspiracy or of its nonexistence, probabilities are suggestive, if not conclusive. And it was for obtaining, in such fashion, possible light on such presence or nonexistence of conspiracy that Exhibits 5, 6, and 7, and others later on (Exhibits 17, 18 and 19; 21, 22, and 23; and 26, 27, and 28) were designed as they were. If large corporations appeared individually or in groups where they might not be expected to, or otherwise in patterns that contrasted with "common sense" or other presumption or prejudice, a whiff of conspiracy might be detected. If not, at least a Scotch verdict of "Not proven," if not of "Not guilty" might be a reasonable outcome.

The data in these exhibits, as they turn out, stand at least as knots, if not as clouds of witnesses, that order—stemming from underlying circumstances, rather than happenstance or conspiracy—was a better explanation, in a large majority of instances, for the emergence and rise of large corporations in some industries and not in others.

For example, as shown in Exhibit 5, by 1929, 43 of the 200 Largest Corporations had arisen among the railroads, and 39 among the utilities. Apart from any knowledge whatever of economics or technologies of these industries, their capital requirements, or their regulatory environments, one's sense of reasonability prompts the thought that something other than happenstance or idiosyncratic behavior was at work. Moreover, such numbers of conspirators would present considerable practical problems of security, discipline, and distribution of booty; conspiracy, as the explanation, seems not very plausible. An underlying order, rather, has appeal as a better explanation.

As to the occurrence of 20 of the 200 Largest Corporations of 1929 in Petroleum, 11 in Iron and steel, and 8 in Nonferrous metals, again with no reference whatever to the fundamentals of these industries, one may reasonably tilt toward order as the explanation, albeit in decreasing degree as the numbers decline.

In any case, although there is no magic to the number seven in this kind of analysis —as there is in crapshooting—the occurrence of that many of the biggest corporations in any one of 54 Industry Categories gives one pause, at least, to consider the possibility of an underlying order.

When it comes to smaller numbers of firms, one may entertain less certain inclinations. If there are, say four, five, or six of the largest firms in an industry where, in light of industry "basics," large scale seems a likely outcome of industry dynamics over time, a predisposition to believe in order is not clearly unreasonable, although that prejudice might be less in the presence of smaller numbers. If such numbers should occur where there appear to be no such basics, one might reasonably think of conspiracy or, even, happenstance.

When it comes to still smaller numbers—say one or two, or even three—one's prejudices might reasonably lean toward an explanation in terms of idiosyncratic results of the actions of particular founders or the peculiar aptitudes or validity of particular management traditions, or more or less singular monopoly positions. Or, with the numbers two or three, one's presumptions of conspiracy might be telling shots of intuition.

In any event, looking at the whole cloth of data in these exhibits, and at the list of Industry Categories in Table 1, in which none of The 200 occurred, one may reasonably feel disposed to a presumption that neither happenstance nor conspiracy was the most probable explanation for the occurrence, in their particular industries, of at least the large majority of the number of the 200 Largest Corporations of 1929 and the even much larger preponderance of their "presences" as measured by asset values.

One might reasonably keep an open mind as to the preferable explanations in the cases of a number of the industries listed in Exhibit 7, as to some of the industries in Exhibit 6, and even as to one or two listed in Exhibit 5. In these instances, more than in others, direct evidence, one way or the other, would be particularly welcome. These same issues of logic, evidence, and inference will be encountered in course of the analysis of the occurrence and presence among industries of the largest corporations of 1971. See Chapters 7 and 8.

7. "Entry" is a vague concept whose lack of clear meaning bedevils antitrust litigation. It is possible, literally, to "enter" an industry, say like soup, frozen fish, laundry bleach, automobile components, even computers on a very small, perhaps local, scale, perhaps with only one or two customers. That has been done thousands of times, and with better than average returns. If one equates "entry" with *quick, profitable* expansion to a scale of national, "ubiquitous," distribution—perhaps with a "full line" of products —with large numbers of customers—that is something else, again. To persist, to grow, even to a scale of $1 million of assets or sales, to survive as long as five to ten years, is hard in a free, competitive society. If it were easy, the number of millionaires would be a thousand times larger than it is.

What do you mean, concretely, by "entry"? Guaranteed success on a large scale?

8. Table 1, taken too literally, can be somewhat misleading. Bethlehem Steel had been engaged in shipbuilding. General Electric and Westinghouse had been in household

appliances and measuring instruments. Ford had even been in aircraft. The seeming "absence" of very large firms from some of these Industry Categories is a consequence of categorizing whole companies in accord with their principal, broad lines of business—actually, in accord with the one Industry Category in which they had the largest volume of sales.

The point does remain, however, that none of the Largest Corporations had its principal line of business in these particular industries and that, with exceptions of the sort mentioned, the *presence* of the Largest Firms in these industries was not major.

In recent years, with the rise of "conglomerates," that situation has changed somewhat. See Chapter 13.

9. The association of numbers (occurrence), mass (presence), and average size of corporations in 1971 is demonstrated and discussed in Chapter 8.

4

The Largest Nonfinancial Corporations of 1929-1930; the advancing Industrial Revolution in America

The notable clusters of big companies in some industries, the scatter of big companies in others, and their absence from still others were all *about* something; an underlying, powerful, persistent something. The pattern and order in the occurrence and presence of The 200 Largest Nonfinancial Corporations of 1929-30 were manifestations of the advance and spread of the continuing Industrial Revolution in America. This was not widely recognized at the time. It is not generally recognized even now.

Large business corporations—companies so large that their capital had to be provided by numerous stockholders; companies managed by people who owned only a small part of the equity—had emerged in the 18th century and became numerous early in the 19th century: turnpikes and canals, at first; railroads later. About the time of the Civil War, their numbers had grown and so had the scale of the largest. From the 1870s through the 1920s, they thrived in increasing numbers and growing scale, flourishing in a systemic, symbiotic, mutually affecting relationship with the rest of the nation. The growing and developing country was a nurturing environment for all sorts of enterprise, especially so for well-adapted organizations in rapidly growing and evolving, mostly, then, newer industries. America was a place of vast fertile spaces; of great natural waterways; of rich deposits of ores, and endless forests; of low-cost energy in wood, falling water, coal, oil and, in time, gas; a continent being peopled by a growing and spreading, hopeful and even confident population—a population becoming rich enough to generate, and to risk, capital in astonishing amounts; a nation whose laws, politics, and customs permitted and actively fostered *development*. Large and growing corporations, as well as individual farmers and entrepreneurs, drew heavily upon these favoring "externalities" for labor, intelligence, capital, resources, and encouragement. Large and growing corporations, especially, were prime movers in the development of the country during the half-century. Most notably in "newer" burgeoning industries, they assembled and organized available inputs on a scale seldom, if ever, seen before, and they applied the nascent technologies of the late 19th and early 20th centuries to produce the goods, services, and tools of an increasingly complex "Industrialism." And back in that environment, for the disposition of their outputs, these corporations found a free and open and receptive market of growing size and wealth, such as business had never even dreamed of before.

During the five decades from the 1870s to the 1920s, America's people grew from under 50 to over 120 million. In the 1870s and 80s, the country was still agrarian and rural, as it had been for 250 years from its beginning in the early 17th century. By the late 1920s, it had become the world's largest industrial and increasingly urban nation. America was becoming, very largely, a secular and "technological" state. From a relatively poor, heavily indebted nation, it became one of the world's richest and a major creditor. Total production had increased more than ninefold. Per capita income had more than tripled.[1] What had taken place was nothing less than a revolution.

In the very midst of such swirling changes, large numbers of citizens were deeply alarmed by much of what was going on. Few aspects of those revolutionary times were more troubling, and more dissonant with American tradition, than the rise of Big Business, of *very* large—in those days "colossal"—corporations. These new entities, so out of keeping with what had been, were in the forefront of the more visible changes of the times; they were also, in fact, although that was not widely understood, among the principal instruments and engines of those changes.

As it happens in circumstances of turbulent, revolutionary change, the economic, industrial, and social transformations going on in the United States in the half-century or so before 1929 engendered more than mere alarm. These trends and happenings elicited strong reactions. Much of the hostile reaction was directed at Big Business. Some of that was aimed at individuals: people like John D. Rockefeller, Andrew Carnegie, and others mentioned earlier. Some was aimed at faceless groups—"trusts"—such as the cornstarch, sugar, tobacco, and whiskey trusts. It was widely believed—and with some reason—that such men and groups, in a relentless drive toward "consolidation" and the like, were using unfair means to weaken or browbeat competitors and to force them to sell out at artificially low prices to the emerging "combinations." Second, it was widely believed—and again there was reason—that promoters of consolidations and such engaged in dishonest and unsound financial practices and manipulations to further their personal as well as corporate purposes.[2] Third, a major objective of consolidation having been, indeed, to build up combinations, far larger than most existing competitors, through mergers, trusts, holding companies, nonvoting stock, and other devices, it was not surprising that they were widely thought—again with some reason—to engage in various monopolistic practices.

In any event, many large fortunes were made in the process, and movers and shakers behind the rise of large corporations decreed Renaissance palazzi on Fifth Avenue, and stately pleasure domes in Tuxedo Park, Newport, and Pride's Crossing. The display and ostentation, the moneyed vulgarity, went badly with the strong hankering for simplicity and egalitarianism that were still so much a part of American culture. Not for no reason did Theodore Roosevelt's "Malefactors of Great Wealth" become bugbears of American politics in the years before World War I. (Such targets were still visible and popular, during Franklin Roosevelt's presidential campaigns many years later, even in 1940.)

Many critics were persuaded that the large corporations coming upon the scene during that half-century prior to 1929 were actually restructuring the American industrial order. They saw the growth of large corporations as *displacing* or *supplanting* prototypical small businesses, and *concentrating* them into larger and larger, and *fewer* big entities. This thought of the critics had many examples to go on.

Many, not all, large corporations of the times did indeed have beginnings in the putting together of numbers of smaller companies into a much larger one. This was true, for instance, in the early days of Standard Oil. It was true of the companies assembled and created by Carnegie and put together to form United States Steel Corporation. Even much later, into the 1920s, a number of corporations listed among the largest of 1929, including General Motors and Chrysler Corporation, early on had followed strategies of acquiring the *assets*—not the stocks—of numerous smaller companies, bringing together into one increasingly tightly integrated corporate whole the resources of numbers of heretofore independent, smaller companies.

In some cases, as in General Motors and Chrysler, that strategy of "consolidation" served well in establishing a base for successful competition with other large companies (as with Ford, then much the largest)—and with numerous smaller companies that, mostly unsuccessfully, tried to follow a strategy of paddling their own canoes. The combinations opened up possibilities for economies of scale, integration, for access to large amounts of capital needed by such industries, and, in time, for developing and applying advances in technology.

A public policy had already taken form in opposition to the rise of large corporations. In 1890, Congress passed the Sherman Act in an effort to strike at the trusts and contracts and conspiracies that restrained trade and competition. The Interstate Commerce Commission was created by Act of Congress in 1890 to protect users from discriminatory and exploitive actions of railroads. In 1914, Congress passed the Clayton Act. One provision of this act was to outlaw concentration through the acquisition by one corporation of the *stock* of another, where such action would impair competition. Another provision of the Clayton Act was to outlaw the kinds of price discrimination that had so operated to the advantage of some of the trusts, including Standard Oil. In that same year, Congress, by another act, established the Federal Trade Commission, which was to suppress unfair competition—presumably, mostly on the part of large corporations.

The federal government brought some notable antitrust suits whose objective was the dissolution of combinations and large corporations. Some of these were successful; those, for instance, against Standard Oil, DuPont, and American Tobacco. The courts ordered dissolution or divestiture of major portions of the business in each case. One major action failed, that against United States Steel Corporation, when the Supreme Court said, among other things, that "mere size" was not an antitrust offense. This was a momentous decision. Great size, in itself, was held not to be an offense, only certain *means* of achieving size. Bigness, as such, through this decision, achieved a certain legitimacy, if not popularity. But that legitimacy is still in question.

Despite Congress, attorneys general, and courts, and widespread popular dismay, large corporations kept growing in size and numbers, all the same. And the reason was that, behind the growth of big corporations, something more basic was happening than mere combination and consolidation of existing, smaller firms; more basic than fortune-making through financial frenzy, flummery, chicanery or otherwise; more basic, even, than the knowing, willful creation of monopoly positions for making profits through dominating size. All these captured attention and gave rise to much sound and much fury. Of far greater and more lasting moment, the continuing development of America was entering a new era, and was gathering speed and mass.

American industry was, indeed, developing a *new* structure. It was not *re*structuring the old.

I have mentioned critics of Big Business. Not only did they criticize large corporations, as such. They went further, especially vehement in their strictures against the industrial-urban, "mass" civilization growing up around them. Many recognized full well that this was the environment of, by, and for *large* organizations: big corporations, to be sure, but big unions also, and big government. America was coming to need large—*very* large—enterprise to supply the material base, wherewithal, and support for growing aggregations of millions of industrial urban dwellers: railroads, utilities, automobiles, petroleum, chemicals, iron and steel, nonferrous metals, mass transit. It was equally true, although not much remarked upon, that the traditional towns of American life, small and quiet in rural settings, were not environments where the productive establishments of Big Business could reside.

The most common charges against the large corporations of Big Business were that they (*a*) were inefficient; (*b*) controlled the politicians and political institutions of the country; (*c*) were immoral and amoral, or at least were not governed by, and according to, the benign values of responsible citizens brought up in the Judaeo-Christian tradition.[3]

We hear less, these days, about the first count in the presentment: inefficiency. But we hear as much or more than ever about the other two: the political power and the lack of morality of large corporations. We shall get back to these matters a bit later on.

THE CHANGING NATURE AND STRUCTURE OF AMERICAN INDUSTRY; EMERGENCE OF LARGE CORPORATIONS

The critics did not clearly see nor firmly grasp the fact that a *new* industrial order was coming into being, an order in several sectors of which, not all, *very* large scale and vertical integration were inherent and intrinsic. Underlying much of their thinking was the notion, scarcely ever articulated, that large corporations were merely aggregations, concentrations—rather artificial puttings-together, or something like that—of *small* corporations; that *big* corporations were adventitious creations of a few irresponsible and not very likable people; that somehow, as by breaking up the big corporations into numerous small ones, America could return to its more familiar and congenial industrial order of small, bourgeois, entrepreneurial firms, and to the social and political order which that connoted.

Adolf A. Berle, Jr., and Gardiner C. Means were among the most insightful, original, thorough, and, in some ways, useful critics of the "modern corporation." But even they did not clearly perceive and understand the nature of the emergent industrial order and the niches in that system that were being created and occupied by corporations that were large and, especially important, growing. Leitmotivs running through their work were "concentration"; "dispersion of stock ownership"; and "divergence" or "separation" between "ownership and control." Throughout their influential and, in some particulars, valuable book, they affirmed the notion that industry structures and corporate relationships, which in some historical past, had *not* been concentrated, dispersed, or separated, had now become so, or were in the process.

Their words portrayed the rise of large corporations as coming about through a process of reorganization of the previous industrial order. Central to this process, as Berle and Means talked about it, was the *concentration* of numbers of smaller, heretofore independent firms into fewer, larger corporate aggregates. This, it would appear, was accompanied by two other related processes: (*a*) the *dispersion* of the ownership of these resultant larger corporations (This took place, it would seem, as small groups of former manager-owners who had held the stocks of the predecessor small companies became, and were *replaced* by, larger numbers of stockholders who, inevitably, held smaller fractions of the ownership of the successor big companies. As these stockholdings, in turn, were sold off or bequeathed, they were dispersed even further.); and (*b*) the corollary process of *separation* of ownership from control. (This separation transformed men who had been manager-owners into hired employees—who had relatively little financial interest in the larger corporations—and replaced owner-managers with passive, distant, and for practical purposes anonymous investors.)

This is how they put it:

> These corporations (". . . whereby the wealth of innumerable individuals *has been concentrated* into huge aggregates and whereby control . . . *has been surrendered* to a unified direction . . .") have arisen in field after field as the myriad independent and competitive units of private business *have given way* to the few large groupings of the modern quasi-public corporations. The typical business unit of the 19th century was owned by individuals or small groups; was managed by them or their appointees; and was, in the main, limited in size by the personal wealth of the individuals in control. These units *have been supplanted* in even greater measure by great aggregates in which tens and even hundreds of thousands of workers and property worth hundreds of millions of dollars, belonging to tens or even hundreds of thousands of individuals, *are combined* through the corporate mechanism into a single producing organization under unified control and management. Such a unit is the American Telephone and Telegraph Company, perhaps the most advanced development of the corporate system . . . . (Italics added.)[4]

Embedded in the quoted phrasing (language quite like that of many other commentators) is a subtle but basic misapprehension of what had been, and still was, going on—and still is, to this day. Taking place were the coming on the scene, the *inception, growth,* and the *spread* of *new* corporations in *new* industries. This brought about, and was accompanied by, *qualitative* changes, as well as great quantitative *growth* in the industrial structure. Processes were going on that, in some dimensions, were far more important than mere *concentration* of preexisting firms. The new and growing corporations were producing *new* products and *new* services. They were applying new knowledge—of electricity, thermodynamics, metallurgy, chemistry, for instance; or new management techniques in manufacturing, marketing, finance, control, organization. Intrinsic in these industries—indeed, of overpowering technological and commercial significance—were requisite large-scale productive operations, and opportunities for economies of vertical integration, that is, the tightening linkage of successive producing units into larger and larger "conversion" *systems.*

The individual corporations of Big Business, themselves, were not merely, as has been said earlier, quantitatively larger than traditional small firms, not mere magnifications of them. In manning and organization structure; in control processes; in application of new technological and managerial techniques and knowledge; in methods of raising capital; in these as well as in their productive "hardware," the big corporations were *new kinds* of entities, not simply aggregations of smaller ones, and certainly not simply *bigger* specimens of the same kinds as the small. New kinds of productive units had been erected—often by combination of consolidation, as first step—and then grew and flourished because they were peculiarly well adapted to a whole environment that was evolving.

Large Corporations and the developing industrial infrastructure

Consider the railroads. There were more of them on the 1929 roster of Largest Corporations than of any other kinds of companies. In total, and on the average (with the exception of the telephone and telegraph companies) they were larger than the rest of The 200. In their day, the railroads were the very epitome of Big Business. From their beginnings, before the Civil War, the railroads were among the earliest and most prominent of the capital-intensive, new-technology-using, large-scale industries of the continuing Industrial Revolution. In fact, there were never, in any meaningful way, *"small*-business," proprietor-owned-and-operated, atomistic railroads. Even the first roads, tiny to be sure by the yardsticks of 1929, represented what were in those early days, *very large* aggregates of capital, larger than the private fortunes of their promoters, bigger than family fortunes, large enough to require joint-stock financing. Almost from the very outset, ownership of the railroads was widespread—dispersed—among numerous owners; and the ownership and control of them were separate.

From their beginnings, the railroads grew with gathering speed. The growth of railroad mileage in the United States is shown by the figures of Table 3, which approximately describe a classic sigmoid (S-shaped) growth curve. For more than four-score-and-seven years, the promoters and builders of railroads were hard at work. If there was ever a "go-go," *growth* industry, it was the railroads in their salad days.

The managements of the railroads, naturally enough, pursued efficient utilization of great overhead investments in ways (in tracks, cuts, fills, bridges, and tunnels) and in rolling stock; economies of scale in design, construction and operations, and in the use of managerial talents. Much of the growth was what we now call "internal growth," financed by retention of earnings. Even more was financed by expanded borrowings, and flotation of additional shares of ownership.

But also, almost from the very beginning, there was great movement toward integration of individual lines and companies into

TABLE 3
The growth of American railroads, 1830-1930

Year	Road mileage*	Increase in mileage, previous decade
1830	23 miles	23 miles
1840	2,800	2,880
1850	9,000	6,200
1860	30,600	21,600
1870	52,900	22,300
1880	93,300	40,400
1890	166,700	73,400
1900	206,600	39,900
1910	266,200	59,600
1920	296,800	30,600
1930	303,200	6,400

*1830-80, miles of road operated; 1890-1930, first main, and other main tracks operated. Round numbers.
Source: U.S. Department of Commerce, Bureau of the Census, *Historical Statistics of the United States, Colonial Times to 1957* (Washington, D.C.: U.S. Government Printing Office, 1960), pp. 427 and 429.

larger and larger *systems*. Part of this impetus came from the pursuit of economies and advantages of efficient utilization of equipment and crews, and convenience of continuous movement, especially between increasingly distant points. And in this process of consolidation, probably inevitable in any event because of the objective gains to be had, there were also immensely alluring possibilities for financial manipulation and, sometimes, raw skulduggery. And these kinds of opportunities were often pursued at least as energetically.

The rise of the railroads and the large railroad corporations, behind all the hugger-mugger of frenzied finance, represented the advent and growth and diffusion of a new technology of transportation, and the development of an utterly new industry with an utterly new structure. The tremendous investments, the large economic power, the widespread ownership, and the *separateness* (a *state* of affairs)—not separation (a *process*)—of ownership and control were inherent in the very nature of railroads on a continental scale, and implicit from the beginning. So, also, was the monopolistic position of the railroads, which also characterized them from the beginning and which had achieved a climax of sorts by 1929.

Granted that consolidation and combination did, to be sure, take place among the railroads, the outstanding aspect of their history was not that. The outstanding aspect was *growth*, far rather than concentration. Consolidation was a matter of form. Growth was a matter of substance.[5]

After the railroads, the most numerous large corporations in 1929 were the Electric, gas, and sanitary utilities. Of these, 39 were among The 200 Largest Companies. The processes of growth of the electric and gas utilities, begun long after the railroads, had much in common with them. As was true of the early decades of the railroads, the

TABLE 4
The growth of American electric utilities, 1902-1929

Year	Generating capacity of central stations (000 kilowatts)	Increase in capacity, previous period (000 kilowatts)
1902	1,212	1,212*
1907	2,709	1,497
1912	5,165	2,456
1917	8,994	3,829
1922	14,192	5,198
1927	25,079	10,887
1929	29,839	4,760†

*From the beginning.
†Two years.
Source: U.S. Department of Commerce, Bureau of the Census, *Historical Statistics of the United States, Colonial Times to 1957* (Washington, D.C.: U.S. Government Printing Office, 1960), p. 509.

growth of the electric utilities, as measured in thousands of kilowatts of installed generating capacity in central stations, also showed rapid and increasing rates of *growth*. From "ground zero" in the 1870s, the installed capacity of the industry grew to what we see now was a very modest level by the close of the 19th century. But from the beginning of the 20th century to the Great Crash, the industry grew by leaps, increasing by a factor of 25. By the early 1920s, the industry was adding each year more capacity—twice as much—as had existed in total in 1902, when Teddy Roosevelt successfully brought a dissolution suit against Northern Securities Company, one of the first holding companies, a form of financial organization that came to be characteristic of the electric utilities. (In this instance, the company was organized to hold stock of railroad corporations, the Northern Pacific and Great Northern, roads which, to an extent, were in competition.) Unlike that of the railroads, the growth of the "utilities" had not "topped out" by 1929-30. Far from it, as we know and shall see statistically, later on.

It was not by chance that, after the railroads, there were more electric and gas utility companies on the list of Largest Nonfinancial Corporations in 1929 than of any other sort, and that, second to the rails, they had the next largest share of the total assets of The 200. The utilities, too, from their beginnings, even as local enterprises, required relatively great amounts of capital for their construction and expansion. The economics of their overhead costs were similar. They, also, had a legally monopolistic position. It was said and believed that the generation and distribution of gas and electric power were "natural monopolies." That belief was not wrong. There were objective reasons, inherent in the technology, the hardware, economies of scale, and in the nature of their markets, for linking purely local utilities together into larger and larger operating systems. (These reasons still exist.) And, again, there were enormous profits to be made by promoters and insiders in the course of putting these systems together.

Some of the utility "systems" that were put together were largely *financial* arrangements, structures of interwoven holding companies, devices useful, in all truth, for getting and allocating to operating entities almost unprecedented amounts of capital. It was in the financing and refinancing of these systems that arose some of the most highly publicized, if not the greatest, opportunities for financial gain and for dazzling financial sleight of hand and, on occasion, outrageous dishonesty. But, again, the electric and gas utilities *did* grow. Their growth *after* 1929 was even more spectacular. But that is another story. We shall come to it later.

A key point to be grasped in an effort to understand the development of the nation, and not to be lost sight of because of all the distracting brouhaha, was that the *growth* of the electric utilities was far more than merely the *concentration* of what had been. Concentration was a means to an end, and not a major one at that. Growth, again, was the substance. From small beginnings, often mere "seeds" of enterprise, large corporations grew.

It is clear—certainly from the perspective of today—that the growth of huge electric and gas utilities, like the growth of the railroads, was part and parcel of the Industrial Revolution as it advanced into the 20th century. And, again, it was a matter of the emergence of a *whole new industry* with a whole new structure. The rise of the utilities was not merely a restructuring of something that had existed earlier in simpler form. The rise of large utilities was an integral part of a new chapter in the historical development of the United States.

Then there were the telephone and transit utilities. And here, again, there were similarities: large, and growing, even huge minimum scale; capital-intensivity; monopolistic franchise; pressures toward integration of single companies into systems; enormous growth from small beginnings. They, also, were part and parcel of that Industrial Revolution. They, also, represented the *new,* and not merely a restructuring of what had been.

The growth and, in the process, the transformation of telecommunications in the United States were two of the more spectacular strands in the history of the United States. Telegraphy, founded in 1842, was already "big" business by the Civil War. But telephony, from a single, primitive, jury-rigged circuit in 1876, streaked ahead of telegraphy some years before the turn of the century. Drawing inputs in growing flows from the American environment—technology, materials, capital, people—the telephone system grew as few industries have ever done since. The service it provided was not merely incrementally better than letter post or even telegraphy. It was an identifiable, if not a discrete innovation, a "discontinuity." The data in Table 5 measure the growth. Not measured are the reciprocal effects that vastly improved communication had upon the whole of American development and the possibilities and opportunities opened up, year after year, by that development.

TABLE 5
The growth of the American telephone industry, 1880-1929

Year	Number of telephones (000)	Increase in number over previous period (000)	Miles of wire (000)	Increase in mileage over previous period (000)
1880	54	54*	34	34
1885	156	102	156	122
1890	234	78	240	84
1895	340	106	675	435
1900	1,356	1,016	1,962	1,287
1905	4,127	2,771	5,780	3,818
1910	7,635	3,508	11,642	5,862
1915	10,524	2,889	23,721‡	12,079†
1920	13,329	2,805	30,112	6,391§
1925	16,936	3,607	49,519	19,407
1929	20,068	3,132§	74,542	25,023†

* From the beginning.
† Six years.
‡ 1916; prior years, "Bell" system only; from 1916, includes "Bell" and independent companies.
§ Four years.
Source: U.S. Department of Commerce, Bureau of the Census, *Historical Statistics of the United States, Colonial Times to 1957* (Washington, D.C.: U.S. Government Printing Office, 1960), pp. 480, and 482 and 483. The figures given by *Historical Statistics of the United States from Colonial Times to 1970*, p. 783, for the years 1920, 1925, and 1929 are negligibly different.

In 1929, of the 20 million telephones in the country, the Bell system had over 15 million. Another 4.5 million phones of other companies were connected with that system and, through it, with each other. No doubt about it. As many observers noted, often with alarm, American Telephone and Telegraph Company in 1929 did (and does, even more, now) represent a large aggregate of capital, operated by hundreds of thousands of employees (364,402 in 1929; more now). The people who controlled it (and those who do, now) surely owned altogether no significant fraction of it. This corporation, and the system that had (and has) been organized under its aegis bear no resemblance to the idealized, or even the real individual family business of the 19th century, competing in an unstructured market with a dust of other small companies. In these matters, the critics were not wrong. But they erred and missed *the* point of its growth in expressing the notion that the company had *supplanted* a host of small companies that had, unfortunately, *given way.*

In point of fact, in its early chapter AT&T did merge into itself and acquire a number of local operating companies with a view to building up a nationwide, monopoly system. But that means of growth came to a halt in 1913, by agreement with the attorney general.[6] From then on, the company accounted for all its growth. In the next 16 years to 1929, however measured, the company grew several times over. The growth of the Bell System since 1929 has been even more notable than before.

The process of the growth of AT&T, from its commercially—and socially—insignificant beginnings, followed a very different course from that of mere concentration. It was a dynamic process of *development,* both qualitative as well as quantitative.

The history of the mass transit companies, by now, is a sad one, and need not long detain us. In 1929, there were 8 transit companies among The 200 Largest Corporations. Some, if not all of these did, indeed, have their 19th-century origins in independent companies that were franchised exclusively for particular routes in cities. Such franchises were given for Fifth Avenue in New York, for example, and to individual cable car companies on particular hills of San Francisco. At various points in the stories of the biggest transit companies, consolidation did figure. In 1929, four separate transit companies in New York City, alone, were among the very largest nonfinancial corporations of the country. Over the years, economies of scale and integration, and public convenience, together no doubt with opportunities for promoters' gains, operated to foster corporate consolidations. But it is hard to remember, now, that, in their day also, these companies were *growth* companies. In any case, at least the largest of these companies have long since disappeared from the private sector.

In sum, the very large companies producing rail transportation, electrical energy, communication, and mass transit were the means through which large assemblages of capital and human resources were brought together to exploit technologies heretofore unknown and to operate on scales without precedent, and to serve demands that seemed to grow without limit. These companies represented—they *were,* concretely—key elements in the developing infrastructure of the American Industrial Revolution as it evolved and gathered mass and momentum. That burgeoning revolution was the environment in which they appeared and grew. In systemic and reciprocal relationships with that environment, they helped make possible its growth and development and were in turn, themselves, made possible by the new and expanding markets and sources of necessary inputs: capital, equipment, educated personnel.

It is no wonder that, of the 200 Largest Companies, 95 of them were in these five industries; that these particular companies held almost two-thirds of all the assets of the 200 Largest Corporations; that they held about two-thirds of all the assets invested in *all* transportation and *all* utility companies; and that they held over 25 percent of *all* assets of *all* nonfinancial corporations.

Large Corporations and the development of new manufacturing industries

In that same roiling half-century from 1880 to 1930, growth and change were going on even more rapidly, if possible, in manufacturing and mining than in the regulated industries. Again, concentration, consolidation, combination, and such, did, indeed, happen; but they were minor developments as compared to substantive expansion and development. The biggest and most rapid growths and change, the most dramatic developments in American industry—not surprisingly, really—were unrolling in what were then, in still largely agrarian America, newer industries.

One way of gauging growth and development in our industries over that period is to look at values of capital investments in them at various points in time. In Exhibits 11 and 12 are displayed illustrative data for selected industries, in selected years from 1880 to 1929, that measure "capital invested in manufacturing." That figure excludes cash, receivables, inventories, and other current assets and investments in securities. It does, however, understate capacity growth where there were improvements in processes and equipment, as there were in many industries, especially newer ones, during those years.

The data displayed in Exhibit 11 relate to industries characterized by rapid growth, emerging large-scale organization, and continuing surges of technological change. Exhibit 12 relates to selected industries characterized by smaller-scale organizations and relative technological maturity as of the closing decades of the 19th century. In the first category are Iron and steel and products, Nonferrous metals, Petroleum refining, Paper, pulp, and products, Chemicals and allied substances, Rubber products, Electrical machinery, and Motor vehicles. In the second, typical of their broad category, are Textiles and textile products, Leather products, Forest products (other than paper, pulp, and their products), and Printing and publishing.

The data reflect much more rapid growth in the former than in the latter group of industries. The data in these exhibits almost speak for themselves. Using "capital invested in manufacturing" in "Total manufacturing" as a benchmark (Exhibit 12), the analyst sees that the relative growths in the "newer" industries were greater and faster than in then more "mature" industries; of the newer industries, the absolute growths were also larger, except for Textiles and textile products.

Exhibit 13 presents some summary data based on Exhibits 11 and 12, that illustrate how much more rapidly newer manufacturing industries were growing than older ones, and how the "mix" of manufacturing—apart from the magnitude of manufacturing output—was changing. By 1929, industries that had been negligible, or even nonexistent, in 1880 had grown to a point where they were clearly important.

In 1880, capital invested in manufacturing in the eight "newer" industries accounted for about 19 percent of all capital then invested in manufacturing. By 1929, after almost 50 years of generally extraordinary industrial growth, these particular industries had come to account for about 43 percent. In some instances, these industries

EXHIBIT 11
Growth of selected larger-scale Big Business industries in America, 1880-1929: Capital invested in manufacturing (values in millions of 1929 dollars; index numbers, 1880 = 100.0)

Year	Iron and steel and products			Nonferrous metals			Petroleum refining			Paper, pulp, and products		
	Capital	Increase for period	Index numbers	Capital	Increase for period	Index numbers	Capital	Increase for period	Index numbers	Capital	Increase for period	Index numbers
1880*	$ 472	$ 472	100.0	$ 116	$ 116	100.0	$ 37	$ 37	100.0	$ 90	$ 90	100.0
1890	1,143	671†	242.2	276	160†	237.9	151	114†	408.1	200	110†	222.2
1900	1,599	456†	338.8	610	334†	525.9	195	44†	527.0	453	253†	503.3
1904	2,886	1,287‡	511.4	804	194‡	693.1	254	59‡	686.5	670	217‡	744.4
1909	4,305	1,419‡	912.1	1,203	399‡	1,037.1	327	73§	883.8	1,002	332§	1,113.3
1914	5,166	861§	1,094.5	1,365	162§	1,176.7	552	225§	1,491.9	1,246	244§	1,384.4
1919	6,735	1,569§	1,426.9	1,808	443§	1,558.6	1,380	828§	3,729.7	1,524	278§	1,693.3
1929	6,666	−69†	1,412.3	2,364	556†	2,037.9	6,092	4,712†	16,464.9	2,239	715†	2,478.8
Increase, 1880-1929		$6,194			$2,248			$6,055			$2,149	

Year	Chemicals and allied products			Rubber products			Electrical machinery ‖			Motor vehicles		
	Capital	Increase for period	Index numbers	Capital	Increase for period	Index numbers	Capital	Increase for period	Index numbers	Capital	Increase for period	Index numbers (1890 = 100.0)
1880*	$ 206	$ 206	100.0	$ 10	$ 10	100.0	$ 3	$ 3	100.0	–	–	–
1890	478	272†	206.0	36	26†	360.0	40	37†	1,333.3	$ 4	$ 4	100.0
1900	869	391†	421.8	74	38†	740.0	180	140†	6,000.0	73	69†	1,825.0
1904	1,134	265‡	650.5	93	19‡	930.0	379	199‡	12,633.3	57	−16‡	1,425.0
1909	1,531	397§	743.2	139	46§	1,390.0	554	175§	18,466.7	267	210§	6,675.0
1914	2,078	547§	1,008.7	265	126§	2,650.0	718	164§	23,933.3	616	349§	15,400.0
1919	2,777	699§	1,348.1	704	439§	7,040.0	1,146	428§	38,200.0	1,936	1,320§	48,400.0
1929	4,221	1,444†	2,049.0	1,131	427†	11,310.0	1,600	454†	53,333.3	2,742	806†	68,550.0
Increase, 1880-1929		$4,015			$1,121			$1,597			$2,742	

* For 1880, cumulative capital to date.
† Increase during previous decade.
‡ Increase during previous four years.
§ Increase during previous five years.
‖ Electrical machinery and equipment; radios.

Source: *Historical Statistics of the United States . . .*, p. 412; Daniel Creamer, et al., *Capital in Manufacturing and Mining* (Princeton: Princeton University Press, 1960), pp. 241-47. See Note 7, Chapter 4. Data for 1880 and 1890 include "custom and neighborhood shops." Data for 1900, 1904, 1909, 1914, 1919 include "Factories producing annual value of $500 or more." Data for 1929 include "Factories producing annual value of $5,000 or more."

EXHIBIT 12
Growth of selected smaller-scale industries in America, 1880-1929: Capital invested in manufacturing (values in millions of 1929 dollars; index numbers, 1880 = 100.0)

Textile and textile products

Year	Capital	Increase for period	Index numbers
1880*	$ 998	$ 998	100.0
1890	2,024	1,026†	202.8
1900	2,876	852†	288.2
1904	3,482	606‡	348.9
1909	4,636	1,154§	464.5
1914	5,163	527§	517.3
1919	6,752	1,589§	676.6
1929	8,195	1,443†	821.1
Increase, 1880-1929		$7,197	

Leather products

Year	Capital	Increase for period	Index numbers
1880*	$ 328	$ 328	100.0
1890	640	312†	195.1
1900	809	169†	246.6
1904	1,066	257‡	325.0
1909	1,359	293§	414.3
1914	1,351	-8§	411.9
1919	1,411	60§	430.2
1929	1,213	-198†	369.8
Increase, 1880-1929		$ 885	

Forest products ‖

Year	Capital	Increase for period	Index numbers
1880*	$ 847	$ 847	100.0
1890	1,950	1,103†	230.2
1900	2,253	303†	266.0
1904	2,662	409‡	314.3
1909	3,591	929§	424.0
1914	3,475	-116§	410.3
1919	3,155	-320§	372.5
1929	4,083	928†	482.1
Increase, 1880-1929		$3,236	

Printing, publishing, and allied products

Year	Capital	Increase for period	Index numbers
1880*	$ 144	$ 144	100.0
1890	466	322†	323.6
1900	801	335†	556.3
1904	939	138‡	652.1
1909	1,265	326§	874.5
1914	1,444	179§	1,002.8
1919	1,556	112§	1,080.6
1929	2,737	1,184†	1,900.7
Increase, 1880-1929		$2,593	

Total manufacturing

Year	Capital	Increase for period	Index numbers
1880*	$ 4,821	$ 4,821	100.0
1890	11,157	6,336†	231.4
1900	17,452	6,295†	362.0
1904	23,295	5,843‡	483.2
1909	31,563	8,268§	654.7
1914	36,737	5,174§	762.0
1919	46,094	9,357§	956.1
1929	63,292#	17,198†	1,312.8
Increase, 1880-1929		$58,471	

* For 1880, cumulative capital to date.
† Increase during previous decade.
‡ Increase during previous four years.
§ Increase during previous five years.
‖ Excludes paper, pulp, etc.; includes sawmill products, furniture, etc.
Given in Creamer as 63,022.

Source: *Historical Statistics of the United States*, p. 412; Creamer et al., *Capital in Mining and Manufacturing*, pp. 241-47. Data for 1880 and 1890 include "custom and neighborhood shops"; data for 1900, 1904, 1909, 1914, 1919 include "Factories producing annual value of $500 or more"; data for 1929 include "Factories producing annual value of $5,000 or more." See Note 7, Chapter 4.

EXHIBIT 13

Relative growth of capital invested in manufacturing, 1880-1929; Selected larger-scale
Big Business and smaller-scale industries in America

	Percentage of total assets, 1880	Percentage of total manufacturing growth, 1880-1929	Percentage of total assets, 1929
Iron and steel and products	10.0%	10.6%	10.5%
Nonferrous metals	2.4	3.8	3.7
Petroleum refining	0.8	10.4	9.6
Paper, pulp, and products	1.9	3.7	3.5
Chemicals and allied substances	4.3	6.7	6.7
Rubber products	0.2	1.9	1.8
Electrical machinery	*	2.7	2.5
Motor vehicles	*	4.7	4.3
Textiles and textile products	20.7	12.3	12.9
Leather products	6.8	1.5	1.9
Forest products.	17.6	5.5	6.5
Printing, publishing, and allied products . .	3.0	4.4	4.3
Total manufacturing	100.0%	100.0%	100.0%

*Less than $\frac{1}{10}$ of 1 percent.
Source: Exhibits 11 and 12.

grew from truly negligible beginnings, notably Petroleum refining, Paper, pulp, and products, Electrical machinery, and Motor vehicles—to become *major* industries. The growth of investment in manufacturing in these eight industries—about $27 billion of 1929 dollars—accounted for almost half of all growth in investment in manufacturing over those five decades—which was about $58 billion. While total manufacturing investment increased 12-fold, from $4.8 billion of 1929 dollars to $58.5 billion, manufacturing investment in these eight large-scale Big Business industries increased almost 30-fold, from $935 million to over $27 billion of 1929 dollars. *Growth,* not simply nor even primarily "consolidation," was what was going on.

Behind such quantitative growth, enormous *changes* were happening. Time can be spared to mention only a few. In 1880, practically all steel making in the United States involved the Bessemer process, which accounted for about 1.1 million long tons out of 1.2 million. By 1929, out of *56* million tons of steel ingots and casting produced—there's growth!—48 million came from open-hearths, a process that had accounted for only 10 percent of the production of 1880.[8]

At the turn of the century, electrical machinery was still a very minor industry. Automobiles, such as they were, were gentlemen's toys and diversions. Petroleum refining in the 1880s and 90s was certainly primitive as compared to what was to come; by 1929, it had evolved into an enormously complex, massive operation. Up until World War I, the United States was largely dependent on European sources for chemicals other than the simplest. By 1929, the domestic industry was producing large amounts of dyes, pigments, and the early synthetics and plastics. The Rubber products industry that produced tires for America's millions of automobiles in 1929 bore little recognizable relationship to that which, in the 1880s and 90s, produced "elastic" for corsets and early tires for bicycles. The growth of these industries was spectacular, and we all know something of how their outputs evolved.

A couple more observations will highlight the substantive growth and change of two key industries. The first "billion dollar" corporation was the United States Steel Corporation. The sheer size of the company was a source of apprehension to many. Yet, in invested dollar and tonnage terms, the steel industry grew more than fourfold with the next 20 years, and almost sixfold in the next 30.

Petroleum refining (only the "manufacturing" part of the whole petroleum industry) seemed so large in the opening decade of the century, and was so completely dominated by Standard Oil, that it was the prime target for government efforts at dissolution. The effort succeeded in 1911. Thirty-three companies were "disaffiliated." But by 1919, growth of the industry was such that eight formerly affiliated companies of the Standard Oil Trust were among the 100 largest "industrial" corporations in their own right. The refining end of the business, alone, more than doubled, and by 1929 had increased over 20-fold.[9]

This is not the place to attempt to interpret the reasons and means of growth of all the other kinds of companies on the 1929 list of Largest Nonfinancial Corporations. But a few more comments are in order. Some of the "manufacturing" companies on the list had, indeed, put together a number of smaller companies, but then had grown by new means for satisfying long-established consumer wants: those in meat and tobacco, for instance. The rise of large companies in these industries depended upon automation, economies of scale, integration of manufacturing and distribution, economies of mass promotion. Sometimes their growth was aided by other less admirable accomplishments, such as the exercise of sheer power in market places, and the exploitation of labor—unorganized, often immigrant, even child labor.

Some of the largest companies of 1929 represented cumulating results of early efforts to bring technologies of the Industrial Revolution to distribution: division and integration of labor; general purpose and specialized materials-handling equipment; time and motion studies; budgets and control mechanisms; applications of new techniques for site selection, unit layouts, media selection, etc. These included general merchandise and mail order companies and the then biggest chain of food stores: Sears Roebuck; Montgomery Ward; Woolworth's; the A&P. Some of these companies also had extraordinary power in buying as well as in selling, and were not loath to use it.[10]

Six of the largest companies produced manufactured food products that still, well after the turn of the century, represented innovations in the diets of increasingly urban Americans: canned goods, factory-made jams, jellies, ice cream, bread, cakes. In the words of *The Music Man,* "the Uneeda Biscuit in the air-tight sanitary package . . . made the cracker-barrel obsolete, obsolete." Prepared foods were the basis for a social, as well as a dietary, revolution. That revolution is still flowing fast, as a visit to any supermarket in the country will reveal.

The fact should again be noted that *none* of the very largest companies had arisen in several of the very oldest categories of industry: Agriculture and fisheries; Construction; Apparel; Furniture and fixtures; Printing and publishing; Wholesale trade; and Services (other than motion pictures). In contrast to other industries, such as railroads, petroleum, and automobiles, there were in these older industries no scale barriers to "entry" nor to healthy survival on a small, even individualistic "proprietorship-operated" scale. In these particular industries, factors simply did not prevail that had made possible and attractive the building up and growth of very large corporations in other fields: economies of large scale and integration; of mechanization; inherent promise, as well as complexities of developing technology, organization, and control systems.

GROWTH AND CHANGE IN THE BUSINESS COMMUNITY; GROWTH AND CHANGE IN THE GROSS NATIONAL PRODUCT

The history of the products and services that were produced by the use of those investments and that flowed out of American industry is generally too well known to rehearse here in any great detail. Overall, the output (GNP) of the American economy increased, as has been said, more than ninefold, from about $11 billion in 1874 (in 1929 dollars) to over $104 billion in 1929. And the greatest increases in production within that stream, always relatively, and mostly even absolutely, came about in those industries that epitomized the new industries that characterized our industrial growth in the decades after the Civil War.[11] According to data prepared by Professor Simon Kuznets, a Nobel prizewinner, the Gross National Product (in 1929 dollars) rose over fivefold (5.6 times) from an annual average of about $14.8 billion in the decade 1874-83 to an annual average of about $82.8 billion in the decade 1924-33. In per capita terms, the Gross National Product more than doubled (it increased 2.3 times), rising from $304 (in 1929 dollars) to $687.[12] During those 50 years, the U.S. population somewhat more than doubled (it increased 2.3 times), rising from a bit over 50 million in 1880 to a bit over 123 million early in 1930.[13]

Absolutely and relatively, the expansion of the American economy in those two generations from the 1870s to the 1920s remains without parallel—except, perhaps, its own growth in the following half-century. Not only did the Gross National Product and the National Income *increase*—that was important and dramatic. At least as important, if not more so, and really more dramatic, the *composition* and the *sources* of the Product and the Income were transformed. The qualitative *changes* tell more about what was going on in America than the quantitative *increases.*

Investment and capacity were generally increasing in American industries, more rapidly, as we have seen, in newer industries than in old. So also, of course, was physical production and output. Production in manufacturing as a whole, measured by index numbers of physical output, increased by about 3.6 times from 1899 to 1929. Some industries—the newer ones—increased more rapidly than the average of the overall, some more slowly—the older ones. Trends of these sorts are depicted in Table 6. These data are, especially, suggestive of the changes that were taking place in the composition of "mix" of the outputs of American industry and of consequent changes in the composition of its National Product and of the sources of its National Income.

TABLE 6
Increase in physical output, all manufacturing and selected industries, 1899-1929 (index numbers, 1929 = 100)

	Index numbers, 1899	Ratio, 1929 output to 1899 output
All manufacturing	28.0	3.6
Textile products	38.0	2.6
Leather products	64.0	1.6
Iron and steel products	21.0	4.8
Chemical products	19.0	5.3
Transportation equipment	7.3	13.7
Petroleum refining	5.9	16.9

Source: Solomon Fabricant, *The Output of Manufacturing Industries, 1899-1937* (New York: National Bureau of Economic Research, 1940), pp. 60-61, 72, 110, and 517. Over the years, "transportation equipment" includes an increasing proportion of motor vehicles.

The foregoing figures sketch out a major story line, the changing composition of the production-income streams in America during those four decades. Other data that measure *rates of change* may convey a further, and perhaps better, feel of the dynamics of development in various sectors of the economy. In Exhibit 14 are given the *average annual rates of growth* of production from 1885 to 1929 for a number of selected products and product groups. These data were compiled quite a few years ago by Arthur F. Burns, not long ago the chairman of the Board of Governors of the Federal Reserve System. The reader may be helped to grasp the significance of these differences in rates of growth if reminded that a quantity that increases at a compound rate of 1 percent per annum will double in about 67 years; at a compound rate of 5 percent, will double in 14 years; at 10 percent, will double in 8 years. Over a 45 year period—as from 1885 to 1929—a 1 percent annual growth rate will result in an aggregate growth of 1.6 times; at 5 percent, a growth of 9.2 times; and at 10 percent, a growth of about 75 times.

EXHIBIT 14
Selected rates of output growth in America, 1885-1929

Products and product groups	Average annual rate of growth, 1885-1929	Ratio, 1929 output to 1885 output
Wheat (millions of bushels)	1.1%	1.9
Corn (millions of bushels)	0.9	1.3
Cotton (thousands of bales)	1.9	2.5
Petroleum (crude, millions of barrels)	8.5	46.0
Chemical materials		
Sulphur (thousands of long tons)	24.6	*
Phosphate rock (thousands of long tons)	5.4	9.5
Salt (millions of barrels)	4.9	8.7
Cotton (consumption in manufacture, thousands of bales) . . .	3.0	3.4
Wood (consumption in manufacture, millions of pounds)	1.0	1.6
Steel (thousands of long tons)	7.2	33.0
Aluminum (thousands of pounds)	24.3	*
Copper (consumption, millions of pounds)	6.0	34.2

*Because of the extremely small bases in the very early years, these figures are not very meaningful. Between 1900 and 1929, sulphur production grew by a factor of over 750; even between 1910 and 1929, it grew by a factor of 9.6. Between 1900 and 1929, aluminum output grew by a factor of 31 times.

Source: Arthur F. Burns, *Production Trends in the United States since 1870* (New York: National Bureau of Economic Research, 1934), pp. 55, 57-59; and Table 44.

It is quite clear from these data, which are but a sampling of those put together by Mr. Burns, that the average annual rates of growth were higher, even much higher, among newer, large-scale, Big Business industries than elsewhere in the economy, whether in agriculture or in manufacturing.

As Mr. Burns said, even these data fail to convey the full import of the growth of then new industries. They do not, for example, show the growths of outputs of such new industries as telephones, telegraph, automobiles, pipelines, and aircraft, which appeared only in later years. He might have added, also, all kinds of electrical apparatus, motion pictures, and electric power. Nor do the data presented here reflect the contribution to the transformation of American industry of the *disappearance* of older, small-scale industries of an earlier era: whale oil lamps, wagons and carriages, for instance.

ECONOMIC DYNAMICS AND CULTURAL LAG AMONG ECONOMISTS

In the decade following 1929, despite such facts, many observers, including many professional economists, held views to the effect that the rise of big corporations was due to mergers, consolidations, and the like combined with predatory, unfair, and other antisocial practices. A whole body of theory grew up and gained rather widespread acceptance that these mergers, and so on, were responsible for reducing the numbers of competitors in industry after industry, creating powerful, noncompetitive, oligopolistic industries under the control of a few large sellers. Such industry structures were held to so operate as to stultify expansion; to raise prices; to suppress competition; and (to the extent that technological change was considered) to suppress or retard innovation; to misallocate resources into socially less valuable and less productive uses; and, generally, to depress or slow down increases in the standard of living. In oligopolistic, Big Business industries, it was held, price was higher, output smaller, quality inferior, and investment less than would have been the case were the industries made up of large numbers of small, anonymous "competitive" producers. A whole generation of professional economists was exposed to ideas of this sort.[14]

In one especially influential treatise of the thirties, concerned with the "decline of competition," the author put it forth as a fact that American industry was characterized by a decline in the numbers of sellers. He said, "It is a commonplace that the number of firms in many industries has been falling." He was much concerned by what he took to be "the reduction of the number of firms and their increasing size over the past half century." This particular author did allow that there could well be, and probably were, economies in large scale; but he was clear in his mind that large corporate size had been achieved by socially reprehensible methods:

> The increased volume of business necessary to permit the utilization of these ["methods of production which are economical only if large quantities are produced under a single organization"] has been attained in part by price cutting; the largest firms, however, have more frequently attained their present size either by direct attacks upon rivals in the form of temporary or local price cutting aimed at destroying them, by defaming their products and the like, or by mergers. . . .[15]

There is no point in raking over old coals and trying all over again these kinds of charges, so commonly made. But it is significant that in the rather substantial volume from which this quotation is taken, no discussion—literally, *none*—appears that deals with the enormous expansion of the Gross National Product and of the National Income in total and per capita; with the extraordinary changes in the compositions of the Gross National Product and the industry sources of National Income; with the extraordinary increases in outputs of utterly new industries, and the amazing changes in industrial technologies coming to be applied—all of which characterized the half-century preceding its publication. Capitalism, the writer was persuaded, had failed to preserve its competitive quality.

As one studies—and now, again, from the perspective of many years later, studies anew—the rather mournful literature of "monopolistic" and "imperfect" competition that told in loving detail of the shortcomings of the American industrial structure of the early 1930s, one is left wondering why the American economy had not actually rather withered away, fossilized with a static technology, doomed to an output unable to keep up with a growing population. One may, perhaps, be forgiven if one wonders if something significant had not been overlooked in the casting up of hypotheses.

One wonders anew how the easily perceivable dynamic features of the American economy came to be so little noted and remarked upon. Mergers there were. Big companies did appear; and despite all—including government efforts to stop them (not always with much help from the courts), and the supposed inherent incapacities of their own managements—big companies grew even bigger. But, for better or for worse, that was scarcely *the* major story line of the American economy over the decades before The Crash.

Arthur F. Burns, some of whose data were cited a few pages back, was prominent among those economists who found on the American scene different matters to interest them. He was struck not only by the growth of the American economy but, even more, by the changes that had taken place. He said:

> The outstanding characteristics of the economic progress in the United States since the Civil War have been increase and change in wants and activities. The total volume of national production has increased rapidly, as has the volume of production of major industrial groups. But the rate of advance has been uneven in the various individual industries, and in any one industry at various times. The growth of general production has therefore been accompanied by a continual transformation of its pattern. With the incessant introduction of new commodities and services, disappearance of old commodities, and shifts in the relative importance of continuing products, vast changes have occurred in the qualitative composition of national industry . . . . [16]

A bit later on, Mr. Burns says:

> The very causes which have determined the rapid advance of general production in this country since the Civil War have also determined the divergence in the trends of its separate industries. Progress in the general economy has been marked by the invention of new commodities, development of new raw materials, and discovery of new mineral resources; by changes in the methods of production, transformation of industrial equipment, recovery of waste products, and changes in the forms of industrial organization; by an increase in the number of uses to which given raw materials are put, and in the number of materials put to given uses; and by an emergence of a variety of luxury products and style goods. These changes have resulted in an increasing divergence of production trends, for they have served to stimulate or depress, but to an unequal extent, the development of the various industries . . . . [17]

Burns did not say so, but he might well have, that higher rates of growth were far more often and more strongly, and changes revealed by his statistics were much more prominently, associated with those industries in which large corporations had become influential than with those industries in which they had not.

My own favorite economics professor, the late Joseph A. Schumpeter, was among the small number of professional, academic economists who rejected the static notions of monopolistic, oligopolistic, and imperfect competition, together with the hypotheses of the decline of competition, as failing to grasp essential and demonstrable realities of the dynamics of production and consumption, of their developing sources and evolving contents, and of the rising level of living. I quoted him earlier to the effect that, if proponents and adherents of hypotheses of monopolistic and imperfect competition had taken recourse in facts (as did Mr. Burns and Schumpeter, himself) the "shocking suspicion" might have dawned upon them "... that big business may have had more to do with creating that standard of life than with keeping it down."

Schumpeter saw the rising and changing streams of outputs and consumption as part and parcel of the inherently evolutionary processes of "capitalism." A few paragraphs later, he said

> ... the contents of the laborer's budget, say from 1760 to 1940, did not simply grow on unchanging lines but they underwent a process of qualitative change. Similarly, the history of the productive apparatus of a typical farm, from the beginnings of the rationalization of crop rotation, plowing and fattening to the mechanized thing of today—linking up with elevators and railroads—is a history of revolutions. So is the history of the productive apparatus of the iron and steel industry from the charcoal furnace to our own type of furnace, or the history of the apparatus of power production from the overshot water wheel to the modern power plant, or the history of transportation from the mailcoach to the airplane. The opening up of new markets, foreign or domestic, and the organizational development from the craft shop and factory to such concerns as U.S. Steel illustrate the same process of industrial mutation—if I may use that biological term—that incessantly revolutionizes* the economic structure *from within*, incessantly destroying the old one, incessantly creating a new one. This process of Creative Destruction is the essential fact about capitalism. It is what capitalism consists in and what every capitalist concern has got to live in. . . .[18]

By 1929-30, America was well into what was really a whole new chapter in the Industrial Revolution. And that chapter in this continuing Revolution—it *was*, and still *is*, truly, a Revolution!—was largely characterized by, it was largely brought about by, new kinds of human organizations: *very* large business corporations. *Big* organizations that did new things in new ways. These were the devices, in the American system, whereby new technologies of production, distribution, communication, and management could be organized and employed to produce the material base of an utterly new kind of civilization: highly urban, highly industrial; a complex, large-scale, highly integrated, mass-production, technology-advancing civilization. The rise of large corporations—of Big Business—was not a thing apart from that Revolution. They were of its essence. For better or for worse, for richer or for poorer—really, *much* richer—that Revolution was not and, indeed, it could not have been brought about by a community of small, petit-bourgeois, proprietor-owned-and-managed

---

*Those revolutions are not strictly incessant; they occur in discrete rushes that are separated from each other by spans of comparative quiet. The process as a whole works incessantly, however, in the sense that there always is either revolution or absorption of the results of revolution, both together forming what are known as business cycles.

businesses. The emergent, new America was no nation of shopkeepers, of artisan industry, of atomistic competition in unstructured, ephemeral markets.

The 322,000 nonfinancial corporations of 1929 tabulated in Exhibit 3 produced a lion's share of the material support of a nation then of 123 million people, of whom the nation could afford to keep almost 30 million of the young in schools, getting more—and usually better—education than the mass of any people had ever had. In 1929 dollars, the Gross National Product of that year was $103.1 billion; in 1971 dollars, $300 billion; in 1977 dollars, $450 billion. This stream of goods and services required for its production a labor force of about 49 million, made up of 14 million white-collar workers, 19 million blue-collar workers, 5 million service workers, and 11 million farm workers. The support of all this activity required, among other inputs, 450 *billion* ton-miles of rail freight; 22,900 *trillion* BTUs (British thermal units) of energy; and over 56 million tons of steel.[19]

The world had never seen the like. The American Industrial Revolution, in which, over the years, Big Business played an increasingly leading role, was nothing less than a transformation of an entire human *system,* of a whole civilization. Still more growth and change was yet to come.

In the nature of things, not by happenstance, the tremendous aggregates of capital employed by large corporations were supplied by millions of individuals, largely unknown even to the intermediary financial organizations that assembled and allocated so much of the needed capital. For practical purposes, the ultimate suppliers of capital were unknown to those who managed and controlled the nonfinancial corporations that employed that capital. No longer were the characteristic productive organizations of the country owned and run by independent "bourgeois" proprietors and "capitalists." Those who ran these big companies were of a class newly emerged, mostly in the course of the preceding generation: salaried, essentially unpropertied professional managers. Not only did they run these big companies, these people *controlled* them in their every dimension. They held and exercised literal life and death powers over those companies. These managers controlled their own selection and that of their successors. More, they controlled the selection of their own nominal overseers and hypothetical superiors, the directors. In blunt fact, they constituted a self-perpetuating oligarchy. These relatively few men made decisions that touched the lives of millions. They decided upon prices—as best they could, especially in the face of dynamic competitive forces. They allocated resources. They decided to build or to move or to tear down factories. They decided what to produce and how much. They often seemed to have an "in" with presidents and governors, legislators and justices.

In 1929, in a corporate community of 322,000, The 200 Largest Nonfinancial Companies—less than $\frac{1}{10}$ of 1 percent of the number of business corporations—held about 41 percent of all corporate assets. The rise of these corporations had taken place in a relatively short time. Excepting what had become a negligible fraction of the earliest beginnings, this corporate growth had taken place after the Civil War. Indeed, something like two-thirds to three-quarters of the whole growth of these large companies took place within a single generation, the first 30 years of the 20th century. Much of the growth, perhaps a third, came about in the decade between the end of World War I and The Crash of 1929. While academics discussed and politicians declaimed, a new breed of businessmen had actually revolutionized the industrial structure, and through it the entire American economic system. In fact and in deed—men of action, not words—*they* were the *real radicals* of the era. *They* were the ones who, for better or worse, were really changing the fact, fabric, and substance of America. That they really were "radicals," in the sense of seeking and *achieving radical change* in the established order, probably never occurred to any of them.

INDISCIPLINE AMONG LARGE CORPORATIONS

The rise of Big Business and of the industrial urban civilization that were developing in a mutually affecting, symbiotic relationship was troublesome. These enormous corporate productive entities were anomalies, *hundreds of thousands* of times larger than the ideal family-owned, owner-operated business; hundreds of times larger even than their smaller, corporate would-be rivals. Their workings, more than any other force, were bringing about an economic revolution. This *economic* revolution, with no explicit *political* mandate from the sovereign people, was bringing about a *social* revolution.* The fact that America was becoming so different from the country's agrarian and rural, small-business, historical past, was a deeply disturbing development in the nation still committed to pluralism, to decentralization of economic and political power, to family independence, even to a rough egalitarianism among individuals. And, here, a whole array of big corporations had arisen as a manifest challenge, even a denial—a seemingly successful rejection—of the idealized order of things as old as the republic itself. That was shocking enough. But then, in 1929 and the years following, came even more and greater shocks. These followed apparent collapse of the new corporate order, exposure of scandal, and renewed attacks on the very legitimacy of these large corporate institutions.

These shocks were to find legislative, executive, and judicial expression in the years of the New Deal.

It was becoming apparent that responsibility for the actions of big corporations and their managers was vague and tenuous, that there was much room for self-serving actions by inside managers. Laws and

---

*One of my readers points out, correctly, I think, that the "big-business-urban-industrial" order, in effect, obtained its "mandate" through uncountable daily "ballots" in the form of millions of daily decisions of millions of consumers over many, many years.

customs of business of earlier times seemed no longer to suffice for the governance of these new entities. By 1929, much seemed wrong with the ways in which many of these large corporations were set up and run. The Crash and The Depression and well-publicized scandals made the point.

If there was no going back to the small-scale, atomistic "bourgeois capitalism" of the 19th century, with all the supposed individual responsibility and all the checks and balances that its ideology had promised, there was now abroad in the land a gathering resolve to develop new means of governance for the large corporations that were now a common, essential, and seemingly permanent feature of the new American system. Had not World War II opened, with the German invasion of Poland, that resolve might have found more extensive expression than it did in the 1930s. That resolve may still find further expression in the years ahead.

*   *   *   *   *

No one in those days, now well over 40 years ago, had much conception of what the continuing American Industrial Revolution would bring in the future by way of growth and change in the corporate community and in the American system more generally, nor by way of new problems for government policy toward Big Business, nor by way of new demands upon corporate policy. In later chapters, we shall talk about some of those problems and demands.

We look next at the Largest Corporations of 40 and more years later—of 1971; and, then, at the changes in the community of Big Business over those decades, and what they signified.

NOTES

1. U.S. Department of Commerce, Bureau of the Census, *Historical Statistics of the United States, Colonial Times to 1957* (Washington, D.C.: U.S. Government Printing Office, 1960), p. 14; also *Long-Term Economic Growth, 1860-1965* (Washington, D.C.: U.S. Government Printing Office, 1966), pp. 14, 16, and 166.

2. See, e.g., Thomas William Lawson, *Frenzied Finance* (New York: The Ridgeway-Thayer Co., 1905).

3. See J. D. Glover, *The Attack on Big Business.*

4. Berle and Means, *The Modern Corporation*, pp. 2-3. The notion that the classic economic order of small, bourgeois, closely held firms was being transformed by a process whereby small companies were being concentrated into large ones was picked up by Mr. Justice Louis D. Brandeis in his dissent in the case of *Louis K. Ligget* v. *Lee*, 288 U.S. 517 (1933), p. 565. This great justice used almost the very words of Berle and Means:

   > The typical business corporation of the last century, owned by a small group of individuals, managed by their owners and limited in size by their personal wealth, is being *supplanted* by huge concerns in which the lives often of hundreds of thousands of employees and the property of tens or hundreds of thousands of investors are subjected, through the corporate mechanism, to the control of a few men. Ownership has been *separated* from control; and this *separation* has removed many of the checks which formerly operated to curb the abuse of wealth and power. And, as ownership of the shares is becoming

increasingly *dispersed,* the *power* which *formerly* accompanied ownership is *becoming* increasingly *concentrated* in the hands of a few .... (Italics added.) Cited by Glover, *Attack on Big Business,* pp. 119-20.

5. For discussion of the rise of the railroads, see Chandler, *The Visible Hand,* chaps. 3, 4, and 5.

6. See John Brooks, *Telephone; The First Hundred Years* (New York: Harper & Row, 1976), p. 136, et passim.

7. Conversion of balance sheet data from "current" to "constant" dollars, for years separated by considerable spans of time, is a very tricky business both conceptually as well as practically. One interesting method for doing so is described in some detail in *Capital in Manufacturing and Mining: Its Formation and Financing,* by Daniel Creamer et al. (Princeton: Princeton University Press, for the National Bureau of Economic Research, 1960); Appendix A, Section B, pp. 221-38.

In essence, these authors segregated corporation assets for each of 15 Major Industry Groups into three categories: Machinery and Equipment; Buildings and Land; Cash, Accounts Receivable, and Inventories; together, these made up "Total Capital Invested in Manufacturing." They then endeavored to estimate the average age of the assets on the books in these categories for each major industry group. Next, for each of some 39 "minor industries" they applied an even larger number of varied price indexes to each of these "average-aged" classes of assets in an effort to "deflate" the asset values remaining on the books, so to speak, in each given year, from "current" to "constant" (in this case, 1929) dollars. The resultant data were something like depreciated replacement costs of the assets of each year in each industry in terms of "constant" dollars of the base year.

The many steps employed in the statistical process involved many assumptions and many ingenious devices and manipulations of available and estimated data. The hard-headed analyst can be only grateful for the painstaking and skillful work of these authors. The analyst may nevertheless take the particular resultant values as useful *approximations* that *indicate* trends and relative levels rather than firm measurements. When all is said and done, it may be that less elegantly and elaborately estimated data would be about as useful for practical purposes and at least as sustainable as to rigors of logic, given the nonhomogeneity over time of the underlying concrete phenomena— e.g. machinery, inventories, and buildings and improvements to real estate. See Creamer, *Capital in Manufacturing and Mining,* pp. 19-21; et passim.

The data of "capital" investments "in manufacturing" as given in *Historical Statistics of the United States* are not strictly comparable to those given by the Treasury's *Statistics of Income* as shown in Exhibits 3 and 14. For the years prior to 1929, the *Historical Statistics* are based on the *Census of Manufactures,* which, presumably, includes all forms of enterprise, corporate and noncorporate, whereas the Treasury data are based only on *corporate* income tax returns. *Census* data relate to "establishments"—say, individual plants, offices, distribution centers, and other *places of employment.* For the vast majority of firms, which typically have only one "establishment," the data for the establishment and for the firm as a whole are one and the same, or nearly so. Large-scale corporations are likely to have more than one establishment. Moreover, large firms do tend to have establishments of different *kinds.* Treasury data relate to *corporate* assets, which include their total investments in all sorts of establishments: their mines, if any, warehouses, offices, as well as factories and other kinds of manufacturing establishments. For the years of 1929 and thereafter, the *Historical Statistics* figures are based on corporation balance sheet data of the Treasury. The *Historical Statistics* data of *capital in manufacturing* exclude investment *in securities,* which, of course, are included among corporate assets as reported on balance sheets.

Another reason why the data are not strictly comparable would seem to be in the fact that the *Historical Statistics* data try to estimate investments in *manufacturing,* whereas the Treasury corporate balance sheet data relate to their assets of all kinds, say the ore deposits of metal companies ("Mining") and the pipelines of petroleum companies ("Transportation"). The *Historical Statistics,* accordingly, also exclude "capital" in investments in securities. Although these investments, by their nature, are not capital in *manufacturing,* they are, of course, assets reported on balance sheets of corporations that are in manufacturing.

The greatest apparent disparities between the two sets of data for 1929 are to be found in the data for Chemicals and allied substances and Metal and metal products. The Treasury data for Chemicals and allied products include reported assets of petroleum companies, which include assets of integrated companies in petroleum extraction, transportation, and distribution. The Treasury data for Metal and metal products include, for example, the mineral deposits and mining assets of integrated iron and steel and nonferrous metals companies. (See Exhibit 3, Footnotes c, d, e.)

Considering the innate disparities between the two sets of data, the actual differences, except for Chemicals and Metal are not great, certainly not in relation to the inherent inexactitudes of such measurements as aggregate *Census* and *Treasury* data. That they are as close as they are could, indeed, be a result of "compensating errors."

One takes on faith the homogeneity and comparability of the *Historical Statistics,* or any such data, over a 50-year span. We know that the concreteness of productive assets changed greatly over those years—as they have since. The nonhomogeneity over time of the underlying phenomena being measured casts a haze over the meaning of the numbers. We probably can take the data as *indicative of trends,* if not as precise measures of capital invested in various sectors, as long as we do not push our analyses and conclusions too far.

The primary source of the data from *Historical Statistics* is Creamer, *Capital in Manufacturing and Mining.*

8. U.S. Department of Commerce, *Historical Statistics.*

9. See Ralph W. Hidy and Muriel E. Hidy, *History of Standard Oil Company (New Jersey): Pioneering in Big Business, 1892-1911* (New York: Harper & Brothers, 1955); see, also, J. D. Glover, "Rise and Fall of Corporations: Challenge and Response"; a note prepared for instruction at the Harvard Business School; Boston, Mass.; (file 4-367-017). See, also, Chandler, *The Visible Hand,* Chapter 11.

10. See Alfred D. Chandler, chap. 7.

11. U.S. Department of Commerce, *Long Term Economic Growth, 1860-1965,* pp. 166 and following.

12. Simon Kuznets, *National Product Since 1869* (New York: National Bureau of Economic Research, 1946), p. 119.

13. U.S. Department of Commerce, *Historical Statistics,* p. 7.

14. Notably, Edward H. Chamberlin, *The Theory of Monopolistic Competition* (Cambridge: The Harvard University Press, 1933); and Joan Robinson, *The Theory of Imperfect Competition* (London: Macmillan and Co., Ltd., 1933). These were seminal works. They were followed by many, many others, which added their own variants and extensions to the basic hypotheses.

The hypotheses of "monopolistic" and "imperfect" competition were snapped up at an "unprecedented pace" by economists, reformers, and politicians almost immediately upon their appearance. (Robert Triffin, *Monopolistic Competition and General Equilibrium Theory,* Harvard University Press, 1940, p. 17.) Within three years of their appearance, one economist proclaimed with guileless candor their real significance for critics, not only of *big* business, but of private, free-market enterprise generally:

"In the sphere of ethico-economic thought . . . the prospect of widespread recognition of the new theoretical developments is certain, for in them the groping of social welfare advocates for a rationale of public interference in private capital enterprise effectively to combat that of laissez-faire finds glorious realization." (Horace G. White, Jr., "A Review of Monopolistic and Imperfect Competition Theories," *American Economic Review,* vol. 26, no. 4, December 1936, p. 649.)

Now, at last, the ambitions, prejudices, sentiments, emotions, and misreadings of history and fact by critics of a free society and advocates of *dirigiste* statism had a "rationale." The rhetoric and strictures had preceeded rationale for almost a half-century.

This sort of Alice-in-Wonderland verdict *before* trial is not unique in human history. What is extraordinary—but very understandable—is the way large numbers of pamphleteers, politicians, bedazzled jurists and many professionals eager for leading roles in "public interference in private capital enterprise" have clung to these hypotheses concerning the anatomy, physiology, and evolution of American industry despite the visible, palpable denials of them all about us—there to be seen, felt, and measured, year after year! (See J. D. Glover, *The Attack on Big Business,* op. cit., p. 76.)

15. Arthur Robert Burns, (not to be confused with Arthur F. Burns), *The Decline of Competition* (New York: McGraw-Hill Book Company, Inc., 1936).

16. Arthur F. Burns, *Production Trends in the United States Since 1870* (New York: National Bureau of Economic Research, 1934), p. 49.

17. Ibid., p. 63.

18. Schumpeter, *Capitalism, Socialism, and Democracy,* p. 83.

19. U.S. Department of Commerce, *Historical Statistics,* pp. 431, 355, 416.

5

The Largest Nonfinancial Corporations of 1971; the rise of a new industrial order

Now, for Big Business on the contemporary scene.

In a later chapter, we shall look more systematically at some of the economic, social, and other changes of the last 40 years, and where our Largest corporations fitted in those dynamics. For the moment, our account will be helped by a sketch of a few of the outstanding features of the American community of 1971 and of a very few of the changes that took place along the way, as we came to where we are. This will help our mind-set vault the four decades from the times we have been thinking about so far, and give us something of a common context in which to see the biggest companies of the day.

THE FOUR DECADES, 1929-1971

The Israelites, fleeing from slavery in Egypt, wandered for 40 years in the desert, living from day to day, before they entered the promised land. Whether 40 years is a *long* time depends. For the adult generation of those Jews who died away in the wilderness—even Moses himself—never setting foot upon the goal, the years must have felt interminable, each year—each day—an agony of time without end. But, for the young, born and growing up in a space stark and seemingly without bounds, one year must have seemed much like the one before, time passing scarcely sensed or measured.

In retrospect, looking back if we can more than 40 years from the 1970s, the year 1929 must seem remote indeed, merging and fusing in our impressions, perceptions, and recollections with images, myths, and legends of high and far off times, so different was it from what we now see and know. Those who have come later can have little or no conception of it at all.

How was 1971 different? Let me count the ways.

The year that ended *The* Boom was a time before antibiotics, and latter-day immunizing agents and programs; when Americans still died in hundreds of thousands from infectious diseases. Before television, the present opium of the people. Before Civil Rights legislation with its bright promise and, now, something more than token fulfillment. Before *The* Depression and its lasting traumatic impacts on American dreams. Before what is still thought of as *The* War by so many—with its 16 million Americans in arms, its 400,000 dead. Before missiles of ocean-spanning range. Before *The* Bomb. Before bloody and corrupting "police actions"—can we now call them wars?—far away on the mainland of Asia. When automobiles, refrigerators, telephones, air conditioners, and air travel were status symbols of the well-to-do rather than necessities of life, even for the humble. Before plastics had become a way of life. Before *The* Computer, linear accelerators, and cyclotrons. Before *The* Pill and its resultant Unproclaimed Emancipation that started the overturn of mores as old as the cave peoples. Before superhighways and supermarkets.

So *many* ways. Too many to count.

The most obvious features: in 1971, we were 207 million; two-thirds of us living in metropolitan areas. We had become one of the world's most urban peoples. Our Gross National Product was over *a trillion* dollars—over a *thousand billion: $1,063.4* billion in 1971 dollars; about $1,500 billion in 1977 dollars.[1] There is scarcely any meaningful way to measure our 1971 income in 1929 dollars, so profoundly different were the compositions of the products and incomes, and the "market baskets" produced and consumed in the two years.

We had become one of the largest nations; certainly, the most opulent. Again, what is truly remarkable is not that our total output and total income were bigger than heretofore and elsewhere—of course they were. More dramatic, and far, far more important, they were made up of, and went for different, so *very* different things.

The dynamics of the American system were qualitative as well as quantitative. And qualitative changes give rise to far more problems and issues of public and corporate policy than do quantitative ones—a subject to which we shall return.

The American *community* of 1971—the collectivity of all the component entities of the American human ecological system—was composed of many *more* entities: more individuals and households; more business proprietorships, partnerships and corporations; more non-profit organizations; more labor unions; more government agencies and instrumentalities. Of households, there were almost 65 million;

of business proprietorships, 9.7 million; and of partnerships, 950,000. The number of employed persons ranged about 80 million. A farm population of 8.9 million worked 2.9 million farms. Of nonprofit organizations, national in scope, almost 12,000: thousands of trade groups, fraternal organizations, religious and educational organizations, national labor unions, political action groups, and all the rest. And there were well over 100,000 units, agencies and instrumentalities of government at the federal, state, and local levels: regulatory agencies; regular departments of government; the military establishment; public hospitals and other types of institutions; fire districts, school districts, irrigation districts—all with various powers to do things, to tax, to borrow, and to say yes or no and how much and where and when. Of business corporations, we had about 1.7 million, of which 140,000 were active in various finance and insurance fields, and 1.6 million teemed in scores—hundreds—of "nonfinancial" genera and species.[2]

This community, as mentioned a moment ago, generated a Gross National Product of $1,063 billion—over a *trillion* dollars. Allowing for $91 billion of capital consumption allowances (depreciation, depletion, and write-offs), and for other items including indirect taxes (collected by business and paid over to governments), and business transfer payments (receipts for, and paid over to, others), the National Income came to $858 billion.[3] Of this National Income, as shown in Table 7, $693 billion originated in "business"; of this, in

TABLE 7
Sources of National Income, 1971 (values in billions of 1971 dollars)

Business	
Corporations	$468.1
Sole proprietorships and partnerships	155.2
Other private businesses	57.1
Government enterprises	13.0
Subtotal	$693.3
Households and institutions	33.7
General government	124.6
Rest of the world	6.0
Total	$857.7

Source: *Survey of Current Business* (July 1974), pp. 15, 17.

turn, $468 billion originated in *corporate* business (as distinct from sole proprietorships and partnerships; government enterprises; and "other businesses").[4] Households and institutions generated National Income of $34 billion; $124.6 billion originated in "general government"; $6 billion originated in net consequences of international production and income-generating transactions.[4] In addition to $468 billion of National Income, corporations contributed to the Gross National Product the large majority of an additional $94 billion (as measured by deductions for "capital consumption allowances"). In addition, $4.3 billion "transfer payments" (e.g. company benefit plans) flowed through corporation accounts. The 1971 Gross Product of nonfinancial corporations was reported by the Department of Commerce as $555.1 billion.[5] National Income per capita, overall, came to over $4,100, or $13,200 per household, on the average.

In this ambient environment, as we said, operated 1.6 million nonfinancial corporations, employing $1.4 *trillion* of assets. And in this corporate subpopulation of the American community functioned The 200 Largest, which held assets whose total reported book value stood at $538 billion, which is to say 38 percent of the assets of all nonfinancial corporations. The 559 Largest, the smallest of which was as large as the smallest of The 200 of 1929, held $707 billion, accounting for 50 percent of all reported assets of all nonfinancial corporations in 1971. (See Exhibit 15.)

During the 42 years separating the close of 1929 from the end of 1971, the human population had grown from 120 million to 207 million, an increase of almost 75 percent. The nonfinancial corporate population had grown almost fivefold, from 332,000 to 1,592,000 (Exhibits 3 and 15). In terms of 1971 dollars, the assets of nonfinancial corporations had increased $2\frac{1}{3}$ times, from something like $600 billion to $1,400 billion. (In 1977 dollars, over $2,000 billion.) In the four decades, the Gross National Product increased—insofar as one can make such comparisons over such long periods of great change—had increased 3.6 times. "Real" income per capita had more than doubled. The American community—people, households, productive entities, including corporations—was not only far more numerous; so also was its "mass." Its physical impact upon its habitat had increased mightily. One very rough way to gauge such a thing is to look to the energy required to extract materials from the habitat, to drive the flow of many different inputs through the productive community that converted them into usable goods and services. The energy from all sources consumed in 1929, as mentioned, stood at 22.9 *quadrillion* (!) BTUs. The figure for 1971 stood at 68.7! This was the energy equivalent of 2.9 *billion* tons of coal, or 12 *billion* barrels of oil! Our energy use rose almost three times.[6]

Our apparatus for converting all this energy into heat, light, motion; for moving things and people; giving shape and form to materials; for rearrangement of atoms and molecules, increased even more, as shown in Table 8.

That the heat and motion hinted at by these rather incomprehensible figures had a real physical impact is only vaguely suggested by the tangible artifacts we have strewn around the American landscape over the past 40 years or so: our cities, highways, airports, harbor and river works and levees; our sullied and often stinking waterways.

But, we are in danger of getting ahead of our story. The purpose of presenting these data was to sketch out something of the American system of 1971 in which the corporate population had a place.

TABLE 8
Horsepower of prime movers, 1930 and 1971 (millions)

	1930	1971
Electric central stations	43	473
Railroads	110	56
Aircraft	3	179
Other nonautomotive	81	421
Total nonautomotive	237	1,130
Automotive	1,427	20,732
Total	1,664	21,862

Sources: For 1930, *Historical Statistics of the United States*, p. 506. For 1971, *Statistical Abstract of the United States, 1974*, p. 514.

We shall come back to the changes that swept over us from 1929 to 1971, and the parts our Largest Corporations played in those changes.

THE CORPORATE COMMUNITY, 1971

Our interest now is the Largest Corporations of 1971 and where they fitted in the corporate community. Before we get on, two questions need answering. Why the year 1971? And when we say "Largest Corporations" in that year, what do we mean?

As to the first, when the basic data for this study were being assembled, 1971 was the latest year for which the Internal Revenue Service had made available the comprehensive corporate financial data that it compiles annually from income tax returns.[7] These are the figures that tell so much about the American corporate population of which Big Business is part.

The answer to the second question is a little more involved. The roster of largest nonfinancial corporations of 1929 lists 200 companies. "Largest" was defined as the "Top 200." As arbitrary definitions go, that is not a bad one. With that as a definition, we shall look at The 200's that stood at the very pinnacle of the corporate pyramids of 1929 and 1971.

But there is this difficulty: defining "largest" that way results in a 200th company for 1971 that is more than three times larger than the 200th of 1929. This means that the groups, although strictly comparable as to number—200, in each case—are not strictly comparable as to size of firms.

We can also define "largest" arbitrarily in terms of minimum asset size; that would make the two groups a bit more comparable. A minimum size of $250 million is not a bad arbitrary definition of "largest." In fact, that is the lower limit of the biggest size class in the IRS tabulations of corporate data. If the minimum is set at $250 million, then we have a group of 200 in 1929 so defined, and one of 559 in 1971. For many purposes of studying the position of "very large" corporations in American industry, this definition and comparisons based upon it are more meaningful. For one thing, we can more readily relate the data to IRS statistics. Accordingly, we shall have occasion to look *both* at the Top 200 corporations, and at the corporations with assets of more than $250 million (in 1971 dollars) in the two years.

So. We go on to look at the whole nonfinancial corporate community of 1971, and at both The 200 Largest Nonfinancial Corporations, and at The Next 359 as well, altogether The 559 Largest Companies of that year, and where they fitted in that community. Later, in Chapter 9, we shall compare this later population to that of 1929, and consider the changes that took place over the 40-odd years between those two countings.

All corporations, large and small

A summary statistical snapshot of the corporate community of 1971 is given in Exhibit 15.

All told, this community of 1971 numbered 1.7 million business corporations of all kinds, sizes, and locations—of all varieties, species, genera, and orders. Of these, 141,000 were engaged in financial and insurance operations. The rest, 1.6 million, were engaged in agriculture, mining, manufacturing, providing public utility services, trade, services, and real estate operations. Here were the entities that produced over half of the Gross National Product and the National Income of 1971. The vast majority were each linked at first hand in a complex network of interdependences with anywhere from a handful to tens of thousands of others in roles of buyers, downstream, and sellers, upstream; as competitors, actual or potential, for inputs and for sales. Indirectly, at one or more removes, each was connected with all, as are the living things in an ecological system of nature—say, a deciduous forest or, better, a freshwater pond. Upstream, providing human inputs, were more than a third of all the gainfully employed. Downstream from these corporations, linked directly and indirectly with them, were the 65 million households and the 200-plus million consuming individuals of America. Related to these corporations, also, were the thousands of union locals, and tens of thousands of governmental units of all the many kinds and sizes they come in. Such was the community milieu of the Largest Nonfinancial Corporations.

Altogether, nonfinancial corporations, as mentioned, held assets reported at $1,410 billion. The occurrence of corporations—large or small—among various Major Industry Groups (as measured in numbers) and their presence (as measured by asset values) varied widely. In the Major Industry Groups so notably characterized by "small" business—Agriculture, Construction, Wholesale and retail

EXHIBIT 15
The 200 and The 559 Largest Nonfinancial Corporations of 1971 compared to all U.S. nonfinancial corporations, by Major Industry Groups (numbers of firms and values of assets)

Major Industry Groups	All corporations		The 200 Largest Corporations			The 559 Largest Corporations		
	Number of firms	Value of assets ($ millions)	Number of firms	Value of assets ($ millions)	Assets held by The 200 as percent of assets of all corporations, by Major Industry Groups	Number of firms	Value of assets ($ millions)	Assets held by The 559 as percent of assets of all corporations, by Major Industry Groups
Agriculture	39,932	$ 11,800	0	$ 0.0	0.0%	0	$ 0.0	0.0%
Mining and quarrying ...	12,613	26,042	0	0.0	0.0	3	1,413.6	5.4
Construction	143,092	48,243	0	0.0	0.0	3	1,201.2	2.5
Manufacturing								
Food...	16,394	63,332	15	19,555.0	30.9	43	35,048.2	55.3
Textiles..........	22,883	26,616	2	2,323.7	8.7	14	7,050.2	26.5
Lumber...wood...paper...	20,888	39,141	8	12,506.9	32.0	17	17,385.7	44.4
Printing, publishing....	26,541	20,910	0	0.0	0.0	7	2,702.1	12.9
Chemicals........	10,825	155,924	35	128,528.9	82.4	82	152,691.1	97.9
Rubber and tires	6,235	13,071	5	9,149.0	70.0	5	9,149.0	70.0
Leather	2,269	3,809	0	0.0	0.0	2	696.7	18.3
Stone, clay, and glass...	8,580	15,762	2	2,708.4	17.2	17	9,831.7	62.4
Metal and metal products ...	69,461	286,315	39	102,975.8	35.9	113	137,322.3	48.0
Other and misc. mfg.....	16,897	21,767	12*	40,115.8*	N.M.	34†	49,750.2†	N.M.
Subtotal manufacturing ...	200,973	$ 646,647	117	$317,863.5*	49.2%	332	$421,627.2†	65.6%
Transportation...utilities..	71,104	309,902	71	197,450.3	63.7	160	240,469.4	77.6
Wholesale and retail trade...	538,664	210,884	12	22,926.5	10.9	38	33,553.1	15.9
Services	287,780	62,226	0	0.0	0.0	17	6,899.1	11.1
Nature of business not allocable	21,438	847	0	0.0	0.0	0	0.0	0.0
Real estate	276,597	93,920	0	0.0	0.0	6	2,031.2	2.2
Total nonfinancial corporations	1,592,193	$1,410,511	200	$538,240.3	38.4%	559	$707,194.8	50.1%
Finance, insurance	141,139	1,487,710						
Total, all industries ...	1,733,332	$2,889,221						

*For comparative purposes, includes Western Electric and its assets as separate company in subtotal and total. Company not counted as separate corporation. See Appendix A, "Notes to Exhibit 1," Note 53.

†For comparative purposes, includes Western Electric and manufacturing subsidiaries of General Telephone & Electronics as separate corporations. Companies not counted as separate companies in subtotal and total. See Appendix A, "Notes to Exhibit 1," Notes 53 and 54.

N.M. means "not meaningful." Of The 559 corporations of 1971, a total of 34 companies in 5 Industry Categories were included here under "Other and miscellaneous manufacturing." These included 11 companies in "Office...computing machines," 14 in "Radio...communication equipment," 2 in "Scientific...control...devices...measuring...," 2 in "Photographic equipment," 5 in "Metal and metal products." These companies and their assets, however, seem to have been classified by the IRS under one or more other Major Industry Groups or subgroups, such as "Metal and metal products." Accordingly, comparison of the assets of these 34 companies with the IRS data for "Other and misc. mfg." is not meaningful.

The shortcomings of "Major Industry Groups" as a way of categorizing corporations are alluded to in Exhibit 3, Note c, *supra*.

Sources: (*a*) United States Department of the Treasury, Internal Revenue Service, Statistics Division; *Source Book, Statistics of Income, 1971; Corporation Income Tax Returns*; (*b*) Exhibit 1; (*c*) see, also, Appendix B. See also Exhibits 34, 35, and 36. "All corporations" includes firms reporting "Zero Assets." This is consistent with the data for 1929, which includes "corporations reporting no net income."

trade, and Services—more than 1 million firms out of the 1.6 million total functioned, with $333 billion of assets. These smaller companies in these five numerous Groups of businesses comprised almost two-thirds of the total corporate population. They worked with something less than a quarter of all the corporate assets.

In two other Major Industry Groups, relatively fewer firms worked with relatively more assets: in Manufacturing of all kinds, 201,000 firms worked with $647 billion of assets; in Transportation . . . utilities, 71,000 worked with $310 billion. The companies in these two groups accounted for a bit less than one-fifth of the number of all corporations. The $957 billion of assets they worked with accounted for more than two-thirds of all corporate assets. These were the Major Industry Groups where Big Business was to be found.

This striking unevenness in the distribution of the numbers and the masses of corporations among the Major Industrial Groups was associated, naturally, with notable differences as to the average sizes of firms. (See Table 9.) The "average" firm (a purely abstract concept!) in the utilities field was over 20 times the size of the average firm in "trade." The average firm in Manufacturing was 11 times the size of the average in Agriculture. In a few pages, we shall return for a more detailed look at sizes of firms in different industries.

Some pretty important implications flow quickly from the data: America had already left its agrarian past far behind it, in 1929. It was now, in 1971, a "hyper-industrial" community. Of nonfinancial corporate investments, almost half were in the many branches of Manufacturing. It was a community that required enormous private investments in the infrastructure components of transportation and energy; over 20 percent of all corporate assets, in fact. It was a community of such aggregate mass and intricate complexity as to call for 539,000 corporations with $210 billion of assets (to say nothing of more than a million proprietorships and partnerships) to handle the wholesale and retail marketing and physical distribution of its out-

TABLE 9
Relative distributions of nonfinancial corporations among Major Industry Groups:
Occurrence and presence; average sizes of firms; 1971

Major Industry Groups	Percentage of number of all firms	Percentage of assets of all firms	Average size of firms ($000)
Agriculture	2.5%	0.8%	$ 295.5
Mining and quarrying	0.8	1.8	2,064.7
Construction	9.0	3.4	337.1
Manufacturing	12.6	45.8	3,217.6
Transportation . . . utilities	4.5	22.0	4,358.4
Wholesale and retail trade	33.8	15.0	391.5
Services	18.1	4.4	216.2
Real estate	17.4	6.7	339.6
Other	1.3	0.1	39.5
Totals	100.0%	100.0%	$ 885.9

Source: Exhibit 15.

puts. The corporate community included almost 300,000 corporations with $62 billion of assets whose purposes were the provision of an increasing flow of ever more varied services necessary for efficient production by large, complex industries and for more comfortable living in urban agglomerations.

So much for the overview.

THE LARGEST NONFINANCIAL CORPORATIONS OF 1971

Within the whole corporate community were very small numbers of very particular kinds of companies—the very largest. Although they were few, their "presence"—mass—was very large, indeed. The 200 very biggest of these, the frequency of their occurrence being only 126 per million firms of all kinds and sizes, held about $538 billion of assets—38 percent of the aggregate of all corporate holdings. The next tier of 359 companies, the smallest of which had assets of $250 million, held another $169 billion. Together, these 559 Largest Corporations, about $3/100$ of 1 percent of the total number of companies, held $707 billion of assets. Those holdings of those very few companies accounted for about half of the total "mass" of all corporate assets.

Those global figures, necessary as they are for perspective, scarcely even begin to give an understanding of where our biggest companies fitted in the scheme of things, or why, or with what consequences.

The distribution of Largest Corporations among Major Industry Groups

The very largest companies occupied very particular niches in the corporate community. We shall see this in considerably more detail in a few moments. But we sense the first intimations of that fact in looking at the structures of the Major Industrial Groups. Of The 200 Largest Firms, none was to be found in Agriculture, Construction, or Services among the Major Industry Groups. In contrast, 118 of these 200 very largest companies were in Manufacturing and 71 were in Transportation and other utilities.

Of the Next 359 Largest Nonfinancial Corporations, each with assets of $250 million or more, none was in Agriculture; 3 were in Construction; 17 in various kinds of Services (5 in motion pictures; 4 in hotels-motels). As with The 200 very largest, the Next 359 were also to be found primarily in Manufacturing—222 of them—and among the Transportation and other utilities companies—89 in number.

Altogether, 500 of The 559 Largest Nonfinancial Corporations, holding assets reported at $664.6 billion, were in the fields of manufacturing and utilities. The rest—59 companies, holding $42.6 billion of assets—were scattered among Mining and quarrying, Construction, Wholesale and retail trade, and Services.

Again, in 1971 as in 1929, the important occurrence and presence of big companies in some fields, the scattering of big companies in others, and their absence from still others, were *about* something; the same "something," in fact as in 1929; but in a later state of its ongoing development: the continuing Industrial Revolution in America.

The "Major Industrial Groups" that appear in Exhibits 3 and 15 are not as useful for analytical purposes as one could wish, except in very broad-brush ways, such as we have just been through. Unfortunately, for 1929, revealing and important disaggregations of these Group statistics cannot be constructed. For 1971, however, Industry Categories can be constructed from corporate and IRS data that correspond much more usefully to the ways American industries are actually structured, although even so, one could hope for better data for analyzing the positioning of multidivisional corporations in the industrial structure. Nevertheless, the data reveal a great deal.

The distribution of the Largest Corporations among Industry Categories. In Exhibit 1, the identities and assets of The 559 Largest Nonfinancial Corporations of 1971, segregated as between The Top 200 and The Next 359, are listed and classified according to 54 Industry Categories. Exhibits 16-24 present data that analyze the somewhat different structures of the group of The 200 Largest and that of the Next 359 Largest.

In brief, although the numbers of firms and the assets of both The Top 200 and The Next 359 were notably clustered in Utilities, regulated industries and in Integrated industries, The 200 were considerably more so. Beyond those clusters, The Next 359 were spread much more widely throughout other Industry Categories than was the case with The 200. For example, among The Next 359 companies, 75 occurred in 14 Industry Categories where there was none of The 200.

The differences in the distributions of The 200 and The Next 359 contain important suggestions as to qualitative differences between the natures of large and of *very* large companies. Readers who have detailed interests in the structures of industries may be interested to peruse the next few pages and to scan Exhibits 16-24. Others may skip to the section entitled "The 559 Largest Corporations of 1971," and to Exhibits 25-30, which follow thereafter.

The 200 Largest Corporations of 1971, by Industry Category. In Exhibit 16 are tabulated The 200 Largest Nonfinancial Corporations of 1971. The exhibit shows, for each Industry Category the numbers present of The 200 and their assets. The exhibit also shows the per-

EXHIBIT 16
Industry distribution of the numbers and assets of The 200 Largest Nonfinancial Corporations, 1971

Industry Category	Number of firms	Assets held ($ millions)	Numbers of firms as percentage of The 200	Assets as percentage of total assets held by The 200
1. Agriculture...	0	$ 0.0	0.0%	0.0%
2. Iron and steel	7	18,319.2	3.5	3.4
3. Nonferrous metals	8	12,707.9	4.0	2.4
4. Coal	0	0.0	0.0	0.0
5. Petroleum	20	100,425.4	10.0	18.7
6. Construction	0	0.0	0.0	0.0
7. Food...	3	3,537.4	1.5	0.7
8. Meat...	3	4,173.9	1.5	0.8
9. Dairy...	3	3,356.0	1.5	0.6
10. Alcoholic beverages	1	932.2	0.5	0.2
11. Soft drinks...	1	1,107.9	0.5	0.2
12. Tobacco...	4	6,447.6	2.0	1.2
13. Textiles	1	1,390.2	0.5	0.3
14. Apparel...	1	933.5	0.5	0.2
15. Lumber... wood... paper... products	8	12,506.9	4.0	2.3
16. Furniture and fixtures	0	0.0	0.0	0.0
17. Printing and publishing...	0	0.0	0.0	0.0
18. Chemicals...	10	21,761.5	5.0	4.0
19. Pharmaceuticals...	4	4,329.0	2.0	0.8
20. Soaps, cleaners...	1	2,013.0	0.5	0.4
21. Rubber and tires	5	9,149.0	2.5	1.7
22. Leather...	0	0.0	0.0	0.0
23. Nonmetallic mineral products...	0	0.0	0.0	0.0
24. Glass...	2	2,708.4	1.0	0.5
25. Fabricated metal products...	1	1,183.2	0.5	0.2
26. Metal cans...	2	3,062.5	1.0	0.6
27. Machinery...	0	0.0	0.0	0.0
28. Farm, construction... machinery	2	3,269.7	1.0	0.6
29. Office... computing... machines	7	19,970.0	3.5	3.7
30. Electrical machinery...	2	10,425.7	1.0	0.9
31. Household appliances	1	1,669.7	0.5	0.3
32. Radio... communication equipment	3*	14,664.7*	1.5	2.7
33. Scientific... control... devices... measuring...	1	2,183.1	0.5	0.4
34. Photographic equipment...	1	3,298.0	0.5	0.6
35. Motor vehicles...	8	40,329.2	4.0	7.5
36. Aircraft...	8	12,008.7	4.0	2.2
37. Ship... building...	0	0.0	0.0	0.0
38. Railroad equipment...	0	0.0	0.0	0.0
39. Other and miscellaneous manufacturing	0	0.0	0.0	0.0
40. Rail transportation	11	27,660.6	5.5	5.1
41. Transit...	0	0.0	0.0	0.0
42. Motor transportation	2	2,665.1	1.0	0.5
43. Water transportation	0	0.0	0.0	0.0
44. Air transportation	6	9,154.3	3.0	1.7
45. Electric, gas... sanitary...	47	91,799.1	23.5	17.1
46. Telephone, telegraph... services...	5	66,171.2	2.5	12.3
47. Radio and TV broadcasting	0	0.0	0.0	0.0
48. Wholesale trade...	0	0.0	0.0	0.0
49. Retail...	1	1,571.8	0.5	0.3
50. General merchandise...	9	19,411.3	4.5	3.6
51. Food stores	2	1,943.4	1.0	0.4
52. Motion pictures...	0	0.0	0.0	0.0
53. Services...	0	0.0	0.0	0.0
54. Real estate	0	0.0	0.0	0.0
Totals	200	$538,240.3	100.0%	100.0%

*Includes Western Electric; see Appendix A, "Notes to Exhibit 1," Note 53.
Source: Exhibit 1.

centage of The 200 in each Industry Category and the percentage of the *total* assets of The 200 that are present in each.

The most apparent fact is that these 200 firms and their assets were distributed very unevenly among the 54 Industry Categories. In 18 of the Industry Categories, including Agriculture, Construction, Furniture and fixtures, and Leather, for instance, there were none of The 200. In Wholesale trade, also, there were none. In Retail trade there was one. In contrast, of The 200 Corporations, with their assets of $538 billion, substantial numbers and assets were clustered in certain other industries, for instance, Petroleum, Chemicals, Rail transportation, Electric, gas and sanitary services; and substantial fractions of the total assets of The 200 were also concentrated in those Industry Categories.[8]

Of The 200 Companies, 20—that is, 10 percent of The 200—showed up in Petroleum; these companies held over $100 billion of assets; almost 19 percent of the total assets of The 200 were present in that one industry complex. In Electric, gas and sanitary services, there were 47 of the largest companies, or 23.5 percent of the largest companies. These 47, together, held about $92 billion in assets, about 17 percent of all the assets of The 200. In Rail transportation there were 11 of The 200; together, they held assets of over $27 billion, which is to say 5.1 percent of the assets of The 200.

As in 1929—with some important differences we shall take up in a later chapter—a majority of The Top 200 of 1971 were to be found in the utilities and regulated industries, and in four industry complexes or "systems" notable for the occurrence and the asset masses of large companies integrated across broad spans of specific industries ranging from the production of raw materials to manufactured products, in some cases ready for consumption. Exhibit 17 shows 71 of these 200 as located in utilities and regulated industries and another 43 in integrated industries. Together, these 114 companies in nine out of the 54 Industry Categories held almost two-thirds of all the assets of The 200. There were none in Water transportation or in Broadcasting. (See Exhibit 17.) Another 42 companies were to be found in five additional industries in which the occurrence of very large companies was rather common—that being defined as the appearance of seven or more firms. In these 14 industries, 156 of The 200 appeared; these corporations reported almost 85 percent of the aggregate assets of The 200 largest. (See Exhibit 17.)

Anticipating, for a moment, a topic of a later chapter (differences between the industry distributions of The 200 of 1929 and of The 200 of 1971), we will make a few quick and contrasting references from Exhibit 16 back to Exhibit 2. Some of the industries of major importance in 1929 had become relatively, or even absolutely, less prominent: the railroads, above all, and railroad equipment; the urban transit companies; leather; motion pictures. In contrast, very large companies had emerged out of some industries that had scarcely existed in 1929 or, if so, only in primitive form: Pharmaceuticals;

EXHIBIT 17
Regulated and integrated industries and industries with seven or more of The 200 Largest Nonfinancial
Corporations, 1971

Industry Category	Number of companies	Percentage of The 200 Companies	Assets held ($ billions)	Average value of assets per company ($ billions)	Percentage of the total assets held by The 200 Companies
Utilities, regulated industries					
Railroad transportation	11	5.5%	$ 27.66	$ 2.51	5.1%
Transit	0	0.0	0.0	–	–
Electric, gas . . . sanitary	47	23.5	91.80	1.95	17.1
Telephone, telegraph	5	2.5	66.17	13.23	12.3
Air transportation	6	3.0	9.15	1.53	1.7
Motor transportation	2	1.0	2.67	1.34	0.5
Water transportation	0	0.0	0.0	–	0.0
Radio and TV broadcasting	0	0.0	0.0	–	0.0
Subtotals	71	35.5%	$197.45	$ 2.78	36.7%
Integrated industries					
Petroleum	20	10.0%	$100.43	$ 5.02	18.7%
Iron and steel	7	3.5	18.32	2.62	3.4
Nonferrous metals	8	4.0	12.71	1.59	2.4
Lumber . . . wood . . . paper	8	4.0	12.51	1.56	2.3
Subtotals	43	21.5%	$143.97	$ 3.35	26.7%
Regulated and integrated industries, totals	114	57.0%	$341.42	$ 2.99	63.4%
Other industries with 7 or more of The 200 Largest Nonfinancial Corporations, 1971					
Chemicals	10	5.0%	$ 21.76	$ 2.18	4.0%
Office . . . computing . . . machines	7	3.5	19.97	2.85	3.7
Motor vehicles	8	4.0	40.33	5.04	7.5
Aircraft	8	4.0	12.01	1.50	2.2
General merchandise	9	4.5	19.41	2.16	3.6
Subtotals	42	21.0%	$113.48	$ 2.70	21.1%
Totals	156	78.0%	$454.90	$ 2.92	84.5%

Source: Exhibit 1.

Office . . . computing . . . machines . . .; Radio . . . communication
equipment; Aircraft; Air transportation. Very large companies had
grown enormously in both number and mass in other industries:
Petroleum; Lumber . . . wood . . . paper . . . products; Chemicals,
Motor vehicles.

The clusters in 1971 of the very largest corporations in the utilities
and the integrated industries were not dissimilar to those of 1929.
The biggest differences were these: (a) the decline, absolute and
relative, of the railroads; (b) the rise of the utilities, mostly electric;
(c) the absolute and relative growth of the very large corporations in
the petroleum industry.

In 1971, there was another difference as to the bunching of the
biggest companies in certain industries. Seven or more—something of
a flock—of the largest companies, to the number of 42, occurred in
five other industries; these 42 held 21.1 percent of the assets of The

200. In two of these five industries, Aircraft and Office . . . computing . . . machines, now both distinguished by the presence of a cluster of the very biggest companies, there had been none of The 200 of 1929. In three other industries, Chemicals, Motor vehicles, and General merchandise and mail order, notable increases had taken place in the numbers present of the very largest companies and, allowing for inflation, in the total values of their assets and average size. In each of these five industries—Motor vehicles, especially—the growth of large companies was a major factor in the change of the composition of the roster of the very largest companies.

In three "regulated" industries, the very large corporation was not a visible commonplace: Motor transportation, Water transportation, and Radio and TV broadcasting. In fact, some very large corporations categorized elsewhere were present in both motor and water transportation: railroads in piggyback, bimodal, truck-rail transport; large petroleum companies, which both owned and chartered barges and vessels, in inland and coastal waterways and ocean transport. Regulation by the Federal Communications commission had operated to inhibit the growth of very large companies in broadcasting.

As we shall see in a moment, a number of the second-tier companies of The Next 359 had grown up in these three industries.

The occurrence of 156 of the very large corporations in these 14 big-company industries was not happenstance. These were all industries in which very large scale has been pretty much the rule since the turn of the 20th century, at least. Not just large but, obviously, growing scale. In each of these industries, excepting only the railroads—about which, more later on—there has been tremendous growth since 1929. Whether because of the antitrust laws—which have been invoked with varying frequency, intensity, zeal, and effectiveness—or for reasons of corporate policy and strategy, very little of their growth over these past 40 years and more came from consolidation, combination, or plain mergers. The growth of these industries came very largely from internal growth.[9]

To say that these industries expanded overall is not, as we shall see in a later chapter, to say that each and every company grew. Far from it. A number of them disappeared in various ways—doleful or dramatic.

These 156 companies that occurred in industry clusters of seven or more were not just "large." By any reasonable standard, they were *very* large.

Beyond these 14 industries in which the presence and masses of very large corporations were notable, 13 very large companies occurred with some frequency—that is, 4 or 5 of them per industry—in three other industries: Rubber and tires, Tobacco, and Pharmaceuticals. See Exhibit 18.

EXHIBIT 18
Other industries with four to six of The 200 Largest Nonfinancial Corporations, 1971

Industry Category	Number of companies	Percentage of The 200 Companies	Assets held ($ billions)	Average value of assets per company ($ billions)	Percentage of the total assets held by The 200 Companies
Rubber and tires	5	2.5%	$ 9.15	$1.83	1.7%
Tobacco	4	2.0	6.45	1.61	1.2
Pharmaceutical	4	2.0	4.33	1.08	0.8
Totals	13	6.5%	$19.93	$1.53	3.7%

Source: Exhibit 1.

Spreading still further, a scattering—1, 2, or 3 companies, to the number of 32—showed up in 19 other industries. See Exhibit 19.

A story, of course, lies behind the rise to high visibility of each of these companies. More indicative, however, of what was going on in America in those years was the fact that in most—not all—of the industries listed in Exhibits 18 and 19—the ones in which there were only scatterings of the very largest companies—considerable numbers of other companies had arisen, just below The 200 in size, that were all at least as large as the smallest of The 200 of 1929. Examples would be the 16 second-tier companies in Food; 6 each in Electrical

EXHIBIT 19
Other industries with one to three of The 200 Largest Nonfinancial Corporations, 1971

Industry Category	Number of companies	Percentage of The 200 Companies	Assets held ($ billions)	Average value of assets per company ($ billions)	Percentage of the total assets held by The 200 Companies
Food	3	1.5%	$ 3.54	$1.18	0.7%
Meat	3	1.5	4.17	1.39	0.8
Dairy	3	1.5	3.36	1.12	0.6
Alcoholic beverages	1	0.5	0.93	0.93	0.2
Soft drinks	1	0.5	1.11	1.11	0.2
Textiles	1	0.5	1.39	1.39	0.3
Apparel	1	0.5	0.93	0.93	0.2
Soaps, cleaners	1	0.5	2.01	2.01	0.4
Glass	2	1.0	2.71	1.36	0.5
Fabricated metal	1	0.5	1.18	1.18	0.2
Metal cans	2	1.0	3.06	1.53	0.6
Farm, construction . . . machinery	2	1.0	3.27	1.64	0.6
Electrical machinery	2	1.0	10.43	5.22	1.9
Household appliances	1	0.5	1.67	1.67	0.3
Radio . . . communication equipment . . .	3*	1.5	14.66*	4.89*	2.7*
Scientific . . . control	1	0.5	2.18	2.18	0.4
Photographic equipment	1	0.5	3.30	3.30	0.6
Retail trade	1	0.5	1.57	1.57	0.3
Food stores	2	1.0	1.94	0.97	0.4
Totals	32	16.0%	$63.41	$1.98	11.8%

*Includes Western Electric, the manufacturing subsidiary of American Telephone & Telegraph, not counted among The 200.
Source: Exhibit 1.

EXHIBIT 20
Industry distribution of the numbers and assets of The Next 359 Largest Nonfinancial Corporations, 1971

Industry Category	Number of firms	Assets held ($ millions)	Numbers of firms as percentage of The 359	Assets as percentage of total assets held by The 359
1. Agriculture...	0	$ 0.0	0.0%	0.0%
2. Iron and steel	12	5,088.5	3.3	3.0
3. Nonferrous metals	10	5,052.2	2.8	3.0
4. Coal	3	1,413.6	0.8	0.8
5. Petroleum	10	5,420.9	2.8	3.2
6. Construction	3	1,201.2	0.8	0.7
7. Food...	16	8,784.5	4.5	5.2
8. Meat...	2	1,151.2	0.6	0.7
9. Dairy...	3	1,709.0	0.8	1.0
10. Alcoholic beverages	5	2,422.9	1.4	1.4
11. Soft drinks...	1	827.7	0.3	0.5
12. Tobacco...	1	597.9	0.3	0.4
13. Textiles	8	3,189.5	2.2	1.9
14. Apparel...	4	1,537.0	1.1	0.9
15. Lumber...wood...paper...products	9	4,878.8	2.5	2.9
16. Furniture and fixtures	0	0.0	0.0	0.0
17. Printing and publishing...	7	2,702.1	1.9	1.6
18. Chemicals...	16	8,654.9	4.5	5.1
19. Pharmaceuticals	17	7,729.0	4.7	4.6
20. Soaps, cleaners...	4	2,357.4	1.1	1.4
21. Rubber and tires	0	0.0	0.0	0.0
22. Leather...	2	696.7	0.6	0.4
23. Nonmetallic mineral products...	13	6,089.6	3.6	3.6
24. Glass...	2	1,033.7	0.6	0.6
25. Fabricated metal products...	9	4,709.1	2.5	2.8
26. Metal cans...	2	680.3	0.6	0.4
27. Machinery...	9	3,300.5	2.5	2.0
28. Farm, construction...machinery	5	3,400.6	1.4	2.0
29. Office...computing...machines	4	1,493.1	1.1	0.9
30. Electrical machinery...	6	2,285.9	1.7	1.4
31. Household appliances	6	2,689.8	1.7	1.6
32. Radio...communication equipment	11*	5,302.4*	3.1	3.1
33. Scientific...control...devices...measuring...	1	270.9	0.3	0.2
34. Photographic equipment...	1	617.1	0.3	0.4
35. Motor vehicles...	9	4,232.1	2.5	2.5
36. Aircraft...	2	774.5	0.6	0.5
37. Ship...building...	0	0.0	0.0	0.0
38. Railroad equipment...	4	2,133.0	1.1	1.3
39. Other and miscellaneous manufacturing	5	1,950.9	1.4	1.2
40. Rail transportation	10	4,686.9	2.8	2.8
41. Transit...	0	0.0	0.0	0.0
42. Motor transportation	3	915.5	0.8	0.5
43. Water transportation	3	1,110.1	0.8	0.7
44. Air transportation	6	3,044.9	1.7	1.8
45. Electric, gas...sanitary...	59	29,092.7	16.4	17.2
46. Telephone, telegraph...services...	6	2,842.8	1.7	1.7
47. Radio and TV broadcasting	2	1,326.2	0.6	0.8
48. Wholesale trade...	1	318.3	0.8	0.2
49. Retail trade...	6	1,978.5	1.7	1.2
50. General merchandise...	11	5,079.6	3.1	3.0
51. Food stores	8	3,250.2	2.2	1.9
52. Motion pictures	5	1,946.8	1.4	1.2
53. Services...	12	4,952.3	3.3	2.9
54. Real estate	6	2,031.2	1.7	1.2
Total...	359	$168,954.5	100.0%	100.0%

*Includes manufacturing subsidiaries of General Telephone & Electronics, counted here as one company; see Appendix A, "Notes to Exhibit 1," Note 54. This company not included in the total number of The 359.
Source: Exhibit 1.

EXHIBIT 21
Regulated and integrated industries and industries with seven or more of The Next 359 Largest Nonfinancial
Corporations, 1971

Industry Category	Number of companies	Percentage of The 359 Companies	Assets held ($ billions)	Average value of assets per company ($ billions)	Percentage of the total assets held by The 359 Companies
Utilities and regulated industries					
Railroad transportation	10	2.8%	$ 4.69	$0.469	2.8%
Transit	0	0.0	0.0	–	0.0
Electric, gas . . . sanitary	59	16.4	29.09	0.493	17.2
Telephone, telegraph	6	1.7	2.84	0.473	1.7
Air transportation	6	1.7	3.04	0.507	1.8
Motor transportation	3	0.8	0.92	0.307	0.5
Water transportation	3	0.8	1.11	0.370	0.7
Radio and TV broadcasting	2	0.6	1.33	0.665	0.8
Subtotals	89	24.8%	$ 43.02	$0.483	25.5%
Integrated industries					
Petroleum	10	2.8%	$ 5.42	$0.542	3.2%
Iron and steel	12	3.3	5.09	0.424	3.0
Nonferrous metals	10	2.8	5.05	0.505	3.0
Lumber . . . wood . . . paper products	9	2.5	4.88	0.542	2.9
Subtotals	41	11.4%	$ 20.44	$0.499	12.1%
Totals, regulated and integrated industries	130	36.2%	$ 63.46	$0.488	37.6%
Other industries with 7 or more of The Next 359 Largest Nonfinancial Corporations, 1971					
Food	16	4.5%	$ 8.78	$0.549	5.2%
Textiles	8	2.2	3.19	0.399	1.9
Printing and publishing	7	1.9	2.70	0.386	1.6
Chemicals	16	4.5	8.65	0.541	5.1
Pharmaceuticals	17	4.7	7.73	0.455	4.6
Nonmetallic mineral . . . products	13	3.6	6.09	0.468	3.6
Fabricated metal	9	2.5	4.71	0.523	2.8
Machinery	9	2.5	3.30	0.367	2.0
Radio . . . communication equipment . . .	11*	3.1	5.30*	0.482	3.1
Motor vehicles	9	2.5	4.23	0.470	2.5
General merchandise	11	3.1	5.08	0.462	3.0
Food stores	8	2.2	3.25	0.406	1.9
Services	12	3.3	4.95	0.413	2.9
Subtotals	146	40.7%	$ 67.96	$0.465	40.2%
Totals	276	76.0%	$130.31	$0.477	77.1%

*Includes GTE Manufacturing subsidiaries, counted here as one company.
Source: Exhibit 1.

machinery and Household appliances; and the 11 in Radio . . . communication equipment.

The Next 359 Largest Corporations of 1971. And so we come to look at the second tier of largest companies, The Next 359. Several features stand out in the composition of that stratum. See Exhibits 20 and 21.

First, and most important, the composition of the roster of The 359 was patterned, not random. And this ordering casts light on factors that affect the structures of industries.

Second, the companies of the second tier were *much* smaller on the average than those of the first: $471 million to $2.7 billion. The Next 359 held only 12 percent of the assets of the largest companies, in contrast to the 38 percent held by The 200.

Third, significant clusters of second-tier companies occurred in the "regulated" and integrated industries, as was true of The Top 200. Of these companies, 59 of them, with 17 percent of the assets of the whole group, showed up in Electric, gas . . . sanitary services.

Fourth, generally speaking, however, the distribution of The 359 shows wider occurrence and considerably less "bunching" than The 200 did, in a limited number of industries. There was much more industrial diversity among The 359. For example, about 80 percent of the number of The 200 and more than 80 percent of their assets showed up in only 14 industries. See Exhibit 17. But as for The 359, even 24 industries accounted for smaller fractions of their number and their assets. And, whereas there were 4 to 6 of The 200 in only four industries (13 in all, 6.5 percent of their number with 3.7 percent of their assets; see Exhibit 18), companies among The 359 occurred in clusters of 4 to 6 in 12 industries. See Exhibit 22. These smaller but significant clusters accounted for 60 of The 359 companies, one-sixth of their number, and about the same proportion of their assets.

Fifth, as a manifestation of the wider spread of The 359 among industries, there were only five industries in which there was none of their number, whereas there were 18 in which none of The 200 occurred.

Despite the generally greater spread of The 359 among industries, as compared to The 200, fewer of The 359 showed up scatterings of

EXHIBIT 22
Other industries with four to six of The Next 359 Largest Nonfinancial Corporations, 1971

Industry Category	Number of companies	Percentage of The 359 Companies	Assets held ($ billions)	Average value of assets per company ($ billions)	Percentage of the assets held by The 359 Companies
Alcoholic beverages	5	1.4%	$ 2.42	$0.48	1.4%
Apparel	4	1.1	1.54	0.39	0.9
Soaps, cleaners	4	1.1	2.36	0.59	1.4
Farm, construction . . . machinery	5	1.4	3.40	0.68	2.0
Office . . . computing . . . machines	4	1.1	1.49	0.37	0.9
Electrical machinery	6	1.7	2.29	0.38	1.4
Household appliances	6	1.7	2.69	0.45	1.6
Railroad equipment	4	1.1	2.13	0.53	1.3
Other and miscellaneous manufacturing	5	1.4	1.95	0.39	1.2
Retail trade	6	1.7	1.98	0.33	1.2
Motion pictures	5	1.4	1.95	0.39	1.2
Real estate	6	1.7	2.03	0.34	1.2
Totals	60	16.7%	$26.23	$0.44	15.5%

Source: Exhibit 1.

one, two, or three companies. This was the case in only 13 industries, as compared to 19 in which there were such scatterings of The 200. And only 24 companies of The 359 were thus scattered diffusely in comparison to 32 of The 200. (See Exhibits 23 and 19.)

Industry profiles of the distribution of The 200 and The 359. The industry profiles of the Top 200 and of The Next 359 were significantly different. The two sets of large companies, the *very* large and the large, were distributed among the Industry Categories in very different patterns. In a number of important instances, the two sets of companies were concentrated—or sparse, as the case may be—in different industries. In a way of speaking, because of such concentrations, some Industry Categories were first-tier industries; some were second-tier. In others, of course, representatives of the largest companies were exceptional or totally lacking; these were characteristically "smaller" or "small" company industries.

In first-tier industries, companies from among The 200 were far more prominent than those from among The 359. In other industries, the reverse was true: companies of The Next 359 predominated. This predomination was most clearly evident as gauged by relative asset masses. Data to this effect are displayed in Exhibit 24.

For example, in Petroleum, companies of The 200 held assets of about $100 billion; companies in the industry from The 359 held only $5.4 billion. Of the assets of the companies in the industry that were among The 559, those among The 200 held 94.9 percent ($100.4 billion of the $105.8), while those from among The 359 held 5.1 percent. The ratio of the two sets of holdings was almost 20:1.

EXHIBIT 23
Other industries with one to three of The Next 359 Largest Nonfinancial Corporations, 1971

Industry Category	Number of companies	Percentage of The 359 Companies	Assets held ($ billions)	Average value of assets per company ($ billions)	Percentage of the assets held by The 359 Companies
Coal	3	0.8%	$ 1.41	$0.47	0.8%
Construction	3	0.8	1.20	0.40	0.7
Meat	2	0.6	1.15	0.58	0.7
Dairy	3	0.8	1.71	0.57	1.0
Soft drinks	1	0.3	0.83	0.83	0.5
Tobacco	1	0.3	0.60	0.60	0.4
Leather	2	0.6	0.70	0.35	0.4
Glass	2	0.6	1.03	0.52	0.6
Metal cans	2	0.6	0.68	0.34	0.4
Scientific...control... devices...measuring...	1	0.3	0.27	0.27	0.2
Photographic equipment	1	0.3	0.62	0.62	0.4
Aircraft	2	0.6	0.77	0.39	0.5
Wholesale trade	1	0.3	0.32	0.32	0.2
Totals	24	6.7%	$11.29	$0.47	6.7%

Source: Exhibit 1.

EXHIBIT 24

Some illustrative differences in the Industry Profiles of The 200 Largest (first-tier) and The Next 359 Largest (second-tier) Corporations

Industry Category	Number of firms		Assets ($ billions)		Average size of firms ($ billions)		Percentage of The 559 assets held in Industry Category by companies among:	
	The 200	The 359	The 200	The 359	The 200	The 359	The 200	The 359
First-tier industries								
Petroleum	20	10	$100.4	$ 5.4	$ 5.0	$0.5	94.9%	5.1%
Tobacco	4	1	6.4	0.6	1.6	0.6	91.4	8.6
Rubber and tires	5	0	9.0	0.0	1.8	0.0	100.0	0.0
Office...machines	7	4	20.0	1.5	2.9	0.4	93.0	7.0
Motor vehicles	8	9	40.3	4.2	5.0	0.5	90.6	9.4
Aircraft	8	2	12.0	0.8	1.5	0.4	93.8	6.2
Rail transportation	11	10	27.7	4.7	2.5	0.5	85.5	14.5
Telephone, telegraph	5	6	66.2	2.8	13.2	0.5	95.9	4.1
General merchandise	9	11	19.4	5.1	2.2	0.5	79.2	20.8
Totals and averages	77	53	$301.4	$38.6	$ 3.9	$0.73	88.6%	11.4%
Second-tier industries								
Construction	0	3	$ 0.0	$ 1.2	$ 0.0	$0.4	0.0%	100.0%
Food	3	16	3.5	8.8	1.2	0.5	28.5	71.5
Apparel	1	4	0.9	1.5	0.9	0.4	37.5	62.5
Printing and publishing	0	7	0.0	2.7	0.0	0.4	0.0	100.0
Pharmaceuticals	4	16	4.3	8.7	1.1	0.5	33.1	66.9
Leather	0	2	0.0	0.7	0.0	0.3	0.0	100.0
Fabricated metals	1	9	1.2	4.7	1.2	0.5	20.3	79.7
Machinery	0	9	0.0	3.3	0.0	0.4	0.0	100.0
Household appliances	1	6	1.7	2.7	1.7	0.4	38.6	61.4
Railroad equipment	0	4	0.0	2.1	0.0	0.5	0.0	100.0
Food stores	2	8	1.9	3.3	1.0	0.4	36.5	63.5
Motion pictures	0	5	0.0	1.9	0.0	0.4	0.0	100.0
Services	0	12	0.0	5.0	0.0	0.4	0.0	100.0
Real estate	0	6	0.0	2.0	0.0	0.3	0.0	100.0
Totals and averages	12	107	$ 13.5	$48.6	$ 1.1	$0.45	21.7%	78.3%

In Petroleum, companies of The 200 also outnumbered those of The 359 by 2:1, being 20 of The 200 and but 10 of The 359.

Petroleum was pretty clearly a first-tier industry. Rubber and tires was more so; none of the largest was among The Next 359.

As distinguished in this way, Food (except Meat and Dairy) was a second-tier industry. Of the 19 companies among The 559 Largest that were in Food, 3 were from among The First 200, but 16 were from among The Next 359. The 3 largest firms held assets of $3.5 billion; the next 16 held assets of $8.8 billion. The first 3 held 28.5 percent of The 559 assets present in the industry; the next 16 held 71.5 percent.

In these terms, Pharmaceuticals was also, characteristically, a second-tier industry. More so were Printing and publishing and Motion pictures.

The data in Exhibit 24 suggest the existence of significant differences in underlying industry structures. The data are illustrative only; too much should not be made of them. But a couple of hypotheses do come to mind in the course of examining the different patterns of distribution. One would be to the effect that in certain industries—Petroleum, for example—basics of physical facts and processes (production, transportation, refining, distribution, and marketing to consumers) tend to foster *very* large size in consequence of economies both of (*a*) large scale at each of several points in the whole process, *and* (*b*) integration of these processes into something like continuous, highly coordinated construction and operation.[10] In any case, the very biggest petroleum companies greatly overshadowed those in the second stratum.

The relative predominance of second-tier companies in Food, as a contrasting illustration, suggests that in this industry, as in others, there were, indeed, economies of scale in production, marketing, finance, management, or whatever, but that these economies did not necessarily lead to the emergence of *very* large companies. Even the *largest* of the Food companies (General Foods) was only 60 percent of the size of the *average* of The Top 200.

A second related hypothesis that forms itself is to the effect that there are important differences in *kind* as between the *very big* companies in a given industry and the simply *big*. This hypothesis would suggest, among other things, that "next largest" companies are not mere midgets or "scale-downs" of the same species as those among the very largest, but fit in different kinds of niches in the encompassing productive system.

Among the 77 very largest companies of the nine first-tier industries illustrated in Exhibit 24, the average firm size was $3.9 billion. This was more than five times the average size of the "next largest" companies in these same industries, $730 million. There is basis for a strong hunch that the largest companies were not merely quantitatively different from the next smaller group. The difference in average size as between the 12 largest companies to be found among the 14 illustrative second-tier industries and the 107 next largest in those industries was $1.1 billion compared to $450 million, a factor of 2.4 times. Even this lesser difference is substantial and, more than likely, is significant of real qualitative differences.

The greater quantitative difference between the "very largest" and the next "largest" companies in first-tier industries does suggest, further, a much sharper qualitative differentiation between them than the differentiations between the largest and next largest in second-tier industries. A scrutiny of the particular companies appearing among the very biggest and among the next biggest in a number of industries seems to support that idea: Iron and steel, Nonferrous metals, Petroleum, Motor vehicles, and Aircraft.

The biggest Iron and steel companies of 1971 for the most part were "full-line," highly integrated producers with very large-scale conversion systems—some with interlinked multiple plants for continuous-flow production from blast and basic oxygen furnaces through continuous strip mills for plate sheet and construction shapes. Smaller companies tended to be more specialized, with shorter lines of products.

The largest Nonferrous metals companies were also integrated, broad-line companies—some of them multinational in scope. The second-tier nonferrous companies, again, tended to be more specialized and less fully integrated.

The biggest companies in the Petroleum category were predominantly fully integrated and, again, most were multinational. The smaller companies in this industry complex were far more specialized, several of them being engaged in providing certain kinds of services to the integrated companies.

The first-tier Motor vehicles companies included the three more integrated producers of passenger cars, the more integrated producers of trucks, as well as three producers of broad lines of parts and components. The second-tier companies were rather assemblers of vehicles and producers of shorter lines of products.

The largest of the Aircraft companies were somewhat more diverse, but did include three large producers of varied aircraft, including models widely used for civilian purposes. Also included were large, broader-range companies engaged in production of weapons and space-systems. Three conglomerates were included in the group. The two second-tier companies, however, were primarily both producers of specialized military aircraft.

But the relation between scale and function is a big topic in its own right. It cannot be dealt with as completely in this work as it deserves, although we shall look at some additional data that will offer the same suggestion that, within an industry complex, along the axis of scale, function does change qualitatively, even among the larger companies.

The 559 Largest Corporations of 1971. In any event, we come now to consider as a group The 559 Largest Nonfinancial Corporations of 1971. This is the grouping of corporations that, in ways that count most, corresponds to The 200 of 1929. As mentioned, these companies are all listed in Exhibit 1, together with their assets. Each held $250 million of assets or more. In total, these companies held $707 billion of assets, about half of all assets of all nonfinancial corporations. They are tabulated by Industry Categories in Exhibit 25.

Having now dealt with the distributions of The 200 and The 359 among industries, we can dispose of The 559 fairly quickly. In doing so, we shall do well to recall that, as defined by asset size—$250 million and up—these are the companies that corresponded to the roster of The 200 of 1929. The most obvious observation is that, instead of 200 large firms, there were almost three times as many. Their total assets of $707 billion versus the $244 billion of 1929 (in something

	Industry Category	Number of firms	Assets held ($ millions)	Numbers of firms as percentage of The 559	Assets as percentage of total assets held by The 559
1.	Agriculture...	0	$ 0.0	0.0%	0.0%
2.	Iron and steel	19	23,407.7	3.4	3.3
3.	Nonferrous metals	18	17,760.1	3.2	2.5
4.	Coal	3	1,413.6	0.5	0.2
5.	Petroleum	30	105,846.3	5.4	15.0
6.	Construction	3	1,201.2	0.5	0.2
7.	Food...	19	12,321.9	3.4	1.7
8.	Meat...	5	5,325.1	0.9	0.8
9.	Dairy...	6	5,065.0	1.1	0.7
10.	Alcoholic beverages	6	3,355.1	1.1	0.5
11.	Soft drinks...	2	1,935.6	0.4	0.3
12.	Tobacco...	5	7,045.5	0.9	1.0
13.	Textiles...	9	4,579.7	1.6	0.6
14.	Apparel...	5	2,470.5	0.9	0.3
15.	Lumber... wood... paper... products	17	17,385.7	3.0	2.5
16.	Furniture and fixtures	0	0.0	0.0	0.0
17.	Printing and publishing...	7	2,702.1	1.3	0.4
18.	Chemicals...	26	30,416.4	4.7	4.3
19.	Pharmaceuticals...	21	12,058.0	3.8	1.7
20.	Soaps, cleaners...	5	4,370.4	0.9	0.6
21.	Rubber and tires	5	9,149.0	0.9	1.3
22.	Leather...	2	696.7	0.4	0.1
23.	Nonmetallic mineral products...	13	6,089.6	2.3	0.9
24.	Glass...	4	3,742.1	0.7	0.5
25.	Fabricated metal products...	10	5,892.3	1.8	0.8
26.	Metal cans...	4	3,742.8	0.7	0.5
27.	Machinery...	9	3,300.5	1.6	0.5
28.	Farm, construction... machinery	7	6,670.3	1.3	0.9
29.	Office... computing... machines	11	21,463.1	2.0	3.0
30.	Electrical machinery...	8	12,711.6	1.4	1.8
31.	Household appliances	7	4,359.5	1.3	0.6
32.	Radio... communication equipment	14*	19,967.1*	2.5	2.8
33.	Scientific... control... devices... measuring...	2	2,454.0	0.4	0.3
34.	Photographic equipment...	2	3,915.1	0.4	0.6
35.	Motor vehicles...	17	44,561.3	3.0	6.3
36.	Aircraft...	10	12,783.2	1.8	1.8
37.	Ship... building...	0	0.0	0.0	0.0
38.	Railroad equipment...	4	2,133.0	0.7	0.3
39.	Other and miscellaneous manufacturing	5	1,950.9	0.9	0.3
40.	Rail transportation	21	32,347.5	3.8	4.6
41.	Transit...	0	0.0	0.0	0.0
42.	Motor transportation	5	3,580.6	0.9	0.5
43.	Water transportation	3	1,110.1	0.5	0.2
44.	Air transportation	12	12,199.2	2.1	1.7
45.	Electric, gas... sanitary...	106	120,891.8	19.0	17.1
46.	Telephone, telegraph... services...	11	69,014.0	2.0	9.8
47.	Radio and TV broadcasting	2	1,326.2	0.4	0.2
48.	Wholesale trade...	1	318.3	0.2	†
49.	Retail trade...	7	3,550.3	1.3	0.5
50.	General merchandise...	20	24,490.9	3.6	3.5
51.	Food stores...	10	5,193.6	1.8	0.7
52.	Motion pictures...	5	1,946.8	0.9	0.3
53.	Services...	12	4,952.3	2.1	0.7
54.	Real estate	6	2,031.2	1.1	0.3
	Totals	559	$707,194.8	100.0%	100.0%

*Includes Western Electric and Manufacturing subsidiaries of GTE; see Appendix A, "Notes to Exhibit 1," Notes 53 and 54. These companies are not included in the total number of The 559.

†Less than 0.1 percent.

like constant dollars) represented similar growth. The average size of firms in the two years was roughly the same, $1.2 billion in 1929 and $1.3 billion in 1971. The differences in the make-ups of the two rosters of companies are dramatic; they will be the focus of a chapter unto themselves. (See Chapter 9.)

Again, as in the case of The 200 in both 1929 and 1971 and in the case of The 359 of 1971, the distribution of The 559 among the 54 Industry Categories was strongly patterned. Far from being spread evenly, these large companies tended to be clustered in certain industries, to be sparse in others and totally absent from a few. Where they did tend to occur, they did so in significant numbers and in relatively great mass. Exhibit 25 reveals substantial numbers of these companies, and masses of assets in certain Industry Categories, as in Iron and steel, Petroleum, Nonferrous metals, Lumber, Chemicals, Office ... computing ... machines, Motor vehicles, the rails, the utilities. Representatives of The 559 were few or absent in Agriculture, Furniture, Wholesale trade, and Real estate.

Where these 559 companies tended to cluster, and where they did not, is revealed in Exhibits 26, 27, and 28.

Of The 559 Largest Firms of 1971, the largest clustering—160 of them—occurred in the seven "regulated" industries; these particular companies held one-third of all the assets of our Largest Corporations, and one-sixth of all assets of nonfinancial corporations. Another 84 companies clustered in four characteristically "integrated" industries. These 84 companies, together, held almost one-quarter of the assets of the Largest Corporations. These 244 companies, in 11 industries, held well over half of the assets of our biggest companies and well over one-quarter of *all* assets of *all* nonfinancial corporations.

These were *big* organizations. The average assets of the 160 firms in the "regulated" industries amounted to $1.5 billion. The average of the firms in the "integrated" industries stood at almost $2 billion. It is no exaggeration to say that the infrastructure of American industry was largely in the hands of these companies. They were the major sources of energy, the raw materials of industrialism, and major carriers of people and things. Just by themselves, they towered over The 200 largest "modern corporations" of 1929. (See Exhibits 5, 6, and 7.)

Numbers of other notable clusterings of our biggest companies also occurred. Another 237 of the Largest Corporations clustered in "coveys" of 7 or more in 19 other industries. These 237 also held about one-third of the total assets of The 559. Some of these clusters were numerous, indeed: 26 in Chemicals, 21 in Pharmaceuticals, 17 in Motor vehicles, and 20 in General merchandise and mail order. See Exhibit 26.

In short, 481 of the 559 largest companies, holding over 90 per-

EXHIBIT 26
Regulated and integrated industries and industries with seven or more of The 559 Largest Nonfinancial
Corporations, 1971

Industry Category	Number of companies	Percentage of The 559 companies	Assets held ($ billions)	Average value of assets per company ($ billions)	Percentage of the total assets held by The 559 companies
Utilities, regulated industries					
Railroad transportation	21	3.8%	$ 32.35	$1.54	4.6%
Transit	0	0.0	0.0	–	0.0
Electric, gas . . . sanitary	106	19.0	120.89	1.14	17.1
Telephone, telegraph	11	2.0	69.01	6.27	9.8
Air transportation	12	2.1	12.20	1.02	1.7
Motor transportation	5	0.9	3.58	0.72	0.5
Water transportation	3	0.5	1.11	0.37	0.2
Radio and TV broadcasting	2	0.4	1.33	0.67	0.2
Subtotals	160	28.6%	$240.47	$1.50	34.0%
Integrated industries					
Petroleum	30	5.4%	$105.85	$3.53	15.0%
Iron and steel	19	3.4	23.41	1.23	3.3
Nonferrous metals	18	3.2	17.76	0.99	2.5
Lumber . . . wood . . . paper	17	3.0	17.39	1.02	2.5
Subtotals	84	15.0%	$164.41	$1.96	23.2%
Totals, regulated and integrated industries	244	43.6%	$404.88	$1.66	57.3%
Other industries with 7 or more of The 559 Largest Nonfinancial Corporations, 1971					
Food	19	3.4%	$ 12.32	$0.65	1.7%
Textiles	9	1.6	4.58	0.51	0.6
Printing and publishing	7	1.3	2.70	0.39	0.4
Chemicals	26	4.7	30.42	1.17	4.3
Pharmaceuticals	21	3.8	12.06	0.57	1.7
Nonmetallic mineral . . . products	13	2.3	6.09	0.47	0.9
Fabricated metal	10	1.8	5.89	0.59	0.8
Machinery	9	1.6	3.30	0.37	0.5
Farm, construction . . . machinery	7	1.3	6.67	0.95	0.9
Office . . . computing . . . machines	11	2.0	21.46	1.95	3.0
Electrical machinery	8	1.4	12.71	1.59	1.8
Household appliances	7	1.3	4.36	0.62	0.6
Radio . . . communication equipment . . .	14*	2.5	19.97*	1.43	2.8
Motor vehicles	17	3.0	44.56	2.62	6.3
Aircraft	10	1.8	12.78	1.28	1.8
Retail trade	7	1.3	3.55	0.51	0.5
General merchandise	20	3.6	24.49	1.22	3.5
Food stores	10	1.8	5.19	0.52	0.7
Services	12	2.1	4.95	0.41	0.7
Subtotals	237	42.4%	$238.05	$1.00	33.7%
Totals	481	85.5%	$641.82	$1.34	90.8%

*See footnote *, Exhibit 25.

cent of the assets of the group, were to be found in 30 "Industry Categories."

An additional 80 companies (14.3 percent of The 559) were to be found in scatterings of anywhere from one to six companies in 20 other industries. These companies beheld about 9 percent of the assets of The 559. See Exhibits 27 and 28.

EXHIBIT 27

Other industries with four to six of The 559 Largest Nonfinancial Corporations, 1971

Industry Category	Number of companies	Percentage of The 559 companies	Assets held ($ billions)	Average value of assets per company ($ billions)	Percentage of the total assets held by The 559 Companies
Meat	5	0.9%	$ 5.33	$1.07	0.8%
Dairy	6	1.1	5.07	0.85	0.7
Alcoholic beverages	6	1.1	3.36	0.56	0.5
Tobacco	5	0.9	7.05	1.41	1.0
Apparel	5	0.9	2.47	0.49	0.3
Soaps, cleaners	5	0.9	4.37	0.87	0.6
Rubber and tires	5	0.9	9.15	1.83	1.3
Glass	4	0.7	3.74	0.94	0.5
Metal cans	4	0.7	3.74	0.94	0.5
Railroad equipment	4	0.7	2.13	0.53	0.3
Other and miscellaneous manufacturing	5	0.9	1.95	0.39	0.3
Motion pictures	5	0.9	1.95	0.39	0.3
Real estate	6	1.1	2.03	0.34	0.3
Totals	65	11.6%	$52.34	$0.81	7.4%

EXHIBIT 28

Other industries with one to three of The 559 Largest Nonfinancial Corporations, 1971

Industry Category	Number of companies	Percentage of The 559 Companies	Assets held ($ billions)	Average value of assets per company ($ billions)	Percentage of the total assets held by The 559 Companies
Coal	3	0.5%	$ 1.41	$0.47	0.2%
Construction	3	0.5	1.20	0.40	0.2
Soft drinks	2	0.4	1.94	0.97	0.3
Leather	2	0.4	0.70	0.35	0.1
Scientific control devices measuring	2	0.4	2.45	1.23	0.3
Photographic equipment	2	0.4	3.92	1.96	0.6
Wholesale trade	1	0.2	0.32	0.32	0.05
Totals	15	2.7%	$11.94	$0.80	1.7%

The fact that, in the global picture of Big Business, these 80 companies, rather scattered among 20 industries, were less in numbers and bulk as compared to the more massive aggregations listed in Exhibit 26, should not obscure a fact of importance: in several of these particular industries, the scatterings of members of The 559 really loomed large on local industry scenes. This was notably true, as we shall see in more detail in the next chapter, in Dairy, Tobacco, Rubber and tires, Glass, Metal cans, and Photographic equipment. Each of these, with the possible exception of Rubber and tires, which, in a very real way, was a specialized part of the Motor vehicles industry, was a relatively small industry; certainly as compared to the metals, petroleum, chemicals, and utilities, for instance. In them,

representatives of The 559 necessarily ranked relatively more important than companies of comparable size in large industries.

The distributions of The 200, The 359, and The 559 of 1971 are
summarized in Exhibit 29. These Largest Companies are no less
"ubiquitous" on the American scene of 1971 than The 200 of 1929.
More than merely ever-present, these corporations and their works
characterize the American way of life. The food we eat; the clothes
we wear; the homes we live in; the vehicles we move in; the energy
that illumines, propels, and warms us; the tools we use, of production and communication—all—embody in irreplaceable fashion the
outputs of these firms.

And yet, this ubiquity does not extend to their places within the
business community and the nation's productive system. In that
sense, the sitings of our Largest Corporations are very special.

The most numerous and the biggest clusters of our Largest Corporations were localized in very particular Industry Categories: in the 7
regulated industries, in the 4 integrated industries and in 19 other
industries—30 in all. In these industries, were to be found 481 of the
big corporations and over 90 percent of their assets. In 24 other
Industry Categories, the large corporations occurred infrequently or
not at all. Altogether, in those industries only 80 of The 559—14
percent of their number—were to be found; and these held but 9 percent of the assets of the whole group.

But these data do not fully measure and convey the particularity

EXHIBIT 29
Industry distributions of The 200, The 359, The 559 Largest Nonfinancial Corporations, 1971; Summary

	Utilities and other regulated industries	Integrated industries	Other industries with 7 or more companies	Other industries with 4 to 6 companies	Other industries with 1 to 3 companies	Industries with no companies		Totals
						"Older" industries	"Newer" industries	
Number of companies								
The 200*	71	43	42	13	32	—	—	200
The 359†	89	41	146	60	24	—	—	359
The 559‡	160	84	237	65	15	—	—	559
Number of industries where occurring								
The 200	5	4	5	3	19	17	1	54
The 359	7	4	13	12	13	5	0	54
The 559	7	4	19	13	7	4	0	54
Value of assets ($ billions)								
The 200	$197.5	$144.0	$113.5	$19.9	$63.4	—	—	$538.2
The 359	43.0	20.4	68.0	26.2	11.3	—	—	169.0
The 559	240.5	164.4	238.1	52.3	11.9	—	—	707.2
Percentage of assets								
The 200	36.7%	26.7%	21.1%	3.7%	11.8%	—	—	100.0%
The 359	25.5	12.1	40.2	15.5	6.7	—	—	100.0
The 559	34.0	23.2	33.7	7.4	1.7	—	—	100.0

*See Exhibits 17-19.
†See Exhibits 21-23.
‡See Exhibits 26-28.

of the natures of our biggest corporations. Even in those industries where they did cluster—a rather particular phenomenon of itself—they occupied a special place. This was mentioned a few pages back in connection with Petroleum, Metals, Motor vehicles, and Aircraft, for example. To this listing could be added Rubber and tires and Office...computing...machines, for further instances. Even among the electric utilities, the big utilities occupied a special place: the provision of power for our great urban agglomerations. Scarcely any productive entity of any sort occupies a more specialized—or vital—niche than a billion-dollar urban utility. Not only are these companies—about 50 in number—physically, economically, politically, socially different from corporations in other industries, they are qualitatively, as well as quantitatively, different from the smaller utilities, even from those large enough to be listed among The Next 359.

Of especial interest, because of both its intrinsic importance and because of what it indicates as to the development of the American system, is the appearance, in 1971, of large and very large corporations in industries in which none of The 200 of 1929 had occurred. No less than 119 of The 559 of 1971 were to be found in 16 industries in which *none* of The 200 of 1929 had occurred. Of these, 49 were in eight "older" industries; 70 were in eight "newer" industries. See Exhibit 30.

As to the "older" industries, 3 of The Top 200 of 1971 occurred

EXHIBIT 30
Largest Companies appearing by 1971 in older and newer industries where none had been in 1929

	Companies among The 200	Companies among The 359	Companies among The 559
Older industries			
Construction	0	3	3
Alcoholic beverages	1	5	6
Bottled and canned soft drinks	1	1	2
Apparel	1	4	5
Printing and publishing	0	7	7
Nonmetallic mineral products	0	13	13
Wholesale trade	0	1	1
Services other than motion pictures	0	12	12
Subtotals	3	46	49
Newer industries			
Pharmaceuticals	4	17	21
Office...computing....machines	7	4	11
Household appliances	1	6	7
Scientific...devices	1	1	2
Radio and TV broadcasting	0	2	2
Aircraft...	8	2	10
Motor transportation	2	3	5
Air transportation	6	6	12
Subtotals	29	41	70
Totals	32	87	119

Note: Individual Large Corporations had been active in these Industries, but none had been primarily identified with them. See Chapter 3, Note 8.

in three of the industries. In these same industries, there were now also 10 of The Next 359. Beyond these, there were 36 second-tier companies in five other "older" industries.

No doubt, over the intervening four decades, economies of scale had been devised that permitted or even encouraged growth in these industries of companies with assets of $250 million. Scrutiny of the particular "older" industries listed in the upper portion of Exhibit 30, such as Construction, Apparel, Printing and publishing, and Wholesale trade, leads to the thought that the developments that lay behind the rise of these large companies were probably as much conceptual, managerial, and strategic in nature as technological. Such developments would include the development of organization structures, information and control systems, means of access to capital markets, strategic definitions of corporate roles and functions, that were appropriate to meeting, on very large scale, growing and changing demands. In any case, these companies of 1971 were surely not mere scale-ups of companies as they had existed in 1929.

Even more interesting and revealing was the fact that 70 of The 559 Largest Corporations had appeared in eight "newer" industries that had scarcely existed in 1929 and in which, of course, none of The 200 of that year had occurred. Again, scrutiny of the particular industries and of the particular companies quickly leads to appreciation of the importance of technological advance in the rise of large corporations in these sectors. But more was at work than technological change per se, say the development of knowledge in laboratories, and even in pilot plants. Present also were developments in "hardware" and in knowledge and concepts that implied economies of scale in production. More: developments had taken place in economies of scale in research and development; in the engineering of large, complex production systems; and other important staff work, such as planning, human resources management, procurement, and quality control. One perceives the presence of such developments in Pharmaceuticals, Office . . . computing . . . machines, and Aircraft, for example.

In other newer industries, still other factors were present that led to large optimal, even *large minimal* scale, for instance, Air transportation and Household appliances.

In Air transportation, the individual "production" unit, the airplane, had, itself, become large. A single "smaller" commercial jet transport now represented an investment of the order of $6 to $8 million; just one such plane represented a mass of assets larger than the assets of the 98 percent of all our corporations, those which reported assets of less than $5 million. When several, even scores of such planes were organized into a single productive *system,* the result was inevitably a very large corporation, indeed.

In Household appliances, economies of scale in production combined with economies of scale in distribution and marketing to foster the growth of a limited number of companies whose managements understood more than a little how to achieve the economies that were possible. Those companies whose managements understood these basic facts could formulate strategies consonant with those facts, could devise concrete plans and programs to implement those strategies, and operate effectively the large and complex organizations that worked. Those companies flourished.

In a later chapter, we shall return to examine some of the dynamics that influenced the rise—and in some cases, the fall—of large corporations in various industries. For the moment, we need but recognize that the growth and transformation of our Largest Corporations over those 40-some years was a complex of processes far more profound and intricate than mere mergers and "consolidations." These processes were part and parcel of the continuing Industrial Revolution, of the continuing development of America. And in that literally *radical* development, these Largest Corporations were among the very prime movers.

The community of Big Business of 1971 was more numerous and much bigger than that of 1929. In wandering through history for 40 years, the American people had left still farther behind, never to be recaptured, their agrarian, rural, artisan, bourgeois, individualistic, family- and neighborhood-centered mode of life. In some ways, these had been the longest 40 years in our history, so far had they carried us, so different did our whole way of life become. The humanistic world of Currier and Ives, even the raucous, grating world of the Roaring Twenties, had become no less distant than that of the Crusades or the Arthurian legends. The community of our Largest Corporations, by then, was of, by, and for the closing decades of the 20th century and the opening ones of the 21st—which will be upon us sooner than we think.

Foreign corporations in the United States

So far, we have taken a fairly nationalistic, not to say isolationist or jingoistic view of the occurrence and presence of Large Corporations in American industry. We have ignored large foreign corporations. In fact, they were numerous and, in some Industry Categories, their presence was large. Some were present in the United States, in terms of ownership of productive entities; some were present in terms of significant export positions. Not only were important foreign firms actually present, there were also, in 1971, many *potential* entrants, some of which have since then entered the American arena in a big way.

For now, just by way of suggestion, we list just a few of the more obvious entities:

Shell Oil Company, a subsidiary of the Royal Dutch/Shell Group.
Lever Brothers, a subsidiary of Unilever Ltd. and Unilever N.V.

Alcan, a Canadian producer of aluminum.

International Nickel, the Canadian-based largest producer of nickel.

Brown & Williamson Tobacco, a subsidiary of British American Tobacco.

Hoffmann-La Roche, a subsidiary of a Swiss pharmaceutical company.

Ciba-Geigy, a subsidiary of a Swiss pharmaceutical-chemical company.

Hoechst, a large German chemical company.

Bayer, A. G., another large German chemical company.

Volkswagen, a German auto maker.

In addition, by way of further example, subsidiaries of Pechiney and Rio Tinto and national companies of foreign nations are important in several of the nonferrous metals.

In actuality and potentiality, the total influence of foreign firms was large, especially so in particular sectors. But that is another story, just in itself.

*   *   *   *   *

In the next chapter, we now go on to consider matters having to do with nagging questions as to relative presence or "concentration" of our present-day Largest Corporations among the several industries.

NOTES

1. *Economic Report of the President (1979),* Tables B-1 and B-3.

2. *Statistical Abstract of the United States, 1974,* pp. 5, 40, 44, 350, 476; *Source Book, Statistics of Income, 1971;* Exhibit 15.

3. *Economic Report of the President,* p. 203.

4. *Survey of Current Business;* July 1974, June 1975.

5. *Survey of Current Business* (July, 1974), p. 18.

6. *Statistical Abstract of the United States, 1974,* p. 514.

7. By the summer of 1979, when the manuscript of this book was completed, federal data for 1975 were available. See Chapter 12.

   A major part of the lag between the filing of corporate income tax returns and the eventual publication of data based upon them by the Internal Revenue Service stems from the fact that corporate tax returns remain "open" after their filing for three years for possible amendments. The rest of the time, presumably, is taken up by the clerical and data processing task of getting the data together in publishable form.

   In compiling the data, the IRS generally tallies returns of *all* corporations with assets of $10 million or more, but relies on *samples* of returns of corporations smaller than that. This sampling no doubt introduces some error. Overall, the error is probably less than one might suppose. As the IRS points out, statistics for whole industries are generally governed by the returns of these larger companies, which, as to numbers rather than mass, are a small minority of the corporate community. In 1971, nonfinancial corporations with assets of $10 million or more held a reported total of about $1,030,800 million, about 73 percent of all assets of all nonfinancial corporations. (See *Source Book, Statistics of Income, 1971,* pp. 8, 18, 69.)

   The data for The 559 Largest Nonfinancial Corporations listed in Exhibit 1 and tabulated in Exhibits 15, etc., defined as those publicly held companies with assets of more than $250 million, do not correspond exactly either as to numbers or as to assets with the data given by the Internal Revenue Service for nonfinancial corporations similarly defined. The figures given by the IRS for nonfinancial corporations with assets of $250 million and over, derived from balance sheets of reporting corporations, are 615 companies, versus 559, and $772.6 billion of assets versus $707.2 billion. (See *Source Book, Statistics of Income, 1971*, pp. 8, 18, and 69.)

Several factors work to produce the differences. In the first place, of course, corporate financial data reported publicly and data included in tax returns are different matters. Naturally, corporations—like individuals—are interested in minimizing their tax liabilities. This *may* result in a tendency to "write down" assets as rapidly as possible in order to maximize charges against income and, accordingly, to reduce tax liabilities. The same motivations do not necessarily apply to published data, where efforts may be in the direction of maximizing reported income, with consequent decreases in charges against income and increases in reported asset values.

Second, the data for The 559 corporations in Exhibit 15 are publicly reported, *consolidated* data. In consolidated statements, the data for any number of subsidiaries of a parent corporation are brought together. In this process assets and liabilities, of course, are not simply added; intracompany data (which includes intersubsidiary and parent-subsidiary investments and obligations) are cancelled out. It is probable that some large companies file separate, rather than consolidated, tax returns and balance sheets for certain subsidiaries; this results in an apparent increase in the total number of corporations and the total value of assets reported by the IRS as compared to consolidated data.

Some of the subsidiaries for which separate returns are filed may have assets of *more* than $250 million. For each of these, the IRS number of corporations and the reported assets in that largest size class would be increased. Some of the subsidiaries for which separate returns are filed have assets of *less* than $250 million. This has the effects of increasing the apparent numbers of corporations in size classes of less than $250 million as well as increasing the reported values of assets therein.

Third, it is, unfortunately, highly likely that some of the largest publicly held corporations escaped our efforts to "discover" them.

Those, I suspect, are the principal causes of the differences. There are two others.

A number of U.S. subsidiaries of foreign firms are surely included in IRS tabulations and are among those classified by the IRS as reporting assets of over $250 million. These data, in general, are not reported publicly. One can only speculate as to their identities or natures. It is possible that important foreign-held companies are included in IRS data for Nonferrous metals, Tobacco, Food, Paper, Chemicals, and Pharmaceuticals, for example.

Finally, a certain number of large corporations, especially in Wholesale trade, are very closely held and issue no public reports. Inclusion of these among IRS compilations also operates, of course, to increase the apparent numbers of corporations and values of assets.

The apparent net effects of these differences, however they work individually, is to increase both the apparent numbers and total assets of corporations reported by IRS over those reported publicly. The two sets of data being as close as they are, one can proceed with reasonable confidence that the realities underlying the data are not importantly misportrayed by either set of figures. In some degree of counterbalance, perhaps, the data shown here do include assets of U.S. firms that are physically located out of the country. In some industries, as Petroleum, the result is to overstate the presence of those companies *in the United States*. For further data and discussion of the differences between IRS and published information concerning corporations with assets of $250,000,000 and more, see Note 1 to Chapter 7.

8. Categorizing whole corporations according to single industries occasionally results in important over- and understatements of their presence in certain industries. For instance, in Exhibits 16-18, the presence of very large steel companies in coal mining is understated as is the presence of certain large companies in ship building. Obversely, their presence in Iron and steel and other industries is overstated.

9. A similar finding for an earlier period was reached by John Lintner and J. Keith Butters, "Effects of Mergers on Industrial Concentration, 1940-1947," *The Review of Economics and Statistics*, vol. 32, no. 1 (February 1950), pp. 30-48. (This article prompted a series of "replies" by John M. Blair, a "comment" by J. Fred Weston, a

"rejoinder" to Mr. Blair by M. A. Adelman, and a "rejoinder" and "further rejoinder" to Mr. Blair, as well as a "rejoinder" to Mr. Weston, by Messrs. Lintner and Butters. See *The Review of Economics and Statistics,* vol. 33, no. 1 (February 1951) and vol. 34, no. 4 (November 1952).

10. One landmark study indicates this was surely true of petroleum: John G. McLean and Robert W. Haigh, *The Growth of Integrated Oil Companies* (Boston: Harvard Business School, 1953).

6

The Largest Corporations in their industry settings; industry systems; Industry Categories; concepts of concentration and presence

In all the discussion of Big Business, the Modern Corporation, and of large companies generally, probably no topic has captured more attention of political leaders, economists, and the general public than "concentration."[1] Where a few large firms loom very large in an industry, the structure of the industry is said to be "concentrated." Stemming from the "concentrated" industrial structure, comes, depending upon the commentator, concentrated political power, economic power, market power. This power, it is said, derives from *size*—absolute size, relative size. Large size, it is widely thought—and not just by critics of business—enables large corporations to "dominate" markets and industries, even political and economic processes, and to make "monopolistic" profits.

The present chapter deals with some concepts that are central to that discussion. The next presents and analyzes data that tell a great deal about the place of large corporations in the several Industry Categories of the American economic system.

"CONCENTRATION" OF POWER IN INDUSTRIES

We have already seen in Chapter 2 something of older, traditional concerns with corporate size. These were concerns with the size of big firms in their generality, such as those of Adam Smith and later critics like Adolf Berle and Gardiner Means. Such preoccupations are but a step away from a somewhat more recent set of concerns with the collective size of particular groups of large corporations, say those in various industry sectors. The thought is often expressed that, because of their collective size, small groups of particular large corporations dominate, or control, specific markets or entire industries. As a consequence of such concentration of structure, the economic behaviors of firms in these industries—particularly of the local "Big Four" or "Big Eight," or such—are believed to be "monopolistic" or "oligopolistic": Prices are higher; costs are higher; utilization of existing capacity is lower—as is investment in new or additional capacity; innovation is slower and moves ahead, if at all, in smaller, perhaps more timid steps; quality of goods and services is inferior; wasteful advertising and other forms of socially unproductive promotion is greater; because of the lure of possible monopolistic or oligopolistic profits, resources are diverted away from socially more desirable uses and into such industries, so that the composition of the Gross National Income is less than "optimal."

All these shortfalls are in comparison with what would be the case were the industry less concentrated, that is, if it were populated by enough *more* and sufficiently *smaller* firms so as to approach a "competitive" structure.

Other misgivings economic in nature have also been expressed. But the foregoing counts in the indictment are probably the high points—if that is the term.

Social and political concerns over concentration follow hard upon the heels of the economic: employment, it is feared, is lower; the nation does not enjoy as much technological advance as it would; public policies toward industries reflect the interests of the largest firms, not of the smaller ones, or of consumers; the economic sector is not as responsive to societal needs—as for instance, greater employee and consumer safety, and protection of the environment from pollution. The economic and political power of groups of large corporations—even of individual corporations—are so great, according to some, that they exercise disproportionate, and presumably undesirable, influence upon the nation's foreign, as well as domestic, policy.

Implicit in much of the concentration literature are several common themes. One major one, we have already seen: industry structures that were once and formerly not concentrated have become so through processes such as consolidations, mergers, and acquisitions. The thought quickly follows that the behaviors of industries now concentrated are less benign than they once were.

Another theme runs to the effect that concentrated industry structures could be made less concentrated through processes of "*de*concentration," as through enforced divestiture or dissolution. The thought, here, is that, whereas the consequences of the first process—the rise of large corporations—were deleterious, those of the second—

unscrambling and cutting down to size—would be beneficial, as the workings of industry became more competitive.

All these things, and more, are thought and said by critics to flow from concentration. But, we have seen, there have been those who doubt that all these things can be so.[2]

Economic concentration—Some summary data

The overall fact as to concentration is that a very few large companies do indeed hold a large fraction of the total value of all of the productive assets in the American economy—the wherewithal, tangible and intangible—for converting inputs into outputs. In total, The 200 Largest publicly held nonfinancial corporations of 1971 owned close to 40 percent of the value of *all* the assets of *all* nonfinancial business corporations. The 559 Largest publicly held companies, each with assets of over $250 million, owned something over 50 percent of that total value.

Our big corporations *are* big. They are *very* big. Much of the nation's productive apparatus is held and run under the aegis of a comparatively few firms. Into this apparatus flows a very large fraction of the entire stream of all inputs—human efforts, among them—and out of it flows a very large fraction of the value of the outputs of our industrial system. Collectively, these companies are a major productive force in the economy. And they are the sources of characteristics of that economy that distinguish it from the economies of other nations. These characteristics include vast aggregations of capital in large-scale, capital-intensive undertakings, and comparatively high per capita consumption of the outputs of those accumulations.

But that is just the beginning. As we have already seen, our large corporations are distributed very unevenly throughout the corporate community. In 1971, none was in Agriculture and fisheries or in Furniture and fixtures, for instance. In the electric and gas utilities, for contrast, there were 106; in petroleum, 30. Their numbers and their assets were distributed—clustered, scattered, or absent, as the case may be—and in very different ways, some here, some there. (See, e.g., Exhibits 16, 20, and 25.)

This disparate concentration, or dispersion of the *numbers* as well as the *assets* of our largest companies is *about* something. This was true in 1971, as it was also in 1929. This remarkably uneven distribution of our large companies had to do with fundamentals of the evolving industrial structure of the country.

Concentration in industries

Concentration of industries in the hands of small numbers of large companies has been the subject of a great deal of statistical study.

Concentration (more correctly, "concentratedness") is generally gauged by means of "concentration ratios."[3] More often than not, those ratios are based upon assets. The most common sort of ratio used in such studies is the percentage of the value of *all* corporate assets in an industry that is held by, say, the largest four or largest eight corporations, or the like. The higher this percentage, the greater is said to be the degree of concentration or, most particularly, the inferred degree of monopoly power. Sometimes, concentration ratios are based on sales or shipments.

Such computations, and even the inferences from them have a seeming straightforwardness: you add up two sets of numbers and divide the total of one by the total of the other. Sad to say, however, such matters are really not so simple. There is a lot of room for confusion and plain misunderstanding. And because we, ourselves, are about to look at some numbers that may *seem* to resemble "concentration ratios," we shall take the precaution of trying to get a few points clear at the outset.

Large Corporations and concentration in industries

The association of particular large corporations with concentration or, as we shall say, *presence* in specific industries involves three steps. First, clarification and definition of the concept of an "industry," or some other aggregation of firms in which the particular large firms have their place. We, ourselves, shall be speaking of Industry Categories. Second, classification of firms in accord with those industries as delineated and described. Third, measurement of what we shall call the relative *presence* of the large corporations in those Industry Categories.

Concentration ratios and the like are based upon two sets of ideas or concepts. One is the concept of an industry or a line of commerce or a market, or some such, that is to be studied for indications of concentration. The other is the measure whereby concentration in some sense—its relative strength, or weakness, or absence—is to be gauged. Both of these sets of ideas are set about by possible sources of confusion and ambiguity.

If particular corporations are to be related to the existence of concentration in individual industries, they must, of course, be sorted out and classified according to those industries. But this process of classification is also beset by conceptual and practical problems of its own. Some large corporations operate in a number of what were formerly, and are still often, thought of as discrete industries. In addition to this inherent problem, the ambiguous data disclosed by a few corporations do not permit the analyst to determine exactly what they are.

202

The basic building block of many concentration analyses is a concept of an industry—i.e., that which is or is not concentrated. And it is precisely at this initial point that significant difficulties of analysis enter. What *is* an industry? Depending upon where those boundaries are drawn that define the particular industry or line of commerce, a market or whatever, and that also define the contents thereof, the resulting measure of concentration will be higher or lower. Moving boundaries just a little, so to speak, this way or that can change concentration ratios mightily. That is a real problem. More important is the question as to whether the boundaries so drawn correspond, in fact, to major concrete realities of managerial decisions and corporate interactions as to investment, employment, production, distribution, and competition—for instance. As it happens, the structures of industries, their boundaries and contents, more often than not are tangled, uncertain matters. And in these matters, as in so many, ordinary custom and habits of thought are less than reliable guides.

A common concept of an industry is a collection of like firms, which, using like methods, produce a limited and defined set of like products that are purchased by a common collection of buyers who have more or less freedom to choose among the like sellers. The behaviors of the producing and consuming groups, and the outcomes of those behaviors, are, further, commonly conceived to be interactive and interrelated in varying ways and degrees, ranging from competitive, if there are many sellers—and, it may be said, many buyers, also—to oligopolistic or monopolistic, if there are few.

Neat as that cluster of ideas seems to be—*because* it is so neat—it falls far short of dealing with the complex realities of most structures of industry. Take two of the seemingly most straightforward examples to test the point: one industry so conceived might appear to be Metal cans. Another might be Rubber and tires.

Offhand, it would seem, everyone knows what metal cans are. And in 1971, there were four large companies commonly identified with such products. Likewise, everyone knows about Rubber and tires, especially the latter. And there were five well-known companies in 1971 commonly associated with *those* products. One might suppose that the definitions and boundaries of these two seemingly familiar industries, and the measurement of the relative positions in them of these large companies would present no great difficulties of understanding or measurement. But when one looks closely, problems do appear.

As it happens, each of the four can companies is involved to an important degree with other sorts of containers—say, paper, paperboard, glass, foils, and plastics. Each of the five tire companies is involved, not only with tires, but, in varying proportions and in varying ways and in significant volumes, with rubber products other than tires. Some have important positions in chemicals (some of which are substitutes for natural rubber, some of which move out into quite other domains); at least one has an important position in natural rubber plantations; some have retail operations.

Each of these companies in what might look like two pretty straightforward industries interacts with like companies in varying ways and to varying degrees in connection with a variety of products and markets, as well as with companies that, at first scrutiny, might appear to be located in other "industries." More: each has had opportunities to integrate both upstream toward inputs, and downstream toward customers. Each has had opportunities to expand horizontally into more or less closely associated fields. And each has done so—all in varying proportions. And, to really complicate the job of the analyst, several of these companies have capitalized on opportunities to move into what seem to be entirely different fields, such as broadcasting.

What do these examples suggest about defining an industry? Products and producers—to say nothing of buyers—are not always neatly defined. The relevant boundaries and arenas of corporate activity and behavior may be very fuzzy. It would seem we need to begin with a different concept if we are to accommodate industrial realities as they are. One possibility is to think about, and work with, a concept of something like "industry systems."

"Motor vehicles and equipment" as a complex industry system

In brief, an "industry system"—or, approximately, an Industry Category in the terminology we shall use—is a constellation or collectivity of companies, large and small, that are importantly interrelated, whose behaviors are significantly interactive because they are mutually affecting to an important degree.* They may be closely interrelated and interactive as buyers and sellers and/or as actual or potential competitors. Their action, both strategic and operational, or even potential or supposed actions, such as capital expansion or withdrawal, price increases or decreases, are mutually affecting. Unlike, even seemingly uncompetitive, corporations may, in fact, as through the actual or potential substitutability of their output and/or their inputs, be indirectly, but importantly, interrelated because of their mutual direct relationships with a common set of customer or supplier companies. The key words in trying to delineate and describe an "industry" are "interrelated" and "interactive"—and those are matters of practical fact.

It is in industry *systems* of that sort—not in simple "industries" of homogeneous, "like" companies producing, if not homogeneous, then very "like" products—that our large corporations have their

---

*For further discussion of the concept of Industry Categories, see Note 6. For the composition of the Industry Categories used in this work, see Appendix B.

existence and operate. The companies in Motor vehicles and equipment provide an example of such an industry system or Industry Category.

Presumably, General Motors, Ford, Chrysler, and American Motors operate in a common industrial milieu. They affect each other. They all turn out automobiles. General Motors and Ford are also major producers of trucks and off-highway equipment. In this, they compete with each other and with International Harvester and with White, among others. The buyers of the outputs of these producers are varied sorts: individuals, fleet operators (car rental companies, government units, large utilities, companies with traveling sales forces), farmers, contractors, etc., etc. The kinds of cars and other vehicles they buy tend to vary. There is no one, easily identified "market" for the outputs of the companies. There are identifiable "submarkets." In these, the relative positions of the companies can and do vary. They compete for sales. To complicate matters, all of these companies *do,* or *can,* or—and this is important—*may* either make or buy parts, components, and subassemblies.

Several other major companies—they are listed in Exhibit 1—are purveyors to the "automobile" companies, often selling to two or more of them simultaneously. The major companies, at any given time, may be both making, themselves, and buying from vendors the very same parts, components, and subassemblies. In addition to larger supplying companies, like Bendix and Borg-Warner, there are dozens, perhaps scores of smaller companies that live and function in a symbiotic, systemic way with the major "automobile" companies, with motor truck companies, and with each other. Many of these purveyors sell also to customers in quite other industries—in aircraft, for example.

There is more to the story, still: the companies that constitute this complex are mutually affecting, not only through actual behaviors and relationships, but in consequence of *potential* actions and relationships. The perception, as well as the fact, that a company—especially a major one—*may* decide to do this or that, to make or to buy, can affect the behaviors of others—suppliers and competitors—about as much as any actual, overt behavior.

What is involved here is a real, functioning, more or less clearly identifiable *system* of organically interrelated members. It is not possible to understand the behavior of any one of the firms of the complex in isolation, be it large or small. All and each can be understood only as members of an interacting and interdependent group or system. This subcommunity includes, in principle, all producers who manufacture and assemble vehicles and equipment and parts, components, and subassemblies thereof. This whole *system* is the Industry Category labeled "Motor vehicles and equipment."

Even that is not all. This subcommunity, it can be reasonably argued, really includes, also, the wholesale and retail distributors who sell and service vehicles, components, and parts. These distributors and retailers have their existence and operate in a symbiotic relationship with each other, of course; but so they do also with the producers of the flow of the products they depend upon for their existence. Changes in supply factors upstream affect wholesale and retail distributors no less concretely than do changes in demand factors downstream, among their own customers or potential customers. Motor vehicle wholesalers and retailers have no function, not even meaning, except as part of a chain of interrelated entities that reaches, through them, all the way from the production of parts to buyers of the end items. What happens at the distribution levels of this industry feeds effects back upstream to influence vehicle and components producers alike.

The wholesale and retail distribution stages of what can be thought of as an extended "Motor vehicle" *system*, or subcommunity, are no small matters, themselves, when it comes to numbers and mass: see Table 10.

TABLE 10
Numbers of firms and values of assets in the wholesale and retail distribution of motor vehicles: 1971

	Number of firms	Value of assets ($ millions)
Motor vehicles and automotive equipment—wholesale	13,417	$ 6,145.4
Automotive and truck dealers	30,529	15,079.7
	43,946	$21,225.1

Source: U.S. Internal Revenue Service, *Statistics of Income—1971, Corporation Income Tax Returns,* Tables 181 and 196.

An understanding of what happens in the distribution stages of these vehicles, in some ways, is indispensable to an understanding of what is going on in the "production" segment of this inter-linked system—and vice versa. Technological and style changes and innovations affect the *whole* system, qualitatively. Seasonal and cyclical oscillations—surges—in volumes of movement of products through the system affect the whole, quantitatively. A reasonable case could be made for including these firms and their assets in the Motor vehicle industry.

Where to draw the boundaries around this system is not a mere theoretical matter. Ideally, that should be done in consequence of rigorous factual research. Failing that, for present purposes, we shall define the Industry Category by sheer personal judgment, and exclude very arbitrarily—and only for present purposes—the wholesale and retail distribution stages.[4] The definition of the Industry Category here labeled Motor vehicles and equipment is given in Appendix B in terms of Standard Enterprise Classification, and Standard Industry Classification industries.

Nonferrous metals: an example of a complex, integrated Industry Category

Some other examples of industry systems—Industry Categories—may clarify the point.

Nonferrous metals companies can, do, and *may* produce any one or several of the metals aluminum, copper, nickel, molybdenum, zinc, lead, and various alloy metals. Horizontal growth, actual or potential does, can, and may come about in any one of several ways: some nonferrous metals often occur together in nature or in close proximity; to produce one is to produce one or more others. Companies with a strong base in one metal have sometimes developed positions in others, either by acquisition of proven reserves or by locating and opening up new mines on their own.

The metals can and do compete—aluminum and copper in electric power transmission; aluminum, and its alloys, with chromium in finishes and trims; manganese, tungsten, and vanadium in hardening steel.

Vertical integration, to various degrees, has also been, and remains, a strategic option for nonferrous metals companies. They can, do, or may—or may not—engage in mining, smelting, refining; in production of ingot, sheet, rods, semifinished, even finished goods. They may market through agents or brokers, or through their own efforts; they sell either on a spot basis or under supply contracts, or both.

Not only are there companies of American nationality operating in the American economy and competing in international arenas. Present, also, are foreign multinationals. Imports from abroad are, or may be, major factors in American markets: products of Alcan and International Nickel come from Canada; Pechiney, a French company, holds an American subsidiary that produces aluminum, and is, itself, at all times a potential, if not actual, presence in the American market. Rio Tinto, a major British nonferrous multinational, operates worldwide and produces important amounts of several nonferrous metals that find markets on every continent, including the United States. National companies, such as those of Zaïre, Zambia, Peru, and Chile, compete with privately owned companies and are major factors in copper, worldwide, including in the United States.

In consequence of global ongoing and potential actions and interactions of and among these companies—and between them and their major customers, at least—worldwide networks exist of competitive, and vendor-user relationships, and of patterns of prices.

Again, what is before us is a complex, organic industry *system.* One cannot get a real grasp of what is going on in any one isolated sector of this complex, considered by itself. It is the whole that works and that counts, and that must be the unit of study.

Other Integrated Industry Categories

Large corporations figure importantly in at least three other integrated industry complexes: Iron and steel, Petroleum, and Lumber and wood products and paper and allied products. In each of these, a number of large corporations operate over a broad spectrum, ranging from production of primary raw materials, through the production of intermediate or semifinished products of several kinds, and through to production of diversified arrays of products far downstream. In some instances, they provide some of their own ancillary services along the line, such as transportation. The larger companies are integrated to varying degrees, being more or less self-sufficient at each of several levels for inputs from upstream, and integrated to varying degrees as regards disposition of various outputs downstream. In varying ways and to varying degrees, the larger companies do, or may, compete among themselves for inputs or for customers at various stages of the production stream. At any of the several levels along the way companies do and may even buy from, or sell particular products to, each other, regularly or intermittently.

Operating alongside of the Largest Companies in each of these Industry Categories, and just about at every level of the chain, from raw materials to finished products, are numbers of smaller, sometimes quite small "independent" companies. These smaller companies—themselves often partly integrated—may be suppliers and/or customers and/or competitors, of larger, as well as of smaller, companies.

At some stages of production, within each of these integrated industries, current technologies or innovative aspects or processes offer greater opportunities for economies of scale, even of very large scale, than at others. In some instances, great economies of scale or of integration seem to be present. In others, perhaps because of special circumstances, relatively small-scale, independent operations appear to coexist with very large.

In Iron and steel, for example, data seem to show that there are general and substantial economies of large scale of individual plants in several steel-making processes. Other economies seem to be achievable through integration of some successive processes into more or less continuous production, or "conversion" systems. Multiplant companies are likely to be able to achieve additional, if smaller, economies of integration and flexibility of operations. Steel companies represent a variety of permutations and combinations of specialization, large scale, varying degrees of integration, and production of steel products downstream from steel-making itself. Such factors tend to make for large, integrated, multiplant, multiproduct corporations. On the other hand, smaller plants and companies, for instance those based on local supplies of scrap, and serving local and/or specialized markets, are able to find niches in the overall system where they seem to be altogether viable.[5]

In Lumber and wood products and paper and allied products, woodland operations apparently can be, and are, carried on economically at almost any scale, from very small to extremely large. Production of pulp tends to be on a large scale, and is often, but not always, directly linked in a continuous process with the production of paper or board. Some pulp is shipped great distances, even internationally, to be used as a prime purchased input for papermaking. Production of kraft and newsprint paper and fiberboard also require comparatively large scale. Converting paper and paper products into end-items, such as bags, printed folding cartons, paper tablets, and boxes of stationery apparently can be done on both large and small scales. In some instances, later steps in the production process are linked directly, and on large scale, with papermaking. In this industry, as in others, companies, even those which are more or less integrated, may buy and sell intermediate products among themselves.

In Petroleum, exploration for oil and/or gas can be done on both relatively small and large scale. Offshore drilling is, of its nature, a large-scale operation. Production of crude oil is carried on by small "independents" as well as by large integrated "majors." An interstate pipeline such as those owned and operated by some of the large integrated companies is, by its very nature, a large-scale undertaking. A single refinery—now really a chemical complex, in contrast to the old small-scale "skimmers" of early days—is of very large minimum size. This is due, in part, to the versatility and flexibility of equipment and multiplicity of processes now built into refineries, as well as to efforts to optimize simultaneously combined economies of transportation, storage, and processing. Because of economies of continuous flows and interlinked and coordinated operations, significant economies of integration exist, as well as economies of scale. But in particular circumstances, nonintegrated, smaller-scale operations can and do coexist with those of the very largest companies. The whole network is interconnected by all kinds of actual and potential relationships among companies of all sizes and kinds.

"Trans-industry" systems

Our illustrating sampler of a few different industry systems would be incomplete without mention of an example where a system of interacting producers cuts across several industries as traditionally conceived. A prime instance is containers. These, of course, are made out of metals (sheet and foil), paper products, glass, plastics, wood. There is a wide range of buyers, large and small, each of whom has some choice—perhaps a great deal of latitude—as to what kind of container to use, made out of what kind of material. Some large users of containers produce some or all of their own needs. Others, who do not, might do so should circumstances warrant. In this complex, as in other industry systems, behaviors and outcomes, to varying degrees, are, or may be, influenced, not only by producers currently in place, but by incipient, or even *potential* entrants, both foreign and domestic.

In a very real sense, at any given time, there *is* a "container industry," although it would be hard to state categorically what its boundaries and contents might be. In any event, these boundaries and contents are constantly in flux in consequence of such trends and events as changing technologies and relative costs, changes in relative rates of returns and in comparative advantages among the various categories of products; plant expansion, changing tastes, price changes, and enactment of new laws and regulations (such as those which, at one time, were intended to prevent or hinder the substitution of cartons for glass bottles in the retail distribution of milk).

A number of trans-industry systems seem to be emerging and gaining importance—"recreation" being another example currently. However, insuperable practical problems of getting "industry" data compiled in this fashion, to say nothing of data for individual corporations, really precludes any treatment of them in this present work.

System of systems: "Food" as a complex of industry systems

The various food industries—especially "processed foods"—present a tremendously interesting and challenging set of conceptual and intellectual problems of definition and study, to say nothing of practical problems of public policy and strategies of individual corporations. To be sure, there are any number of categories of food products definable in terms of their intrinsic, physical properties, manufacturing processes, provenance, and uses. But all of these categories overlap, and the behaviors of consumers, distributors, and manufacturers crisscross and zigzag through these categories as though they are well-nigh interchangeable and as though, for many practical purposes, boundaries between them scarcely exist.

The housewife or other buyer wanders through the modern supermarket, up and down hundreds of feet—or yards—of passageways stocked on both sides up to six feet high. Spread before her—or him—are literally thousands of items: six to eight or ten thousand in the many stores of national and regional chains. In this marketplace all items compete against all for the purchaser's weekly budget. This is no "Mom-Pop" corner store with a few hundred different items at best. Never in the history of the world has the household been presented with such a menu and a baffling spread of alternatives. What to have for breakfast? Dry or cooked cereals? Sausages? Eggs? Pancakes? Grits? Lamb stew? Yogurt? Toast, "danish," or muffins? Fruit or juices, and if so which? Or, at least in New England, clam chowder and/or pie? For lunch: peanut butter, bologna, tuna fish, cheese, ham sandwiches? Soups? Cottage cheese? Milk or soda pop? Dinner: canned, frozen, or dehydrated soups? Meat, fish, macaroni and cheese, baked beans? If fish, then fresh, frozen, canned, or "full course" meal, ready-to-heat-and-eat? Fresh, canned, or frozen vegetables? Steak tonight, or, maybe, hamburger and fresh-cut flowers for a bit of glamor on a limited budget? Ice cream; cakes (ready-to-eat, or some cake mix for a do-it-yourself project); frozen straw-berries? Cheese—foreign or domestic? Butter or margarine? Or, less fattening, perhaps, jam or jelly?

"Lines of commerce" or "relevant markets" defined by complaining litigants with axes to grind or by lawyers trying to prove cases for clients, or by confused juries or harried judges trying to reach a sustainable, if not meaningful opinion—none of this means anything to the buyer who is considering meals, menus, and budgets; nor to chain managers who are trying to maximize their returns over the whole spectrum of offerings.

The alternatives—the permutations and combinations available, and chosen, are almost literally infinite. The studious stroller observing customers making their choices—sometimes in a funk of indecision amidst such cornucopian cascades of possibilities—scrutinizing the contents of the filling push-carts—can get a liberal, clinical education as to the realities of a dynamic marketplace. Much more realistic than reading legal briefs or judicial opinions or academic treatises.

As one watches consumer behavior, one becomes less certain, not more confident, as to where to draw the boundaries among the "industries." Looking upstream at the sources of these goodies does not help much. There are many suppliers—large, medium, and small. Some produce a few products; some, literally hundreds. Others stand in the wings of this churning marketplace, debating with themselves whether to produce this or that item—or a whole category of items—or to withdraw and devote their efforts elsewhere.

To complicate matters still further, some of the large retailers also manufacture some of the items that appear on their shelves: canned fish, bread, cakes, pasteurized milk, canned fruits and vegetables. Or they stand ready to do so, if they figure that there is a worthwhile profit to be made.

And then there are companies that, normally, are wholesalers, but who also are manufacturers of particular items, and that, at any time, may decide to produce fewer or more. And there are manufacturers who do their own wholesaling.

There are companies that are normally packers and producers of meat and meat products, but that also produce poultry and poultry products, butter, eggs, peanut butter, and edible oils. Others produce dairy products, canned fruits and vegetables, frozen foods, and soft drinks. What "industry" are they in?

In Exhibit 1, companies are categorized as among Food and kindred products, Meat and meat products, and Dairy and dairy products. Clearly, these categorizations are more than a little arbitrary. A good argument could be made for lumping them all together under one heading, Food. And a good argument could be made that, what-

ever government agencies, economists, and lawyers—or businessmen—
might say, these companies are all, essentially in a *single* line of commerce or industry.

At very least, they are each and all linked with everyone else in a
network of competition; they all compete with all for the consumer's
dollar; they each and all have varying opportunities for extending or
contracting their product lines. If not a single industry or a line of
commerce in the traditional, legalistic, or hypothetical senses of
those words, they live in a very real system of dynamic, interacting
relationships. Or should we say "a system of systems of industries"?
And, let it be noted that it is the biggest companies that reach this
way and that across the widest ranges of individual products, acting
as forces that hold the individual products together in a *system* of
interrelated parts. And let it be further noted that it is primarily the
biggest companies that, by trial and error, or through rigorous tough-
minded research, have introduced most of the thousands of items
that are now offered the consumer in lieu of the barrels and tubs of
flour, sugar, molasses, lard, and the few other staples that grand-
mother had at her disposal.

Just recently, this whole picture of the Food industry has been
complicated and churned up with the advent and almost explosive
growth of "fast-food" chains. By 1978, according to some estimates,
about 20 percent of America's food budget was being spent in these
new outlets. An utterly new form of *competition*—real, honest-to-
goodness competition—has arisen. New alternatives were available to
consumers: "Shall we—I—cook dinner at home (with all the fuss of
preparation and cleaning up) or go around the corner and for a
modest amount have the leisure of 'eating out.'?"

Industry Categories

The purposes of this study require the placing and assessment of
large corporations in their industry contexts. This implied the definition of a number of industry systems.

In an ideal sense, as mentioned a few pages back, determination of
the contents and boundaries of industry systems is not simply a theoretical proposition. On the contrary, their boundaries and contents
should reflect ascertainable and demonstrable facts. The included
contents of such defined systems should reflect actual patterns of
major interactions that take place among companies, within recognized interrelationships. Industry-system boundaries and contents
should reflect, also, patterns of corporate strategies and major investment and operating decisions that are expressive of managerial awareness of, and response to, such interrelationships and interactions.
Boundaries, ideally, would be set along the "edges" of such documented patterns of interactions, where they diminish to "negligible,"
or at least to a level of "not very important."

212

In actuality, of course, data for doing this for the whole nonfinancial sector simply do not exist. A practical surrogate for such a mosaic of industry systems had to be found. This approximation had to meet three requirements. First, it had to accommodate business realities of The 559 Largest Corporations of 1971, which were to be sited within meaningful industry systems. Second, the schema had to permit, for purposes of comparison, accommodation of industry data generally available, especially government data from the Internal Revenue Service and the Census. Third, it had to cover, in total, the entire nonfinancial industrial sector of the American economy.

The result was the system of Industry Categories that appears in Exhibit 1 and others derived from and based upon it, such as Exhibit 2. The boundaries and contents of these Industry Categories are set forth in Appendix B.[6] The boundaries and contents of these Industry Categories reflect the lines of business of large firms as revealed and described in annual reports and filings with the Securities Exchange Commission. They are defined in terms of the Standard Enterprise Classification and the Standard Industry Classification schema composed of literally hundreds of industries that have been devised by the federal government for categorizing business establishments for a variety of administrative purposes, including various compilations of statistics. Collectively, the industries of this classification cover the entire economy, including the nonfinancial sector.

CLASSIFICATION OF CORPORATIONS INTO INDUSTRY CATEGORIES

For the purposes of this study, individual corporations were classified into Industry Categories according to the largest single fraction of their sales. (This is the practice of the Internal Revenue Service for compiling published corporate financial statistics; it is also used by the Securities Exchange Commission in preparing its compilations of industry data.) In most cases, classification was a simple matter. Some cases were obvious—airlines, railroads, motor vehicles, iron and steel, chemical, petroleum, and nonferrous metals companies, for examples. Others were tougher. In some cases, disclosures were not sufficiently informative to permit sure classification. In a few cases, disclosures, it turned out after further study, were positively misleading. Comments on classification problems presented by certain corporations are given in Appendix A.

Variety among companies within an industry

No assumption or representation is made to any effect that the companies classified in the same "Industry Category" are closely alike when it comes to the natures and proportions of the different kinds of inputs and assets they employ; degrees of integration; of the specific natures and breadth of product lines. On the contrary:

although they are similar in some ways, it is a fact that there are often *major* differences among them, such as among the several companies placed in Iron and steel, Nonferrous metals, Chemicals and allied products, and Motor vehicles and equipment.

Not only are the largest companies in most of the Industry Categories not necessarily closely alike even as among themselves; they tend to be *very different* in important particulars from smaller and small companies in the same industry system. We shall see in a moment some illustrative data on the point, drawn from the Iron and steel industry. And in the next chapter, the point will be more than amply documented.

These rather obvious points have important practical, as well as theoretical, implications, as will emerge as we go along.

DYNAMISM OF INDUSTRY SYSTEMS AND CORPORATIONS

Having gone through the process of setting up Industry Categories for study and comparisons, and having classified all companies in accordance with them, we must yet bear in mind the fact that whole industry systems are dynamic in their very natures, as are individual corporations. Boundaries and contents do not, and will not, stay put very long. Whole new particular industries, whole new Industry Categories come into being. Some disappear. All seem to have a life cycle of birth and early stirrings, growth during exuberant youth, stolid maturity, shriveling senescence, and death in their twilight. More important: the life-cycle of industries and of Industry Categories is not merely quantitative. Industries *change* over time. They change their outputs; their inputs; their conversion processes; their markets. More. Their membership changes: individual companies come and companies go; some falter and fail; some flourish. Of this, we have seen something already. In the following two chapters we shall consider some of the major changes that have swept through American industries over the past 40 years and more. All of our industries, in their own phases, have passed through various landmark states of their cycles. Some of our bellwether industries of times past have "topped out." Some industries have been restructured in consequence of technological changes, government intervention, changing markets, or because of dynamic institutional factors. The structures, contents, and boundaries of industries are sometime things.

Individual corporations often change their "personalities" over time; aggressive and brawling in youth, they may become staid and bureaucratic in their middle age and dull and unresponsive in advancing years. Over time, they may change their very nature and function, as have more than a few of the companies on our rosters.[7]

So much for the "locale" in the economy or, in the terminology used here, the Industry Categories *in which* business corporations occur and function, be they large or small.

THE RELATIVE PRESENCE OF LARGE COMPANIES

We come, now, to deal with concentration or, much rather, with the matter of *presence* of large corporations in the several Industry Categories. Just as conceptual and practical problems arise in defining the industry or Industry Category that is to be measured for concentration, so also do problems arise in defining and interpreting the ratio or degree of concentration. A common, conventional measure, as mentioned, is the percentage of the total assets of corporations of the industry that is held by some specified group of the largest, say the "Big Four" or "Big Eight," or some such. The trouble is that this ratio, unless carefully interpreted, can be, and often is, very misleading. In order to set the stage for looking at a lot of seemingly similar ratios in the next chapter, we are now going to consider what such ratios mean and what they do *not* mean.

The word concentration and the implied concept lying behind it tend from the outset to obscure and mislead discussion of what is a very serious matter. In a culture as attached as ours to pluralism and egalitarianism, the very word concentration has strong and prejudicial overtones. Concentration in *any* degree much more than zero chafes our ideological sensibilities. Beyond this matter of entangled feelings, the word carries an implication that is in deep error and stands in the way of objective analysis of the structures of some of our key industries.

Instead of concentration, we need, if possible, a word both neutral and accurate. The word we are going to use is "presence." It is the *presence* of large corporations in Industry Categories that we are going to measure and study.

The reasons that the word concentration and the ratios purporting to measure it have an inherent capacity to mislead are twofold: they suggest, first, the unambiguous existence of a total body of assets held by corporations that operate within a set of boundaries clearly demarking and encompassing an industry, or the like. But we have seen that the delineation of an industry or even an Industry Category is by no means a clear-cut process, which, having been once performed, stays put over time. Second, the implication is left that this body of assets is held by corporations of the industry in allotments of varying sizes but of essentially homogeneous composition. This is to say, the implication is given that, although some companies hold considerably more or less than an arithmetically pro rata share of the aggregate "pile" of the assets of the industry, the makeups of the numerous separate collections of assets held by big and small companies are pretty uniform. Some companies, it might seem, have lots of assets, some have less; but the implication lurks around the edges of the discussion to the effect that the "portfolio mix" of assets in each case, large or small, is just about the same from one company to another.

That implication is essentially false. The concrete natures of the assets of very large, medium-size, and small corporations in an industry are *not* the same. They are more different than oranges are from apples. They are as unlike as fish, fowl, and good red herring. To lump together all the different kinds of assets of an Industry Category and then to compute that these companies, here, own X percent of the total and that those corporations, there, own Y percent—suggesting that the shares are similar as to composition—glosses over deep qualitative differences in the natures of corporations of different asset "masses" or *presence* that are of the essence in our industrial structure.

Presence of large corporations in Iron and steel

Some figures as to the numbers and sizes of firms in the Iron and steel Industry Category will illustrate the point. This Industry Category, in the language of the Standard Industry Classification, is made up of firms in "metal mining: iron ores" and in "Ferrous metal processing and basic products, and primary metal products not elsewhere classified."

The Iron and steel Industry Category, which is based upon the structures of integrated companies and is compatible with the Standard Industry Classification, includes "establishments" (individual plants and production and employment units) and corporations coming under the following headings:

Iron ore mines; plants for beneficiating, sintering, and otherwise preparing ores.

Blast furnaces, steel works, and rolling and finishing mills (establishments primarily engaged in producing hot metal, pig iron, ferroalloys, etc., from iron ore and iron and steel scrap; hot rolling iron and steel into basic shapes such as plates, sheet, strips, rods, bars, and tubing, and producing a wide variety of other semi-finished and finished items).

Electrometallurgical installations.

Firms and establishments primarily engaged in drawing wire from purchased iron or steel rods, bars, or wires; also establishments primarily engaged in making steel nails and spikes from purchased materials.

Cold-roll mills producing steel sheet, strip, and bars (from purchased hot rolled sheets and bars).

Mills fabricating steel pipe and tubes (from purchased materials).

Iron and steel foundries, primarily engaged in producing iron and steel castings, generally on a job or order basis (some produce for sale to others, some for intracompany uses), both gray iron and malleable iron castings.

Logically, because such is the organization of large companies and of the nature of the industry, the Industry Category should include also transportation facilities especially adapted to the needs of iron and steel production, including, especially, Great Lakes water transportation. However, inasmuch as the IRS does not show such data separately, that portion of the iron and steel industry system is not included.

Plants described as "blast furnaces, steel works, and/or rolling and finishing mills" are typically more or less integrated, reaching from furnaces of one kind or another (in which crude pig iron and/or steel ingot is produced from ore and/or sinter and/or scrap) through production of steels, to an enormous range of scores of possible semi-finished and finished products such as plate, sheet, rods, tubes, structural shapes, even nails and galvanized products, all in various permutations and combinations. Such plants are of very large scale, in the range of $100 million and up to hundreds of millions.

Operating in the same Industry Category, along with a limited number of huge, integrated complexes of large iron and steel companies, are literally hundreds of corporations ranging in size down from "large" (representing investments in, say, the $50 million–$100 million range), to "small" (say in the range of $1 million–$5 million), to "very small" (say, with assets of less than $250,000 or even less than $100,000). Most of these corporations, probably, operate single plants that, using purchased pig iron and steel, produce a galaxy of particular products. Some of these products are in regular, others in intermittent, competition with like products coming out of integrated mills. Other outputs of small plants and companies are highly specialized, as for instance, custom-made gray iron and malleable iron castings that require very special equipment and trained personnel.

These facts are reflected in the data of Table 11.[8] The reported values of assets of 16 reporting firms in the largest size category ($250 million and up) averaged about $1.4 *billion*. This was about *500 times* the $2.8 *million* average size of the other 2,206 smaller reporting firms in the Iron and steel Industry Category. Half of the firms in the industry had assets of less than about $250,000; about three-quarters had assets of less than $5 million.

The point need not be labored: the concrete natures of the assets of Iron and steel firms of greatly different size, and the particular and special niches in which they fit in the web of the American industrial structure, are tremendously varied. Big iron and steel companies are not merely small iron and steel companies scaled up; small companies are not even medium-size ones scaled down. As one moves along the spectrum of size, up or down, one encounters very differ-

TABLE 11
Iron and steel Industry Category, 1971; Distribution of firms and assets, number of firms, value of assets, average size of firms, and relative presence of firms, by size class

Size class of firms ($000)	Number of firms	Value of assets ($000)	Average size of firms ($000)	Indexes of relative "presence" of firms
Zero assets	51	—	—	—
$0-100	704	$ 27,372	$ 38.9	0.1
100-250	394	65,732	166.8	0.2
250-500	336	115,073	342.5	0.4
500-1,000	218	156,773	719.1	0.6
1,000-5,000	339	806,704	2,379.7	2.8
5,000-10,000	68	468,143	6,884.5	1.6
10,000-25,000	50	766,789	15,335.8	2.7
25,000-50,000	20	778,632	38,931.6	2.7
50,000-100,000	10	711,169	71,116.9	2.5
100,000-250,000	16	2,320,263	145,016.4	8.2
More than $250,000	16	22,176,875	1,386,054.7	78.1
Totals/average	2,222	$28,393,526	$ 11,877.8	100.0
Totals/average of firms, excluding those with assets of over $250 million	2,206	$ 6,216,651	$ 2,818.1	

Source: U.S. Internal Revenue Service, *Corporation Source Book of Statistics of Income, 1971,* Tables 79 and 135.

ent species of assets, operations, and industrial and economic functions. There is no way in the world, technically, economically, and administratively speaking, that *small* companies can produce what the biggest companies do. And *vice versa.*

And this is why it is that one must be careful in talking about concentration. In 1971, the 16 largest tax-reporting iron and steel corporations held about 80 percent of the total *value* assets of all corporations classified as being in industries that have been defined as constituting the Iron and steel Industry Category. This does *not* mean, of course, that they held 80 percent of the total value of each *kind* of assets. Indeed, of some kinds of assets—such as continuous, integrated mills—the very biggest firms surely held 100 percent; of other assets of more specialized natures, no doubt they held far less, perhaps even zero, or close to it. Nor can it be said that they held a weighted average of 80 percent of the assets; there is no way that a weighted *average* of assortments of anything as disparate as the assets of corporations in iron and steel can be really meaningful in a concrete way.

The figures of Table 11 mean this: about 80 percent of the total *value* (not of *kinds*) of assets of corporations in iron and steel are of the *sorts* that are owned and operated by *very large* companies, which is to say, those that held assets with reported values of over $250 million. Conversely, something less than 1.5 percent of the assets of the Industry Category were of the *sorts* that are owned and operated by various kinds of *small* companies with assets of less than $1 million. The remainders of the assets were of sorts held by companies in size brackets ranging from $1 million to $250 million.

Another very different kind of example, this time, a very large industry in terms of the total assets and one of the most numerous, with a very unconcentrated structure: Construction. Of course, there are all sorts of construction firms, ranging from local electrical contractors and plumbers, all the way to firms operating on an international scale and that may undertake construction of vast hydroelectric projects, pipelines, whole cities. Many of the smallest firms are not even incorporated. Over half of those that were incorporated in 1971 had assets of less than $100,000. At the other end of the size spectrum, there is a handful of construction corporations holding assets of over $250 million. Of these, several are closely held.[9]

The structure of this Industry Category is sketched statistically in Table 12, which shows the distributions of the numbers and assets of the corporations, together with the average size of firm and relative presence of firms in each of the several size classes.

This Construction Industry Category, like other industries, is a *complex system* in which *different kinds* of firms of different sizes are interlinked into a vastly complex tissue. Firms are related directly and indirectly, each with many others, as competitors and in various combinations and recombinations of prime contractors, subcontractors, sub-subcontractors, and so on. As one scans the profile of this industry, passing from smallest to largest, one must be struck with how very *different* the firms must be that constitute the membership of the system. The average size of the largest, but least

TABLE 12
Construction Industry Category, 1971; Distribution of firms and assets, number of firms, value of assets, average size of firms, and relative presence of firms, by size class

Size class of firms ($000)	Number of firms	Value of assets ($000)	Average size of firm ($000)	Indexes of relative "presence" of firms
Zero assets	3,064	–	–	0.0
$0-100	82,811	$ 2,771,499	$ 33.5	5.7
100-250	26,794	4,277,404	159.6	8.9
250-500	15,100	5,310,229	351.7	11.0
500-1,000	8,112	5,615,312	692.2	11.6
1,000-5,000	6,229	12,037,657	1,932.5	25.0
5,000-10,000	594	4,044,325	6,808.6	8.4
10,000-25,000	259	3,875,145	14,962.0	8.0
25,000-50,000	65	2,215,313	34,081.7	4.6
50,000-100,000	38	2,569,859	67,627.9	5.3
100,000-250,000	20	3,274,542	63,727.1	6.8
More than $250,000	6	2,251,581	375,263.5	4.7
Totals/average	143,092	$48,242,866	$ 337.1	100.0
Total/average of firms, excluding those with assets of over $250 million	143,086	$45,991,285	$ 321.4	

Source: U.S. Internal Revenue Service, *Corporation Source Book of Statistics of Income, 1971*, Table 26.

numerous firms was over 10,000 times the average size of the smallest, most numerous. Clearly, the largest firms were something quite different from something merely a 10,000-fold scale-up of the smallest firms. Even as compared to the average-size firm, the largest were 1,000 times as large.

The three largest publicly held firms of 1971, classified under Construction, (Dillingham, McDermott, and Kaiser) reported their numbers of employees, respectively, as 12,300, 7,400, and 8,300; their reported assets (see Exhibit 1) were $529 million, $374 million, and $299 million, respectively. Their assets *per employee* figure out to $43,000, $51,000, and $36,000. In concrete terms, these large construction firms were productive organisms in which large numbers of people, with many specialized skills and jobs, were organized, along with large amounts of capital, into functioning wholes. Their assets *per employee* were about as large as, or larger than, the *total* assets of more than half of all construction firms.

In the encompassing American productive system, the constituent members of this industry complex called Construction fitted into a wide range of very different niches. Different as they were in both sizes and functions, they yet made up a system for all that, inextricably interlinked in an organic oneness.

The profile of the relative presence of Construction firms in the several size classes is very different from that of Iron and steel. Less than 5 percent of the total mass, so to speak, of the assets in Construction was to be found in the largest size class—appreciably less than the total presence of the smallest firms. About 40 percent of the aggregate presence of Construction firms was accounted for by firms with assets of less than $1 million; 25 percent of the total mass of assets was in the single size class of $1 million to $5 million. In Iron and steel, by contrast, only a bit more than 10 percent of the total asset value was held by firms smaller than $1 million; and only 2.8 percent of the asset value was held by firms of the size $1 million to $5 million. And, as mentioned, almost 80 percent of the asset total was held by the largest corporations with assets of more than $250 million.

These sketches of the structures of these two very different kinds of industry systems, taken singly and taken together, further illustrate the nature of industry systems: complexes of very *unlike* entities interlinked more by virtue of their differences, and consequent interdependence, than by their similarities, into functioning wholes. These data also illustrate what is meant by *presence*. Unlike the concept of concentration, which vaguely—and incorrectly—hints at different-sized aggregations of assets of common natures and purposes, the concept of *presence* has to do with relative *masses* of assets that, of a certainty, are of *unlike* natures and functions within the industry complex of which they are part.

Relative presence is not "market share"

The relative presence in an Industry Category of corporations of a certain size class, say, those with assets valued at more than $250 million, represents nothing more, to repeat, than the fraction of the total value of the assets of the Industry Category that is of the sorts operated by corporations of that size. That fraction is *not* "market share."

Concentration ratios and market shares and the like are often constructed on a tacit assumption to the effect that the products of an industry fall comfortably in a single line of commerce or the like. For most Industry Categories, and even for most industries narrowly defined, this is not the case. Many industries, including Iron and steel, for instance, or Chemicals, or Food, or Nonferrous metals, or Meat, or Railroad equipment, or Aircraft or even Motor vehicles, produce many individual products—in some industries, scores of individual products (sometimes joint-products, sometimes by-products) sold and bought in as many or more identifiable markets. Because different kinds of products, as mentioned in connection with Iron and steel, generally require different kinds of plant, equipment, tools, technical and managerial skills, the percentages of the sales of different specific products accounted for by corporations of any given size may range from 100 percent to zero. Although about 80 percent of the assets of the Iron and steel industry were of sorts held by corporations with assets of $250 million and up, as shown in Table 11, the shares of sales of individual products or groups of products, at any given time, could easily range from 100 percent, in the case of hot-rolled shapes, for example, down to zero in the cases of certain special kinds of castings. And distinctions of these sorts would be found in most industries.

Just one more example: something over 50 percent of the assets of the Industry Category Aircraft, guided missiles, and parts were of sorts held by the ten aircraft companies with more than $250 million of assets. None of these companies produced any light, private aircraft. On the other hand, the three largest (the smallest of which had assets of about $1.5 billion) produced 100 percent of the jumbo jets: the Boeing 747's, the McDonnell Douglas DC-10's, and the Lockheed 1011's. Many, however, were competitive and/or interdependent in aerospace and defense programs.

Within overall shares of sales of products of various categories, the fractions accounted for by individual companies in an Industry Category, at any one time, can vary widely depending on needs for, and relevance of, presently available special equipment, existing patent positions, current marketing skills, and other key strategic variables. Not only that. Many markets have more or less definite geographical boundaries. These can be related to freight advantages enjoyed by the more favorably located plants of particular companies. Situations of this kind exist commonly enough in markets for heavy and bulky products, such as petroleum, iron and steel, and chemicals and fertilizers.

Accordingly, at any one time, down underneath figures of relative presence, so to speak, the market shares of individual companies and of groups of corporations can, and do, vary greatly depending on the very specifics of the products and regions in question. Add to this the actual and potential dynamics of important strategic variables, and the concern of so many managements over the volatility and precariousness of specific "market shares" becomes readily understandable.

All the same, and for these reasons, relative *presence* in industries is not to be confused with market share, however defined. The indexes of relative presence are indicative of the presence in Industry Categories of the relative amounts of certain *kinds* of assets. Our particular interest lies in the relative presence of assets held by the very biggest companies.

* * * * *

With these concepts and caveats in mind, we now move on to consider the *relative presence* of the largest companies among the several Industry Categories and the suggestions these data carry as to differences in industry structures and some of the underlying reasons therefore.

NOTES

1. Some recent examples of this enormous and still growing body of literature are the following, each of which contains extensive bibliographies and/or numerous references.

   John M. Blair, *Economic Concentration; Structure, Behavior, and Public Policy* (New York: Harcourt Brace Jovanovich, 1972).

   Harvey J. Goldschmid et al., eds., *Industrial Concentration: The New Learning* (Boston: Little, Brown and Company, 1974).

   Joseph P. Mulholland and Douglas W. Webbinte, *Concentration Levels and Trends in The Energy Sector of the U.S. Economy* (Staff Report to the Federal Trade Commission) (Washington, D.C.: Superintendent of Documents, 1974).

   Steven Lustgarten, *Industrial Concentration and Inflation* (Washington, D.C.: American Enterprise Institute for Public Policy Research, 1975).

   Samuel Richardson Reid, *The New Industrial Order; Concentration, Regulation, and Public Policy* (New York: McGraw-Hill Book Company, 1976).

2. Among those holding more constructive views about large-scale enterprise have been Schumpeter, Kuznets, and Arthur F. Burns, referred to in Chapter 4. Some of the recent discussion is also considerably more sophisticated and objective. See, e.g., Goldschmid, *Industrial Concentration.*

3. Some subtle misapprehensions enter the discussion through the use of the noun "concentration," which primarily denotes a *process,* that of *becoming* concentrated, rather than the more exact, although clumsy word "concentratedness," which would denote a *state* of being "concentrated." The use of the word "concentration," in itself, somehow suggests that parts of the economy that formerly were *not* concentrated have become so through some *process* of "concentration."

4. A reasonable and analogous case could be made for including petroleum wholesaling and retailing in the Petroleum Industry Category. In both Motor vehicles and Petro-

leum, distribution is inextricably linked with production: volumes flowing through various parts of the system, whether of one or the other, fluctuate together; technological change has impacts upon both production and various levels of distribution (e.g., when Petroleum moved to three grades of gasoline and, more recently, to no-lead gasoline. Similar system-wide impacts occur whenever there are significant model or technological changes in automobiles.)

Moreover, the presence of Petroleum companies is probably significant in bulk stations and terminals.

The additional data for firms engaged, and for assets employed, in distribution, were Petroleum to be redefined so as to include them, would be as follows (data from *Source Book,* Tables 188 and 197):

Distribution of petroleum and petroleum products

	Number of firms	Value of assets ($ millions)
Wholesale petroleum and petroleum products	7,885	$4,869.3
Gasoline service stations	11,185	1,858.6
Totals	19,070	$6,727.9

The total data for Petroleum, restated so as to include wholesale and retail distribution (corporations, only) would then appear as follows, in contrast to industry data shown in Exhibits 34, 35, and 36:

Number of firms	26,791
Value of assets ($ millions)	$122,482.7

Recalculated in accord with such restatement, the presence indexes for Petroleum shown in Exhibits 34, 35, and 36 would be as follows:

Presence, The 200	82.0%
Presence, The 359	4.4
Presence, The 559	86.4

Such restatement would not affect the presence indexes materially. For Petroleum, as shown above, the indexes would be somewhat lower than indicated in Exhibits 34, 35, and 36. For Wholesale and retail trades, the indexes would be slightly higher.

The decision was made, arbitrarily and only for present purposes, not to include wholesaling and retailing in Petroleum.

5. See, e.g., Anthony Cockerill and Aubrey Silberston, *The Steel Industry; International Comparisons of Industrial Structure and Performance* (London: Cambridge University Press, 1974), especially Chaps. 7 and 10.

6. Most Industry Categories fell into place fairly easily; setting boundaries that correspond to the ways companies and industries are defined and work in practice was no great problem. In a few cases, this was not true. The prime example was the clusterings of companies in Office, computing . . . machines, Radio, communication equipment . . . electric components, and Aircraft, guided missiles. . . . Interdependence for subcontracts and supplies of components and subassemblies is extensive among these three industry systems. Several of the leading companies are active in more than one of the categories. But for the most part, even these categories worked out tolerably well for the present "broad-brush" purposes.

Food and Pharmaceuticals are further examples of complex industry systems or Industry Categories.

The Food Industry Category is one of the more complex. Some companies, such as General Foods, have very broad product lines; the lines of others, Kellogg for instance, are much shorter. At various times, some of the companies try with greater or less success to extend their lines. Or they may withdraw from this one or that. At any one time various companies compete with various particular others as to certain products or product groups but not as to still others. The pattern of any moment may, and does, change.

Moreover, as mentioned, competition cuts across product lines, even product categories. The consumer may have cereal for breakfast, or ham and eggs, or yogurt, or muffins, or kippered herrings, or clam chowder, or apple pie. For dinner, the working couple may have canned or frozen soup, TV dinners based on meat, fish, pasta, etc. The alternatives they may consider range broadly across many product groups. They may cook up their own meals, using endless permutations and combinations chosen from among literally thousands of packaged and unpackaged food items. To complicate matters, in certain food lines, retail chains—the A&P, for instance—are also to be counted among the largest manufacturers. And to complicate matters still further, at least two non-U.S. firms, Unilever and Nestlé, are also major factors in certain lines.

Pharmaceuticals is another very complex system of companies, making various kinds of products: antibiotics, ataractics, antihistamines, analgesics, biologicals, hormones, diagnostics, fungicides, bacteriostats, vitamins—just for instance. Some also produce operating room and hospital supplies. No one company produces the whole "line."

Unlike different kinds of foods that may be substituted for one another, pharmaceuticals are fairly, or very, specific in their application. And yet, even so, there are important relationships. For example, effective use of immunizing agents may reduce demands for antibiotics, diagnostics, and analgesics.

Some pharmaceutical companies (and chemical companies, as well) sell "fine chemicals"—such as various vitamins, antibiotics, steroids—to other companies, including competitors and potential competitors, who incorporate them into their own pharmaceutical end-items. Some of these paired sellers and buyers are sometimes actual or potential competitors as to some of these items or, if not these, then others. Again, important non-U.S. companies are active in American markets. Some of these are *very* large: Hoffman-La Roche, Ciba-Geigy, and Sandoz, for example, all of which are Swiss; Bayer and Hoechst are both German and are both among the world's largest chemical companies. Many of the American companies have important positions in other countries. To complicate matters, some of the pharmaceutical companies have important positions in other fields quite removed, food, for instance, and plastics.

Companies enter and leave these areas of products, each of which has certain recognizable subdivisions. In varying degrees, and in varying ways, all the pharmaceutical companies listed in Exhibit 1 affect each other, as do many smaller pharmaceutical companies and large companies, sited primarily in other industry complexes—meat packing and chemicals, for instance—which also produce various pharmaceutical products.

Some Industry Categories, because of their nature, were defined primarily in terms of generally similar functions performed in generally similar fashion under generally similar constraints. These include the regulated industries: electric and gas utilities, airlines, railroads, motor transportation, and telephone and telegraph services. These industries, in concept and in fact, are different from industries that operate as interlinked systems of diverse kinds of companies, their systemic nature arising from supportive, competitive, investment, and operational interrelationships and interactions.

Let it be noted that the concept of industry *system* or Industry Category, as used here, is very different from the concept of "industry" often used in economic theory that is defined in terms of a group of *given* competing sellers that offer *given* generically, if not specifically, "like" products to a defined body of buyers, as to whom the sellers, in their behavior, are indifferent. Such a concept is far too narrow to be a useful model of the real world. In that world, seemingly very unlike parties can be interrelated and interactive in many varied and complex ways. Even more important, in the real world, "givens" are *given* for only short periods of time. All significant variables are, in fact, more or less dynamic: outputs, inputs, conversion processes; sellers, buyers, and actual and potential competitors; comparative costs of labor and capital; comparative international advantages; regulatory constraints; just to name a few. See Appendix B for further comments and the contents of Industry Categories.

7. See John D. Glover, "Rise and Fall of Corporations: Challenge and Response," a note prepared for use at the Harvard Business School; [PR-6-A(I)]. In Chapter 11, we shall consider some cases of persistence and impermanence among the Largest Corporations as between 1929 and 1971.

8. The data in Table 11 do not correspond exactly to those relating to Iron and steel in Exhibit 1 and Exhibits 34, 35, and 36 and exhibits based thereon. Table 11 is based upon income tax returns. Exhibit 1 is based on public reports. For tax purposes, tax

returns of corporations may consolidate all or some of their subsidiaries, or consolidate their returns in ways different from published reports. Tax accounting, especially as regards write-downs and write-offs, together with possibly different treatments of depreciation and depletion, can result in estimates of revenues, costs, net income, and asset values that are somewhat different from those in published reports. Given such possible differences, the data of Table 11 are quite consistent with those of Exhibit 1. IRS data, such as those in Table 11 and Exhibits 31, 32, and 33, cover privately held corporations whereas, of course, Exhibit 1 does not.

Similar differences arise as regards tax-reported and publicly reported data for other Industry Categories.

9. See, e.g., Lawrence Minard, "In Privacy They Thrive," *Forbes* (November 1, 1976), pp. 38-49.

7

The modern corporation
in modern America;
occurrence and presence
of large corporations

The community of productive organizations, in any society, is part, a literally essential part, of the total human *ecosystem*. Upon it, and of it, individuals, households, and families depend for their way of life, in fact, for their very lives. One cannot really understand the larger embracing system without a grasp of the composition, structure, and workings of the productive community within it. The productive community, in turn, has no existence, purpose, or meaning apart from the rest of the encompassing human ecosystem of which it is part.

Among the world's many cultures and political systems, of varying ideologies, degrees of technological and structural development, and sophistication, the indispensable productive community is organized in many different ways. The American productive system includes government and other public instrumentalities in their hundreds, private nonprofit organizations in their thousands; family-owned and -run farms and businesses in their millions; a million and a half small-ish businesses organized in corporate form; and a few thousand larger to very large corporations either closely held by small groups of associated stockholders or publicly owned by widely scattered, "anonymous" stockholders.

This pluralistic productive "subsystem" of the "American Way" is wondrously diverse in its hundreds of different kinds—"species"—of its millions of producing entities; bewilderingly complex in its structure; mystifying in its workings: A living, sensate organic whole. The functioning of the flowing processes of this massive tissue of human organizations is well nigh as intricate as that of the earthly "web of life," itself.

What a piece of work is our economy!

We shall understand it a mite better for having studied the nature and structure and development of our corporate population.

In the American economy, as was pointed out early in Chapter 5, the business corporations of the private sector generated over half of the country's National Income. And of that, a further half, more than a quarter of the total—a very special fraction in its makeup—was produced by a handful of our very largest corporations; the especial center of attraction for this book.

In that earlier chapter, we looked at the disposition of the numbers and assets of those Largest Corporations among the Major Industry Groups and the several Industry Categories. The strongly patterned distributions of numbers and asset masses of the biggest corporations, as shown, for instance, in Exhibit 26, give out powerful indications of *order* in the incidence of those organizations and in the national development of which their emergence was a component. The appearance, growth, disposition, and arrangement ("taxis" is the technical term in ecology) of our largest companies are not random or casual phenomena.

The data we are now about to examine abound with even more and stronger suggestions that explanation of the evolution and present place of large corporations in the American system must run in terms of basic, objective trends, factors, and exigencies of demand, production, and distribution: evolving "know-how"; development of resources; population growth and advancement in health and education, desires and aspirations; a myriad organizational and institutional facts that have facilitated and constrained productive activity and economic choice; advance in material well-being; the workings of a society, an economy, a polity, characterized by the presence and workings of hundreds, thousands, millions of centers of initiative, decision-making, and resource-allocation—driven and molded by changing values, rising expectations, unfolding and spreading knowledge, and exploding technologies.

The sense can hardly be avoided—so compelling are the data—that, in looking at our corporate population—the whole of it, small and large units alike—we are beholding something of essence in an entire human ecological system in process of growth and transformation. In particular, the data indicate strongly that the occurrence—numbers—and the presence—asset masses—of our Largest Corporations among the several industry systems (Industry Categories) were in very large measure—not entirely—consequences of the expanding scales and magnitudes of tasks to be carried out in the developing American System, and the means developed and necessary for their performance. Economies of scale, changing and expanding over time, were surely present, calling forth, by virtue of their dynamically evolving technologies, growing aggregations of capital and organizations of growing size. In the broadly inclusive scheme of things called the American System, large corporations have been key elements, prime instruments of support and change.

Large, even enormous scale—in business, government, unions, education, health care—has become more American than apple pie itself. *Bigness* is a very postulate or cornerstone of the American System. A consummate irony is that our traditional, accepted ideology, the one we know and find comfortable, makes no provision for it. The business community, for its part, is awkward rather than recalcitrant in conceding that its key, vital role in our System clothes it with overriding public interest and implies great and grave responsibilities for the general welfare of the American people and the environment in which we, all of us, live.

A later chapter will take up some of the implications of these findings and conclusions.

THE PRESENCE OF THE LARGEST CORPORATIONS IN AMERICAN INDUSTRY—SUMMARY

The *presence* of the largest corporations in different sectors of American industry, as gauged by their *asset masses,* is as strongly patterned as is their *occurrence,* as indicated by the distribution of their *numbers.* This patterning of their assets is even more revealing of the very different natures of the several industry *systems* that, together, make up our productive community, and in which corporations large and small have their places.

To put the matter in a nutshell: the *occurrence* (i.e., the numbers) of very large corporations that appear in various Industry Categories (or Groups or other industry sectors) is strongly associated with their *relative presence* (i.e., the fraction of the respective total asset-masses held by them). This is to say, the frequency of their appearance in various Industry Categories is positively associated with the *degree* to which the asset-masses of those industries are characterized by the *kinds* of assets held by large companies. Very large companies occur less frequently or not at all in Industry Categories whose asset-masses are more characterized by the *kinds* of assets held by smaller and small companies.

This describes in general terms the *where* and throws light on the *why* of the greater occurrence of large corporations in some Industry Categories than in others.

In Chapter 8, we shall see further suggestions that relative occurrence of very large corporations among Industry Categories is associated with differences among *kinds* of assets characteristic of corporations of different scales.

Big companies have *their* place in the industrial scheme of things; smaller companies have theirs; small companies have *theirs*. And they are different *kinds* of places—each and all indispensable in their own ways in our contemporary industrial order.

In 1971 as in 1929, the assets of the Largest Corporations were strongly clustered in the Utilities and other regulated industries and in Manufacturing. Only small fractions, if any, of the total assets of the Largest Companies were present in other whole broad sectors of American industry: in Agriculture, Construction, Wholesale and retail trade, for instance. The asset-masses of these Industry Categories are characteristically of kinds held by smaller and small companies.

Among the Industry Categories and clusters of these Categories that are more particularly defined than the Major Industry Groups, the assets of the Largest Corporations were likewise distributed very unevenly. But this very unevenness betokens order and reason, and says a great deal about the compositions of our industry systems. Of all the assets of The 559 Largest Corporations, over 34 percent were present in the Industry Categories labeled collectively as Utilities and other regulated industries. The electric and gas utilities, alone, contained 17 percent of those assets. These are notably Industry Categories whose asset-masses are characterized by assets of kinds held by large and very large corporations.

Among the Industry Categories that composed the broad Major Industry Groups labeled Manufacturing, the distribution and presence of the assets of The 559 bore additional witness to the existence of order and reason. That Group contained altogether about 60 percent of all the assets of The 559. About 23 percent were located in the four integrated industries; Petroleum, by itself, accounted for 15 percent.

In contrast to such notable clusters in some industries, few, if any, of the assets of The 559 were to be found in a number of other manufacturing Industry Categories. For example, none was located in Furniture and fixtures; and only two corporations, holding about $700 million of assets, which is to say less than $\frac{1}{10}$ of 1 percent of all of the assets of The 559, were present in Leather. . . .

The *relative* presence of the Largest Corporations as compared to the presence of other firms, and as measured by "presence index," was equally patterned. Corporations numbered among The 559 Largest held almost two-thirds of all corporate assets in Manufacturing. Others held almost four-fifths of all corporate assets in Transportation and other utilities. In contrast, members of The 559 held only minor or negligible fractions of the total assets reported by corporations classified as being engaged in the Major Industry Groups—Agriculture, Construction, and Real estate.

Among individual Industry Categories, the relative presence of The

559 ranged from zero or close to zero in Agriculture, Furniture and fixtures, and Wholesale trade, to over 80 percent in 11 of the 54 Industry Categories. Companies among The 559 held over 90 percent of the total corporate assets in Petroleum, Metal cans, and Photographic equipment.

In sum, the aggregate values of asset masses of kinds held by the Largest Corporations and their relative "weight" therein, in comparison to other firms, were major in some sectors, minor in others, and absent in still others. The patterns reflect in large measure the relative effectiveness or absence of forces making for, and opportunities giving rise to, large scale in production processes and corporate organization. Large corporations arose and became notable primarily in industries where large scale was called for by the tasks to be performed and made possible by evolving technologies of production, distribution, and organization. Their presence was roughly proportional to those underlying forces at work.

This broad generalization does not dismiss the likelihood that other systemic forces were at work. We shall discuss some of these later on. But it is reinforced by certain facts relating to sizes of corporations. Large corporations tended to be particularly notable in Industry Categories where the sizes of corporations *other* than themselves tended *also* to be relatively large. Their presence was lower, or nonexistent, in Industry Categories where the sizes of *other* corporations were smaller. For example, in Industry Categories where the presence index numbers of The 559 were greater than 60 percent, the average size of all *other* firms was $1,198,000. In Industry Categories where the presence index was between 10 percent and 20 percent, the average size of all *other* firms was $801,000.

From a different perspective, and speaking very generally, the average sizes of the Largest Corporations, just *among themselves,* were smaller in those Industry Categories where they, the biggest firms, were smaller than the average sizes of the largest firms located in other Industry Categories where their relative presence was more notable. For instance, the average size of the members of The 559 was $1.6 billion in Industry Categories where their relative presence was over 60 percent. In Industry Categories where the relative presence index was between only 10 percent and 20 percent, the average size of the very largest firms was $372 million. (We shall inquire into this matter further in the next chapter.)

This is to say that the Largest Corporations were not only the biggest among all others within their respective Industry Categories. They were relatively numerous and larger where the *next* largest and, on the average, the other corporations also tended to be relatively large. These Industry Categories were those where forces and opportunities making for large scale were operating more powerfully. The Largest Corporations were relatively less numerous and smaller—even absent—in those Industry Categories where the next largest and, on the average, the other corporations tended to be smaller. Those were the Industry Categories where the forces and opportunities making for bigness were weaker.

In broad general terms, the patterns of occurrence and presence of our Largest Corporations were consequences of forces present and implicit in the whole evolution of The American System. They were products of the workings and development of that system. For their part, they were also prime engines of change and evolution in that system.

THE LARGEST COMPANIES IN THE CORPORATE POPULATION AS A WHOLE

As we begin our review of the place of the Largest Corporations in the corporate population, we shall look, first, at where and how they fitted in among *all* corporations ranked simply according to asset size, irrespective of where, more particularly and "logically," they fitted in the structure of industry. Next, we shall look at where they fitted among very broad Major Industry Groups. Thereafter, we shall consider where they fitted among our 54 Industry Categories.

The Largest Corporations among all companies ranked by size

Bigness of our largest corporations has been their most remarked-upon feature. And, as we have said, they *are* very big, indeed. *How* big they are, and where and how they fit in with other corporations of lesser size is perhaps less familiar. That is a good place to start our overview.

In Exhibit 31, data appear that describe the profile of the American corporate community obtained from sorting out our companies, so to speak, and ranking and categorizing them by asset size. In 1971, there were, as we have seen, 1,592,000 nonfinancial corporations (including 277,000 firms in Real estate). The vast majority of these firms were "small" by any yardstick. More than half of our companies, almost 900,000, had assets reported at less than $100,000. Of this corporate population, 1,211,000—over three-quarters of all corporations—reported assets valued at less than $250,000 each. All corporations reporting assets up to $5 million numbered somewhat more than 1,533,000, 96 percent of all nonfinancial corporations.

Among these smaller firms, presumably, were to be found "worthy men," independent heads of their own establishments—no "mere servants" of corporations—who support themselves and their families from the "small profits" realized therein. The heads of these firms, surely, must have been the kinds of men Mr. Justice Douglas and Judge Hand had in mind when they spoke of "resident proprietors beholden to no one," and "small producers, each dependent for his success upon his own skill and character."

Asset size classes ($000)	Number of corporations	Assets of corporations ($ millions)	Percentage of the number	Percentage of assets	Average asset size of corporation ($000)
Zero	44,199	–	2.8%	–	–
Zero to $100	891,576	$ 31,289	56.0	2.2%	$ 35
$100-250	319,676	51,217	20.1	3.6	160
$250-500	164,737	57,682	10.3	4.1	350
$500-1,000	90,505	62,819	5.7	4.5	694
$1,000-5,000	67,339	130,296	4.2	9.2	1,935
$5,000-10,000	6,764	46,407	0.4	3.3	6,861
$10,000-25,000	3,978	60,692	0.2	4.3	15,257
$25,000-50,000	1,423	49,023	0.1	3.5	34,450
$50,000-100,000	766	53,316	0.05	3.8	69,603
$100,000-250,000	615	95,201	0.04	6.7	154,798
$250,000 or more	615	772,570	0.04	54.8	1,256,211
Totals*	1,592,193	$1,410,511	100.0%	100.0%	$ 886
The 559 Largest Nonfinancial Corporations†	559	$ 707,195	0.04%	50.1%	$1,265,107

*All tax-reporting corporations.
†According to published information of publicly held United States corporations.
Source: *Corporation Income Tax Returns; Corporation Source Book, Statistics of Income, 1971.*

Altogether, these small companies with assets of less than $5 million held about one-quarter of the reported value of the assets of all nonfinancial corporations. There can be no doubt that hundreds of thousands of small companies filled many vital niches and performed many indispensable roles in the workings of The American System.

At the other end of the spectrum of our companies arrayed according to assets size were a few hundred firms, each reporting assets of $250,000,000 and up.* These *really big* corporations accounted for a negligible percentage of the number of all corporations—less than $4/100$ of 1 percent. They did, however, hold over half of the total *value* of corporate assets.

In between the smaller firms, with assets up to $5 million, and the largest, with assets of more than $250 million, were about 14,000 firms. These represented less than 1 percent of the number of corporations. They held something over one-fifth of the reported value of

---

*The Internal Revenue Service counted 615 such firms, holding a total of $773 billion of assets. Both of these figures are somewhat greater than the 559 firms—publicly-owned corporations, reporting assets of $707 billion—which are listed in Exhibit 1 and which are the base of much of the statistics of this work. The differences are discussed at some length in Note 7 to Chapter 5 and in Note 1 to the present chapter.

The total assets of the 615 corporations of the IRS that reported assets of more than $250 million came to $772.6 billion; their average size was $1.256 billion. The total assets of The 559 Largest Corporations listed in Exhibit 1 came to $702.2 billion; their average size came to $1.265 billion. The figures are not so disparate as to lead to different conclusions.

Whatever the differences in numbers and assets, and the causes of these differences, the two sets of data relating to our Largest Corporations tell the same story, with only minor variations of detail.[1]

all assets of nonfinancial corporations. About one-third of these "mid-range" companies were publicly owned, with shares more or less frequently traded in national, regional, local, and over-the-counter stock exchanges.

The *asset* profile of this array of all nonfinancial firms was utterly different from the *numbers* profile. The smallest and most numerous companies, with assets reported at less than $100,000, over half of the total number of all companies, held only 2.2 percent of the reported assets. The next most numerous, those with assets between $100,000 and $250,000—one-fifth of the number—held only 3.6 percent. Altogether, the firms with assets of less than $5,000,000—over 96 percent of the entire corporate community—held less than one-quarter (23.6 percent) of all nonfinancial corporate assets.

The Largest Companies—constituting a tiny fraction of the number of firms—held more than half of all corporate assets.

All of those firms in between, from $5 million to $250 million, being less than $\frac{1}{10}$ of 1 percent of the total number, held over one-fifth of the assets (21.6 percent).

Speaking of drama, one of the impressive ways of trying to perceive the various and profoundly different natures of firms of different sizes is to consider the sizes of the average firm in the several size classes. The "average" firm in the size class of assets up to $100,000 reported assets of $35,000. This figure—the *total* assets of the average firm in the smallest group—was less than the investment *per employee*—for a single job—among the largest firms in such large-scale, capital-intensive industries as Iron and steel ($35,600), Non-ferrous metals ($52,000), Petroleum ($114,000), Electric and gas utilities ($206,000), and Telephone and telegraph ($68,000).

At the other end of the array, the *average* reported value of assets of the very largest firms was $1,256,211,000. Measured by asset value, the average of the biggest firms was *tens of thousands* of times as large as the average of the smallest corporations. (See Exhibit 31.) Even if we look at the *average* size of the very largest companies in comparison to the larger ones among the smaller companies, we still see a vast difference. The average size of firm in the size bracket of $1 million to $5 million was $1.9 million. In contrast even to this figure, the *average* size of the largest firms was *hundreds* of times—almost 1,000 times—as large. And, of course, there were scores and more of the very largest firms that were far, far larger than the average of them.

We shall refer again to some of the facts and implications of the extraordinary range of differences in size or between smaller and larger firms.*

---

*Smaller corporations come in for further mention in Chapters 8 and 9.

Corporations, like other entities, can be described and measured in terms relating to a number of different aspects and dimensions. In the data that immediately follow, corporations large and small are classified by Major Industry Groups. Later, we shall see what their picture looks like when we classify them by Industry Categories. Elsewhere and for other purposes, corporations are sometimes described and measured in terms of location (particularly when they operate small single "establishments"), age, nature of ownership, and stage of development in their life-cycles. Often, especially when they are single-product firms (almost invariably, small), they are categorized in terms of individual particular outputs.

The taxonomy of corporations—that is, the science of classification of companies—is almost undeveloped, as compared to the development of the science of taxonomy of living things for the purposes of biology and ecology, or the taxonomy of human beings for the purposes of demography. In fact, as in the case of Major Industry Groups, or even in the cases of many "industries," some schemes of classification are of limited use. But we must work with what we have. And the categories and dimension we have for this study are Major Industry Groups, Industry Categories, and reported asset sizes.

One statistical overview of the corporate population of 1971 was given in Exhibit 15. Those data show something of the disposition, among Major Industry Groups, of the numbers and assets of all companies, and of The 200 and The 559 Largest Nonfinancial Corporations. A somewhat different, more summary picture of the corporate community and of the largest corporations therein is given in Exhibit 32; other related perspectives are given in Tables 13 and 14.

The summary data of Exhibit 32 and Tables 13 and 14 must be used with caution. They are subject to numerous qualifications and *caveats* that need not be repeated here. These limitations stem from the very haziness of the contents and boundaries of Major Industry Groups, and from problems of categorizing whole industries, to say nothing of individual firms, according to this lattice-work. These data can serve only to give one highly abstract, broad-brush overview of our corporate community and the places within it of our largest corporations. They should not be scorned, however, for their shortcomings. The broad overview that these figures give—a very large-scale "map"—should help us from getting lost in the forest of numbers we shall soon enter.

Patterns of occurrence and presence of all corporations

The first observation to be made of Exhibit 32, as of Exhibit 15, is that the *numbers* and the *assets* of all corporations vary enormously among the several Major Industry Groups, and are distributed

EXHIBIT 32
The distribution, among Major Industry Groups, of the numbers and assets of all nonfinancial corporations, and of The 200 and 559 Largest, 1971

Major Industry Groups	All corporations				The 200 Largest Corporations				The 559 Largest Corporations			
	Number of firms (000)	Value of assets ($ billions)	Percentage of firms	Percentage of assets	Number of firms	Value of assets ($ billions)	Percentage of The 200 firms	Percentage of The 200 assets	Number of firms	Value of assets ($ billions)	Percentage of The 559 firms	Percentage of The 559 assets
Agriculture	39.9	$ 11.8	2.5%	0.8%	0	$ 0.0	0.0%	0.0%	0	$ 0.0	0.0%	0.0%
Mining and quarrying . .	12.6	26.0	0.8	1.8	0	0.0	0.0	0.0	3	1.4	0.5	0.2
Construction	143.1	48.2	9.0	3.4	0	0.0	0.0	0.0	3	1.2	0.5	0.2
Manufacturing	201.0	646.6	12.6	45.8	118#	317.9	59.0	59.1	334#	421.6	59.7	59.6
Transportation . . . utilities . . .	71.1	309.9	4.5	22.0	71	197.5	35.5	36.7	160	240.5	28.6	34.0
Wholesale and retail trade . . .	538.7	210.9	33.8	15.0	12	22.9	6.0	4.3	38	33.6	6.8	4.8
Services	287.8	62.2	18.1	4.4	0	0.0	0.0	0.0	17	6.9	3.0	1.0
Real estate	276.6	93.9	17.4	6.7	0	0.0	0.0	0.0	6	2.0	1.0	0.3
Nature of business not allocable	21.4	0.8	1.3	*	0	0.0	0.0	0.0	0	0.0	0.0	0.0
Total nonfinancial corporations	1,592.2	$1,410.5	100.0%	100.0%	200	$538.2	100.0%	100.0%	559	$707.2	100.0%	100.0%
Finance, insurance	141.1	1,487.7										
Total, all industries . . .	1,733.3	$2,889.2										

Note: Interpretations of these data are subject to observations set forth in Footnote 3 to Exhibit 3, in Chapter 3.
#The 200 include Western Electric; the 559 include Western Electric and the electronic and communications subsidiaries of General Telephone & Electronics, counted as one firm. Assets, but not firms, are included in column totals.
* Less than 1/10 of 1 percent.
Source: U.S. Internal Revenue Service, Statistics of Income—1971, Corporation Income Tax Returns; Corporation Source Book of Statistics of Income, 1971.

TABLE 13
Relative distributions among Major Industry Groups of the
number of The 559 Largest Corporations and of all other
corporations: 1971

	The 559	All others*
Agriculture	0.0%	2.5%
Mining and quarrying	0.5	0.8
Construction	0.5	9.0
Manufacturing	59.7	12.6
Transportation . . . utilities	28.6	4.5
Wholesale and retail trade	6.8	33.8
Services	3.0	18.1
Real estate	1.0	17.4
Nature of business not allocable	0.0	1.3
Total	100.0%	100.0%

*Excluding The 559.

TABLE 14
Distributions among Major Industry Groups of the assets of The 559 Largest Corporations
and of all other firms: 1971

	Assets held by The 559 Largest Firms ($ billions)	Assets held by other firms ($ billions)	Relative distribution of the assets of The 559	Relative distribution of the assets of all other firms
Agriculture	$ 0.0	$ 11.8	–	1.7%
Mining	1.4	24.6	0.2%	3.5
Construction	1.2	47.0	0.2	6.7
Manufacturing	421.6	225.0	59.6	32.0
Transportation . . . utilities	240.5	69.4	34.0	9.9
Wholesale and retail trade	33.6	177.3	4.8	25.2
Services	6.9	55.3	1.0	7.9
Real estate	2.0	91.9	0.3	13.1
Not allocable	–	0.8	–	*
Total, nonfinancial corporations	$707.2	$703.3	100.0%	100.0%

*About $\frac{1}{100}$ of 1 percent.

according to very different profiles. Of all corporations, almost 70
percent of the *number*—1.1 million—were in Wholesale and retail
trade, Services, and Real estate. These industry Groups, speaking
very generally, were bailiwicks of "small" business. Add Agriculture
and Construction, also typically "small-business" sets of industries,
and the number of firms goes up to 1,280,000, which is to say, 80
percent of the number of all nonfinancial corporations.

When it comes to the profile of the disposition of corporate *assets,*
the picture is very different: the reported value of assets came to
almost a *trillion* dollars in just two large Groups of industries, Manufacturing and Transportation . . . utilities. These figures amount to
more than two-thirds of the values of all the assets of all nonfinancial
corporations.

A broad generalization takes form as to the distributions of numbers and assets of corporations: aggregations of asset values tend to be smaller in very broad industry Groups where the numbers of firms are larger; conversely, aggregations of asset values tend to be larger where the numbers of firms are smaller. Some industry Groups are characterized by large numbers of smaller firms; others, by smaller numbers of larger firms. Our Largest Corporations are most conspicuous as to their numbers and their presence in those latter groups.

This is an intriguing fact.

In the animal world, one law of life seems to be that, among the different species, the *numbers* of individual members of species vary inversely with their individual *sizes.* According to this pattern, there are fewer individuals of large species—say, elephants—and more individuals of smaller species—say, field mice. Similarly, in the human ecosystem, there are fewer, say, electric utilities and petroleum and computer companies than there are, say, retail outlets, incorporated farms, or personal service organizations. This, it would seem, is in the nature of things, a "law of life" in human affairs.

The numbers and assets of The 559 Largest Corporations were distributed very differently from those of the rest of the corporate community, as may be seen in Exhibit 32 and Tables 13 and 14.

Occurrence and presence of The Largest Corporations in the community of all corporations. The profiles of the occurrence of The 200 and of The 559 were very different from those of other corporations. The Largest Corporations occurred primarily in two Major Industry Groups. Of The 200 Largest, 188—94 percent—occurred in Manufacturing and Transportation... utilities. Twelve companies appeared in Wholesale and retail trade; actually, nine of them were in General merchandise and two were in Food stores. The 559 were spread out a bit more; but, even so, 492—88 percent of them—occurred in the same two broad categories, Manufacturing and the Utilities. About 10 percent of The 559 occurred in wholesale and retail trade and services.

Other and, of course, smaller corporations were, relatively speaking, far less common in the two Industry Groups where the Largest Corporations tended to occur. Smaller companies were relatively, as well as absolutely, much more common in trade, services, real estate, construction, and, of course, agriculture.

The distributions of the *assets* of larger and smaller firms were also different from each other; with exceptions, these distributions followed patterns generally similar to the distribution of their respective numbers. This appears in the data of Table 14. Of the assets of The 559, about 94 percent were present in Manufacturing and the Utilities. Of the assets of all other corporations, about 42 percent were present in those two Major Industry Groups, 32 percent being in

Manufacturing and 10 percent being in Utilities. On the other hand, almost 60 percent of the assets of all other corporations were present in Industry Groups in which relatively few of the assets of The 559 were present.

Another perspective on the differences in the patterns of the presences of The 559 Largest corporations and of all others is provided by Table 15. These data show the *relative* presence in Major Industry Groups of The 559 Largest Corporations in comparison to that of all other firms.

TABLE 15
Indexes of the *relative presence* in Major Industry Groups of
The 559 Largest and of all other corporations: 1971

| Major Industry Groups | Presence index | |
	The 559 Largest Corporations	All other firms
Agriculture	0.0%	100.0%
Mining.	5.4	94.6
Construction.	2.5	97.5
Manufacturing	65.2	34.8
Transportation . . . utilities	77.6	22.4
Wholesale and retail trade	15.9	84.1
Services	11.1	88.9
Real estate	2.1	97.9
Not allocable	0.0	100.0
All Industry Groups other than Finance	50.2%	49.8%

These data, for reasons we have discussed, should not be taken as precise measures of the relative asset masses of the largest, and of all the other corporations in the Major Industry Groups. But the story they tell is clear enough: overall, about half of the total value of the assets of all corporations was accounted for by the very largest corporations; the other half was held by all other corporations. But, among the Major Industry Groups, it was only in Manufacturing and Transportation . . . utilities that the relative presences of the biggest corporations accounted for more than half of the reported value of the assets. Among all the other Groups, it was the presence of smaller corporations in the "All other" category that was most prominent. More, it is fair to say that these other Groups were predominantly the "turf" of smaller business.

Large corporations did, indeed, have their "place" in the scheme of things. And, so, also, did smaller ones.

Occurrence and presence of the Largest Corporations and average company size. As we shall see later in some detail, there is a broad-brush association of size of corporations in industries and their occurrence: the Largest Corporations tend to appear more frequently in industries where the average size of *other* firms is relatively large than in industries where the average size of other firms is relatively small. This broad tendency shows up in data relating to Major Industry Groups as well as in the more detailed data relating to Industry Categories.

This broad tendency suggests that the relatively greater occurrence and presence of the largest firms in certain industries is associated with, and related to objective industry-specific factors that make for relatively large size not only among the very largest companies, but among smaller companies as well.

First, let it be noted, in Exhibit 33, that the average sizes of the firms among The 559 that occur in Manufacturing and Transportation... utilities are notably larger than the average sizes of members of The 559 that occur in other Groups. A similar—roughly similar—pattern appears among "All other" firms. Although on a much

EXHIBIT 33
Average sizes of The 559 Largest and all other nonfinancial corporations among Major Industry Groups: 1971

	Average size of all firms ($ millions)	Average size of The 559 ($ millions)	Average size of all other firms ($ millions)	Ratio of average size of The 559 to size of all other firms
Agriculture	$0.295	–	$0.295	–
Mining.	2.060	$ 470	1.950*	240
Construction	0.340	400	0.330	1,210
Manufacturing	3.220	1,260	1.120	1,125
Transportation...utilities...	4.360	1,500	0.980	1,530
Wholesale and retail trade . . .	0.390	885	0.330	2,680
Services	0.215	405	0.190	2,130
Real estate	0.340	340	0.330	1,030
Other	0.040	–	0.040	–
All industries†	$0.885	$1,265	$0.440	2,875

Note: Figures are rounded somewhat more than usual as a signal of limitations of the data.
*This figure may be strongly biased upward because of inclusion of large nonferrous metals companies and perhaps even some petroleum companies that more comparably might have been categorized among Manufacturing, as was done with members of The 559.
†Includes Agriculture and "Not allocable."

smaller scale, the average sizes of the much smaller firms among the "All other" that occur in Manufacturing and the Utilities are notably larger (with exception of Mining) than the average sizes of all other firms in the other Major Industry Groups. Setting aside, for the moment, the great differences in scale as between The 559 and all other firms, the implication takes form to the general effect that some factors, at least, that gave rise to relatively larger scale among The 559 in those two Groups, as compared to the average sizes of "559" firms in other Industry Groups, operated also among the much smaller "All other" corporations.

We shall see further suggestions of this tendency when we come in a few moments to examine the "relative presence" of the largest companies among the several Industry Categories.

Large and small companies; Difference in scale and differences in kind. One other overall observation to be made of the data in Exhibit 33 is that of the *enormous* differences between the sizes of the largest companies and the rest of the corporate community. Those differences were touched upon earlier while we were looking at Exhibit 31. Excluding the Major Industry Group Mining, for which the data may be somewhat skewed artificially and, hence, may be misleading, The 559 Largest Corporations were many *hundreds* of times larger, on the average, than the average sizes of "All other" firms. In Manufacturing, the representatives of The 559 were about *1,000* times the size of all the other companies. In Wholesale and retail trade, The 559 were well over *2,000* times as large. And these comparisons include companies that, in terms of asset size, were just under The 559, including some hundreds of firms in the asset bracket of $100 million to $250 million.

As noted earlier, these enormous differences in size strongly indicate that, among all of the several Major Industry Groups, The 559 Largest Companies were very *different in kind* from the vast majority of firms, and not simply members of the same "genus," as it were—let alone the same "species"—only much larger.

So. To recap what we have seen so far of the occurrence and presence of the largest corporations in American business: a relatively short list of companies held about half of the total value of all corporate assets. These largest institutions were not just somewhat larger than others; they were tens, hundreds, thousands of times larger than the 1.6 million other firms with which they coexisted in symbiotic, complex industry systems. The large majority of these largest firms occurred in two broad industry Groups: Manufacturing and Transportation and other public utilities.

In Manufacturing, 334 of The 559 Largest Corporations held about two-thirds of the total reported value of all assets. Among the utilities, 160 of The 559 held over three-quarters of the value of all assets; 71,000 other firms held the rest. Elsewhere, representatives of The 559 occurred and had perceptible, even significant, but not predominant presence. This was the case in retail distribution—especially in General Merchandise and Mail Order and among Food Store chains—and in Motion Pictures and Services. (The "services" in which The 559 were engaged were of very particular kinds, as a glimpse at Exhibit 1 will reveal.)

At the same time, other broad sectors of American business were domains of *small* companies, including hundreds of thousands of *very small* firms: Agriculture, Construction, Wholesale and retail trade, Services, and Real estate.

We move ahead now, using a finer "screen," to examine the presence of the Largest Corporations among the 50-odd Industry Categories that correspond more or less closely to the more or less distinct, but interdependent, productive *systems* that make up the nation's industrial structure.

OCCURRENCE AND PRESENCE OF THE LARGEST CORPORATIONS AMONG "INDUSTRY CATEGORIES"

In Chapter 5, data and analyses were presented that showed the distribution of the Largest Companies among the 54 Industry Categories. These corporations manifest strong tendencies to be clustered in a limited list of industries. To recall, almost 90 percent of The 559 occurred in 30 Industry Categories, almost half of the companies being in the 7 regulated and 4 integrated industries:

Utilities and other regulated industries	160 firms
Four characteristically integrated industries	84 firms
Nineteen other industries in which seven or more of the companies occurred	237 firms

As we shall see in some detail, these 481 companies held over 90 percent of the total reported value of the assets of The 559 Largest Corporations.

In broad terms, to summarize and repeat an earlier finding, the Largest Companies tended to occur primarily in industries in which economies of scale and integration were inherent and common, and where the tasks to be performed were large, as the supply of utility services to large metropolitan areas. They were scarce in industries in which such factors were absent or weak.

Beyond this notable tendency toward patterned, clustered occurrence, two other significant sets of facts were noted (in Exhibit 30) as to the appearance of the Largest Companies: First, 70 of The 559 occurred in eight "newer" industries—pharmaceuticals, computers, aircraft, and air transportation, for example—where none of The 200 Largest of 1929 was to be found. Second, another 49 had arisen in eight "older" industries where none of the biggest had been in 1929. The emergence of these companies in these 16 industries were manifestations of significant dynamics operating in the American System.

Exhibits 34, 35, and 36 display straightforward data that measure the relative *presence* of the largest corporations among the 54 Industry Categories. Exhibit 34 relates to The 200 Largest; Exhibit 35, to The Next 359; Exhibit 36, to The 559 Largest Corporations of 1971. These three exhibits served as sources of data for analytical presentations, as in Exhibits 15, 32, and 33 and in Tables 13, 14, and 15. They will also serve as sources for a number of later exhibits and tables, in which they are summarized.

EXHIBIT 34
The 200 Largest Nonfinancial Corporations compared to all nonfinancial corporations, numbers and assets, by Industry Category: 1971

	All corporations		200 Largest Corporations		
Industry Category	Number of firms	Value of assets ($ millions)	Number of firms	Value of assets ($ millions)	Presence index, 200 Largest Companies
1. Agriculture....................	39,932	$ 11,800.4	0	$ 0.0	0.0%
2. Iron and steel................	2,222	28,393.6	7	18,319.2	64.5
3. Nonferrous metals	3,055	32,064.3	8	12,707.9	39.6
4. Coal	1,766	3,819.5	0	0.0	0.0
5. Petroleum	7,721	115,754.8	20	100,425.4	86.8
6. Construction	143,092	48,242.9	0	0.0	0.0
7. Food...	8,991	27,035.4	3	3,537.4	13.1
8. Meat...	2,543	8,687.9	3	4,173.9	48.0
9. Dairy...	2,137	5,885.7	3	3,356.0	57.0
10. Alcoholic beverages	426	9,115.6	1	932.2	10.2
11. Soft drinks...	2,220	4,656.0	1	1,107.9	23.8
12. Tobacco...	77	7,952.0	4	6,447.6	81.1
13. Textiles...	5,846	15,204.0	1	1,390.2	9.1
14. Apparel...	17,037	11,411.9	1	933.5	8.2
15. Lumber... wood... paper... products	14,133	34,897.4	8	12,506.9	35.8
16. Furniture and fixtures	6,755	4,243.7	0	0.0	0.0
17. Printing and publishing...	26,541	20,909.9	0	0.0	0.0
18. Chemicals...	6,684	39,768.8	10	21,761.5	54.7
19. Pharmaceuticals...	4,113	13,732.2	4	4,329.0	31.5
20. Soaps, cleaners...	2,167	5,492.0	1	2,013.0	36.7
21. Rubber and tires	6,235	13,071.4	5	9,149.0	70.0
22. Leather...	2,269	3,808.5	0	0.0	0.0
23. Nonmetallic mineral products...	11,064	15,034.9	0	0.0	0.0
24. Glass...	946	4,842.7	2	2,708.4	55.9
25. Fabricated metal products...	22,720	23,568.1	1	1,183.2	5.0
26. Metal cans.................	138	3,966.9	2	3,062.5	77.2
27. Machinery...	22,168	22,518.4	0	0.0	0.0
28. Farm, construction... machinery	2,925	15,097.6	2	3,269.7	21.7
29. Office... computing... machines	556	24,805.7	7	19,970.0	80.5
30. Electrical machinery...	4,664	20,649.7	2	10,425.7	50.5
31. Household appliances	457	5,049.9	1	1,669.7	33.1
32. Radio... communication equipment	5,741	25,909.1	3	14,664.7	56.6
33. Scientific... control... devices... measuring...	1,612	5,199.0	1	2,183.1	42.0
34. Photographic equipment...	633	4,145.3	1	3,298.0	79.6
35. Motor vehicles...	2,392	57,913.8	8	40,329.2	69.6
36. Aircraft...	815	24,204.7	8	12,008.7	49.6
37. Ship... building...	1,015	2,916.7	0	0.0	0.0
38. Railroad equipment	1,345	6,317.7	0	0.0	0.0
39. Other and miscellaneous manufacturing	11,678	9,694.8	0	0.0	0.0
40. Rail transportation	18,132	43,421.8	11	27,660.6	63.7
41. Transit	9,073	4,286.7	0	0.0	0.0
42. Motor transportation	27,452	13,427.7	2	2,665.1	19.8
43. Water transportation	6,385	6,482.6	0	0.0	0.0
44. Air transportation	3,428	16,595.8	6	9,154.3	55.2
45. Electric, gas... sanitary...	8,235	137,168.0	47	91,799.1	66.9
46. Telephone, telegraph... services...	3,453	80,044.5	5	66,171.2	82.7
47. Radio and TV broadcasting	3,923	5,278.5	0	0.0	0.0
48. Wholesale trade...	168,150	90,917.7	0	0.0	0.0
49. Retail trade...	320,656	68,136.0	1	1,571.8	2.3
50. General merchandise...	22,853	38,859.6	9	19,411.3	50.0
51. Food stores	27,005	12,970.1	2	1,943.4	15.0
52. Motion pictures...	10,061	6,424.2	0	0.0	0.0
53. Services	277,719	55,801.6	0	0.0	0.0
54. Real estate	267,399	92,066.1	0	0.0	0.0
55. Nature of business not allocable	21,438	847.1	0	0.0	0.0
56. All industries other than finance and insurance	1,592,193	$1,410,510.9	200	$538,240.3	38.2%

Sources: (All corporations) U.S. Internal Revenue Service, *Statistics of Income–1971, Corporation Income Tax Returns; Corporation Source Book, Statistics of Income, 1971;* (200 Largest Corporations) Exhibit 1.

EXHIBIT 35
The Next 359 Largest Nonfinancial Corporations compared to all nonfinancial corporations, numbers and assets, by Industry Category: 1971

		All corporations		Next 359 Largest Corporations		
	Industry Category	Number of firms	Value of assets ($ millions)	Number of firms	Value of assets ($ millions)	Presence index, 359 Largest Companies
1.	Agriculture...	39,932	$ 11,800.4	0	$ 0.0	0.0%
2.	Iron and steel	2,222	28,393.6	12	5,088.5	17.9
3.	Nonferrous metals	3,055	32,064.3	10	5,052.2	15.8
4.	Coal	1,766	3,819.5	3	1,413.6	37.0
5.	Petroleum	7,721	115,754.8	10	5,420.9	4.7
6.	Construction	143,092	48,242.9	3	1,201.2	2.5
7.	Food...	8,991	27,035.4	16	8,784.5	32.5
8.	Meat...	2,543	8,687.9	2	1,151.2	13.3
9.	Dairy...	2,137	5,885.7	3	1,709.0	29.0
10.	Alcoholic beverages	426	9,115.6	5	2,422.9	26.6
11.	Soft drinks...	2,220	4,656.0	1	827.7	17.8
12.	Tobacco	77	7,952.0	1	597.9	7.5
13.	Textiles...	5,846	15,204.0	8	3,189.5	21.0
14.	Apparel...	17,037	11,411.9	4	1,537.0	13.5
15.	Lumber... wood... paper... products	14,133	34,897.4	9	4,878.8	14.0
16.	Furniture and fixtures	6,755	4,243.7	0	0.0	0.0
17.	Printing and publishing...	26,541	20,909.9	7	2,702.1	12.9
18.	Chemicals...	6,684	39,768.8	16	8,654.9	21.8
19.	Pharmaceuticals	4,113	13,732.2	17	7,729.0	56.3
20.	Soaps and cleaners...	2,167	5,492.0	4	2,357.4	42.9
21.	Rubber and tires	6,235	13,071.4	0	0.0	0.0
22.	Leather...	2,269	3,808.5	2	696.7	18.3
23.	Nonmetallic mineral products...	11,064	15,034.9	13	6,089.6	40.5
24.	Glass...	946	4,842.7	2	1,033.7	21.3
25.	Fabricated metal products...	22,720	23,568.1	9	4,709.1	20.0
26.	Metal cans...	138	3,966.9	2	680.3	17.1
27.	Machinery...	22,168	22,518.4	9	3,300.5	14.7
28.	Farm, construction... machinery	2,925	15,097.6	5	3,400.6	22.5
29.	Office... computing... machines	556	24,805.7	4	1,493.1	6.0
30.	Electrical machinery...	4,664	20,649.7	6	2,285.9	11.1
31.	Household appliances	457	5,049.9	6	2,689.8	53.3
32.	Radio... communication equipment	5,741	25,909.1	11	5,302.4	20.5
33.	Scientific... control... devices... measuring	1,612	5,199.0	1	270.9	5.2
34.	Photographic equipment	633	4,145.3	1	617.1	14.9
35.	Motor vehicles...	2,392	57,913.8	9	4,232.1	7.3
36.	Aircraft...	815	24,204.7	2	774.5	3.2
37.	Ship... building...	1,015	2,916.7	0	0.0	0.0
38.	Railroad equipment...	1,345	6,317.7	4	2,133.0	33.8
39.	Other and miscellaneous manufacturing	11,678	9,694.8	5	1,950.9	20.1
40.	Rail transportation	18,132	43,421.8	10	4,686.9	10.8
41.	Transit	9,073	4,286.7	0	0.0	0.0
42.	Motor transportation	27,452	13,427.7	3	915.5	6.8
43.	Water transportation	6,385	6,482.6	3	1,110.1	17.1
44.	Air transportation	3,428	16,595.8	6	3,044.9	18.3
45.	Electric, gas... sanitary...	8,235	137,168.0	59	29,092.7	21.2
46.	Telephone, telegraph... services...	3,453	80,044.5	6	2,842.8	3.6
47.	Radio and TV broadcasting	3,923	5,278.5	2	1,326.2	25.1
48.	Wholesale trade...	168,150	90,917.7	1	318.3	0.4
49.	Retail trade...	320,656	68,136.0	6	1,978.5	2.9
50.	General merchandise...	22,853	38,859.6	11	5,079.6	13.1
51.	Food stores	27,005	12,970.1	8	3,250.2	25.1
52.	Motion pictures...	10,061	6,424.2	5	1,946.8	30.3
53.	Services...	277,719	55,801.6	12	4,952.3	8.9
54.	Real estate	267,399	92,066.1	6	2,031.2	2.2
55.	Nature of business not allocable	21,438	847.1	0	0.0	0.0
56.	All industries other than finance and insurance	1,592,193	$1,410,510.9	359	$168,954.5	12.0%

Sources: (All corporations) U.S. Internal Revenue Service, *Statistics of Income—1971, Corporation Income Tax Returns; Corporation Source Book, Statistics of Income, 1971;* (359 Next Largest Corporations) Exhibit 1.

EXHIBIT 36
The 559 Largest Nonfinancial Corporations compared to all nonfinancial corporations, numbers and assets, by Industry Category: 1971

	Industry Category	All corporations		559 Largest Corporations		Presence index, 559 Largest Companies
		Number of firms	Value of assets ($ millions)	Number of firms	Value of assets ($ millions)	
1.	Agriculture...	39,932	$ 11,800.4	0	$ 0.0	0.0%
2.	Iron and steel	2,222	28,393.6	19	23,407.7	82.4
3.	Nonferrous metals	3,055	32,064.3	18	17,760.1	55.4
4.	Coal	1,766	3,819.5	3	1,413.6	37.0
5.	Petroleum	7,721	115,754.8	30	105,846.3	91.4
6.	Construction	143,092	48,242.9	3	1,201.2	2.5
7.	Food...	8,991	27,035.4	19	12,321.9	45.6
8.	Meat...	2,543	8,687.9	5	5,325.1	61.3
9.	Dairy...	2,137	5,885.7	6	5,065.0	86.1
10.	Alcoholic beverages	426	9,115.6	6	3,355.1	36.8
11.	Soft drinks...	2,220	4,656.0	2	1,935.6	41.6
12.	Tobacco	77	7,952.0	5	7,045.5	88.6
13.	Textiles...	5,846	15,204.0	9	4,579.7	30.1
14.	Apparel	17,037	11,411.9	5	2,470.5	21.6
15.	Lumber...wood...paper...products	14,133	34,897.4	17	17,385.7	49.8
16.	Furniture and fixtures	6,755	4,243.7	0	0.0	0.0
17.	Printing and publishing...	26,541	20,909.9	7	2,702.1	12.9
18.	Chemicals...	6,684	39,768.8	26	30,416.4	76.5
19.	Pharmaceuticals...	4,113	13,732.2	21	12,058.0	87.8
20.	Soaps, cleaners...	2,167	5,492.0	5	4,370.4	79.6
21.	Rubber and tires	6,235	13,071.4	5	9,149.0	70.0
22.	Leather...	2,269	3,808.5	2	696.7	18.3
23.	Nonmetallic mineral products...	11,064	15,034.9	13	6,089.6	40.5
24.	Glass...	946	4,842.7	4	3,742.1	77.3
25.	Fabricated metal products...	22,720	23,568.1	10	5,892.3	25.0
26.	Metal cans...	138	3,966.9	4	3,742.8	94.4
27.	Machinery...	22,168	22,518.4	9	3,300.5	14.7
28.	Farm, construction...machinery	2,925	15,097.6	7	6,670.3	44.2
29.	Office...computing...machines	556	24,805.7	11	21,463.1	86.5
30.	Electrical machinery...	4,664	20,649.7	8	12,711.6	61.6
31.	Household appliances	457	5,049.9	7	4,359.5	86.3
32.	Radio...communication equipment	5,741	25,909.1	14	19,967.1	77.1
33.	Scientific...control...devices ...measuring	1,612	5,199.0	2	2,454.0	47.2
34.	Photographic equipment	633	4,145.3	2	3,915.1	94.4
35.	Motor vehicles...	2,392	57,913.8	17	44,561.3	76.9
36.	Aircraft...	815	24,204.7	10	12,783.2	52.8
37.	Ship...building...	1,015	2,916.7	0	0.0	0.0
38.	Railroad equipment...	1,345	6,317.7	4	2,133.0	33.8
39.	Other and miscellaneous manufacturing	11,678	9,694.8	5	1,950.9	20.1
40.	Rail transportation	18,132	43,421.8	21	32,347.5	74.5
41.	Transit	9,073	4,286.7	0	0.0	0.0
42.	Motor transportation	27,452	13,427.7	5	3,580.6	26.7
43.	Water transportation	6,385	6,482.6	3	1,110.1	17.1
44.	Air transportation	3,428	16,595.8	12	12,199.2	73.5
45.	Electric, gas...sanitary...	8,235	137,168.0	106	120,891.8	88.1
46.	Telephone, telegraph...services...	3,453	80,044.5	11	69,014.0	86.2
47.	Radio and TV broadcasting	3,923	5,278.5	2	1,326.2	25.1
48.	Wholesale trade	168,150	90,917.7	1	318.3	0.4
49.	Retail trade...	320,656	68,136.0	7	3,550.3	5.4
50.	General merchandise...	22,853	38,859.6	20	24,490.9	63.0
51.	Food stores	27,005	12,970.1	10	5,193.6	40.0
52.	Motion pictures...	10,061	6,424.2	5	1,946.8	30.3
53.	Services...	277,719	55,801.6	12	4,952.3	8.9
54.	Real estate...	267,399	92,066.1	6	2,031.2	2.2
55.	Nature of business not allocable	21,438	847.1	0	0.0	0.0
56.	All industries other than finance and insurance	1,592,193	$1,410,510.9	559	$707,194.8	50.1%

Sources: (All corporations) U.S. Internal Revenue Service, *Statistics of Income—1971, Corporation Income Tax Returns; Corporation Source Book, Statistics of Income, 1971;* (559 Largest Corporations) Exhibit 1.

The presence of the Largest Corporations among the Industry Categories; summary

The aggregate "presence" of our 559 Largest Corporations, as measured by reported values of assets, was over $700 billion. This represented more than one-half of the total reported value of all nonfinancial corporate assets. As we shall put it, the aggregate "presence index" of these largest units among all nonfinancial corporations (which came to something over 50 percent) indicates that something over half of the value of all reported nonfinancial corporate assets were of kinds held by our 559 Largest Corporations.*

The overall "presence index" of The 200 Largest among the 1,600,000 nonfinancial corporations of all sorts came to about 38 percent. Put another way, about 40 percent of the reported total

---

*In the interest of clarity, it may be useful to restate what "presence indexes" mean. Whether for a particular Industry Category or group of industries or even for the corporate community overall, a presence index indicates the percentage of the *value* of assets, in a *system* of corporations of different but interrelated corporations, that are of kinds held by corporations of given size. In cases of corporations among The 200 Largest, the index shows the percentage, if any, of the total value of corporate assets that is of sorts held by corporations with assets valued at upwards from $900 million. In the cases of The 359, the index measures the relative amount, if any, of the total value of corporate assets that is of sorts held by corporations reporting assets in the bracket from $250 million to $900 million.

These index do *not* measure "market share" or anything like it. *Very large* corporations, at any given time, are likely to be actually present, individually, to widely varying degrees among several or many "markets" for very particular products, none or few of which, at most, may be served by even somewhat smaller, let alone much smaller, corporations.

These indexes measure the relative presence of large corporations in *complex industry systems* that comprise many corporations of very different kinds and of very different sizes, that may produce very different products in very different ways for very different users, both outside the particular system as well as within.

It is symbiotic mutual dependence among *different* kinds of entities in a system that characterizes the relationships between *large* and *small* corporations, not competition among *like* kinds.

For the purpose of trying to discern broad patterns, as distinct from fine-tuned observations, a very rough assumption is made in the following pages to the effect that, although the *specific* sorts of assets held by The 200 and by The 359 may, and in some cases certainly do, differ significantly in *kind,* they have much more in common than they do with the assets of smaller and small firms. Accordingly, despite the more rigorous hypothesis expressed in the subsection "Industry profiles of the distribution of The 200 and The 359" in Chapter 5, it is tacitly and generally assumed in the following pages and exhibits that the assets of The 200 and of The 359 are sufficiently "similar," or at least "similar" in their *differences* from small companies in their respective Industry Categories; that their presence indexes may be added in order to obtain an inclusive index that measures the relative total presence of The 559 as compared to all other corporations. What that summed percentage means is that, overall, about 50 percent of all nonfinancial corporate assets were of *kinds* held by very large corporations as compared to assets held, commonly, or even likely to be held by smaller and small corporations.

Among many Industry Categories, this crude assumption is probably sufficiently valid as to result, for present purposes, at least in no great misapprehensions. But in a few instances, such an assumption of at least rough "homogeneity" or "similarity" is surely questionable. In some Industry Categories, there are important qualitative differences as between The 200 and The 359. Examples would be Petroleum; Telephone and telegraph; Office... computing machines; Motor vehicles...; and Aircraft....

It is *probably* true, I think, that although there may be, and probably are, significant differences as between assets of The 200 Largest and those of The Next 359, these differences are less than the differences between them, collectively, and those of the rest of the firms in the given Industry Category.

If conclusions requiring great precision are avoided, a few possible disparities will probably not lead us too far astray.

See also Chapter 6, Note 6.

value of all nonfinancial corporate assets was accounted for by assets of the sorts held by corporations reporting $900 million *and up,* each. Together, their reported assets came to $538 billion.

The overall presence index of The Next 359 Largest Corporations was about 12 percent. These second-tier Largest Companies each held assets reported at anywhere from $250 million up to about $900 million; in total, they reported assets of $169 billion.

The combined overall presence index of The 559 Largest Corporations stood at over 50 percent. As mentioned on several occasions and shown, in Exhibit 31 most dramatically, these few companies, with assets ranging up from $250 million, held over half of the reported assets of all nonfinancial corporations.

Exhibits 37, 38, and 39, drawing upon the detailed data of Exhibits 34-36, summarize significant occurrence and relative presence data of The 200 Largest, The Next 359, and The 559 Largest Nonfinancial Corporations of 1971.

EXHIBIT 37
Occurrence and relative presence of The 200 Largest Nonfinancial Corporations among groups of Industry Categories: 1971

	Number of Industry Categories	Number of The 200	Assets held ($ billions)	Presence indexes, The 200*
Utilities and regulated industries	8*	71	$197.5	64.4%
Integrated industries	4	43	144.0	68.2
Other industries with 7 or more of The 200	5	42†	113.5	61.2
Other industries with 4 to 6 of The 200	3	13	19.9	57.5
Other industries with 1 to 3 of The 200	19	32†	63.4	33.9
Industries with *none* of The 200‡	19	–	–	–
Totals	55‡	200	$538.2	38.2%

* Includes three utilities and regulated industries in which the presence of The 200 was zero: Transit, Water transportation, and Radio and TV broadcasting.
† Includes Western Electric, the manufacturing subsidiary of American Telephone & Telegraph.
‡ Includes "Not allocable."

Presence of The 200 Largest Corporations, 1971

Of The 200 Largest companies, 71 occurred among the eight Utilities and other regulated industries. Their assets of $197.5 billion accounted for 64.4 percent of the reported assets of these industries. In these industries, the presence of The 200 ranged up to 82.7 percent in Telephone and telegraph, down to zero in Transit and Water transportation.

Forty-three of The 200 occurred in the four characteristically integrated industries; their $144 billion of assets accounted for something over two-thirds of the total value of assets in these key industries. The relative presence of The 200, as shown in Exhibit 34, stood at 86.8 percent in Petroleum (oil and gas, that is); 64.5 percent in Iron and steel and lower concentrations of something under 40 percent in Nonferrous metals and Lumber and wood products (including paper and paper products).

In each of five other industries, clusters of 7 or more of The 200 occurred. These industries included Chemicals, Computers, Motor vehicles, Aircraft, and General merchandise. Together, the 42 companies concerned held assets reported at $113.5 billion. As has been observed on several occasions heretofore, such sizable clusters suggest the existence of underlying objective factors that foster or at least permit the growth of very large companies; the very natures of the specific industries carry suggestions as to what some of these factors are. The relative presence of these groups of companies ranged up from 49.6 percent in the case of Aircraft to 80.5 percent in Office and accounting machines and computers.

Altogether, these 156 companies of The 200, occurring in 17 Industry Categories, held by far the lion's share of the assets, $455 billion, out of the total of $538 billion held by our largest companies (see also Exhibit 17). Their presence among the 17 Industry Categories averaged over 60 percent.

In three other industries, 13 very large companies occurred in smaller but still notable clusters of 4 to 6: Tobacco, Pharmaceuticals, and Rubber and tires. In two of these, Tobacco and Rubber, the relative presence of the largest companies stood at 81 percent and 70 percent. In these 13 industries—tires and tobacco aside—forces operating toward very large size have not—as yet—been as powerful as in industries where the relative presence of very large corporations in more numerous and larger clusters was more remarkable.

In 19 other industries, 32 of the companies occurred, either individually or in clusters of two or three. In some of these Industry Categories, as in Soaps and cleaners and Photographic equipment, single companies stood out. The largest soap company had a relative presence of about 37 percent; that of the largest photographic company stood at almost 80 percent. In others, pairs of companies vied for prominence: Metal cans and Electrical machinery. The two largest can companies accounted for a combined presence index of 77 percent; the largest electrical equipment companies, about 50 percent.

To wind up, none of The 200 occurred in 19 other Industry Categories, and their relative presence, of course, was zero.

Overall, the presence index of The 200 among all Industry Categories stood at 38 percent. But, as documented in Exhibit 17, their numbers and masses were clustered within a very special list of industries.

Presence of The Next 359 Largest Corporations, 1971

The Next 359 Largest Nonfinancial Corporations were much smaller than The 200, both individually and in total. They ranged in size from $250 million to about $900 million, averaging about $470 million as compared to the average of almost $2.7 billion for The 200. In total, their assets came to about $169 billion, as compared to $538 billion for The 200. Their overall presence index among all nonfinancial corporations, much lower than that of The 200, stood at 12 percent. Nevertheless, the aggregate presence of The 359 did represent roughly one-eighth of the value of the reported assets of *all* nonfinancial corporations.

Summary data relating to occurrence and relative presence of The 359 Next Largest appear in Exhibit 38.

The distribution of the numbers and the asset masses of The 359, as we shall see, is a bit more complex than that of The 200. For that reason, the relative presence of The 359 in each of the several industries is calculated on two bases: first, in relation to the assets of *all* corporations, including The 200 that may be present, if any; second, among the assets of corporations remaining after the exclusion of those of The 200.

The Next 359 were more widely dispersed, both as to numbers and asset masses, among the Industry Categories than were The 200.

EXHIBIT 38
Occurrence and relative presence of The Next 359 Largest Nonfinancial Corporations among groups of Industry Categories: 1971

	Number of Industry Categories	Number of The 359	Assets held ($ billions)	Presence index among all corporations other than The 200*	Presence index among all corporations*
Utilities and regulated industries	8†	89	$43.0	39.4%	14.0%
Integrated industries	4	41	20.4	30.4	9.7
Other industries with 7 or more of The 359	13	146‡	68.0	26.1	18.4
Other industries with 4 to 6 of The 359	12	60	26.2	11.2	9.6
Other industries with 1 to 3 of The 359	13	24	11.3	6.4	5.2
Industries with *none* of The 359 §	6	0	–	0.0	0.0
Totals	55	359	$169.0	19.4%	12.0%

* See text for explanation.
† Includes Transit, in which none of The 359 occurred.
‡ Includes electronics and communications subsidiaries of GTE counted as one firm, not included in the total number; see Appendix A, Note 54.
§ Includes "Not allocable."

With one exception, Rubber and tires, they were to be found in each of the industries where occurred representatives of The 200. In addition, members of The 359 showed up in 13 other Industry Categories where none of The 200 had appeared. Whereas 57 percent of the number and 63 percent of the assets of The 200 appeared in the eight utilities and other regulated industries and the four integrated industries, only 36 percent of The 359 did so, and they held only 38 percent of the aggregate asset value of The 359. (See Exhibits 21 and 38.)

In contrast to The 200, clusters of 7 or more of The 359 occurred in 13 Industry Categories rather than in just 5. In these Industry Categories occurred 276 of The 359, holding 40 percent of their assets. And 60 of The Next 359 companies occurred in clusters of 4 to 6 in 12 industries, as compared to 13 companies in 3 industries for The 200.

In consequence of that more widespread dispersion of The 359, there were only 13 industries in which occurred small clusters of them, numbering 1 to 3, and these held but 6.7 percent of their assets. As to the small clusters of The 200, these occurred in 19 industries, containing 32 of the very largest corporations and these held 12 percent of the total assets of The 200. (See Exhibits 19 and 37.) These scatterings of The 200, for the most part, represented the "summits" of what were the occurrence and presence in those industries of large companies primarily from the list of The 359.

Overall, The 359 were far overshadowed in sizes and masses, if not in simple numbers, by The 200. And yet, certain industries were far more characterized by the occurrence and presence of the second-tier companies than by the first tier. Of this, we have already seen something in Exhibit 24, in Chapter 5.

The last column of Exhibit 38 displays the presence index among all corporations of The 359 in groups of industries. In the Utilities and regulated industries, this index was 14.0 percent. Added to the index for The 200 occurring in those industries, this brought the total presence of The 559, as shown in Exhibit 39, to 78.4 percent. In the four integrated industries, the overall presence index of The 359 came to 9.7 percent, which, added to the index of The 200, brought the index of The 559 to 77.8 percent.

Among The 200, there were clusters of 7 or more companies in five industries other than the Utilities and integrated industries, where the 42 companies concerned had a combined dollar presence of $113 billion and presence index of over 60 percent. Among The 359, clusters of 7 or more, including 146 corporations, occurred in 13 industries. (Only 3 of these 13 industries were among the 5 in which there were clusters of 7 or more of The 200.) The overall dollar presence of The 359 in these industries, however, came only to $68 billion, and their combined presence index to only 18.4 percent.

The number of clusters of 4 to 6 among The 359 corporations involved was substantially greater than for The 200 (13 against 3), and the numbers of companies in those clusters were much more numerous, 60 as compared to 13. Nevertheless, the combined presence index of The 359 in these clusters came to only 9.6 percent in contrast to the combined presence index of The 200 in their clusters of similar size, which came to 57.5 percent.

What this all means, of course, is that below The 200, there was (a) a substantial increase in the *number* of companies with assets of more than $250 million; (b) a notable decrease in their average *size;* and (c) far less compact clustering in a limited number of industries, or, expressed otherwise, far greater dispersion among the several Industry Categories.

The *industry* profiles of the two groups of companies, The 200 and The 359, were very different.

The *size* profiles also were different. The sizes of individual companies among The 200 ranged in size from $900 million to over $54 billion. Over a dozen had assets valued at more than $5 billion. The size profile of The 359 was contained within the limits of $250 million to $900 million. About 160 held assets of $500 million or more, of which over 20 were among the electric and gas utilities.

One way of trying to observe the pattern of The 359 in their own right is to examine them after the exclusion of, or apart from, the occurrence and presence of The 200. That effort to do so is summarized numerically in the fourth column of Exhibit 38. What these data show is a pattern not dissimilar from that of The 200, albeit on a much reduced scale: in very general terms, the relative presences of The 359 (after giving effect to the exclusion of representatives of The 200), like those of The 200, tended to be greatest among the Utilities and other regulated industries and the characteristically integrated industries. Among utilities and regulated industries, The 200 apart, the relative presence index of The 359 was 39.4 percent. Among the integrated industries, the overall average presence index was a bit over 30 percent. These, of course, as has been mentioned, are industries in which pressures toward, and comparative advantages of, large scale are particularly noticeable.

Then there were notable clusters of The 359 in certain industries: groups of 7 or more in 13 industries (146 companies), and sets of 4 to 6 in another 12 (60 companies). In all of these categories, particularly in the more numerous clusters, there were widespread and *commonly* felt forces making for sizable scale. In the 13 industries with 7 or more of The 359, there were more than 10 companies in 7 of them. The average presence index of The 359 in these 13 industries, exclusive of The 200, was over 26 percent.

What this means is that, setting aside the assets of members of The 200, companies among The 359 held an average of something over a quarter of the assets of all the other corporations in these 13 Industry Categories. The most notable relative presence of The 359 on this basis was in Pharmaceuticals, where, after allowing for the presence of the 4 largest companies, all included among The 200, the 17 next largest companies included among The 359 accounted for over 89 percent of all the rest of the assets of that Industry Category. This is unusual, although, among those industries in which there were clusters of 4 to 6 of The 359, the relative presence of The 359, after removing the presence of The 200, stood at about 69 percent of the remaining assets in Soaps and cleaners and 82 percent in Household appliances.

By and large, however, the relative presence of The 359, although minor compared to that of The 200, was very considerable in a number of industries. But these presences fall off quite rapidly beyond those 25 industries included among the utilities, the integrated industries, and those in which occurred sizable clusters—7 or more—of The 359. This falling off, as with clustering, was associated with general, underlying, and persisting conditions.

Presence of The 559 Largest Corporations, 1971

The occurrence and presence of The 559 Largest Corporations were, of course, the sums of the occurrences and presences of The 200 and The Next 359. Data that summarize the numbers and presence profiles of these corporations appear in Exhibit 39.

As with the two component groups, there were notable clusters of The 559 among the utilities and other regulated industries, among the integrated industries, and among industries in which clusters of numerous companies had appeared.

EXHIBIT 39
Occurrence and relative presence of The 559 Largest Nonfinancial Corporations among groups of Industry Categories: 1971

	Number of Industry Categories	Number of The 559	Assets held ($ billions)	Presence indexes, The 559
Utilities and regulated industries	8*	160	$240.5	78.4%
Integrated industries	4	84	164.4	77.8
Other industries with 7 or more of The 559	19	237‡	238.1	45.2
Other industries with 4 to 6 of The 559	13	65	52.3	28.2
Other industries with 1 to 3 of The 559	7	15	11.9	7.4
Industries with *none* of The 559	4†	—	—	—
Totals	55	559	$707.2	50.1%

* Includes Transit, in which occurred none of The 559.
† Does not include Transit, in which occurred none of The 559.
‡ Includes manufacturing subsidiaries of American Telephone & Telegraph and General Telephone & Electronics. These are not included in the total of 559.

Among the utilities and other regulated industries, 160 companies (about 30 percent of The 559) had emerged; they held $240.5 billion of assets (34 percent of the aggregate assets of The 559) and rose to an average presence of 78 percent in these eight Industry Categories. The growth of these regulated industries, especially the electric and telephone utilities, over the 40-some years from 1929 are important aspects of the development of American industry in those turbulent decades.

In the four integrated Industry Categories, the presence of The 559 was similarly prominent, averaging almost 78 percent—over 90 percent in oil and gas (Petroleum), and over 80 percent in Iron and steel. The aggregate reported assets of the 84 companies in these four integrated industries stood at $164 billion.

Again, a sizable number of The 559 Largest companies—237 or 42 percent of their number—appeared in industries where sizable clusters of large companies were noteworthy features, as they were in 19 industries other than the utilities and the integrated industries. Together, these 237 companies reported assets at over $238 billion, or about one-third of all of the assets of The 559. The relative presences of these numerous clusters of seven or more large firms ranged down from more than 80 percent in Pharmaceuticals, Office...computing machines, and Household appliances to less than 9 percent in Services and 5.4 percent in Retail trade.

The presence indexes among the several Industry Categories for The 559 Largest Corporations are set forth in Exhibit 40, which shows how these indexes were composed of the respective indexes of The 200 and The 359.

The data of Exhibit 40 reveal, in broad, general terms, an association between (a) tendency for clusters of large corporations to emerge in Industry Categories and (b) their relative presence in those industries. In simple terms, this means that where very large corporations are more *numerous,* their collective *mass* tended to be relatively larger, compared to smaller corporations.

As mentioned before, this assertion of association might appear to have a certain circularity about it: if there are *more,* certainly their relative *mass,* compared to others, must be greater? Not necessarily.

Consider the Pharmaceutical industry: it contained 21 of The 559 Largest companies. Their combined relative mass, to be sure, stood at almost 90 percent. A rather obvious, self-defining association? Yes. And, no. The matter is not so simple. It was quite a different matter in other industries. Consider further: Food...contained 19 of the large companies, whose collective presence was only 46 percent; Fabricated metal products contained 10 of the large companies, but their relative presence was no greater than 25 percent; Retail trade contained 7, and their presence index came to only 5.4 per-

EXHIBIT 40
Relative presence in Industry Categories of clusters of The 559, and of The 200 and The
359 Next Largest Corporations: 1971

Industry Categories	Presence index, The 559 Largest Corporations	Presence index, The 200 Largest Corporations	Presence index, The Next 359 Largest Corporations
Part 1.			
Utilities, regulated industries			
Electric, gas,...	88.1%	66.9%	21.2%
Telephone, telegraph...	86.2	82.8	3.5
Rail transportation	74.5	63.8	10.8
Air transportation	73.5	55.4	18.1
Motor transportation	26.7	20.1	6.7
Radio and TV...	25.1	–	25.1
Water transportation	17.1	–	17.1
Transit	0.0	0.0	0.0
Totals, utilities and regulated industries	79.5%	65.3%	14.2%
Integrated industries			
Petroleum	86.4%	82.0%	4.4%
Iron and steel	82.4	64.5	17.9
Nonferrous metals	55.4	39.6	15.8
Lumber...wood...paper	49.8	35.8	17.8
Totals, integrated industries	75.4%	66.0%	9.4%
Part 2.			
Other industries with 7 or more of The 559 Largest Corporations			
Pharmaceuticals...	87.8%	31.5%	56.3%
Office...computing machines	86.5	80.5	6.0
Household appliances	86.3	33.1	53.3
Radio...communication equipment	77.1	56.5	20.5
Motor vehicles	76.9	69.6	7.3
Chemicals...	76.5	54.7	21.8
General merchandise	63.0	50.0	13.1
Electrical machinery	61.6	50.5	11.1
Aircraft...	52.8	49.6	3.2
Food...	45.6	13.1	32.5
Farm, construction machinery	44.2	21.7	22.5
Nonmetallic mineral products	40.5	–	40.5
Foodstores	40.0	15.0	25.1
Textiles	30.1	9.1	21.0
Fabricated metal products	25.0	–	20.0
Machinery	14.7	–	14.7
Printing and publishing	12.9	–	12.9
Services	8.9	–	8.9
Retail trade	5.4	2.4	3.0
Totals, industries with 7 or more of The 559	45.4%	30.0%	15.4%
Part 3.			
Industries with 4 to 6 of The 559 Largest Corporations			
Metal cans	94.4%	77.2%	17.1%
Tobacco	88.6	81.1	7.5
Dairy...	86.1	57.0	29.0
Soaps, cleaners	79.6	36.7	42.9
Glass	77.3	55.9	21.4
Rubber and tires	70.0	70.0	–
Meat	61.3	48.0	13.2
Alcoholic beverages	36.8	10.2	26.6
Railroad equipment	33.8	–	33.8
Motion pictures	30.3	–	30.3
Apparel	21.7	8.2	13.5
Other and miscellaneous manufacturing	20.1	–	20.1
Real estate	2.2	–	2.2
Totals, industries with 4 to 6 of The 559	28.2%	17.7%	10.5%

EXHIBIT 40 *(continued)*

Industry Categories	Presence index, The 559 Largest Corporations	Presence index, The 200 Largest Corporations	Presence index, The Next 359 Largest Corporations
Part 4.			
Industries with 1 to 3 of The 559 Largest Corporations			
Photographic equipment	94.5%	79.6%	14.9%
Scientific . . . control . . . devices	47.2	42.0	5.2
Soft drinks	41.6	23.8	17.8
Coal	37.0	–	37.0
Leather	18.3	–	18.3
Construction	2.5	–	2.5
Wholesale trade	0.4	–	0.4
Totals, industries with 1 to 3 of The 559	7.6%	4.2%	3.4%
Totals, industries with 1 or more of The 559	50.1%	38.2%	11.9%
Part 5.			
Industries with *none* of The 559 Largest Corporations			
Agriculture	–	–	–
Furniture	–	–	–
Ship . . . building	–	–	–
Transit	–	–	–
Nature of business not allocable	–	–	–
Totals, industries with *none* of The 559	–	–	–

cent. On quite the other side of things, only four companies in Metal cans had a presence index of 94 percent; and only two companies in Photographic equipment had a combined presence of 96 percent.

Industry systems do have different "profiles" when the companies are arranged according to size. More on this in Chapter 8.

Numbers and relative presence, industry by industry, were not *necessarily* associated. But, *statistically,* in broad perspective, there *was* an association, as shown in Table 16. And the basis of this association ran in this wise: forces and inducements operating to foster and admit of large scale functioned with varying strength from one Industry Category to another. No doubt, these forces had to do with such basics as comparative advantage, currently available technology, and present stages of industries in their respective life-cycles.

TABLE 16
Clusters and presence indexes of Largest Companies

Clusters of the largest companies*	Number of Industry Categories	Number of companies	Average presence index
7 or more	19	237†	45.4%
4 to 6	13	65	28.2
1 to 3	7	15	7.6

*Excludes Utilities . . . , etc.

†Includes manufacturing subsidiaries of American Telephone & Telegraph and General Telephone & Electronics.

Where such tendencies were strong and ubiquitous, numbers of large corporations emerged, and their masses attained prominence; where less strong or absent, fewer or no large corporations emerged, and the mass of the productive assets in the industry system was in the hands of smaller or small corporations.

Exceptions granted—as illustrated in cases just cited—there was a broad-brush association between the emergence in industries of *numbers* of large corporations and their attainment of relatively important *presence*.

The rise of large corporations, granted interventions of individuals, was basically a systemic phenomenon whose etiology lay in the advance of the continuing Industrial Revolution in Modern America.

An aside on understanding economic values in large numbers

It is not easy to comprehend the meaning nor the magnitude of the capital investments in these, some of our large, indispensable industries, several of them largely "peopled" by *very* big corporations. The $700 billion of assets of The 559 Largest corporations represented investments that worked out to over $3,000 for every man, woman, and child in America.

One way of trying to grasp the magnitudes involved is to line up these figures with those of public expenditures.

In 1971, federal government outlays totaled $220 billion, of which $75 billion, for example, went for national defense, $76 billion for health, labor, and welfare (of which $68 billion went for "social security and special welfare services"), and $146 billion went for interest payments on the federal debt. State expenditures in 1971 amounted to $149 billion, of which $58 billion went for education, $48 billion for health, labor, and welfare, and $17 billion for highways.

It does put matters into some sort of perspective to realize that the $220 billion of expenditures of the federal government for a *single* year—1971—was about the same as the *total accumulated net investment of* our *138 large companies* in *railroads, electric utilities,* and *telephone and telegraph, combined, built up over more than 100 years!* Or that our national defense budget of $75 billion for the *one* year 1971 was a figure larger than the *combined* asset values built up, over decades, by our 63 largest companies in Iron and steel, Nonferrous metals, and Chemicals. Or that the $48 billion of state expenditures on health, labor, and welfare for the year of 1971 was *more* than the combined assets, built up over the years from original capitalization, reinvestment of earnings, and from additions of capital from borrowings and issues of new securities, of the 17 largest corporations in the industry system of Motor vehicles, or of the 55 largest companies in five other important Industry categories: Textiles..., Fabricated metals..., Farm, construction machinery..., Household appliances..., Aircraft..., and Air transportation.

Considerations aside as to international prudence, humanitarian inclinations and constraints, and prevailing consensus as to national priorities, the magnitudes of such expenditures—on what, from a strictly economic point of view partake of the nature of nonproductive capital outlays and current consumption expenditures—must operate as a "drag" on economic *development*. Some portions of those expenditures allocated to formation of *productive* new *capital* outlays could have significant consequences for making available more, and more productive jobs, increasing productivity, and *increasing*—as distinguished from redistributing—total economic welfare.

One question implicit in these figures may not be so much, "How do we cut back on these particular expenditures?" but "How do we accelerate capital formation?"

More of this in a later chapter.

Some important caveats

Before passing on to other matters, two important *caveats* should be recorded. Presence indexes and other measures, such as traditional concentration ratios depend very much upon how Industry Categories, industries, markets, and such-like are defined. The more specific and narrow the definition, the higher will be the presence index or concentration ratio, or whatever, of any given group of companies.

A good example is Metal cans. In the collection of Industry Categories of this study, four companies are listed under that industry and are shown as having a relative presence index of 94.4 percent. Conceivably, these companies might have been thrown in with the Industry Category labeled Fabricated metal products. If so, a whole Industry Category would have disappeared; the number of companies in Fabricated metal products would have been increased from 10 to 14; the assets of that reconstituted Industry Category would have increased from $5.9 billion to $9.6 billion; and the two presence indexes of The 559 therein would have been recomputed from 25 percent for Fabricated metals and 94.4 percent for Metal cans to a single new index of 41.2 percent.

There can be little doubt that the presence index of large firms in Metal cans was *high;* and that it appeared to be higher, for instance, than in Railroad equipment. Nevertheless, if we were so moved, it is quite likely that we could, with some reason, define one or more particular sectors of Railroad equipment as separate industries, perhaps, even as Industry Categories for which the presence index might well be over 90 percent. Contrariwise, as suggested earlier, if we lumped Metal cans together with all sorts of other, and competing types of containers, of whatever materials, it is certain that the overall presence index of the firms among The 559 would be far less than 90 percent.*

The purpose of this *caveat* is not to apologize for this, nor, necessarily, to criticize any other system of defining industries and calculating presence indexes and the like. It is simply to serve as reminder that the taxonomy of industries is pretty elusive—even crude—and that data and ratios based upon them are to be used and interpreted with the reserve called for by objective inquiry into important matters.

A related *caveat* is this: presence indexes are not measures of monopoly or oligopoly, or any such. Some economists have hypothesized that the *intensity,* perhaps even the *kinds,* of competition in industries—not to talk of their capability for innovation, not to mention their "evolution" and development—are determined by their structure, that is, the numbers, concentration ratios, and such, of large firms. This is a big and red-hot topic in its own right. But, retrospective search back over the decades in quest of explanation of evolution of our industry systems must lead to dissatisfaction with simple, mechanistic, short-run models of industries and markets as commonly conceived. Explanation of evolution of industry systems and of individual firms—their inputs, their outputs, their conversion processes, the inner workings of human decision-making and managerial control of large complex undertakings, their changing niches in the growing and developing scheme of things—must surely take into account their several stages of unfolding and growth and their mutually affecting relationships with the dynamic, organic, evolving ecosystem that is America.

* * * * *

We now proceed to consider more systematically some relationships between occurrence, presence, and scale of corporations.

*In fact, since 1971, there has been some movement of can companies into other forms of containers, such as folding cartons. And other forms of containers, such as glass, are now competing successfully with cans in the packaging of fruits, vegetables, and soups.

1. See Footnote 7 to Chapter 5.

For those with an interest in the matter, an analysis of the principal differences between The 559 corporations that form the basis of this study and the 615 largest corporations included in the Internal Revenue Service corporate data for 1971 is summarized in the following table:

Analysis, principal apparent reported net differences between IRS and published data of The 615 Largest Corporations and The 559 Largest Publicly held Corporations*

		Assets ($ millions)			Numbers of firms		
Industry Category		The 615	The 559	The 615 greater than The 559	The 615	The 559	The 615 greater than The 559
1.	Iron and steel	–	–	†	16	19	–(3)
3.	Nonferrous metals	$ 26,549	$ 17,760	$ 8,789	–	–	§
5.	Petroleum	102,623	105,846	–(3,223)	34	30	4
6.	Construction	–	–	†	6	3	3
9.	Food	–	–	†	24	19	5
10.	Alcoholic beverages	5,444	3,355	2,089	–	–	§
14.	Apparel.	–	–	†	2	5	–(3)
15.	Lumber	20,037	17,386	2,651	–	–	§
17.	Printing and publishing	5,405	2,702	2,703	14	7	7
18.	Chemicals	–	–	†	32	26	6
19.	Pharmaceuticals	9,899	12,058	–(2,159)	–	–	§
23.	Nonmetallic products	3,953	6,090	–(2,137)	9	13	–(4)
25.	Fabricated metal products	–	–	†	7	10	–(3)
27.	Machinery.	6,538	3,301	3,237	–	–	§
28.	Farm, construction . . . machinery. .	9,496	6,670	2,826	–	–	§
30.	Electrical machinery	–	–	†	4	8	–(4)
35.	Motor vehicles	53,088	44,561	8,527	14	17	–(3)
36.	Aircraft	21,987	12,783	9,204	16	10	6
38.	Railroad equipment	4,283	2,133	2,150	–	–	§
40.	Railroad transportation	36,466	32,348	4,118	–	–	§
41.	Transit	2,757	–	2,757	–	–	§
45.	Electric, gas, sanitary	123,431	120,892	2,539	–	–	§
46.	Telephone and telegraph	76,508	69,014	7,494	–	–	§
48.	Wholesale trade	12,571	318	12,253	22	1	21
49.	Retail trade	1,465	3,550	–(2,085)	–	–	–
50.	Retail merchandise	27,209	24,491	2,718	3	7	–(4)
54.	Real estate	–	–	†	11	6	5
	(Other, total, and net)	22,862	221,937	925‡	401	380	21
	Totals and net differences	$772,571	$707,195	$65,376	615	559 ‖	56 ‖

*"Principal differences" defined arbitrarily as greater than $2 billion and/or three firms.
†Difference less than $2 billion.
‡Net difference.
§Difference less than three firms.
‖Excludes manufacturing subsidiaries of two telephone companies.

Of the net difference of 56 companies between the list of The 559 Largest (publicly held) nonfinancial corporations of 1971 and the 615 largest corporations reported by the IRS, the principal difference was 21 companies located in Wholesale trade. This Industry Category as reported by the IRS probably included large privately-held ordinary "wholesalers" of hardware, pharmaceuticals, etc. These companies may also include separately reporting sales and distribution subsidiaries of large manufacturing companies, say in Motor vehicles and Petroleum, and, perhaps, also in Food. Arguably, these should be included, were the data available, in the latter Industry Categories of the parent firms.

Some of the larger numbers of certain industries, such as Nonferrous metals and Chemicals companies, reported by the IRS, may well be wholly owned U.S. subsidiaries of non-U.S. corporations, as might well be the case also in Petroleum and Food.

The greatest difference in values of assets is also to be seen in Wholesale trade. This is followed by the greater reported assets reported by the IRS for Nonferrous metals and Motor vehicles.

Some of the differences in the two lists are probably accounted for by accounting differences in corporate reporting to the Treasury and corporate disclosures to the public. Other differences are likely to be due to differences in classifying corporations by Industry Category.

Despite energetic efforts and the general usefulness of secondary sources, it is certain that some corporations were not "discovered" and therefore not included in Exhibit 1 and other exhibits and tables based upon it.

Other possible causes of differences have already been touched upon. See also Chapter 5, Note 7.

The net difference of the 56 more companies included among The 615 can be summarized thus:

	The 559	The 615
Industry differences greater than three companies	24	57
42 other Industry Categories with differences of less than three companies	—	25*
Net differences in number of companies		56†

*Includes manufacturing subsidiaries of telephone companies.
†Excludes those companies.

The *net* difference of the $65 billion or more reported assets of The 615 was composed as follows:

	$ billions	
	The 559	The 615
Industry differences greater than $2 billion	$9.6	$74.2
38 other Industry Categories (net)	—	0.9
Net difference in apparent asset values	—	$65.4

8

The modern corporation in modern America; the association of occurrence, presence, and scale

A major *leitmotiv* of the book is this: the growth and distribution of large corporations throughout the structure of American industry has been, and is, an integral aspect of the expansion and transformation of the whole American System over the past century. The efflorescence of the community of large—*very* large—corporations was not an aberration; not an anomaly; not an "-oma" of something gone wrong in the body socio-politico-economic. The growth of large corporations, when, and where, and how large they grew, were of the very essence of the nation's evolution from a modest, agrarian, rural, insular country into a massive, urban, industrial one and an economic and technological world power.

Certain is that the Largest Corporations are particularly numerous and loom especially large among certain industries. Just as we have needed, and fortunately have had, men—and women—to match our towering mountains and reaching, fruited plains, we have needed and have had organizations in scale to the tasks of providing infrastructure to our whole community of productive organizations and for providing important fractions of needed daily physical support of our 220 million people, their almost 80 million households, and their millions of places of employment and other forms of productive activity.

It is no great simplification, as we shall show, to perceive some industries as characterized by Big Business and others as typified by "small." These differences are part of the *order* in which, for better or worse, we now live.

The large corporations of today, as has been stated several times, are not mere scale-ups of small corporations. With exceptions of a few conglomerates, our very large companies are not mere aggregations—combinations or consolidations—of small or smaller corporations stuck together with a glue of common ownership.[1] The large and very large modern corporations, as we know them now, fit into the encompassing ecological system of American life in their own very special niches, doing their own special things, living in symbiotic relationships within, and with, systems of other corporations of all kinds and sizes. Small firms are not merely scale-downs of large companies, performing the same functions, on a reduced scale, but after their own miniature fashion. They too, have their own special niche and interrelationships in the web of American productive life.

Under some circumstances and in some productive systems, large corporations can and do flourish. Under others, they do not. The same is true of small enterprises. As ecologists and others interested in our natural environment can understand, the very conditions that permit and foster the growth of small corporations may—and generally do—inhibit the growth of larger ones. And, not surprisingly, the reverse is true: different habitats are congenial to different forms of life. And different forms of corporate life flourish in different parts of the American productive system.

That is how things are.

Modern America is an integrated political, social, and economic—physical—*whole*. One nation indivisible. This has become a material *fact*—no mere ideological rhetoric, canted daily by children. That is no accident. Its wholeness is made possible—literally made possible—by our vast networks of transportation and communication, and by enormous flows across our republic of goods, services, energy, people, ideas, and capital that move and are transmitted through vast productive systems, and among the several systems that, collectively, are the productive apparatus of the American people.

Large corporations are integral and indispensable elements in that apparatus.

The existence and the future of our large corporations, integral as they are to modern American life, pose great new questions of public and corporate policy. These will rank high on America's agenda for years to come.

More of that later.

The occurrence and distribution of large corporations among industry systems are, essentially, consequences of basic, persistent factors. The very large corporations occur in—and are absent from—various Industry Categories pretty much according to where economies, technology, phases of industry life-cycles, and processes of national development would indicate. Occurrence of large corporations, clusterings of their *numbers* in industry systems, are associated with their *relative presence,* the fraction of total asset masses present in those systems held by those companies. Broadly speaking, this pattern is to be observed in American industry: the greater the numbers of the largest companies occurring in an industry system, the larger their relative presence. And vice versa.

Of this we have seen clear indications in the data presented so far.

In addition, we have seen intimations that the *occurrence* of large corporations and their *relative presence* in industry systems are also associated with corporate *size.*

Two collections of data remain to be examined that support further the observation that the emergence and locations of our biggest companies in the private sector are products of observable order and understandable reason deep within the American system and its dynamics.

First, in this chapter, we shall look at a collection of data relating to varying *sizes* of corporations—both larger and smaller—in the several industry systems. Second, in the next two chapters, we shall examine the emergence and growth of large corporations over the past 40 years and the relationships of that development to growth—and change—of the American business community and the System of which it is part.

OCCURRENCE, PRESENCE, AND SCALE OF LARGE CORPORATIONS: SUMMARY

In the pages and exhibits of this chapter, data are presented that indicate that not just two, but three, measures relating to the positioning and scale of large corporations in the several industry systems tend, all, to be associated: (*a*) their numbers; (*b*) their relative presence; and (*c*) their size. Where (*a*) large corporations are more numerous and (*b*) their relative presence is more pronounced, (*c*) they tend also to be larger than the large corporations in other Industry Categories. Not only that: the *other* corporations—other than the largest, that is—in those same Industry Categories tend to be larger than the "other" corporations in those Industry Categories where the Largest Corporations are less numerous, their relative presence lower, and *their* sizes smaller. Relative "bigness" or "smallness" of the *largest* firms tends to be associated with relative bigness or smallness of "other" firms.

What this patterning suggests is this: underlying, basic conditions in the several Industry systems have tended, in varying degrees (and in varying degrees at different times) to permit or encourage the emergence of numbers of larger companies, their attainment of relative importance in those industry systems, as measured by relative mass, and their growth to large and very large size.

These basics have included such factors as objective economies of scale in production, economies of integration, economies of multi-plant, multiproduct operations, and benefits from such other matters as easier access to significant inputs, and economies of scale in the several processes of marketing and financing and in the development and application of managerial and technical skills. In some instances, in varying degrees, and at different times, public policy, through legislation, executive regulation, and judicial opinions and decisions, have also fostered growth in some industries: federal, state, and local tax advantages; protective tariffs; legality of certain kinds of monopolies and mergers, but not of others. Sometimes, the pressures and incentives stemming from public sources were deliberate; sometimes they were side effects of other measures; sometimes they were quite inadvertent, and even unnoticed.

The more pronounced—on a net basis—these embedded conditions in various industries and sectors have been, the more pronounced has been the lifting up of large companies.

The patterning and association—and their origins and impacts—have not been confined just to the biggest companies. They have extended to other and smaller companies as well.

In some industry systems, pressures and opportunities did not exist similar to those that gave rise to bigness elsewhere; or, if they did, worked with no great strength in the contexts of other factors relevant to the structure, technologies, and development of those industries. In these Industry Categories, few, if any, of the largest companies have appeared. Their relative presence is low, or lacking. The sizes of corporations in such industries—even of such "large" ones as there may be—have been comparatively small. Detailed data that show the patterned association of numbers, relative presence, and size are displayed in Exhibits 44, 45, and 46, which are to be found toward the end of this chapter. These figures are summarized for the more general reader in Exhibits 41, 42, and 43.

A metaphor may illustrate the point of the association of numbers, relative presence, and size of corporations: our biggest corporations, these soaring elevations on the industry landscape, are not isolated monoliths, sprung up in awesome, freestanding solitude from surrounding flatlands, like the famous Ship Rock near the "Four Corners" of Arizona, Utah, Colorado, and New Mexico. Instead, they are but the highest of numerous peaks pushed up in ranging massifs by systems of forces deep underneath. In these configurations, the relatively lower heights may be enormous, even though they be up-staged by the very tallest, the way lesser crests of the Colorado Rockies—many of them over 13,000 or even 14,000 feet—are over-shadowed by Mt. Elbert, the very highest. Even the smaller of those lesser peaks would tower over the highest points of the Great Smokies—to say nothing of the Ozarks—which arose with few truly outstanding prominences, in their own, but lower and smaller masses.

Where the pinnacles are *higher,* other peaks are also *more numerous.* Even secondary mounts are lifted higher than elsewhere. Their total masses are far greater than those of lesser systems. Where the summits are lower, their numbers are fewer, the surrounding hills are lower in proportion, and their aggregate masses are smaller in comparison.

The "profiles" of ranges are very different. Some rise abruptly above low-lying areas, like the Andes above the Peruvian deserts to the west and the vast flat jungles of the Amazon to the east. Some rise almost as abruptly from flat but high plains, like the Rampart range, with its Pike's Peak, above the stretching distances of the altiplano of eastern Colorado. Some systems are low and rounded, ill-defined rolling uplands, like western ridges of the Appalachians.

In all these configurations, whatever their differences, the high and higher points are parts of *systems.* High, medium, and lower points were all individual manifestations of the same basics that gave rise to the whole. The highest "elevations" in industry systems, the sorts of things we are particularly interested in, are not solitary eruptions springing up randomly or idiosyncratically from nowhere, or merely from some curious particularity.

OCCURRENCE AND PRESENCE OF THE LARGEST COMPANIES AND THE SCALE OF CORPORATIONS IN INDUSTRY CATEGORIES

This chapter, let it be conceded, is heavy laden with statistics. A primary purpose is to give factual documentation to some important propositions about the structures of American industry. To ease the reader's burden, the underlying data have been summarized in a few exhibits. The statistical underpinnings are also given, set apart, at the end of this chapter, for those who may find them interesting.

The general reader's attention will be directed toward the limited number of exhibits that put together the essence. He and others may prowl about the statistical backup if and as they please.

First, we shall look at the four-way relationships among occurrence, presence, size of The 200 Largest Corporations, and size of other corporations. These data, in Exhibit 41, summarize the considerable detail of Exhibit 44, which is to be found, along with other basic data, toward the end of the chapter.[2]

So, now, turning to the data, we look, first, at the association of the occurrence, presence, and scale of The 200 Largest Corporations in the several Industry Categories, together with the association of occurrence and presence with sizes of both the largest and "other" corporations. We then look at data relating to The 359 Next Largest Companies. Finally, we look at patterns of association relating to The 559 Largest Corporations combined.

The association of occurrence, presence, and scale
of The 200 Largest Corporations

In Exhibits 41 and 44, the several Industry Categories have been grouped in five clusters according to the relative presence in them of The 200 Largest Corporations. In 11 Industry Categories, the relative presence of companies included among The 200 was greater than 60 percent. A total of 117 of The 200 occurred in those Industry Categories. In ten Categories, the relative presence in their respective industries of companies among The 200 was in the range of 40 percent to 60 percent. In these ten industry systems, 47 of The 200 Largest companies showed up. And so on. In eight Industry Categories where presence indexes were less than 20 percent, the number of "representatives" of The 200 was only 12 in total. In 19 Industry Categories, as we have seen, there were none of The 200.

As one's eye runs down the columns of Exhibit 41, line by line, corresponding to the decline in the average relative presence of The 200 Largest Corporations, one cannot help observing the concurrent and unbroken declines, both in the occurrence (the numbers) of these large companies *and* in their average size, and in the average sizes of other corporations. The average size of The 200 declined from $3.3 billion, in industries where they were most numerous and their relative presence greatest, down to about $1.2 billion in those industries where—aside from the 19 Industry Categories where none occurred—their numbers were smallest and their relative presence least.

This pattern was set in a context in which the average size of *all* corporations in the several groups of Industry Categories also declined, along with the decline in the occurrence, presence, and size of The 200. These average sizes of *all* corporations declined steadily from $10,376,000 in those Industry Categories in which the presence index of The 200 was 60 percent and more, down to $399,000 in those Industry Categories where the presence of The 200 was zero.

Of course, this latter pattern was weighted by the presence of The 200 in the several groups of industries. And this weighting varied; it was as high as 74.8 percent, in the group of greatest cluster of The 200, down to zero, at the "bottom." In order to make allowance for this fact, the average sizes of firms *other* than The 200 in these several Industry Categories were also calculated, and are shown in the last column of Exhibit 41.

These average sizes of all corporations other than The 200 also fell, rather irregularly, from $2,617,000 to $399,000. This is not an unbroken line, to be sure. Unblemished association is probably too much to ask for in complex human data. But the overall pattern is clear enough, of decline in the size of *other* companies in association with decline in the size of The 200 Largest.

Presence index of The 200 Largest Corporations in Industry Category	Number of Industry Categories	Occurrence (number of The 200 Largest Firms)	Presence index (assets of 200 Largest Firms as percentage of all corporate assets)	Average size of all firms* ($000)	Average size of The 200 Largest Firms ($ millions)	Average size of All Other Firms† ($000)
Greater than 60%. 11		117‡	74.8%	$10,376	$3,304	$2,617
40%-60% 10		47	52.4	3,709	2,124	1,769
20%-40% 7		25	33.9	2,841	1,504	1,879
Zero-20% 8		12	7.8	431	1,180	397
Zero § 19		–	–	399	–	399
55		200	38.2%	$ 886	$2,691	$ 548

*Includes The 200.
†Includes The 359 Next Largest.
‡Includes manufacturing subsidiary of American Telephone & Telegraph.
§Includes "Not allocable."
Source: Exhibit 44.

Of course, it must be remembered that we are talking about averages. We are speaking in broad terms. But as economic data go, the general picture holds: among the several industry systems, there *is* a pattern of association between the average sizes of the *largest* corporations and the average sizes of *other* firms in those same Industry Categories.

The altitudes of the highest peaks in various systems are associated with the heights of the relatively lower prominences in those same systems.

The association of occurrence, presence, and scale of The Next 359 Largest Corporations

We turn now to look at The Next Largest 359 corporations, to determine whether the patterns of association of occurrence, presence, and size that are present among The 200 Largest may also hold as regards them. The answer is a qualified affirmative.

In order to see this, we crop out of the picture, so to speak, of each group of Industry Categories the data that relate to The 200. We do this in the interest of trying to see how The 359 in the several Industry Categories stand in relation to each other and to all "other" corporations *smaller* than they.

The summary data as to The 359 are in Exhibit 42; the details are set down in Exhibit 45, located at the end of the chapter.

As the presence index of The 359 among groups of Industry Categories declines—setting aside The 200 Largest—the average size

Presence index of The Next 359 Largest among corporations (other than The 200) in Industry Category	Number of Industry Categories	Occurrence (number of Next 359 Firms)	Presence index (assets of 359 Next Largest Firms among firms excluding The 200)	Average size of all firms other than The 200 ($000)*	Average size of The 359 Next Largest firms ($ millions)	Average size of "smaller" firms excluding The 559† ($000)	Presence index of The Next 359 among all corporations
Greater than 60% 7	7	92‡	68.1%	$3,699	$488	$1,187	25.6%
40%-60% 6	6	60	45.7	2,127	487	1,158	22.4
20%-40% 23	23	149	27.0	1,517	490	1,108	12.1
Zero-20% 13	13	59	4.9	346	369	329	4.3
Zero § 6	6	–	0.0	332	–	332	0.0
Total/average 55	55	359	19.4%	$ 548	$471	$ 442	12.0%

* Includes The 359.
† See Note 2, Chapter 8.
‡ Includes electronic and communications manufacturing subsidiaries (counted as one) of General Telephone & Electronics.
§ Includes "Not allocable."
Source: Exhibit 45.

of "all" (remaining) corporations declines without interruption from $3,699,000 down to $332,000. These "all" corporations are the corporate demographic context of The 359 after The 200 have been blanked out of the picture. These "all" corporations include, of course, The 359, themselves.

As the presence index of The 359 declines, the average sizes of The 359 tend to be rather stable at around $487–490 million until that group of those Industry Categories is reached where the presence indexes of The 359 have dropped to the level where they are greater than zero but less than 20 percent. In the group of industries at those levels of presence, the average size of The 359 falls rather dramatically to $369 million.

At the same time, the average size of the other remaining, and smaller corporations (excluding The 359) declines rather regularly, from $1,187,000 to $332,000. This decline, at first, is not great. But, as was true of The 359, when the group of industries is reached where the presence indexes of The 359 lie between zero and 20 percent, the average size of the "other" corporations—other than The 359, that is—falls abruptly, in this instance, from $1,100,000 to $329,000.

Again we see indications—pretty unmistakable—that corporate *size* among the several industry systems is essentially a phenomenon of order. Not of rigid, tightly linked, mechanistic one-for-one order, to be sure, but patterned far from randomness. And this matter of corporate size is associated with frequency of occurrence of large corporations with degree of relative presence of the Largest Corporations.

Comment on the independence of conclusions based upon indications of association among occurrence, presence, and size among The 200 and The 359

The sets of data that relate to the association among occurrence, relative presence, and average sizes of The 200 and other corporations among Industry Categories (Exhibits 41 and 44) and those that relate to The 359 (Exhibits 42 and 45) both give support to the existence of that association. This fact takes on particular significance because the sets of data cast light upon the matter from different perspectives: for instance, as may be seen from looking at the detailed statistics of Exhibits 44 and 45, these patterns of association emerge from data that relate to quite different sets of industries. For example, Part 1 of Exhibit 44 and Part 1 of Exhibit 45, which relate to those industries in which the respective relative presences of The 200 and The 359 were greater than 60 percent, are composed of very different sets of Industry Categories. Only one industry—Metal cans—is found on both lists. The two companies in Metal cans that were among The 200 held 77.2 percent of the total assets of that Industry Category. The two companies among The 359 held 75.2 percent of what assets in the industry remained after deducting those of the two largest. Other than that, the compositions of the lists of industries in the respective two first parts of Exhibits 44 and 45 were different.

When it comes to the respective second parts of those two exhibits, where the presence indexes of The 200 and of The 359 were, respectively, between 40 percent and 60 percent, only three of the ten industries listed in Part 2 of Exhibit 44 showed up among the six industries in Part 2 of Exhibit 45.

As to the third parts of Exhibits 44 and 45, again the lists of industries, upon which the patterns of association are based in part, are quite different. The list of Industry Categories in which the relative presences of The 200 were between 20 percent and 40 percent contained seven industries. For The 359, the list contained 23 industries. That is to say, of the seven industries in Part 3 of Exhibit 44, only four show up among the 23 Industry Categories of Part 3 of Exhibit 45.

In short, although some very small amount of autocorrelation, or "duplication," may exist among the patterns of association of occurrence, relative presence, and size revealed by the data related to The 200 and The 359, the association of these three dimensions holds good for the two groups of companies across very different collections of Industry Categories.

The association of occurrence, presence, and scale of The 559 Largest Corporations

We look now at the data for The 559 Largest Corporations for possible further light on this patterned association among occurrence, presence, and size of large corporations in industry systems. The summary data are displayed in Exhibit 43; the underlying details are contained in Exhibit 46.

In looking at these data, it is important to note that the particular Industry Categories that are contained in tabulation groups where the several presence indexes are labeled as "Greater than 60 percent"; "40 percent–60 percent"; and so on, vary as among Exhibits 41, 42, and 43. For example, in Exhibit 41, the presence indexes of The 200 in industries where they were "Greater than 60 percent" refer, of course, solely to companies among The 200. These include corporations holding assets of something more than $900 million each. In Exhibit 42, the group of industries where the presence indexes were "Greater than 60 percent" pertains solely to the relative presence of The 359. These include companies reporting assets of between $250 million and $900 million. The compositions of the several industry groupings vary greatly as between Exhibits 41 and 42.

In Exhibit 43, the presence indexes measure the relative presence of The 559, which figure, of course, combines The 200 and The 359. These companies, as we have seen, include all of those that held assets of more than $250 million. The resultant presence indexes of The 559 in all Industry Categories, "move upward," so to speak, as compared to those of The 200 and The 359, reflecting as each of these indexes do, in Exhibit 43, the combined presence in the several groups of Industry Categories of *all* corporations on our list of *the* Largest Companies of 1971.

Exhibit 43 summarizes the data on association of occurrence, presence, and size among The 559. The details are contained in Exhibit 46, located at the end of the chapter.

In Exhibits 43 and 46, the group of greatest relative presence of The 559 has been subdivided into "Greater than 80 percent" and

EXHIBIT 43
Occurrence, relative presence, and size, The 559 Largest Nonfinancial Corporations: 1971; summary

Presence index of The 559 Largest Corporations in Industry Category	Number of Industry Categories	Occurrence (number of The 559 Largest Firms)	Presence index (assets of 559 Largest Firms as percentage of all corporate assets)	Average size of all firms ($000)	Average size of The 559 Largest Firms ($ millions)	Average size of other firms ‡ ($000)
Greater than 80% 11		222	88.3%	$14,355	$1,697	$1,697
60%-80% 11		137*	72.4	3,632	1,455	1,004
40%-60% 9		98	47.7	2,383	833	1,249
20%-40% 10		54	27.5	1,020	531	740
Zero to 20% 9		50	4.9	331	397	315
Zero . . . . 5†		—	0.0	308	—	308
Totals and averages, all Industry Categories 55		559	50.1%	$ 886	$1,265	$ 442

* Includes the subsidiaries of American Telephone & Telegraph and General Telephone & Electronics mentioned heretofore.
† Includes "Not allocable."
‡ Excludes The 559 Largest Corporations. See Note 2, Chapter 8.
Source: Exhibit 46.

"60 percent–80 percent." The greater number of firms included in each of those Groups, as compared to the numbers of The 200 and The 359, permits such segregation to be statistically meaningful.

Again, as with The 200 and The 359, the occurrence and the relative presence of The 559 decline in association. Along with those associated declines, the average size of *all* firms in those groups of Industry Categories declines steadily from an average of $14,353,000, in those Industry Categories where the presence indexes of The 559 are greater than 80 percent, down to $308,000 in those Categories where none of The 559 was present. More meaningful, the average sizes of firms other than The 559 also tend to decline.

The average size of The 559 declines steadily along with their occurrence and presence. This four-way association gives further affirmation to the proposition that, among the whole community of largest corporations, the very largest, averaging almost $1.7 billion, are to be found where the largest firms are both most numerous and their relative presence greatest. Conversely, the "smallest" of the Largest Corporations, whose average size was $397 million, were found among those Industry Categories in which—aside from total absence—the numbers of The 559 were smallest (50) and the relative presence of The 559 was least (4.9 percent). (See Exhibit 43.)

Taking The 559 out of the picture, as was done in the other tabulations, the average sizes of "all other" corporations also were closely associated with the occurrence, relative presence, and average sizes of The 559. There was one "interruption" in that association. The average size of "all other" corporations was larger in those Industry Categories where the average presence indexes of The 559 fell between 40 percent and 60 percent than was true of the group of industries where the average presence indexes fell between 60 percent and 80 percent, and where the indexes were lower.

Despite this exception, the general pattern was clear: the smaller "other" corporations, which among the several Industry Categories were the "foothills" of the several massifs of corporations, tended, on the whole, to be greatest in those Industry Categories where the numbers and masses and sizes of the Largest Corporations tended to be greatest, and vice versa.*

Occurrence and presence of very large and large, and of smaller and small, corporations tend to be associated with asset masses

---

*When, in order to allow for more direct comparison of Exhibit 43 with Exhibits 41 and 42, the groups of industries are combined in which the presence indexes of The 559 were *Greater than 60 percent,* the following results are obtained:

Occurrence of The 559	359
Average presence index	82.1%
Average size of *all* corporations	$6,653,000
Average size of The 559	$1,198,000,000
Average size of all other corporations	$1,179,000

See Exhibit 46, Parts 1 and 2.

characterized, respectively by the *kinds* of assets held by very large and large, and the *kinds* of assets held by smaller and small corporations. Q.E.D.

Some further comments on the data

Two other comments probably should be made concerning the data in this chapter. First, the reader will surely have noticed, as was pointed out earlier, how *much* larger the Largest Companies are than "other" corporations. Overall, on the average, The 200 were 4,900 times larger than the arithmetic average of "other" corporations, *including* even The 359, and more than *6,000* times larger, excluding The 359. In turn, on the average, The 359 were over 1,000 times the average size of all "other" corporations, excluding The 559.

Clearly, when we are talking about the *largest* and "all other"—to say nothing of "the smaller," let alone "the smallest"—we are talking about entities that must be quite unlike as to nature. They are not of the same species or even of the same genera or orders, differing only as to scale.

We shall return to this topic a few pages later on.

A second comment is related to that made a few moments ago. When we put the lists and the data of The 200 and of The 359 together, in order to get data relative to The 559, we, in effect, "smooth out" the data. In doing so, we "smooth over," to a degree, some of the statistical vagaries that arise from "imperfections" in the operation of the underlying forces that give rise to bigness. The data that relate, respectively, to observable actualities in the occurrence, presence, and sizes of The 200 and The 359 in individual Industry Categories are probably at least somewhat, if not considerably, different from what they might be expected to be, were the underlying forces to operate "perfectly." Combining them to get the data for The 559 does result in larger "samples," and this *may* give us a somewhat better picture of the community of largest corporations as it is distributed among industries than we might get from looking at either of the subsets of data alone.

Again, the reader is reminded that Exhibits 44, 45, and 46 are located at the end of this chapter.

INDUSTRY "PROFILES" OF THE POPULATION OF NONFINANCIAL CORPORATIONS

Further insight into the occurrence, and presence and size of large—and of *small*—corporations comes from examination of "profiles" of corporations grouped according to size classes. These profiles will be the subject of our attention in the next few pages. Exhibit 47 sets forth the profiles, by size classes, of the total population of *all nonfinancial* corporations as to numbers of firms, values of assets, average sizes of assets, and percentages of assets located in each size class. The underlying data that give the corresponding profiles for each of the Industry Categories are contained in Exhibits 48, 49, 50, and 51, and these are located at the end of this chapter. These show, for each Industry Category, by size classes, (1) the number of firms; (2) value of assets; (3) average size of firm; (4) percentage of industry assets.

These data will enable us to understand even more about the place of large corporations, as well as throw light on the place of small corporations, an important topic in its own right, which has been largely set to one side in this study of *very big* corporations.

The "profiles" of the several Industry Categories, of course, are very different from one industry to another, as can be inferred from such data as those in Exhibits 34, 35, and 36. For instance, the "masses" of the assets in Petroleum and the Utilities are far greater than those in Construction and Services, and the distributions of the asset masses among size classes are very different. Very small numbers of the corporations in Petroleum and the Utilities occur in the size class of more than $250 million of assets; but the masses of the assets of those two industries present in that size class are very great, indeed, both relatively and absolutely. The numbers of small corporations in Construction and Services are far more numerous than those in Petroleum and the Utilities. The numbers of firms in Construction and Services, for example, that are located in the smallest size class—assets of less than $100,000—are also very great, but the masses of the assets of those two "small business" industries are distributed far more evenly than the assets of "big business" industries such as Petroleum and the utilities.

The data of Exhibits 48–51 are summarized in Exhibit 47.[3] The highlights of this Exhibit, which tell a great deal about our corporate population, are these:

1. Over half (56 percent) of all our nonfinancial corporations had assets of less than $100,000; over 86 percent had assets of less than $500,000.

2. The *assets* of nonfinancial corporations were, on the whole, distributed almost exactly inversely to their *numbers*. The three smallest size classes—those up to $500,000—contained less than 10 percent of total corporate assets despite the fact that they contained 86 percent of the number of firms.*

---

*The profiles of individual Industry Categories, as mentioned, vary tremendously as regards asset values, percentages of industry assets, and numbers of firms located in the several size classes. As shown in Exhibits 48-51, about 90 percent of the assets of both Petroleum and the Utilities, for instance, were massed in a single size class—the largest. By contrast, the greatest relative presence in any one size class for Services was about 18 percent in the "mid-range" size class $1 million to $5 million. In Construction, about 25 percent of the assets were in that same size class.

EXHIBIT 47
Profiles of the population of nonfinancial corporations in the United States; 1971, by size classes

Nonfinancial corporations	Totals	Zero	Zero to $100	$100 to $250	$250 to $500	$500 to $1,000	$1,000 to $5,000	$5,000 to $10,000	$10,000 to $25,000	$25,000 to $50,000	$50,000 to $100,000	$100,000 to $250,000	Over $250,000
							Assets of corporations ($000)						
Numbers of corporations	1,592,193	44,199	891,576	319,676	164,737	90,505	67,399	6,764	3,978	1,423	766	615	615
Assets of corporations ($ millions)	$1,410,511	—	$31,289	$51,216	$57,682	$62,819	$130,296	$46,407	$60,691	$49,023	$53,316	$95,201	$772,571
Percentages of corporations	100.00%	2.78%	55.98%	20.07%	10.35%	5.68%	4.23%	0.42%	0.25%	0.09%	0.05%	0.04%	0.04%
Percentages of total assets of all nonfinancial corporations	100.00%	—	2.22%	3.63%	4.08%	4.45%	9.22%	3.29%	4.30%	3.47%	3.78%	6.75%	54.77%
Percentages of total assets, excluding those with assets greater than $250 million	100.00%	—	4.90%	8.03%	9.04%	9.85%	20.42%	7.27%	9.51%	7.68%	8.36%	14.92%	—
Average size of all corporations ($000)	$885.9	—	$35.1	$160.2	$350.1	$694.1	$1,934.9	$6,860.9	$15,256.8	$34,450.5	$69,602.7	$154,797.7	$1,256,212.5
Average size of all corporations other than those with assets greater than $250 million ($000)*	$400.8												

*See Note 2, Chapter 8.
Source: Exhibits 48, 49, 50, and 51.

3. Nonfinancial corporations with assets of more than $250 million, although they accounted for a mere $^4/_{100}$ of 1 percent of the number of firms, held over half of all nonfinancial corporate assets.

4. The average sizes of all nonfinancial corporations in the several size classes ranged from $35,000 (for those with assets of less than $100,000) up to over $1.2 billion for those with assets of more than $250 million. The *average* corporation in the largest size class was over *36,000* times the size of the average corporation in the smallest size class. Even as compared to the average corporation in the size class from $250,000 up to $500,000, the very biggest corporations, averaged almost 3,600 times larger.

The diversity of our corporations with respect to size was just as great as the diversity of the natures of the several industry systems of which they are components. What is involved in visualizing, in really useful terms, the quantitative, let alone the qualitative, differences between two corporations, one of which is *36,000,* or even 3,600 times larger than the other? The complexity of the corporate community in the human ecosystem of America is so vast, so intricate, that it surely cannot be grasped, let alone understood, in terms of commonly used simple, mechanistic stereotypes of corporations and industry structures. The striking differences in the profiles of the various industry systems reflect great *qualitative* differences among them. And the farther one gets down into the details of the composition of industry systems, the more one has to be impressed that very different basic factors were at work in their formation, development, and evolution.

OCCURRENCE AND PRESENCE OF SMALLER CORPORATIONS

The patterning of smaller-business and bigger-business industries

So far, in our study of the demography of corporations, we have concentrated upon industry distribution, occurrence, and presence of the very largest companies. Even in the pursuit of that specific interest, there is another useful perspective: What does our corporate population look like when viewed, so to speak, "from below"? Building on the data we have already seen, including figures set forth in Exhibit 47, we are now ready to examine them in just that way. In particular, we are going to look at the relative occurrence and relative presence of our smaller corporations, especially as they are to be found in the several Industry Categories in which the relative presence of the Largest Corporations ranges downward from massive to total absence.

Data that will serve that purpose are set forth in Exhibit 52. These figures summarize the more detailed data contained in Exhibits 48-51 and 53, in their several parts. These exhibits are placed at the end of the chapter.

The structure of Exhibit 53 corresponds to the structure of Exhibit 46, in which Industry Categories are grouped according to presence indexes of The 559 Largest Corporations: Industry Categories in which the indexes were, respectively, Greater than 80 percent; between 60 percent and 80 percent; between 40 percent and 60 percent; between 20 percent and 40 percent. In Exhibits 52 and 53, the groupings of indexes of zero and of zero to 20 percent have been combined in the interest of getting as good a fix as possible on the occurrence and presence of *small* business.

In Exhibit 52 (as well as Exhibit 53), smaller corporations have been classified into three groups: corporations (*a*) with assets of less than $1 million; (*b*) with assets of from $1 million to $5 million; and (*c*) with assets of from $5 million to $10 million.

The first observation to be made in Exhibit 52 is that the vast majority of the *number* of corporations in *all* Industry Categories—without exception—are comparatively "small." As may be seen in Exhibit 53, in 49 out of 55 Industry Categories, 80 percent or more of the firms have assets of less than $1 million; and in *all* industries, over 90 percent have less than $5 million.

The next observation to be made is that the relative presences of the largest and of the smaller corporations vary inversely. In those Industry Categories in which the presence indexes of The 559 Largest firms were greatest, and averaged 88.3 percent (see Exhibits 46 and 53, Parts 1), the presence indexes of smaller firms—with assets up to $10 million—came typically to less than 3 percent. In contrast, as can be seen in Exhibit 52 (and in the details of Exhibit 53), where the presence indexes of the largest firms were below 20 percent, averaging less than 5 percent (see Exhibit 46 and Exhibit 53, Parts 5 and 6), the presence indexes of smaller firms, with assets up to $1 million, were typically about 26 percent; the presence indexes of firms with assets of from $1 million to $5 million were typically 20 percent; and the presence indexes of firms with assets of $5 million to $10 million were typically about 6.6 percent.[2] In total, in Industry Categories where the presence of the largest firms was least, the presence of smaller firms, with assets of up to $10 million, was greatest, being typically over 50 percent.

The Industry Categories in which the presence of the Largest companies was lowest were typically *small*- and *very-small*- company industries, not even "medium-size company" industries. In the two last columns of Exhibits 52, there is, again, clear, if imperfect, demonstration that the "typical" (median) size, as well as the (arithmetic) "average" size, of all firms in the several Industry Categories tends to decline along with declines in the *occurrence* and *presence* of The Largest firms.

Industry systems tend to be colored by the presence of big companies or small companies in varying degrees in consequence of basic technological, economic, and other factors that are operating.

For our purposes of understanding the very large—the "modern"—corporation, a revealing fact is that an inverse relationship exists in the several Industry Categories between the relative *occurrence*—and

EXHIBIT 52
Relative occurrence and relative presence of smaller firms among nonfinancial corporations: 1971; summary (values are *medians*; see Exhibit 53)

	(1)	(2)	(3)	(4)	(5)	(6)	(7)	(8)	(9)	(10)
					Assets of corporations ($ millions)				*Average size of firms, excluding The 559 ($000)*	*Median size, all firms ($000)**
Presence index of The 559 Largest Corporations in Industry Category	*$0-$1*		*$1-$5*		*$5-$10*		*$0-$10*			
	Percentage of firms	*Percentage of assets*	*Percentage of firms*	*Percentage of assets*	*Percentage of firms*	*Percentage of assets*	*Percentage of firms*	*Percentage of assets*		
Greater than 80%	81.8%	0.9%	13.5%	1.3%	2.0%	0.7%	97.3%	2.9%	$1,697	$236
60%-80%	87.9	3.5	7.9	3.9	1.4	1.8	97.8	9.2	1,004	125
40%-60%	83.5	5.9	12.2	7.5	1.5	3.7	97.2	17.1	1,249	187
20%-40%	89.5	13.8	8.5	11.4	1.1	5.9	99.1	31.1	740	146
Zero-20%	94.3	26.0	4.4	19.5	0.6	6.6	99.3	53.6	315	94
All Industry Categories. . . .	87.9%	5.9%	8.5%	7.5%	1.4%	3.7%	97.8%	17.1%	$ 442	$146

Column 9 is arithmetic averages.
*Medians are "raw" medians, not interpolated or weighted medians. See Note 2, Chapter 8.
Source: Exhibit 53.

relative *presence*—of *big* firms and the relative *presence* of *small* firms. In industry systems, where there are small *numbers* of very large firms, the largest *presence* of assets is accounted for by the smaller corporations.

And the opposite also holds: an inverse relationship exists between the relative *occurrence*—that is, typical percentages of *numbers* of small firms—and relative *presence* of biggest firms. It is in Industry Categories where the *numbers* of smaller firms represent the lowest percentages of the industries' populations that the relative *presence* of the biggest firms is greatest. In Industry Categories where the *asset masses* of big firms are relatively greatest—the *numbers* of smaller firms are lowest.

As one compares the second column of Exhibit 43 (the absolute *numbers* of *biggest* firms) with the relative *presence* (the asset percentages) of *smaller* firms (columns 2, 4, 6, and 8 of Exhibit 52), the pattern becomes unmistakable that these inverse, not so very obvious relationships do exist. As the average size of *small* firms declines, their relative aggregate presence in their respective Industry Categories increases.*

What these inverse relationships show is this: certain industries, on the face of the facts, have been more congenial to the appearance, emergence, and growth of *big* firms than have others. Other industries have been relatively more encouraging of smaller, and relatively more inhibitory to bigger, firms. Some industries are more characterized by numbers and presence of *big* firms. Others are more characterized by numbers and presence of small firms.

The strong patterning of such relationships confirms that industry systems are arrayed over a spectrum ranging from characteristically big-business industries to typically small-business industries.

The strong patterning of tendencies of this sort gives further support to the idea that present "profiles" of Industry Categories are consequences of basics deep within individual industries in particular eras, and deep in the American system: stages of life-cycles of industries, circumstances and conditions of available technology; economies—or diseconomies—in scale and in multiplant, multiproduct operations; institutional arrangements, such as tax provisions, and other matters of public policy, operating either through the executive or legislative branches of government, particularly at the federal level.

OCCURRENCE, PRESENCE, AND SCALE IN CHARACTERISTICALLY "MODERN" INDUSTRIES

In the next two chapters, we shall take a look at where and how the development of very large corporations fitted in with the eco-

*Again, it should be recalled that "average size" in this context is more an index of difference in *kind* than a quantitative measure of difference merely in size.

nomic and technological development of the nation over the past 40-some years. But as a prelude to that, a couple of observations should act as "curtain raisers" and pique our interest.

Even the nonstatistically-minded reader might take a quick look, toward the end of this chapter, at Parts 1 and 2 of Exhibit 46. These relate to those Industry Categories in which The 559 Largest Corporations accounted, respectively, for more than 80 percent, and between 60 percent and 80 percent of total assets. Of the 11 Industry Categories in Part 1 of Exhibit 46, at least 8 are among those that are among the most "characteristic," and/or "newest" in a "modern" industrial structure, as the world currently understands those terms: Iron and steel, Petroleum, Pharmaceuticals, Computers, Electric utilities, and Telephone and telegraph services, for example. Of the 11 Industries covered in Part 2, no less than 8 were of that sort: Chemicals, Electrical machinery, Radio and communication equipment, Motor vehicles, Rail transportation, Air transportation, for instance. The 20 large corporations categorized under "General merchandise" have been in the forefront of companies that have led the way in bringing the Industrial Revolution to distribution and marketing. (Alas for W. T. Grant!)

Now, look at the other end of the spectrum of the presence of big companies, at Part 5 of Exhibit 46. This Part 5 includes those industries where the largest corporations accounted for between 0.4 percent and 18.3 percent of total industry assets; and look at Part 6, where the largest corporations accounted for none of the assets of the Industry Category. As we have noted before (see Exhibit 30), with perhaps an exception or two—say Transit, maybe—these are "old" industries. These are not industries that characterize the present-day American economy, or that of any other modern industrial state. These are surely *not* industries that have led the way over the past 40 years in advancing known and applied technology. They include, and mostly *are,* however, those industries that most nearly approach the stereotype of competitive industries as held forth by received economic doctrine. These 14 industries, characterized as much by the absence of the Largest Corporations as any other factor, comprised 1.3 million, or 82 percent of the number of *all* nonfinancial corporations, and held about 31 percent of the assets.

It may seem ironic, at first sight, that those industries that according to "received" economic theory, are most "monopolistic" and therefore, presumably the least innovative, are, in fact, precisely those that *have* come to be most characteristic of "modernity" and, let it be admitted, indispensable to the physical support of life as we in the Western world now know it.

The irony, of course, lies not in the facts, but in persistence of an orthodoxy that could not—and cannot—explain some of the most salient and obvious economic facts of "modern" human existence, in which about 10 percent of the world's population—mostly in the

NATO countries—presently participate and to which the rest of the earth's population desperately aspires.[4]

One does not have to be a paraclete of bigness, not even of a "free enterprise" system, to feel a need for some new thinking about the economic, political, and societal processes that make for movement up and away from the appalling Malthusian margin of bare existence, whose proximity characterized life even in America in its early days, and which is still an ever-present, daily, concrete reality—no mere abstraction—for billions of our fellow human beings in the Third and Fourth worlds.

CONCLUSIONS

We have now completed our survey of the strongly patterned occurrence and presence of very large corporations in the structure of American industry. The distributions of numbers and assets of both large and small corporations, to a major degree, are interim outcomes, to date, of intrinsic and dynamic etiological processes at work, interacting in mutually affecting fashion with the growth and evolution of the whole American System. These patternings of the occurrence and presence of large corporations are no mere consequences of the "concentration" of what were, once upon a time, scattered small and family enterprises.

In studying *big* business, we are studying nothing less than evolution of America as a *developing* nation—a system that has not yet "arrived," but that is still in process of transformation and, let us hope, human and humane advancement.

In the next chapter, we are going to look all too briefly at where the development of the community of very large corporations fitted in with the development of America, in general, over the past four decades. Before we do, it may be useful to review a few of the findings of facts and at a few of the major hypotheses that have been put forward so far.

1. The composition of the list of Largest Corporations is obviously very "selective." The composition, or "mix," of the collective assets of those Largest Companies, in 1971, as in 1929, reflects impressive tendencies for large aggregations of corporate assets to appear in certain industries far more than in others. (See, e.g., Exhibit 25.)

2. Our Largest Corporations and their assets are not randomly diffused among the several industry *systems* that make up our industrial structure. They are visibly clustered in certain, particular industry systems. These systems include, especially, the electric and gas utilities; the telecommunications systems; rail and air transportation; petroleum, and other characteristically integrated industry systems; and some 19 other Industry Categories where circumstances had permitted and encouraged the growth of *numbers*—not just a few—of

the Largest Corporations. (See, e.g., Exhibit 26.) In other industries, the numbers of The 559 which occurred were small or zero. (See, e.g., Exhibits 27, 28, and 30.)

3. In some 27 Industry Categories altogether, in great contrast to others, it was not only the *numbers* of the Largest Corporations present that were the most notable features of those industry systems. The mere sizes of their asset masses imply a great deal about the abilities of those industries—of those very corporations—to gather in and convert inputs into outputs and to distribute these—and thus to contribute enormously to the "mix" as well as to the sizes of the Gross National Product and the National Income.

4. In these big-business industries, more than 450 of The 559 occurred. In the Utilities and regulated industries, the overall presence index of The 559 was almost 80 percent. In the integrated industries, the overall presence index of The 559 was about 75 percent. In the 19 other industries in which numbers of The 559 were common, their overall presence index was about 45 percent. (See Exhibits 29 and 40.)

5. These data, presented earlier, powerfully suggest, of themselves, systemic forces at work. In the present chapter, the data that illustrate strong association of occurrence, presence, and size—both as to small as well as to large corporations—further confirm the existence of operating *order*. (See, e.g., Exhibits 43 and 52.)

6. These four-way relationships, in particular, give strong suggestion that some industry systems and the potentialities that they offered for development, and what economists tend to call favorable "externalities," constituted, over the past four decades and more, milieux or "environments" that favored bigness or smallness, as the case may be, in varying degrees. And the occurrence, presence, and scale of corporations among industry systems reflect those basics.

7. It is not, by the way, a foregone conclusion that circumstances of the past will continue into the future, and that present industry structures will persist. On the contrary, our own history provides evidence of comings, restructurings, and even goings of whole industries. We shall see something of those processes in the very next chapter.

* * * * *

There follow a number of pages of detailed statistical backup for various exhibits interspersed through the text of Chapter 8. The general reader can dip into these figures if so minded; if not, he or she may skip over them to Chapter 9. The more specialized reader may find these detailed tabulations to be of some interest.

Exhibits 44-46 contain the data summarized in Exhibits 41-43.

Exhibits 48-51 contain the basic data underlying Exhibit 47.

Exhibit 53 carries the details on which is based Exhibit 52.

EXHIBIT 44

Occurrence, relative presence, and size of The 200 Largest Nonfinancial Corporations among Industry Categories; 1971

Part 1. Industry Categories in which the presence index of The 200 Largest Corporations was greater than 60 percent

Industry Category	Total number, all corporations	Total assets, all corporations ($ millions)	Average size of firm* ($000)	Average size of firm, excluding The 200† ($000)	Average size of The 200 Firms ($ millions)	Occurrence of The 200 Largest Firms (numbers of firms)	Presence of The 200 Largest Firms (value of assets in $ millions)	Presence index (assets of 200 Largest Firms as percentage of total industry assets)
2. Iron and steel	2,222	$ 28,394	$ 12,779	$ 4,549	$ 2,617	7	$ 18,319	64.5%
5. Petroleum	7,721	115,755	14,992	1,991	5,021	20	100,425	86.8
12. Tobacco	77	7,952	103,273	20,603	1,612	4	6,448	81.1
21. Rubber and tires	6,235	13,071	2,096	630	1,830	5	9,149	70.0
26. Metal cans	138	3,967	28,746	6,647	1,532	2	3,063	77.2
29. Office...computing machines	556	24,806	44,615	8,809	2,853	7	19,970	80.5
34. Photographic equipment	633	4,145	6,548	1,340	3,298	1	3,298	79.6
35. Motor vehicles	2,392	57,914	24,212	7,376	5,041	8	40,329	69.6
40. Rail transportation	18,132	43,422	2,395	870	2,515	11	27,661	63.7
45. Electric, gas...sanitary	8,235	137,168	16,657	5,541	1,953	47	91,799	66.9
46. Telephone, telegraph	3,453	80,045	23,181	4,024	13,234	5	66,171	82.7
Totals and averages, these industry categories	49,794	$516,639	$ 10,376	$ 2,617	$ 3,304	117	$386,632	74.8%

Part 2. Industry Categories in which the presence index of The 200 Largest Corporations was between 40 percent and 60 percent

Industry Category	Total number, all corporations	Total assets, all corporations ($ millions)	Average size of firm* ($000)	Average size of firm, excluding The 200† ($000)	Average size of The 200 Firms ($ millions)	Occurrence of The 200 Largest Firms (numbers of firms)	Presence of The 200 Largest Firms (value of assets in $ millions)	Presence index (assets of 200 Largest Firms as percentage of total industry assets)
8. Meat	2,543	$ 8,688	$ 3,416	$ 1,777	$ 1,391	3	$ 4,174	48.0%
9. Dairy	2,137	5,886	2,754	1,186	1,119	3	3,356	57.0
18. Chemicals	6,684	39,769	5,950	2,698	2,176	10	21,762	54.7
24. Glass	946	4,843	5,119	2,262	1,354	2	2,708	55.9
30. Electrical machinery	4,664	20,650	4,428	2,193	5,213	2	10,426	50.5
32. Radio...communication equipment	5,741	25,909	4,513	1,960	4,888	3	14,665	56.6
33. Scientific...control...devices...measuring	1,612	5,199	3,225	1,872	2,183	1	2,183	42.0
36. Aircraft	815	24,205	29,699	15,113	1,501	8	12,009	49.6
44. Air transportation	3,428	16,596	4,841	2,175	1,526	6	9,154	55.2
50. General merchandise	22,853	38,860	1,700	851	2,157	9	19,411	50.0
Totals and averages, these industry categories	51,393	$190,605	$ 3,709	$ 1,769	$ 2,124	47	$99,848	52.4%

Part 3. Industry Categories in which the presence index of The 200 Largest Corporations was between 20 percent and 40 percent

Industry Category	Total number, all corporations	Total assets, all corporations ($ millions)	Average size of firm* ($000)	Average size of firm, excluding The 200† ($000)	Average size of The 200 Firms ($ millions)	Occurrence of The 200 Largest Firms (numbers of firms)	Presence of The 200 Largest Firms (value of assets in $ millions)	Presence index (assets of 200 Largest Firms as percentage of total industry assets)
3. Nonferrous metals	3,055	$ 32,064	$ 10,496	$ 6,352	$ 1,589	8	$12,708	39.6%
11. Soft drinks	2,220	4,656	2,097	1,599	1,108	1	1,108	23.8
15. Lumber...wood...paper products	14,133	34,897	2,469	1,585	1,563	8	12,507	35.8

No.	Industry								
19.	Pharmaceuticals	4,113	2,288	3,339	13,732	1,082	4	4,329	31.5
20.	Soaps, cleaners	2,167	1,606	2,534	5,492	2,013	1	2,013	36.7
28.	Farm, construction machinery	2,925	4,047	5,162	15,098	1,635	2	3,270	21.7
31.	Household appliances	457	7,412	11,050	5,050	1,670	1	1,670	33.1
	Totals and averages, these industry categories	39,070	$ 1,879	$ 2,841	$110,989	$ 1,504	25	$37,605	33.9%

Part 4. Industry Categories in which the presence index of The 200 Largest Corporations was between zero and 20 percent

No.	Industry								
7.	Food	8,991	$ 2,614	$ 3,007	$ 27,035	$ 1,179	3	$ 3,537	13.1%
10.	Alcoholic beverages	426	19,256	21,399	9,116	932	1	932	10.2
13.	Textiles	5,846	2,363	2,601	15,204	1,390	1	1,390	9.1
14.	Apparel	17,037	615	670	11,412	934	1	934	8.2
25.	Fabricated metal products	22,720	985	1,037	23,568	1,183	1	1,183	5.0
42.	Motor transportation	27,452	392	489	13,428	1,333	2	2,665	19.8
49.	Retail trade	320,656	208	212	68,136	1,572	1	1,572	2.3
51.	Food stores	27,005	408	480	12,970	972	2	1,943	15.0
	Totals and averages, these industry categories	420,133	$ 397	$ 431	$180,869	$ 1,180	12	$14,156	7.8%

Part 5. Industry Categories in which the presence index of The 200 Largest Corporations was zero

No.	Industry				
1.	Agriculture	39,932	$ 11,800	$ 296	0.0%
4.	Coal	1,766	3,820	2,163	0.0
6.	Construction	143,092	48,243	337	0.0
16.	Furniture and fixtures	6,755	4,244	628	0.0
17.	Printing and publishing	26,541	20,910	788	0.0
22.	Leather	2,269	3,809	1,679	0.0
23.	Nonmetallic mineral products	11,064	15,035	1,359	0.0
27.	Machinery	22,168	22,518	1,016	0.0
37.	Ship building	1,015	2,917	2,874	0.0
38.	Railroad equipment	1,345	6,318	4,697	0.0
39.	Other and miscellaneous manufacturing	11,678	9,695	830	0.0
41.	Transit	9,073	4,287	473	0.0
43.	Water transportation	6,385	6,483	1,015	0.0
47.	Radio and TV broadcasting	3,923	5,279	1,346	0.0
48.	Wholesale trade	168,150	90,918	541	0.0
52.	Motion pictures	10,061	6,424	639	0.0
53.	Services	277,719	55,802	201	0.0
54.	Real estate	267,399	92,066	344	0.0
55.	Nature of business not allocable	21,438	847	40	0.0
	Totals and averages, these industry categories	1,031,773	$ 411,415	$ 399	0.0%
	Totals and averages, all industry categories	1,592,193	$1,410,511	$ 886	$ 548	$ 2,691	200	$538,240	38.2%

*Includes The 200 and The 359.
†Includes The 359 Next Largest Corporations.

EXHIBIT 45
Occurrence, relative presence, and size of The Next 359 Largest Nonfinancial Corporations among Industry Categories; 1971

Part 1. Industry Categories in which the presence index of The Next 359 Largest Corporations among corporations other than The 200 Largest was greater than 60 percent

Industry Category	Total number, corporations other than The 200	Total assets, corporations other than The 200 ($000)	Average size of firms, other than The 200 ($000)	Average size of firms, excluding The 559 ($000)	Average size of The Next 359 Firms ($ millions)	Occurrence of The Next 359 Largest Firms (numbers of firms)	Presence of The Next 359 Largest Firms (value of assets in $ millions)	Presence index of The Next 359 among corporations excluding The 200	Presence index of The Next 359 among all corporations
9. Dairy	2,134	$ 2,530	$ 1,186	$ 385	$570	3	$ 1,709	67.5%	29.0%
19. Pharmaceuticals	4,109	9,403	2,288	409	455	17	7,729	82.2	56.3
20. Soaps, cleaners	2,166	3,479	1,606	519	589	4	2,357	67.7	42.9
26. Metal cans	136	904	6,647	1,672	340	2	680	75.2	17.1
31. Household appliances	456	3,380	7,412	1,533	448	6	2,690	79.6	53.3
34. Photographic equipment	632	847	1,340	365	617	1	617	72.8	14.9
45. Electric, gas ... sanitary	8,188	45,369	5,541	2,002	493	59	29,093	64.1	21.2
Totals and averages, these industry categories	17,821	$ 65,912	$ 3,699	$ 1,187	$488	92	$ 44,875	68.1%	25.6%

Part 2. Industry Categories in which the presence index of The Next 359 Largest Corporations among corporations other than The 200 Largest was between 40 percent and 60 percent

Industry Category	Total number, corporations other than The 200	Total assets, corporations other than The 200 ($000)	Average size of firms, other than The 200 ($000)	Average size of firms, excluding The 559 ($000)	Average size of The Next 359 Firms ($ millions)	Occurrence of The Next 359 Largest Firms (numbers of firms)	Presence of The Next 359 Largest Firms (value of assets in $ millions)	Presence index of The Next 359 among corporations excluding The 200	Presence index of The Next 359 among all corporations
2. Iron and steel	2,215	$ 10,075	$ 4,549	$ 2,263	$424	12	$ 5,089	50.5%	17.9%
18. Chemicals	6,674	18,007	2,698	1,405	540	16	8,655	48.1	21.8
23. Nonmetallic mineral products	11,064	15,035	1,359	809	468	13	6,090	40.5	40.5
24. Glass	944	2,135	2,262	1,169	517	2	1,034	48.4	21.0
32. Radio ... communication equipment	5,738	11,244	1,960	1,038	482	11*	5,302	47.2	20.5
44. Air transportation	3,422	7,442	2,175	1,287	508	6	3,045	40.9	18.3
Totals and averages, these industry categories	30,057	$ 63,938	$ 2,127	$ 1,158	$487	60	$ 29,215	45.7%	22.4%

Part 3. Industry Categories in which the presence index of The Next 359 Largest Corporations among corporations other than The 200 Largest was between 20 percent and 40 percent

Industry Category	Total number, corporations other than The 200	Total assets, corporations other than The 200 ($000)	Average size of firms, other than The 200 ($000)	Average size of firms, excluding The 559 ($000)	Average size of The Next 359 Firms ($ millions)	Occurrence of The Next 359 Largest Firms (numbers of firms)	Presence of The Next 359 Largest Firms (value of assets in $ millions)	Presence index of The Next 359 among corporations excluding The 200	Presence index of The Next 359 among all corporations
3. Nonferrous metals	3,047	$ 19,356	$ 6,352	$ 4,710	$505	10	$ 5,052	26.1%	15.8%
4. Coal	1,766	3,820	2,163	1,365	471	3	1,414	37.0	37.0
5. Petroleum	7,701	15,329	1,991	1,288	542	10	5,421	35.4	4.7
7. Food	8,988	23,498	2,614	1,640	549	16	8,785	37.4	32.5
8. Meat	2,540	4,514	1,777	1,325	576	2	1,151	25.5	13.3
10. Alcoholic beverages	425	8,184	19,256	13,717	485	5	2,423	29.6	26.6
11. Soft drinks	2,219	3,548	1,599	1,226	828	1	828	23.3	17.8
12. Tobacco	73	1,504	20,603	12,583	598	1	598	29.8	7.5
13. Textiles	5,845	13,814	2,363	1,820	399	8	3,190	23.1	21.0
15. Lumber	14,125	22,390	1,585	1,241	542	9	4,879	21.8	14.0
25. Fabricated metal products	22,719	22,385	985	778	523	9	4,709	21.0	20.0
28. Farm, construction machinery	2,923	11,828	4,047	2,888	680	5	3,401	28.8	22.5

No.	Industry								
29.	Office...computing... machines	549	4,836	8,809	6,134	373	4	30.9	6.0
30.	Electrical machinery	4,662	10,224	2,193	1,705	381	6	22.4	11.1
35.	Motor vehicles	2,384	17,585	7,376	6,442	470	9	24.1	7.3
38.	Railroad equipment	1,345	6,318	4,697	3,121	533	4	33.8	33.8
39.	Other and misc. manufacturing	11,678	9,695	830	663	390	5	20.1	20.1
40.	Railroad transportation	18,121	15,761	870	611	469	10	29.7	10.8
46.	Telephone, telegraph services	3,448	13,874	4,024	3,205	474	6	20.5	3.6
47.	Radio and TV broadcasting	3,923	5,279	1,346	1,008	663	2	25.1	25.1
50.	General merchandise	22,844	19,449	851	629	462	11	26.1	13.1
51.	Food stores	27,003	11,027	408	288	406	8	29.5	25.1
52.	Motion pictures	10,061	6,424	639	445	389	5	30.3	30.3
	Totals and averages, these industry categories	178,389	$ 270,642	$ 1,517	$ 1,108	$490	149	27.0%	12.1%

Part 4. Industry Categories in which the presence index of The Next 359 Largest Corporations among corporations other than The 200 Largest was between zero and 20 percent

No.	Industry								
6.	Construction	143,092	$ 48,243	$ 337	$ 329	$440	3	2.5	2.5
14.	Apparel	17,036	10,478	615	525	384	4	14.7	13.5
17.	Printing and publishing	26,541	20,910	788	686	386	7	12.9	12.9
22.	Leather	2,269	3,809	1,679	1,373	348	2	18.3	18.3
27.	Machinery	22,168	22,518	1,016	867	367	9	14.7	14.7
33.	Scientific...control... measuring	1,611	3,016	1,872	1,705	271	1	9.0	5.2
36.	Aircraft	807	12,196	15,113	14,188	775	2	6.4	3.2
42.	Motor transportation	27,450	10,763	392	359	305	3	8.5	6.8
43.	Water transportation	6,385	6,483	1,015	842	370	3	17.1	17.1
48.	Wholesale trade	168,150	90,918	537	539	318	1	0.3	0.4
49.	Retail	320,655	66,564	214	201	330	6	3.0	2.9
53.	Services	277,719	55,802	201	183	413	12	8.9	8.9
54.	Real estate	267,399	92,066	344	337	339	6	2.2	2.2
	Totals and averages, these industry categories	1,281,282	$ 443,766	$ 346	$ 329	$369	59	4.9%	4.3%

Part 5. Industry Categories in which the presence index of The Next 359 Largest Corporations among corporations other than The 200 Largest was zero

No.	Industry								
1.	Agriculture	39,932	$ 11,800	$ 296	$ 296	$ 296		0.0%	0.0
16.	Furniture and fixtures	6,755	4,244	628	628	628		0.0	0.0
21.	Rubber and tires	6,230	3,922	630	630	630		0.0	0.0
37.	Ship...building	1,015	2,917	2,874	2,874	2,874		0.0	0.0
41.	Transit	9,073	4,287	473	473	473		0.0	0.0
55.	Nature of business not allocable	21,438	847	40	40	40			
	Totals and averages, these industry categories	84,443	$ 28,017	$ 332	$ 332	$471	359	19.4%	0.0%
	Totals and averages, all Industry Categories	1,591,993	$872,271,000	$ 548	$ 442	$471	359	19.4%	12.0%

*Includes, counted as one company, the electronic and communications subsidiaries of General Telephone & Electric Corporation and estimated assets thereof. See Exhibit 1.

EXHIBIT 46
Occurrence, relative presence, and size of The 559 Largest Nonfinancial Corporations among Industry Categories; 1971

Part 1. Industry Categories in which the presence index of The 559 Largest Corporations was greater than 80 percent

Industry Category	Total number, all corporations	Total assets, all corporations ($ millions)	Average size of firm by assets ($000)	Average size of firm, excluding The 559 ($000)	Average size of The 559 Firms ($ millions)	Occurrence of The 559 Largest Firms (numbers of firms)	Presence of The 559 Largest Firms (value of assets in $ millions)	Presence index (assets of The 559 Largest Firms as percentage of total industry assets)
2. Iron and steel	2,222	$ 28,394	$ 12,779	$ 2,263	$1,232	19	$ 23,408	82.4%
5. Petroleum	7,721	115,755	14,992	1,288	3,528	30	105,846	91.4
9. Dairy	2,137	5,886	2,754	385	844	6	5,065	86.1
12. Tobacco	77	7,952	103,273	12,583	1,409	5	7,046	88.6
19. Pharmaceuticals	4,113	13,732	3,339	409	574	21	12,058	87.8
26. Metal cans	138	3,967	28,746	1,672	936	4	3,743	94.4
29. Office ... computing ... machines	556	24,806	44,615	6,134	1,951	11	21,463	86.5
31. Household appliances	457	5,050	11,050	1,533	623	7	4,360	86.3
34. Photographic equipment	633	4,145	6,548	365	1,958	2	3,915	94.5
45. Electric, gas ... sanitary	8,235	137,168	16,657	2,002	1,140	106	120,892	88.1
46. Telephone, telegraph ... services	3,453	80,045	23,181	3,205	6,274	11	69,014	86.2
Totals and averages, these industry categories	29,742	$ 426,900	$ 14,353	$ 1,697	$1,697	222	$376,810	88.3%

Part 2. Industry Categories in which the presence index of The 559 Largest Corporations was between 60 percent and 80 percent

Industry Category	Total number, all corporations	Total assets, all corporations ($ millions)	Average size of firm by assets ($000)	Average size of firm, excluding The 559 ($000)	Average size of The 559 Firms ($ millions)	Occurrence of The 559 Largest Firms (numbers of firms)	Presence of The 559 Largest Firms (value of assets in $ millions)	Presence index (assets of The 559 Largest Firms as percentage of total industry assets)
8. Meat	2,543	$ 8,688	$ 3,416	$ 1,325	$1,065	5	$ 5,325	61.3%
18. Chemicals	6,684	39,769	5,950	1,405	1,170	26	30,416	76.5
20. Soaps, cleaners	2,167	5,492	2,534	519	874	5	4,370	79.6
21. Rubber and tires	6,235	13,071	2,096	630	1,830	5	9,149	70.0
24. Glass	946	4,843	5,119	1,169	936	4	3,742	77.3
30. Electrical machinery	4,664	20,650	4,428	1,705	1,589	8	12,712	61.6
32. Radio ... communication equipment	5,741	25,909	4,513	1,038	1,426	14	19,967	77.1
35. Motor vehicles	2,392	57,914	24,212	5,622	2,621	17	44,561	76.9
40. Rail transportation	18,132	43,422	2,395	611	1,540	21	32,348	74.5
44. Air transportation	3,428	16,596	4,841	1,287	1,017	12	12,199	73.5
50. General merchandise	22,853	38,860	1,700	629	1,225	20	24,491	63.0
Totals and averages, these industry categories	75,785	$ 275,214	$ 3,632	$ 1,004	$1,455	137	$199,280	72.4%

Part 3. Industry Categories in which the presence index of The 559 Largest Corporations was between 40 percent and 60 percent

Industry Category	Total number, all corporations	Total assets, all corporations ($ millions)	Average size of firm by assets ($000)	Average size of firm, excluding The 559 ($000)	Average size of The 559 Firms ($ millions)	Occurrence of The 559 Largest Firms (numbers of firms)	Presence of The 559 Largest Firms (value of assets in $ millions)	Presence index (assets of The 559 Largest Firms as percentage of total industry assets)
3. Nonferrous metals	3,055	$ 32,064	$ 10,496	$ 4,710	$ 987	18	$ 17,760	55.4%
7. Food	8,991	27,035	3,007	1,640	649	19	12,322	45.6
11. Soft drinks	2,220	4,656	2,097	1,226	968	2	1,936	41.6
15. Lumber ... wood ... paper ... products	14,133	34,897	2,469	1,241	1,023	17	17,386	49.8
23. Nonmetallic mineral products	11,064	15,035	1,359	809	468	13	6,090	40.5
28. Farm, construction ... machinery	2,925	15,098	5,162	2,888	953	7	6,670	44.2

#	Industry Category								
33.	Scientific...control...devices measuring	1,612	5,199	3,225	1,705	$ 1,227	2	2,454	47.2
36.	Aircraft	815	24,205	29,699	14,189	1,278	10	12,783	52.8
51.	Food stores	27,005	12,970	480	288	519	10	5,194	40.0
	Totals and averages, these industry categories	71,820	$171,159	$ 2,383	$ 1,249	$ 833	98	$ 81,595	47.7%

Part 4. Industry Categories in which the presence index of The 559 Largest Corporations was between 20 percent and 40 percent

#	Industry Category								
4.	Coal	1,766	$ 3,820	$ 2,163	$ 1,365	$ 471	3	$ 1,414	37.0%
10.	Alcoholic beverages	426	9,116	21,399	13,717	559	6	3,355	36.8
13.	Textiles	5,846	15,204	2,601	1,820	509	9	4,580	30.1
14.	Apparel	17,037	11,412	670	525	494	5	2,471	21.7
25.	Fabricated metal products	22,720	23,568	1,037	778	589	10	5,892	25.0
38.	Railroad equipment	1,345	6,318	4,697	3,121	533	4	2,133	33.8
39.	Other and miscellaneous manufacturing	11,678	9,695	830	663	390	5	1,951	20.1
42.	Motor transportation	27,452	13,428	489	359	716	5	3,581	26.7
47.	Radio and TV broadcasting	3,923	5,279	1,346	1,008	663	2	1,326	25.1
52.	Motion pictures	10,061	6,424	639	445	389	5	1,947	30.3
	Totals and averages, these industry categories	102,254	$104,264	$ 1,020	$ 740	$ 531	54	$ 28,650	27.5%

Part 5. Industry Categories in which the presence index of The 559 Largest Corporations was between zero and 20 percent

#	Industry Category								
6.	Construction	143,092	$ 48,243	$ 337	$ 329	$ 400	3	$ 1,201	2.5%
17.	Printing and publishing	26,541	20,910	788	686	386	7	2,702	12.9
22.	Leather	2,269	3,809	1,679	1,373	349	2	697	18.3
27.	Machinery	22,168	22,518	1,016	867	367	9	3,301	14.7
43.	Water transportation	6,385	6,483	1,015	842	370	3	1,110	17.1
48.	Wholesale trade	168,150	90,918	540	539	318	1	318	0.4
49.	Retail trade	320,656	68,136	212	201	507	7	3,550	5.2
53.	Services	277,719	55,802	201	183	413	12	4,952	8.9
54.	Real estate	267,399	92,066	344	337	339	6	2,031	2.2
	Totals and averages, these industry categories	1,234,379	$408,885	$ 331	$ 315	$ 397	50	$ 19,862	4.9%

Part 6. Industry Categories in which the presence index of The 559 Largest Corporations was zero

#	Industry Category								
1.	Agriculture	39,932	$ 11,800	$ 296	$ 296				0.0%
16.	Furniture and fixtures	6,755	4,244	628	628				0.0
37.	Ship...building	1,015	2,917	2,874	2,874				0.0
41.	Transit	9,073	4,287	473	473				0.0
55.	Nature of business not allocable	21,438	847	40	40				0.0
	Totals and averages, these industry categories	78,213	$ 24,095	$ 308	$ 308				0.0%
	Totals and averages, all industry categories	1,592,193	$1,410,511	$ 886	$ 442	$1,265	559	$707,195	50.1%

EXHIBIT 48

Numbers of nonfinancial corporations by asset size classes, by Industry Category; 1971

Industry Category	All corporations, number of firms	Zero	Zero-$100	$100-$250	$250-$500	$500-$1,000	$1,000-$5,000	$5,000-$10,000	$10,000-$25,000	$25,000-$50,000	$50,000-$100,000	$100,000-$250,000	$250,000 or more*	The 559 Firms	Difference between The 615 and The 559
1. Agriculture	39,932	983	19,367	9,732	5,466	2,654	1,551	115	46	10	2	6	—	—	—
2. Iron and steel	2,222	51	704	394	336	218	339	68	50	20	10	16	16	19	-3
3. Nonferrous metals	3,055	125	1,015	707	413	285	361	54	39	12	13	12	19	18	1
4. Coal	1,766	184	572	408	180	194	164	24	19	9	8	1	3	3	—
5. Petroleum	7,721	282	3,437	1,518	969	497	668	111	103	48	26	28	34	30	4
6. Construction	143,092	3,064	82,811	26,794	15,100	8,112	6,229	594	259	65	38	20	6	3	3
7. Food	8,991	80	3,376	1,802	1,236	1,010	1,097	152	118	44	31	21	24	19	5
8. Meat	2,543	13	657	750	296	385	331	51	36	13	5	3	3	5	-2
9. Dairy	2,137	—	548	526	344	330	313	42	20	5	1	3	5	6	-1
10. Alcoholic beverages	426	9	51	25	98	81	84	15	22	12	12	9	8	6	2
11. Soft drinks	2,220	39	595	286	418	411	394	37	31	3	3	1	2	2	—
12. Tobacco	77	—	—	20	—	20	15	8	3	2	2	1	6	5	1
13. Textiles	5,846	126	1,736	1,133	811	725	992	144	105	37	12	14	11	9	2
14. Apparel	17,037	335	8,217	3,322	2,113	1,472	1,317	143	70	23	12	11	2	5	-3
15. Lumber....wood...paper products	14,133	333	5,162	3,740	1,884	1,286	1,334	189	96	36	28	26	19	17	2
16. Furniture and fixtures	6,755	208	2,773	1,796	720	640	486	76	37	8	10	1	—	—	—
17. Printing and publishing	26,541	415	15,288	5,056	2,768	1,488	1,160	133	107	62	31	19	14	7	7
18. Chemicals	6,684	185	2,601	1,159	1,042	656	764	90	68	46	20	21	32	26	6
19. Pharmaceuticals	4,113	55	2,615	568	325	304	131	47	22	11	7	9	19	21	-2
20. Soaps, cleaners	2,167	55	1,320	237	232	145	119	20	15	7	5	6	6	5	1
21. Rubber and tires	6,235	11	2,372†	1,334	1,081	615	662	87	42	12	8	4	7	5	2
22. Leather	2,269	9	636	445	412	346	353	30	19	9	3	5	2	2	—
23. Nonmetallic mineral products	11,064	324	3,728	2,360	1,869	1,398	1,122	141	58	21	15	19	9	13	-4
24. Glass	946	51	471	142	117	51	75	13	11	4	4	3	4	4	—
25. Fabricated metal products	22,720	160	8,931	5,068	3,651	2,239	2,180	248	128	54	35	19	7	10	-3
26. Metal cans	138	—	—	40	25	25	59	4	3	3	—	—	4	4	2
27. Machinery	22,168	308	11,485	4,838	2,603	1,249	1,245	224	119	36	28	22	11	9	2
28. Farm, construction machinery	2,925	134	703	469	548	458	467	61	40	17	6	13	9	7	2
29. Office computing machines	556	3	152	104	57	108	75	15	13	8	4	6	11	11	—
30. Electrical machinery	4,664	130	2,063	827	615	513	340	63	49	33	12	15	4	8	-4
31. Household appliances	457	—	191	20	84	49	71	14	11	4	3	4	6	7	-1

Asset size classes ($000)

No.	Industry															
32.	Radio communication equipment	5,741	63	2,575	1,053	800	511	497	97	75	28	15	12	15	14	1
33.	Scientific control devices measuring	1,612	10	785	283	147	108	204	24	25	10	8	7	1	2	-1
34.	Photographic equipment	633	-	348	150	66	29	24	5	4	1	3	1	2	2	
35.	Motor vehicles	2,392	22	988	465	202	300	282	48	36	15	9	11	14	17	-3
36.	Aircraft	815	1	254	121	168	94	115	12	14	7	6	7	16	10	6
37.	Ship building	1,015	1	495	202	61	123	96	20	9	4	-	3	1	-	1
38.	Railroad equipment	1,345	31	467	234	325	88	132	23	21	11	6	2	5	4	1
39.	Other and misc. mfg.	11,678	164	6,744	1,725	1,357	836	657	92	55	23	15	5	5	5	-
40.	Rail transportation	18,132	375	11,919	3,240	1,416	650	378	54	42	10	13	12	23	21	2
41.	Transit	9,073	421	6,825	977	466	218	133	19	8	2	2	1	1	-	1
42.	Motor transportation	27,452	403	16,025	5,412	2,802	1,463	1,106	106	83	27	15	6	4	5	-1
43.	Water transportation	6,385	149	3,584	1,126	765	396	259	48	26	10	12	5	5	3	2
44.	Air transportation	3,428	111	2,226	635	197	114	83	14	12	11	7	5	13	12	1
45.	Electric, gas sanitary	8,235	133	4,689	1,624	885	304	278	48	58	35	30	45	106	106	-
46.	Telephone, telegraph services	3,453	192	1,509	515	396	286	452	36	30	15	6	4	12	11	1
47.	Radio and TV broadcasting	3,923	175	1,367	1,406	371	289	222	43	26	12	2	7	3	2	1
48.	Wholesale trade	168,150	3,210	75,007	38,718	23,562	14,810	11,082	952	529	167	57	34	22	1	2
49.	Retail trade	320,656	7,646	182,737	74,705	31,788	14,845	8,298	365	161	54	35	19	3	7	-4
50.	General merchandise	22,853	889	12,043	4,782	2,812	1,218	859	90	73	28	18	20	21	20	1
51.	Food stores	27,005	818	17,265	5,249	2,136	856	494	77	54	20	16	10	10	10	-
52.	Motion pictures	10,061	327	6,512	1,771	730	372	253	57	19	6	5	3	6	5	1
53.	Services	277,719	8,415	204,665	35,712	15,001	7,754	5,195	476	309	99	48	32	13	12	1
54.	Real estate	267,399	9,109	133,032	62,951	32,063	16,728	11,687	1,045	549	154	44	26	11	6	5
55.	Nature of business not allocable	21,438	3,862	15,928	1,000	433	149	55	10	1	-	-	-	-	-	-
56.	All industries other than finance and insurance	1,592,193	44,199	891,576	319,676	164,737	90,505	67,339	6,764	3,978	1,423	766	615	615	559	56
57.	Finance and insurance	141,139	6,517	66,513	20,461	10,957	8,051	11,226	5,177	6,373	2,692	1,501	937	734		
58.	All industries	1,733,332	50,716	958,089	340,137	175,694	98,556	78,565	11,941	10,351	4,115	2,267	1,552	1,349		

*In 1971 IRS reported 615 firms in "all industries other than financial and insurance" as having assets of $250 million or more. See Chapter 7, Note 1.

†IRS reported 2,382, which seems to have been an error.

EXHIBIT 49

Assets of nonfinancial corporations by asset size classes, by Industry Category; 1971

Industry Category	All corporations, total value of assets of firms ($ millions)	Asset size classes ($000)												Value of assets, The 559
		Zero	Zero-$100	$100-$250	$250-$500	$500-$1,000	$1,000-$5,000	$5,000-$10,000	$10,000-$25,000	$25,000-$50,000	$50,000-$100,000	$100,000-$250,000	$250,000 or more	
1. Agriculture	$ 11,800.4	—	803.6	1,597.5	1,936.2	1,801.4	2,999.5	785.1	694.1	324.3	107.6	751.2	—	—
2. Iron and steel	28,393.6	—	27.4	65.7	115.1	156.8	806.7	468.1	766.8	778.6	711.2	2,320.3	22,176.9	23,407.7
3. Nonferrous metals	32,064.3	—	39.9	117.4	138.6	200.7	727.1	375.4	623.3	398.4	920.3	1,974.6	26,548.6	17,760.1
4. Coal	3,819.5	—	23.7	69.2	62.6	129.5	338.1	169.4	275.6	327.8	522.2	218.3	1,683.2	1,413.6
5. Petroleum	115,754.8	—	121.1	254.3	328.2	334.5	1,471.3	793.9	1,557.8	1,691.6	1,871.2	4,707.8	102,623.1	105,846.3
6. Construction	48,242.9	—	2,771.5	4,277.4	5,310.2	5,615.3	12,037.7	4,044.3	3,875.1	2,215.3	2,569.9	3,274.5	2,251.6	1,201.2
7. Food	27,035.4	—	148.8	287.6	441.2	715.3	2,275.0	1,021.5	1,897.8	1,478.1	2,177.5	3,193.8	13,398.8	12,321.9
8. Meat	8,687.9	—	37.1	117.8	96.1	263.0	649.3	340.7	526.6	505.9	372.5	512.4	5,266.5	5,325.1
9. Dairy	5,885.7	—	20.9	87.4	114.3	243.3	666.7	262.6	265.8	166.5	58.9	433.2	3,566.1	5,065.0
10. Alcoholic beverages	9,115.6	—	3.3	2.9	32.4	59.3	196.1	114.8	351.1	433.3	861.5	1,616.9	5,443.8	3,355.1
11. Soft drinks	4,656.9	—	24.5	52.1	149.9	283.4	705.0	248.1	441.6	106.9	190.2	151.3	2,303.0	1,935.6
12. Tobacco	7,952.0	—	—	3.3	—	14.3	36.2	53.7	46.1	63.8	143.3	144.0	7,447.3	7,045.5
13. Textiles	15,204.0	—	78.4	180.1	293.5	508.5	2,138.2	1,006.1	1,612.8	1,324.7	936.9	2,071.6	5,053.4	4,579.7
14. Apparel	11,411.9	—	283.6	536.5	768.6	1,019.2	2,622.5	981.0	1,073.6	778.5	818.6	1,771.0	758.9	2,470.5
15. Lumber...wood...paper...products	34,897.4	—	209.6	609.5	652.8	887.6	2,601.3	1,304.9	1,527.0	1,186.6	1,925.3	3,955.7	20,037.0	17,385.7
16. Furniture and fixtures	4,243.7	—	118.4	285.0	244.2	456.4	952.0	546.8	580.5	265.1	651.7	143.6	—	—
17. Printing and publishing	20,909.9	—	527.2	801.8	970.3	1,045.9	2,425.3	952.9	1,604.8	2,100.2	2,104.8	2,972.0	5,404.1	2,702.1
18. Chemicals	39,768.8	—	104.3	190.3	374.4	459.2	1,573.6	624.0	1,045.5	1,524.4	1,432.7	3,141.9	29,298.5	30,416.4
19. Pharmaceuticals	13,732.2	—	87.5	95.1	118.5	212.4	302.2	302.7	359.8	404.5	491.7	1,460.4	9,899.2	12,058.0
20. Soaps, cleaners	5,492.0	—	31.4	36.2	83.5	102.4	268.5	145.3	251.8	251.0	374.6	919.6	3,027.6	4,370.4
21. Rubber and tires	13,071.4	—	80.6	217.0	392.5	412.8	1,333.3	525.8	629.6	409.5	562.4	603.1	7,904.8	9,149.0
22. Leather	3,808.5	—	29.4	71.6	144.4	250.1	743.2	206.4	293.4	324.3	228.8	812.9	703.9	696.7
23. Nonmetallic mineral products	15,034.9	—	160.9	410.5	673.8	981.2	2,201.4	965.9	840.5	719.1	1,087.1	3,041.2	3,953.4	6,089.6
24. Glass	4,842.7	—	16.4	23.0	43.8	39.4	163.2	89.1	190.6	126.4	291.0	482.2	3,377.6	3,742.1
25. Fabricated metal products	23,568.1	—	342.9	828.5	1,305.3	1,566.7	4,184.2	1,725.4	1,963.7	1,873.4	2,489.1	2,830.0	4,458.8	5,892.3
26. Metal cans	3,966.9	—	—	6.7	—	18.1	156.5	20.7	45.0	95.2	—	—	3,624.7	3,742.8
27. Machinery	22,518.4	—	451.1	799.3	919.7	881.5	2,532.5	1,483.4	1,891.9	1,314.4	1,973.4	3,733.1	6,538.3	3,300.5
28. Farm, construction machinery	15,097.6	—	26.9	75.6	195.6	310.2	908.4	429.7	635.2	601.2	420.8	1,997.6	9,496.4	6,670.3
29. Office...computing machines	24,805.7	—	8.3	18.4	20.2	76.9	153.4	99.7	227.9	288.8	294.4	927.5	22,690.2	21,463.1
30. Electrical machinery	20,649.7	—	70.9	137.4	221.2	380.0	759.8	443.7	731.4	1,115.5	845.2	2,515.3	13,429.3	12,711.6
31. Household appliances	5,049.9	—	7.3	4.6	30.1	39.3	183.6	100.5	192.4	131.9	214.6	439.2	3,706.4	4,359.5

No.	Industry	(1)	(2)	(3)	(4)	(5)	(6)	(7)	(8)	(9)	(10)	(11)	(12)	(13)	Total
32.	Radio communication equipment	19,967.1	18,148.6	2,027.4	943.9	980.0	1,216.6	681.8	1,009.5	343.6	287.8	175.7	94.3	—	25,909.1
33.	Scientific control devices measuring	2,454.0	2,162.8	959.2	609.1	340.6	362.3	163.1	406.3	75.7	48.1	45.1	26.6	—	5,199.9
34.	Photographic equipment	3,915.1	3,496.3	190.1	201.6	28.7	71.7	36.3	40.0	22.7	23.8	21.8	12.3	—	4,145.3
35.	Motor vehicles	44,561.3	53,088.1	1,800.3	587.4	541.5	583.5	316.6	590.4	217.4	76.0	74.4	38.0	—	57,913.8
36.	Aircraft	12,783.2	21,987.0	976.0	334.0	238.5	223.3	77.6	206.1	69.3	63.0	19.2	10.7	—	24,204.7
37.	Ship building	—	1,822.5	367.5	—	143.0	157.0	121.3	147.4	81.8	25.7	29.7	20.8	—	2,916.7
38.	Railroad equipment	2,133.0	4,282.6	247.1	453.3	396.9	345.9	144.8	224.0	60.1	116.3	36.8	9.9	—	6,317.7
39.	Other and misc. manufacturing	1,950.9	2,598.6	748.0	1,092.1	818.5	860.8	666.8	1,342.9	594.1	468.5	289.3	215.3	—	9,694.8
40.	Rail transportation	32,347.5	36,465.5	2,042.7	966.2	392.0	642.4	376.0	696.4	442.5	483.5	521.9	392.8	—	43,421.8
41.	Transit	—	2,756.6	102.9	165.1	79.4	140.6*	128.2	278.0	140.1	159.2	147.3	189.3	—	4,286.7
42.	Motor transportation	3,580.6	2,908.0	829.1	1,077.1	848.5	1,346.8	701.9	2,280.6	996.7	984.4	855.6	599.0	—	13,427.7
43.	Water transportation	1,111.0	2,284.4	827.0	904.2	321.6	387.7	339.3	561.0	278.7	273.7	185.4	119.6	—	6,482.6
44.	Air transportation	12,199.2	14,084.2	801.1	551.2	391.5	210.9	106.1	147.4	79.1	75.1	95.6	53.6	—	16,595.8
45.	Electric, gas, sanitary	120,891.8	123,430.7	7,411.3	2,201.8	1,297.3	955.0	356.0	574.2	216.5	296.2	262.7	166.3	—	137,168.0
46.	Telephone, telegraph services	69,014.0	76,508.1	501.3	423.1	536.7	432.9	246.0	901.5	211.9	140.9	81.0	61.1	—	80,044.5
47.	Radio and TV broadcasting	1,326.2	1,933.0	1,036.4	115.0	412.6	400.5	297.8	463.2	197.6	138.0	222.5	61.9	—	5,278.5
48.	Wholesale trade	318.3	12,571.3	5,325.2	3,902.5	5,624.5	7,930.9	6,515.7	21,189.5	10,374.2	8,348.3	6,352.2	2,783.6	—	90,917.7
49.	Retail trade	3,550.3	1,464.9	2,768.0	2,463.8	1,839.9	2,393.9	2,435.6	14,330.0	10,129.4	11,048.2	11,854.5	7,407.8	—	68,136.0
50.	General merchandise	24,490.9	27,209.3	2,912.0	1,219.1	1,002.5	1,132.1	640.6	1,730.3	842.1	990.6	737.1	443.9	—	38,859.6
51.	Food stores	5,193.6	4,774.8	1,393.9	1,114.5	658.4	826.3	505.3	936.8	571.7	735.6	830.3	622.6	—	12,970.1
52.	Motion pictures	1,946.8	3,273.4	427.7	303.4	179.7	303.6	389.3	523.5	251.8	255.3	290.9	225.6	—	6,426.2
53.	Services	4,952.3	5,327.5	4,708.4	3,144.2	3,399.1	4,604.9	3,287.0	9,877.0	5,391.1	15,156.6	5,641.8	5,263.8	—	55,801.6
54.	Real estate	2,031.2	3,920.5	3,681.8	2,893.5	5,226.6	8,124.5	7,166.8	22,628.1	11,660.6	11,161.0	10,033.5	5,569.1	—	92,066.1
55.	Nature of business not allocable						18.4	75.7	100.3	105.0	149.3	152.4	246.0	—	847.1
56.	All industries other than finance and insurance		31,289.1	51,216.4	57,682.0	62,818.5	130,296.1	46,407.0	60,691.4	49,023.0	53,315.7	95,200.6	772,570.7	—	$1,410,510.5
57.	Finance and insurance		2,037.2	3,280.6	3,872.9	5,653.1	27,299.6	37,626.7	100,784.5	93,873.7	103,765.6	143,787.5	956,729.6	—	$1,478,711.0
58.	All industries		33,326.3	54,497.0	61,554.9	68,471.6	157,595.7	84,033.7	161,475.9	142,896.7	157,081.3	238,988.1	1,729,300.3	—	$2,889,221.5

EXHIBIT 50

Average assets, nonfinancial corporations, by asset size classes, by Industry Category: 1971

Industry Category	All corporations, average value of assets ($000)	Zero	Zero–$100	$100–$250	$250–$500	$500–$1,000	$1,000–$5,000	$5,000–$10,000	$10,000–$25,000	$25,000–$50,000	$50,000–$100,000	$100,000–$250,000	$250,000 or more
1. Agriculture	$ 295.5	—	41.5	164.1	354.2	678.7	1,933.9	6,827.0	15,089.1	32,430.0	53,800.0	125,200.0	—
2. Iron and steel	12,778.4	—	38.9	166.8	342.6	719.3	2,379.6	6,883.8	15,336.0	38,930.0	71,120.0	145,018.8	1,386,056.2
3. Nonferrous metals	10,495.6	—	39.3	166.1	336.6	704.2	2,014.1	6,951.9	15,982.1	33,200.0	70,792.3	164,550.0	1,397,294.7
4. Coal	2,162.8	—	41.4	169.6	347.8	667.5	2,061.6	7,058.3	14,505.3	36,422.2	65,275.0	218,300.0	561,066.7
5. Petroleum	14,992.2	—	35.2	167.5	338.7	673.0	2,202.5	7,152.3	15,124.3	35,241.7	71,969.2	168,135.7	3,018,326.4
6. Construction	337.1	—	33.5	159.6	361.7	692.2	1,932.5	6,808.6	14,961.8	34,081.5	67,628.9	163,725.0	375,266.7
7. Food	3,006.9	—	44.1	159.6	357.0	708.2	2,073.8	6,720.4	16,083.0	33,593.2	70,241.9	152,085.7	558,283.3
8. Meat	3,416.4	—	56.5	157.1	324.7	683.1	1,961.6	6,680.4	14,627.8	38,915.4	74,500.0	170,800.0	1,755,500.0
9. Dairy	2,754.2	—	38.1	166.2	332.3	737.3	2,130.0	6,252.4	13,290.0	33,300.0	58,900.0	144,400.0	713,220.0
10. Alcoholic beverages	21,398.1	—	64.7	116.0	330.6	732.1	2,334.5	7,653.3	15,959.1	36,108.3	71,791.7	179,655.6	680,475.0
11. Soft drinks	2,097.3	—	41.2	182.2	358.6	689.5	1,789.3	6,705.4	14,245.2	35,633.3	63,400.0	151,300.0	1,151,500.0
12. Tobacco	103,272.7	—	—	165.0	—	715.0	2,413.3	6,712.5	15,366.7	31,900.0	71,650.0	144,000.0	1,241,216.6
13. Textiles	2,600.8	—	45.2	158.9	361.9	701.4	2,155.4	6,986.8	15,360.0	35,802.7	78,075.0	147,971.4	459,400.0
14. Apparel	669.8	—	34.5	161.5	363.6	692.4	1,991.3	6,861.0	15,337.1	33,847.8	68,216.7	161,000.0	379,450.0
15. Lumber...wood ...paper... products	2,469.2	—	40.6	163.0	346.5	690.2	1,950.0	6,904.2	15,906.2	32,961.1	68,760.7	152,142.3	1,054,578.9
16. Furniture and fixtures	628.3	—	42.7	158.7	339.2	713.1	1,958.8	7,194.7	15,689.2	33,137.5	65,170.0	143.6	—
17. Printing and publishing	787.8	—	34.5	158.9	350.5	702.9	2,090.8	7,164.7	14,998.1	33,874.2	67,896.8	156,421.0	386,050.0
18. Chemicals	5,949.8	—	40.1	164.2	359.3	700.0	2,059.7	6,933.3	15,375.0	33,139.1	71,635.0	149,614.3	915,578.1
19. Pharmaceuticals	3,338.7	—	33.5	167.4	364.6	698.7	2,306.8	6,440.4	16,354.5	36,772.7	70,242.9	162,266.7	521,010.5
20. Soaps, cleaners	2,534.4	—	23.8	152.7	359.9	706.2	2,256.3	7,265.0	16,786.7	35,857.1	74,920.0	153,266.7	504,600.0
21. Rubber and tires	2,096.0	—	33.9	162.7	363.1	671.2	2,014.0	6,043.7	14,990.5	34,125.0	70,300.0	150,775.0	1,129,257.1
22. Leather	1,678.5	—	46.2	160.9	350.5	722.8	2,105.4	6,880.0	15,442.1	36,033.3	76,266.7	16,258.0	351,950.0
23. Nonmetallic mineral products	1,358.9	—	43.2	173.9	360.5	701.8	1,962.0	6,850.3	14,491.3	34,242.8	72,473.3	160,063.2	439,266.7
24. Glass	5,119.1	—	34.8	162.0	374.4	772.5	2,176.0	6,853.8	17,327.2	31,600.0	72,750.0	160,733.3	844,400.0
25. Fabricated metal products	1,037.3	—	38.4	163.4	357.5	699.7	1,919.3	6,957.3	15,341.4	34,692.6	71,117.1	148,947.4	636,971.4
26. Metal cans	28,745.6	—	—	167.5	—	724.0	2,652.5	5,175.0	15,000.0	31,733.3			906,175.0
27. Machinery	1,015.8	—	39.3	165.2	353.3	705.8	2,034.1	6,622.3	15,898.3	36,511.1	70,478.5	169,686.3	594,390.9
28. Farm, construction machinery	5,161.6	—	38.3	161.2	356.9	677.3	1,945.2	7,044.3	15,880.0	35,364.7	70,133.3	153,661.5	1,055,155.5
29. Office...computing ...machines	44,614.6	—	54.6	176.9	354.4	712.0	2,045.3	6,646.7	17,530.8	36,100.0	73,600.0	154,583.3	2,062,745.4
30. Electrical machinery	4,427.4	—	34.4	166.1	359.7	740.7	2,234.7	7,042.8	14,926.5	33,803.0	70,433.3	167,686.7	3,357,325.0
31. Household appliances	11,050.1	—	38.2	230.0	358.3	802.0	2,585.9	7,178.5	17,490.9	32,975.0	71,533.3	109,800.0	617,733.3

No.	Industry												
32.	Radio communication equipment	1,209,906.6	168,950.0	62,926.7	35,000.0	16,221.3	7,028.9	2,031.2	672.4	359.8	166.9	36.6	—	4,513.0
33.	Scientific control devices measuring	2,162,800.0	137,028.6	76,137.5	34,060.0	14,492.0	6,795.8	1,991.7	700.9	327.2	159.4	33.8	—	3,225.7
34.	Photographic equipment	1,748,150.0	190,100.0	67,200.0	28,700.0	17,925.0	7,260.0	1,666.7	782.8	360.6	145.3	35.3	—	6,548.7
35.	Motor vehicles	3,792,021.4	163,663.6	65,266.7	36,100.0	16,208.3	6,595.8	2,093.6	724.7	376.2	160.0	38.5	—	24,211.4
36.	Aircraft	1,374,187.5	139,428.6	55,666.7	34,071.4	15,950.0	6,466.7	1,792.1	737.2	375.0	158.7	42.1	—	29,699.0
37.	Ship...building	1,822,500.0	122,500.0	—	35,750.0	17,444.4	6,065.0	1,535.4	665.0	421.3	147.0	42.0	—	2,873.6
38.	Railroad equipment	856,520.0	123,550.0	75,550.0	36,081.8	16,471.4	6,295.6	1,696.9	683.0	357.8	157.3	21.2	—	4,697.1
39.	Other and misc. manufacturing	519,720.0	149,600.0	72,806.7	35,586.9	15,650.9	7,247.8	2,043.9	710.6	345.2	167.7	31.9	—	830.2
40.	Rail transportation	1,585,456.5	170,225.0	74,323.0	39,200.0	15,295.2	6,962.9	1,842.3	680.7	341.4	161.1	32.9	—	2,394.7
41.	Transit	2,756,600.0	102,900.0	82,550.0	39,700.0	17,575.0	6,747.3	2,090.2	642.6	341.6	150.8	27.7	—	472.5
42.	Motor transportation	727,000.0	138,183.3	71,806.6	31,425.9	16,226.5	6,621.7	2,062.0	681.3	351.3	158.1	37.4	—	489.1
43.	Water transportation	456,880.0	165,400.0	75,350.0	32,160.0	14,911.5	7,068.7	2,166.0	703.8	357.8	164.6	33.4	—	1,015.3
44.	Air transportation	1,083,400.0	160,220.0	78,742.8	35,590.9	17,575.0	7,578.5	1,775.9	693.8	381.2	150.5	24.1	—	4,841.2
45.	Electric, gas, sanitary	1,164,440.5	164,695.5	73,393.3	37,065.7	16,465.5	7,416.7	2,065.5	712.1	334.7	161.8	35.5	—	16,656.7
46.	Telephone, telegraph services	6,375,675.0	125,325.0	70,516.7	35,780.0	14,430.0	6,833.3	1,994.5	740.9	355.8	157.3	40.5	—	23,181.1
47.	Radio and TV broadcasting	644,333.3	148,057.1	57,500.0	34,383.3	15,403.8	6,925.6	2,086.5	683.7	372.0	158.3	45.3	—	1,345.5
48.	Wholesale trade	571,422.7	156,623.5	68,464.9	33,679.6	14,992.2	6,844.2	1,912.1	700.5	354.3	164.1	37.1	—	541.0
49.	Retail trade	488,300.0	145,684.2	70,394.3	34,072.2	14,868.9	6,672.9	1,726.9	682.3	347.6	158.7	40.5	—	212.5
50.	General merchandise	1,295,680.9	145,600.0	67,727.8	35,803.5	15,508.2	7,117.8	2,014.3	691.4	352.2	154.1	36.8	—	1,700.4
51.	Food stores	477,480.0	139,390.0	69,656.2	32,920.0	15,300.0	6,562.3	1,896.3	667.8	344.4	158.2	36.1	—	480.3
52.	Motion pictures	545,566.7	142,566.7	60,680.0	29,250.0	15,978.9	6,829.8	2,069.2	676.9	349.7	164.2	34.6	—	638.5
53.	Services	409,807.7	147,137.5	65,504.2	34,334.3	14,902.6	6,905.5	1,901.3	695.2	343.8	158.0	25.7	—	201.0
54.	Real estate	356,409.0	141,607.7	65,761.4	33,938.9	14,798.7	6,858.2	1,936.2	697.1	348.1	159.4	41.9	—	344.3
55.	Nature of business not allocable	—	—	—	—	18,400.0	7,570.0	1,823.6	704.7	344.8	152.4	15.4	—	39.6
56.	All industries other than finance and insurance	1,256,212.5	154,797.7	69,602.7	34,450.5	15,256.8	6,860.9	1,934.9	694.1	350.1	160.2	35.1	—	885.9
57.	Finance and insurance	1,303,446.3	153,455.2	69,131.0	34,871.4	15,814.3	7,268.1	2,431.8	702.2	353.5	160.3	30.6	—	$ 10,477.1
58.	All industries	1,281,912.7	153,987.2	69,290.4	34,725.8	15,600.0	7,037.4	2,005.9	694.7	350.4	160.2	34.8	—	$ 1,666.9

EXHIBIT 51

Percentage distributions of assets, nonfinancial corporations, by asset size classes, by Industry Category; 1971

Industry Category	All corporations, total assets ($ millions)	Total percent	Asset size classes ($000)											
			Zero	Zero-$100	$100-$250	$250-$500	$500-$1,000	$1,000-$5,000	$5,000-$10,000	$10,000-$25,000	$25,000-$50,000	$50,000-$100,000	$100,000-$250,000	$250,000 or more
1. Agriculture	$ 11,800.4	100.0%	—	6.81%	13.54%	16.41%	15.26%	25.42%	6.65%	5.88%	2.75%	0.91%	6.36%	—
2. Iron and steel	28,393.6	100.0	—	0.09	0.23	0.40	0.55	2.84	1.64	2.70	2.74	2.50	8.17	78.10%
3. Nonferrous metals	32,064.3	100.0	—	0.12	0.36	0.43	0.63	2.26	1.17	1.94	1.24	2.87	6.16	82.79
4. Coal	3,819.5	100.0	—	0.62	1.81	1.64	3.39	8.85	4.43	7.22	8.58	13.67	5.72	44.06
5. Petroleum	115,754.8	100.0	—	0.10	0.22	0.28	0.29	1.27	0.68	1.34	1.46	1.61	4.06	88.65
6. Construction	48,242.9	100.0	—	5.75	8.86	11.00	11.64	24.95	8.38	8.03	4.59	5.32	6.78	4.66
7. Food	27,035.4	100.0	—	0.55	1.06	1.63	2.65	8.41	3.78	7.02	5.47	8.05	11.81	49.56
8. Meat	8,687.9	100.0	—	0.43	1.36	1.11	3.03	7.47	3.92	6.06	5.82	4.29	5.89	60.62
9. Dairy	5,885.7	100.0	—	0.36	1.48	1.94	4.13	11.33	4.46	4.51	2.83	1.00	7.36	60.59
10. Alcoholic beverages	9,115.6	100.0	—	0.04	0.03	0.35	0.65	2.15	1.26	3.85	4.75	9.45	17.74	59.72
11. Soft drinks	4,656.0	100.0	—	0.53	1.12	3.22	6.08	15.14	5.32	9.48	2.29	4.08	3.25	49.46
12. Tobacco	7,952.0	100.0	—	—	0.04	—	0.18	0.46	0.68	0.58	0.80	1.80	1.81	93.65
13. Textiles	15,204.0	100.0	—	0.52	1.18	1.93	3.34	14.06	6.61	10.61	8.71	6.16	13.63	33.23
14. Apparel	11,411.9	100.0	—	2.49	4.70	6.73	8.93	22.98	8.60	9.41	6.82	7.17	15.52	6.65
15. Lumber...wood...paper...products	34,897.4	100.0	—	0.60	1.75	1.87	2.54	7.45	3.74	4.38	3.40	5.52	11.33	57.42
16. Furniture and fixtures	4,243.7	100.0	—	2.79	6.72	5.75	10.75	22.43	12.88	13.68	6.25	15.36	3.38	—
17. Printing and publishing	20,909.9	100.0	—	2.52	3.83	4.64	5.00	11.60	4.56	7.67	10.04	10.06	14.21	25.85
18. Chemicals	39,768.8	100.0	—	0.26	0.48	0.94	1.15	3.96	1.57	2.63	3.83	3.60	7.90	73.67
19. Pharmaceuticals	13,732.2	100.0	—	0.64	0.69	0.86	1.55	2.20	2.20	2.62	2.95	3.58	10.63	72.08
20. Soaps, cleaners	5,492.0	100.0	—	0.57	0.66	1.52	1.86	4.88	2.65	4.58	4.57	6.82	16.74	55.13
21. Rubber and tires	13,071.4	100.0	—	0.62	1.66	3.00	3.16	10.20	4.02	4.82	3.13	4.30	4.61	60.47
22. Leather	3,808.5	100.0	—	0.77	1.88	3.79	6.56	19.51	5.42	7.70	8.52	6.01	21.34	18.48
23. Nonmetallic mineral products	15,034.9	100.0	—	1.07	2.73	4.48	6.53	14.64	6.42	5.59	4.78	7.23	20.23	26.29
24. Glass	4,842.7	100.0	—	0.34	0.47	0.90	0.81	3.37	1.84	3.94	2.61	6.01	9.96	69.75
25. Fabricated metal products	23,568.1	100.0	—	1.45	3.52	5.54	6.65	17.75	7.32	8.33	7.95	10.56	12.01	18.92
26. Metal cans	3,966.9	100.0	—	—	0.17	—	0.46	3.95	0.52	1.13	2.40	—	—	91.37
27. Machinery	22,518.4	100.0	—	2.00	3.55	4.08	3.91	11.25	6.59	8.40	5.84	8.76	16.58	29.04
28. Farm, construction machinery	15,097.6	100.0	—	0.18	0.50	1.30	2.05	6.02	2.85	4.21	3.98	2.79	13.23	62.90
29. Office...computing...machines	24,805.7	100.0	—	0.03	0.07	0.08	0.31	0.62	0.40	0.92	1.16	1.19	3.74	91.47
30. Electrical machinery	20,649.7	100.0	—	0.34	0.67	1.07	1.84	3.68	2.15	3.54	5.40	4.09	12.18	65.03
31. Household appliances	5,409.9	100.0	—	0.14	0.09	0.60	0.78	3.64	1.99	3.81	2.61	4.25	8.70	73.40
32. Radio...communication equipment	25,909.1	100.0	—	0.36	0.68	1.11	1.33	3.90	2.63	4.70	3.78	3.64	7.82	70.05

No.	Industry	Amount	%												
33.	Scientific...control devices...measuring	5,199.9	100.0	—	0.51	0.87	0.93	1.46	7.81	3.14	6.97	6.55	11.71	18.45	41.59
34.	Photographic equipment	4,145.3	100.0	—	0.30	0.53	0.57	0.55	0.96	0.88	1.73	0.69	4.86	4.59	84.34
35.	Motor vehicles	57,913.8	100.0	—	0.06	0.13	0.13	0.38	1.12	0.55	1.00	0.94	1.01	3.11	91.67
36.	Aircraft	24,204.7	100.0	—	0.04	0.08	0.26	0.28	0.85	0.32	0.92	0.99	1.38	4.03	90.84
37.	Ship...building	3,916.7	100.0	—	0.71	1.02	0.88	2.80	5.05	4.16	5.38	4.90	—	12.60	62.48
38.	Railroad equipment	6,137.7	100.0	—	0.16	0.58	1.84	0.95	3.55	2.29	5.48	6.28	7.18	3.91	67.79
39.	Other and misc. manufacturing	9,694.8	100.0	—	2.22	2.98	4.83	6.13	13.85	6.88	8.88	8.44	11.26	7.72	26.80
40.	Rail transportation	43,421.8	100.0	—	0.90	1.20	1.11	1.02	1.60	0.87	1.48	0.90	2.23	4.70	83.98
41.	Transit	4,286.7	100.0	—	4.42	3.44	3.71	3.27	6.49	2.99	3.28	1.85	3.85	2.40	64.31
42.	Motor transportation	13,427.7	100.0	—	4.46	6.37	7.33	7.42	16.98	5.23	10.03	6.32	8.02	6.17	21.66
43.	Water transportation	6,482.6	100.0	—	1.84	2.86	4.22	4.30	8.65	5.23	5.98	4.96	13.95	12.76	35.24
44.	Air transportation	16,595.8	100.0	—	0.32	0.58	0.45	0.48	0.89	0.64	1.27	2.36	3.32	4.83	84.87
45.	Electric, gas...sanitary	137,168.0	100.0	—	0.12	0.19	0.22	0.16	0.42	0.26	0.70	0.95	1.60	5.40	89.98
46.	Telephone, telegraph...services	80,044.5	100.0	—	0.08	0.10	0.18	0.26	1.13	0.31	0.54	0.67	0.53	0.63	95.58
47.	Radio and TV broadcasting	5,278.5	100.0	—	1.17	4.22	2.61	3.74	8.78	5.64	7.59	7.82	2.18	19.63	36.62
48.	Wholesale trade	90,917.7	100.0	—	3.06	6.97	9.18	11.41	23.30	7.17	8.72	6.19	4.29	5.86	13.83
49.	Retail trade	68,136.0	100.0	—	10.87	17.40	16.21	14.87	21.03	3.57	3.51	2.70	3.62	4.06	2.15
50.	General merchandise	38,859.6	100.0	—	1.14	1.90	2.55	2.17	4.45	1.65	2.91	2.58	3.14	7.49	70.02
51.	Food stores	12,970.1	100.0	—	4.80	6.40	5.67	4.41	7.22	3.90	6.37	5.08	8.59	10.75	36.81
52.	Motion pictures	6,424.2	100.0	—	3.51	4.53	3.97	3.92	8.15	6.06	4.73	2.80	4.72	6.66	50.95
53.	Services	55,801.6	100.0	—	9.43	10.11	9.24	9.66	17.70	5.89	8.25	6.09	5.63	8.44	9.55
54.	Real estate	92,066.1	100.0	—	6.05	10.90	12.12	12.66	24.58	7.78	8.82	5.68	3.14	4.00	4.26
55.	Nature of business not allocable	847.1	100.0	—	29.04	17.99	17.62	12.40	11.84	8.94	2.17	—	—	—	—
56.	All industries other than finance and insurance	$1,410,510.5	100.0	—	2.22	3.63	4.08	4.45	9.22	3.29	4.30	3.47	3.78	6.75	54.77
57.	Finance and insurance	$1,478,711.0	100.0	—	0.14	0.22	0.26	0.38	1.85	2.54	6.81	6.35	7.01	9.72	64.67
58.	All industries	$2,889,221.5	100.0	—	1.15	1.89	2.13	2.37	5.45	2.91	5.59	4.94	5.44	8.27	59.83

EXHIBIT 53

Relative occurrence and relative presence of smaller firms among Industry Categories, 1971

Part 1. Industry Categories in which the presence index of The 559 Largest Corporations was greater than 80 percent

| | Assets of corporations ($ millions) | | | | | | Average size of firms, excluding The 559 ($000) | Median size all firms* ($000) |
| | $0-$1 | | $1-$5 | | $5-$10 | | | |
Industry Category	Percentage of firms	Percentage of all assets	Percentage of firms	Percentage of all assets	Percentage of firms	Percentage of all assets		
2. Iron and steel	76.6%	1.3%	15.3%	2.8%	3.1%	1.6%	$ 2,263	$ 236
5. Petroleum	86.8	0.9	8.7	1.3	1.4	0.7	1,288	114
9. Dairy	81.8	7.9	14.6	11.3	2.0	4.5	385	248
12. Tobacco	51.9	0.2	19.5	0.5	10.4	0.7	12,583	963
19. Pharmaceuticals	94.0	3.7	3.2	2.2	1.1	2.2	409	77
26. Metal cans	47.1	0.6	42.8	4.0	2.9	0.5	1,672	1,339
29. Office...computing...machines	76.3	0.5	13.5	0.6	2.7	0.4	6,134	333
31. Household appliances	75.3	1.6	15.5	3.6	3.1	2.0	1,533	302
34. Photographic equipment	93.7	2.0	3.8	1.0	0.8	0.9	365	91
45. Electric, gas...sanitary	92.7	0.7	3.4	0.4	0.6	0.3	2,002	85
46. Telephone, telegraph...services	83.9	0.6	13.1	1.1	1.0	0.3	3,205	107
Median values*	81.8%	0.9%	13.5%	1.3%	2.0%	0.7%	$ 1,697	$ 236

Part 2. Industry Categories in which the presence index of The 559 Largest Corporations was between 60 percent and 80 percent

Industry Category	Percentage of firms	Percentage of all assets	Percentage of firms	Percentage of all assets	Percentage of firms	Percentage of all assets		
8. Meat	82.6	5.9	13.0	7.5	2.0	3.9	$ 1,325	$ 220
18. Chemicals	84.4	2.8	11.4	4.0	1.3	1.6	1,405	172
20. Soaps, cleaners	91.8	4.6	5.5	4.9	0.9	2.6	519	78
21. Rubber and tires	86.8	8.4	10.6	10.2	1.4	4.0	630	183
24. Glass	87.9	2.5	7.9	3.4	1.4	1.8	1,169	90
30. Electrical machinery	88.9	3.9	7.3	3.7	1.4	2.1	1,705	125
32. Radio...communication equipment	87.1	3.5	8.7	3.9	1.7	2.6	1,038	133
35. Motor vehicles	82.7	0.7	11.8	1.0	2.0	0.5	5,622	160
40. Rail transportation	97.1	4.2	2.1	1.6	0.3	0.9	611	73
44. Air transportation	95.8	1.8	2.4	0.9	0.4	0.6	1,287	72
50. General merchandise	95.1	7.8	3.8	4.5	0.4	1.6	629	87
Median values	87.9%	3.5%	7.9%	3.9%	1.4%	1.8%	$ 1,004	$ 125

Part 3. Industry Categories in which the presence index of The 559 Largest Corporations was between 40 percent and 60 percent

Industry Category	Percentage of firms	Percentage of all assets	Percentage of firms	Percentage of all assets	Percentage of firms	Percentage of all assets		
3. Nonferrous metals	83.3%	1.5%	11.8%	2.3%	1.8%	1.2%	$ 4,710	$ 182
7. Food	83.5	5.9	12.2	8.4	1.7	3.8	1,640	187
11. Soft drinks	78.8	11.0	17.7	15.1	1.7	5.3	1,226	364
15. Lumber...wood...paper...products	87.8	6.8	9.4	7.5	1.3	3.7	1,241	163
23. Nonmetallic mineral products	87.5	14.8	10.1	14.6	1.3	6.4	809	194
28. Farm, construction...machinery	79.0	4.0	16.0	6.0	2.1	2.8	2,888	321
33. Scientific...control...devices...measuring	82.7	3.8	12.7	7.8	1.5	3.1	1,705	106
36. Aircraft	78.3	0.7	14.1	0.9	1.5	0.3	14,189	297
51. Food stores	97.5	21.3	1.8	7.2	0.3	3.9	288	73
Median values	83.5%	5.9%	12.2%	7.5%	1.5%	3.7%	$ 1,249	$ 187

Part 4. Industry Categories in which the presence index of The 559 Largest Corporations was between 20 percent and 40 percent

4.	Coal	87.1%	7.5%	$ 147	9.3%	1.4%	8.9%	4.4%	$ 1,365
10.	Alcoholic beverages	62.0	1.1	685	19.7	3.5	2.2	1.3	13,717
11.	Textiles	77.5	7.0	240	17.0	2.5	14.1	6.6	1,820
14.	Apparel	90.7	22.9	100	7.7	0.8	23.0	8.6	525
25.	Fabricated metal products	88.2	17.2	167	9.6	1.1	17.8	7.3	778
38.	Railroad equipment	85.1	7.1	212	9.8	1.7	2.3	5.5	3,121
39.	Other and miscellaneous manufacturing	92.7	16.2	84	5.6	0.8	13.9	6.9	663
42.	Motor transportation	95.1	25.6	145	4.0	0.4	17.0	5.2	359
47.	Radio and TV broadcasting	92.0	11.7	83	5.7	1.1	8.8	5.6	1,008
52.	Motion pictures	96.5	15.9	72	2.5	0.6	8.1	6.1	445
	Median values	89.5%	13.8%	$ 146	8.5%	1.1%	11.4%	5.9%	$ 740

Part 5. Industry Categories in which the presence index of The 559 Largest Corporations was zero or between zero and 20 percent

6.	Construction	95.0%	37.3%	$ 83	4.4%	0.4%	25.0%	8.4%	$ 329
17.	Printing and publishing	94.3	16.0	84	4.4	0.5	11.6	4.6	686
22.	Leather	81.4	13.0	277	15.6	1.3	19.5	5.4	1,373
27.	Machinery	92.4	13.5	94	5.6	1.0	11.2	6.6	867
43.	Water transportation	94.3	13.2	85	4.1	0.8	8.7	5.2	842
48.	Wholesale trade	92.4	30.6	123	6.6	0.6	23.3	7.2	539
49.	Retail trade	97.2	59.4	84	2.6	0.1	21.0	3.6	201
53.	Services	97.8	38.4	64	1.9	0.2	17.7	5.9	183
54.	Real estate	91.5	41.7	94	4.4	0.4	24.6	7.8	337
1.	Agriculture	95.7	52.0	98	3.9	0.3	25.4	6.7	296†
16.	Furniture and fixtures	90.9	26.0	133	7.2	1.1	22.4	12.9	628†
37.	Ship . . . building . . . †	86.9	5.4	109	9.5	2.0	5.1	4.2	2,874‡
41.	Transit	98.2	14.8	60	1.5	0.2	6.5	3.0	473†
55.	Nature of business not allocable	99.7	77.1	43	0.3	0.0	11.8	8.9	40
	Median values	94.3%	26.0%	$ 94	4.4%	0.6%	19.5%	6.6%	$ 315

*Except averages of The 559. Medians are interpolated medians arrived at by estimating the size of the hypothetical firm at the mid-point of the range of corporate sizes.

†Occurrence and presence of The 559 were zero.

‡Includes one corporation listed by the IRS among the 615 corporations with assets of more than $250 million. See Exhibit 49 and Chapter 7, Note 1. Without that corporation, the average size of the other firms was $1,079 thousand.

1. In recent years, a number of "conglomerates" have come into being; and a few hitherto merely *large* corporations have been in a fair way to becoming "conglomerates." A few comments on this phenomenon will be made in Chapter 13. For the moment, we can note that very few of The 559 Largest Corporations of 1971 had come into being through processes of, or reasons for, "conglomeration." The reasons for, and processes of, development of "conglomerates" were quite distinct from those of corporations that merely became big, or even very big, through processes of *growth* as distinguished from "combinations" and the like.

2. Because of the highly skewed distribution among Industry Categories of the numbers and the asset values of corporations (see, e.g., Exhibit 47), arriving at "typical" or "average" values presents problems. For that reason, in Exhibits 41-46, for example, the "average" asset values of firms are calculated on two bases: one that includes *all* corporations; another that excludes the Largest. In some Industry Categories, the asset values of the Largest Corporations are so large relative to the rest of the industry system as to completely overshadow, from a simple arithmetic point of view, the values of the assets of all other firms. "Average" values that include these large asset masses can be misleading. Even when several industries are grouped, some of this effect still persists. (See Exhibit 44, Part 1, for example.) For this reason, among others, the data should be handled gingerly.

   On the other hand, the *numbers* of firms in some industries—Services, for example—are so great that they far outweigh the numbers of firms in others—Leather, for instance. The number of firms in *five* out of 54 Industry Categories—Retail trade, Services, Real estate, Wholesale trade, and Construction—account for over 1,170,000—over 70 percent—of a total of *all* of the 1,592,000 nonfinancial corporations. Any calculation relating to *percentages* of the *numbers* of firms based on straightforward calculation will be heavily colored by the numbers of firms in such populous industries.

   Accordingly, in Exhibits 52 and 53, data are given for both *average* sizes of firms included among The 559 and for *median* sizes of firms.

   Because these "typical" figures are medians rather than arithmetic averages, they—like medians, generally—will only "accidentally," if ever, add up to 100 percent. They are none the less useful, for all that.

3. The reader will note that Exhibits 47-51 and 48 include *615* nonfinancial firms with assets of $250 million or more, whereas we have been talking all along about The *559* Largest. (See Chapter 7, Note 1.)

4. The classical formulation of that orthodoxy was *The Theory of Monopolistic Competition,* by Edward Chamberlin (Cambridge: Harvard University Press, 1933) (and later editions). In general, this received doctrine holds that, if only—somehow—industries were made up of large numbers of small firms producing essentially and easily substitutable, if not identical, products (more often than not in minimum-optimum-size plants), instead of small numbers of large firms trying to differentiate their products, then prices and costs would be lower, and outputs would be greater; quality of goods would be higher, and social welfare, in general terms, would be optimized; i.e., things would be "better" in many important dimensions than the results produced by the industrial structure we actually have.

   This doctrine has received more sophisticated formulation in recent years; but its core, as just stated, remains the same. See, e.g., F. M. Scherer, *Industrial Market-Structure and Economic Performance* (Chicago: Rand McNally & Co., 1970); and F. M. Scherer et al., *The Economics of Multi-plant Operation, an International Comparisons Study* (Cambridge: Harvard University Press, 1975).

   The trouble is that the doctrine is still preoccupied with the hypothetical working out of a limited set of variables that are explicitly or tacitly assumed to be *given* and *static.* The analysis continues to be cross-sectional. Dynamic, "longitudinal" phenomena are slighted or ignored.

9

The Largest Corporations and American development, 1929-1971;

Part I: The dynamic demographics of American corporations

Earlier, as in Chapter 5, various references have been made to times past, such as 1929, and to changes over years since then. In this chapter, we shall take a further look at some of the major aspects of the development of the United States over the last four decades and at the parts that the business community and our Largest Corporations, in particular, have played in that development, and at what that history may tell us about the transforming structure of the American System and where "big business" fits in that emergent scheme of things.

Our large corporations have been a major source of impetus, of driving force in making America what it is. Forty-some years ago, Adolf Berle and Gardiner Means were struck by how "ubiquitous" were the large corporations of the day, and their products and services. Nowadays, our Largest Corporations and their outputs are far more than merely ubiquitous. Now, they are among those elements of living and producing that are most *characteristic* of the "American System." In a literal sense, they are of the *essence* of that System.

Our Largest Corporations have grown in numbers and in mass. They have changed in their character. This expansion and development of our corporate population have gone ahead, interacting in reciprocal relationships with the general growth and evolution of the nation and its economy.

The expansion and development of America have provided "externalities" that, on the whole, with important exceptions, have fostered growth of, and change in, corporations; growing and better educated populations of workers and consumers; rising levels of incomes and expanding savings; expanding and improving networks of transportation and communication; growing and more accessible technology; even certain means of taxation and particular laws—these latter, more by the way they have operated than by deliberate policy.

The growing streams of the outputs of business organizations—automobiles, metals, pharmaceuticals, machinery, electric power, petroleum, the thousands of materials of all kinds that flow from the chemicals industry, telecommunications, mass distribution, and all the rest—have both responded to the nation's growth and made it possible.

The whole American *system* has grown and changed—expanding and evolving *as a system,* not as unrelated elements, independently following unrelated, isolated trajectories.

Growth is only part of our nation's story of the past forty-odd years. More important by far have been the processes and facts of *change.* The "American System" is not only much larger than it was. It is *very different:* not only from what it was; but different, even, from the handful of other leading industrial nations.

We know that. But we are seldom aware of how much of those differences of American life and ways of doing things are due to the workings of our large corporations. Directly, by themselves, and through massive industry systems of which they are nuclei, our large corporations have been leading actors in the *transformation* of the American System. From these large corporations, interacting with thousands upon thousands of even very small companies, flow the lion's share of what are the most typical tools, products, and services of "modernity."

Other institutions, of course, have also had their own effects on growth and change in America: governments, universities, unions, churches, foundations, associations of all sorts, for instances. But their influences, speaking generally, have been of rather intangible and indirect sorts. They have often expressed, and have helped determine "rules of the game," values and priorities, allocations of resources. Occasionally, intervention of government has been paramount, as in World War II.

Increasingly, throughout the whole period, the federal government, especially, but state and local governments as well, intervened in the workings of the "system." This they have done both directly and indirectly. In World War II, of course, the federal government all but took over the whole industrial apparatus. State and local governments have greatly expanded their social services, such as education, health care, and, along with the federal government, have developed vast "welfare" programs that entail massively growing "transfer payments," such as Social Security. Indirectly, governments have intervened in the allocation of resources and flows of products by means of provisions of tax laws and rulings, subsidies and "supports," tariffs and quotas, permits and a variety of other kinds of leverage increasingly available to them.

Unions, through efforts to gain recognition; through bargaining over contract provisions as to wages, hours, seniority, work rules, and working conditions, among other matters; through grievance actions and otherwise, have also affected the structure and workings of the system. The outcomes of these actions have worked to make some sorts of economic activities relatively more or less attractive than others, have hastened or retarded any number of developments in industry and commerce.

Universities have made possible advancement of knowledge and thought in arts, sciences, and technologies, and the emergence of new senses of "what ought to be."

But constraints, incentives, knowledge, "demands," aspirations—even visions—are all intangible in their nature. These are forces that shape what happens. Their actual effects, however, if there were—and are—to be any, had to be made manifest, and expressed *concretely*. It is one thing to think, and write and talk—even legislate—about changing values, about new policies and priorities, about new insights and knowledge; to voice "demands"; to encourage, discourage, or even prohibit. But something else is called for if these intangibles are to find tangible expression and to become realities.

A principal instrumentality through which these forces have achieved realization and concreteness has been the business community, composed, as it is, of the several industry systems. And as we have seen, in many of these industry systems, the nuclei that do so much to condition what they do, and how they do it, are made up of our Largest Corporations. The tangible, concrete America we see, live in, and cope with—the best we can—is, to a very large degree, the joint and cumulating product of the workings of hundreds of thousands of corporations, which have been making and doing—changing —things day after day, all these years.

As one looks about a room—a living room, a classroom, an operating room—about a factory; as one walks or drives through our cities, even the countryside, it requires no great sensitivity or knowledge of history to *see* how America and its way of life have been literally revolutionized, not merely transformed. We may be a little slower in coming to realize that among the chief "engines of change" in making this revolution a reality have been our large corporations.

Not so obvious, but no less real, is that many of the chief "revolutionaries" have been the thousands upon thousands of managers of these firms who have labored day after day for forty years to bring about change: to introduce new products; to find, mobilize and utilize new inputs, new means of production and distribution, new means of communication, new means of transportation. Managers, in the last four decades, have made innumerable decisions committing billions of dollars and billions of labor-years of human endeavor to bring about such changes. With all that going on, it would be unthinkable that America could have remained as it was. Or that the working out to equilibrium positions of sets of givens, or the attainment of "dynamic stability" could have been, in any sense, historic realities.

Whether these changes have produced a "better" nation is a metaphysical question. Theologians may have something to contribute to a discussion of that topic; but, ultimately, every individual will act as her or his own judge of that. Whether these changes have produced a "happier" nation is a socio-psycho-anthropological question, although some have tried to treat it as a philosophical one. Having left behind in history the Romanticism of Rousseau and the Transcendentalism of Thoreau, with all of their presuppositions, perhaps we can now approach that important matter with more intellect, if less fervor. And as we do, we, as a people, may well resolve to set new goals, new priorities, a new course.

Those matters, significant as they are, nevertheless, are afield from our present, more pedestrian objective. That purpose is to unearth and understand better some key facts about our national productive apparatus. This is composed primarily of business corporations that have played a decisive role both in making us what we are and in enabling us to become what we now find ourselves.

That is the burden of this chapter.

THE LARGEST CORPORATIONS IN THE TOTAL CORPORATE COMMUNITY, 1929-1971: SUMMARY

In 1929, there were 322,084 corporations in the United States. Over the 42 years from 1929 through 1971, this number grew by 1,270,101 to a total of 1,592,193. The number of incorporated firms almost quintupled.

The total asset mass of the community of corporations, measured in something like 1971 dollars, had amounted to just under $600 billion in 1929. By 1971, this productive apparatus had increased in value by a factor of 2.35 to about $1,411 billion. Of that increase of $811 billion, some $463 billion—about 57 percent—was accounted for by the growth of corporations with assets (in 1971 dollars) of $250 million or more.

In consequence of the relatively faster growth of the assets of the Largest Corporations, the fraction of the total of corporate assets held by them grew from about 40 percent to about 50 percent. This growth was accounted for in very large measure, as we shall see, by the expansion of industries most characteristic of what we think of in connection with such concepts as modernity, urbanization, and industrialism. It did not, again as we shall see, represent to any important degree a concentration of anything that heretofore had been unconcentrated. Nor did the growth of large corporations mean that small business was disappearing.

On the contrary, small business, far from moribund or disappearing, was flourishing. Over the 40-some years, the number of small corporations had grown by almost 1.3 million. As we shall see, small corporations were becoming far more varied in nature; they were responding to hosts of new opportunities opening up as the American people became more and more opulent, more urban, more cosmopolitan, and as they became more and more imaginative in consumption as well as in production. Small business grew, also, in response to literally hundreds of thousands of new opportunities opening up with the advance of technologies and in consequence of the growth in scale and complexity and sophistication of industry systems particularly and increasingly characteristic of the recent decades of the continuing Industrial Revolution in America. The *nature* of the community of small business had evolved along with the rest of the American System.

EXHIBIT 54
The largest nonfinancial corporations in the total corporate community, 1929-1971 (values in billions of 1971 dollars)

	All corporations	The 200	The 559*	All corporations other than The 559 Largest
Number of nonfinancial corporations				
1929	322,084	200*	200*	321,884
1971	1,592,193	200	559*	1,591,634
Increase in number of corporations	1,270,109	–	359†	1,269,750
Index of the number of firms				
1929	100.0	100.0	100.0*	100.0
1971	494.3	100.0	279.5†	494.5
Assets				
1929	$598.3	$244.5*	$244.5*	$353.8
1971	$1,410.5	$538.2*	$707.2*	$703.3
Increase in value of assets	$812.2	$239.7†	$462.7†	$349.5
Index of asset values				
1929	100.0	100.0	100.0*	100.0
1971	235.8	220.1	289.2†	198.8
Percentage of total assets				
1929	100.0%	40.8%	40.8%*	59.1%
1971	100.0%	38.2%	50.1%*	49.9%
Average size of firm, thousands of 1971 dollars				
1929	$1,858	$1,222,500	$1,222,500	$1,099
1971	$886	$2,691,000	$1,265,116	$442

*Corporations with assets of $250 million and more in 1971 dollars.
†Compared to The 200 of 1929.
Source: Exhibits 1, 2, 15, 32, etc.

A couple of other measures reflect the vitality of small business over these 40-some years. The total assets of all corporations other than the largest almost doubled, from about $354 billion to about $703 billion. At the same time, because of the fivefold increase in the *number* of corporations, the average size of corporations declined by almost 60 percent. In relative terms, it took far less to be in business—in corporate form—in 1971 than it had in 1929.

As for *large* corporations, they were not only more numerous. They were far more diverse, and far less tightly clustered in those industries that had been particularly characterized by the presence of large corporations in 1929. The growth and increasing variety of large corporations stand as testimony, as we said, to the key roles they played as energizing forces in both the expansion and transformation of American industry and the American economy.

A statistical summary of the changing "demographics" of American corporations is set forth in Exhibit 54.

GROWTH AND CHANGE OF THE CORPORATE COMMUNITY

Now, we shall look at and contemplate some of the detailed data relating to growth and change of the corporate business community. The dynamics of that community is the context in which the subpopulation of Largest Corporations has grown and evolved. Our first device for this study is a compilation of corporate data classified according to Major Industry Groups. Parts 1 and 2 of Exhibit 55, which follow, do two things: (*a*) they sketch profiles of the corporate community as a whole, both as it was at the end of 1929 and as it was at the end of 1971; and (*b*) they set forth data that measure the net changes that took place in those profiles between the two terminal years. These data tell us a great deal about the history of America as a developing nation over four decades of swirling change.

Before we get into analyzing the numbers, we should note a few *caveats* about the data.

First, as has been noted earlier, data based on the so-called Major Industry Groups leave much to be desired. These difficulties are compounded in looking at sets of data separated by more than 40 years. But, on the ground that something is better than nothing, we use these groupings for asset data simply because, for the year 1929, no other comprehensive data as to corporate assets are available. Second, as also has been noted, there are real problems in converting values of assets expressed in 1929 dollars into values expressed in 1971 dollars. Third, and most important, is the simple fact that the concrete assets behind the reported values of 1929 and 1971 were *very* different in kinds. For example, the power-generating equipments of the electric utilities in 1971 were far different, and more efficient, from those of 1929. In the Chemicals and allied products group, for instance, great values of assets existed in 1971 that had no counterparts in 1929: plants for making antibiotics and antihistamines, for instance. Although petroleum refineries existed in 1929, to be sure, the catalytic, reforming, and other kinds of apparatus commonly used in 1971 for producing gasoline, nylon, synthetic rubber, ammonia, and other petrochemicals—all in a single "refining" complex—were all artifacts of a much later technology.

EXHIBIT 55
Growth and change, the U.S. corporate community; All corporations, 1929-1971
(Part 1: Numbers of firms, values of assets)

Major Industry Groups	1929				1971			
	Number of firms	Percentage of firms	Value of assets ($ millions)*	Percentage of assets	Number of firms	Percentage of firms	Value of assets ($ millions)*	Percentage of assets
Agriculture, forestry, and fisheries	9,430	2.9%	$ 6,564	1.1%	39,932	2.5%	$ 11,800	0.8%
Mining and quarrying	12,502	3.9	36,295	6.1	12,613	1.0	26,042	1.8
Construction	18,358	5.7	9,494	1.6	143,092	9.0	48,243	3.4
Manufacturing								
Food and kindred products, beverages and tobacco	14,845	4.6	30,062	5.0	16,394	1.0	63,332	4.5
Textiles and textile products	14,340	4.5	20,316	3.4	22,883	1.4	26,616	1.9
Lumber and wood products and allied products	9,568	3.0	19,157	3.2	20,888	1.3	39,141	2.8
Printing, publishing, and allied products	11,170	3.5	8,706	1.5	26,541	1.7	20,910	1.5
Chemicals and allied products	7,071	2.2	43,040	7.2	10,825	0.7	155,924	11.1
Rubber and tires	614	0.2	4,362	0.1	6,235	0.4	13,071	0.9
Leather and leather products	2,433	0.8	3,675	0.1	2,269	0.1	3,809	0.3
Stone, clay, and glass products	4,561	1.4	7,341	1.2	8,580	0.5	15,762	0.1
Metal and metal products. .	20,156	6.3	70,795	11.8	69,461	4.4	286,315	20.3
Other and misc. mfg.	7,472	2.3	8,141	1.4	16,897	1.1	21,767	1.5
Subtotal, manufacturing	92,230	28.6%	$ 215,595	36.0%	200,973	12.6%	$ 646,647	45.8%
Transportation and other public utilities	21,608	6.7	238,627	39.9	71,104	4.5	309,902	22.0
Wholesale and retail trade . .	129,089	40.1	67,000	11.2	538,664	33.8	210,884	15.0
Services	35,967	11.2	23,988	4.0	287,780	18.1	62,226	4.4
Nature of business not allocable	2,900	0.9	773	0.1	21,438	1.3	847	— ‖
Real estate	—†	—	—†	—	276,597	17.1	93,920	6.7
Totals, nonfinancial corporations‡	322,084	100.0%	$ 598,336	100.0%	1,592,193	100.0%	$1,410,511	100.0%
Financial corporations § . . .	133,937		431,671		141,139		1,478,710	
Total, all industries	456,021		$1,029,999		1,733,332		$2,889,221	

Note: See Exhibit 3, Footnote c and Note 1, Chapter 9. Numbers of firms of 1929 are those "reporting net income" and "reporting no net income."

* 1971 dollars. See Chapter 1, Note 4 and Appendix A, General Note 7.

† Data for 1929 not available.

‡ Excludes real estate in 1929; includes real estate, 1971.

§ In 1929, includes real estate, together with banking, insurance, and other financial industries; in 1971, excludes real estate.

‖ Less than $1/10$ of 1 percent.

Major Industry Groups	Net increases/decreases 1929-71		Relative changes 1929-71 (1929 = 100)		Percentages of the net increases/decreases, all nonfinancial corporations	
	Number of firms	Value of assets ($ millions)*	Number of firms	Value of assets	Of the number of fims	Of the assets
Agriculture, forestry and fisheries	30,502	$ 5,236	423	183	2.4%	0.6%
Mining and quarrying	111	−10,253	101	72	− ‖	−1.3
Construction	124,734	38,749	779	508	9.8	4.8
Manufacturing						
Food and kindred products, beverages and tobacco	1,549	33,270	110	211	0.1	4.1
Textiles and textile products	8,543	6,300	160	131	0.6	0.8
Lumber and wood products and paper and allied products	11,320	19,984	218	204	0.9	2.5
Printing, publishing, and allied products	15,371	12,204	238	240	1.2	1.5
Chemicals and allied substances	3,754	112,884	153	362	0.3	13.9
Rubber and tires	5,621	8,709	1,015	300	0.4	1.1
Leather and leather products . .	−164	134	93	104	− ‖	−
Stone, clay, and glass products	4,019	8,421	188	215	0.3	1.0
Metal and metal products	49,305	215,520	345	404	3.9	26.5
Other and miscellaneous manufacturing	9,425	13,626	226	267	0.7	1.7
Subtotal, manufacturing	108,743	431,057	218	300	8.6	53.1
Transportation and other public utilities	49,496	71,275	329	130	3.9	8.8
Wholesale and retail trade	409,575	143,884	417	315	32.2	17.7
Services	251,813	38,238	800	259	19.8	4.7
Nature of business not allocable	18,538	74	739	110	1.5	− ‖
Real estate	−†	−†	−†	−†	21.8‡	11.6‡
Totals, nonfinancial corporations ‡	1,270,109	812,183	494	236	100.0%	100.0%
Financial corporations §	7,202 §	1,047,039 §	105	343		
Total, all industries	1,273,311	$1,859,222	380	281		

Note: See Exhibit 3, Footnote *c*. Because of substantial questions as to close comparability of the data of the terminal years, overly specific conclusions should not be drawn from this exhibit.

* 1971 dollars. See Chapter 1, Note 4 and Appendix A, General Note 7.

† Data for 1929 not available.

‡ Excludes real estate in 1929; includes real estate, 1971; accordingly, increases in real estate corporations between 1929 and 1971 are overstated.

§ In 1929, includes real estate, together with banking, insurance, and other financial industries; in 1971, excludes real estate; accordingly, increases in financial corporations between 1929 and 1971 are understated.

‖ Less than $\frac{1}{10}$ of 1 percent.

The switching apparatuses of telephone systems of 1929 were largely manual; in 1971, they were, with exceptions of small rural companies, totally electromechanical; and microwave relays, even satellites, were rapidly displacing wire on many major telephone traffic routes. A number of electronic-switching centrals, the precursors of hundreds of new units scheduled for installation over the next decades, were already in place. One has to be very reserved and very general in thinking about these numbers.

Not only were the assets of large corporations vastly different in kinds, so also were the assets of small business, as we shall note in just a moment.

Bearing those qualifications in mind, let us turn to the figures, such as they are.

As one scans Exhibit 55, Parts 1 and 2, one quickly sees several principal facts. First, between 1929 and 1971, the population of corporations in America had increased by a factor of almost *five*. Their numbers had grown from 322,000 to almost 1,600,000. Second—bearing all the qualifications in mind—the total dollar book value of the assets of these corporations had more than doubled, from about $600 billion (1971 dollars) to $1,410 billion.[1]

The corporate population of 1971—viewed in very broad-brush terms—was not only more numerous and more "massive" than that of 1929; it was notably *different* in its composition. Of the increase in the "census" total of corporations from 322,000 to 1,600,000, almost two-thirds of the growth in numbers had come about in three Major Industry Groups: Wholesale and retail trade, Services, and Construction.

Equally remarkable was the difference in the composition of the aggregate asset mass—quite apart from the qualitative differences as between the kinds of assets employed within industries, as mentioned above. Of the $812 billion of increase in assets—assuming the conversion of 1929 dollars of assets into 1971 dollar terms was somewhere near accurate for gauging asset growth—almost 40 percent of that growth was in two Major Industry Groups that characterize modern, large-scale industrialism: more than 25 percent had been in Metal and metal products; 14 percent had been in Chemicals and allied substances. To this might be added the 8.8 percent increase in the broad utilities Group—about which, more later. At the same time, significant, although lesser, growth had taken place in three typically small business groups. Almost 18 percent of the total growth had been in Wholesale and retail trade; more than 11 percent in Real estate; almost 5 percent in both Construction and Services.

Tables 17 and 18 may help focus attention on the major differences in the two populations.

What is most notable here is that the greater part, over 80 percent, of the increase in the *numbers* of corporations took place in typically

TABLE 17
Principal increases in the corporation population, 1929-1971
by Major Industry Groups

	Increase in number of firms (000)	Percentage of the total increase in number of firms
Construction	124.7	9.8%
Wholesale and retail trade	409.6	32.2
Services	251.8	19.8
Real estate	260.0 (?)	20.5 (?)
All other	224.0	17.6
Total	1,270.1	100.0%

Source: Exhibit 55, Part 2. See footnotes to that exhibit concerning real estate.

TABLE 18
Principal increases in asset values, 1929-1971; by Major Industry Groups and selected subgroups

	Increase in values (billions of 1971 dollars)	Percentage of the total increase in value of assets
Construction	$ 38.7	4.8%
Chemicals and allied substances	112.9	13.9
Metal and metal products	215.5	26.5
Transportation and other public utilities	71.3	8.8
Wholesale and retail trade	143.9	17.7
Services	38.2	4.7
Real estate	90.0 (?)	11.1 (?)
All other	101.7	12.5
Total	$812.2	100.0%

Source: Exhibit 55, Part 2. See footnotes to that exhibit concerning real estate.

small-business industry Groups. We shall return to this interesting phenomenon in a moment.

As mentioned, almost half of the total *asset* growth had taken place in three Groups: Chemicals and allied products (13.9 percent), which includes the Petroleum industry, of course; in Metal and metal products (26.5 percent), which includes, among other Industry Categories, basic Iron and steel, Nonferrous metals, and most notably, Motor vehicles; and, about 9 percent, in Transportation and other public utilities. (This latter figure, as we shall shortly see, is *net* of a sizable actual *decline* in the asset values of Rail transportation.)

The growth of the assets in the Major Industry Group Wholesale and retail trade, along with the growth in the *numbers* of corporations, is quite a story, in itself.

In any event, the facts stand out that dynamic processes had brought about large absolute and relative increases in the *numbers* and *assets* of *small* firms, and large absolute and relative growth in the *asset masses* of *big* firms.

The net result was that, even in broad-brush terms, let alone concrete detail, the structure and the composition of the American corporate community in 1971 were very, very different from those of 1929.

These developments did not occur in isolation. Again, they were part and parcel of the growth and evolution of the whole American System.

A NOTE ON THE DYNAMICS OF THE COMMUNITY OF SMALL BUSINESS

This book is preoccupied with the places and roles of *large* corporations. But here is another instance where a few comments on *small* business are not merely an interesting digression, but add meaning to our chosen topic.

As we have seen, the numbers of small firms increased, as did the asset masses of small firms, between 1929 and 1971. But the dynamics were not merely quantitative. Again, far more important and far more interesting are the qualitative dynamics. Exhibit 55, Parts 1 and 2, do not record merely that there were *more* of the *same kinds* of small firms, using more of the same kinds of assets, than there had been in 1929. Highly detailed "demographic" censuses of small firms in these two terminal years would reveal very different kinds of populations.

Systemic evolutionary processes had been taking place all the while that resulted in an utter transformation of the nature and composition of the community, and subcommunities of *small* business. And that transformation was directly, as well as indirectly, connected with the transformation of the *big* business community, and was an integral part of the transformation of the whole American System, including its technology and other aspects of its culture, its way of life and means of living.

A few minutes of wandering through the Yellow Pages of the telephone directory in any city of the United States will suggest just *how* different were the populations of small business in 1929 and 1971, and in what ways, and why they were different.

An outstanding example is to be found in the case of the automobile and its companion and, on the highways, its competitor, the truck. Although the Motor vehicles industry, narrowly conceived, is pretty much a Big Business industry (as indicated in Chapter 7), its rise has been accompanied by a rise just about as dramatic, although perhaps less visible, in small businesses that, in a *systemic* sense, are really just as much a part of the Automobile industry as the Big 4 auto-makers, themselves. Motor vehicles, still something of a novelty in 1929, in 1971 were of the very essence of the American Way of Life.

The IRS data for 1971 listed 10,604 corporations engaged in the wholesale trade of motor vehicles and equipment; 41,483 corporate firms under "Retail trade: Automotive dealers and service stations"; and 23,211 corporations in "Automobile services and miscellaneous repair service"—for a total of more than 75,000 companies.

In the Yellow Pages, aside from "Automobile Dealers—New Cars," these myriads of auto-related firms are found under such categories as "Automobile Repairing and Service," "Automobile Electric Equipment," "Automobile Electric Service," "Automobile Parts and Supplies—Retail," "Automobile Racing and Sport Car Equipment," "Automobile Radios and Stereo Systems—Retail," "Automobile Rental and Leasing," "Automobile Washing and Polishing Equipment and Supplies," and on and on, page after page, to "Automobile Wrecking." Then there were firms in businesses of selling, repairing, and rebuilding automobile batteries and bearings; providing "Limousine Service"; selling and retreading tires.

And that is just a sampling of the entries.

Then one finds entries in contracting, distribution, sale, and service of items and needs stemming from new technologies: "Acoustical Consultants"; "Audiovisual Consultants"; "Audiovisual Equipment and Supplies"; "Automation Systems" (including contractors, distributors, retailers and consultants); "Controls, Control Systems and Regulators" (again contractors, distributors, retailers, and consultants); "Data Processing Equipment," "Data Processing Services," and "Data Systems—Consultants and Designers"; "Electric Appliances—Major" and "Electric Appliances—Small, Repairing"; and such enterprises as "Photoelectric Cells and Equipment" and "Ultrasonic Equipment and Supplies."

During World War II and since, we have learned more about manipulating and producing molecules than in all prior time. So, we now have large numbers of businesses under the headings of "Chemicals—Manufacturers and Distributors," "Chemists—Analytical and Consulting." And then scores of wholesale and retail dealers specializing in plastic products: bags, boxes, bindings, bottles, envelopes, furniture, letters, novelties, scrap, shower curtains, and on and on. And columns of "Pharmaceutical Products—Wholesalers and Manufacturers" and "Pharmaceutical Research Laboratories."

Then there are all the sorts of "Contractors": "General," "Concrete—Prestressed"; "Electric"; as well as "Contractors' Equipment and Supplies," distributors and rental services; and firms that sell, install, and service heating and illuminating, as well as air-conditioning and other kinds of equipment, furnishings, and various amenities of easier living.

Come *pages* of firms engaged in various aspects of television: "Television Program Producers," "Television and Radio Dealers and Service," "Television Rental," "Television Systems and Equipment—Closed Circuit" (installed and maintained by "security" services!). Under the general heading of "Real Estate," comes column after column of lists of brokers, realty corporations, apartment buildings, office buildings, industrial sites and parks, "relocation specialists," followed by columns of "Real Estate Appraisers," "Real Estate Developers," "Real Estate Consultants," and "Real Estate Management."

An incredible array of enterprises and businesses, almost invariably small, catering to ways of life unknown to 1929—and maybe or maybe not preferable: "Cocktail Lounges," "Liquor Stores," "Wine Shops," "Burglar Alarm Systems," "Abortion and Abortion Alternatives, Information," and "Drug Abuse and Addiction Information and Treatment Centers," "Snow Vehicles," "Outboard Motors," and "Barbecue Equipment and Supplies."

All the way to "X-ray Laboratories—Industrial"; "Yoga Instruction" (having passed by "Judo, Karate and Jiu-Jitsu Instruction"), and "Zippers—Repairing."

The day of the village blacksmith is long gone. But small business is alive and well and flourishing in Modern America!

What a topic, in its own right, would be the growth and transformation of the community of *small* enterprise—corporate and otherwise, profit-seeking and eleemosynary—as an integral part of the growing and evolving American System!

From the standpoint of our present topic of *large* corporations, it is easy enough to see outlines of all sorts of symbiotic, interdependent relationships with smaller firms—smaller firms as suppliers, as distributors, as sources of service to large corporations and to the users of their products, and as competitors for the discretionary-spending dollars of opulent consumers and for such critical input factors as managerial talent.

The increasing numbers of firms, in all their diversity, were both consequence and cause of the increasing complexity and diversity of American life—of life styles, of production, of consumption. The "simple" human ecological system of "frontier," almost Spartan, life, based upon small-scale industry and, broadly speaking, agrarian production and life in smaller towns, has been replaced by an utterly different system. And much of that transformation has taken place over the past 40 years.

In Exhibit 56, Parts 1 and 2, are displayed data that relate to the community of Largest Corporations as it was in 1929 and as it was in 1971, and to the *growth* of, and *differences* in the compositions of, that community as between the terminal years of 1929 and 1971.

As between those years, the community of our Largest Corporations had undergone three important changes. Their numbers had increased; there were 559 corporations in 1971 that were as large as any included among The 200 of 1929. The aggregate asset masses had grown. And the composition of that community had become very different. In these dimensions, the community of the Largest Corporations was one of the most dynamic components of the entire American system.

Again, we shall have to remind ourselves how *different* also were the *individual* firms of 1971 from those of 1929, even those that had persisted over the whole time span and were included in the same Major Industry Groups, in the two terminal years—say, General Electric—let alone entirely new kinds of firms that had arisen in industries not then yet born.

The 200 Largest of 1929 and 1971 among all corporations

The 200 Largest firms of 1929 were the largest among 322,000; those of 1971, among almost 1,600,000. The asset mass of all corporations, as mentioned, had increased from something like $600 billion of 1971 dollars to about $1,411 billion—a factor of about 2.4; that of The 200 Largest of the respective years had increased from $244 billion to $538 billion—by a somewhat smaller factor, say, 2.2. (See Exhibit 55, Part 1, and Exhibit 56, Part 1.) In consequence, the relative share, or "presence index," of all corporate assets held by The 200 Largest seems to have declined somewhat, from 40 percent to 38 percent. (With all the questions one can raise about strict comparability of the data, one cannot be too sure of that comparison. The "real" share of The 200 Largest, conceivably, could have either decreased more than that, or, actually, even increased to some extent.)

About two other matters, however, there seems to be greater certainty: the *average* size of The 200 Largest does appear to have more than doubled, from $1.2 billion to about $2.7 billion; second, the average size of all *other* corporations (still in 1971 dollar terms) seems to have been reduced by something like 50 percent, falling from $1,800,000 to $886,000.

In short, the total asset mass of The top 200 grew about in step with that of all other corporations, say, by doubling, or something more. But the *number* of all other corporations grew by such a

EXHIBIT 56

Growth and change, the Largest Nonfinancial Corporations, 1929-1971, by Major Industry Groups

(Part 1: Numbers of firms and values of assets; The 200 Largest Corporations of 1929 and 1971, and The 559 Largest Corporations of 1971)

Major Industry Groups	The 200 Largest Corporations, 1929				The 200 Largest Corporations, 1971				The 559 Largest Corporations, 1971			
	No. of firms	No. of firms, as percentage of The 200	Value of assets ($ millions)	Assets held by The 200 as percentage of all corporations, by Major Industry Groups	No. of firms	No. of firms, as percentage of The 200	Value of assets ($ millions)	Assets held by The 200 as percentage of all corporations, by Major Industry Groups	No. of firms	No. of firms, as percentage of The 559	Value of assets ($ millions)	Assets held by The 559 as percentage of all corporations, by Major Industry Groups
Agriculture	0	0.0%	$ 0.0	0.0%	0	0.0%	$ 0.0	0.0%	0	0.0%	$ 0.0	0.0%
Mining and quarrying	4	2.0	2,130.4	5.8	0	0.0	0.0	0.0	3	0.5	1,413.6	5.4
Construction	0	0.0	0.0	0.0	0	0.0	0.0	0.0	3	0.5	1,201.2	2.5
Manufacturing												
Food	13	6.5	8,073.0	26.9	15	7.5	19,555.0	30.9	43	7.7	35,048.2	55.3
Textiles	1	0.5	349.4	1.7	2	1.0	2,323.7	8.7	14	2.5	7,050.2	26.5
Lumber...wood...paper...products	4	2.0	3,100.0	16.1	8	4.0	12,506.9	32.0	17	3.0	17,385.7	44.4
Printing, publishing	0	0.0	0.0	0.0	0	0.0	0.0	0.0	7	1.3	2,702.1	12.9
Chemicals	25	12.5	28,915.5	67.1	35	17.5	128,528.9	82.4	82	14.7	152,691.1	97.9
Rubber and tires	4	2.0	2,687.7	61.6	5	2.5	9,149.0	70.0	5	0.9	9,149.0	70.0
Leather	1	0.5	347.5	9.4	0	0.0	0.0	0.0	2	0.4	696.7	18.3
Stone, clay, glass	1	0.5	311.7	4.2	2	1.0	2,708.4	17.2	17	3.0	9,831.7	62.4
Metal and metal products	36	18.0	35,226.9	49.8	39	19.5	102,975.8	35.9	113	20.2	137,322.3	48.0
Other and misc. mfg.	2	1.0	1,360.1	16.7	12*	6.0	40,115.8*	N.M.§	34†	6.1	49,750.2†	N.M.§
Subtotal, manufacturing	91	45.5%	$ 82,502.3	38.3%	118	59.0%	$317,863.5*	49.2%	340†	60.8%	$424,242.0†	65.6%†
Transportation utilities	95	42.5	154,534.5	64.6	71	35.5	197,450.3	63.7	160	28.6	240,469.4	77.6
Wholesale and retail trade	9	4.5	4,341.1	6.4	12	6.0	22,926.5	10.9	38	6.8	33,553.1	15.9
Services	4	2.0	2,723.9	11.3	0	0.0	0.0	0.0	17	3.0	6,899.1	11.1
Nature of business not allocable	0	0.0	0.0	0.0	0	0.0	0.0	0.0	0	0.0	0.0	0.0
Total nonfinancial corporations excluding real estate	109	99.5%	$244,103.1	40.8%	200‡	100.0%	$538,240.3	38.2%	553‡	98.9%	$705,163.6	50.0%
Real estate	1	0.5	382.2	—	0	0.0	0.0	N.M.	6	1.1	2,031.2	2.2
Total nonfinancial corporations	200	100.0%	$244,485.3	—	200‡	100.0%	$538,240.3	38.2%	559‡	100.0%	$707,194.8	50.1%

Note: Values in 1971 dollars.

* Includes Western Electric Corporation, a manufacturing subsidiary of American Telephone & Telegraph; see Appendix A, "Notes to Exhibit 1," Note 53.

† Includes manufacturing subsidiaries of American Telephone & Telegraph and General Telephone & Electronics; see Appendix A, "Notes to Exhibit 1," Notes 53 and 54.

‡ Although indicated separately above, the foregoing subsidiaries are not counted separately in the total numbers of firms.

§ "N.M." signifies "not meaningful."

EXHIBIT 56 *(continued)*
(Part 2: Comparisons of numbers of firms and values of assets; The 200 Largest Corporations of 1929 and 1971, and The 559 Largest Corporations of 1971)

Major Industry Groups	The 200 Largest Corporations of 1971 compared to The 200 Largest of 1929						The 559 Largest Corporations of 1971 compared to The 200 Largest of 1929					
	Net increases/decreases 1929-71		Relative changes 1929-71 (1929=100)		Percentages of the increases/decreases		Net increases/decreases 1929-71		Relative changes 1929-71 (1929=100)		Percentages of the increases/decreases	
	Number of firms	Value of assets ($ millions)	Number of firms	Value of assets	Of the number of firms	Of the assets	Number of firms	Value of assets ($ millions)	Number of firms	Value of assets	Of the number of firms	Of the assets
Agriculture	–	$ 0.0	–	–	–	–	0	$ 0.0	–	–	–	–
Mining and quarrying	-4	-2,130.4	–	–	–	-0.7%	-1	-716.8	75	66	-0.3%	-0.2%
Construction	–	0.0	–	–	–	–	3	1,201.2	N.M.§	N.M.§	0.8	0.3
Manufacturing												
Food	2	11,482.0	115	242	–	3.9	30	26,975.2	331	434	8.4	5.8
Textiles	1	1,974.3	200	665	–	0.7	13	6,700.8	1,400	2,018	3.6	1.4
Lumber...wood....												
paper...products	4	9,406.9	200	403	–	3.2	13	14,285.7	425	561	3.6	3.1
Printing...publishing	–	0.0	–	–	–	–	7	2,702.1	N.M.	N.M.	1.9	0.6
Chemicals	10	99,613.4	140	444	–	33.9	57	123,775.6	328	528	15.9	26.8
Rubber and tires	1	6,461.3	120	340	–	2.2	1	6,461.3	125	340	0.3	1.4
Leather	-1	-347.5	–	–	–	-0.1	1	349.2	200	200	0.3	0.1
Stone, clay, glass	1	2,396.7	200	869	–	0.8	16	9,520.0	1,700	3,154	4.5	2.1
Metal and metal products	3	67,748.9	108	292	–	23.1	77	102,095.4	314	390	21.4	22.1
Other and miscellaneous manufacturing	10*	38,755.7	600	2,949	–	13.2	32†	48,390.1	1,700	3,658	8.9	10.5
Subtotal, manufacturing	31	$237,491.6	136	395	–	80.8%	249	$341,739.7	374	514	69.4%	73.9%
Transportation...utilities	-24	42,914.6	75	129	–	14.6	65	85,934.9	168	156	18.1	18.6
Wholesale and retail trade	3	18,585.4	133	528	–	6.3	29	29,212.0	422	773	8.1	6.3
Services	-4	-2,723.9	–	–	–	-0.9	13	4,175.2	425	253	3.6	0.9
Nature of business not allocable	–	0.0	–	–	–	–	0	0.0	–	–	–	–
Total nonfinancial corporations excluding real estate	1*	$294,137.2	–	220	–	100.1%	354‡	$461,060.5	278	289	98.6%	99.6%
Real estate	-1	-382.2	–	–	–	-0.1	5‡	1,649.0	600	531	1.4	0.4
Total nonfinancial corporations	–	$293,755.0	–	220	–	100.0%	359	$462,709.5	280	289	100.0%	100.0%

Note: Values in 1971 dollars.
*Includes Western Electric; not included in the total number of corporations. See Appendix A, "Notes to Exhibit 1," Note 53.
†Includes manufacturing subsidiaries of American Telephone & Telegraph and General Telephone & Electronics; not included in the total number of corporations. See Appendix A, "Notes to Exhibit 1," Notes 53 and 54.
‡Although indicated separately above, the foregoing subsidiaries are not counted separately in the total numbers of firms.
§"N.M." signifies "not meaningful."

factor that The 200 of 1971 were now surrounded by almost five times as many, and considerably smaller, corporations as had been The 200 of 1929.

In ecological terms, the subcommunity of the Largest Corporations now was set in, and was interdependent with, and was part of, a far more diverse and far more populous and, therefore, a far more complex ambient corporate community than had been the case 40-some years earlier.

As the total corporate community had grown in numbers and sheer mass, far more significantly, it had evolved in kind. *Change, evolution, transformation*—not "equilibrium"—was a (perhaps *the*) central fact in the major productive apparatus of our private sector: the corporate community.

The implications of facts relating to the changing structure and composition of the community of corporations must stand as challenge no less to businessmen, political leaders, and other thinking people than to economists. Some of those implications will be raised in Chapter 13.

The 200 Largest of 1971 compared to those of 1929

As was true of *all* corporations, the compositions of the two rosters of The 200—in 1929 and 1971—were different; so, also, were the relative distributions of their assets among industry Groups.

The biggest shift in the makeup of the largest firms, as categorized by those Groups, was their greater representation in Manufacturing, up from 91 companies to 118. There were 10 more in each of Chemicals and allied products and Other and miscellaneous manufacturing. Of the 10 more in Chemicals and allied products, leaving aside for the moment the identities of individual companies, the net increase of 10 was entirely in *chemicals,* as distinct from Petroleum, including 4 corporations in Pharmaceuticals that had been a long, long way from inclusion among The 200 Largest of 1929.

The growth of very large integrated companies in Lumber... wood ...paper is attested by the net increase from 4 to 8 corporations in the representation of that Industry Group among The 200. The asset mass of the largest integrated Lumber... wood... paper companies of 1971 had quadrupled as compared to those of 1929.

The net increase of ten firms in Other and miscellaneous manufacturing included seven in Office, computing and accounting machines, one in Scientific, measuring, and control devices, two in Radio, TV, and communication equipment. The net increase of three firms in Metal and metal products among The 200 of 1929 conceals more than it reveals, as we shall soon see, when we look at what happened within individual Industry Categories—such as, for instance, the decrease in the number of Iron and steel companies included among The 200 Largest and the increase in the number of companies in Motor vehicles.

The same can be said of the apparent net decrease of 24 in the number of firms among The 200 Largest in Transportation . . . utilities. In this instance, to anticipate, the data given for Major Industry Groups utterly gloss over the restructuring of the railroads and the utilities and the rise of the airlines—three very important chapters in our industrial history of the past 40 years. But we are coming back to those developments in just a few pages.

As to assets, as distinguished from numbers, the relative position, or presence index, of The 200 Largest Corporations apparently declined, as mentioned, from about 41 percent to about 38 percent of the total. This is to say, not to put too much reliance on numbers that may be a bit "spongy," that the share of the total value of *all* corporate assets held by The 200 Largest was *about* the same in 1971 as in 1929.

As to changes in the *distribution* of the assets of The 200's in the two terminal years, some of these changes paralleled changes in the corporate community as a whole; some did not. The representation of the largest firms in the Manufacturing Group, for instance, increased, but at a considerably faster rate than for corporations as a whole. The country was, indeed, becoming more industrialized as Manufacturing grew, and much of this process was carried forward by the very largest firms. The relative growths of the largest corporations in Chemicals and allied products, and in Other and miscellaneous manufacturing were far greater than among The 200 Largest Corporations than among corporations as a whole.

The asset-share of The 200 in Metal and metal products apparently dropped (from something like 50 percent of the total assets of all corporations in those industries to about 36 percent), even though *within* and among The 200 the asset growth in those industries was one of the largest—from $35 billion to $103 billion. (See Exhibit 56, Parts 1 and 2.) The explanation, of course, lies in the even greater growth of *all* companies, generally, in that Industry Group. (Exhibit 55, Part 1, shows an overall growth for *all* corporations in Metal and metal products from $70.8 billion to $286.3 billion and an increase in the number of firms from about 20,000 to over 69,000.) Clearly, in certain branches of metal and metal products industries, smaller firms had grown relatively faster than the larger firms.

As our technology and national product increased in sophistication, so also did our production and consumption of metals, not only of iron and steel and alloy metals, but of items using aluminum, copper, tin, zinc, and all the other nonferrous metals. Increasing use of metals is a facet of the syndrome of advancing industrialization—and has been since the opening of the copper mines in the Sinai and the Negev, thousands of years ago. And smaller corporations, in their own fashion, were participating in the growth and advance of metal-related industries.

In contrast to the relatively great growth of The 200 in certain industry Groups, the relative growths of assets among smaller companies were much faster than among The 200's in Agriculture; Mining; Construction; and Services.

These differentials as between the very largest and all other corporations in rates and masses of growth are further indications of existing, and probably increasing, ecological-type specialization, by size of corporation in different industry niches of the industry structure considered as an entire system, organic and dynamic in its nature.

Broad conclusions to be drawn from these particular data are not too clear, but it does seem that the asset-shares of the very largest corporations tended especially to grow in more modern groups where new opportunities were emerging for economies of scale, multi-plant operations, and capital-intensivity.

More detailed examination of the Largest Corporations classified by Industry Categories, rather than by Major Industry Groups, will throw more light on significant developments in the structure of industry. We shall come to that analysis in a moment.

The 559 Largest Corporations of 1971 compared to The 200 Largest of 1929—by Major Industry Groups

An element of the arbitrary is involved in the comparison of The 200 Largest of one year with The 200 of another, especially when separated by such a span of years. Less arbitrary and more revealing is a comparison of the populations of corporations of comparable *size,* irrespective of numbers. Relating data of the corporations with assets of $250 million and over, in 1971, to those of comparable size in 1929 provides a basis for that sort of comparison: hence, "The 559" of 1971 versus "The 200" of 1929. (See Exhibit 56, Parts 1 and 2.)

The two rosters were very different, indeed. First, of course, was the mere fact that there were 359 more corporations of that size in 1971 than in 1929, an increase in number by a factor of 2.8. Second, whereas the aggregate asset mass of The 200 of 1929 (in an approximation of 1971 dollars) was $244.5 billion, the asset mass of The 559 was $707.2 billion, an increase of $462.7 billion—an increase by a factor of 2.9. Incidentally—or *was* it only "incidentally?"—the average size of The 200 of 1929 was about $1.2 billion, as we saw; the average size of The 559 of 1971 was almost the same: $1.3 billion.

Third and by far more important, the composition of the two rosters, in terms of Major Industry Groups, was *very* different.

Fourth, and related, the relative shares among *all* corporations of assets held by The 559—the presence indexes—were *very* different from the presence indexes of The 200 of 1929.

Before going on with the comparison of The 559 of 1971 with The 200 of 1929, it is useful to see something of the growth and change in the roster of the Largest Corporations in the context of the growth and change of the entire corporate community.

In the corporate community as a whole, over half of the aggregate asset growth from 1929 to 1971—about $800 billion—appears to have taken place in Manufacturing. Other lesser, but important, changes in aggregate corporate assets included the following: something like 9 percent of the growth had occurred in Transportation and other public utilities; 17.7 percent in Wholesale and retail trade; something like 5 percent in both Construction and in Services; and a sizable (although uncertain) portion in Real estate.

In comparison, almost three-quarters of the total asset growth of the very Largest Corporations took place in Manufacturing. There was also significant net growth in the utility field, and some, but not great, growth in Wholesale and retail trade.

Putting these few observations together, we can draw a few notable conclusions as to the growth of the very Largest Corporations in the context of the whole corporate community. Most notable, it would seem, was that the corporate community as a whole had become far more industrial in consequence of the fast relative growth of Manufacturing. Within this important Major Industry Group, the asset growth of the Largest Corporations—some 340 or so, in 1971—had accounted for a significant majority—perhaps close to four-fifths. And Manufacturing, very broadly speaking, had become much more large-scale than it had been.

In contrast, whereas sizable increases had occurred in assets, overall, in Construction, in Wholesale and retail trade, and in Services, comparatively little of these growths were accounted for by corporations included among The Largest. These Major Industry Groups, along with Agriculture, were still largely sectors of small-scale enterprise.

Beyond these general observations, one hesitates to go because of lack of close comparability in the available data.

Of the net increase of 359 corporations with assets of $250 million or more, 249 were in Manufacturing; 65 were in Transportation ... utilities (and this took place, as we shall see, despite a significant decrease in the number of railroads!); 29 were in Wholesale and retail trade; and 13 were in quite a variety of Services.

Within Manufacturing, the largest single increase in numbers of the biggest companies came in Metal and metal products; this increase included increases of companies related to Motor vehicles and a variety of other kinds of mechanical equipment and machinery. The next largest increase, of 57 corporations, came in Chemicals and allied products, and this increase included, primarily, companies in petroleum, in chemicals proper, and in pharmaceuticals.

Next came increases, respectively, of 32 in Other and miscellaneous manufacturing, and 30 in Food and kindred products of all sorts. The former included, as we have mentioned, numbers of "high-technology" companies in computing, controls, and communications and electronics. The latter reflected growth of a variety of companies engaged in many kinds of food processing. This particular growth reflected, of course, certain kinds of technological changes such as the advent of quick-freezing, which made possible the addition of numbers of new foods to the everyday, year-round diets of the American people. Perhaps even more, the growth of the Food companies reflected economic and social changes: rising levels of income, more singles living alone, more working wives. Then, too, cultural changes opened opportunities for adding new items to traditional diets: prepared ethnic foods, cheeses, different kinds of ready-to-eat breakfast cereals, and so on.

The changing, as well as rising, "demographic" profile of our large corporations, in terms of their numbers among the Major Industrial Groups, was both cause and consequence of several different kinds of changes taking place throughout the American system.

As to asset masses and presence indexes, there were still different changes in the makeup of the community of our Largest Corporations and their places in the structure of industry.

Outstanding is the fact that whereas 42.5 percent of the assets of The 200 of 1929 was in the Transportation . . . utilities Group—railroads and electric utilities, mainly—this fraction had fallen to 28.6 percent despite a net increase in asset mass of $86 billion. (See Exhibit 56, Part 1.) In contrast, the proportion of the asset mass of The 559 in Manufacturing had increased to 60.8 percent as compared to 45.5 percent among The 200 of 1929. This came about in consequence of an increase in the asset mass in Manufacturing of $342 billion, from $82.5 billion to $424.2 billion in the hands of the Largest. A similar situation was to be observed in the Stone, clay, glass . . . Group (see Exhibit 56, Part 1).

A more notable increase in the relative presence of Largest Corporations occurred in the Group labeled Wholesale and retail trade: the increase of $29.2 billion of assets in the hands of the Largest firms was sufficient to increase their relative presence from 6.4 percent to 15.9 percent.

Overall, the net increase in the aggregate asset mass of the Largest Corporations of $462.7 billion was sufficient to raise their relative presence among all nonfinancial corporations from a weighted average of about 41 percent to one of over 50 percent.

In very truth, among the several industry Groups, and overall, the Largest Corporations had, indeed, become more "ubiquitous" than they had been 40 years earlier.

No doubt, some of the increases in the relative presence of the Largest Corporations had come about through mergers and acquisitions—through literal concentration, that is—especially prior to the passage of the Kefauver Amendment of 1950 to the Clayton Act. This statute prohibited the acquisition of the *stock* of one corporation by another where such acquisition would impair competition in "any line of commerce." (An earlier provision had prohibited purchase of *assets.*)

But when one looks more closely at the growth of the Largest Corporations—firms, as classified into narrower and more specific Industry Categories and, second, in even greater detail, by looking at the growth of individual firms—it becomes clear that by far the greater part of this growth had come about through, and because of, processes more fundamental than the sorts of financial transactions that are involved in mergers and acquisitions.

There were, indeed, numerous instances of corporate growth brought about largely through mergers and acquisitions. Some of these were of ·the nature of "conglomerates"—puttings-together of corporations having little or nothing in common, and presenting few, if any, opportunities for economies of scale, of integration, or of multi-plant operation. In Chapter 13, there will be a few comments about the causes and consequences of conglomeration.

In short and overall: the 559 biggest "peaks" of American non-financial corporations were almost three times as numerous and more than twice as massive as The 200 of 1929. Corporations with assets of $250 million or more had grown in number; more important, they had increased relatively more in aggregate mass than other corporations. Their overall relative share of total corporate assets had grown from about 40 percent to about 50 percent. This growth had occurred far more in some industry sectors than in others. Again, as we have seen earlier and from different perspectives, the growth of large corporations was not spread evenly nor randomly throughout the corporate community. This absolute and relative growth was an integral aspect of the spreading and advancing industrialization of America, a process that had been—and still is—underway since the birth of the republic, and especially since the Civil War.

We shall now go on to get a "finer grain" picture of the changes in the community of Big Business when we look at the rosters of 1929 and 1971 classified by Industry Categories.

We went about as far as we can in comparing the community of
Largest Corporations in the *total* corporate community of 1971
against the Largest in the *total* corporate community of 1929. It
really is too bad that we cannot trace growth and change in the
whole corporate community back to 1929 in terms of Industry
Categories rather than in terms of Major (and Minor) Industry
Groups. The necessary data are simply not available. The IRS
Groups, as has been mentioned on several occasions, are too uneven
in scope and size. Far worse, they do not correspond with the way
industry systems are—or ever were—really structured.

We can, however, make comparisons among the Largest Corporations of then and now in terms of the more meaningful Industry
Categories. And these comparisons tell a great deal about the development, not only about large corporations—which they do—but,
more, about American industry as a whole and the larger System of
which it is part.

From time to time, references have been made to differences as
between the Largest Corporations of 1929 and those of 1971. (See,
e.g., Exhibit 30, as well as Exhibit 56.) Now it is time to deal with
the topic in earnest and in some detail. The data make clear the particular and indispensable roles of large corporations in the making of
our economy.

Statistical analyses of the changing compositions of the rosters of
the Largest Corporations of 1971 versus those of 1929 and of the
changes in the distributions of the net increases in the dollar values
of their assets are displayed in Exhibit 57, Parts 1 and 2, which are
placed at the end of this chapter. The highlights of those data are
set down in Tables 19 and 20, Exhibits 58 and 59.

Changes among The 200 Largest Nonfinancial Corporations of 1929 and 1971; the rosters of the companies

The principal changes in the rosters of The 200's of 1929 and
1971 are shown in Table 19. The decrease in the number of railroad
corporations is, of course, the single biggest difference. How the
mighty had fallen! In 1929, of the then 200 Largest, 43 were railroads. Of The 200 of 1971, this number had fallen to 11. From before the turn of the century, up until The Crash, the large railroad
was the archtype of Big Business. More ominous, perhaps, in the
minds of Populists, even than The Money Trust, The Sugar Trust—
rivaling or exceeding the Standard Oil Trust—the rails stood as symbols of an order of things that violated the innate idealization of
egalitarianism in the American tradition. These large corporations
were regarded as the creations of "Robber Barons"; they were widely

TABLE 19
Changes in the composition of the roster of The 200 Largest
Nonfinancial Corporations, 1929-1971

	Number of companies lost
Industry Categories *losing* Large Corporations	
Rail transportation	32
Transit	8
Iron and steel	4
Coal	4
Motion pictures	4
Railroad equipment	3
Others (7)	8
Total, 13 Industry Categories	63

	Number of companies gained
Industry Categories *gaining* Large Corporations	
Electric, gas, sanitary	8
Aircraft	8
Office, computing machines	7
Air transportation	6
Chemicals	6
Pharmaceuticals	4
Lumber . . . wood . . . paper	4
Motor vehicles and equipment	4
General merchandise	3
Others (12)	14*
Total, 21 Industry Categories	63*

*Does not include Western Electric.

thought to—and, perhaps, often did—control state legislatures. They had been put together and fought over in the era of "frenzied finance." The Crash brought the whole structure down. Few were the rails that escaped bankruptcy and reorganization. Not even Adolf Berle and Gardiner Means—even while they were writing their book—seemed to understand how vulnerable, under the shocks of the extraordinary Depression, were the flimsy financial structures of the railroads.

Out of the debris emerged some pretty battered phoenixes. And some of these had a second go-around in bankruptcy and reorganization in the late 1960s and early 1970s. Reorganized and re-reorganized, the railroads are still with us. But, as is all too well known, they have continuing grave problems. With a few bright exceptions, their future is hazy.

The disappearance of the big Transit companies has already been mentioned. They really did disappear from the private sector, victims of technological and social change, aggravated by political footballing.

Iron and steel companies also had been bugbears to those who feared bigness. The United States Steel Corporation, if memory serves, was the first Billion Dollar company, put together at the turn of the century by J. P. Morgan in defiance of the Sherman Act. The Big Steel decision, which two decades later held that bigness was not, of itself, an offense, opened the door to many later mergers through the acquisition of the *properties* rather than the stock of other corporations, as had been arranged in the case of "*The* Steel Company." More recently, as mentioned, a new Section 7 of the Clayton Act sought to close that loophole, by outlawing the acquisition by one company of the *stock* of another when an effect would be to impair competition in any "line of commerce." But mergers are nowadays simply of a different sort. More about that in Chapter 13.

But again, mere bigness did not guarantee persistence, status, or even vitality—not even survival—as we shall see in Chapter 11. In any case, the surging growth of companies in new industries shouldered some of the old steel companies aside and out of the Top 200. A number of those large steel corporations that gave Berle and Means qualms are still around; some of them have slipped down among The Next 359 and are still with us. Some became white chips in maneuvers of mergers and acquisitions.

The dynamics of the American System did more to channel, if not to "tame" large steel companies than statutes and litigation.

Coal companies, again, once-upon-a-time giants in the corporate community, came upon lean times, thanks in large measure to the devastating competition of oil and gas. No doubt, also, the economic and social advancement of the miners, who, in the years following the Depression achieved some of the highest pay scales in American industry, did much to erode whatever comparative advantage the industry had had, based, in considerable measure, on wages and working conditions that would nowadays be an affront to American sensibilities.

The motion picture companies were broken up in a landmark successful antitrust action that compelled the separation of ownership of picture production and picture showing.

The relative subsidence of railroad equipment companies, even their disappearance, again was a consequence of changes bigger than they—changes to which they could not, or in any event did not, adapt.

For more cheerful reading, we now turn to industries more strongly represented among The 200 in 1971 than in 1929. Here, the dynamism of the American System again is demonstrated—in these instances, upbeat rather than downbeat.

The large electric utilities were almost totally reorganized in consequence of the Public Utility Holding Company Act. The effect of that act was to break up the crazy quilt—it was not really a quilt; more like a cat's cradle—of the holding companies that had been thrown up during the 1920s. In these holding companies, widely scattered intermediate holding and actual operating companies, all over the country, were brought under common control through layer upon layer of companies holding minority but controlling financial interests in the underlying operating companies.

From this process of reorganization, which also entailed the squeezing of lots of "water"—write-down in the reported values of assets—out of the industry, there emerged a whole new set of companies that, at least, had the virtue of controlling "contiguous," interconnected operating companies. The contiguity of these companies in some instances, however, was not much more than would just satisfy the administrators of the act. One result of the reorganization was the setting up, or restoration, of a large number of relatively and, actually, very small operating companies. In consequence, the industry, as it is now organized, is no doubt far sounder financially than it was; but it probably falls short of what a rational structure might be were the companies both free and willing to become consolidated into stronger, more compact regional entities, capable of achieving full economies of scale in power generation, transmission, load distribution, multiplant operations, management, and so on. But that is a long story in itself.

In any event, the growth of the electric utilities was, again, a phenomenon of the dynamism of an America with almost insatiable needs for electric energy.

Other increases in numbers among the Top 200 were consequences of that same sort of dynamism that came from technological change combined with enterprising drive: Aircraft, airlines, computers, chemicals, pharmaceuticals. Prototypes of companies in these industries—in some cases, lineal ancestors—had indeed existed in 1929, or even before. But their growth to the scale we see now came much later—even after World War II.

The increased number of big integrated companies producing lumber and all the products that come from trees simply continued the trend of companies seeking economies of vertical integration, from forest to finished products, that was well under way in the 1920s.

The increased number of companies in Motor vehicles came in large part through the growth of large component producers, who, over the years, as sources of supply to the big automobile companies, became large enough, themselves, to be included in the list of The 200 of 1971.

Whether steel companies, also large suppliers of the automobile companies, might have profitably integrated forward to produce automobile components poses a nice question for business strategists with a liking for historical might-have-beens.

The coming on to the list of The 200 of a net increase of 3 companies, from 6 to 9, in General merchandise was a consequence of successful efforts to bring the Industrial Revolution to marketing and distribution. Actually, there were 5 companies on The 200 list of 1971 that had not been there in 1929. Two that had been on the list of 200 in 1929 were no longer among The 200 in 1971; both of these, we shall see, were among The Next 359 in 1971. But one of these, even though it had more than doubled in its size, simply hadn't kept up with the parade, so rapid was the pace of growth and change. The other firm was not only relatively smaller in size; it seems actually to have shrunk despite the growth going on around it. And that's another interesting study in corporate policy and strategy.

The topic of persistence and turnover among large corporations will be the focus of Chapter 11.

The increases and a few decreases in the assets of The 200 Largest Companies, 1929-1971. The principal increases and decreases in the asset holdings of companies among The 200 Largest in 1929 and 1971 are shown in Table 20.

TABLE 20
Principal changes in the industry distribution of the assets of The 200 Largest Nonfinancial Corporations, 1929-1971

	Value of decreases ($ billions) *
Industry Categories *losing* assets	
Rail transportation	$ 49.8
Transit	4.3
Motion pictures	2.7
Coal	2.1
Others (5)	1.5
Totals, 9 Industry Categories	$ 60.4

	Value of increases ($ billions) *
Industry Categories *gaining* assets	
Petroleum	$ 75.9
Telephone, telegraph … services	50.3
Electric, gas … sanitary	35.3
Motor vehicles and equipment	32.6
Office … computing … machines	20.0
Chemicals	17.7
General merchandise	16.5
Radio … communication equipment	13.8
Aircraft	12.0
Lumber … wood … paper …	9.4
Air transportation	9.2
Electrical machinery	8.0
Nonferrous metals	6.7
Rubber and tires	6.4
Iron and steel	4.3
Tobacco	4.3
Pharmaceuticals	4.3
Others (18)	27.4
Totals, 35 Industry Categories	$354.1

*1971 dollars.

The aggregate asset values of The 200 Largest nonfinancial corporations of 1971 were well over twice the figure of 1929, in approximate 1971 dollar terms. And this increase was achieved despite a shrinkage of almost $50 billion in the reported assets of the largest railroads among the very largest companies of the two years and a shrinkage or disappearance from the list of another $10 billion: $4.3 billion that had been held by Transit companies, over $2 billion in each of Motion pictures and Coal, and $1.5 billion in five other Industry Categories.

The increases in asset values, not surprisingly, came in Industry Categories that were in the forefront of the continuing development of the United States as a modernizing, industrializing, urbanizing, technology-exploiting nation. Almost two-thirds of the net asset growth came from six Industry Categories alone: Petroleum ($76 billion); Telephone and telegraph ($50 billion); Electric, gas and other utilities ($35 billion); Motor vehicles ($33 billion); Office... computing... machines ($20 billion); and Chemicals ($18 billion).

The growth in numbers and in asset *masses* of these industries helped to transform the composition of our largest companies to a degree that they bore little relationship to The 200 of 1929.

To these six industries, whose growth did so much to change the American economy, can be added another half-dozen industries whose growths—both in numbers as well as in asset mass—also made their own contributions to changing not only the composition and structure of the economy and its industry structure, but its very life: the mass-merchandisers, General merchandisers ($17 billion); Radio ...communication equipment ($14 billion); Aircraft ($12 billion); integrated companies in Lumber... wood... paper... ($9 billion); and Electrical machinery ($8 billion).

The very largest companies in these 12 Industry Categories—those included among the respective 200's of 1929 and 1971—grew in asset mass by a total of $300 billion. The very largest companies in another 23 Industry Categories, between 1929 and 1971, grew by another $50 billion.

This thoroughgoing transformation of the composition of our 200 very largest corporations surely manifested something far deeper than mere concentration. This transformation was part of the whole syndrome of national development. It flowed from the same underlying etiology of developments that was driving America in a *system* of processes of change, imperfectly perceived, even less well understood—even, actually, *mis*understood, to this very day.

Changes among the largest companies—The 200 of 1929 and The 559 of 1971

Just how great and how extensive were the changes in the community of large corporations is even better grasped through a comparison of The 559 of 1971 to The 200 of 1929. Not only was the composition of the roster of our Largest companies vastly different. There were many more of them—going on three times as many companies of the size that captured the attention and concern of astute observers of 40 years ago.

The rosters of the companies. The principal differences between the list of The 200 of 1929 and the list of The 559 of 1971 are set forth in Exhibit 58.

The declines in the numbers of railroads, transit, and coal companies need no further comment, except to note that some of the railroads that had been among The 200 of 1929 were still around but, now, among The Next 359. This was also the case with one of the coal companies.

The *increases* in numbers of companies, a gross figure of 390 and a net figure of 359, are far more interesting. Bear in mind, now, that these companies were each at least as large as any that had been on the list of The 200 of 40-some years earlier.

The biggest net growth in number of firms, of course, was among the Utilities. Some part of this may have resulted from the breakup of the old holding companies. But there can be little question that most of this growth in numbers was real and was the result of real growth of the Utilities during those decades. These companies were indispensable elements in the nation's infrastructure. As the economy grew, as technologies of production evolved, as consumers desired more energy in the home—as all this happened—more and more energy and, correspondingly, more and more investment was called forth. Companies grew in size. More and more of them passed over the lower size limit of $250 million, which was the lower boundary of the roster of companies we have been studying.

A more direct and telling index—be it all that simple—of the development of the nation could hardly be found than the increase in the number of sizable Utilities.

It is hard to know which other notable Industry increases in numbers of firms to pick out for comment: surely, Chemicals, with an increase of 22 corporations among the largest, and Pharmaceuticals, with 21. Both of these industries have had their critics, sometimes, perhaps, deservedly so. In both of these large systems of industry, companies pushed hard to develop and apply technologies; sometimes, perhaps, faster, as subsequent events have suggested, than their real mastery of all of the relevant sciences and knowledge. On the other side of things, there can be no doubt that demand in marketplaces, often urgent, for the new, promising fruits of these industries acted as powerful attractions for introduction of new products and rapid expansion. And there can be little objective, historical doubt that the material and personal welfare of the American people has been far advanced through the development of these

EXHIBIT 58
Changes in the composition of the rosters of The 200 Largest
Nonfinancial Corporations of 1929 and The 559 of 1971

	Number of companies lost
Industry Categories *losing* Large Corporations	
Railroad transportation	22
Transit	8
Coal	1
Total, 3 Industry Categories	31

	Number of companies gained
Industry Categories *gaining* Large Corporations	
Electric, gas ... sanitary	67
Chemicals	22
Pharmaceuticals	21
Food	15
General merchandise	14
Lumber ... wood ... paper	13
Nonmetallic mineral products	13
Radio ... commmunication equipment	13*
Motor vehicles and equipment	13
Air transportation	12
Services	12
Office ... computing ... machines	11
Nonferrous metals	10
Petroleum	10
Aircraft	10
Food stores	9
Iron and steel	8
Textiles	8
Fabricated metal products	8
Printing and publishing	7
Machinery	7
Household appliances	7
Telephone, telegraph ... services	7
Alcoholic beverages	6
Electrical machinery	6
Apparel	5
Farm, construction ... machinery	5
Other and miscellaneous manufacturing	5
Motor transportation	5
Retail trade	5
Real estate	5
Others (17)	33
Total, 48 Industry Categories‡	390†

*Includes manufacturing subsidiaries of AT&T and GTE.
†Excludes manufacturing subsidiaries of AT&T and GTE.
‡In four Industry Categories, there was none of The Largest
Corporations in either year.

industries. The growth and change of these two key industries,
together with all the pullings and haulings which they have felt,
could be subjects of whole books, in their own rights.

The expansion of the number of Food companies among the
Largest Corporations—most of them among The Next 359—also

could justify a volume in itself. These companies were both cause and effect of changes in American eating habits. Some of these have had to do with economic advance, whereby consumers were able, in effect, to pay for a certain amount of food processing by others—the shelling of peas, as a single homely example; or perhaps the preparation of a full, multicourse meal. Probably more important were the changes in social customs: more people living alone, more women in the work force, and upgrading of diet preferences, to name just a few.

Companies in this industry, too, have come in for their share of criticism and problems, perhaps again, in some instances, brought upon themselves. But, surely, there is no turning back to the diet and food habits of long ago. Americans now, for sure, want a much more varied diet, with a lot of processing before it comes into the pantry.

Not surprisingly, in view of what we have seen of the Largest Companies, further significant increases in numbers of corporations, beyond the Top 200, show up also in other new technology industries: Radio . . . communication equipment . . . electronics . . . ; Air transportation; Office . . . computing . . . machines; Aircraft. Even in Petroleum, an additional ten made the list, bringing the total number up to 30.

Perhaps more intriguing—for being less expected—is the fact that now, among The 559 Largest companies of 1971 are many engaged in industries in which few or none appeared among The 200 of 1929, industries that heretofore were bailiwicks of smaller, if not *small*, business: Services; Food stores; Textiles; Printing and publishing; Apparel—just to name a few. These increases accounted for no very great numbers of the total increase of companies from 200 to 559 that were above the $250 million level. But these companies did represent efforts, more or less successful, to bring large scale into industries once characterized, almost exclusively, by relatively small firms.

This, too, was part of the whole pattern of development. What it portends for the future makes one wonder. If the past is prologue, then we can expect further successful efforts of imaginative enterprises to bring the Industrial Revolution to yet other sectors that are still domains of "smallness."

The increases (and a few decreases) in the assets of the Largest Companies, 1929-1971. Table 20 set forth the highlights of the increases—and a few decreases—in the asset masses of the companies included in the lists of The 200 Largest in 1929 and 1971. Exhibit 59, among other matters, compares the asset masses of The 200 Largest of 1929 and The 559 Largest of 1971. (See Column 1.) In effect, with those data, we are comparing the aggregate asset masses of corporations of $250 million or more (in 1971 dollars) active in the two terminal years.

EXHIBIT 59
Principal changes in the industry distribution of the assets of The 200 Largest Nonfinancial Corporations of 1929 and The 559 of 1971; the presence indexes of The 559 in those Industry Categories in which occurred the largest net changes in assets of The 559 of 1971 over those of The 200 of 1929

	Net changes		Percentage of total assets held by The 200 of 1929	Percentage of total assets held by The 559 of 1971	"Presence index"; The 559 of 1971
	($ billions)*	(Percentage)			
Principal Industry Categories with decreasing assets					
Rail transportation	$−45.2	−9.8%	31.7%	4.6%	74.5%
Transit	−4.3	−0.9	1.8	0.0	0.0
Motion pictures	−0.8	−0.2	1.1	0.3	30.3
Coal	−0.7	−0.2	0.9	0.2	37.0
Totals, 4 Industry Categories	$−51.2	−11.1%	35.5%	5.1%	−
Principal Industry Categories with increasing assets					
Petroleum	$ 81.3	17.6%	10.0%	15.0%	91.4%
Electric, gas . . . sanitary	64.4	13.9	23.1	17.1	88.1
Telephone, telegraph . . . services	53.1	11.5	6.5	9.8	86.2
Motor vehicles	36.9	8.0	3.1	6.3	76.9
Chemicals	26.3	5.7	1.7	4.3	76.5
General merchandise	21.6	4.7	1.2	3.5	63.0
Office . . . computing . . . machines . . .	21.5	4.6	0.0	3.0	86.5
Radio . . . communication equipment	19.1	4.1	0.4	2.8	77.1
Lumber . . . wood . . . paper	14.3	3.1	1.3	2.5	49.8
Aircraft	12.8	2.8	0.0	1.8	52.8
Air transportation	12.2	2.6	0.0	1.7	73.5
Pharmaceuticals	12.1	2.6	0.0	1.7	87.8
Nonferrous metals	11.8	2.6	2.5	2.5	55.4
Food	10.3	2.2	0.8	1.7	45.6
Electrical machinery	10.3	2.2	1.0	1.8	61.6
Iron and steel	9.4	2.0	5.7	3.3	82.4
Rubber and tires	6.4	1.4	1.1	1.3	70.0
Nonmetallic mineral products	6.1	1.3	0.0	0.9	40.5
Farm, construction . . . machinery . . .	5.2	1.1	0.6	0.9	44.2
Services	5.0	1.1	0.0	0.7	8.9
Subtotals, 20 Industry Categories .	(440.1)	(95.1)	(59.0)	(82.6)	(71.8) ‖
Others (27)†	73.8	15.8	5.5‡	12.3	25.8§
Totals, 47 Industry Categories† . .	$513.9	111.1%	64.5%	94.9%	49.6%#

* 1971 dollars

†Does not include three Industry Categories with none of The 200 in 1929 or of The 559 of 1971: Agriculture, Furniture and fixtures, and Shipbuilding.

‡Includes 14 Industry Categories with none of The 200 in 1929 and 16 others.

§Median value; range is 0.0 to 94.4% in both "Metal cans" and "Photographic equipment."

‖Median value: 71.8%.

#Weighted arithmetic average.

Source: Exhibit 57, Part 2; Exhibits 2, 25, 36, etc.

Exhibit 59, beyond analyzing the principal net increases and decreases of the asset masses of certain Industry Categories, also sets forth other data that will help braid several strands of the analysis together in a sort of summary.

In 1929, the aggregate asset mass of The 200 came to $244.5 billion. The aggregate asset mass of The 559 of 1971 came to $707.2 billion. This represents a *net* increase of $462.7 billion, accumulated over more than 40 years. This *net* figure was, as shown in Exhibit 59, the resultant of total net increases in 47 Industry Categories of $513.9 billion and net *decreases* in four that amounted to a total of $51.2 billion. Exhibit 59 shows that big corporations in Rail transportation, Transit, Motion pictures, and Coal figure less importantly even among The 559 of 1971 than among The 200 of 1929. These data give further support to those in Table 20 that showed these industries were not the Big Business domains of enormous vitality they once had been.

Concerning these data, a couple of points can be made: the figures probably do reflect real *disinvestment* among the railroads. Miles and miles of rusting rails and deteriorating roadbeds; crumbling, malodorous stations and depots; decaying rolling stock give all too tangible evidence to that effect.

It is not clear that there had been a corresponding *real* disinvestment in Transit, now that much of the industry has been moved into the public sector; the actual value of assets could now be even more, but the public transit systems of most large cities do give the impression of a winding down of what had once been a growing, thriving industry.

As for Motion pictures and Coal, it is hard to know whether there has been real disinvestment or real expansion of investment by the biggest of companies. The facts are concealed behind a haze of mergers and probable differences between published figures and income tax data, differences as to the consolidation or separate returns for subsidiaries, and such. These are only two of many instances where we know really very little about corporations in our midst.

As for the reported *increases* in asset holdings by the Largest Corporations between 1929 and 1971, the aggregate gross total came to $514 billion. As indicated in Exhibit 59, the bulk of this increment in investment had occurred in industries that had played lead roles in the transformation of America over the past four decades. About half of the increase had come in just five industries: Petroleum; the Utilities; Telephone and telegraph; Motor vehicles; and Chemicals and allied products. Another quarter—bringing the figure to over 75 percent—had been added by another eight industries, strongly characterized by change, themselves, and also heavily contributory to changes in our whole system: General merchandise—the mass merchandisers; Computers and office machines; Radio, communication and electronic equipment; integrated Lumber, wood, and paper companies; Aircraft and Airlines; Pharmaceuticals; and the Nonferrous metals.

At this point, one does have to remind oneself that the figures in Exhibit 59 (and Exhibit 57, Part 2) represent only the increases of assets of the Largest Companies, those with assets of more than $250 million. (Pictures of the total increases in corporate assets were given in Exhibit 55.)

Just the same, the figure of $462.7 billion for the net increase in assets of corporations bigger than $250 million does represent 57 percent—more than half, anyway—of the *total* net increase of $812.2 billion, over 42 years, for *all* corporations.

Even more importantly, we have to remind ourselves that these increases in asset values, like the large corporations themselves, were not just distributed evenly or randomly throughout the whole industrial structure. The 57 percent is simply an overall "average" sort of figure. In many industry systems, the figures shown in the lower portion of Exhibit 59, for the Largest Companies, represented a far greater fraction than 57 percent of whatever increase in investment did take place. In the dozen or so industries where the increased investment of the largest companies was greatest, a conservative estimate of *their* fraction of the *total* increase in investment in those industry systems would be of the order of 80 percent, and in some cases more.

Exhibit 59 brings together other data that help locate the place of our Largest Corporations in our present industry structure and in the developments that, in recent decades, have operated to shape it. The Largest Corporations are notably more widespread than they were among the several Industry Categories. Corporations with assets of $250 million and more are to be found in many more industries than was true in 1929. The greatest relative shares of the assets of these Largest Corporations are to be found—as shown in Exhibit 36 and in Column 4 of Exhibit 59—in those Industry Categories especially to be identified with modernity. The greatest net increases in dollar values of asset masses among them over the four decades, and the greatest increases in the relative proportions of those assets were to be found in those industries. By and large, with the exceptions noted in Exhibit 36 and as shown again in Column 5 of Exhibit 59, the relative presences of The Largest Corporations were greatest among those very industries and least among the older industries. These were industries that earned, raised, and borrowed major amounts and shares of the net allocations of capital between 1929 and 1971. These capital growths enabled them to be major engines of change. These were changes and allocations that reflected implicit and explicit priorities of the American people. They reflect *hundreds of billions* of allocations of consumption and investment expenditures, day after day, for 40 years. These accumulations of capital now help make it possible for these Industry Categories to produce flows of particular kinds of goods and services that contemporary Americans wish to have—apparently insist upon having.

The advance and growth—in some cases the very appearance on the scene—of these industries have been identifying characteristics of the continuing Industrial Revolution in America.

These are industries of *big* business.

NOTE

1. Values expressed in 1929 dollars, as in Exhibit 3, have been multiplied by a factor of 3.0675 as a measure for expressing those values in something like 1971 dollars. See Chapter 1, Note 4 and Appendix A, General Note 7.

EXHIBIT 57
Growth and change in the Largest Nonfinancial Corporations, 1929-1971; by Industry Categories
(Part 1: Changes in the composition of the roster of the Largest Nonfinancial Corporations)

Industry Category	(1) Number of firms among The 200 of 1929*	(2) Number of firms among The 200 of 1971†	(3) Increase/decrease number of firms among Top 200	(4) Number of firms among The Next 359, 1971‡	(5) Percentage of firms among The Next 359, 1971	(6) Number of firms among The 559, 1971§	(7) Percentage of firms among The 559, 1971	(8) Increase/decrease number of firms among The 559 versus number of firms among The 200 of 1929†
1. Agriculture	0	0	0	0	0.0%	0	0.0%	0
2. Iron and steel	11	7	-4	12	3.3	19	3.4	8
3. Nonferrous metals	8	8	0	10	2.8	18	3.2	10
4. Coal	4	0	-4	3	0.8	3	0.5	-1
5. Petroleum	20	20	0	10	2.8	30	5.4	10
6. Construction	0	0	0	3	0.8	3	0.5	3
7. Food	4	3	-1	16	4.5	19	3.4	15
8. Meat	3	3	0	2	0.6	5	0.9	2
9. Dairy	2	3	1	3	0.8	6	1.1	4
10. Alcoholic beverages	0	1	1	5	1.4	6	1.1	6
11. Soft drinks	0	1	1	1	0.3	2	0.4	2
12. Tobacco	4	4	0	1	0.3	5	0.9	1
13. Textiles	1	1	0	8	2.2	9	1.6	8
14. Apparel	0	1	1	4	1.1	5	0.9	5
15. Lumber...wood...paper...products	4	8	4	9	2.5	17	3.0	13
16. Furniture and fixtures	0	0	0	0	0.0	0	0.0	0
17. Printing and publishing	0	0	0	7	1.9	7	1.3	7
18. Chemicals	4	10	6	16	4.5	26	4.7	22
19. Pharmaceuticals	0	4	4	17	4.7	21	3.8	21
20. Soaps, cleaners	1	1	0	4	1.1	5	0.9	4
21. Rubber and tires	4	5	1	0	0.0	5	0.9	1
22. Leather	1	0	-1	2	0.6	2	0.4	1
23. Nonmetallic mineral products	0	0	0	13	3.6	13	2.3	13
24. Glass	1	2	1	2	0.6	4	0.7	3
25. Fabricated metal products	2	1	-1	9	2.5	10	1.8	8
26. Metal cans	2	2	0	2	0.6	4	0.7	2
27. Machinery	2	0	-2	9	2.5	9	1.6	7
28. Farm, construction ...machinery	2	2	0	5	1.4	7	1.3	5
29. Office...computing...machines	0	7	7	4	1.1	11	2.0	11
30. Electrical machinery	2	2	0	6	1.7	8	1.4	6
31. Household appliances	0	1	1	6	1.7	7	1.3	7
32. Radio...communication equipment	1	3‖	2	11#	3.1	14‖#	2.5	13‖#
33. Scientific...control...devices...measuring	0	1	1	1	0.3	2	0.4	2

	Col1	Col2	Col3	%	Col5	%	Col7
34. Photographic equipment	1	0	1	0.3	2	0.4	1
35. Motor vehicles	4	4	9	2.5	17	3.0	13
36. Aircraft	0	8	2	0.6	10	1.8	10
37. Ship...building	0	0	0	0.0	0	0.0	0
38. Railroad equipment	3	−3	4	1.1	4	0.7	1
39. Other and miscellaneous manufacturing	0	0	5	1.4	5	0.9	5
40. Rail transportation	43	−32	10	2.8	21	3.8	−22
41. Transit	8	−8	0	0.0	0	0.0	−8
42. Motor transportation	0	2	3	0.8	5	0.9	5
43. Water transportation	1	−1	3	0.8	3	0.5	2
44. Air transportation	0	6	6	1.7	12	2.1	12
45. Electric, gas, sanitary	39	8	59	16.4	106	19.0	67
46. Telephone, telegraph services	4	1	6	1.7	11	2.0	7
47. Radio and TV broadcasting	0	0	2	0.6	2	0.4	2
48. Wholesale trade	0	0	1	0.8	1	0.2	1
49. Retail trade	2	−1	6	1.7	7	1.3	5
50. General merchandise	6	3	11	3.1	20	3.6	14
51. Food stores	1	1	8	2.2	10	1.8	9
52. Motion pictures	4	−4	5	1.4	5	0.9	1
53. Services	0	0	12	3.3	12	2.1	12
54. Real estate	1	−1	6	1.7	6	1.1	5
Totals	200	0	359	100.0%	559	100.0%	359

* See Exhibit 2.
† See Exhibit 16.
‡ See Exhibit 20.
§ See Exhibit 25.
‖ Includes Western Electric; not included in total.
Includes electronics and communications subsidiaries of GTE, counted as one company; not included in total.

EXHIBIT 57 *(continued)*
(Part 2: Changes in the industry distribution of the assets of the Largest Nonfinancial Corporations)

	(1)	(2)	(3)	(4)	(5)	(6)	(7)	(8)
	Assets, The 200 Largest		Change, 1929-71		Assets, 1971		Change in assets of The 559 Largest of 1971 over assets of The 200 Largest of 1929	
Industry Category	1929 ($ billions)*†	1971 ($ billions)*‡	($ billions)*	(percentage)	The 359 Next Largest ($ billions)*§	The 559 Largest ($ billions)*‖	($ billions)*	(percentage)
1. Agriculture	$ 0.0	$ 0.0	$ 0.0	0.0%	$ 0.0	$ 0.0	$ 0.0	0.0%
2. Iron and steel	14.0	18.3	4.3	1.5	5.1	23.4	9.4	2.0
3. Nonferrous metals	6.0	12.7	6.7	2.3	5.1	17.8	11.8	2.6
4. Coal	2.1	0.0	-2.1	-0.7	1.4	1.4	-0.7	-0.2
5. Petroleum	24.5	100.4	75.9	25.8	5.4	105.8	81.3	17.6
6. Construction	0.0	0.0	0.0	0.0	1.2	1.2	1.2	0.3
7. Food	2.0	3.5	1.5	0.5	8.8	12.3	10.3	2.2
8. Meat	2.8	4.2	1.4	0.5	1.2	5.3	2.5	0.5
9. Dairy	1.2	3.4	2.2	0.7	1.7	5.1	3.9	0.8
10. Alcoholic beverages	0.0	0.9	0.9	0.3	2.4	3.4	3.4	0.7
11. Soft drinks	0.0	1.1	1.1	0.4	0.8	1.9	1.9	0.4
12. Tobacco	2.1	6.4	4.3	1.5	0.6	7.0	4.9	1.1
13. Textiles	0.3	1.4	1.1	0.4	3.2	4.6	4.3	0.9
14. Apparel	0.0	0.9	0.9	0.3	1.5	2.5	2.5	0.5
15. Lumber…wood…paper products	3.1	12.5	9.4	3.2	4.9	17.4	14.3	3.1
16. Furniture and fixtures	0.0	0.0	0.0	0.0	0.0	0.0	0.0	0.0
17. Printing and publishing	0.0	0.0	0.0	0.0	2.7	2.7	2.7	0.6
18. Chemicals	4.1	21.8	17.7	6.0	8.7	30.4	26.3	5.7
19. Pharmaceuticals	0.0	4.3	4.3	1.5	7.7	12.1	12.1	2.6
20. Soaps, cleaners	0.3	2.0	1.7	0.6	2.4	4.4	4.1	0.9
21. Rubber and tires	2.7	9.1	6.4	2.2	0.0	9.1	6.4	1.4
22. Leather	0.3	0.0	-0.3	-0.1	0.7	0.7	0.4	0.1
23. Nonmetallic mineral products	0.0	0.0	0.0	0.0	6.1	6.1	6.1	1.3
24. Glass	0.3	2.7	2.4	0.8	1.0	3.7	3.4	0.7
25. Fabricated metal products	1.0	1.2	0.2	0.1	4.7	5.9	4.9	1.1
26. Metal cans	0.8	3.1	2.3	0.8	0.7	3.7	2.9	0.6
27. Machinery	0.9	0.0	-0.9	-0.3	3.3	3.3	2.4	0.5
28. Farm, construction machinery	1.5	3.3	1.8	0.6	3.4	6.7	5.2	1.1
29. Office…computing machines	0.0	20.0	20.0	6.8	1.5	21.5	21.5	4.6
30. Electrical machinery	2.4	10.4	8.0	2.7	2.3	12.7	10.3	2.2
31. Household appliances	0.0	1.7	1.7	0.6	2.7	4.4	4.4	1.0
32. Radio…communication equipment	0.9	14.7	13.8	4.7	5.3	20.0	19.1	4.1
33. Scientific…control…devices …measuring	0.0	2.2	2.2	0.7	0.3	2.5	2.5	0.5
34. Photographic equipment	0.5	3.3	2.8	1.0	0.6	3.9	3.4	0.7
35. Motor vehicles	7.7	40.3	32.6	11.1	4.2	44.6	36.9	8.0
36. Aircraft	0.0	12.0	12.0	4.1	0.8	12.8	12.8	2.8
37. Ship…building	0.0	0.0	0.0	0.0	0.0	0.0	0.0	0.0

38. Railroad equipment	1.0	0.0	-1.0	-0.3	2.1	2.1	1.1	0.2
39. Other and miscellaneous manufacturing	0.0	0.0	0.0	0.0	2.0	2.0	2.0	0.4
40. Rail transportation	77.5	27.7	-49.8	-17.0	4.7	32.3	-45.2	-9.8
41. Transit	4.3	0.0	-4.3	-1.5	0.0	0.0	-4.3	-0.9
42. Motor transportation	0.0	2.7	2.7	0.9	0.9	3.6	3.6	0.8
43. Water transportation	0.3	0.0	-0.3	-0.1	1.1	1.1	0.8	0.2
44. Air transportation	0.0	9.2	9.2	3.1	3.0	12.2	12.2	2.6
45. Electric, gas...sanitary	56.5	91.8	35.3	12.0	29.1	120.9	64.4	13.9
46. Telephone, telegraph...services	15.9	66.2	50.3	17.1	2.8	69.0	53.1	11.5
47. Radio and TV broadcasting	0.0	0.0	0.0	0.0	1.3	1.3	1.3	0.3
48. Wholesale trade	0.0	0.0	0.0	0.0	0.3	0.3	0.3	0.1
49. Retail trade	1.0	1.6	0.6	0.2	2.0	3.6	2.6	0.6
50. General merchandise	2.9	19.4	16.5	5.6	5.1	24.5	21.6	4.7
51. Food stores	0.5	1.9	1.4	0.5	3.3	5.2	4.7	1.0
52. Motion pictures	2.7	0.0	-2.7	-0.9	1.9	1.9	-0.8	-0.2
53. Services	0.0	0.0	0.0	0.0	5.0	5.0	5.0	1.1
54. Real estate	0.4	0.0	-0.4	-0.1	2.0	2.0	1.6	0.3
Totals	$244.5	$538.2	$293.7	100.0%	$169.0	$707.2	$462.7	100.0%

* 1971 dollars.
† See Exhibit 2.
‡ See Exhibit 16.
§ See Exhibit 20.
‖ See Exhibit 25.

10

The Largest Corporations and American development, 1929-1971;

Part II: Dynamic "externalities"; the environment of corporations

The previous chapter was a look at the corporate business community as a whole and how it grew and changed from 1929 to 1971. That community was, and is, the immediate context—the close-in environment—of the Largest Corporations. That was, and is, the encompassing productive system in which they, and the industry subsystems of which they were a part, have their existence.

Out beyond the corporate community was, and is, the rest of the productive economy—the family farms, the individual proprietorships and partnerships, government enterprises, and other non-profit-producing instrumentalities. In, among, and around the economic structure, as we have seen, are the tens, hundreds of thousands of voluntary organizations and associations that have worked to further, to obstruct, or to shape this or that cause, trend, or development. On the receiving and consuming side of the economy are the tens of millions of individual consumers and households that consume outputs of that economy. These individuals, we and our fellow citizens, also constitute our work force, whose services constitute major inputs into our production. Other entities consumed parts of that output: corporations, which invested in tangible and intangible assets; and government agencies of all levels, whose purchases and consumption ranged from school books to bombers.

Scattered through the American community are literally tens of thousands of units and agencies of government at federal, regional, state, and local levels, with powers to act, to regulate, to tax, to do, to incur debts and obligations.

The sum total of all these entities of many different sorts—interrelated and interactive in so many different ways—is the American community. Its material base and support is the production of its economic sector.

That community, or society, over the past decades, has had ups and downs, extraordinary triumphs and defeats. But all the while, it has continued to *develop.* Whether or not it was working out a Manifest Destiny is hard to say; but it *grew*—greatly. Far more: it *changed.* And, to repeat the point, our Largest Corporations were principal actors in that evolution. As part of the economy, the Largest Corporations, all along, have provided a major and distinct fraction of the material support of the society as a whole. They have contributed enormous motive power to the evolution of the American society. The Largest Corporations, evolving along with other uniquely American institutions, have made, and are making, conspicuous and observable and, indeed, distinct contributions to what is most characteristically "American" and most dynamic in the American Way of Life. And, reciprocally, their own existence and development were made possible by the presence of the other elements and components of the American system around them. Collectively, the many elements and components of the American System, in their thousands and millions, and in all their diversity, constitute the "externalities" and the teeming environment of the corporate community.

Over the past 40 and more years these other elements and components of the American System have also experienced growth and change. These changes have come about in systemic and reciprocal fashion with growth and change in the corporate community. The corporate community could not have grown and changed as it did, had it not been for the other developments going on about them. And the rest of the American System could not evolve as it did, had not the American corporate community functioned as engines of change and producers of very particular elements of the material basis and support of the System.

The growth and evolution of the American corporate community, and the evolutions of the American society and economy were not separate phenomena, each going its own way and doing its own thing. They were, all, aspects of a single, comprehensive, unified and unifying *system,* growing and developing under dynamic tensions over time, in the course of its unfolding history.

The Industrial Revolution lives! And wherever one looks, its manifestations strike the eye. And The Largest Corporations—large-scale, *very* large-scale enterprises—have been, and are, key elements, indispensable instrumentalities, in our continuing evolution as a nation. As such, whether We the People or They the Corporations will it or no, and no matter how "private" they and we may think they are, they are inescapably clothed with the public interest. For better or for worse, our welfare and theirs are no longer—if they ever were—separate independent matters. We and They, to emphasize, are parts of a single system.

Some implications of that basic fact will be touched upon in Chapter 13.

Search for the lost past

The burden of this chapter is going to be carried by a handful of numbers. These will give a few revealing, statistically measurable indications of trends that have been under way since the shock of 1929. But a few remembrances of some of the high- and low-lights of the years of change may provide a qualitative sketch of the times as a setting for the numerical data to come.

As we all know, the climax of 1929 was followed by years of depression, faltering, and revival. More important by far than the slowdown and disarray of economic activity, and of far more lasting consequence, was the restructuring of the American society and many of its institutions that came about in those years and thereafter.

The relative roles of, and the relationships between, the federal and state and local governments were restructured in ways that would have astounded the Founding Fathers. Localism and states' rights have given much ground to advancing federalism.

The changing relationships among the various levels of government were only part—perhaps a smaller part—of the restructuring of American society. The relationships between government and the individual became far more interactive and intimate. The individual came to receive far more support from the community, through government, and at the same time became far more dependent and constrained. This was also true of the relationship between the corporations and government.

This restructuring of governmental roles and growing government power seems destined to continue for yet a while longer. This historic extension has touched almost every aspect of American life. Some call it creeping socialism; some regard it as an inevitable consequence of development; some welcome it with enthusiasm.

Consider just a few of the areas in which federal power is now great or even paramount: Social Security, unemployment insurance, medical care, welfare; transportation policies and facilities—or their lack—rail, highway, and air; communication and energy, in which there is much intervention, but no clear policy; agriculture; housing; education; employment standards and safety; extension and guarantee of civil rights and of equal protection of individuals and groups under law; relationships between employees and employers; finance and banking; and corporate governance.

We became involved far more deeply in world events and struggles than we ever had been before. We were totally committed to, and involved in, the world's most terrible war. Millions of Americans were scattered over the entire globe. We were engaged twice in deeply divisive interventions of doubtful outcomes on the mainland of Asia. We had minor armed excursions into the Middle East and Latin America. We took on major responsibilities in the development and workings of new international institutions, arrangements, and conventions: the United Nations, the International Monetary Fund, the World Bank, and international regulation of telecommunications and air transport. We tried, with uncertain results, to help stabilize "friendly" national governments around the world and to arbitrate new and, mostly, old disputes among peoples.

This was an era of increasing application of technological changes advancing at exponential rates. Much of the new technologies came out of efforts started during World War II: aviation; radiation phenomena; electronics; atomic energy; molecular biology, biochemistry, and organic and physical chemistry; life sciences; applied and theoretical mathematics.

And, ironically, in the midst of human progress on some fronts and generally increasing prosperity, we have seen the hearts of our great cities east of the Mississippi sink into decay and suffer malign neglect—human despair and confusion; surging crime; chronic underemployment of our youth and our Black and Hispanic minorities; and episodic chaos—now far less beautiful for patriot's dreams than ever they were before.

It is almost impossible to look back through this tangle of movements and events and see any clear picture, get any real comprehension of what we were and how things were, back then, before all that. There were, indeed, Americans living in quiet small towns with shady broad streets and white-painted churches. Some enjoyed quiet and private lives, under their own vines, with far more plowshares and pruning hooks than swords and spears.

But millions more did live in slum-like ghettos and impacted ethnic enclaves, such as in the Lower East Side of New York and its many counterparts around the country and on the wrong and untidy side of the railroad tracks of not-really-so-content smaller communities. And our people knew racial, ethnic, religious, and sexist discrimination, poverty, and the threat of dispossession and cyclical and secular unemployment, and underemployment, ill-health, stricken and penniless old age, and young lives snuffed out by disease—all more than we now can really know or feel.

EXHIBIT 60
Selected indicia, social and economic growth and development in the United States, 1929-71

Indicators	1929	1971	Index number for 1971; (1929 = 100.0)
Human population			
Number (000)*	121,770	207,053	170.0
Urban†	56.2%	73.5%	130.8
Rural (farm and nonfarm)	43.8%	26.5%	60.5
Death rates, per 1,000‡			
Total	11.8	9.3	78.2
White	11.3	9.3	82.3
Black	16.9	9.2	54.4
Expectation of life at birth, years§			
Total	57.1	71.1	124.5
White	58.6	72.0	122.9
Black	46.7	65.6	140.5
Work force			
"Civilian labor force" (000)‖	49,180	84,113	171.0
Agricultural	10,450	3,387	32.4
Nonagricultural	37,180	75,732	210.1
Unemployed	1,550	4,993	322.1
Corporations, nonfinancial#			
Total number of corporations	322,084	1,592,793	494.5
Total value of corporate assets ($ billions)	$598.3	$1,410.5	235.8
Number of publicly held corporations with more assets than $250 million	200	559	279.5
Assets of publicly held corporations with assets more than $250 million ($ billions, 1971)	$244.5	$707.2	289.2

Note: For some statistics series, data are not readily available for the years 1929 and 1971; in such instances, data for 1930 and 1970 are used.

*In 1929, "Resident Population"; in 1971, "Total Population," *Statistical Abstract of the United States, 1976*, p. 5.

†*Historical Statistics of the United States from Colonial Times to 1957*, p. 9; and *Statistical Abstract*, p. 25. Years are 1930 and 1970.

‡*Historical Statistics*, p. 27; and *Statistical Abstract*, p. 62.

§*Historical Statistics*, p. 25; and *Statistical Abstract*, p. 60.

‖*Historical Statistics*, p. 70; and *Statistical Abstract of the United States, 1974*, p. 336.

#See, e.g., Exhibits 3, 15 and 56.

Amelioration did not come about through neglect, benign or otherwise. Not so very *good* old days. Not so *very* long ago.

Not even a Homer, in vivid compact prose, could do justice to the continuing epic of emergent America, from 1929 to 1971. How inadequate a few statistics must be! But they do sketch a story-line of our recent past.

Some of those data are displayed in Exhibit 60; and we shall look at them and others as we go.

WE, THE PEOPLE OF THE UNITED STATES, 1929-1971

How different we are from what we were two-score years, and more, ago! In numbers we grew. In 1929 we were 122 million; in the spring of '71, we were 207 million. Over those years, we had grown at an average compound rate of 1.277 percent. So, there were more of us; more than half as many again; 170 percent of our numbers of the earlier year. Quantitative growth in head-count is, of course, a major facet of national development. In earlier stages of our country, population growth was an objective much sought as national policy. Many people are less sure, these days, that population growth is a good thing. Multiplying as unto the sands of the sea does give rise to major problems, not to say possible catastrophe. Be that as it may, national *development* also—and especially—implies *change,* as distinct from sheer growth. And *change* we did!

Growth in numbers; declining growth rate

The *rate* and roots of our population growth over these past four decennial periods have been quite different from what they were, say, over the preceding years, from the turn of the century. And those dynamic demographic variables were related to, and were, themselves, aspects of our continual Industrial Revolution.

Our average compound rate of growth over the years 1901-30 was 1.603 percent. That does not sound so very much different from the average rate of later years, 1.27 percent. But *if* we had continued to grow at that earlier rate for the next 41 years, we would have come to number some 236 million, which is to say, more than 30 million more than we actually were! That difference comes to about the 1970-71 combined population of New York and California, or the combined population of New York, New Jersey, and Pennsylvania!

This decline in the rate of population growth occurred despite the fact that technological, cultural, environmental, and other kinds of changes had dramatically decreased our death rates for all ages, both sexes, and all races. The consequent increase in life expectancy was but one consequence of the continuing Industrial Revolution.

The slowing down in our rate of population growth that took place, despite our lengthening life expectancy, was also a phenomenon of our development. Several factors were at work. The inflow of immigration was slowed down. As we became more urban and industrial, as land was taken up, there came a time when, as a people, we wished to close down the influx of potential workers, whose increasing numbers constantly added to the supply of labor. A major point, aside from social and political considerations, was to protect the wage levels of those who had already come. In the three decades, from 1901 to 1930, more than 18 million immigrants entered the country. These hopeful arrivals not only added directly to the numbers of our people; in following years, the growing stream of their posterity was a major factor in our national growth. But in the next 40 years after 1930, the inflow of immigrants dwindled to about 7.4 million.[1]

Birth rates dropped.[2] And for this, no doubt, there were many reasons. But some of the principal reasons were related directly to the continuing Industrial Revolution: urbanization and a consequent de-emphasis on the desirability of large families to do the work of farm and rural people. Advancing availability and more widespread use of methods of contraception, including new products of the pharmaceutical industry, itself an emergent large-corporation industry system and a prime product of the ongoing Industrial Revolution, enabled people as never before to control the size of their families.

Urban and rural America

Aside from the fact that we were far fewer in number than we might otherwise have been, had not systemic changes slowed our growth, the *composition* of that population came to be far different from what it might have become, had not processes of development been at work. One way of grasping the magnitudes and significance of some of those key differences is to compare what we actually did become to what, hypothetically, we might have been had developmental changes *not* taken place.

For instance, granting that our population was, in fact, smaller in 1971 than it would have been had our earlier rate of growth continued, that population was far more urban (and, accordingly, far less rural) than would have been the case had the urban/rural ratio of 1929 continued in effect. In 1930, we were 56.2 percent urban; in 1970, the figure was 73.5 percent. In numbers, in 1971 we were 207 million, of whom 152 million were urban and 55 million were rural. If the urban-to-rural ratio of 1930 had still been in effect, those numbers would have been, instead, 116 million urban and 91 million nonurban. In other words, given our 1971 population of 207-odd million, about 36 million of us, hypothetically, who were now urban would now have been nonurban or rural, instead. That is about the equivalent of the total population of Minnesota, Iowa, Missouri, North and South Dakota, Nebraska, Kansas, Kentucky, Tennessee, Alabama, Mississippi, Arkansas, and Louisiana, and you could throw in Montana to round it out.[3] The increase of urbanism and the corresponding decline of ruralism were prime aspects of the social evolution of the American System. This social change had political consequences as well. Fewer of our people had direct agrarian economic interests. More now had urban and industrial interests.

An even more dramatic way of getting a sense of the magnitude of change in a major shift in the makeup of our people may be this: in 1930, our farm population was 30.5 million. These good people, living close to the soil, accounted for 25 percent of our total population. By 1971, our people living down on the farm had actually dwindled by 70 percent; in numbers, by 21.1 million down to 9.4 million.[4] Our farm people, by then, had come to account for only 4.5 percent of our people. If, hypothetically, as in 1929, 25 percent of our 1971 population of 207 million had been farm population, instead of the 4.5 percent it actually was, that population would have come to over 50 million. One way of expressing the magnitude of this shift is to try to realize that over *40 million* of us, now, in 1971, who were actually urban in residence and "nonfarm" in calling, might otherwise have been part of a greatly larger farm population. It would be hard for those 40 million of us urban people—whoever we are—to imagine what it would be like to be rural, sociologically, and farm people, economically.

The social, political, economic, and personal implications of that particular change in mix of our people must be as profound in our historical development as a people as was the Passing of the Frontier in an earlier generation.

This shift was a consequence of—more exactly, it came about hand in hand with—the sum of processes of industrialization.

Our changing age distribution

Technological change in health care—more biologicals and other agents and programs for immunization, greatly improved technologies of diagnosis, far more numerous and varied agents of chemotherapy, better instrumentation and techniques of surgery—and rising standards of public health because of higher incomes, better nutrition, and better sanitary services, were among the major factors that changed life expectancy. All these factors were associated with *development*. In consequence, our age profile changed dramatically between 1929 and 1971, and more of us were living longer.

If we had had the same age profile, on a percentage basis, in 1971 as we did in 1929, we would have had millions fewer of older people: about 6.6 million fewer in the age bracket 45-64 and about 9.5 million fewer in the group 65 years and older. Sixteen million of our middle-aged and elderly, who actually were living in 1971, would never achieved those ages had the life expectancies continued that were in effect when they were younger, back in 1929. They would already have died, somewhere along the way. See Exhibit 61.

On the other side, and this, of course, is equally hypothetical, we might otherwise have had millions more young people if we had had the same age profile in 1971 as in 1929, especially in the productive age bracket of 25-44.

Among the attributes of urbanization, industrialization, and social, organizational, and technological development, was a notably smaller and older population than we would otherwise have had. This change, also, has to be accompanied by further social, political, and economic consequences that fan out through the community and reach forward in time.

EXHIBIT 61
Our changing age distribution, 1929-1971

Age groups	Population, 1929 (millions)	Percentage of population, 1929	Population, 1971 (millions)	Percentage of population, 1971	Hypothetical population of 1971 based on distribution of 1929 (millions)	Difference of 1971 actual from 1971 hypothetical (millions)
Under 5	11.7	9.6%	17.2	8.3%	19.9	− 2.7
5-15	26.8	22.0	44.4	21.4	45.5	− 1.1
16-19	9.1	7.5	15.6	7.5	15.5	+ 0.1
20-24	10.7	8.8	18.1	8.7	18.2	− 0.1
25-44	35.9	29.5	48.8	23.6	61.1	−12.3
45-64	21.1	17.3	42.4	20.5	35.8	+ 6.6
65 and over	6.5	5.3	20.5	9.9	11.0	+ 9.5
Totals	121.8	100.0%	207.1	100.0%	207.1	0.0

Source: *Economic Report of the President, 1974,* Table C23.

The changing profile of Americans at work

Along with our population growth and the quantitative growth of the rest of our economy, the number of Americans at work has likewise increased. The "civilian labor force"—a measure of the number of people presumably at work or available for work—had risen from 49.2 million in 1929 to 84.1 million in 1971. (That figure does not include 2.5 million military personnel on active duty.) Including the military, the *total* labor force had increased to about 87 million.* That total labor force had increased slightly more than the population as a whole. And thereunto hangs a tale of changing personal mores and of changing allocation of resources by the people.

Aside from the *growth* of our labor force, interesting enough in its own right, the composition of that work force has changed in ways of profound social and human significance. What we now do for our livings—and who it is who work—fall into very different patterns from what was true of the generations of 40 years ago. The occupational profile of the American labor force has been a dynamic element in our continuing evolution as a people.

Some of the high spots of those changes: large numbers of women have entered the labor force; indeed, in such numbers did they go that they more than replaced the great withdrawal of younger people who stayed on longer in schools and colleges in order to get the education needed to staff modern productive entities.

---

*Measurements of "labor force," "employment," "gainfully employed," "economically active," etc. are a thicket of differences of concepts, definitions, of methods of data collection, and the like. It is extremely difficult, if not impossible to find or to develop data that are strictly comparable as between 1929/30 and 1970/71, or even as among various categories as of any given time. Accordingly, "broad-brush" methods are required and conclusions must need be general.

For information on different statistical series relating to work and labor, see *Historical Statistics of the United States from Colonial Times to 1970,* pp. 121-25.

We are far more *industrial*. We work at jobs requiring greater skills and greater education. We have upgraded our work.

In broad terms, 10.5 million, or 21 percent of the civilian labor force of 1929 were identified with agricultural pursuits; 37.2 million, 76 percent, were identified with nonagricultural callings; 1.6 million nominally "in" the civilian labor force were unemployed as of the time the data were compiled. By 1971, Americans in the civilian labor force identified with agriculture had declined by almost 70 percent from that figure of 10.5 million, down to about 3.4 million. This was, then, about 4 percent of that civilian labor force.

In contrast, people identified with nonagricultural employment had more than doubled from roughly 37 million to about 76 million. By 1971, we were 95 percent or more identified with nonagricultural callings.[5] (It is a curious example of "cultural lag" that we were—and are—still defining our callings with reference to an early common and "ideal" way of life that had, in fact, become a small fraction of our national scene, in a manner reminiscent of the way deep-dyed Nantucketers divide the world's people into "Islanders" and "Off-islanders," which category includes people from Cape Cod, Boston, Iowa, Cairo, and Hong Kong.)

What shock would that transformation of the American people be to our Founding Fathers, with their pro-agrarian predilections!

The expansion of the nonagricultural labor sector, which is to say, industrial-urban, where the vast majority of us are now occupied—was distributed far from evenly. The mix of our industrial-urban employments—"nonagricultural"—has changed markedly over the years: relatively fewer were in Mining; Manufacturing; and Transportation and public utilities. Relatively more were employed in Wholesale and retail Trade, in Services, in Financial establishments and, especially, in Government. See Exhibit 62.*

These changes, also, were part and parcel of the continuing evolution and development of our country.

An indicated absolute *decrease* in Mining was no doubt largely real (not just a statistical quirk) and due in large measure to the mechanization of our coal mines, where human resources and raw human energy were displaced by increasingly sophisticated mechanical equipment. Of those employed in the industry, more came to be engaged in the maintenance, as well as the direct handling, of that equipment, both above and below ground.

The absolute increase, but indicated *relative* decline, in the fraction of our people employed as wage and salaried workers in Manufacturing and in Transportation and public utilities was due to both increasing productivity of labor in those broad sectors and to the

---

*These data are not strictly comparable with the data of Exhibits 60 and 63.

EXHIBIT 62
Employees on payrolls in nonagricultural establishments, 1929 and 1971; by Major Industry Groups and Government

	1929		1971		Hypothetical number employed, 1971, based on 1929 distribution (000)	Differences, actual from hypothetical* (000)
	Number employed (000)	Percentage	Number employed (000)	Percentage		
Mining	1,087	3.5%	602	0.9%	2,473	−1,871
Contract construction . . .	1,497	4.8	3,411	4.8	3,391	+20
Manufacturing	10,702	34.2	18,529	26.2	24,161	−5,632
Transportation and public utilities	3,916	12.5	4,442	6.3	8,831	−4,389
Wholesale and retail trade	6,123	19.5	15,142	21.4	13,776	+1,366
Services	3,440	11.0	11,869	16.8	7,771	+4,098
Finance, insurance and real estate	1,509	4.8	3,796	5.4	3,391	+405
Government	3,065	9.8	12,856	18.2	6,923	+5,933
(State and local)	(2,532)	(8.1)	(10,079)‡	(14.3)	(5,722)	(+4,357)
(Federal) §	(533)	(1.7)	(2,777)‡	(3.9)	(1,201)	(+1,576)
Totals	31,339	100.0%	70,645	100.0%	70,645	−
Others†	5,841	−	5,087	−	−	−

Note: Figures are rounded. Data for the separate years are not strictly comparable because of changed definitions, etc. Data are also not strictly comparable with "Civilian Labor Force" data shown in Exhibit 60.

* Actual minus hypothetical.

† A calculated *net* figure to balance with total "Nonagricultural" figure in "Civilian Labor Force," Exhibit 60. Includes proprietors, self-employed persons, unpaid family workers and domestic servants, and other differences.

‡ Estimated; based on proportions of 1970; see *Statistical Abstract . . . , op. cit.,* p. 349.

§ Does not include the Armed Forces.

Source: For 1929, *Historical Statistics of the United States, from Colonial Times to 1970,* p. 137. For 1971, *Statistical Abstract of the United States, 1974,* p. 345. The figures for employees on nonagricultural *payrolls* exclude proprietors, self-employed person, unpaid family workers, domestic servants, etc., all of whom are included in the data for the aggregate "Civilian labor force." As so defined, the data for "employees on nonagricultural payrolls" are, probably, a rough but usable surrogate, probably somewhat overstated, for a count of employees of corporations (as distinct from unincorporated family businesses, proprietorships and partnerships).

relatively greater increase in employment in Trade, Services, Finance, and Government.

The growth of employment in Government was but one index of the increasing and proliferating roles of public intervention in American life.

Note should also be taken of the tremendous increase in the size of our military establishment. In 1929 our military counted about 260,000. In 1971, 2.5 million were in the military. Beyond that, another 1.1 million were employed as civilians working for the armed services, bringing total people in the military establishment to over 3.6 million. This was one of the consequences of the "Cold War" and some not-so-cold engagements overseas.[6]

Again, some hypothetical figures of "what might have been" may help us grasp the magnitudes of these changes. Granting that the numbers of employed workers had increased, if we had had the same broad occupational profile in 1971 as we did in 1929, almost 2 million more of us would have been employed in Mining than was the fact—mostly in coal mines. It is not too much to say that almost 2 million of us had been liberated from tough, difficult work underground. About 5.6 million more of us—now employed elsewhere—would have been employed in Manufacturing and about 4.4 million more in Transportation (e.g., the Railroads and Transit systems) and other public utilities.

In contrast, 1.4 million *fewer* would have been employed in Trade, and another 400,000 fewer in Finance, than actually were. Most important, about 4 million fewer would have been employed in Services than actually were, and about *6 million fewer* would have been employed in Government: about 1.5 million fewer in federal government and about 4.5 million in state and local governments!

The shifts in the broad industrial composition of our employed workers were further products and manifestations of our *development* over those churning years. Our more complex society, with greater capacity for production and with higher levels of income, could both afford, and *needed,* relatively as well as absolutely, more of our efforts in Services, Trade, Finance, and Government.

In the latter instance, the fraction of our nonagricultural employed who were in Government rose from 10 percent to 18 percent of our people "on payrolls." And on this latter topic, a few comments more, later on.

The upgrading of our callings

Karl Marx and numerous other earnest commentators of the 19th and 20th centuries have feared and predicted that a major consequence of industrialization would be the downgrading of the worker to the role of a simple automaton, functioning to provide sheer muscle power with a minimum of skill or exercise of human intelligence. Overall, the American experience has, in fact, been decisively to the contrary. The occupational profile of the American working population, far from being downgraded, was significantly upgraded over the 40 years of our study. Our labor force has been upgraded, that is, in the sense that *more* jobs, both absolutely and relatively, now require *more* skill and offer *more* opportunity for our self-realization as *people,* and for exercise of our human intelligence and skill, as distinct from simple muscle power. That upward shift is documented by the data in Exhibit 63.

An analysis in any depth of the changes outlined in Exhibit 63 would take us far afield, indeed. A few obvious and pertinent facts stand out: the greatest shifts in the occupational profile are directly associated with processes of industrialization, generally, and with the development of large-scale, capital-intensive, multiplant enterprise in particular.

Consider the dramatic decrease in farm employment. This decrease has come about hand in hand with enormous increases in agricultural productivity. Many factors have contributed to the extraordinary

EXHIBIT 63
Distribution of the "Experienced Civilian Labor Force" or the "Economically Active
Population," by "Major Occupation Group," 1930 and 1970

Major Occupation Group	1930 (percentage)		1970 (percentage)	
White collar workers		29.4%		47.4%
Professional, technical	6.8%		14.5%	
Managers	7.4		8.1	
Clerical	8.9		17.8	
Sales	6.3		7.1	
Blue collar workers		39.6%		36.6%
Craftsmen, foremen	12.8%		13.9%	
Operatives	15.8		18.0	
Laborers	11.0		4.7	
Service workers		9.8%		12.9%
Private household	4.1%		1.5%	
Other	5.7		11.3	
Farmworkers		21.2%		3.1%
Totals		100.0%		100.0%

Note: The data are not strictly comparable with those of either Exhibit 60 or 62; they do include the self-employed, etc., but not the unemployed. In 1930, the data relate to persons 14 years and over; in 1970, the base is persons 16 years old and over. The totals respectively for 1930 and 1970, not shown above, were 48,686,000 and 79,802,000. The changed profile of occupation is clear, nonetheless.

Source: *Historical Statistics of the United States from Colonial Times to 1970*, p. 139.

increases in agricultural productivity: plant genetics, better soil management, irrigation, crop rotation. But farm mechanization and synthetic fertilizers have also been of prime importance, and these are products primarily of very large corporations. The timeless Man with the Hoe, bent from years at grinding labor, has all but disappeared, his place taken by skilled operatives of modern tools and methods.

Exhibit 63 documents tremendous increase, relatively as well as absolutely, in persons following white-collar occupations. Numbers of persons in blue-collar occupations did increase, but the proportion, overall, of such jobs declined. The absolute *number* of laborers actually declined (from over 5 million in 1930 to about 3.5 million in 1970); and the *fraction* of our people so occupied declined from 11 percent to 4.4 percent.[7] The numbers of "Craftsmen, foremen, and kindred workers" held about constant; the proportion of "Operatives and kindred workers" increased somewhat.

What happened among "Service workers" tells a story of its own. The number of service workers in private households—servants, that is—actually declined from about 2 million to a little over 1 million. This shift, not very significant in an absolute sense, bespeaks deep social change: progessing democratization of our society and the opening up of more and, especially, new job opportunities.

The great absolute and relative growth in numbers of "Service workers, except private household" serves as a scanning device to detect social changes—some desirable, but not all: increases in numbers of firemen, food service workers, and such "Personal service" people as barbers and beauticians. Sad and ominous, and no doubt associated with our neglected urbanization, were relative, as well as absolute, increases in the numbers of guards, watchmen, policemen, and detectives.

Looking at our occupational profile in greater detail, we see other indicia of technological and industrial development; for instance, the presence in 1970 of 258,000 "Computer specialists"—an occupation not shown in earlier years—51,000 of them female; "Engineers, technical," up from 217,000 in 1930 to 1,210,000 in 1970. Other occupations now appear: "Life and physical scientists," in 1970 to the number of 217,000, of whom 39,000 were female; of these latter, 12,000 were "mathematical specialists"; 110,000 "social scientists," of whom 21,000 were female. The increase in accountants from 192,000 in 1930 to 713,000 (among whom were 187,000 females) is an interesting index of the increasing complexity of organizations and regulations.[8] The point is evident: the continuing Industrial Revolution required, called forth, and was made possible by a far *more*—not less—sophisticated work force.

Women at work

One of the most dramatic and telling changes in the work force of America has been the absolute and relative growths of female employment, and the opening of many new kinds of jobs for our womenfolk. In 1930, the female fraction of the work force was 21.9 percent. That percentage had risen to 38.2 percent in 1971. The participation rate, the fraction of women who could be regarded as being part of the labor force, rose from 23.6 percent (of the women aged 14 and over) in 1930 to 42.8 percent (of the women 16 and over) in 1971. In numbers, we are talking of about 10 million women in 1929 and about 32 million in 1971.[9]

This opening up of employment of women was, of course, associated with many factors—cultural, social, political, economic. It was also associated with processes of development and technological change that called for more and more workers with intelligence and skill as distinct from sheer physical strength. Of our female workers, over 60 percent were in white-collar jobs as compared to 39 percent of our males. Again, it is in modern industries—with their mechanization, with their complexities of scale, technology, multiple-plant operations, and the attendant growing needs for increasingly sophisticated research and development, management control, internal communications, marketing operations—that women have been particularly successful in finding employment. Industries, that is, characterized by modernity and the presence of very large corporations.

The availability of a growing supply of increasingly educated women has been a major factor in making possible the continuing industrial development of America.

That brings us to the next point.

The changing educational profile of Americans

One is hard put to think of any factor more directly associated with the continuing Industrial Revolution in America than the rising educational level of our people. This relationship is reciprocal. The increasing efficiency of the productive apparatus and its expanding flow of wealth enable our society to support larger numbers of young people in years of postponed productive life while they get education and training. The increasingly complex productive apparatus of our times, including government, simply could not function without an increasingly educated labor force to make it work, to design and manage its operations, to direct its evolution.

Exhibit 64 presents selected indicators that trace the growth and development of education in the United States. The data speak for themselves. More of our people get more education. As a nation, we have been willing to allocate an increased percentage of our rising

EXHIBIT 64
Selected indicators of education in America, 1930 and 1970

Indicator	1930	1970	Index number (1930 = 100.0)
School enrollments (000)			
Total	29,652	59,138	199.4
Kindergarten	786	2,770	352.4
Grades 1-8	22,953	34,078	148.5
Grades 9-12	4,812	14,744	306.4
Higher education	1,101	7,545	685.3
School expenditures			
Total ($ billions)	$3.23	$76.3	–
Distribution of expenditures (%)			
Elementary and secondary	80.6%	64.1%	80.0
Higher education	19.4	35.9	183.0
Total	100.0%	100.0%	–
Percentage of Gross National			
Product, *total*	3.1%	7.2%	232.3
Elementary and secondary	2.5	4.6	184.0
Higher education	0.6	2.6	433.3
Percentage of population enrolled			
Ages 14-17	73.1%	94.1%	128.8
Ages 18-19	25.4	47.7	187.8
Degrees conferred			
Total	138,752	1,140,292	821.8
Male	84,486	676,814	801.1
Female	55,266	463,478	838.6
Masters and Doctors	17,268	262,616	1,520.8
Male	10,871	165,676	1,524.0
Female	6,397	96,940	1,515.4

Sources: *Statistical Abstract of the United States, 1974*, pp. 109, 139; *Abstract... 1976*, p. 120.

Gross National Product to education. It has been a real growth industry for several decades. In 1929, only half of our people received as much as a grammar school education; now, more than half go at least through high school. But beyond that, the sector of greatest growth has been in higher education. Although these particular data do not register it, as others clearly do, the underlying figures show that the education of women and minorities has been advancing to a level where, now, both groups typically receive more education than did the more privileged white males only a few years ago. This tremendous growth in education has been transforming our population. Each year, a cohort of our older people—not so well educated—pass from the scene. Their place is taken by a younger class whose education exceeds that of their passing elders by several years. The summation of these annual changes—subtractions from and additions to our adult population—over a period of years has resulted in a community whose education has risen along with the advance of industrialization. Education, beyond being technologically necessary, has been a great facilitator for "social circulation" and notable movement toward a truly open society.

Whether that new population—and those of us who are still around—are wiser or happier is hard to say. That the oncoming cohorts *know* more than predecessors is indisputable. That our people *need* to know more in order to cope with more complex productive activities and more complex circumstances of life and living is clear—doomsayers and educational elitists to the contrary notwithstanding.

THE WEALTH OF THE NATION, 1929-1971

Getting and spending, perhaps we do lay waste our powers. Perhaps we do take too much thought for the morrow and lay up for ourselves too many treasures upon earth. Perhaps we, as a people, really are too materialistic. Those are metaphysical issues, beyond the scope of this work. It is a pragmatic fact, however, that the civilization—if that is the right word—we now know depends utterly, as all societies do, upon its material base. That material base of ours has been expanding far faster than our population. Our annual stream of wealth per capita, already by far the highest in the world in 1929, far from being in "equilibrium," has doubled over the past 40 years, even as our numbers were increasing by over two-thirds. Not only that, much of the increase came notably in consequence of the development of industries particularly characterized by large and very large corporations. Transformations, more spectacular than sheer growth, have taken place not only in the totality of what we *produce,* including raw materials and other upstream elements, but in all that finally comes out of the production process, ready for personal *consumption,* for *investment,* and for governmental uses. And, again, the sources of those transformations, more than others, are industries characterized by large-scale enterprise.

The flow of wealth: Production, allocation, and consumption

The production, allocation, and consumption of wealth are all parts of a continuous systemic process. Human resources and assets, tangible and intangible, are employed in extraction and agricultural production; that which is produced is utilized downstream to produce wealth closer in condition to being consumable or usable for production. Flows of outputs upstream in the flow are taken in by all the varied kinds of entities as inputs. In turn, outputs by them are recycled back into the system.[10] That which, in course, becomes consumable, sustains and edifies—according to individual tastes—the human population. That which is usable for production is recycled back into the productive apparatus. Governments take a fraction to sustain them and to enable them to perform functions designated by legislative bodies.

In mechanical terms, the flow follows a circling, moving spiral. In ecological terms, it is a system of scores of millions of interlinked entities of thousands of different kinds. The ultimate linkage among them is in large measure the production, flow, and consumption and use of wealth. These are entities whose numbers and varieties have been increasing; whose natures and relationships, in consequence, have been changing. In strictly functional terms—in terms of what they are and what they do—our individuals, our organizations, our corporations, our governments have been evolving. What they desire and need for their support, what they are able to do and to produce, what they desire and demand as to circumstances of life and doing—all have been changing.

We have looked at changes in our human and corporate communities. Now we examine the growing and changing flow of wealth these communities produce and consume. We have been told: by their fruits shall ye know them. To the extent that we can enhance our knowledge and understanding of that flow—the "fruits" of our production—we can enhance our knowledge and understanding of the society of which we are part.

Sources of the flow of wealth

A prime indicator of our national wealth is our Gross National Product. In value terms, this is a measure of the mass of the wealth generated, say, in a year. We know a good bit about where that wealth comes from, but not so much as one could wish.

In Exhibit 65 are displayed data that summarize, in terms of 1971 dollars, the magnitudes and portions of the wealth—Gross National Product—that flowed from principal productive sectors of the American community in the years 1929, 1947, and 1971.

Between 1929 and 1947, the GNP increased, net, in constant 1971

EXHIBIT 65
Sources of the flow of wealth: the Gross National Product as the sum of "values added" by major sectors;
1929, 1947, and 1971 (values in billions of 1971 dollars)

	1929		1947		1971	
Gross National Product	$302.2		$449.7		$1,063.4	
Business	$262.2		$379.8		$ 896.9	
Nonfarm		$236.9		$359.6		$867.9
Farm		20.1		20.2		27.7
Statistical discrepancy		5.2		−		1.3
Households and institutions	14.8		15.2		34.7	
Government*	24.0		53.3		125.2	
Federal		4.6		26.6		46.8
State and local		19.6		26.4		78.5
Rest of the world	1.2		1.5		6.6	

Note: Figures are rounded.
*Compensation of employees in general government and government enterprises.
Sources: *The National Income and Product Accounts of the United States, 1929-1974;* Tables 1.7, 1.8 and 7.5. The data in the sources are given in 1972 dollars; these were converted into 1971 dollars, using appropriate "deflators."

dollars, by about 50 percent, or at an average compound annual rate of 2.214 percent. In the 24 years between 1947 and 1971, the GNP increased by 237 percent, rising by an annual average compound rate of 3.60 percent. Over the whole period, 1929-71, the GNP increased by 350 percent, at an average annual compound rate of 3.01 percent. Growing faster than the population, the GNP in per capita terms more than doubled between 1929 and 1971 from about $2,500 to about $5,000, measured in 1971 dollars.

As to major sector sources of wealth generated, "Business-nonfarm" and "Households and institutions" both increased—the latter more than doubling—but declined in relative importance between the terminal years 1929 and 1971. "Business-nonfarm" more than doubled and showed a relative increase from 78 percent of the GNP to about 82 percent.

The GNP originating in governments is taken, by conventional but arbitrary methods of national income accounting, to be measured by the compensation paid to employees. So measured, GNP generated by the federal government increased more than tenfold, rising from $4.6 billion in 1929, in 1971 dollars, to $46.8 billion in 1971, and increasing from 1.5 percent to 4.4 percent. GNP originating in state and local governments increased by a factor of 4, rising from 6.5 percent to 7.4 percent of the total.

Net exports rose from $1.2 billion to $6.6 billion—a far cry, incidentally, from our current vast net deficits, due in large measure to petroleum imports. A major share of these net exports was provided by "Business-nonfarm," and by large-company industries, in particular.

No doubt about it, the business community—the "nonfarm" segment, especially—is the prime source of the flow of our wealth. We are an industrial nation.

Exhibit 66 sketches in some detail the sources of the GNP in various "industries" and "sectors" in the years 1947 and 1971. Exhibit 67, drawing upon and highlighting important facts of Exhibit 66, displays some of the notable *increases* in "Gross Product Originating" in industries and sectors characterized, respectively, by (*a*) the presence of The Largest Corporations and (*b*) the presence of smaller and small companies.

Unfortunately, such detailed data cannot be extended back to 1929. Nor do the data of those exhibits dovetail perfectly with those of Exhibit 65; but the correspondence between the two sets of figures is close enough for our rather general purposes. More unfortunate—for our purposes and for understanding the place of large corporations in the American economy—is the fact that Gross National Product and National Income accounts are based on "establishments" —individual places of employment—rather than on corporations. Nor do the data in Exhibits 66 and 67 tie in directly with *corporate* financial data, such as those in Exhibit 46. Even so, the data give general indications as to where large and small corporations fit in when it comes to tracing the sources of the wealth we produce each year.

Some of the most notable absolute-dollar increases in the Gross National Product between 1947 and 1971 came from industries characterized by smaller and small corporations: Agriculture; Contract construction; Printing and publishing; Machinery (other than electrical); Wholesale trade; Retail trade; and Services. Together, these seven sectors accounted for 42.1 percent of the GNP of 1947 and 39.7 percent in 1971. These sectors accounted for 37.8 percent of the overall increase in the GNP between those terminal years.

The notable relative increases in Wholesale trade and Services no doubt reflected the increasing complexity of American industry and the opulence of the American way of life. The relatively lesser, but nonetheless very large, increase in Retail trade perhaps reflected increasing efficiency of retail marketing, stemming from the continuing extension into that sector of the ongoing Industrial Revolution.

In any event, the tremendous expansion of these three large small-business "industries" had presented hundreds of thousands of opportunities for small enterprises of the kinds now listed in thousands of the Yellow Pages around the country. (See Exhibit 48 in Chapter 8.)

Especially interesting, for purposes of understanding where very large corporations fit in the American economy, are increases in Gross Product Originating in industries heavily characterized, to the extent of more than 60 percent, by the presence of The Largest Corporations. In 1947, nine of these industries, listed in Exhibit 66,

EXHIBIT 66
Sources of the flow of wealth: "Gross Product Originating" in industries and other sectors, including governments; 1947 and 1971
(values in billions of 1971 dollars)

Industries; sectors	1947[1]	1971[1]	Percentage of total, 1947	Percentage of total, 1971	Increases/ decreases[1]	Index, 1971 (1947=100.0)
Agriculture, forestry and fisheries	$ 22.2	$ 30.7	4.9%	2.9%	$ 8.5	138.3
Metal mining and primary metal industries[2]	17.1	20.2	3.8	1.9	3.1	118.1
Coal mining	3.4	2.6	0.8	0.2	−0.8	76.5
"Petroleum"[3]	8.5	19.6	1.9	1.8	11.1	230.6
Contract construction	27.1	51.6	6.0	4.9	24.5	190.4
Food and kindred products[4]	14.5	27.3	3.2	2.6	12.8	188.3
Tobacco	2.3	4.2	0.5	0.4	1.9	182.6
Textile mill products	3.9	8.2	0.9	0.8	4.3	210.3
Apparel and related products	4.9	9.3	1.1	0.9	4.4	189.8
"Lumber . . . wood . . . paper products"[5] . . .	8.3	15.8	1.9	1.5	7.5	190.4
Furniture and fixtures	1.9	4.0	0.4	0.4	2.1	210.5
Printing and publishing	6.3	13.4	1.4	1.3	7.1	212.7
Chemicals and allied products[6]	3.7	20.4	0.8	1.9	16.7	551.4
Rubber and miscellaneous plastic products	2.3	7.4	0.5	0.7	5.1	321.7
Leather and leather products	2.6	2.2	0.6	0.2	−0.4	84.6
Nonmetallic mineral mining; and stone, clay, and glass products[7]	5.2	10.4	1.2	1.0	5.2	200.0
Fabricated metal products[8]	8.1	16.4	1.8	1.5	8.3	202.5
Machinery, except electrical[9]	12.1	26.1	2.7	2.5	14.0	215.7
Electrical machinery[10]	4.7	22.4	1.1	2.1	17.7	476.6
Transportation equipment and ordnance[11]	3.5	14.6	0.8	1.4	11.1	417.1
Motor vehicles and equipment[12]	6.8	22.8	1.5	2.1	16.0	335.3
Instruments and related products[13]	1.7	6.5	0.4	0.6	4.8	382.4
Miscellaneous manufacturing industries . . .	2.1	4.1	0.5	0.4	2.0	195.2
Railroads and transportation services[14] . . .	12.4	12.0	2.8	1.1	−0.4	96.8
Local and highway transportation	9.1	3.4	2.0	0.3	−5.7	37.4
Motor freight transportation and warehousing	3.8	16.2	0.9	1.5	12.4	426.3
Water transportation	2.6	2.5	0.6	0.2	−0.1	96.2
Air transportation	0.4	7.0	0.1	0.7	6.6	1,750.0
Electric, gas, and sanitary services	4.8	25.0	1.1	2.4	20.2	520.8
Telephone and telegraph[15]	4.3	23.6	1.0	2.2	19.3	548.8
Radio and TV broadcasting	0.5	2.1	0.1	0.2	1.6	420.0
Wholesale trade[16]	23.4	72.6	5.2	6.8	49.2	310.3
Retail trade[17]	51.3	110.3	11.4	10.4	59.0	215.0
Services, total	47.2	117.0	10.5	11.0	69.8	247.9
Total, nonfinancial business, except real estate	$333.0	$ 751.9	74.0%	70.7%	$418.9	225.8
Finance, insurance and real estate[18]	53.4	155.8	11.9	14.7	102.4	291.8
Total business, before adjustments	$386.4	$ 907.7	85.9%	85.4%	$521.3	−
Adjustments, net (see Note)	−6.6	−10.8	−1.4	−1.1	4.2	−
Business, adjusted	$379.8	$ 896.9	84.5%	84.3%	$517.1	236.2
Household and institutions	15.2	34.7	3.4	3.3	19.5	228.3
Net exports	1.5	6.6	0.3	0.6	5.1	440.0
Private sector	$396.5	$ 938.2	88.2%	88.2%	$541.7	236.6
Government[19]	53.3	125.2	11.9	11.8	71.9	234.9
Federal	(26.6)	(46.8)	(5.9)	(4.4)	(20.0)	175.9
State and local	(26.4)	(78.5)	(5.9)	(7.4)	(52.0)	297.3
Total Gross National Product	$449.7	$1,063.4	100.0%	100.0%	$613.7	236.5
Population (millions)	144.7	207.1	−	−	−	143.1

Note: The industry data in this Exhibit are based upon an unpublished study by the Bureau of Economic Analysis, " 'Gross Product Originating,' in Current and Constant (1958) Dollars"; Work File 1205-02-01 (July 8, 1972). According to an official of the Bureau, some of the data do not meet usual quality standards for statistics published more formally by the Bureau.

The data have been adjusted by use of "deflators" used in the study, itself, and in the later source mentioned just below, so as to express the values in terms of 1971 dollars.

EXHIBIT 66 *(continued)*

Some of the data shown, including "Adjustments, net" are designed to bring the collection of figures into a degree of conformity with data published subsequently, as in *The National Income and Product Accounts of the United States, 1929-1974,* Tables 1.8 and 7.5. These "adjustments" are simply balancing numbers to conform the data to official later figures for the Gross National Product. See Exhibit 65.

In interpreting Gross National Product data, it is important to bear in mind that these are not *sales* dollars. They are akin to *value added,* as measured by the sum of employee compensation, net interest costs paid, capital consumption allowances, "profit-type income," and indirect business taxes. They exclude the values of purchased goods and services.

The nomenclature, except in a few instances, is that of the unpublished study. In a few instances, such as "Petroleum," the industries used by the unpublished study have been combined by the author in order to obtain categories that would correspond as closely as possible to the Industry Categories used elsewhere in this book. The SIC codes used by this unpublished study are those of the 1957 edition of the Standard Industry Classification Manual. These codes are slightly different from those used elsewhere in this study.

These data are compiled on the basis of "establishments," i.e., individual places of employment, generally speaking, rather than on the basis of corporations. The difference is material in cases of integrated companies, e.g., in "Iron and steel" and "Lumber...paper... wood...," which include "establishments" counted under a number of different SIC Codes.

Despite these differences, the data are useful for our present purposes, providing unduly precise analysis and interpretation are avoided.

[1] Values in billions of 1971 dollars.

[2] Includes industries included in "Metal mining," and in "Primary metal industries," SIC Codes 10 and 33.

[3] Includes SIC Codes 13, 29, and 46: "Crude petroleum and natural gas," "Petroleum and related industries," and "Pipeline transportation."

[4] SIC Code 20.

[5] Includes SIC Codes 26 and 24: "Paper and allied products" and "Lumber and wood products except furniture."

[6] SIC Code 28.

[7] Includes "Mining and quarrying of nonmetallic minerals," SIC Code 14; and "Stone, clay and glass products," SIC Code 32.

[8] SIC Code 34.

[9] SIC Code 35.

[10] SIC Code 36.

[11] SIC Code 7 plus 19 minus 371: "Transportation equipment," plus "Ordnance and accessories," minus "Motor vehicles and equipment."

[12] SIC Code 371: "Motor vehicles and equipment."

[13] SIC Code 38.

[14] SIC Codes 40 and 47: "Railroads" and "Transportation services."

[15] SIC Codes 481, 482, and 489: "Telephone communication," "Telegraph communication," and "Communication services..."

[16] SIC Code 50.

[17] SIC Codes 52-59.

[18] SIC Codes 60-67; i.e., "Finance, insurance, and real estate."

[19] The figure given here for "Total government" is to be distinguished from "Government Purchases of Goods and Services," which measure "final demand" or ultimate allocation of the Gross National Product.

were the sources of a total of $39.0 billion (in 1971 dollars), or 8.7 percent of the Gross National Product. Although these nine industries accounted for only 8.7 percent of the Gross Product Originating in 1947, by 1971 they accounted for $162.8 billion, or 15.3 percent of the Gross National Product. Together, these nine industries accounted for more than 20 percent of the increase in the flow of GNP between those years. With the exception of Petroleum, the Gross Product Originating in each of these industries had increased far more rapidly than the Gross National Product as a whole; even so, Petroleum increased relatively more than the total of Nonfinancial business. See Exhibit 67.

The seven Industry Categories characterized by small business had accounted for something like 43 percent of the GNP in 1947, but about 38 percent of the increase from 1947 to 1971.

Far from lagging, these big-business industries clearly outstripped the growth of industry as a whole. The products of these industries were among those that most especially characterized modernity— capital-intensivity, technology-intensivity, multiplant operations, and the rest—in the more developed economies around the world. The product streaming from the several sectors of the industrial structure was not only growing; the mix was *changing* as output items such as

	Value increases, 1947-71 ($ billions)	Index, 1971 (1947 = 100.0)	Percentage of total increase
Gross National Product	$613.7	236.5	100.0%
Industries characterized by presence of The Largest Corporations*			
Petroleum	$ 11.1	230.6	1.8%
Chemicals	16.7	551.4	2.7
Rubber and miscellaneous plastics	5.1	321.7	0.8
Electrical machinery	17.7	476.6	2.9
Transportation equipment	11.1	417.1	1.8
Motor vehicles and equipment	16.0	335.3	2.6
Air transportation	6.6	1,750.0	1.1
Electric, gas	20.2	520.8	3.3
Telephone and telegraph	19.3	548.8	3.1
Total, these industries	$123.8	–	20.2%
Industries characterized by presence of smaller and small corporations†			
Agriculture	$ 8.5	138.3	1.4%
Contract construction	24.5	190.0	4.0
Printing and publishing	7.1	212.7	1.2
Machinery (excluding Electrical)	14.0	215.7	2.3
Wholesale trade	49.2	310.3	8.0
Retail trade	59.0	215.0	9.6
Services	69.8	247.9	11.1
Total, these industries	$232.1	–	37.8%

*Presence of Largest Corporations 60 percent and more.
†Presence of Largest Corporations less than 20 percent.

these increased rapidly in relative importance, transforming production processes and living patterns. How much more rapidly they *might* have increased is another matter.

In any case, the dynamism of industries characterized by the presence of The Largest Corporations in the years 1947-71 would surely have intrigued Adam Smith.

The Largest Corporations and the Gross National Product

One can "guesstimate" that something of the order of 25 percent of the Gross National Product, and about one-third of the GNP generated by the nonfinancial business sector was generated by The 559 Largest Corporations in 1971: about 24 percent of the GNP apparently was generated in 16 of the industries of Exhibit 66 in which the largest corporations held something like an average 75 percent of the assets, industries such as Petroleum, Metals, Food, Chemicals, Electrical machinery, Motor vehicles, Rail and Air transportation, Electric services, and Telephone. Another 8.0 percent was generated in 8 industries in which the presence index of The 559 ranged around 30 percent. Finally, about 38 percent of the GNP was indicated to have originated in 10 industries in which The 559 held, on an average, something like 5 percent of the assets.

Making the rather cavalier assumption that contribution to the GNP in those industries was roughly proportional to asset values (an assumption that is more likely to lead, in the case of large corporations, to an understatement than to an overstatement), one comes to a figure of about 25 percent of the GNP as flowing from the activities of The 559 Largest Corporations. This is something like one-third, or something over, of the total GNP derived from nonfinancial business.

In any event, and whatever the real fraction may be, The Largest Corporations certainly generated a very important fraction of the total wealth that flowed from our production apparatus.

More important, by far, than any such overall quantitative measure is the fact that the large majority—say 75 percent and more—of the "product originating" in particular industries indispensable to our urban-industrial way of life and standard of living, such as Iron and steel, Nonferrous metals, Petroleum, Chemicals, Pharmaceuticals, Computers, Household appliances, Electric power, Telephonic Communications, Electrical machinery, Radio communication equipment, Motor vehicles, and Air transportation, came from our Largest Corporations.

One can assert categorically that in the overall and, more importantly, in many outstanding specific instances, our whole American society and the way we have chosen to live depend heavily—utterly is perhaps not too strong a word—for material support upon our Largest Corporations. Strikes, or even threatened strikes, in steel, automobiles, railroads, airlines, and telephones, the problems in petroleum, and power brownouts and blackouts give irrefutable testimony to that proposition.

Further insight into this verity comes from examination of how we allocate and spend our wealth.

The allocation of the flow of wealth

In Exhibit 68 are displayed data that measure (in 1971 dollars) the Gross National Product for the years 1929, 1947, and 1971 and indicate the allocations of that flow as among major uses: "Personal consumption expenditures"; "Gross private domestic investment"; exports and imports; and "Government purchases of goods and services" (federal and state and local).

Aside from the obvious overall increases in the magnitudes of these allocations, the most notable development was the allocation of a significantly larger share of the flow to uses of government and

EXHIBIT 68
Allocation of the flow of wealth; The Gross National Product; summary; 1929, 1947, and 1971

	1929		1947		1971	
	$ billions	Percentage of total	$ billions	Percentage of total	$ billions	Percentage of total
Gross National Product	$302.2	100.0%	$449.7	100.0%	$1,063.4	100.0%
Personal consumption expenditures	208.3	68.9	295.8	65.8	668.2	62.8
Gross private domestic investment	53.6	17.7	67.2	14.9	160.0	15.0
Net exports	2.6	0.9	16.5	3.7	1.6	0.2
Exports	(+15.1)	(+5.0)	(+29.2)	(+6.5)	(+65.6)	(+6.2)
Imports	(−12.5)	(−4.1)	(−12.7)	(−2.8)	(−64.0)	(−6.0)
Government purchases of goods and services*	38.3	12.7	70.6	15.7	233.7	22.0
Federal	(6.4)	(2.1)	(33.4)	(7.4)	(96.2)	(9.0)
State and local	(32.0)	(10.6)	(37.1)	(8.2)	(137.5)	(12.9)

Note: Figures are rounded.
*Does not include "transfer payments" such as Social Security, welfare, etc.
Source: *The National Income and Product Accounts of the United States, 1929-1974*, Tables 1.2 and 7.1.

corresponding reductions in relative allocations to personal consumption expenditures and to gross private domestic investment.

The increased relative allocation of GNP to purchases of goods and services by governments, in the face of smaller relative increases of contributions to the GNP as measured by compensation of government employees, in those years, probably reflects the relative growth of government functions that require tangible inputs: military "hardware"; expenditures for health care, including "hardware," such as buildings and equipment; materials for highways; and the like. In constant 1971 dollars, these allocations of wealth to all uses of government were greater by almost $200 billion a year in 1971 than in 1929. The fraction of the GNP so allocated rose from 12.7 percent to 22 percent. This growth and this shift in allocation, both, reflected changes of the times, including the increasing costs for increasing tangible wherewithal required for the performance of expanded and new public functions.

The relative proportions of Personal Consumption Expenditures and Gross Private Domestic Investment have held fairly steady. It seems to be the case, however, that in both 1947 and 1971, as compared to 1929, the relative share going into Gross Private Domestic Investment had declined relatively more than personal Consumption Expenditures.

In per capita terms, government purchases of goods and services had increased in 1971 over 1929 by a factor of 3.6. Personal Consumption Expenditures per capita had increased by a factor of 1.9; i.e., it had almost doubled. Gross Private Domestic Investment per capita had increased by a factor of about 1.75. Given the increasingly capital-intensive nature of the productive apparatus of modern civilization, there is serious question as to whether our capital replacement and expansion is sufficient to maintain full employment over the years ahead of a growing and younger population in modern employments.

This is a point to which we shall return.

The changing pattern of personal consumption expenditures, 1929-1971

One final set of data will complete this effort to perceive and track major facets of the development of the American environment over the past two generations and the place of our Largest Corporations in that development. Exhibit 69 outlines in "constant" 1971 dollars, in percentage, and in index-number terms some of the major features of growth and change in our Personal Consumption Expenditures.

We Americans of today allocate our income among our several kinds of personal consumption expenditures very differently from the way we used to. Those differences are systemically related to the

EXHIBIT 69
Allocation of the flow of wealth: Personal consumption expenditures in the United States, 1929, 1947, and 1971

Personal consumption expenditures	1929		1947			1971		
	Expenditures ($ billions)*	Percentage	Expenditures ($ billions)*	Percentage	Index number (1929 = 100.0)	Expenditures ($ billions)*	Percentage	Index number (1929 = 100.0)
Total	$208	100.0%	$296	100.0%	142.3	$668	100.0%	321.2
Durable goods	21	10.1	30	10.3	144.3	97	14.5	461.9
Motor vehicles and parts	10	4.8	11	3.9	114.0	44	6.6	440.0
Furniture and household equipment	9	4.3	14	4.8	156.7	39	5.8	433.3
Kitchen and other household appliances	1	0.5	3	0.9	260.0	7	1.0	700.0
Radio, television receivers	1	0.5	1	0.4	110.0	9	1.3	900.0
Other	7	3.4	10	3.5	148.6	23	3.4	328.6
Other durable goods	2	1.0	5	1.6	240.0	14	2.1	250.0
Nondurable goods	95	45.7	150	50.5	157.4	278	41.6	292.6
Food	50	24.0	86	29.1	172.2	141	21.1	282.0
Clothing and shoes	25	12.0	29	9.7	115.2	51	7.6	204.0
Gasoline and oil	3	1.4	7	2.3	223.3	23	3.4	766.7
Other nondurable	17	8.2	28	9.4	164.1	63	9.4	370.6
Drug preparations and sundries	1	0.5	2	0.6	170.0	7	1.0	700.0
Other	16	7.7	26	8.9	163.8	56	8.4	350.0
Services	92	44.2	116	39.1	125.8	293	43.9	318.5
Housing	20	9.6	31	10.4	154.0	103	15.4	515.0
Household operation	12	5.8	15	5.1	125.8	42	6.3	350.0
Electricity and gas	1	0.5	2	0.6	200.0	17	2.5	1,700.0
Telephone and telegraph	1	0.5	2	0.7	210.0	11	1.6	1,100.0
Domestic service	9	4.3	6	2.0	66.7	5	0.7	55.5
Other household operation	1	0.5	5	1.8	520.0	9	1.3	900.0
Transportation	8	3.8	16	5.3	196.3	24	3.6	300.0
User-operated	2	1.0	6	2.0	300.0	18	2.7	900.0
Purchased, local	5	2.4	8	2.6	154.0	3	0.4	60.0
Airlines	—	—	—	0.1	NMF†	2	0.3	NMF†
Other purchased, intercity	1	0.5	2	0.6	170.0	1	0.1	100.0
Other services	52	25.0	54	18.3	104.0	125	18.7	240.4
Medical care	8	3.8	14	4.6	168.8	46	6.7	575.0
Other	44	21.1	40	13.7	92.3	79	11.8	179.5

Note: Figures are rounded. Population of the United States in 1929 was 121.8 million; in 1947, 144.7 million (118.8% of 1929); in 1971, 207.1 million (170.0% of 1929).
*1971 dollars.
†NMF = not a meaningful figure.
Source: *The National Income and Product Accounts of the United States, 1929-1974*, Tables 2.7 and 7.12.

surging changes of our continuing development. Not only do we have more money to spend—per capita, about double what it was in 1929 —but we spend it on a very different stream of goods and services from what used to be, and in very different proportions. Some of the most notable increases in the way we spend on personal consumption have been for goods and services that flow out of industries especially characterized by the presence of our Largest Corporations.

As mentioned, on a per capita basis, our Personal Consumption Expenditures, overall, almost doubled. Down below this aggregate, our per capita expenditures increased in all three major categories: Durable goods, Nondurable goods, and Services. They increased in all secondary categories, e. g., Motor vehicles and parts, Food, Housing, Household operation, Transportation, and Other services. Only at the level of what might be called tertiary categories of expenditures do per capita declines appear. Notably these included "Domestic service" and "Transportation—Purchased, local" and "Transportation—Other purchased, intercity" (other than airlines).

We have already seen the decline in employment in domestic service. In per capita "constant" dollar terms, these were at a level of about one-third of what they had been 40-some years earlier. Despite substantial increases in our general capacity to *buy* and to *pay for,* we were, in fact, buying far less domestic service; other more rewarding, more socially and personally acceptable, employments had preempted those who might otherwise have entered domestic service.

The declines in the use of urban transit facilities and of intercity railroad passenger traffic accounted for the declines in those Transportation categories. Transit expenditures per capita fell to about one-third of what they had been, and spending on rail transportation fell to less than two-thirds of what they had been just before the Depression, still in the early years of the automobile.

The relatively greater increases in per capita expenditures in Durable goods and in Services, generally (other than Domestic service, of course), were in accord with Engels' Law, according to which, as income rises, individuals and households tend to spend *relatively less* (although, perhaps, absolutely more) on necessities such as food and clothing, and relatively and absolutely more in other ways. Purchase of Durable goods is one of those ways. In our times, these have included motor vehicles and appliances and other "hardware" for the home. Both of these categories of products, be it noted, were outputs of industries in which the presence of our Largest Corporations was particularly noteworthy. (See Exhibit 36.)

Among Nondurable goods, significant increases in constant-dollar *per capita* purchases took place in Gasoline and oil and in Drug preparations. Expenditures on Gasoline and oil increased by a factor of 4.5. This was the obverse of the decline in expenditures on urban transit and rail transportation. Expenditures on Drug preparations and sundries increased by a factor of 4, reflecting the tremendous growth of the pharmaceutical industry during the first post-World War II generation, following the discovery and mass production of penicillin. It was in those years that other antibiotics were developed, as were antihistamines, steroids, ataractics, vitamins, new analgesics, anesthetics, and all the rest.

Again, these two categories of products were outputs of industries characterized by the presence of our Largest Corporations: Petroleum and Pharmaceuticals.

The increases in personal and household use of Electricity and Telephone and telegraph servcies were among the most conspicuous changes. Expenditures on the former, per capita, increased by a factor of *10!* Expenditures, per capita, on telephone (and to a lesser extent, telegraphic) services increased by a factor of about 6.5. Again (I fear this may be getting somewhat monotonous, but the point really does have to be gotten across!), these were the products of two industries especially characterized by *very* large scale and the presence of companies among the *very* Largest.

Finally, our expenditures for medical care, in something like real terms, increased by a factor of almost 3.5. This reflects the fact that more of our people got more medical care—not just more of the "software" of the services of medical personnel, but also more use of the "hardware" of medical care: hospital beds in hospital buildings, therapeutic and diagnostic X-ray equipment, multiphasic analyzers of all sorts, and the like.

Despite all the controversy over difficult questions in the area of health-care delivery, it is certain that one aspect of our continuing national development was that our people were, indeed, getting more and better medical care than back in the "good old days," when the medical profession, with such means it had, could do precious little for the really ill. Being ill, to be sure, was inexpensive. Spontaneous healing, *if* it occurred, was cheap. Dying, if that was the eventual outcome—as it was, even in cases of pneumonia and other infectious diseases that are no longer killers—incurred practically no cost, either for the victim or for the community. But that, also, was long ago and far away. And most of us have no desire to return.[11]

THE LARGEST CORPORATIONS AND AMERICAN DEVELOPMENT, 1929-1971; CONCLUSION

In this chapter and the one before, we have seen that, without a doubt, the growth in numbers and mass of our Largest Corporations was not a thing apart from growth and change in the American society and the American economy. They developed together in systemic, symbiotic fashion. Still less was the growth of the community of very large corporations associated with economic constraint, with lowered outputs and higher prices and the like, or with technological drag—the kinds of economically hurtful, counterproductive results commonly attributed to Big Business, to large scale, and vertical integration, to smallness of numbers, and such. The facts run clearly to the contrary. Speaking generally of the four decades 1929-71, our large and *largest* corporations (with only a few outstanding exceptions, such as the Railroads and the Transit companies of yesteryear) have been sources of, forces for, and direct associates with major changes and advance, social as well as economic.

As has been said and suggested in earlier chapters, it is inconceivable that the continuing development of the American System as we know it could have been brought about by, or in association with, an industrial structure characterized by vast numbers of petty and individually inconsequential firms. It is equally clear that the growth and development of these large firms was utterly dependent upon developing externalities—human, social, political—that made *possible* and *relevant* the growth of modern industry as we now know it, in this country, in this area.

To insist upon recognition of the strong economic performance of business is not, by any means, to assert that all the acts and fruits of large corporations were good, especially in dimensions other than economic. Individual cases of criminal conspiracy in restraint of trade have been sources of grave doubts, widely held, about the intents and values of businessmen *in general!* Mischievous actions of particular business executives—unlawful political contributions at home; bribery overseas of officers of government, political parties, and unions; various dismal forms of shenanigans for violating the laws of friendly nations—have corrupted not only the recipients and other "beneficiaries," but, no doubt, the perpetrators themselves and their corporations. Such violations of law and common standards of ordinary propriety have woefully damaged the image of business in the perceptions of peoples around the world.

Connivings, petty and otherwise, with competitors by underlings, and sometimes by topmost executives, have brought certain corporations under antitrust fire by government and private parties. Whether such conspiracies and other "monopolistic" practices had significant effects as to prices and outputs is not always clear. Often, viewed in perspective, they were fruitless in the face of major market realities. But they have served to put the whole business community under clouds of doubt.

It is not possible to estimate the price the whole corporate community must pay for such lapses, in terms of lessened credibility and heightened suspicions of business in the minds of governments and citizenry, at home and abroad, because of the wearisome and wretched behavior of a few executives and a few corporations. And that carries its own high, if imponderable, price.

In the two concluding chapters of this work, as mentioned earlier, some of the possible implications of these facts will be explored.

One implication must be that the discipline of economics must look to itself and endeavor to examine the places and roles of large corporations with greater objectivity, with greater methodological rigor, and in greater depth than has been common heretofore. And, it is clear, this has to be done in the context of efforts to explain the qualitative, as well as the quantitative, *development* of our American System, with which the development of large corporations has been so intimately associated.

Another and major general implication must be that corporations will have to set and abide by standards of being and doing that are appropriate to important institutions of whom much is expected.

* * * * *

Before going on to such weighty topics we are going to take a look at persistence and turnover among The Largest Corporations over our 42-year time span. In 1929, The 200 Largest Corporations of the day must have seemed to some as permanent on the landscape as the pyramids. In fact, the rosters and order of precedence of our Largest Corporations display a startling degree of impermanence. Large corporations, even as small ones, come and go, rise and fall. Size is no assurance of continuity. And that fact also has some powerful implications, especially for directors and managers of these important economic institutions.

NOTES

1. *Statistical Abstract of the United States, 1976,* p. 102.

2. Ibid., p. 51.

3. Ibid., p. 11.

4. Ibid., p. 631.

5. *Economic Report of the President, 1976,* Table B-27.

6. *Statistical Abstract of the United States, 1976,* p. 334.

7. See *Historical Statistics of the United States from Colonial Times to 1970,* p. 139.

8. *Historical Statistics of the United States from Colonial Times to 1957,* p. 77; *Statistical Abstract of the United States, 1976,* p. 375.

9. *Historical Statistics of the United States from Colonial Times to 1957,* p. 71 (the year is 1930); for 1971, *Statistical Abstract of the United States, 1976,* p. 355.

10. A concept of "circular flow" *("Kreislauf")* was developed by Joseph A. Schumpeter, back in 1911, in his doctoral dissertation, *The Theory of Economic Development.* This work was translated by Redvers Opie and was published by the Harvard University Press, Cambridge, Mass. in 1936. The concept of the economy as an "output-input" system was developed by Wassily W. Leontief; *Studies in the Structure of the American Economy: Theoretical and Empirical Exploration in Input-Output Analysis* (New York: Oxford University Press, 1953); and *Input-Output Economics* (New York: Oxford University Press, 1966).

11. For an extraordinary empirical study of national development in a number of different countries, see Simon Kuznetz, *Economic Growth of Nations* (Cambridge: Harvard University Press, 1971). His concluding Chapter 7, especially pp. 343-54, treats of key relationships among such variables as demographic changes, and changes in industrial structure, law, social philosophy, innovations and spread of applied technology, and institutions of government.

11

Corporate strategies,
1929-1971; persistence,
decline, disappearance—
emergence and growth of
large corporations

A Greek philosopher, I think, said you cannot bathe twice in the same river. A contemporary ecologist might say that you cannot walk twice through the same woods. A demographer might say you cannot tally twice the same community—including a community of corporations. What this is about is that change seems common enough to be a law of life and the universe. Things come and things go. Those that come are not the same as those that leave. Nor are the numbers that come identical to those that go. As a result, change takes place. So, also, growth and regression.

That is how it is with rivers, forests, and human communities.

The American population of today is very different in many ways from that of 40 years ago. Each year, each month, each day of the past, some—mostly elderly—have passed from the scene; their places have been taken by younger people brought up in a very different milieu, itself changing day by day. A consequence, as we have seen, is an American people now very different from what we were.

This we understand. Long ago we were told that we are as grass. In our mornings we flourish and grow up; in our evenings we are cut down and wither. And we have seen this truth with our own eyes. And have felt its ecstasy and its agony in our own hearts. We know it all too well.

We are, perhaps, less aware that the lot of business corporations is also transient. Companies come; companies go. Companies are born; companies die. Even very large ones. And that is why the membership of the community of corporations, like the makeup of a forest or the composition of the human community, itself, is dynamic—changing and, in our times, growing.[1]

Few of our elders in 1929 foresaw, or could have foreseen, that many of the big companies then towering above the rest of the business community would pass away, and that others, even though they might still live on, would no longer be the young corporate lions they then were. At the time—and this is so of their modern-day counterparts—the Largest Corporations were not only "ubiquitous," as has been said; they were so much vaster, seemingly so much more powerful, than the rest of the business community, they might well have appeared as everlasting, permanent features of the American system. But they were not.

Half of those Largest Corporations are with us yet. Some do seem hale and hearty. But who is to say they will be still, 10, 20, 40 years hence? Some have slipped down among The Next 359; some seem less than vigorous, already. Half of the largest companies of 1929, lest we forget, have passed from the scene, or at least disappeared from view.

Impermanence of corporate fortune and existence, and dynamics of condition in the corporate community are facts. And they are facts of moment for both public policy and business management. Those matters we shall discuss in Chapter 12.

This chapter surveys data relating to living, aging, dying, to emergence and growth—turnover—among our Largest Corporations between 1929 and 1971.

TURNOVER AMONG THE LARGEST CORPORATIONS, 1929-1971; SUMMARY

Of The 200 Largest Corporations of 1929, 100 were identifiably still part of the business community of 1971. The others—another 100—had disappeared. Of the 100 that were still among the Largest Corporations of 1971—those holding assets of $250 million or more —only 75 were still among The 200 Largest as of 1971. The rest—25 of them—had declined in relative ranking according to asset size, so that, in 1971, they appeared only among the then Next 359 Largest. Even among those that were still among The 200 Largest of 1971— the 75—a number of eye-catching shifts in relative ranking had occurred. Most—but not all—of the surviving firms had grown, in constant-dollar terms; some much more than others. Others had even shrunk.

Time and the consequences of their own decisions had dealt very unevenly with our Largest Corporations.

Over those same years a whole new generation of very large corporations appeared to view. By 1971, we had 559 corporations as large as, or larger than, The 200 of 1929. Of these, 459 had not been on the roster of The 200 of 1929. Of The 200 Largest of 1971, a majority—125—had not been among The 200 Largest of 1929. Of The Next 359 of 1971, 334—93 percent—had not been among The 200 of 1929. Some of the 459 large corporations that had grown and emerged into the light of prominence had not even existed in 1929 or if so, were small, obscure companies that few people had ever even noticed or cared about.

Table 21 summarizes the "persistence" of certain of The Largest Corporations of 1929 into 1971 and the emergence into visibility of others.

TABLE 21
"Persistence" of corporations from 1929 and emergence of "newly visible" corporations among The Largest Corporations of 1971

	Among The 200	Among The 359	Among The 559
"Persisting" companies, from 1929	75	25	100
"Newly visible" companies	125	334	459
Totals	200	359	559

In 22 of our 54 Industry Categories, all—100 percent—of The Largest Corporations of 1971 had come on to the roster since 1929. In another 13 Industry Categories, between 80 percent and 100 percent of The Largest Corporations were, so to speak, new arrivals. In another eight Industry Categories, between 50 percent and 80 percent of The Largest Corporations were newly on the list of The Largest since 1929.*

In sum, a mere half of The Largest Corporations of 1929 had persisted into 1971, remaining still among the largest; they accounted for only a bit more than one-sixth of the community of the Largest Corporations of 1971. This later roster was made up to the extent of 82 percent of firms—459 out of 559—that had not made the list compiled 40-some years earlier by Adolf Berle and Gardiner Means.

With the waning and the passing of the old and the arrival, growth, and emergence of the others into easy view, the nature and the structure of American industry had undergone a profound transformation.

A tale worth telling lies behind the fortune or misfortune of each

---

*See Exhibit 72.

of the companies on the rosters of the terminal years. In some instances, on the somber side, what happened to individual companies was but a piece of larger history—the lives and hard times of coal companies, railroads, and transit companies, for instance, as they were overtaken and overwhelmed by events and trends beyond their grasp. In others—the utilities and motion pictures, for example—what happened to individual companies was, on the face of things, at least, a consequence of particular, explicit national policy. But it is fair to argue that these industries had done much to bring Draconian public action upon themselves through unacceptable policies and actions of their own.

For many among the rest, the subsidence or disappearance of individual companies was surely and primarily a consequence of the unwisdom or ineptitude of their own directors and managements.

On the other side—the happier one—hundreds of companies rose into view, sometimes spectacularly. No doubt, they were helped by strong tides of technological, economic, social, and political change. But so also were—or might have been—hundreds, or even thousands, of others who also were "starters" but who were outdistanced, or who could not "make it," who sooner or later reached a modest ceiling of achievement or just disappeared. In the business world, it simply is not true that a rising tide lifts all boats. For every corporate success, the passages of history are littered by many, perhaps dozens of, failures. The development of the automobile industry in the 1920s and the electronics and pharmaceutical industries in the years since World War II give ample illustration of the proposition.

Corporate emergence, growth, survival, and success are not matters of happenstance. Strategies and policies well adapted to changing external realities and exigencies, and tides of opportunity taken at the flood, lead on to corporate fortune. The ill-suited—obsolescent, premature, or doggedly mistaken—lead down; and out.

Be that as it may, and we shall come back to these matters in a moment, the moral should not be lost in a thicket of particulars: the strategies and policies of corporations are set by directors and executives. Accountability, if not responsibility, rests upon them for the consequences of their decisions, commitments, and acts of omission. For better or worse, they set the objectives, policies, and strategies of their corporations and shape the courses of action that their companies pursue.

THE 200 LARGEST CORPORATIONS OF 1929: PERSISTENCE, DECLINE, AND DISAPPEARANCE

A detailed statistical tabulation is given in Exhibit 70, Part 1, of the persistence, decline, or disappearance of the corporations that were among The 200 Largest of 1929.[2] Exhibit 70 appears at the end of this chapter. Some of the highlights of those data are given in Exhibit 71.

Of The 200 of 1929, as was mentioned, 75 were still among The 200 of 1971. Twenty-five had lost relative position and had declined in rank, to be counted among The Next 359 of 1971. One hundred of The 200 of 1929 were still in the community of largest corporations, some in Industry Categories different from those they had been in 1929. Another hundred had disappeared.

Persistence

As one can see in Exhibit 71, those of The Largest companies of 1929 that were situated in Iron and steel, Nonferrous metals, Petroleum, Tobacco, and General merchandise showed considerable persistence in terms of both numbers and survival rate. Smaller numbers (four each) of survivors, but higher rates of survival (100 percent) are to be seen in Chemicals and in Rubber and tires. Still smaller numbers (three each) and somewhat lower, but still high, survival rates (75 percent) can be seen in Food and Motor vehicles. In these nine Industry Categories were to be found 50 of the 100 survivors of The 200 of 1929. Beyond these, some interesting pairs of Largest Corporations survived, still among The 200 of 1971, indeed still in leadership positions: American Can and Continental Can, and General Electric and Westinghouse. Some preeminent and somewhat lonely leaders of 1929 were still preeminent in their industries 40-some years later: Procter & Gamble and Eastman Kodak.

These particular surviving companies were all in Industry Categories that, whatever their ups and downs, were no less basic in 1971 than in 1929. Indeed, some of these companies, back in 1929, were survivors of earlier periods of industrial development—in some cases reaching back well before World War I, as in the cases of steel and the nonferrous metals. In any event, they had remained in the forefront of industries that, between 1929 and 1971, showed strong long-run growth.

In a way, more remarkable was the persistence of a handful of companies in industries that had suffered greatly from technological change, economic change, social and political change. For example, of the "Big Three" meat packers of 1929, one—Swift—was still visibly around; the other two, no longer the young, robust giants of earlier years, had been taken over and merged into "Johnny-come-lately" conglomerates. Of the three large Railroad equipment builders of 1929, one—ACF, successor to American Car & Foundry—was still present among The Largest; but, like Swift, it was no longer one of The 200. The other two had disappeared. Like the empire of Belshazzar, Armour and Wilson and Baldwin Locomotive and American Locomotive had been weighed in the balances and found wanting, and their kingdoms were divided and given to Medes and Persians.

EXHIBIT 71
Persistence, decline, and disappearance among The 200 Largest Corporations of 1929; 1929-1971; summary

Industry Category	Number of firms, 1929	Cases of persistence among The 200 of 1971*	Cases of decline into the ranks of The Next 359 of 1971*	Cases of persistence plus cases of decline*	Cases of "disappear-ance"†	Percentage of The 200 of 1929 that persisted among The 559 of 1971*
1. Industry Categories with notable cases of persistence‡						
Iron and steel	11	7	2	9	2	81.8%
Nonferrous metals	8	6	1	7	1	87.5
Petroleum	20	11	0	11	9	55.0
Food.	4	1	2	3	1	75.0
Meat.	3	2	1	3	0	100.0
Dairy.	2	2	0	2	0	100.0
Tobacco.	4	3	1	4	0	100.0
Lumber.	4	2	0	2	2	50.0
Chemicals.	4	3	1	4	0	100.0
Soaps, cleaners	1	1	0	1	0	100.0
Rubber and tires	4	4	0	4	0	100.0
Leather	1	0	1	1	0	100.0
Glass	1	1	0	1	0	100.0
Fabricated metal products . .	2	1	1	2	0	100.0
Metal cans	2	2	0	2	0	100.0
Machinery.	2	0	1	1	1	50.0
Farm, construction. . . machinery	2	1	0	1	1	50.0
Electrical machinery	2	2	0	2	0	100.0
Radio. . . communication equipment	1	1	0	1	0	100.0
Photographic equipment . . .	1	1	0	1	0	100.0
Motor vehicles	4	3	0	3	1	75.0
Telephone, telegraph.	4	2	0	2	2	50.0
General merchandise	6	3	2	5	1	83.3
Food stores	1	1	0	1	0	100.0
Subtotals	94	60	13	73	21	77.7%
2. Industry Categories with notable cases of disappearance ‖						
Coal	4	0	0	0	4	0.0%
Textiles	1	0	0	0	1	0.0
Railroad equipment	3	0	1	1	2	33.3
Railroad transportation	43	6	7	13	30	30.2
Transit	8	0	0	0	8	0.0
Water transportation	1	0	0	0	1	0.0
Electric, gas. . . sanitary	39	5§	0§	5§	34§	12.8
Retail trade.	2	0	0	0	2	0.0
Motion pictures	4	0	1	1	3	25.0
Real estate	1	0	0	0	1	0.0
Subtotals	106	11	9	20	86	18.9%
Totals	200	71 ‖	22 ‖	93 ‖	107‖	46.5%
Companies persisting, but in different Industries.	–	+4 ‖	+3 ‖	+7 ‖	–7 ‖	–
Net changes	200	75 ‖	25 ‖	100 ‖	100	50.0%

*In same Industry Category.

†Includes company moved to different Industry Category.

‡Industry Categories in which 50 percent or more of The Largest Corporations of 1929 were among The 559 Largest of 1971.

§See text, the section of Chapter 11 entitled "Persistence," and Exhibit 70, Part 1, Footnote 11, concerning "persistence" and "disappearance" among the Utilities as between 1929 and 1971.

‖See Exhibit 70, Part 1, Footnotes 14, 15, and 16.

Source: Exhibit 70, Part 1.

One of the four largest motion picture companies of 1929, Warner Brothers, like Armour and Wilson, had survived, in a fashion; but, like them, it was now merely the largest unit in another recent conglomerate arrival on the business scene.

Granted that the meat-packing, railroad equipment, and motion picture industries had suffered from powerful external trends and developments bigger than they, the visible persistence of Swift, American Car and Foundry, demonstrated that identifiable survival—at least, of a sort—*was* possible. What was it that these companies had that the others who disappeared did not? Clearly, greater powers of adaptation to a changing environment must have been a major factor, whatever other quality may have been present.

Therein lies a moral.

Some other instances of persistence are worth comment. The whole railroad industry, as already noted, was utterly restructured, as were the electric utilities. Yet, in both industries, there were a few survivors.

The railroads were restructured mainly in two or three traumatic waves of reorganization: that occasioned by the bankruptcies of the Thirties, and the more recent consolidations, after World War II. By 1971, the 43 railroads that made up such a large part—a major part—of The 200 Largest corporations of 1929 had been consolidated into a dozen or so surviving lines and systems. To be sure, these survivors, with only one or two exceptions, were shadows of their former selves, and mostly tottery at that. But survival *is* survival, and where most others have disappeared in one way or another, that is no mean feat. As an old gaffer once explained to his grandson, years after the events, his greatest accomplishment during the French Revolution was to have survived.

Why that particular handful of survivors among the railroads? Location of routes was no doubt a major factor: The long lines of the West and South, by and large, had fared better than the eastern roads. But financial acumen and flexibility of organizing concepts and of human will, and greater vision—perhaps even honesty—were also present to a greater degree in a fortunate few, such as the Norfolk and Western. And, maybe, some luck.

Of the 39 electric, gas, water, and sanitary utilities of 1929, it is hard to say how many survived, so great and so general were the reorganizations that took place under pressure coming from the Public Utility Holding Company Act. Of these few survivors, whatever their number, it is safe to say that one thing of major importance that they had in common was that the corporate structures of these companies corresponded to concrete, meaningful realities of reasonably compact, physically integrated operating systems. They were more than the flimsy, opportunistic financial tracery of the holding companies of the Roaring Twenties that corresponded to no system realities. It was to their great credit that the directors and managements of these particular surviving companies were not caught up in the feverish financial pyramiding and manipulation whereby holding companies were created, and which, aside from making fortunes for some of their promoters, served no great real purpose. When Judgment Day came to the industry, these very few persisting companies were in order and are more or less happily still with us.*

Decline and growth among survivors

As with all organisms, there were *degrees* of surviving among The 200 of 1929 that were still around in 1971. Some had survived in healthier, more energetic states than others.

Among corporations, as among other organisms, *degrees* of living, so to speak, can be measured by various vital signs. Among living organisms such signs are available as pulse, metabolism, body temperature, blood pressure, and weight gain or loss. Among corporations, life-signs include profitability and levels and trends of sales and asset values. Of all possible measures of corporate vitality and health, we have at hand for the scope and purposes of this study only asset values. For some companies, we have these observations as of two widely separated dates. There are limits as to what one can infer from such data. But, being all we have, the levels and trends indicated by these figures will have to serve the turn as best they can.

Of the 100 Largest Companies of 1929 that had survived into the 1970s, 25 had slipped from among the Top 200 down among The Next 359. Among the other 75, some had grown markedly. These instances give rise to challenging thoughts.

Steel. The steel industry, which was a real *growth* industry from the Civil War to the Great Depression, provides intriguing examples of individual corporate growth and decline over the years 1929 through 1971. The aggregate "mass" of the very largest steel companies that were among The 200 in 1929 and in 1971, respectively, had increased by about 30 percent, from about $14 billion (in something like 1971 dollars) to about $18 billion. The aggregate mass of *all* steel companies with assets of over $250 million in 1971 dollars, including two that had slipped down among The 359, had risen by two-thirds, from $14 billion in 1929 to $23.4 billion. Clearly, the growth of some of the largest companies had not kept pace with the growth of the industry system of which they were components. A good bit of churning had been taking place in this system.

In this milieu, although the assets of Wheeling-Pittsburgh Steel, for example, had increased by 55 percent in terms of 1971 dollars over

---

*I, personally, have serious doubt that the present structure of our utilities, highly fragmented as it is, is anywhere near optimal from the point of view of rational management, allocation of capital, reliability of networks, intelligent—and intelligible—regulation, etc.

the years, its rank among the largest steel companies had declined from Number 6 to Number 9. Its relative presence among the largest steel companies had declined slightly, from 2.8 percent in 1929 to 2.6 percent in 1971. But it had been overtaken and far surpassed by three of its erstwhile smaller rivals—National, Armco, and Inland. These had grown by 497 percent, 639 percent, and 435 percent, respectively. Among its larger rivals, Republic had grown by 72 percent.

In the churning relationships among the largest steel companies, what happened to the two largest companies quite clearly illustrates the proposition that size, alone, gives no assurance of corporate health and vitality. In 1971, Bethlehem was still Number 2. Its asset mass had grown by something like 40 percent, over the 40-odd years—a compound annual growth rate of 0.85 percent—considerably less than the industry as a whole. And its relative presence among the largest steel companies had declined from about 18 percent to about 15 percent. No great record.

The performance of United States Steel—"*The* Steel Company"— was more thought-provoking still: in terms of asset values, this once-largest of all corporations had pretty much stood still over all those years, if, indeed, it had not actually shrunk. Its relative presence among the largest steel companies in 1929 had stood at just over 50 percent. In 1971, its relative presence had declined to about 27 percent. A faltering giant.

Others of the once largest steel companies had fallen on hard times indeed: Jones & Laughlin, as a corporation, had disappeared, along with the formerly large and independent meatpacker, Wilson & Co., into the conglomerate Ling-Temco-Vought. Crucible Steel was the largest component of another, smaller conglomerate, Colt Industries. But even this surviving acquirer, in total, was only about 40 percent larger than Crucible, itself, alone, had been, 40 years earlier. Cliffs Corporation, the smallest of the largest steel companies of 1929, despite its subsequent merging with another iron and steel company, was no longer even among The 559 of 1971.

Under more creative, and more activist, direction and management, three steel companies, as mentioned—National Steel, Inland Steel, and Armco—had achieved very healthy growth over the years. In fact, the growth of these three much smaller companies, alone, was about equal to the total net growth of the very largest steel companies between 1929 and 1971.

In a mature industry, healthy growth and advance was still possible, given appropriate strategies and policies and determined leadership.

Nonferrous metals. The vicissitudes of the one-time largest nonferrous metals companies, no less than those of the steel companies, give one to think about the differences that direction and management make in the unfolding fortunes of corporations. The aggregate asset value of nonferrous metals companies with assets greater than $250 million in 1971 dollars had increased threefold between 1929 and 1971. But the fortunes of individual companies varied greatly. In 1929, 8 of The 200 Largest Corporations were in nonferrous metals. In 1971, among The 200 Largest, 8, again, were in nonferrous metals. But they were not the same eight. Two on the earlier list were not there in 1971; two companies, which had not even existed in 1929, were now on the list. Of the two that had dropped off the list of The 200, one had dropped down into the ranks of The Next 359; one had been merged, as a lesser component, into a conglomerate, and had thus disappeared from view.

In this system of companies, there were also examples of growth: American Metal Company (renamed AMAX and now including Climax Molybdenum, which was later acquired) grew almost fivefold in size, from $252.7 million to $1,253.3 million. Alcoa grew almost threefold, from $920.3 million to $2,644.6 million. Phelps Dodge had more than doubled, from $382.5 million to $988.7 million.

There were instances of far slower growth. Kennecott Copper had grown from $1,036.2 million to $1,843.2; American Smelting and Refining had grown at an average annual compound rate of 0.48 percent from $739.3 million to $905.9 million.

In this context of industry growth, which, in total, had pretty much kept pace with the growth of the American economy, Anaconda, once by far the largest of the nonferrous metals companies, had actually shrunk 30 percent in asset values, from $2,087.7 million to $1,454.1 million. This put Anaconda, in asset value terms, well below two utter newcomers, Reynolds Metals and Kaiser Aluminum & Chemical. Not a notable record for what had once been a vital, leading company. (What remained of Anaconda—not a great deal, in all truth—was acquired for stock and a small amount of cash by Atlantic Richfield Company, in early 1977.)

Petroleum. Over the years 1929-71, as our industrial and economic development continued in growing mass and changing nature, our total consumption of energy increased threefold from about 23,000 *trillion* British thermal units to about 69,000 trillion. Of those totals, petroleum in 1929 provided about 6,000 trillion, or something over 25 percent, and about 28,000 trillion, or about 40 percent, in 1971.[3] Petroleum was one of our great growth industries during those turbulent years of economic expansion and manifold changes. The aggregate assets of the largest companies in Petroleum grew by a factor of 4.3, from $24.5 billion of 1971 dollars in 1929, to $105.8 billion in 1971. There was lots of room for growth for individual petroleum companies, as total American petroleum output, alone, increased by a factor of about 4.7.

Some of the largest petroleum companies of 1929 grew in even greater proportion; but some did not. Some disappeared through mergers—some, like Richfield, through a positive strategy of growth.

For absolute growth, Standard Oil Company (New Jersey), now Exxon, was surely a standout. Its assets grew by almost $15 billion between 1929 and 1971; but in relative terms, this growth by a factor of about 3.8 was at a rate lower than that of the aggregate of petroleum companies among The 200 largest of the two terminal years. In relative terms, the greatest internal growth was achieved by Gulf, which grew by over $8 billion, which represented a factor of over 7. Phillips grew by a factor of more than 7. What had been Atlantic Refining in 1929, a nonintegrated company with no production, became through mergers Atlantic Richfield, an integrated company, growing by a factor of over 9. Texaco grew by more than $9 billion of 1971 dollars, and by a factor of about 5.7.

Three of the largest petroleum companies of 1929 lagged well behind the overall growth of that industry system: Standard Oil of California grew by a factor of just over 4; Shell (the United States subsidiary of Royal Dutch Shell) grew by a factor of only 3.1; Standard Oil Company (Indiana) grew by a factor of less than 2.2.

Some of the leading petroleum companies of 1929 went on to great things. Some rather drifted. Others really missed the tide.

General merchandise. One last group of companies will serve to illustrate the fact of varying fortunes of large companies over a span of years: the general merchandisers. By 1929, a half-dozen of the then 200 Largest companies were those that had gone a long way, as was said in the last chapter, in bringing rational methods of the Industrial Revolution and economies of scale to mass merchandising and marketing. These were Sears Roebuck, Montgomery Ward, Woolworth, Marshall Field, Kresge, and Macy's.

The aggregate assets of those companies in 1929 stood at about $2.9 billion, in 1971 dollars. Forty-two years later, the aggregate assets of the General merchandise companies then among The 200 Largest stood at $19.4 billion—a growth of about 670 percent. The total assets of all General merchandisers holding assets valued at more than $250 million had risen to $24.5 billion—a growth of about 840 percent. Indeed, the continuing extension of the Industrial Revolution in mass marketing was one of the more notable features of our industrial and economic development over those years. And the more than tenfold growth of Sears Roebuck from 1929 to 1971 was an outstanding demonstration of what was possible during that Revolution, whose time had come. Other large General merchandisers had also grown, although by no means at the same rate: Montgomery Ward, under far less creative and adaptive leadership, had merged, following, no doubt, practical reasons of asset management, but no powerful substantive "business" strategy, with a container company. Kresge had grown by a factor of about 3.3; Woolworth had grown by a factor of about 3.1.

With such opportunities to be grasped—and which were, in fact, grasped by some—one might think that all of the mass merchandisers of 1929 could have made similar records, rising with a common tide. Macy's did, indeed, double its assets; but, clearly, this was only a fraction of what might have been achieved. Marshall Field, far from capitalizing upon tremendous opportunities, had actually shrunk substantially. One must wonder what the directors and executives of that once great and leading organization could have been thinking of, during all those years of developments going on about them.[4]

The enormous disparities among the fortunes of generally similar and systemically interrelated large corporations in these and other Industry Categories are living refutations of theories that seek to explain individual, or even group, corporate behavior in deterministic, structuralist terms.

EMERGENCE AND GROWTH OF NEW LARGE CORPORATIONS

Just as there is no suggestion in the work of Berle and Means and in received economic theory that large corporations can regress or even disappear and that bigness is no guarantee of permanence, so also is there no suggestion that smaller corporations, including newly born companies, can appear, grow, and achieve such a mass, in both older and even entirely new industries, that they may come to be counted among the very largest. But 125 of The 200 Largest Corporations of 1971 had not been on the List of 1929. Of the 559 corporations holding assets valued at more than $250 million in 1971, 459 of them—82 percent—were not among The 200 of 1929.*

Despite long-standing concern about the possibility that the existence and workings of large companies might inhibit economic development and growth of smaller companies—a concern that is understandable—in fact, literally hundreds of companies did emerge from relative obscurity, or even from scratch, to become prominent members of the business community.

Of the new Largest companies of 1971, few, if any, were born great. Surely none had had greatness thrust upon it. And in the world of business, "empires" are not acquired during fits of inadvertence.

A statistical tabulation is given in Exhibit 70, Part 2, of the emergence and growth of companies that had moved into the ranks of The 200 Largest and The 359 Next Largest of 1971. This tabulation also appears at the end of this chapter. In Exhibit 72 are summarized some of those data that focus on the growth and emergence of indi-

---

*See Table 21 and Note 2 at the end of this chapter.

EXHIBIT 72
Emergence and growth among The Largest Corporations; 1929-1971; summary

Industry Category	Number of firms among The 200 Largest in 1971 but not among The 200 Largest of 1929[2]	Number of firms among The Next 359 in 1971 but not among The 200 Largest of 1929[3]	Number of firms among The 559 Largest in 1971 but not among The 200 Largest of 1929[4]	Percentage of The 559 Largest of 1971 not among The 200 Largest of 1929[5]
1. Industry Categories with notable cases of emergence[1]				
Iron and steel	0	10	10	52.6%
Nonferrous metals	2	9	11	61.1
Coal	0	3	3	100.0
Petroleum	9	10	19	63.3
Construction	0	3	3	100.0
Food	2	14	16	84.2
Dairy	1	3	4	66.7
Alcoholic beverages	1	5	6	100.0
Soft drinks	1	1	2	100.0
Textiles	1	8	9	100.0
Apparel	1	4	5	100.0
Lumber... wood... paper ... products	6	9	15	88.2
Printing and publishing	0	7	7	100.0
Chemicals	7	15	22	84.6
Pharmaceuticals	4	17	21	100.0
Soaps, cleaners	0	4	4	80.0
Nonmetallic mineral products	0	13	13	100.0
Glass	1	2	3	75.0
Fabricated metal products	0	8	8	80.0
Machinery	0	8	8	88.9
Farm, construction... machinery	1	5	6	85.7
Office... computing... machines	7	4	11	100.0
Electrical machinery	0	6	6	75.0
Household appliances	1	6	7	100.0
Radio... communication equipment	2[6]	11[7]	13[6,7]	92.9
Scientific... control devices	1	1	2	100.0
Motor vehicles	5	9	14	82.4
Aircraft	8	2	10	100.0
Railroad equipment	0	3	3	75.0
Other and miscellaneous manufacturing	0	5	5	100.0
Motor transportation	2	3	5	100.0
Water transportation	0	3	3	100.0
Air transportation	6	6	12	100.0
Electric, gas... sanitary...[8]	42	59	101	95.3
Telephone, telegraph	3	6	9	81.8
Radio and TV broadcasting	0	2	2	100.0
Wholesale trade	0	1	1	100.0
Retail trade	1	6	7	100.0
General merchandise	6	9	15	75.0
Food stores	1	8	9	90.0
Motion pictures	0	4	4	80.0
Services	0	12	12	100.0
Real estate	0	6	6	100.0
Subtotals	122	330	452	92.1%
2. Other Industry Categories				
Seven industries[9]	8	8	16	39.0%
Totals, as above	130	338	468	
Less companies not to be counted among net new increases[10]	−5	−4	−9	
Net "new appearances"	125	334	459	82.1%

EXHIBIT 72 (continued)

[1] Industry categories in which *more than 50 percent* of The 559 of 1971 had not been among The 200 of 1929.

[2] See Exhibit 70, Part 2; Column 1.

[3] See Exhibit 70, Part 2; Column 3.

[4] See Exhibit 70, Part 2; Column 5.

[5] See Exhibit 70, Part 2; Column 9.

[6] Includes Western Electric; not included in totals.

[7] Includes one or more communication equipment subsidiaries of General Telephone & Electronics, counted as one company; not included in totals.

[8] See text, the section of Chapter 11 entitled "Persistence," and Exhibit 70, Part 1, Note 11.

[9] Industry Categories—seven—in which "newly emerged" companies, i.e. those which were *not* on list of 1929, represented *50 percent or less* of The 559 of 1971: Meat; Tobacco; Rubber and tires; Leather; Metal cans; Photographic equipment; Railroad transportation.

[10] Among The 200, Western Electric and four companies that moved in from other industries; among The 359, one or more subsidiaries of General Telephone & Electronics and three companies that moved in from other industries. See Exhibit 70, Part 2, Notes 12, 13, 14, and 15.

vidual companies that were not visible, or even not in existence in 1929, onto the list of largest corporations of 1971.

Emergence of Large Companies in newer industries

We have already taken note of emergence of newly visible, or altogether new Large companies in some of our newer industries. Table 22 summarizes data that give measure to those appearances. Of The 559 Largest Corporations of 1971, about 1 in 6, or 93, were to be found in these six newer industry systems; 90 of those companies had not been on the list of Largest in 1929. The increase in the total value of the assets in these Industry Categories—about $105 billion—accounted for about 22.5 percent of the total increase in assets of the Largest Companies.

These particular corporations were not alone in their respective industry systems, of course. But they did account for the lions' shares of the assets of those Industry Categories, ranging up to almost 90 percent in the case of Pharmaceuticals.

TABLE 22
Emergence of Large Corporations in selected newer industries, 1929-1971

Industry Category	Firms among The 559 Largest of 1971	Firms of The 559 of 1971 not on the list of 1929	Values of assets, 1929 ($ billions)	Values of assets, 1971 ($ billions)	Presence index, Largest Companies in total Industry Category†
Chemicals	26	22	$4.1	$ 30.4	76.5%
Pharmaceuticals	21	21	–	12.1	87.8
Office... computing	11	11	–	21.5	86.5
Radio... communication equipment	13*	14*	0.9	20.0	77.1
Aircraft	10	10	–	12.8	52.8
Air transportation	12	12	–	12.2	73.5
Totals	93	90	$5.0	$109.0	

*See Exhibit 70, Part 2, Notes 6 and 7.

†See Exhibit 36.

These 90 new Largest Corporations were merely the most visibly successful of all the companies that had entered the lists in these particular Industry Categories. These were the ones, among all the starters, that, confronting the new opportunities made possible by new technologies, new concepts of management, and economic and social change, had been most successful in designing and carrying out strategies and policies best adapted to the evolving realities around them.

These very companies were prime engines of change that pushed back outer edges of technologies and brought massive increments of real, concrete, manifest change—*progress,* if one be allowed an old-fashioned word—into the American, the world scene. How hard it is, now, to think of a world without them and their products: synthetics—plastics, fibers, fertilizers; antibiotics and all the hundreds of new items in the armamentarium of modern medicine; computers; television and radar; aircraft; and rapid continental and intercontinental air transport.

As we look at these companies in these industries, a point arises too important to pass by: strong, surging forward trends are not enough, of themselves, to carry every corporation along. They do provide a favoring current. But directors and managers have to point their companies in the right direction, establish strategic plans, set upon well chosen courses of research and development, allocate resources, find and develop managers and technicians, and set up organizations well-calculated to take advantage of the tide. Not all the companies in these six great growth industries did so, certainly not with anything like equal effectiveness. Missing from the 1971 list of Largest Corporations in Aircraft, for example, were the names of Curtiss-Wright, Republic, and Chance-Vought, relative giants in the industry well before World War II.

The Chemical and allied products Industry Category also offers interesting documentation of the point.

Chemicals and allied products. The complex industry system of Chemicals and allied products has been one of the most distinctive sources of expansion and innovation in our economy. The development and evolution of this complex has touched every aspect of our daily life. This dynamic Industry Category has been the locale of the emergence and growth of over 20 major corporations unheard of or nonexistent in 1929.

The number of chemical companies among The 200 of 1929 was 4. Of these, 3 were still among The 200 in 1971. One of the companies —Koppers—had not only moved down among The Next 359; it had actually shrunk to something about half the size it had achieved in 1929. The two largest chemical companies of 1929, Du Pont and Union Carbide, were still the largest in 1971. But the third, Allied Chemical, although it had about doubled in size, had been overtaken by five "new arrivals" among The 200 Largest of 1971: Dow, Monsanto, 3M, Celanese, and Grace, which, by the way, had grown greatly while transforming itself from the shipping company it used to be.

The persisting and the newly arrived chemical companies had not merely grown. They had done so, as had scores of companies in other Industry Categories, not primarily just by making and selling more of what they had before, but in consequence of innovations of many kinds, including unrelenting competition for technological leadership.

Dynamism, qualitative as well as quantitative, has been the most noteworthy characteristic of this industry system, as it has of others. In no way can its, and their, development and evolution be described, let alone understood or explained or evaluated, in terms of hypotheses and hypothetical models that posit as given, or that even *ignore,* those variables, that, in their very natures, have been *essential* sources, subjects, and vehicles of expansion, contraction and change, trial and error: evolving and entirely new products; expanding and contracting scales and changing kinds of productive methods and apparatus—including vertical integration of successive processes and development of complex multiplant, multiproduct production systems; changing natures and volumes of inputs and of outputs; emergence, growth, disappearance and changing identities, natures, numbers, and workings of suppliers, producers, and customers, and dynamic symbiotic relationships among them, to name a few.

Question: Granted that companies could grow from modest beginnings to preeminence in *new* fields, was it possible for smaller companies to grow to greatness in the shadows of towering, long-established Largest Companies, with all their alleged dark, forbidding, "monopolistic" powers?

Answer: Yes.*

Growth in the presence of large corporations

Growing up in the shadow of large established companies is certainly not the easiest accomplishment in the business world. But many companies were able to do just that. Beyond those new arrivals in the newer Industry Categories we have just looked at, scores of new arrivals had reached the ranks of Largest Companies in industries where very large companies were already present as far back as 1929. Exhibit 73 registers the emergence of 139 large corporations in 11 Industry Categories in which 64 of The 200 Largest were already located in 1929. Especially noteworthy is the fact that the exhibit also reflects the disappearance in one way or another of 17 of those erstwhile Largest Firms, which were faltering while newer, smaller firms were thriving greatly.

*See Chapter 13 for recent examples.

Industry Category	Number of firms among The 200 Largest, 1929	Number of firms persisting among The 559 of 1971	Number of firms among The 559 not among The 200 of 1929	Total number of firms among The 559 of 1971
Iron and steel	11	9	10	19
Nonferrous metals	8	7	11	18
Petroleum	20	11	19	30
Food...	4	3	16	19
Lumber...wood.	4	2	15	17
Chemicals...	4	4	22	26
Soaps...cleaners	1	1	4	5
Electrical machinery.	2	2	6	8
Household appliances	0*	0	7†	7†
Motor vehicles...	4	3	14	17
General merchandise	6	5	15	20
Totals	64	47	139	186

*General Electric and Westinghouse, classed in Electrical machinery in 1929, were actually relatively large elements in Home appliances, although this was not their primary line of business.
†Does not include General Electric and Westinghouse.

A few comments round out the data.

Iron and steel. Of the 19 corporations in Iron and steel on the list of The 559 Largest of 1971, 10 had not been on the list of 200 in 1929. Although considerably smaller than the very largest companies in this industry complex, these new arrivals accounted for more than half ($5.1 billion) of the total net increase in the total value of the assets—the net growth ($9.4 billion)—of the largest Iron and steel companies of 1971 over the corresponding 1929 figure.

Nonferrous metals. The total asset value of the largest nonferrous metals companies in 1971 was $11.8 billion more than in 1929, in 1971 dollars. Of this increase, $7.9 billion—two-thirds of the growth— were accounted for by the assets of the 11 companies that had not been on the list in 1929, including 2 new arrivals among The 200 Largest, Reynolds Metals and Kaiser Aluminum & Chemical.

Petroleum. Even Petroleum, so often an object of concern as to the size of its component companies and their possibly monopolistic conduct, had had a number of new arrivals among its Largest Corporations. Not counting Union Oil of California, which was a successor to a company already on the list of 1929, nor Cities Service, which had become a petroleum company in the course of its reorganization in accord with the Public Utility Holding Company Act, 7 of the 20 very largest petroleum companies of 1971 had not been on The 200 list of 1929. Beyond these, there were now, in 1971, among The Next 359, another 10 companies in the Petroleum Industry Category that had not been on the list in 1929.

The reported assets of the largest petroleum companies in 1929 had stood at $24.5 billion, in 1971 dollars. In 1971, the assets of petroleum companies with assets of more than $250 million stood at $105.8 billion. The increase amounted to $81.3 billion. Of this, $21.6 billion, or 27 percent, was accounted for by 19 new arrivals, 9 among The 200 and 10 among The Next 359.

Lumber. Another older, established Industry Category in which numbers of smaller companies grew and emerged into prominence was Lumber and wood products and paper and allied products. . . . Of the 8 companies among The 200 Largest of 1971, 6 had not been on the list of 1929. They held $9.4 billion, or 75 percent of the $12.5 billion of assets of the very largest corporations in that industry system in 1971. Two companies among the new arrivals in Lumber . . . wood . . . paper were larger in 1971 than the two companies still on the list that had been among The 200 of 1929. Four of the new arrivals were larger than the second of the two companies that had been on the list of 1929. Moreover, in the Lumber . . . wood . . . paper industry system of 1971, another 9 companies had arrived among The Next 359, along with $4.9 billion of assets, more than half again the total asset value of the Largest companies in the industry in 1929.

Motor vehicles. When Americans think "automobiles" or motor vehicles, most of us probably think of General Motors, Ford, and Chrysler. We may or may not remember the much smaller American Motors, as well. But as the data in Exhibit 1 show, those four companies are merely the most visible—and in the case of American Motors, not even one of the biggest—in one of our largest industry systems, measured in asset values.

The Motor vehicle industry complex included about 2,400 manufacturing companies in 1971 that provided components, parts, and related services to the big automobile companies, to other producers of highway and off-highway equipment, and to the buyers of accessories and replacement parts. Among all of these, in addition to the four *automobile* companies proper, were 13 other companies in the industry system that ranked among The 559 Largest of 1971, including 5 that ranked among The 200. Only 4 of the largest companies in the Motor vehicles Category in 1971 had been among The 200 of 1929.

These other companies had emerged out of the Motor vehicle industry system, as it was in 1929, to become, 42 years later, some of our Largest Corporations. In each case, the company had apparently selected a particularly well-adapted strategy and had developed and maintained some distinctive competences that enabled it to survive in competition with others and to survive and grow in the presence of much larger companies that, as often as not, were actual and potential competitors as well as customers.

The growths of even the largest companies were far from uniform:

Ford and General Motors had each grown by a factor of more than 4. Chrysler had grown by a factor of almost 8. But International Harvester, which had been almost twice as large as Chrysler in 1929, albeit situated primarily in Farm, construction, and mining machinery, had grown, over 42 years, by a factor of less than 2. Studebaker, still alive and doing reasonably well as an automobile company as recently as 1954, eventually had disappeared through merger into another company in another Industry Category.[5]

Along the line, goodness knows how many other companies in the Motor vehicles complex had topped out at scales smaller than $250 million or were simply victims of the shake-out so characteristic of the middle stages of the life cycle of many industries. Antique car buffs, and few others, may remember such names as Cunningham, Maxwell, Overland, Willys-Knight, Essex, Moon, Star, Elcar, Pierce-Arrow, Graham-Paige, and Packard. Only real pros are likely to remember any of the many similarly unsuccessful makers of parts and components. But from among the ranks of suppliers of parts, components, and accessories there emerged a number of companies of substantial size, including Bendix, TRW, and Borg-Warner, now among The Top 200.

In sum, 14 of the 17 Largest Corporations in Motor vehicles in 1971 had not been among The 200 Largest of 1929.

Large and small companies alike may be either the beneficiaries or, as the case may be, the victims of industry-system dynamics that *will* have their way over the years.

* * * * *

The growths of all these companies that have thrived in both newer and more mature industry systems, as is true of so many in other Industry Categories, some of which we have looked at all too briefly, have been characterized by, and are the consequences of, literally hundreds of thousands of individual acts of innovation. In outputs—the much misunderstood and wrongfully maligned "product proliferation." In production processes. In inputs. In physical distribution and marketing—including the development and use of new channels to ultimate industrial and consumer buyers. In methods of financing of their own operations and, often, those of their suppliers and their distributors. In strategic concepts. In organization structures and information and control systems.

Innovations have stemmed out of new technological, social, and economic possibilities opened up by themselves as well as by companies in other industry systems and by public and nonprofit agencies; out of new concepts of products and services; and out of new concepts and techniques of finance and management.

The phenomena manifested by, and related to, the growth of these companies have precious little to do with supposed, hypothetical workings of essentially "given" monopolistic and oligopolistic structures of the sort so often posited in much prevalent economic thought and implicit in so much public policy and court decisions and opinions.

IMPLICATIONS OF A DYNAMIC ECOLOGICAL SYSTEM OF EVOLVING INDUSTRIES

From one year to the next, we are scarcely sensible of the changes that take place in the floral and faunal communities of a regrowing forest. But over a span of 40-some years, idle pasture land in New England can turn into a deciduous forest and be well on its way to becoming the conifer forest that is the longer-run climax state of the region. Persistent forces, working from day to day, bring about changes scarcely observable even in the span of a year. But the summation of such changes over several years results in thoroughgoing transformation. In analogous fashion, over a span of years, as individual corporations come and grow, or regress and disappear in consequence of uncountable thousands of actions patterned by the strategies and policies of individual corporations, the business community can, and does, experience even greater and open-ended transformation. And that is exactly what has happened, and is continuing to happen, in our fluid economic system of which our Largest Corporations are such important components.

Capitalized upon by business leaders, these fateful dynamics in our industrial and business "ecology" have been ignored by business people with short time-horizons and without responsiveness to developments and trends in their environments. They have been ignored also, or slighted by many economists, and by much of our public policy.

Let us remind ourselves, at this point, that a relative few large corporations—out of a total of now more than 1.6 million—hold and operate a majority of the productive assets of the entire corporate business community. The rise and fall, the appearance, persistence and disappearance of large corporations betoken and bespeak the dynamics of the development of our industrial structure and of the entire American system that rests upon that structure.

Many morals, no doubt about it, can be drawn from what has happened over the years in the community of Largest Corporations. From a public standpoint, one clear moral is that poorly directed and managed corporations give rise to social loss just as certainly as corporate health contributes to the general welfare. In recent decades, public preoccupation in other directions and with other matters has resulted in a slighting of the importance to us all of national *development* and of the corporate health and vitality which that evolution requires.

As concerns directors and executives of corporations, a major lesson to be learned is that well-chosen strategies and policies and their vigorous implementation can lead to corporate health and prosperity. Less well-chosen and less effectively pursued strategies and policies can leave a company becalmed and decadent, even one that, in the past, achieved a degree of greatness. Our data document scores of instances where, even in the face of tremendous opportunities, some companies achieved the distinction—if that is the word—of regressing while competitors and other contemporaries moved ahead.

In the next chapter, we consider some of the implications for public and corporate policy of the data we have looked at and the observations we have made along the way.

EXHIBIT 70
Turnover among the Largest Corporations, 1929-1971
(Part 1: Persistence, decline, disappearance; by Industry Category)

	(1)	(2)	(3)	(4)	(5)	(6)
Industry Category	Number of firms among The 200 of 1929	Number of firms among The 200 Largest of both 1929 and 1971	Number of firms among The 200 Largest in 1929 and among The Next 359 in 1971	Number of firms among The 200 Largest in 1929 and among The 559 in 1971	Number of firms among The 200 Largest in 1929 that "disappeared"	Number of firms among The 200 Largest of 1929 that "declined" to The 359 of 1971 or "disappeared"
1. Agriculture	0	—	—	—	—	—
2. Iron and steel	11	7	2[1]	9	2[2]	4
3. Nonferrous metals	8	6	1	7	1	2
4. Coal	4	0	0	0	4	4
5. Petroleum	20	11	0	11	9[3]	9
6. Construction	0	1	—	—	—	—
7. Food	4	1	2	3	1[4]	3
8. Meat	3	2	1	3	0	1
9. Dairy	2	2	0	2	0	0
10. Alcoholic beverages	0	—	—	—	—	—
11. Soft drinks	0	—	—	—	—	—
12. Tobacco	4	3[5]	1	4	0	1
13. Textiles	1	0	0	0	1	1
14. Apparel	0	—	—	—	—	—
15. Lumber . . . wood . . . paper . . . products	4	2	0	2	2[6]	2
16. Furniture and fixtures	0	—	—	—	—	—
17. Printing and publishing	0	—	—	—	—	—
18. Chemicals	4	3	1	4	0	1
19. Pharmaceuticals	0	—	—	—	—	—
20. Soaps, cleansers	1	1	0	1	0	0
21. Rubber and tires	4	4	0	4	0	0
22. Leather	1	0	1	1	0	1
23. Nonmetallic mineral products	0	—	—	—	—	—
24. Glass	1	1	0	1	0	0
25. Fabricated metal products	2	1	1	2	0	1
26. Metal cans	2	2	0	2	0	0
27. Machinery	2	0	1	1	1[7]	2
28. Farm, construction . . . machinery	2	1	0	1	1[8]	1
29. Office . . . computing . . . machinery	0	—	—	—	—	—
30. Electrical machinery	2	2	0	2	0	0
31. Household appliances	0	—	—	—	—	—
32. Radio . . . communication equipment	1	1	0	1	0	0
33. Scientific . . . control devices . . . measuring	0	—	—	—	—	—
34. Photographic equipment	1	1	0	1	0[9]	0
35. Motor vehicles	4	3	0	3	1[9]	1
36. Aircraft	0	—	—	—	—	—
37. Ship . . . building	0	—	—	—	—	—
38. Railroad equipment	3	0	1	1	2	3
39. Other and misc. mfg.	0	—	—	—	—	—
40. Rail transportation	43	6	7	13	30[10]	37
41. Transit	8	0	0	0	8	8
42. Motor transportation	0	—	—	—	—	—
43. Water transportation	1	0	0	0	1	1
44. Air transportation	0	—	—	—	—	—
45. Electric, gas . . . sanitary	39	5[11]	0[11]	5[11]	34[11]	34
46. Telephone, telegraph	4	2	0	2	2[12]	2
47. Radio and TV	0	—	—	—	—	—
48. Wholesale trade	0	—	—	—	—	—
49. Retail trade	2	0	0	0	2	2
50. General merchandise	6	3	2	5	1	3
51. Food stores	1	1	0	1	0	0
52. Motion pictures	4	0	1	1	3[13]	4
53. Services	0	—	—	—	—	—
54. Real estate	1	0	0	0	1	1
Totals	200	71	22	93	107	129
Companies persisting, but in different industries		+4[14]	+3[15]	+7[16]	−7[16]	−4[14]
Net changes	200	75	25	100	100	125

Note: Col. 4 = Col. 2 + Col. 3; Col. 5 = Col. 1 − Col. 4; Col. 6 = Col. 3 + Col. 5; Col. 7 = Col. 2 ÷ Col. 1; Col. 8 = Col. 3 ÷ Col. 1; Col. 9 = Col. 4 ÷ Col. 1; Col. 9 also = Col. 7 + Col. 8; Col. 10 = Col. 5 ÷ Col. 1; Col. 10 also = 100.0 − Col. 9; Col. 11 = Col. 6 ÷ Col. 1; Col. 11 also = Col. 8 + Col. 10; Col. 12 = Col. 2 ÷ Col. 2 of Exhibit 70, Part 2; Col. 13 = Col. 3 ÷ Col. 4 of Exhibit 70, Part 2; Col. 14 = Col. 4 ÷ Col. 6 of Exhibit 70, Part 2.

[1] Includes Crucible Steel, which by 1971 had been merged into Colt Industries, but which determined the categorization of that company.

[2] Includes (a) Jones and Laughlin Steel, merged into Ling-Temco-Vought, whose categorization in 1971 was determined by the sales of meat and meat products of the former Wilson & Co.; and (b) Cliffs Corporation (see Appendix A, Note 6).

[3] All nine Petroleum companies that "disappeared" were merged with or into other Petroleum companies that continued into 1971 at least.

[4] United Fruit was merged into AMK and later into United Brands, whose Industry Category was determined by the sales of the former John Morrell & Co., a meat packer (see Appendix A, Note 24). United Fruit was treated as having "disappeared," and United Brands was treated as a newly emerged company.

[5] Includes Loew's Corporation, whose Industry Category was determined by the sales of the former Lorillard Co.

[6] The two Lumber . . . wood . . . paper companies that disappeared were acquired by other paper companies.

(7)	(8)	(9)	(10)	(11)	(12)	(13)	(14)
Percentage of The 200 of 1929 that persisted among 200 of 1971	Percentage of The 200 of 1929 that "declined" to The 359 of 1971	Percentage of The 200 of 1929 that persisted among the 559 of 1971	Percentage of The 200 of 1929 that "disappeared"	Percentage of The 200 of 1929 that "declined" to The 359 of 1971 or "disappeared"	Percentage of The 200 of 1971 that had been among The 200 of 1929	Percentage of The 359 of 1971 that had been among The 200 of 1929	Percentage of The 559 of 1971 that had been among The 200 of 1929
—	—	—	—	—	—	—	—
63.6%	18.2%	81.8%	18.2%	36.4%	100.0%	16.7%	47.4%
75.0	12.5	87.5	12.5	25.0	75.0	10.0	38.9
0.0	0.0	0.0	100.0	100.0	0.0	0.0	0.0
55.0	0.0	55.0	45.0	45.0	55.0	0.0	36.7
—	—	—	—	—	—	0.0	0.0
25.0	50.0	75.0	25.0	75.0	33.3	12.5	15.8
66.7	33.3	100.0	0.0	33.3	66.7	50.0	60.0
100.0	0.0	100.0	0.0	0.0	66.7	0.0	33.3
—	—	—	—	—	0.0	0.0	0.0
—	—	—	—	—	0.0	0.0	0.0
75.0	25.0	100.0	0.0	25.0	75.0	100.0	80.0
0.0	0.0	0.0	100.0	100.0	0.0	0.0	0.0
—	—	—	—	—	0.0	0.0	0.0
50.0	0.0	50.0	50.0	50.0	25.0	0.0	11.8
—	—	—	—	—	—	0.0	0.0
75.0	25.0	100.0	0.0	25.0	30.0	6.3	15.4
—	—	—	—	—	0.0	0.0	0.0
100.0	0.0	100.0	0.0	0.0	100.0	0.0	20.0
100.0	0.0	100.0	0.0	0.0	80.0	—	80.0
0.0	100.0	100.0	0.0	100.0	—	50.0	50.0
100.0	0.0	100.0	0.0	0.0	50.0	0.0	25.0
50.0	50.0	100.0	0.0	50.0	50.0	11.1	20.0
100.0	0.0	100.0	0.0	0.0	100.0	0.0	50.0
0.0	50.0	50.0	50.0	100.0	—	11.1	11.1
50.0	0.0	50.0	50.0	50.0	50.0	0.0	14.3
—	—	—	—	—	0.0	0.0	0.0
100.0	0.0	100.0	0.0	0.0	100.0	0.0	25.0
—	—	—	—	—	0.0	0.0	0.0
100.0	0.0	100.0	0.0	0.0	33.3	0.0	7.1
—	—	—	—	—	0.0	0.0	0.0
100.0	0.0	100.0	0.0	0.0	100.0	0.0	50.0
75.0	0.0	75.0	25.0	25.0	37.5	0.0	17.6
—	—	—	—	—	0.0	0.0	0.0
—	—	—	—	—	0.0	0.0	0.0
0.0	33.3	33.3	66.6	100.0	0.0	25.0	25.0
14.0	16.3	30.2	69.8	86.1	54.5	70.0	61.9
0.0	0.0	0.0	100.0	100.0	—	—	—
—	—	—	—	—	0.0	0.0	0.0
0.0	0.0	0.0	100.0	100.0	—	0.0	0.0
—	—	—	—	—	0.0	0.0	0.0
12.8	0.0	12.8	87.2	87.2	10.6[11]	0.0	4.7[11]
50.0	0.0	50.0	50.0[12]	50.0	40.0	0.0	18.2
—	—	—	—	—	—	0.0	0.0
—	—	—	—	—	—	0.0	0.0
0.0	0.0	0.0	100.0	100.0	0.0	0.0	0.0
50.0	33.3	83.3	16.7	50.0	33.3	18.2	25.0
100.0	0.0	100.0	0.0	0.0	50.0	0.0	10.0
0.0	25.0	25.0	75.0[13]	100.0	—	20.0	20.0
—	—	—	—	—	—	0.0	0.0
0.0	0.0	0.0	100.0	100.0	—	0.0	0.0
37.5%	12.5%	50.0%	50.0%	62.5%	37.5%	7.0%	17.9%

[7] Includes Singer, categorized in Machinery in 1929, and categorized as being in Household appliances in 1971.

[8] International Harvester, categorized in 1929 as in Farm machinery, was included with Motor vehicles in 1971.

[9] Studebaker of 1929 was merged into Studebaker-Worthington, which was categorized as being in Machinery in 1971.

[10] Includes Pullman Railroad Company which, under the name Pullman Company, was counted in Railroad equipment in 1971.

[11] It is estimated, somewhat arbitrarily, that five of the largest utilities that were among The 200 Largest corporations of 1929 persisted, and were among The 200 Largest Corporations of 1971. See Chapter 11.

[12] Includes International Telephone & Telegraph, which was categorized as being in Radio, TV, communications equipment in 1971.

[13] Loews, Inc., was categorized in Tobacco in 1971 because of the sales of the former P. Lorillard Co.

[14] Four other companies of the Top 200 of 1929 that had persisted among The Top 200 into 1971, but in different Industry Categories from those of 1929: Cities Service, International Harvester, International Telephone & Telegraph, and Pullman.

[15] Three other companies of the Top 200 of 1929 that had "persisted," to be sure, but had moved into different Industry Categories from those of 1929: Singer, Studebaker-Worthington ("descended" from Studebaker), and UV Industries ("descended" from United States Smelting, Refining & Mining Co.).

[16] The seven companies named in 14 and 15, above, were counted as having "disappeared" from the Industry Categories in which they were located in 1929, but were counted as having "persisted" among the *total* of The Largest Corporations of 1971.

EXHIBIT 70 (continued)
(Part 2: Emergence and growth; by Industry Category)

Industry Category	(1) Number of firms among The 200 Largest in 1971 but not among The 200 Largest of 1929	(2) Number of firms among The 200 Largest of 1971	(3) Number of firms among The Next 359 in 1971 but not among The 200 Largest of 1929	(4) Number of firms among The Next 359 of 1971	(5) Number of firms among The 559 Largest in 1971 but not among The 200 Largest of 1929	(6) Number of firms among The 559 Largest of 1971	(7) Percentage of The 200 Largest of 1971 not among The 200 Largest of 1929	(8) Percentage of The Next 359 of 1971 not among The 200 Largest of 1929	(9) Percentage of The 559 Largest of 1971 not among The 200 Largest of 1929	(10) Percentage of The 559 Largest of 1971 that were among The 200 Largest of 1929
1. Agriculture	—	0	—	0	—	0	—			—
2. Iron and steel	0	7	10	12[1]	10	19	0.0%	83.3%	52.6%	47.4%
3. Nonferrous metals	2	8	9	10	11	18	25.0	90.0	61.1	38.9
4. Coal	—	0	3	3	3	3	—	100.0	100.0	0.0
5. Petroleum	9[2]	20	10	10	19	30	45.0	100.0	63.3	36.7
6. Construction	—	0	3	3	3	3	—	100.0	100.0	0.0
7. Food	2	3	14	16	16	19	66.7	87.5	84.2	15.8
8. Meat	1[3]	3	1	2	2	5	33.3	50.0	40.0	60.0
9. Dairy	1	3	3	3	4	6	33.3	100.0	66.7	33.3
10. Alcoholic beverages	1	1	5	5	6	6	100.0	100.0	100.0	0.0
11. Soft drinks	1	1	1	1	2	2	100.0	100.0	100.0	0.0
12. Tobacco	1	4	0	1	1	5	25.0	0.0	20.0	80.0
13. Textiles	1	1	8	8	9	9	100.0	100.0	100.0	0.0
14. Apparel	1	1	4	4	5	5	100.0	100.0	100.0	0.0
15. Lumber...wood...paper products	6	8	9	9	15	17	75.0	100.0	88.2	11.8
16. Furniture and fixtures	—	0	—	0	—	0	—	—	—	—
17. Printing and publishing	—	0	7	7	7	7	—	100.0	100.0	0.0
18. Chemicals	7	10	15	16	22	26	70.0	93.8	84.6	15.4
19. Pharmaceuticals	4	4	17	17	21	21	100.0	100.0	100.0	0.0
20. Soaps, cleaners	0	1	4	4	4	5	0.0	100.0	80.0	20.0
21. Rubber and tires	1	5	—	0	1	5	20.0	—	20.0	80.0
22. Leather	—	0	1	2	1	2	—	50.0	50.0	50.0
23. Nonmetallic mineral products	—	0	13	13	13	13	—	100.0	100.0	0.0
24. Glass	1	2	2	2	3	4	50.0	100.0	75.0	25.0
25. Fabricated metal products	0	1	8	9	8	10	0.0	88.9	80.0	20.0
26. Metal cans	0	2	2	2	2	4	0.0	100.0	50.0	50.0
27. Machinery	—	0	8	9	8	9	—	88.9	88.9	11.1
28. Farm, construction machinery	1	2	5	5	6	7	50.0	100.0	85.7	14.3
29. Office...computing machines	7	7	4	4	11	11	100.0	100.0	100.0	0.0
30. Electrical machinery	0	2	6[4]	6	6	8	0.0	100.0	75.0	25.0
31. Household appliances	1	1	6[5]	6	7	7	100.0	100.0	100.0	0.0
32. Radio...communication equipment	2[6]	3	11[7]	11	13[6,7]	14	66.7	100.0	92.9	7.1
33. Scientific...control...measuring devices	1	1	1	1	2	2	100.0	100.0	100.0	0.0

#	Category	Col. 1	Col. 2	Col. 3	Col. 4	Col. 5	Col. 6	Col. 7	Col. 8	Col. 9	Col. 10
34.	Photographic equipment	0	1	1	1	1	2	0.0	100.0	50.0	50.0
35.	Motor vehicles	5[8]	8	9	9	14[8]	17	62.5	100.0	82.4	17.6
36.	Aircraft	8	8	2	2	10	10	100.0	100.0	100.0	0.0
37.	Ship...building	—	0	0	0	0	0	—	—	—	—
38.	Railroad equipment	—	0	3	4	3[9]	4	—	75.0	75.0	25.0
39.	Other and miscellaneous manufacturing	—	—	—	—	—	—	—	—	—	—
40.	Rail transportation	5[10]	11	3	10	8[10]	21	45.5	30.0	38.1	61.9
41.	Transit	—	0	—	—	0	0	—	—	—	—
42.	Motor transportation	2	2	3	3	5	5	100.0	100.0	100.0	0.0
43.	Water transportation	—	0	3	3	3	3	—	100.0	100.0	0.0
44.	Air transportation	6[11]	6	6	6	12[11]	12	100.0	100.0	100.0	0.0
45.	Electric, gas...sanitary	42[11]	47	59	59	101[11]	106	89.4	100.0	95.3	4.7
46.	Telephone, telegraph...services	3[6]	5	6	6	9	11	60.0	100.0	81.8	18.2
47.	Radio and TV broadcasting	—	0	2	2	2	2	—	100.0	100.0	0.0
48.	Wholesale trade	—	0	1	1	1	1	—	100.0	100.0	0.0
49.	Retail trade	1[2]	1	6	6	7	7	100.0	100.0	100.0	0.0
50.	General merchandise	6[2]	9	9	11	15	20	66.7	81.8	75.0	25.0
51.	Food stores	1	2	8	8	9	10	50.0	100.0	90.0	10.0
52.	Motion pictures	—	0	4	5	4	5	—	80.0	80.0	20.0
53.	Services	—	—	12	12	12	12	—	100.0	100.0	0.0
54.	Real estate	—	0	6	6	6	6	—	100.0	100.0	0.0
	Totals	130[12]	201[13]	338[14]	360[15]	468[12,14]	561[13,15]	62.5%	93.0%	82.1%	17.9%
	Companies moving into different categories and companies not counted in total of "newly emerged"	—5	—1	—4	—1	—9	—2				
	Net "new appearances"	125	200	334	359	459	559	62.5%	93.0%	82.1%	17.9%

Note: Col. 5 = Col. 1 + Col. 3; Col. 6 = Col. 2 + 4; Col. 7 = Col. 1 ÷ 2; Col. 8 = Col. 3 ÷ 4; Col. 9 = Col. 5 ÷ Col. 6; Col. 10 = 100.0 – Col. 9; Col. 10 also = Col. 14, Exhibit 70, Part 1.

[1] Includes Colt Industries, whose Industry Category was determined by the sales of the former Crucible Steel Co. and Wheeling-Pittsburg Steel (see Appendix A, Note 3).

[2] Includes (a) Cities Service, which had been included among Electric, gas, and sanitary services in 1929; and (b) Union Oil of California, which was a reorganization of Union Oil Associates and which, after 1965, included the former Pure Oil Co. (see Appendix A, Note 18).

[3] Includes United Fruit, which had merged into AMK and then into United Brands, and which was classified in Meat and meat products because of the sales of John Morrell & Co., a former meat packing company. (See Appendix A, Note 24.)

[4] UV Industries, which included what had been, in 1929, United States Smelting, was treated as a company that had persisted although in a different Industry category and among The Next 359 of 1971.

[5] Singer, included in Household appliances in 1971, was included among Machinery in 1929.

[6] Includes (a) International Telephone & Telegraph, counted in Telephone, telegraph...services, in 1929 (see Appendix A, Note 52), and (b) Western Electric, a wholly owned subsidiary of American Telephone & Telegraph (see Appendix A, Note 53).

[7] Includes a communication equipment subsidiary of General Telephone & Electronics (see Appendix A, Note 54).

[8] Includes International Harvester, included in Farm...machinery in 1929.

[9] Includes Pullman Inc., formerly Pullman Railroad Company, included in Rail Transportation...in 1929.

[10] Includes companies resulting from extensive reorganizations: Penn Central; Seaboard Coastline; Burlington Northern; Chesapeake & Ohio; Mississippi River Corporation, which controlled Missouri Pacific, an unconsolidated subsidiary.

[11] See Exhibit 70, Part 1, Note 11.

[12] See Exhibit 70, Part 1, Note 14.

[13] Includes Western Electric.

[14] Includes four companies enumerated in Column 3, above: communications equipment subsidiary of General Telephone & Electronics and three companies of The Top 200 of 1929 that had moved down to The Next 359 in different Industry categories by 1971. See Exhibit 70, Part 1, Note 15.

[15] Includes communications equipment subsidiary of General Telephone & Electronics. See Appendix A, Note 54.

NOTES

1. See John D. Glover, "Rise and Fall of Corporations," a note prepared for use in instruction at the Harvard Business School, Boston, Mass. (file 4-367-017).

2. Pesky problems of definition and categorization arise in connection with tallying instances of "persistence" and "disappearance" of merged and reorganized companies.

    If a corporation on the list of The 200 of 1929 was involved in a merger and was the larger partner and the surviving corporate entity, that was a reasonably clear case of "persistence." If a company was merged into another and, although not the surviving corporate entity, was relatively large enough to determine the categorization of the acquiring or merging company (e.g. Crucible Steel into Colt Industries, Armour into Greyhound, and Wilson into L-T-V.) it was counted as "persisting."

    A 1929 corporation merged into another whose Category it did not determine was tallied as having "disappeared," e.g. United Fruit, by various intermediate steps merged into United Brands.

    In recent years, the ongoing process of "conglomeration" has given rise to an increasing number of situations where categorization is difficult, even where there has been informative disclosure.

    Some companies changed their Industry Category over the years, as the source of the largest fraction of their revenues changed, e.g., Cities Service became a Petroleum company after divesting itself of electric utilities; Singer became a Household appliances firm rather than a Machinery company; IT&T, in 1929 categoried under Telephone, telegraph services, became a firm classed as manufacturing Radio and communications equipment. These firms were shown as "disappearing" from their earlier category and as being an "emerged" or "newly arriving" company in the later one. In the *total* figures, however, as in Exhibit 70, Part 2, and Exhibit 71, their numbers were included among the "persisting" corporations, not as "disappeared" or as "newly arriving."

    It is an arguable question whether a *transformed* corporation has "persisted" or whether it is a "new" firm.

    "Persistence" and "emergence" present special difficulties as concepts in the cases of the utilities and railroads. In the course of financial and structural reorganizations of companies in these two industries, physical and intangible properties, obligations and equities, were rearranged, sold, bought, exchanged, liquidated, revalued, and otherwise churned and kneaded to the point where it is now a nightmarish challenge to try to retrace what had happened and to determine what kind or degree of continuity there may have been between original and successor corporations.

    In face of the difficulties, it has been assumed that only 5 of the 39 utilities of 1929 "persisted" among The 200 of 1971 and that the other 34 had "disappeared." It was further assumed that the 42 others of the 47 utilities among The 200 of 1971 were newly emerged and/or grown to the point where they were large enough to be so included. The 59 utilities among The Next 359 were also so regarded.

    As to the 43 railroads of 1929, 13 are counted as "persisting"—6 among The 200 and 7 among The Next 359 of 1971; the 30 others are counted as having "disappeared." Of the ten railroads among The Next 359 of 1971, seven are regarded as "persisting" from 1929 and ten are regarded as "new arrivals" that had moved up over the lower defining limit of $250 million of 1971 dollars.

    A more detailed summary of corporations "persisting" from 1929 and of "newly visible" large corporations, disaggregated as among The 200 and The Next 359 of 1971, and broken down as among Railroads, Utilities, and Other Industry categories is given in Table 23.

3. See *Historical Statistics of the United States from Colonial Times to 1957*, p. 355, and *Statistical Abstract of the United States, 1974*, p. 514.

4. These words were written some months before the attempt of Carter Hawley Hale Stores, Inc., to take over Marshall Field & Co., in late 1977.

5. See Appendix A, Notes 49 and 56.

TABLE 23
Composition of The 559 Largest Corporations of 1971: Corporations "persisting" from
1929 and "newly visible" corporations

	The 200		The Next 359		The 559	
Persisting						
Subtotals		75		25		100
Railroads	6		7		13	
Utilities	7		0		7	
Others	62		18		80	
Newly visible						
Subtotals		125		334		459
Railroads	5		3		8	
Utilities	42		59		101	
Others	78		272		350	
Totals		200		359		559

12

Epilogue: The Industrial Revolution goes on (?)

Four years ago the author and his assistants began to assemble data for this book.* The latest financial statistics then available for the corporate population as a whole were for 1971.[1] In an undertaking like this, concerned with an open-ended, ongoing historical process, one always wants to have up-to-date information, out of natural curiosity, if for no other reason. More to the point, one is likely to wonder whether subsequent events might have taken new and different turns; whether later information might cast doubt on conclusions based on earlier data; or whether, indeed, later data would corroborate and enhance their credibility. Besides, looking at a matter from a different perspective may result in new thoughts.

Following a review of these later data, we shall take a look, in Chapter 13, at some key issues of public and corporate policy that now surround our Largest Corporations. These issues arise out of the uneasy tension between the material necessity of very large-scale productive organizations and Americans' innate fear of size and power.

The following pages present a summary picture of the corporate population of 1975 and of major changes that took place in that population between 1971 and that later year. The chapter also has something to say about the uneven fortunes between 1971 and 1977 of a sample of some 170 of The Largest Corporations in eight important Industry Categories, and about some implications of those data for public and corporate policy.

The first two sets of data about to be presented reflect growth of

---

*These words are being written in August 1979.

the corporate community as a whole, between 1971 and 1975, in both numbers and asset masses.

As to number, great growth in numbers occurred among small corporations in characteristically small-business Major Industry Groups: Services, Trade, and Construction. In value of assets, the major portion of growth took place among large corporations in characteristically big-business sectors: Chemicals and allied products (including petroleum refining); Transportation and public utilities, and in Metal and metal products, which includes Iron and steel, Non-ferrous metals, and Motor vehicles and equipment. (See Exhibits 74 and 75.)

The data give no support to any idea that small business is disappearing or being concentrated. The data, again, reflect the fact that small and big businesses, both, have their own niches in the structure of American industry.

A third set of data for a sample of ten characteristically small-business Industry Categories and a sample of ten characteristically big-business industries, corroborates for 1975 that, as in 1971, broad patterns of association existed, among Industry Categories, between frequency of occurrence of very large corporations, presence index (which measures the relative mass of large company assets in the Industry Category), and average size of the Largest Corporations present and the average size of Other firms. (See Exhibit 76.) The data give further confirmation to the observation that large corporations tend to occur where there are significant advantages, such as economies of large scale; vertical integration; multiplant, multiproduct operations; technology- and capital-intensivity, and the like.

The data also show, again, numbers of Industry Categories where such factors do not obtain, and where the characteristic enterprise is relatively small.

A fourth set of data shows very clearly, but not very remarkably, that, between the years 1971 and 1977, the fortunes of individual companies, even among The Largest, were very different, and that results of strengths and weaknesses in *dynamic* competition among firms *over time* are not merely matters of a few percentage points of margin, but of corporate health and survival. (See Exhibit 77.)

Some managements of very large companies were, and are, far more effective than others in coping with changing opportunities, constraints, and pressures of the real evolving world. What goes on in industries is not merely a matter of "structure" and numbers of firms.

These data, relating to some of our Largest Corporations, also raise serious questions as to whether, in light of the country's needs for continuing growth and development, some sectors of American industry are sufficiently vital and productive of new and additional capital. Even more troublesome is the possibility that, for whatever

EXHIBIT 74

Growth and change in the U.S. corporate community; Nonfinancial corporations and all corporations, 1971-1975; by Major Industry Group; numbers of firms, approximate values of assets

Major Industry Groups	1971 Number of firms* (000)	1971 Estimated "Inflated" value of assets† ($ billions)	1975 Number of firms (000)	1975 Value of assets‡ ($ billions)	Percentage of firms 1971	Percentage of firms 1975	Percentage of assets 1971	Percentage of assets 1975
Agriculture, forestry and fisheries	39.9	$ 15.3	56.3	$ 21.2	2.5%	3.0%	0.1%	0.1%
Mining and quarrying	12.6	33.9	14.2	64.5	0.8	0.8	1.8	3.1
Construction	143.1	62.7	191.2	76.7	9.0	10.2	3.4	3.7
Manufacturing								
Food and kindred products, beverages and tobacco	16.4	82.3	14.5	90.4	1.0	0.8	4.5	4.4
Textiles and textile products	22.9	34.6	21.3	32.9	1.4	1.1	1.9	1.6
Lumber and wood products and paper and allied products	20.9	50.9	24.2	58.1	1.3	1.3	2.8	2.8
Printing, publishing and allied products	26.5	27.2	31.4	27.3	1.7	1.7	1.5	1.3
Chemicals and allied substances	10.8	202.7	11.3	259.6	0.7	0.6	11.1	12.6
Rubber and tires	6.2	17.0	7.4	17.3	0.4	0.4	0.9	0.8
Leather and leather products	2.3	5.0	2.3	4.4	0.1	0.1	0.3	0.2
Stone, clay, and glass products	8.6	20.5	10.1	23.3	0.5	0.5	1.1	1.1
Metal and metal products	69.5	372.2	76.2	399.0	4.4	4.1	20.3	19.3
Other and miscellaneous manufacturing	16.9	28.3	18.6	32.4	0.1	0.1	1.5	1.6
Subtotal, manufacturing	201.0	$ 840.6	217.4	$ 944.6	12.6%	11.6%	45.8%	45.8%
Transportation and public utilities	71.1	402.9	80.7	443.2	4.5	4.3	22.0	21.5
Wholesale and retail trade	538.7	274.1	614.6	323.5	33.8	32.9	15.0	15.7
Services	287.8	80.9	435.7	90.5	18.1	23.3	4.4	4.4
Nature of business not allocable	21.4	1.1	1.7	0.4	1.3	–	–	–
Real estate	276.6	122.1	255.6	97.8	17.4	13.7	6.7	4.7
Totals, nonfinancial corporations	1,592.2	$1,833.7	1,867.4	$2,062.4	100.0%	100.0%	100.0%	100.0%
Financial corporations	141.1	1,922.3	156.2	2,224.2	–	–	–	–
Totals, all corporations	1,733.3	$3,756.0	2,023.6	$4,286.6				

Note: There are questions as to the strict comparability of the data of the terminal years. Accordingly, overly specific conclusions and comparisons should be avoided, especially as regards changes within Groups.

* As reported in *Corporation Source Book... 1971.*

† Reported values of 1971 have been multiplied by a factor of 1.3 in an effort to allow for inflation. Special caution should be exercised in comparisons of values as between the two years. See Note 2 at the end of this chapter. The 1971 dollar values are given in Exhibit 55.

‡ As reported in *Corporation Source Book... 1975.*

EXHIBIT 75
Nonfinancial corporations in the United States, by asset size classes, 1971 and 1975

Asset size classes ($000)	1971		1975		Increase, number of firms, 1971-75 (000)	1971		1975		Increase, value of assets, 1971-75† ($ billions) ‡
	Number of firms (000)	Percentage of the number of firms	Number of firms (000)	Percentage of the number of firms		Value of assets ($ billions) ‡	Percentage of the value of assets	Value of assets ($ billions) ‡	Percentage of the value of assets	
Zero assets	44.2	2.8%	63.5	3.4%	19.3	–	–	–	–	–
Under $100	891.6	56.0	1,030.1	55.2	138.5	$ 40.7	2.2%	$ 35.1	1.7%	*
$100-$250	319.7	20.1	354.6	19.0	34.9	66.6	3.6	56.8	2.8	*
$250-$500	164.7	10.3	191.4	10.2	26.7	75.0	4.1	67.4	3.3	*
$500-$1,000	90.5	5.7	115.4	6.2	24.9	81.6	4.5	80.3	3.9	*
$1,000-$5,000	67.3	4.2	92.0	4.9	24.7	169.4	9.2	181.7	8.8	*
$5,000-$10,000	6.8	0.4	10.3	0.6	3.5	60.3	3.3	70.9	3.4	*
$10,000-$25,000 . . .	4.0	0.2	5.5	0.3	1.5	78.9	4.3	85.7	4.2	*
$25,000-$50,000 . . .	1.4	0.1	1.9	0.1	0.5	63.7	3.5	68.9	3.3	*
$50,000-$100,000 . .	0.8	0.05	1.1	0.06	0.3	69.3	3.8	79.4	3.8	*
$100,000-$250,000 . .	0.6	0.04	0.8	0.04	0.2	123.8	6.7	138.9	6.7	*
$250,000 or more . . .	0.6	0.04	0.8	0.04	0.2	1,004.4	54.8	1,197.3	58.1	*
Totals	1,592.2	100.0%	1,867.4	100.0%	275.2	$1,833.7	100.0%	$2,062.4	100.0%	$224.7

* Figures of increases by size classes are distorted by inflation. See text and Note 3 at end of this chapter.
† See Notes 2 and 3 at the end of this chapter.
‡ 1975 dollars.
Source: *Corporation Source Book, 1971* and . . . *1975.*

reasons, many companies, in real terms, are not even conserving capital they do have.

CORPORATE DEMOGRAPHICS, 1971-1975

Summary

Between 1971 and 1975, the latest year for which comprehensive Treasury financial and demographic data on corporations are presently available, the corporate population of the United States continued to grow. The total number of all corporations increased by about 290,000, from over 1.7 million to over 2.0 million. The population of nonfinancial corporations rose by 275,000, from about 1.6 million to about 1.9 million (See Exhibit 74.) The increase in numbers was accounted for, to the extent of more than 95 percent, by increases of firms in what are primarily small-business Major Industry Groups: a net increase of almost 150,000 in Services; of more than 75,000 in Trade; and of almost 50,000 in Construction.

In 1975, over 1,750,000 nonfinancial firms, which is to say 94 percent of the total number of 1,876,000, had assets of less than $1 million. Something like 90 percent (or more) of the increase in assets occurred among corporations with assets of more than $100 million. (See Exhibit 75.)

Large firms also increased in numbers, but these increases, of course, were much smaller. In 1975, about 600-700 firms had reported assets of $250 million or more.

In total, between 1971 and 1975, the value of corporate assets increased by something like $220 billion in terms of something like "constant" 1975 dollars.[2]

Unfortunately, one cannot make close comparisons as to the respective distributions in the two years of assets by individual size classes, nor as to changes in asset values in size classes.[3] Nevertheless, one can be sure, in a general way, that there were, indeed, significant increases, between 1971 and 1975, in the *numbers* of *smaller* corporations. There were also increases in the *numbers* of *larger* corporations. The majority of the increase in the total *value* of assets of nonfinancial companies surely occurred in assets of *large* corporations.

Changes in composition of the corporate population, by Major Industry Groups

The increase in numbers of small businesses should be reassuring to those who, like Adam Smith, Justices Peckham, Douglas, and Brandeis, and Judge Hand—and this author—have been much interested in the health of small business.

The increase in numbers of firms in Services, Trade, and Construction accounted something over 90 percent of the total increase. Other increases in numbers of firms also bespeak significant increases in numbers of small firms: the increases in number of firms in Agriculture, forestry, and fisheries and Printing and publishing, for example.

Some fractions of the apparent large increases in numbers of corporations in Services, Trade, Construction, and Agriculture, forestry and fisheries, were probably accounted for by the incorporation of businesses previously carried on as proprietorships or partnerships. Even so, in view of substantial increases in Gross National Product originating in the several national income sectors, especially in Services and Trade, it is certain that there were also significant real increases in the numbers of firms in those Major Industry Groups. The apparent increase in numbers is also corroborated by the data of Exhibit 76.

Some apparent decreases in numbers of firms are worth noting, but here one should be careful.[4]

Quite possibly, the number of firms, especially smaller firms in Textiles and apparel really did decline. Because of comparatively high labor costs, some sectors of these industries, as is well known, have been having difficulties against foreign competition. The total reported value of assets in this Major Industry Group also apparently declined, suggesting a real exodus of capital as well as firms. The fact that the number of firms declined somewhat more than the inflated value of assets hints that smaller firms were prominent among those leaving.

The number of firms in Leather and leather products was about the same in 1975 as in 1971. But it appears that the value of assets declined. It is possible that these data indicate a redeployment of capital by larger firms out of this Group into other uses. Such a movement would be compatible with the long-run loss of comparative advantages of this once large and prosperous Industry Group: leather giving way to plastics; American-made shoes and other products giving way to imports.

The apparent decline in the number of corporations in Food and kindred products, tobacco, and beverages, combined with an apparent sizable increase in inflation-adjusted total asset value, is interesting. No doubt, the outputs of processed foods and of beverages have been increasing substantially these past few years, as have capital investments in those industries. The fact that the total inflated value of assets rose while the number of firms declined suggests an exodus of smaller firms. In view of the overall health of this Major Industry Group, one wonders whether at least some part of this apparent movement was accounted for by the recategorization of some firms that were previously classified as being in this manufacturing Industry Group, as becoming more in the nature of distributors, say wholesalers, rather than manufacturers. But that is speculation.

We come now to consider increases in reported *values of assets.* (The apparent declines in assets in Textiles and apparel and in Leather and leather products have already been noted.) And in these comparisons, we must be very cautious.[5] The total increase, in something like 1975 dollars, apparently amounted to something of the order of $220 billion, an increase of something more than 10 percent over the four years, 1971-75. The real increase in constant dollars could be somewhat more or less than that depending on the factor used for allowing for inflation: *more,* if the effect of inflation on reported asset values was really *less* than allowed for; *less,* if the effect was really *greater* than allowed for. In any case, in *real* terms, the aggregate reported value of assets increased over those years by somewhere around 3 percent per annum, or probably less.

The biggest apparent increases seem to have come in Mining, quarrying, etc., Chemicals and allied products, and in Metals and metal products. Together, the apparent, inflation-adjusted increases in these Major Industry Groups came to something more than $100 billion, which accounted for something more than 50 percent of the total apparent increase in all nonfinancial corporation assets. This increase was accounted for by Groups of corporations that, in 1971, numbered a total of about 90,000, which is to say 5 percent of the number of all the then corporations.

These broad figures indicate clearly the quantitative, to say nothing of the qualitative, importance of our big-business industries. In terms of total asset mass of our corporate community, half or more, in 1975 as in 1971 and 1929, was accounted for by a small number of firms in characteristically big-business industries.

This fact is further illuminated by other, more detailed data from the 1975 IRS tabulation.

Patterning of occurrence and presence of large corporations

The patterning of the occurrence and presence of large corporations in 1975, and the association of relative presence with size of corporations, large and small, followed closely those of 1971. In the following pages, sample data illustrate those points.

In interpreting the data, one must bear in mind the distorting effects of inflation, which, along with elements of real growth, no doubt, helped move several, perhaps many, of formerly second-tier companies of 1971 up into the size class of corporations having assets of $250 million or more. Another, but lesser distorting factor, so far as concerns comparisons with 1971, is that the composition of some Industry Categories are slightly different from counterparts of the earlier year.

In Exhibit 76, Parts 1 and 2 are shown, for ten illustrative "low-presence" and ten illustrative "high-presence" industries, data that reflect association among (a) presence index; (b) frequency of occurrence; and (c) average size of the Largest Corporations and the average of other corporations.[3]

In general, these data corroborate the kinds of data and conclusions shown earlier, for 1971, in Chapter 8 and Exhibit 46: high presence-index numbers tend to be associated with frequent occurrence of very large companies, and with larger average size of the Largest Corporations and larger size of other companies. And the inverse is also true of low presence-index numbers; less frequent occurrence of very large companies; and smaller average size of the Largest Corporations present—if any—and smaller size of other companies.

The general drift of the data really does speak for itself, even though the association is less than one-for-one.

Given the underlying forces and factors at work in the evolving structures of corporations and industries, this is in line with what one would expect to find.

The ecological system that is our industry structure does not vary randomly with time, does not oscillate greatly, does not leap up and down, forward and back, year by year.[6] But it *does develop* in scale, complexity, and, especially, in kind—*dramatically,* over time.

PERSISTENCE, DECLINES; GROWTH AND EMERGENCE OF CORPORATIONS: 1971-1977

Over the years 1971-77, the community of Largest Corporations showed growth both in numbers and in mass, as we have seen. Comprehensive data for later years are not yet available; but some pretty good samples of corporate demographic data for 1977 indicate that the growth of large corporations in both numbers and size continued.

Even more interesting is the fact that between 1971 and 1977, turnover and changes in relative rankings of very large corporations also continued—again, as one would expect in a dynamic world. Some companies moved ahead; others seemed to drift; some seem to have regressed. A few disappeared in those six years; they were taken over or merged. Numbers of firms grew to a size that, even allowing for considerable inflation, they had become as large as any included on the roster of Largest Corporations in 1971.[7]

Looked at in "snap-shot" fashion, cross-sectionally in time, the community of Largest Corporations, as is true of any ecological pop-

EXHIBIT 76
Average size, largest and other firms; presence index, largest firms; 1975

Part 1. Ten illustrative "low-presence" industries

Industry Category[1]	Number of firms	Total assets ($ millions)	Number of firms assets more than $250 million[2]	Assets, largest firms ($ millions)	Average size, largest firms ($ millions)	Average size, firms other than largest ($000)	Presence index, largest firms
1. Trucking and warehousing	35,109	$ 19,962.2	10	$ 6,123.1	$ 612.3	$ 394.3	30.7%
2. Fabricated metal products	28,666	38,856.0	16	9,786.9	611.7	1,014.6	25.2
3. Printing and publishing	31,431	27,313.0	12	5,700.7	475.1	687.9	20.9
4. Apparel	15,944	13,772.3	7	2,396.7	342.4	713.8	17.4
5. Services	435,672	90,534.1	27	14,669.6	543.3	197.1	16.2
6. Wholesale trade[3]	143,611	108,275.8	20	14,731.7	736.6	646.7	13.6
7. Construction	191,219	76,691.9	15	7,749.3	516.6	360.6	10.1
8. Retail trade[4]	394,359	92,687.9	4	1,920.0	480.0	230.2	2.1
9. Furniture and fixtures	7,614	5,665.6	–	–	–	744.1	0.0
10. Agriculture, forestry and fisheries	56,280	21,177.9	–	–	–	376.3	0.0

Part 2. Ten illustrative "high-presence" industries

Industry Category[1]	Number of firms	Total assets ($ millions)	Number of firms assets more than $250 million[2]	Assets, largest firms ($ millions)	Average size, largest firms ($ millions)	Average size, firms other than largest ($000)	Presence index, largest firms
1. Telephone, telegraph services	3,691	$116,221.3	12	$110,735.9	$9,228.0	$1,491.0	95.3
2. Electric, gas, and sanitary services	8,634	214,328.9	129	199,114.2	1,543.5	1,788.9	92.9
3. Petroleum[5]	8,054	218,794.3	50	202,123.1	4,042.5	2,082.9	92.4
4. Office and computing machines	446	39,163.4	10	36,083.4	3,608.3	7,064.2	92.1
5. Motor vehicles and equipment	2,107	81,561.6	17	74,596.3	4,388.0	3,332.7	91.5
6. Metal cans	182	4,771.2	4	4,321.2	1,080.3	2,247.2	90.6
7. Pharmaceuticals	1,233	18,674.4	20	15,991.0	799.6	2,212.2	85.6
8. Ferrous metal industries[6]	1,519	42,335.6	20	34,020.3	1,701.0	5,547.2	80.4
9. Chemicals and allied products[7]	6,689	56,396.2	36	43,958.1	1,221.1	1,869.6	77.9
10. Household appliances	490	6,872.3	7	4,970.0	695.7	3,938.5	72.3

[1] Industry Categories may not be identical with Categories of 1971.
[2] See Note 3 at the end of this chapter.
[3] Except Machinery, equipment and supplies; Motor vehicles and equipment; Petroleum and petroleum products. *Corporation Source Book...1975*: pp. 15, 181, 182, 192.
[4] Except Food stores and General merchandise; ibid.; pp. 16, 198, 199.
[5] Oil and gas extraction; Oil and gas field services; Petroleum refining and coal products; Pipelines except natural gas; *Corporation Source Book, 1975*, pp. 085, 086, 128, 172.
[6] Ibid., p. 138.
[7] Industrial chemicals, plastic materials; Paints and allied products; Agricultural and other chemical products; ibid., pp. 123, 126, 127.
Source: *Corporation Source Book, 1975*.

ulation, appears static, given, mechanical, fixed in space and time. Looked at longitudinally, over time, that community reveals itself as organic and dynamic. Some companies (sometimes whole industries) grow, mature, regress; change in natures and characteristics. As they do so, their relative positions change in the entire web of relationships—competitive and supportive—that binds the hundreds of thousands of individual businesses into an integrated, encompassing *system.*

Even in a period as short as six years, the system reveals itself as inherently dynamic. Equilibrium end-states are not of the American industrial structure.

The diligent, questioning analyst would find interest in tracing the fortunes of each of The 559 Largest Corporations of 1971, and the emergence of all the recent newcomers into the ranks of the present Largest. But time, patience, and money run out. And, besides, key points of general interest do take shape in the course of studying some samples of the total population.

In the next several pages, we shall mark the fortunes, between 1971 and 1977, of the companies that were among The 559 Largest in 1971 and that emerged in later years in a very diverse sample of eight Industry Categories: Petroleum, Chemicals and allied products; Iron and steel; in Food and kindred products and two increasingly closely related Categories: Meat and meat products and Dairy and dairy products; in Office, computing and accounting machines; and in Lumber . . . wood . . . paper and allied products.[8]

The reasons for the choices of these sample industries are these:

1. *Petroleum:* A key industry; provides the lion's share of our energy; in terms of capital investment, one of the largest industries; focus of political confusion, controversy, and opportunism; very complex industry structure.

2. *Chemicals and allied products:* Major source of inputs for many industrial and consumer products; typically large-scale, capital-intensive; characterized by technological change and technology-intensivity; focus of increasing popular concern as to environmental impacts, safety, etc.; spotty profitability.

3. *Iron and steel:* Once a bellwether industry; perhaps in stage of disappearing comparative advantage and increasing "maturity"; focus of concerns of public policy.

4. *Food processing:* At center of social revolution and changing life-styles; affected by continuing Industrial Revolution in mass-distribution at Wholesale and retail; focus of concerns of Federal Trade Commission, Food and Drug Administration, Department of Agriculture, etc.; very dynamic, complex industry structure; histori-

cally identifiably separate Meat and Dairy industries seeming to be assimilated into Food generally.

5. *Office, computing, and accounting machines:* Outstandingly dynamic "newer" industry; great and continuing technological changes; intense technological and other forms of competition; increasing foreign competition.

6. *Lumber . . . wood . . . paper and allied products:* An "older," more "mature" industry; typically integrated, large-scale, capital-intensive; many environmental concerns; sustained, but modest growth for some time; spotty profitability; very complex industry structure.

In Exhibit 77, Parts 1-6, are displayed data relating to the growth, or lack thereof, between 1971 and 1977, of individual Largest Corporations of 1971, in those Industry Categories. Shown are their reported assets for the two years, together with an index of *nominal* relative growth and the indicated compound average annual *nominal* growth rate of the book values of those assets. Both of these figures are based on asset data published by the firms, themselves.

Nominal growth of total-asset book-value over a period of years is a crude measure, indeed, of the "vitality" of any one corporation. Comparisons of figures among like—let alone unlike—individual companies, may be dubitable. But this is true also, of course, of net earnings, book value of stockholders' equity, or of a number of other corporate "life signs" in general use. *Caution* is a necessary watchword in any financial analysis.

Problems of comparisons of financial data over time (and among individual companies and industries, also) are compounded, of course, during periods of inflation. Measures of *nominal* growth of assets, during the years 1971-77, and thereafter, necessarily reflect effects of inflation to significant, and perhaps varying, degrees. *Real* growth rates, discounting the effects of inflation, were surely substantially less than the nominal rates reflected in individual company balance sheets. Short of an item-by-item adjustment for each company, there is no way of measuring very closely the relationship between *nominal* growth of assets and *real* growth.[9]

All said, some analysis is better than none, so long as interpretations are restrained and broad-brush.

In interpreting the raw data of Exhibit 77, it may be useful to bear in mind some yardsticks from Table 24. With such yardsticks in mind, the reader may make his own approximate adjustments to individual company and industry data.

The numbers of Table 24 say this: if a company were simply to have kept up with inflation from 1971 through 1977, it would have

TABLE 24
Gross National Product and inflation, 1971-1977

	1971	1977	1971-77
Gross National Product, billions of *current* dollars	$1,063.4	$1,887.2	–
Index, 1971 = 100	100	177	–
Average annual compound growth rate	–	–	10.03%
Gross National Product, billions of *constant* (1972) dollars	$1,107.5	$1,332.7	–
Index	100	121	–
Average annual compound growth rate	–	–	3.13%
GNP Implicit Price Deflator (1972 = 100)	96.02	141.61	–
Index shifted to 1971 = 100	100	147	–
Average annual compound growth rate	–	–	6.69%

Source: *Economic Report of the President...1979;* Tables B-1, B-2, and B-3. See Note 2 at end of this chapter.

had to grow by about 47 percent, at an average annual compound growth rate of about 6.69 percent. If, in addition, it were to have as much "real" growth as, and in step with, the Gross National Product, it would have had to grow by 77 percent at an annual average compound growth rate of 10.03 percent.

Still further, if, in addition to keeping up with inflation, a company were to have achieved real annual average growth of 5 percent, not a terribly exciting result from the point of view of managers of pension and trust funds and other investors, it would have had to grow in current, inflated dollars by 97 percent, at an annual average of about 12.25 percent.

It may be useful to bear such figures in mind while scanning Exhibit 77, keeping always in mind, of course, the possible pitfalls of excessively precise comparisons.

Petroleum industry, 1971-1977

In 1971, the roster of Largest Corporations included 30 companies listed in the Petroleum Industry Category. In 1977, the number had risen to 50, more or less.[9] Two companies had left the ranks of the industry; one moved into Chemicals and allied products; the other simply failed even to maintain its total asset value of 1971.

On the other side of the ledger, 21 additional companies had come on to the roster. All told, these were companies that, in 1977, reported assets in excess of $350 million.[10]

As one scans Exhibit 77, Part 1, Petroleum Industry Category, it would appear that companies that had been among The 559 Largest of 1971 had achieved very different growth records during the following six years. The median growth, as measured by reported asset

EXHIBIT 77
Persistence, decline; growth and emergence of corporations, 1971-1977
(Part 1: Petroleum Industry Category)

Company; in order of reported size, 1977	Reported assets, 1971 ($ millions)	Reported assets, 1977 ($ millions)*	1977 assets, as percentage of 1971 assets†	Apparent average annual compound growth rate, 1971-1977†
A. Companies on 1971 roster				
1. Exxon Corp. (formerly Standard Oil Co., N.J.)	$ 20,315.2	$ 38,453.3	189%	11.2%
2. Mobil Oil Corp.	8,552.3	20,576.0	241	15.8
3. Texaco, Inc.	10,933.3	18,926.0	173	9.6
4. Gulf Oil Corp.	9,446.0	14,225.0	150	7.0
5. Standard Oil Co. of Calif.	7,513.2	14,186.2	189	11.2
6. Standard Oil Co. (Indiana)	5,650.7	12,884.3	228	14.7
7. Atlantic Richfield Co.	4,704.1	11,119.0	238	15.5
8. Shell Oil Co.	4,646.3	8,876.8	191	11.4
9. Tenneco Corp.	4,565.2	8,278.3	181	10.4
10. Standard Oil Co. (Ohio)‡	1,815.2	7,778.0	428	27.5
11. Continental Oil Co.	3,048.7	6,625.2	217	13.8
12. Phillips Petroleum Co.	3,166.7	5,836.5	184	10.7
13. Sun Oil Co.	2,813.3	5,181.0	184	10.7
14. Union Oil of Calif.	2,564.8	4,724.5	184	10.7
15. Getty Oil Co.	2,015.3	4,173.3	207	12.9
16. Occidental Petroleum Co.	2,580.0	4,134.4	160	8.2
17. Cities Service Co.	2,325.3	3,739.6	161	8.2
18. Marathon Oil Co.	1,391.4	3,445.6	248	16.3
19. Halliburton Co.	685.2	3,030.8	442	28.1
20. Amerada Hess Co.	1,328.2	2,998.0	226	14.5
21. Ashland Oil Co.	1,030.2	2,610.4	253	16.8
22. Schlumberger, Ltd.	861.2	2,385.3	277	18.5
23. Pennzoil Company §	(1,545.1)	2,049.7	133	4.8
24. Kerr-McGee Corp.	762.5	1,833.3	240	15.7
25. Murphy Oil Co.	492.1	1,361.0	277	18.5
26. Superior Oil Co.	540.8	1,106.9	205	12.7
27. Fluor Corp.	258.4	970.8	376	24.7
28. Zapata Corp.	464.1	888.8	192	11.4
29. Commonwealth Oil Ref. Co.	357.8	536.6	150	7.0
30. McCulloch Oil Corp. ‖	276.5	263.0	95	−0.8
Totals	$107,391.4	$213,197.6	199%	12.11%
B. Companies not on 1971 roster				
31. American Petrofina Co.	−	$ 854.1	−	−
32. Louisiana Land & Exploration Co.	−	810.8	−	−
33. Mesa Petroleum Co.	−	800.2	−	−
34. Santa Fe International Corp.	−	752.4	−	−
35. Texas Oil & Gas Corp.	−	730.9	−	−
36. Natomas Co.	−	722.6	−	−
37. Ocean Drilling and Exploration Co.	−	682.0	−	−
38. Dillingham Corp.	−	657.8	−	−
39. Baker International Co.	−	640.4	−	−
40. SEDCO, Inc.	−	638.6	−	−
41. MAPCO, Inc.	−	620.6	−	−
42. Tesoro Petroleum Corp.	−	594.5	−	−
43. Houston Oil and Minerals Co. . . .	−	579.8	−	−
44. Belco Petroleum Co.	−	476.3	−	−
45. Reserve Oil & Gas Co.	−	455.4	−	−
46. Mitchell Energy & Development Co.	−	440.6	−	−
47. Home Oil Co.	−	440.5	−	−
48. Tosco Corp.	−	435.9	−	−
49. Quaker State Oil Refining Co. . . .	−	382.4	−	−
Totals		$ 11,715.8		

* For sources of 1977 asset data, see Note 8 at end of this chapter.

† Includes effects of inflation. See text.

‡ Controlling interest was acquired by British Petroleum.

§ As a gas transmission utility, Pennzoil Co., was classified among utilities in 1971. In 1977, the majority of company's assets was in oil and gas production, refining, and marketing. The name was changed from Pennzoil United Co., in 1972. Assets included in total shown for 1971.

‖ McCulloch Oil Corp. experienced substantial write-offs of assets from losses in real estate ventures, etc.

values, was apparently about 200 percent—half grew more, half grew less. The corresponding average annual growth rate, including inflation, was about 12.25 percent. Median company real growth was, it would seem, more than 5 percent. But about half did not grow that much. All but one seem to have at least done better than inflation. It seems that about six of the ten largest companies grew at lesser rates. Throughout the group of companies, numerous changes occurred in relative ranking by asset size in consequence of different growth rates.

Some of the smaller firms that had been on the list in 1971 apparently grew at much higher rates. Some of the companies that had not been on the list in 1971, having then had assets of less than $250 million, had achieved asset growth of the 40 percent or more required to grow from less than $250 million in 1971 to more than $350 million in 1977.[10] Their growths had outstripped other smaller companies of 1971 that did not grow to the $350 million for inclusion on the roster of 1977.

The years 1971-77 were years of turmoil and frustration, even for the petroleum industry companies that did tolerably well. There were great "discontinuities," not of technology, but of government policies around the world: the emergence of the Organization of Petroleum Exporting Countries; nationalization and threats of nationalization—and eventual nationalization—in various countries; actual and developing revolution and insurgency in various countries; increasing government regulation and constraint—often confusing, sometimes arbitrary, always political; increasing management pessimism as to the future of the industry; pressures of growing demand, on one side, *versus* resistances making difficult corresponding increases in supplies. Despite talk about "obscene" profits, compared to inflation, the earnings of most of the larger oil companies and the levels of their stock prices were not, in fact, very exciting.

Some of the companies, for whatever particular reasons, seem to have managed better than others to cope with the complex of events and currents. Differences in percentage growths and relative ranking attest to that.

A fair inference is that, among large and larger companies in Petroleum, the managements of some companies, probably going back before 1971, had been more aggressive, more imaginative—perhaps simply luckier?—than others in having made, in making, and in carrying out basic decisions of policy and corporate strategy. Whatever may have been the particular causes for unusually high or unusually low growth rates of individual firms, it is sure that dynamism in the Industry Category was one of the consequences.

Corporations, after all, are human, social institutions, managed by real people, not mere machines. Over time, their individualities and particular circumstances show up. Competition, growth, health, survival are no mere structural mechanistic matters. And, of course, "industries" are no mere abstractions, but systems of real entities, individual corporations.

Chemicals and allied products

In 1971, the list of the Largest chemical companies included 27 names. In 1977, the number was 32. One company had disappeared. Two companies had moved into this Industry Category from others in consequence of changes in the natures of their business. In addition, five other companies had grown to a point where, in terms of the dollar values of their assets, they were about as large as, or larger than, any of the companies on the roster of 1971.

Overall, the growth rates of the largest chemical companies compare rather unfavorably with those of companies in Petroleum. Of the 26 companies that had been on the list of largest chemical companies in 1971 and were still on the list of 1977, only 12 had reported asset-value growth of as much as 177 percent, the growth of the Gross National Product, including inflation. One company that moved into Chemicals from Petroleum showed very strong growth. Fourteen of the largest chemical companies of 1971 reported growths at less than the GNP in current dollars. The reported growths of seven of the companies, out of 26, were less than inflation, alone (147 percent). On the plus side, the growths of ten of the companies seem to have been larger than those of inflation and real GNP growth combined.

As in Petroleum, numerous changes in relative ranking seem to have been brought about by actions of managements taken during the period or, indeed, in earlier years.

The consequences of basic policy and strategic decisions sometimes take years to work themselves out, for better or for worse. In chemicals, of course, such decisions have related to such matters as how much to spend on research and development and in which particular directions; how to commercialize discoveries, if and when found; whether, how, and to what degree to engage in development of new plastics in films, sheets, fibers and foams, or of new intermediates; arranging for new sources of input materials; development of, and negotiations for, and major allocations of capital into various commodity and speciality chemicals that turn out well rather than poorly; projects for increasing value-added by integrating downstream; investments overseas; mergers and acquisitions; and diversification both within and outside the chemical industry system; coping with environmental and safety problems.

All these many decisions, gifted or poorly taken, as matters have turned out, add up to that extraordinary process of transformational "creative destruction," characteristic of a dynamic, evolving system.

Company; in order of reported size, 1977	Reported assets, 1971 ($ millions)	Reported assets, 1977 ($ millions)*	1977 assets, as percentage of 1971 assets†	Apparent average annual compound growth rate, 1971-1977†
A. Companies on 1971 roster				
1. Dow Chemical Co.	$ 3,078.8	$ 7,675.2	249%	16.4%
2. E. I. Du Pont de Nemours & Co. . . .	3,998.5	7,430.6	186	10.9
3. Union Carbide Corp.	3,554.7	7,423.2	209	13.1
4. Monsanto Co.	2,153.5	4,347.6	202	12.4
5. Minnesota Mining & Mfg. Co.	1,745.2	3,529.6	202	12.4
6. W. R. Grace & Co.	1,647.7	2,941.0	179	10.1
7. Allied Chemical Corp.	1,636.7	2,872.2	176	9.7
8. FMC Corp.	1,095.5	2,141.5	195	11.8
9. Celanese Corp.	1,660.0	2,010.0	121	3.2
10. Williams Cos.‡	(722.3)‡	1,882.8	261	17.3
11. Diamond Shamrock Corp.	702.9	1,810.5	258	17.1
12. Hercules, Inc.	781.8	1,477.5	189	11.2
13. Dart Industries, Inc.	833.6	1,440.2	173	9.5
14. Stauffer Chemical Co.	504.9	1,429.5	283	18.9
15. Olin Corp.§	1,190.9	1,276.1	107	1.2
16. Air Products and Chemicals Inc. . . .	452.8	1,031.8	228	14.7
17. Rohm & Haas Co.	634.3	1,020.9	161	8.3
18. Ethyl Corp.	639.8	974.6	152	7.3
19. Airco, Inc.	583.3	857.5	147	6.6
20. Koppers Co., Inc.	430.7	851.9	198	12.0
21. Armstrong Cork Co.	560.4	822.4	147	6.6
22. GAF Corp.	588.4	762.4	130	4.4
23. Akzona, Inc.	491.2	674.9	137	5.4
24. Pennwalt Corp.	390.6	628.1	161	8.2
25. The Sherwin Williams Co.	390.5	613.4	157	7.8
26. Cabot Corporation	372.9	579.1	155	7.6
27. Chemetron Corp. ‖	296.9	–	–	–
Totals	$31,138.7	$58,594.5	188%	11.08%
B. Companies not on 1971 roster				
28. Big Three Industries	–	$ 515.8	–	–
29. UOP, Inc.	–	450.6	–	–
30. Dow Corning Co.	–	433.2	–	–
31. Gulf Resources & Chemical Co. . .	–	394.1	–	–
32. Reichhold Chemicals Co.	–	387.6	–	–
33. Lubrizol Corp.	–	360.5	–	–
Total	–	$ 2,541.8	–	–

* For sources of 1977 asset data, see Note 8 at end of this chapter.
† Includes effects of inflation.
‡ Williams Cos. included in Petroleum in 1971. Assets included in total for 1971.
§ Olinkraft, a company in Lumber . . . wood . . . paper, spun off; see Exhibit 79, Part 6.
‖ Chemetron acquired by Allegheny Ludlum Industries, November 1977.

Food and kindred products, etc.

In terms of growth of asset values, the food industry complex was not, overall, very exciting—despite, or perhaps because of, all the changes going on in and around it. Of the 31 companies on the list of 1971, only seven reported growths that were equal to, or exceeded, the growth of the Gross National Product, real and inflated combined. Seven of the companies reported growths that were less than inflation alone.

Company; in order of reported size, 1977	Reported assets, 1971 ($ millions)	Reported assets, 1977 ($ millions)*	1977 assets, as percentage of 1971 assets†	Apparent average annual compound growth rate, 1971-1977†
A. Companies on 1971 roster				
1. General Foods Corp.	$ 1,596.8	$ 2,345.0	147%	6.6%
2. Beatrice Foods Co.	934.2	2,128.9	228	14.7
3. Kraftco Co.	1,163.8	2,085.4	179	10.2
4. Ling-Temco-Vought, Inc.	1,961.0	2,066.0	105	0.9
5. The Borden Co.	1,258.0	1,901.6	151	7.1
6. Esmark Inc. (Swift & Co.)	869.3	1,799.9	207	12.9
7. Ralston Purina Co.	897.9	1,766.1	197	11.9
8. CPC International	1,042.7	1,589.2	152	7.3
9. Greyhound Corp.	1,143.2	1,386.5	139	5.6
10. Norton Simon, Inc.	791.4	1,487.2	188	11.1
11. General Mills, Inc.	817.8	1,447.3	177	10.0
12. H. J. Heinz	808.2	1,274.9	158	7.9
13. Carnation Co.	594.6	1,214.6	203	12.5
14. Consolidated Foods Corp.	782.0	1,188.0	152	7.2
15. Standard Brands, Inc.	697.3	1,144.0	164	8.6
16. Pillsbury Co.	407.1	1,105.4	272	18.1
17. United Brands Co.	1,069.2	1,097.8	103	0.4
18. Nabisco, Inc.	633.4	1,063.3	168	9.0
19. Campbell Soup Co.	677.5	1,003.9	148	6.8
20. Foremost McKesson, Inc.	713.0	941.6	132	4.7
21. Quaker Oats Co.	423.7	924.3	218	13.9
22. Kellogg Co.	378.3	839.0	222	14.2
23. Castle & Cooke, Inc.	537.7	817.3	152	7.2
24. Delmonte Corp.	584.2	801.7	137	5.4
25. Anderson Clayton & Co.	329.1	544.6	165	8.8
26. Amstar Corp.	335.0	502.1	150	7.0
27. Pet Inc.‡	401.4	488.3	122	3.3
28. Great Western United Corp. §	313.3	−	−	−
29. General Host Corp. ‖	281.9	(203.3) ‖	(74)	−5.0
30. Libby McNeil & Libby #	268.5			
Total	$22,712.0	$35,361.2	156%	7.66%
B. Companies not on 1971 roster				
31. Archer Daniels Midland Co.	−	$ 732.9	−	−
32. A. E. Staley Mfg. Co.	−	535.6	−	−
33. Central Soya Co.	−	468.7	−	−
34. DeKalb AgResearch Co.	−	426.1	−	−
35. Hershey Foods Co.	−	396.2	−	−
36. Oscar Mayer Co.	−	377.7	−	−
Total	−	$ 2,937.2	−	−

* For sources of 1977 asset data, see Note 8 at end of this chapter.

† Including effects of inflation.

‡ Merged into IC Industries, Inc., 1978.

§ Great Western United, following major losses, was merged into a wholly-owned subsidiary, Hunt International Resources, Inc.

‖ General Host's reported assets of $207.3 million in 1977 were less than the $350 million lower limit for inclusion in the 1977 list. The company had experienced sizable losses and had been engaged in complex transactions in the stocks of two meat packers, Cudahy and Armour.

Merged into Nestlé Alimentana, S.A., 1976.

Several conglomerates entered the field—with mixed results, let it be said. Several companies appeared to turn to conglomeracy as a strategy—also with mixed results.

On the more cheerful side, seven of the companies reported growths that probably represented several percentage points of real growth over and beyond the effects of inflation. Six companies managed the 40 percent or so of asset growth needed to move up onto the list.

Within the group, a number of significant changes were brought about in relative position; more than in either Petroleum or Chemicals. These were turbulent years for some of the companies.

Of companies apparently moving up in rank, four moved up by four or more places. In at least two of these instances, the companies had been engaged in significant acquisitions. Two companies apparently moved up by two ranks. Three companies moved up by one rank. Without a doubt, some of the leading companies in this group had the benefit of outstanding management.

On the down side, four companies moved down by four or more ranks. Two moved down by three ranks. Two companies moved down by one, and two by two ranks. Some of these companies had notoriously lacklustre managements. In one instance, the company's record was highlighted, if that is the word, by Grade-B movie melodrama.

This was a cluster of industries especially characterized by great flux. Companies extended and revised their product lines. Numbers of them moved into fields quite new to them. Some companies participated in the development of whole new categories of processed foods. In face of a large population far above the Malthusian margin, having increasing funds available for discretionary spending, elasticities of substitution among very different kinds of foods—even among nonfood alternatives—became greater and greater. Traditional boundaries and demarcations among varieties, kinds, and categories of foods became more and more blurred and less and less material and relevant. In consequence of demographic and life-style changes, the American people seemed to become more and more interested in change and innovation. Producers and distributors of food products, as of all kinds of consumers' foods, tried to respond—more often than not, not very successfully. Typical life cycles of products became shorter and shorter. It was not always easy to "make a buck" in the food industries.

The reach of new and increasing competition stretched even further. "Eating out" became a growth industry. "Fast foods" consumed on production site or taken away, for a while, was a *super*-growth industry. Both developments offered whole new kinds of competition to both food manufacturers and retailers. Twenty percent or more of America's food budget is now spent outside the home.

These are the kinds of doings and happenings that lay behind the numbers in Exhibit 79, Part 3, Food and kindred products.

Iron and steel

We come to Iron and steel. What happened among companies in Iron and steel in 1971-77 does not make for light summer reading (Exhibit 77, Part 4).

Of the 19 companies on the 1971 list of Largest Corporations, one had disappeared through merger.

Among the 19 on the list of both 1971 and 1977, 4 reported increases in asset values of more than 200 percent, reflecting average annual compound rates of growth in excess of 12.25 percent. These rates of growth were sufficiently high that, simply as numbers, they could have represented real growth beyond inflation and the general advance of the Gross National Product. In fact, the apparent growth of at least two of these companies had come about in large measure through mergers and acquisitions; these companies could reasonably be labeled as conglomerates. The reported assets of another company, which also had become something of a conglomerate, increased by a fraction that just about corresponded to the effect of inflation combined with a 3.2 percent rate of real growth. These companies

EXHIBIT 77 *(continued)*
(Part 4: Iron and steel Industry Category)

Company; in order of reported size, 1977	Reported assets, 1971 ($ millions)	Reported assets, 1977 ($ millions)*	1977 assets, as percentage of 1971 assets†	Apparent average annual compound growth rate, 1971-1977†
A. Companies on 1971 roster				
1. United States Steel Corp.	$ 6,408.6	$ 9,914.4	155%	7.5%
2. Bethlehem Steel Corp.	3,452.3	4,898.9	142	6.0
3. Armco Steel Corp.	2,044.4	2,882.8	141	5.9
4. National Steel Corp.	1,842.9	2,827.6	152	7.4
5. Republic Steel Co.	1,755.3	2,406.3	137	5.4
6. Inland Steel Co.	1,376.6	2,302.4	167	9.0
7. Lykes Corp. (Lykes-Youngstown). .	1,439.1	1,766.6	123	3.5
8. Colt Industries	537.6	1,112.2	207	12.9
9. Allegheny Ludlum Industries	441.9	1,075.9	243	16.0
10. Ogden Corp.	557.5	1,021.7	183	10.6
11. Kaiser Steel Corp.	727.3	961.4	132	4.8
12. Wheeling-Pittsburg Steel Co.	610.8	765.7	125	3.8
13. Chromalloy America Co.	351.3	752.0	214	13.5
14. Interlake Corp.	349.0	559.6	214	13.5
15. Hanna Mining Co.	315.5	478.0	152	7.2
16. McLouth Steel Co.	309.9	437.6	141	5.9
17. Cyclops Corp.	304.5	333.3	109	1.5
18. NVF Co.	270.5	422.7	156	7.7
19. Granite City Steel Co.‡	312.7	—	—	—
Totals	$23,407.7	$34,919.1	149%	6.89%

* For sources of 1977 asset data see Note 8 at end of this chapter.
† Including effects of inflation.
‡ Granite City Steel was merged into National Steel.

may have been none the less socially and economically useful, for all that. (See Chapter 13.)

Five of the companies managed growth only slightly greater, if at all, than might have been accounted for by inflation. Eight of the companies reported asset growth that was less than the effect of inflation.

Compared to other Industry Categories, there were relatively few changes in relative rankings among the companies. Two companies appear to have dropped three ranks and a couple gained two. But the picture, as to rankings, unlike other more turbulent groups of companies, was much more of a steady state. This feature may well be characteristic of a mature industry.

It is surely no accident that no new and formerly much smaller companies emerged to find place in the ranks of the largest steel companies.

In any event, here was a group of the Largest Corporations in a major Industry Category that taken together, appears, at least for the present, to have topped out. The combined reported assets of the seven largest steel companies appears to have increased at a rate no greater than inflation alone. Altogether, the growth of the assets of the 19 companies was just about equal to inflation. It is possible that the real capital values of the assets of some of those companies might even have shrunk.

Altogether, the picture of the American steel industry in the period 1971-77 was, to say the most, not bright. A number of reasons, no doubt, contributed to this pretty bleak record: foreign competition; positive and aggressive commerical and industrial development policies and programs of various foreign countries; passing of historic comparative advantages; slowing down or even disappearance of formerly large markets, foreign and domestic; substitution of other materials, such as prestressed concrete, glass, nonferrous metals, even plastics; perhaps, failure to maintain labor and technological productivity. There are those who say that managements of some of the large steel companies exhibit some of the characteristics of old companies: lack of adaptability to new circumstances as to sources of inputs, methods of production, and opportunities for aggressive marketing; lack of drive and insistence upon better profit performance; lack of imagination and resolution in redeploying capital out of old uses into new.

Whatever be the many reasons, the seeming lack of vitality in this once dynamic and leading industry poses a challenge to both public and corporate policy.

The directors and managers of these uncertain companies, as of others we saw in other industries, would be well advised to give grave and fresh thought as to where they are going to lead their companies in the years ahead.

As to matters of public policy, a few words in a moment.

Office, computing, and accounting machines, 1971-1977

This was one of the great growth industries of the Fifties and Sixties. But during the six years 1971-77 things were slower and different. See Exhibit 77, Part 5. Of the companies on the roster of The Largest of 1971, apparently two grew faster than the Gross National Product. Another one seemingly just about kept abreast. Two others kept ahead of inflation but seem to have had only a very modest real growth. On the other hand, one company, that was far from being on the list in 1971, was well up on the list of 1977, considerably ahead of four companies that had been on the list as early as 1971. Several companies, as was well known in the trade and in financial circles, had been in difficulties.

Among companies of 1971, differential rates of growth, some much greater than others, gave rise to changes in relative positions. Two companies rose by two ranks; one declined by one rank; one declined by three ranks.

EXHIBIT 77 *(continued)*
(Part 5: Office, computing, and accounting machines)

Company; in order of reported size, 1977	Reported assets, 1971 ($ millions)	Reported assets, 1977 ($ millions)*	1977 assets, as percentage of 1971 assets†	Apparent average annual compound growth rate, 1971-1977†
A. Companies on 1971 roster				
1. International Business Machines Corp.	$ 9,576.2	$18,978.4	198%	12.1%
2. Xerox Corp.	2,156.1	4,906.3	228	14.7
3. Sperry Rand Corp.	1,653.8	2,841.5	172	9.4
4. Burroughs Corp.	1,487.8	2,665.5	179	10.2
5. NCR Corp.	1,689.3	2,340.8	139	5.6
6. Litton Industries Corp.‡	1,976.0	2,063.8	104	0.7
7. Control Data Corp.	1,430.8	1,844.0	129	4.3
8. SCM Corp.	542.9	767.9	141	5.9
9. Pitney-Bowes, Inc.	324.5	523.7	161	8.3
10. Addressograph-Multigraph	370.3	470.4	127	4.1
11. Memorex Corp.	255.4	317.8	124	3.7
Totals	$21,463.1	$37,720.1	176	9.85%
B. Company not on 1971 roster				
12. Digital Equipment Co. §	($ 150.1)	$ 1,070.4	713%	31.7%

* For sources of 1977 asset data, see Note 8 at end of this chapter.

† Includes effects of inflation.

‡ Litton recorded substantial write-offs in its Business Systems and Equipment Group. Company has been involved in extensive and complex negotiations with the U.S. Navy.

§ Digital Equipment Co. was not on list of Largest Corporations in 1971; minimum and asset size was $250 million.

Given the earlier dynamism of this industry—in the technology of design of electronic and mechanical equipment and components; of the versatility and scale-capacities of units; in applications and in marketing—a greater overall growth might have been expected. But other factors operated. One, probably, was the enormous increase in the efficiencies of numbers of the products and consequent great reductions in prices in terms of their output capabilities, and, in some instances, in actual dollars. Given quanta of assets could, and did in some instances, produce units with growing processing capacities. On the other hand, some of the competitors could not, or in any event did not, keep up with techological advances.

In a still young industry, some of the earlier competitors seemed to show early signs of maturity.

At least three very large corporations withdrew from the computer field, recording large capital losses in consequence. Whatever the reasons, they were unable and/or unwilling to keep up in the technologies of design and manufacture. Perhaps, also, their marketing was less effective than needed. Perhaps, their alternative uses of capital and talent were greater elsewhere.

Not shown in Exhibit 77, Part 5, of course, were a number of instances of rapid growth of companies not large enough to be included on the list of The Largest Corporations of 1977. These smaller companies seemed to be doing well in fields of smaller-capacity equipment. Also not shown are foreign companies, some quite large, that were beginning to show significant results.

The two largest and most successful companies had been on the receiving ends of troublesome public and private litigation, the outcomes of which are still not certain.

At present, it would appear that although large-capacity equipment requires very large scale and extraordinary technical and managerial abilities, opportunities do exist in particular niches, and that much smaller companies with excellent technology and well-aimed strategies can do very well even in competition with the biggest. What the structure of the industry may look like when and *if* the rate of technological change slows down; when new competitors—some of them very large—develop new technologies of research, manufacture, and marketing, is impossible to say. The growing blurring between communication; computation; data storage, transmission, retrieval, and processing would seem to portend a massive restructuring and merging of several presently distinguishable fields—probably on a global scale.

This is, for sure, no area where the major concerns of either corporate or public policy can be directed at workings and tactics within existing and given frameworks of industry and technology.

The "name of the game" is *transformation.*

Lumber . . . wood products . . . paper and allied products

We come now to the last of the Industry Categories whose histories between 1971 and 1977 constitute our samplings of recent dynamics of the community of our Largest Corporations.

Here is one of the older industries, integrated and diversified relatively early in its development. And yet, several of the companies showed considerable dynamism in the years 1971-77. See Exhibit 77, Part 6. Of the 16 companies on the list in 1971, and continuing through 1977, at least 5 may have grown faster than the Gross National Product, taking into account both inflation and real growth. Another four or five seem to have closely approximated that growth. Only three seemed to fall well below that benchmark.

Although a number of instances showed up of sturdy growth, few instances occurred of substantial changes in relative ranking. Margins

EXHIBIT 77 (continued)
(Part 6: Lumber and wood products and paper and allied products, except Furniture and fixtures)

Company; in order of reported size, 1977	Reported assets, 1971 ($ millions)	Reported assets, 1977 ($ millions)*	1977 assets, as percentage of 1971 assets†	Apparent average annual compound growth rate, 1971-1977†
A. Companies on 1971 roster				
1. Weyerhaueser Co.	$ 2,077.8	$ 4,038.0	194%	11.7%
2. International Paper Co.	2,037.9	3,839.0	188	11.1
3. Georgia Pacific Corp.‡	1,872.7	2,929.0	160	8.1
4. Champion International Co.	1,398.0	2,464.9	176	9.9
5. St. Regis Paper Co.	957.2	1,929.4	201	12.4
6. Boise Cascade Corp. §	2,194.1	1,799.0	82	−3.3
7. Crown Zellerback Corp.	1,030.7	1,736.2	168	9.1
8. Kimberly Clark Co.	938.5	1,651.3	176	9.9
9. Scott Paper Co.	858.6	1,589.5	185	10.8
10. Mead Corp.	868.9	1,374.0	158	7.9
11. Union Camp Corp.	573.4	1,130.1	197	12.0
12. Westvaco Corp.	529.7	885.7	167	9.0
13. Great Northern Nekoosa Corp. . . .	441.1	805.2	183	10.6
14. Potlatch Corp.	328.3	669.4	204	12.5
15. Diamond International Corp.	404.0	636.2	157	7.9
‖ Evans Products Co.	(516.6)	(571.2)	(111)	(1.7)
16. Hammermill Paper Co.	358.2	532.6	149	6.8
Totals	$16,869.1	$28,007.5	166%	8.8%
B. Companies not on 1971 roster				
17. Lousiana Pacific Corp.‡	−	678.2	−	−
18. Olinkraft Co.#	−	460.4	−	−
19. Southwest Forest Industries, Co. . . .	−	397.3	−	−
Total	−	$ 2,038.7	−	−

*For sources of 1977 asset data, see Note 8 at end of Chapter 12; 1977 asset data from *Moody's Industrials.*
†Includes effects of inflation.
‡Louisiana-Pacific Co. formed as 20 percent spinoff from Georgia-Pacific, July 1973.
§Boise-Cascade had very large losses on real estate ventures, etc., in 1972 and following years.
‖In 1977, Evans Products was primarily engaged in retail distribution of building materials. Assets in 1971 and 1977 not included in totals.
#Spinoff from Olin Corp., a chemical company.

of dollar size between certain of the companies did widen or narrow in a number of cases.

Fewer instances do seem to have occurred, as compared to Petroleum and Chemicals, of company growth notably stronger than the growth of the Gross National Product. Some of the integrated Lumber . . . wood . . . paper companies were trying to diversify out of that Industry Category into, among other things, chemicals and real estate. With no more exciting prospects than the performance of recent years, more companies are likely to try to redirect their cash flow and available capital into other areas.

With no extraordinary discontinuities in either production or consumption or technology, the Lumber . . . wood . . . paper and allied products Industry Category seemed, as a whole, to have grown incrementally, but somewhat slower than the economy as a whole. Whether this growth was adequate to contribute significantly to our national development—economic growth, technological advance, and social progress—is something else.

Inflationary and real growth, 1971-77; summary

A summary of the nominal dollar growths and of the growth rates of assets of 170-odd Largest Corporations of 1971 in eight Industry Categories during the years 1971-77 are shown in Table 25.

The 30 largest Petroleum companies of 1971, in total, showed a nominal average annual compound growth rate, including effects of inflation, of about 12 percent. Discounting the effects of inflation, the combined real growth rate may have come to something like 5 percent.

The 27 largest Chemical companies of 1971, combined, showed a

TABLE 25
Growth of the Gross National Product and nominal growth of assets of Largest Corporations in illustrative Industry Categories, 1971-77

	1971 ($ billions)	1977 ($ billions)	1977 as percentage of of 1971*	Average annual nominal compound growth rate 1971-77*
Gross National Product . . .	$1,063.4	$1,887.2	177%	10.03%
Petroleum	107.4	213.2	199	12.11
Chemicals and allied products	31.1	58.5	188	11.08
Food and kindred products	22.7	35.4	156	7.66
Iron and steel	23.4	34.9	149	6.89
Office, computing and accounting machines	21.5	37.7	176	9.85
Lumber, wood . . . paper and allied products	16.9	28.0	166	8.82

*Includes effects of inflation.

book rate of annual average compound growth in assets of about 11 percent. Allowing for inflation, their collective annual average real growth was probably around 4 percent.

The Food and kindred products group showed a combined nominal average annual compound growth rate of 7.7 percent. For the 30 largest companies of 1971 in the three constituent Industry Categories, this could have corresponded to an overall average real growth rate of just about 1 percent. Not very exciting.

The Iron and steel Industry Category had what must be a distressing record. The nominal growth rate of assets for the 19 Largest companies of 1971, all together, was about 6.9 percent. Aside from the effects of inflation, this represents something like a *zero* real growth for the companies taken as a group.

The 11 Largest Office, computing, and accounting machine companies of 1971, combined, recorded an overall nominal annual average rate of growth of assets of about 9.9 percent. Culling out the effects of inflation, these companies, as a group, had a record of real growth of something like 3 percent. This overall result was heavily colored by the strong performances of the two largest firms.

Finally, the 16 Largest corporations of 1971 in Lumber . . . wood . . . and paper and allied products reported in total an annual average compound nominal growth rate in assets of about 8.8 percent. Apart from inflation, this would reflect a real average annual compound growth of something less than 2 percent.

In each industry complex, of course, some companies did better, sometimes much better than others. In each, some companies seem to have suffered *real* losses overshadowed by the effects of inflation. Into the ranks of each group, except Iron and steel, a number of new "Largest," but considerably smaller, companies had emerged to positions on the roster of 1977. By and large, they had done well in *real,* as well as in nominal terms.

The experiences of the several Industry complexes were highly varied. Petroleum and Chemicals, as groups, did well or moderately well. In real terms, Food . . . etc., and Lumber . . . etc., again as groups, recorded small real growths, less than that of the GNP and perhaps less than what is needed over future years, if the economy is to develop at rates necessary for *real* improvement and advancement. Iron and steel seems to have been static.

Altogether, of the 170-odd Largest Corporations of 1971 in the samples, about 90 or more seem to have had at least some, if not much, real growth to show for the six years. Between 70 and 80 probably did not.

Overall, corporation data since 1971 give general corroboration to the data of the period 1929-71. Ours is truly a dynamic ecological system. The fortunes of individual corporations, as of whole industries, are extraordinarily varied. They have their entrances and their exits; and in between, their strange eventful histories. The workings of individual corporations and of whole industries at any one moment, or over a short period of time, be they ever so challenging to executives, academicians, jurists, or government people, are transient in the larger scheme of things that really count most, and of little significance in comparison to the operations of the almost cosmic forces and results of corporate, industry, and national developments that come to pass over periods of years.

PUBLIC POLICY, CORPORATIONS, AND NATIONAL DEVELOPMENT, 1980-

Corporate demographic and performance data for years since 1971 again raise questions and issues of national policy.

For one, how are we to tax corporations, given that so many of them seem to be showing little, or no *real* net income, but only a mirage resulting from inflation? The Securities Exchange Commission is currently much concerned with promoting corporate disclosure of *real* earnings or lack thereof, by moving corporations to "replacement cost" or "current dollar" accounting from "historical cost" accounting. When will an analogous concern spread to the Treasury, as regards rational corporate tax policy? And when, indeed, will regulatory commissions of the several states establish patterns of setting rates that will allow *real* returns to invested capital as an ongoing proposition?

Will awareness that inflation is obscuring widespread losses in the corporate world accelerate the spread of interest in a corporate value-added tax as an alternative to the present corporate net-income tax?

Will we develop a major concern over the fact that *real* capital formation by the corporate community as a whole is probably falling short of what is necessary to provide jobs, competitive by world standards, for an expanding work force and for needed and desirable expansion of Gross National Product and National Income?

Will we begin to take seriously the fact that double taxation of corporate earnings has counterproductive consequences for capital formation and allocation, and is a major drag on national development?

Will we become interested in tax, antitrust-related, and other measures that will permit, perhaps even encourage, redeployment of capital from less profitable, lower-comparative-advantage uses over to more profitable uses, as replacements of policies that impede such conservation, and that now encourage less than optimal allocations of capital?

Will we come to an appreciation that our economy cannot be regulated, constrained, litigated, taxed or jaw-boned into growth and development; that real economic growth and national development require, above all, concrete realities of increased investment and increased production?

Will we come to an appreciation that we have not yet, perhaps by some centuries, reached an inherent end-of-the-line, static state of ultimate development, but that the continuing Industrial Revolution in America will not just happen, inevitably, all by itself, and no matter what we do?

In sum, can we come by a set, or at least a sense, of desirable and feasible goals and objectives for economic growth and national development and then set about working out policies and programs pragmatically designed for their achievement?

CORPORATE POLICY AND DEVELOPMENT, 1980-

The samples of recent financial data have a message for directors and executives of corporations. Performance of many companies over periods of years—perhaps up to half? more, probably, if you include the utilities and other older industries—tends to be less than satisfactory. In times of inflation, this doleful fact can be obscured even from directors and executives, let alone national policy makers. The vision-distorting effect of inflation combined with "historical cost" accounting makes things look better than they really are.

Pressures, constraints, and opportunities of the moment draw attention of managements to current operations. Decisions tend to get made within existing structures of assets; of present lines, and ways of doing business. Need for reexamination of basics is often either not perceived or put off.

But numerous managements, although perhaps still a minority, are now increasingly concerned with redefining, reorienting, even recasting their businesses. Moves are made to integrate upstream or downstream. Not just new products, but whole new lines of business are developed. Older products, assets, and businesses are sold to companies that can do better with them, or they are liquidated. Capital is redeployed from older uses to newer ones. Corporations are acquired that have capital needing redeployment, or because of tax and other considerations. Asset management, management of transformation, and such, characterize the activities and focus of attention of numbers of boards and top managements.

One consequence and symptom of this movement is that, even with increasing disclosure by companies of investments, revenues, and returns by lines of business, classifying and characterizing many companies according to industries is becoming more difficult—even for their own directors and managers—so diverse and multifarious have they become.

Managing such companies, as they evolve and grow, presents problems far different from those whose line or lines of business are, or, more likely, were compact and homogeneous.

In years now ahead, results that give pragmatic sanction to the warrant of directors and executives to manage will include, in many cases will *stress,* ability to get *performance,* to manage assets, to redeploy assets, to *restructure,* to transform companies, from what they have been and are, into what they must become if they are to fulfill their mission as engines of change and to survive well into the next phase of the Industrial Revolution in America.

At the same time, justifying and legitimizing results will include meeting expanding and rising societal expectations as to needs and aspirations of individuals and of the community as a whole.

Directors and executives who are found wanting, and the corporations they run, will falter, perhaps disappear—even as did the unadaptive of the past.

NOTES

1. Department of the Treasury, Internal Revenue Service, *Corporation Source Book, Statistics of Income, 1971; Corporation Income Tax Returns....*

2. In order to make comparisons of asset values as between 1971 and 1975, and as between 1971 and 1977, allowances have to be made, of course, for effects of inflation. Questions arise as to exactly what these allowances should be. Different relevant indexes would justify different allowances, as is indicated by the following data (from *Economic Report of the President, 1979,* Tables B-3, B-57, B-49).

Allowance	Percentage Increase, 1971-75
Implicit Price Deflator, "Gross National Product"	132.45%
Implicit Price Deflator, "Gross Private Domestic Nonresidential Investment".	137.24
Wholesale Price Index, "Industrial Commodities"	150.31
Consumer Price Index, All Items	132.89

In the interests of simplicity and caution, a ratio of 130 was used in Exhibits 74 and 75, for adjusting 1971 asset values into something like 1975 "constant" dollars.

It is possible that 1971 values expressed in the respective estimated 1975 "constant" dollars are somewhat understated. If so, the estimated "real" increases in corporate assets, shown in Exhibits 74 and 75 are overstated. But efforts at greater precision are probably not warranted, for the purposes of this study, in view of the complexity of the data and the whole array of relevant "externalities."

These "inflated" asset values, in no case, should be taken as representing anything like "replacement" values. They represent, exclusively, efforts to express dollar values of heterogeneous masses of "things" in one period in terms of the value of the dollar in other periods.

One recognizes, of course, that inflation affects different sets of prices very differently. These differences are glossed over, even concealed, in broad averages represented by indexes. Accordingly, great restraint is called for, in any case, in making cross-value comparisons at different times during periods of inflation and change.

The problems are amplified as concerns comparisons between 1971 and 1977 because of the greater and, apparently, increasing inflation. See Table 25.

3. The reason why close comparisons cannot be made between periods in times of inflation of distributions of assets by size classes is this: Inflation has a sort of "Doppler Effect" on size distributions of the kind shown in Exhibit 75. Because of inflation, both apparent numbers of firms and apparent values of assets are shifted upward relative to the base year. In consequence, relative to the base year, increases in both numbers of firms and values of assets are relatively "understated" for smaller size classes and relatively "overstated" for larger size classes.

For example, one can be certain that the apparent declines in absolute values and percentage distribution of asset values in the smallest size classes were largely, if not entirely, consequences of upward shift of firms out of those size classes and into larger size classes because of inflation. In the same vein, the apparent increases in numbers and assets for corporations in the largest size classes, by 1975, are surely overstated relative to 1971.

4. The apparent decrease in Exhibit 74, of almost 20,000 firms "not allocable" as to Industry Group was surely due primarily to changes in statistical and/or reporting procedures rather than to any real "disappearance." The large majority of the firms that would have been so classified in 1975, had no changes been made, were probably included in that year in one of the three most numerous Major Industry Groups: Services, Trade, and Construction.

Accordingly, the indicated *increases* for Services, Wholesale and retail trade, and construction, collectively, are probably overstated by about the equivalent of the decrease in the indicated number of "not allocable" firms.

The "IRS" data upon which Exhibits 75 and 76 are based are prepared in part through use of statistical estimation, as through sampling. The procedures used are no doubt sound, but interpretations and conclusions should be appropriately cautious.

5. In order to get even a rough measure of something like "real" changes in asset values, in interests of general comparisons and examination of changes as between 1971 and 1975, the reported values of 1971 have been "inflated."

In Exhibits 74 and 75, asset values of 1971, as mentioned, are multiplied by a factor of 1.3 in order to restate them in terms of something like 1975 dollars. Between 1971 and 1975, various relevant "deflators" used in national income accounting and various price indexes rose by factors of about 1.4 to 1.5. (See, e.g., *Economic Report of the President . . . 1979,* Tables B-3, B-4, B-49, and B-57.) The lower figure of 1.3 was selected, somewhat arbitrarily, to reflect the facts that: (*a*) current assets, because of "roll-over," probably reflect rises in prices pretty currently; (*b*) other assets, however, such as plant and equipment, and various other depreciable and depletable assets, and land roll over more slowly. New and additional "fixed" assets, and such, were acquired by corporations, of course, in various of the years 1972-75 inclusive. Restating revenues, costs, earnings, and assets to reflect the erosion of the dollar, as is urged by the Securities Exchange Commission—but not by the Treasury for tax purposes, nor by state regulatory commissions, for rate-making purposes—is a current bugbear of corporate financial officers and auditing firms.

6. Economists will remember that the motto of Alfred Marshall's *Principles of Economics* was *Natura non fecit saltum*—Nature does not go by leaps. But it does evolve, profoundly, over time, step by finite step.

Marshall, by the way, was the great systematizer of English "classical" economics, as it had been developed in the 19th century by such luminaries as Thomas Malthus, Jeremy Bentham, David Ricardo, and Stanley Jevons.

7. Again, it may be useful to acknowledge limitations in the use of assets as a measure of corporate "size," and growth of assets as some indicator of corporate health. Size, in the writer's opinion, would be better measured by "value added," as would growth. In the absence of value-added data, asset size seems the best alternative. See Chapter 1, Note 3.

Assets can grow, of course, by several means; including retained earnings; raising of new capital by borrowing and issue of new equity securities; acquisitions and mergers. Instances can be found where growth of asset size through mergers and acquisitions has not necessarily been a sign of any great health; some of these show up in Exhibit 77. On the other hand, failure to keep up with inflation, with growth of the Gross National Product (nominal or real, as the case may be) is surely a diagnostic suggestion and lead that all is not well. Alerted by this single "symptom," the diagnostician interested in the particular company can proceed to check other vital signs—and prowl around in the footnotes to the financial statements.

The reader is invited to form his own hunches and questions from the data of Exhibit 77, such as they are.

8. In the several parts of Exhibit 77, the data for 1971 come from Exhibit 1.

The sources of 1977 data for the several parts of Exhibit 77 included (*a*) *Forbes,* May 15, 1978; (*b*) *Fortune,* May 8, 1978, and June 19, 1978; (*c*) *Value Line* data bank via Interactive Data Corporation, Waltham, Massachusetts; (*d*) *Compustat* data bank, via computer facilities of the Harvard Business School. The author gladly acknowledges obligations to these sources. However, no one of these sources is complete or entirely satisfactory, because of errors, omissions, particular definitions, incorrect and dubious classifications of companies, etc. Accordingly, considerable recourse was also had to annual reports, "10-K" statements, etc. For companies merged, etc., the source was *Financial Stock Guide Service, Directory of Obsolete Securities,* 1979 Edition; published by Financial Information, Inc.

Fortune listed about 495 "Industrials" with assets of more than $350 million in 1977. Also listed were 35 "Transportation" companies over that size, as well as 37 in "Retailing." *Forbes, Value Line,* and *Compustat* listed numbers of other firms not picked up by *Fortune.* In addition, there were well over 100 electric and gas utilities, many or most of which were not listed by *Fortune* or the other sources.

Despite best efforts, it is quite likely that some companies that should have been on the roster of 1977 have been overlooked and that other errors of omission and commission have been made.

9. Aside from effects of inflation, there are other reasons why analysts must be careful in making comparisons as to individual corporations over time, among corporations at any one time, and even among industries. Accounting practices and procedures are not necessarily the same over time or even the same as among companies in the same industries. Considerable differences, as is well known, are compatible with accounting "consistency" over time and with "generally accepted accounting principles." Differences, potentially important, also exist, of course, among companies and whole industries as to kinds and "mixes" of assets; as to practices of capitalizing or expensing certain kinds of outlays and costs; as to recognition and measurement of depreciation, depletion, and amortization; as to recognition and write-downs of values of intangibles, and as to recognition and write-offs of losses.

For sizable numbers of corporations and aggregates of assets, some of the idiosyncrasies perhaps cancel out or get smoothed over. Nevertheless, caution is called for in analysis.

The Securities Exhange Commission is currently pushing for "replacement cost" instead of "historical cost" accounting. It is quite likely that "historical cost" accounting gives rise to "inflated" profits; in some cases, "replacement cost" accounting would turn apparent nominal profits into nominal losses. Much ink is being spilled currently as to whether, and if so, how, given a maze of practical problems, "replacement cost" accounting is to be implemented, and if so, what the consequences may be.

10. The minimum size for inclusion in the 1977 roster of Largest Corporations was $350 million, up from $250 million in 1971, up from $81 million in 1929! So much for inflation. Various "deflators" and price indexes rose between 145 percent and 150 percent in the years 1971-77. The figure chosen for adjusting the 1971 minimum of $250 million was 140 percent—a rounded figure and, perhaps, on the conservative side.

13

The large corporation in America: Public and corporate policy

Our large corporations are big; very big. They assemble great aggregates of resources needed to accomplish large-scale results upon which our modern industrial economy depends, indeed, our very civilization, itself. By them are organized into productive entities, thousands of people, worlds of technology, vast amounts of energy and materials, hundreds of millions or billions of dollars of capital embodied in an extraordinary array of productive assets.

Being what they are, these institutions stand at the focus of a central tension in American thought and policy. Their relationship with the "folk" of America is one, so to speak, of love and hate. They are *essential.* But they also rise, awesome, towering in our midst. To millions of Americans, they appear as *powerful,* and therefore *fearsome*.

Fear and loathing of power is an old, persistent strand in American-Anglo-Saxon culture. That strand runs back in time, from ordinary people, intellectuals, ideologues, and politicians of our own day, to Muckrakers of the early 20th century and to Populists of the 19th; to Patriots and Founding Fathers of the American Revolution; to the dissident, emerging middle class and dispossessed crofters of 18th and 17th century England and Scotland and their distaste for the Hanover and Stuart dynasties and their Establishment; back to suspicion, hostility, and fear evoked by the Star Chamber and the chartered monopolies of the Tudors; even back to Plantagenet times, when churls and yeomen of England lived sullenly under the military and growing economic power of Norman overlords, legitimized by Norman bishops and clerics.

Millions from the Continent who passed through the golden door of Ellis Island came to America bringing with them well-founded resentment and, often, dread of the powerful of their Old Countries.

Mistrust of *power*—political, economic, military, ecclesiastical—is deeply rooted in the American spirit.

And yet, in fact, the large corporation—the *very* large corporation —is more American than popcorn. It is as American as Franklin Roosevelt and Herbert Hoover; as George M. Cohan, George Gershwin, George Wallace, George McGovern, and George Washington Carver; and Louisa May Alcott, Susan B. Anthony, Annie Oakley, Jane Addams, Amelia Earhart, and Marian Anderson; as Perth Amboy, Chicago, Dallas, and Puyallup.

The very large corporation has arisen in our midst as part and parcel of the developing American economy, an active, driving, energizing agent: in its own niches, a marvelous engine of production, distribution, and service; of economic and social growth and development. Along with the very smallest of family businesses, the large corporation is an indispensable element in our economy and community.

A preeminently American phenomenon, the very large corporation, for better or worse, depending on one's point of view, has done more than any other institution to render that economy distinct from all others. Far from being aberrant and dissonant, the large corporation—warts and all—is of the essence of American life as we know it.

There, before us, is a major dialectic—a persistent tension—in American thought and fact. It is not to be wondered at that policy concerning this key institution is uncertain, unsettled, ambivalent, even inadvertent, and unintentional. That fuzziness, that ambiguity runs deep.

The implications of this opposition of facts and sentiments are certainly many, and surely complex. Mostly, they lie beyond the purview of this study. A few, however, seem sufficiently important and urgent to warrant some treatment here and now.

PUBLIC POLICY AND THE LARGE CORPORATION

About the only explicit national policy we have as regards very large corporations, as such, is a rather backhanded one: bigness, it would appear, is not an offense, per se; not a violation of the Sherman Act.[1] Backhanded as it is, even that policy, in fact, is less than categorical.

That pronouncement of policy, such as it is, was contained and has been restated in judicial decisions, never in a statute of Congress; and it was first handed down almost 60 years ago. Since then, uncounted clusters of words and thrusts of thought in appellate court decisions and in opinions of lower courts—often no more than *obiter dicta,* to be sure—have cast more than a little haze over even that limited expression of policy.

Scores of bills have been introduced in Congress over the past decades, aimed either directly or tangentially at bigness or at concentration, or the like, or at bigness or certain forms of bigness in particular industries, say, the petroleum industry. None of those bills has yet scored a direct hit on *bigness* as such. But who can say what might come to pass in the course of complex political processes on The Hill?[2]

In regulatory actions and in public and private litigation, a further cloud of dust has been kicked up that has increased the haze. In consent decrees, in judicial decisions and opinions, and in jury verdicts, suggestions have come forth that, although they may not strike directly at bigness as such, tend to sort out *big* firms from small firms in application of laws. For instance, various behaviors as regards patents and common marketing practices that pass for legal and ordinary, even laudable, methods of business, if engaged in by *small* corporations, apparently *may* be held to be unlawful if engaged in by *large* companies—not because they are *large* but because, it is implied, being large, ipso facto, they either are, or *may tend* to be, monopolistc.

Equivocation will not do in the long run. Sooner or later, by means of one procedure or another, We the People, through Congress, have no option but to admit and affirm positively—not just backhandedly, and certainly not just as an incident of litigation, especially of private litigation—that large-scale, vertically-integrated, capital-intensive, massive-overhead, technology-intensive, multiplant, multiproduct organizations are indispensable to the provision of our material support; to the ongoing development and advancement of the American system; to its military defense in a tense and touchy world.

"Have no option," that is, if we aspire even to maintain, let alone to increase and more widely spread, well-being among our citizenry as we grow in numbers from about 220 million, now, to something over 250 million by around the turn of the 21st century. "Have no option," if we wish, beyond that, to produce wherewithal that we may participate with other nations in helping less fortunate peoples to help themselves.

Nostalgia for the technology, the industrial structure, and for the associated ruralism and the fancied simplicity and felicity of frontier and small-town life of the early 19th century, or even the early 20th, may be emotionally warming; but it simply will not cope with global and material realities, the dynamics of our time.

As a nation, we need to face facts and accept the large corporation for what it is, an essential institution and instrument of American life, along with the family, the university, the hospital, the labor union, and the thousands of entities and units of government, great and small.

That resolve made, a host of particulars can then be confronted as to how that institution is to be related to the rest of the community; how it is to contribute to the common wealth; and how it is to be governed, both in its outward behavior and in its inner workings.

That is one implication.

PUBLIC POLICY: HUMAN ECOLOGY AND ECONOMICS

Another related implication is that we stand in need of much more sophisticated *ways of thinking* about the structure, workings, and dynamics of the American *System,* of which large corporations are significant components. Beyond that, we need a more sophisticated and growing body of knowledge and theory, based on research, not mere hypothetical speculations, that will describe and *explain* that System and its development with increasing accuracy and fullness. These achievements will take more time than is comfortable.

The American System: A human *ecological* system

We are gradually learning about ecological systems, with their complexity of interrelated communities of animal and vegetable life that interact with, and are constrained by, physical habitats; about their complex, systemic, interrelated processes of being, of growth, decline, and change. We are becoming aware of the fact that, if we take action in an ecological system for some immediate objective, such as stamping out some insect, animal, plant, or fungus pest, we may slice into the encompassing *system* and upset it in ways that, when all the interacting effects work themselves out, were no part of our plan and far from our liking. We may find that we have upset the balances of the system in perverse ways and have ended up with Springs that are silent, and with more and different, and more disagreeable, problems than we had to begin with.

We are coming to know that. We are developing a *way of thinking* about ecological *systems.*

More recently, we have been gaining an awareness that metropolitan complexes where we live are also *systems,* human ecological systems, surpassing in complexity the ecological systems of nature. We are developing an awareness that simple, direct, well-intentioned actions taken to improve various features of our urban systems may also, when all the impacts and effects work themselves out, bring about dismaying consequences and undesired end-states, leaving us frustrated and mystified. We are coming to know something about the counter-intuitive behavior of complex systems in our human environment.

Our *national* human ecology, comprising our national economy, our whole community, our policy, our culture (in the anthropologist's sense of the word), our Continental physical habitat, is vastly larger and more complex, still. We are probably some generations away from a deep understanding of the structure and dynamics of that "super-system." In the meantime, we can develop a habit of mind, a way of thinking, of striving to look for, to take into account at least major secondary and tertiary impacts and consequences, not just the first-round effects of acts of public and private policy. Unfortunately, a generation may pass before we and our legislatures and other leaders develop such habits of thought and analysis.

Our large corporations, along with our other institutions, are integral and major parts of that national human ecology we call the American System. If they are not healthy, do not function well, the System will be impaired. If the System falters, they will be injured. These economic-social entities have no existence apart from the encompassing System. The System, as we know it, is predicated upon their presence and effective workings. The community of large corporations and the American System have grown up and evolved together.

With that recognition of fact in hand, we can, as rigorously and objectively as we may, accelerate our efforts to enhance our understanding of the structure and interactive, dynamic workings of the many component entities of that System and of the development of the System as a whole.

Public policy and economics

Public policies, as we know, are complex, evolving phenomena, resultants of developments and interactions of traditional ideology and political resolution of many different, differing, and changing interests. Public policies of one sort or another, as they emerge and evolve, are often rationalized, and sometimes affected by thoughts of experts, including economists.

In two areas, the would-be science of economics has not been as helpful as might have been, these past 40 years or so, in advancing our understanding of the American economy and the encompassing American System of which it is a part. For one, the line of economic thought concerned with monopolistic and imperfect competition has been clearly far off the mark by way of explaining observable behaviors and performance of firms and industries.

As to the other area, economic development, our understanding of the dynamics of our System has not been greatly furthered by either of two other lines of economics that have attracted the attention of many economists: (*a*) *Keynesian* economics, with its concern over supposedly cyclical fluctuations in such aggregate variables as total employment and unemployment, savings and investment, money supply and level of interest rates; and (*b*) *development* economics of underdeveloped nations.

Another implication of the present study, accordingly, is that we need *major* advances, even major reorientations, in these fields of economics if we are to do a better job of managing our economy.

"Monopolistic" and "imperfect" competition. Both of these related lines of thought of economics are concerned with the behaviors of groups of sellers (and buyers) when their numbers are few. Both are generally regarded as theories and are so referred to. Both, in fact, are clusters of abstract *hypotheses* and deductions. They are not really *theories* in the sense of that word, which bespeaks reasonably successful, rigorously fact-based and documented efforts to explain observable and observed, and measurable and measured, phenomena. They are both preoccupied with attempts to deduce supposed workings-out of given quanta of given variables and factors from explicitly or, mostly, implicitly given and assumed beginning-states to hypothesized equilibrium end-states. The givens include, explicitly or implicitly, hypothesized firms existing in markets and industries that are well-defined as to contents and boundaries. Implicitly or explicitly, these hypothetical firms produce *given* products, with all of their several and various specifications, in plants of given kinds, numbers, scales, and locations, using, presumably, given technologies of production, distribution and management. They confront given kinds and numbers of buyers, with given demand functions, tastes, preferences, and consumption alternatives. The not-very-competitive sellers (or buyers) have, implicitly, given investment prospects and expectable terms and availabilities of capital funds of various kinds—all, among other things! Given all this, the hypothesizer then speculates as to what the outcomes of given changes would be, given a hypothetical beginning-state.

More than that: aside from these particulars of assumed static givens, analyses of these kinds concern themselves, again explicitly or tacitly, with periods of time sufficiently short that such key variables chosen for consideration show no material change, quantitative or qualitative. In effect, such hypothesizings concern themselves with short-time-span "cross sections" of assumed factors and hypothesized happenings deduced by "logic."

Being *few*, each of the monopolists or oligopolists is hypothesized to take account of probable reactions of each of the others (of whom, of course, he is aware, their number being few) in setting his own price, controlling the level and flow of his output, determining the degree and perhaps the nature of the differentiation, if any, of his particular product among somewhat different but homologous or essentially fungible products, in determining the level of his advertising, if any. Through a series of interactive successive approximations, a static end-state of a group "equilibrium" is supposed eventually to be reached in which no one can improve his position by making any change. That's it. At this point, prices are higher; individual and collective outputs are lower and each has excess capacity; quality is static and inferior; advertising reaches a state of individually and totally unproductive, multilateral, zero-sum checkmate.

If the apparatus of these lines of speculation, with their assumptions, hypotheses, and deductions, had been valid, or were in any way descriptive of reality, we would now observe an economic system that had remained static at best, these past 50 years: among other mournful indicia of the workings of monopolistic or imperfect competition, we would have seen no industrial expansion; prices that in real, constant-dollar terms or, say, in relation to wages and incomes, had been static at best, if not rising; negligible innovation in corporate institutions, in products, in processes of production and distribution; pervasive monopoly profits.

The manifest facts through which we have lived, and now around us, are utterly otherwise, of course. The reason for the stunning disparity between the real world and the hypotheses and conclusions of the economics of monopolistic and imperfect competition is simple and devastating. Far from trying to observe, measure, and explain the extraordinarily complex and varied world of flux in which we find ourselves, these lines of economics have sequestered themselves far from the madding crowd's ignoble strife, there to speculate upon what "must be" rather than upon what *is*. It is not surprising that they end up so far off the mark.

In actuality, as anyone can see for himself, the essence of *real* matters is not their "given-ness" and hypothesized equilibrium end-states; but, on the contrary, their open-endedness; their *dynamism;* their unascertainable present values; let alone their indeterminate future quantitative and qualitative *development,* often at astounding rates of change. The real world of the business firm, large or small, is longitudinal, over time, where everything is subject to changes and moves along. The real world is not cross-sectional, where time, so to speak, is frozen.

Innovations, response, change, reaction—iterated and reiterated, cycled and recycled, endlessly moving—not equilibrium end-states, are central realities. Competition in industry, is, in fact, an endless process entailing innovation, change, and adaptation and response, interaction: changes in mores, preferences, values and expectations; any number of additions and deletions of products and product specifications; extensions, modifications, of whole product lines; changes in such marketing practices as warranties, installation practices, servicing arrangements; experiments in means and methods of distribution and marketing; innovation, modification, expansion, contraction, multiplication and integration of production processes and facilities; the advent of new substitute products and/or services or of radical alternatives offered by other industries; discovery, development, use, and depletion of resources; changing comparative advantages and terms of trade in world markets; to say nothing of mere changes in costs, rates of utilization of existing plants and prices.

Members of industries, industry systems, and Industry Categories do, indeed, try hard to keep track of each other, and, indeed, of firms in other industries and they surely do take into account in determining their own behavior what they perceive, know, and find out. In this perpetual process of monitoring, they are aided by literally hundreds of industry and trade journals and specialized news and market letters. Firms each year spend millions of dollars on market research and market-study services. They monitor trade and industry shows. Executives track *The New York Times, The Wall Street Journal, Business Week, Forbes, Fortune,* and *The Harvard Business Review,* for instance. They follow government publications. They draw upon thousands of consultants.

In consequence of what they learn about competitors, would-be competitors, potential competitors, actual and potential suppliers, distributors and customers, they set prices, redesign, add, and drop products; modify, expand, close plants; make new investments; change advertising messages and media and agencies; seek joint venturers; divest parts of their business; look for acquisitions; change their organization structures and management information and control systems; amend their by-laws and reconstitute their boards of directors. Taking into account their own impacts upon others, and the multilateral, systemic impacts of all upon all, they are inevitably led, not into a catatonic static end-state, but an endless series of challenge-response-challenge-response. Nothing stays put for very long. The essence of modern business and industry is *dynamism,* in which there are losers and winners.

That, not monopolistic or oligopolistic *equilibrium,* is the essential reality.

Through scores, hundreds of processes of innovation and adaptation over time, not just individual firms, but whole industry systems change, grow and develop, or regress. These sorts of *longitudinal* facts are of the real, bottom-line essence of industry behavior and performance: innovation, response; success, error; rise, fall; creative destruction, transformation, evolution, development.

The hypotheses of monopolistic and imperfect competition are in no way descriptive of actuality. Even considered as paradigms or models and not as actual descriptions, they have enormous power to lead serious people far astray.

It is truly amazing how much the dream-like hypotheses of monopolistic and imperfect competition have colored the thinking, not only of many economists, but of legislators, government administrators, and members of the judiciary, as well. And that is a pity.

When economics turns more attention to describing, measuring, and explaining actual developmental features of firms and industries, is more concerned with study of actual, documentable *behavior* and *performance* of firms and industries than with hypotheses about "ideal" industry *structures,* it will have something of greater value to contribute to formulation of public policy.

Keynesian economics. Another branch of economics that has preoccupied numbers of economists for more than a generation is that labeled "Keynesian." As mentioned, this line of economics has been primarily concerned with attempting to explain supposedly cyclical or, in any case, relatively short-run perturbations in levels of such aggregate phenomena as employment; production; savings and investment; level of interest. The apparatus of Keynesian hypotheses implicitly assumes a given economic structure in place, rather than a developing one.

At one time, some Keynesians were persuaded also that the United States had entered a period of long-run, secular stagnation, attributable in considerable measure to supposed passing of investment opportunities. But that particular concern has not been prominent in recent years.

Keynesian economics has been avowedly activist and committed to a concern with current, "on-line" management of government fiscal and monetary operations having a principal objective of offsetting cyclical declines and booms, and maintaining aggregate economic stability at something close to optimal levels.

In any event, this field of economics, like that of monopolistic and imperfect competition, was not greatly concerned with *development* of the economy. It has not been greatly concerned with explaining the course of our economic and industrial history. Aside from the concern of some, almost a generation ago, over the possibility of "secular stagnation," it has not been the purview of Keynesian economics to be much interested in factors of public policies that might foster timely and necessary shifts and changes in the occupational profile of the American people and in the composition of the stream of production, along with needed long-term increases and changes in the aggregates of employment and output. There was little concern, for instance, with (*a*) desirable redeployment of capital, people, and resources out of old employments of eroding comparative advantage; (*b*) attraction of capital, people, and other resources into uses related to the emergent future; (*c*) encouragement of high-risk, high-technology research and development, and their application through education and investment; and certainly no focus on (*d*) matters having to do with evolving structures, behaviors, and performances of firms and industry systems.

As Keynes said, himself, *The General Theory of Employment, Interest, and Money* is "primarily a study of the forces which determine changes in the *scale* of output and employment as a whole...."[3]

Development economics. For quite some time, say, after the American experience in Korea, numbers of economists were much interested in problems of development in underdeveloped countries. There has been hope on the part of some development economists that large multinational corporations (especially, of course, American) might be useful instruments for bringing capital and know-how to those countries. Such things did happen. But it is probably fair to say that there has been little transfer out of this area of economics back into greater understanding of development problems and processes of our own very different, and still developing, evolving, and growing System.

* * * * *

There is plenty of unfinished business lying before the developing science of economics by way of helping our political leadership improve the alignment of public policy with present realities and national objectives, especially as regards the place of large corporations that occupy very special key positions in the American System.

We greatly need rigorous, tough-minded, empirical research into those factors that have shaped and moved our industrial and economic development over at least these past 50 years, if not over the span of the 20th century to date, and that are likely to determine our development at least during the rest of this century.[4]

PUBLIC POLICY: ECONOMIC DEVELOPMENT

As we look through the years, over the rest of the century, we see outlines of our future development and some of its implications. Less easily do we see emergence of national goals and public policy that will accommodate to, or expedite that development. This is especially the case as regards capital formation. Even more so is this the case when it comes to industry sectors and systems characterized by large scale; capital-intensivity; massive-overhead; vertical integration; multiplant, multiproduct operations; technology-intensivity. These sectors have especially to do with infrastructure, such as transportation, communication, and energy and with mass-production; in short, with industry sectors and systems characterized by the occurrence and presence of large corporations.

A few very rough figures indicate something of the magnitude of what lies before us.

Development: 1980-2000

To begin: over the course of the next decade or so, we shall be adding to our population each year about a million and a half souls;

436

in the years beyond, the figure could be about two million. By the year 2000, even at a modest average net growth rate of something like $^{65}/_{100}$ of 1 percent, our population may have increased by about 15 percent, and we may then number over 250,000,000—more than a quarter of a billion! (It could well be more.) Some brood!

If our Gross National Product were to grow at exactly the same rate, so that GNP per capita remained constant, it would have to rise from $1,890 billion (in 1977) to a hypothetical figure of $2,190 billion (in 1977 dollars) in the year 2000; and even this estimate could be low.

A net rise, over the 20-year span, of something like $300 billion in the level of annual GNP, on average, would require vast amounts of additional capital.

In fact, our national goals for development during this period, as yet unformed, will surely call for a higher level of production and, accordingly, for a much higher level of capital formation.

There are many reasons why the GNP per capita should grow. Our people, surely, still aspire to improving their lot and that of their children. We shall wish to improve our environment. We wish to have more public amenities and services. We do wish to improve the lot of our less fortunate people—the least of our brethren. We shall, almost surely, wish, for whatever reasons, to carry a share of the efforts of richer nations to help the poorer to help themselves. So many reasons. Besides, we have shown that our material well-being *can* improve. An average rate of real growth of 3.2 percent for the rest of the 20th century is well within limits of what we have achieved over longer periods in the past. We *could* do better, if we choose. Even at such a rate of growth, if no higher, our GNP in the year 2000 (in terms of 1977 dollars) would more than double to a level of about $3,900 billion!

The achievement of such a level of production would require massive capital investments in productive assets, to say nothing of investments in people, by way of education and training, and in research and development.

A few more rough indicative figures: Gross Private Domestic Investment, representing something like 16 percent of the GNP, would have to rise from about $294 billion, in 1977, to a total annual commitment of something over $600 billion in 2000. Of that investment, based on recent experience, about 60 percent would have to be made by corporations, and, over half of that, in turn, say 60 percent, would have to be made by our then very largest corporations. (By the year 2000, the likelihood is that 1,500 or more corporations will be of a size comparable to The Largest of the early Seventies!) This is to say, by that year, the then largest corporations will have to invest, net of current capital consumption, at an annual rate of something around $220 billion (1977 dollars).

To meet such an objective, our largest corporations in the decade of the Eighties would have to invest, gross, a total of something like $1.4 *trillion* dollars; a total *net,* after "capital consumption allowances," of something like $800 billion! Through the Nineties, the then largest corporations would have to invest, *gross,* a total of something like $2 trillion; *net,* a total of about $1,100 billion.

Those are big numbers. They could well be bigger if we are more ambitious.

In sum, over the next two decades, such a schedule would call for total *gross* investment by the largest corporations, alone, of something more than *$3.4 trillion* (in 1977 dollars) and, by the year 2000, a total *net increase* of invested capital something more than *$1.2 trillion.* The then largest corporations capable of performing the increasingly intricate, massive, global tasks of the times will have to hold an aggregate value of productive assets three to four times that of our present largest firms.

Either that, or we scale back significantly our national and individual aspirations, goals and hopes.

These figures give a measure of other implications for our future economic and industrial development.

Aside from growth in our System, we need transformation and change, also. No small fractions of our invested capital and labor force are now committed to older uses in which our historical comparative advantages are declining. The welfare of the entire national community calls for redeployment of both that capital and that labor into newer applications. That redeployment will require public policy that, if it does not facilitate movement, at least does not inhibit it. The dissipation of the capital invested in our railroads is a prime example of how savings and investments of earlier generations can be frittered away. National policy stood in the way of rational deployment of that capital, to the cost of all of us.

Parts of our older cities and towns are obsolescent and even obsolete. Again, redeployment of capital and labor into new applications is called for—not necessarily, but maybe, in new locations.

Altogether, a major part of the forward push and of the reallocations will have to take place through the workings of large corporations and with encouragement of public authority, i.e., governmental *power.* That is, "will have to," unless, as a matter of national choice, we prefer to generate and to deploy resources away from large corporations in the private sector over to *publicly* owned, large-scale, massive-overhead, high-technology, vertically integrated, capital-intensive, small-marginal-cost, multiplant, multiproduct enterprises of the sorts needed to support a modern civilization.

We have, at the moment, no national goal, no policy for any such achievements. Perhaps we have lost the heart and will to aspire, to *do*. We have but little knowledge as to how we might pursue such objectives. One finds little preoccupation with such matters among politicians, economists, labor leaders, or businessmen.

Our future lies before us, with so much of our country's business for us to be about, so many things to do.

PUBLIC POLICY: TAXATION; CAPITAL FORMATION, ALLOCATION, CONSERVATION

The whole matter of public policies that are expressed in taxes, and of the actual net and total systemic effects of those taxes, is enormously complex, vexatious, and contentious. It is an area where angels and experts fear to tread. But a few points are worth making in connection with an effort to identify some of the major implications of the rise and the place of large corporations in the economy.

Formation, conservation, allocation, and redeployment of capital; economic and industrial development, growth and modernization; income generation and distribution; industry structures—all are profoundly affected by taxation of corporations and individuals, especially by the federal government.

This is scarcely news. What may be worth stressing is how and how far taxation affects the economy as a whole through the nexus of large corporations. An example is the burden of the federal tax on corporate net income. The very Largest Nonfinancial Corporations constitute a minute fraction of the total number of corporations. But, we have seen, they held something more than half of all the assets of the nonfinancial corporate community. These Largest Corporations, in 1971, earned something more than half of the income subject to tax that was earned by all nonfinancial corporations. See Exhibit 78. These few corporations paid almost two-thirds of the *total* income tax bill of *all* nonfinancial corporations. After paying these taxes, they realized significantly less than half of the total *net* income *after* tax. For the very Largest Nonfinancial Corporations, the income tax took 40.3 percent of their income subject to tax; for all other nonfinancial corporations (excluding the very largest), the income tax took 23.1 percent of their income subject to tax. About 60 percent of all the earnings of nonfinancial corporations, net after income tax and after deficits of unprofitable firms, which is to say, available for dividends out of current earnings or for corporate capital formation and allocation, was in the hands of The Largest Corporations.

Clearly, the influences of the corporate income tax are in large measure a matter of its effects on a small number of very large corporations, rather than a widespread and general effect upon the corporate community as a whole. Because of the key position of large corporations in our industry structure, they are also a prime medium

EXHIBIT 78
Incomes and income taxes, nonfinancial corporations, 1971

	All nonfinancial corporations	Nonfinancial corporations with assets of $250 million and more*	Largest Corporations, percentage of all nonfinancial corporations
Number of corporations	1,592,193	615	0.04%
Business receipts	$1,668.5†	$614.9†	36.9%
Assets	$1,410.5†	$772.5†	54.8%
Income subject to tax, after various deductions	$72.9†	$38.0†	52.1%
Income tax, net of credits, refunds, etc.	$23.4†	$15.3†	65.4%
Income tax, net, as percentage of income subject to tax	32.1%	40.3%	34.9%
			(Nonfinancial corporations other than The Largest: 23.2%)
Income after tax, corporations with net income	$49.5†	$22.7†	45.9%
Deficits, corporations without net income	$−15.7†	$−2.5†	15.9%
Total income, net, after tax and deficits, corporations with and without net income	$33.8†	$20.2†	59.8%

*These 615 corporations may, and probably do, include privately held companies, subsidiaries filing separate returns, subsidiaries of foreign corporations, etc. See, Chapter 7, Note 1 and Chapter 8, Note 3.
†Billions.
Source: *Corporation Source Book, Statistics of Income, 1971; Corporation Income Tax Returns...;* Tables 8, 18, 69; 246, 256, 307; Lines 5, 37, 70, 77, 85.

whereby the operations and even the *existence* of taxes on *individual* income and capital gains affect *corporate* capital formation and allocation of corporate capital and the growth of corporations.

Impacts of taxes upon individual and corporate net incomes and capital gains

Apart from raising revenue for purposes of government, which is presumably a principal objective of income and capital gains taxes (aside from redistribution of income), these taxes have a number of important side effects. These were not necessarily intended by Congress. These impacts have to do with such significant phenomena as the growth of corporations; the profile of the corporate community and the structures of industries; the formation, allocation, and dissipation of capital; and with subsidies and burdens arising out of differentials in the assessment of the costs of government upon corporations.

These effects in particular instances are not necessarily bad or benign, as might be judged from a public point of view. But they are surely not necessarily what Congress would desire, given opportunity to choose deliberately. In any case, to repeat, a majority of these side effects find their way into the economy through the impacts of taxes upon very large corporations and their shareholders.

Corporate development, and taxes upon dividend income and capital gains of stockholders*

A major, if unintended, consequence of federal taxes on dividend income and upon capital gains realized by shareholders upon sale of stock of corporations (several states levy similar taxes) is the promotion of growth by existing corporations. First, these taxes, as they work, resulting in double taxation of corporate profits, make retention of corporate earnings a relatively attractive option, not only for corporations desiring additional capital, for whatever reasons, but also for many stockholders as compared to payment of dividends. Second, because capital gains are taxable at rates lower than dividends, this pair of taxes, working together, encourages arrangements that put capital gains rather than dividends in the hands of stockholders, and that keep the underlying corpus of assets as nearly intact as possible. In many instances, provisions of tax law encourage the acquisition of smaller corporations by larger ones.

Taxes on dividend income and corporate growth through reinvestment of earnings. Dividend income received by taxable recipients suffers major shrinkage through the levying of income taxes thereon. Income remaining to the stockholder out of dividends, after taxes, and available for consumption or reinvestment represents a fraction of what is received. In any event, *reinvestment,* if any, of the net proceeds by the stockholder represents investment of *after-tax* dollars.

In contrast, so far as the taxable stockholder is concerned, reinvestment by a corporation of company earnings that remain after payment of the corporation's own income taxes represents, for him, reinvestment of his share of the earnings in the form of *before-tax* dollars. This *can* be a better deal for shareholders. For example, if, in a hypothetical instance, a corporation can earn, say, 8 percent on the *whole amount* of the retained and reinvested earnings that might be paid out in dividends, whereas the hypothetical stockholder could earn, say, 10 percent on an *after-tax half* of his dividends, he could be better off to leave reinvestment to the corporation, even though it earned a somewhat lower *rate* of return than he could realize, after tax, on his own.

In a very real sense, the corporation can do the stockholder a favor by retaining and reinvesting its earnings, after its own income tax, including his share therein, rather than paying them out as dividends. Corporate officials and knowledgeable stockholders are well aware of this, of course.

---

*Statements set forth in the following pages do not take into account the different effects of the many subtle and sometimes significant particularities of individual cases.

Over a period of years, the compounding of retained earnings—*before* shareholders' taxes—on investments by the corporation can be enormously more attractive to stockholders than the compounded returns many of them could realize on investments made by them individually with *after-tax* dollars.

The tax on dividend income in the hands of recipients operates to foster retention by corporations of their earnings. This retention, of course, is a source of growth of corporations, small and large. This tendency to retention also operates to conserve capital. A major portion of dividend income ends up in the hands of the federal government, which, in turn, spends much of it on current public consumption. A sizable fraction of the dividend income remaining in the hands of stockholders also goes for current personal consumption.

Whether the investment allocations of earnings retained by corporations are preferable, from a public point of view, to the investment allocations that would be made by shareholders is an open question. It is clear that they are larger. Whether retention and reinvestment by corporations is preferable to consumption expenditures by government or by recipients of transfer payments can be debated. Our need, on social welfare grounds, for economic expansion and development can scarcely be argued.

Individual capital gains taxes and corporate development. In all the discussion about corporate mergers and acquisitions—much of which is concerned with antitrust and related considerations—relatively little is said about the part played directly and indirectly in these matters by tax considerations. In fact, tax considerations provide a powerful—in some cases, the single most influential—motivating force behind the restructuring and growth of firms, including large ones, by means of mergers and acquisitions. A key factor here is that effective tax rates on capital gains resulting from sale or exchange of stockholders' shares in corporations are considerably less than half of the tax rates on dividends received out of corporate profits.

Taxes and mergers and acquisitions

Inherent in our tax law is strong, persistent, widespread, if not universal pressure or incentive operating on shareholders of corporations, where there are significant potential capital gains, to sell their shares to an acquirer willing and able to pay a price, especially as compared to waiting for future dividends.

It is worth noting in passing that mergers and acquisitions had been a significant, but not a major, factor overall in the growth of The 559 Largest corporations in the period 1948-71. To be sure, some of the very early big corporations were creations of "consolidations"; some of the railroads, United States Steel, and Standard

Oil, for instance. In the 1920s, a few large corporations were first assembled through mergers; General Motors and General Foods, for instance. And in the 1950s and 60s, a few very large corporations were put together: Litton and L-T-V, for example.

Over the years 1948-71, according to the Federal Trade Commission, there were 1,387 acquisitions of firms in mining and manufacturing that had more than $10 million in assets and for which data were publicly available. The total assets of these merged firms came to $68.4 billion in current dollars of the respective years of merger. In addition, there were something like 400 other comparable acquisitions for which data were not publicly available; these companies held something like $10 billion of assets. Over one-third of all these acquisitions, with something over one-half of the total acquired assets of the period, took place in the seven-year period 1965-71. (In the following five years, the pace and volume of such acquisitions fell off substantially.)

Altogether, these 1,800, or so, acquisitions with something like $80 billion of assets could have accounted for something around 10 percent to 20 percent of the assets of The Largest Corporations of 1971.

A number of the acquisitions and mergers involved sizable companies and did, indeed, account for considerable fractions of the growths of the particular acquiring corporations. In the years 1965-71, for instance, 740 mining and manufacturing companies were acquired for which there were data publicly available; their total assets came to $46.8 billion. Of these corporations, 103 had assets of $100 million or more, and their assets came to $28.4 billion in total. The corporations doing the acquiring of these larger merged companies held assets totaling $84.8 billion. These assets acquired, accordingly, and on the average, stood at about one-third of the assets of these particular acquiring firms.[5]

Internal growth from retained earnings and borrowings was far the most important kind and source of corporate development. Since 1971, that has changed somewhat. A very few of the largest corporations of 1971 disappeared into others, still larger: Anaconda into Atlantic Richfield; and Wilson and Jones & Laughlin into L-T-V, for instance. By the late 1970s, a few new names entered the category of largest companies in consequence of mergers. But, far more often, as in earlier years, companies involved in mergers were of far less than the largest size. Circumstances have been changing, however, and mergers of large, if not of the largest, corporations seem to have become somewhat more frequent than in the recent past.

Incentives for disposition of corporations. In effect, the sale of the stock of one company by shareholders to another corporation can make it possible for shareholders to realize, in the form of capital gains rather than as income in the form of dividends, their proportionate shares of accumulated retained earnings of the corporation sold. Where a premium is paid over stockholders' individual purchase prices, they may also realize a further capital gain. A purchase price greater than book value represents, in a way, a portion of even future earnings.

If the stock is exchanged for stock in an acquiring company having a value greater than the cost of the original stock to the stockholder, the individual stockholder may incur liability for a taxable capital gain on which a capital gains tax will have to be paid. This is generally so arranged as to be more attractive than paying taxes on dividends. There may also be estate tax advantages. In general, under the "reorganization" provisions of the Tax Code, the tax is deferred until some future event, such as eventual sale of the stock received in exchange.

This deferral can be very attractive to shareholders. A principal reason is that the stockholder exchanging stock for stock can have his entire share of the equity, now in the acquiring company, working for him during the period before ultimate sale of the stock received, and the resulting tax.

If, and to the extent, cash is paid by the acquiring company for the stock of the acquired company, immediate tax liability is created for the selling stockholder. But, as compared to receipt of dividends taxable as income, even this can be advantageous to the stockholders of the acquired company. This purchase of the acquired company's future earnings can also be attractive for the stockholder of the acquiring company even if, as must be the case, the price is set high enough to be attractive to the shareholders of the acquired company after giving effect to their immediate liability for capital gains tax.

In either case, sale for cash or exchange of stock for stock, the shareholder is likely to fare better by taking his share in past and possible future earnings of the acquired corporation, so to speak, in the forms of return of capital and capital gains rather than as dividends.

In the nature of things, the acquiring company is almost always a larger company. For the stockholder of the acquired company, in the case of sale of stock for stock, this is likely to be a source of greater diversification of his capital risk. For the community, one result is one corporation less and one corporation larger. In many circumstances, this can be a real advantage to the economy at large. (We shall come back to that point in a moment.)

Tax considerations and incentives for acquisition of corporations. On the other side of transactions of mergers and acquisitions, strong incentives also exist. Corporations with substantial earnings retained and accumulated over periods of years often accumulate large amounts of cash, marketable securities and other current assets. Accumulation may continue because of strong cash-flows. This is expecially true if the "recycling" of cash-flows from operations back into the established line or lines of business has become relatively unattractive. If paid out as dividends, such sums, of course, become currently taxable as income in the hands of recipient shareholders. On the other hand, if cash is paid for the stock of another company, that disbursement can inure to the benefit of the shareholders of the acquiring company—through the addition of earnings of the acquired company to the earnings of the acquiring company.

In effect, acquisition of another company for accumulated and/or borrowed cash provides the shareholders of the acquiring company with "tax-shielded" reinvestment of a fraction, at least, of their proportionate shares of values accrued in consequence of retained earnings of both corporations.

Even if the acquiring company borrows to finance the acquisition or gives (as is allowed) a portion of the purchase price in the form of bonds, that can still be advantageous because the interest expense of the incurred debt is a deductible expense. Matters can be, and usually are, arranged so that the cost of the borrowing, after tax, is less than the rate of earnings of the acquired company. (The reader should recognize, of course, that all of this is subject to an extraordinary maze of technical provisions of the Tax Code.)

Incentives also operate to favor acquisitions of the stock of a company through exchange of stock of the acquiring company. If the price-earnings ratio of the stock of the acquiring company is higher than that of the acquired company, matters can easily be so arranged that the subsequent reported earnings per share, and, very commonly, the *market price* of the stock of the acquiring company, both per share and in the aggregate, can be immediately increased.[6] In any event, the capital invested in the acquired company passes into the hands of the acquiring company in consequence of the "exchange of paper."

One other aspect of taxation of corporations has a part in fostering mergers and acquisitions. In spite of various complex limitations, the tax laws, in certain circumstances of "reorganization," do permit deduction of the accumulated losses of one business against the profits of another corporation. Following combination of the firms pursuant to "tax-free" reorganization, past losses can shelter future profits. If such a reorganization can be arranged, past losses can become extremely valuable to both parties—another, and sometimes major, positive force making for mergers and acquisitions.

If it seems that there is something for everyone in corporate mergers and acquisitions, and that it may appear, after all, there *may* be such a thing as a "free lunch," let it be noted that not all of them by any means have worked out well.[7] What the following years might have brought the companies concerned, in the absence of the mergers, is purely hypothetical. Clear is the fact that the *short-run* effects, at least, of merger and acquisition can be, are designed to be, and almost universally have been advantageous to both sets of stock-holders. In some cases, the longer run has been a different story.

Taxation and capital formation and conservation. The fact that tax laws foster corporate growth is, to say the least, not all bad, especially if we are as much or, pragmatically, more concerned with the *performance* of industry and the economy as with its *structure.* The allocation of corporate income to capital formation and productive purposes, in our time, is almost surely socially preferable, from the standpoint of national development, than the payment of dividends or taxes. Consumption is neither intrinsically inferior nor superior to investment and capital formation. At this point in our national evolution, however, we do stand in great need of substantially more capital formation than is actually taking place, if we are to make productive jobs available and to offset inflation, in part, through producing more goods and services.

Retention and reinvestment of corporate earnings is one place where capital conservation and formation come off a bit better than usual in the constant tension between them, on one side, and expenditure on private and public current consumption on the other.

Our present methods of taxation do tend to foster corporate growth. Whether that growth and the particular allocations of capital which it represents are anything like "socially optimal" is another matter. All one can say, now, is that these consequences, whatever they be, are inadvertencies.

PUBLIC POLICY: THE RISE AND GROWTH OF "CONGLOMERATES"

Probably no development in the structures of industry was less of an explicit national objective than the growth of conglomerates—here defined as assemblages of very unlike and unrelated companies put together by merger and acquisition. Few developments are more directly traceable to public policy.

Several principal factors lie at the root of this phenomenon: first, as we have just noted, the several potential advantages of merger to stockholders of both the acquiring and the acquired company; second, attractiveness of opportunities for the redeployment of capital, beyond the long reach of taxes, from less to more promising applications; third, the combination of the two foregoing considerations with the presence and operation of Section 7 of the Clayton Act, as amended.

It is fair to note that promoters of conglomerates have not gone unrewarded. Although their gains in some instances seem to have been large, indeed, in absolute dollars, their compensation relative to the values generated for others often appear modest enough.

Redeployment and preservation of capital

Moving capital out of an older corporation with dimming prospects is not a simple, straightforward matter. In principle, capital could be drained out to the fullest extent possible and given back to stockholders, who could then reallocate that capital to more promising uses. In fact, there are all sorts of practical problems. The legalisms of actual, outright liquidation are horrendous.* Simply winding down a company through distributions of dividends in excess of current earnings, if any, presents its own problems. Professional executives are not much interested in presiding over a winding-down and ultimate liquidation. Besides, one of the major problems is that monies paid out to stockholders that come from retained earnings of *past* years are subject to income tax in the hands of recipients, even if the corporation is experiencing *current* losses. Tax collectors might take up to one-half or more of the proceeds from the dividends; much of the capital accumulated over decades would be consumed in private or public current consumption budgets.

The conglomerate structure offers the possibility of solving practical problems that are entailed, including, importantly, the possibility of preserving the accumulated capital. Companies put together to form conglomerates generally have been not only very different in terms of their industries, but equally so as regards profitability and future prospects. Several of these assemblages have included very profitable, high-technology enterprises with bright futures, put together with elderly, lackluster veterans of earlier and better days, who prospered once upon a time on the basis of comparative advantages now disappearing into history. In principle, given our tax laws, such teaming up of the old with the new, the past with the future, could make sense.

Down within the conglomerate corporate structure, the cash flow (equal to net earnings, if any, plus pretax deductions from revenues that involve no cash outlays, such as depreciation) from less attractive parts of the corporation can by directed over to higher-yielding allocations elsewhere within the structure. Subsidiary corporations with relatively dull or unattractive prospects can be sources of capital for other parts of the total business on more advantageous terms than they or smaller, newer firms might be able to get, going directly on their own to capital markets. Far more important, reallocation of capital from one use to another within the overall corporate structure is sheltered from the erosion that that capital would suffer if it were paid out into the hands of stockholders, there to be taxed before what was left could be reinvested.

In actuality, some conglomerates of this sort seem to have worked out pretty well; others, not.

---

*Receipt of proceeds of outright liquidation in the hands of individual stockholders could result in capital losses or gain, depending upon whether they were less or greater than the investments made by them.

Such conservation of capital is clearly advantageous to its owners. It is advantageous also to the community at large; an all too scarce resource is conserved. Besides that, and this is no mean advantage, entrance into a holding company structure can provide the older corporation with means of dealing with, or even avoiding, practical human, legal, and business problems of winding down or even liquidating an old business.

The rise of conglomerates: The interplay of the tax code and Section 7

Through the combination of the reorganization provisions of the Tax Code with Section 7 of the Clayton Act, as amended, very special forces come into play that foster—"induce" is scarcely too strong a word—the formation of conglomerates.

Section 7 is a piece of the body of antitrust statutes that makes illegal any acquisition by one corporation of the stock or assets of another, where the effect "in any line of commerce in any section of the country may be substantially to lessen competition or to create a monopoly."

Just what this means, either in general or in particular, is a matter of judicial interpretation. A "line of commerce" may be held in public or private litigation to be very narrow, such as bottled liquid laundry bleach, or on the other hand, very broad, such as coal and copper mining, perhaps considered as parts of a single line of commerce or industry, namely, extraction. A "section of the country" may be held to be as small as—literally—Hobbs, New Mexico. In studying the course and outcomes of antitrust litigation, one has reason to detect something of a tendency toward, shall we say, vigorous, if uncertain, interpretations of law.

Just what various judges may hold to constitute a "lessening of competition" is equally obscure. It may be that, under strictest interpretation, *any* advantage that might flow to the merged companies *might* be held to strengthen them *relative to competitors*. This, in turn, *might* be held to constitute a lessening of competition. Whether trying to gain advantage relative to *competitors* (and succeeding in doing so), is logically or in practice synonymous with lessening of *competition,* or is a reasonable, even laudable consequence of competition, much to be encouraged for the good of a dynamic society, is a point that need not be pursued here.

In consequence of the haze of Congressional intent and judicial interpretation that hangs over the matter, companies and their bankers, lawyers, and boards have tried hard to avoid getting involved in mergers that might be vulnerable to attack under Section 7.

This has meant that mergers have been avoided where there were any significant, or even minor economic business or technical gains to be had in the way of economies of scale, of vertical integration, of multiplant operations, or even of "synergism"—a magic word that acquired a powerful mystique of its own in the stock markets of the 1960s.

The safest course of action, given the touchiness of Section 7 in action, has been to arrange mergers of companies where there is only the remotest possibility—if even that—that *any* advantages could be obtained through economies of scale, of vertical integration, of multiplant operations or even of synergy. That is to say, the most clearly legal mergers or acquisitions are those where there are the fewest, the smallest, the most remote possibilities that *any* business operating benefits could arise—aside, presumably, from financial and tax advantages of sorts mentioned previously. Mergers of the most disparate kinds of companies are the most secure from the reach of Section 7 (or of Section 2 of the Sherman Act as regards efforts to monopolize).[8]

A powerful force behind the rise of conglomerates!

Be that as it may, it is a wonder that even more conglomerates—and even *more* "conglomerate" conglomerates, and *larger* conglomerates—have not arisen.

The invocation of Section 7 to prevent pursuit of real economies often amazes legislators, officials, and businessmen of other countries, such as Japan, France, West Germany, Italy, and Spain, where one finds much public policy interest in the "rationalizing" of industry structures—through mergers, among other means—in order, as a matter of public policy, to achieve the very gains that are most clearly vulnerable to attack under our Section 7. As a nation, we shall have to make a clear decision as to whether we are going to permit American companies to restructure themselves in order to enhance their ability to compete with restructured foreign firms, both at home in the United States, as well as abroad.

Conglomerates and the public interest

The rise of conglomeracy, let it be said quickly, has much to be said for it from a community point of view. To repeat, conglomerates may be, and have, in fact, been a major help in speeding reallocation of capital from obsolescent, lower-return, to new, higher-return uses, at the same time sheltering and preserving that capital from dispersion through present taxation and consequent consumption. Moreover, and this is a very different point, conglomerates may work to reduce the risk-cost of the capital employed by them: it is compatible with modern financial theory to suppose that a conglomerate, through diversification of its portfolio of investments, may be able to reduce, to some extent, the total cost of the real "diversifiable risk" of those investments and, accordingly, to reduce the total real *cost* of capital allocated to those uses. If, and to the extent this takes place, benefit redounds to the entire community, as does any other measure that reduces the real cost of inputs into national production.

The actual financial performance of the conglomerates to date has been spotty. But so, alas, has been the profit and performance of the corporate community as a whole, for the past decade. If the profit performances of some of the conglomerates have left something to be desired, the question remains open as to how well the merged corporations would have done as separate companies, especially in view of the fact that numbers of them were of no great strength prior to merger. In many cases, the very weakness of some of the components was a principal reason for their sale to acquiring companies.

Future Congressional or judicial action may put a stop to conglomerate mergers even where there is *no* "lessening of competition in any line of business," simply as an anti-Bigness measure. If that occurs, a new means will have to be devised, in the national interest of development, material progress, and employment, that, in its own way, will facilitate the reallocation and conservation of capital and increase its mobility among alternatives, especially toward more productive uses.

TAX REFORM AND THE LARGEST CORPORATIONS

This is no place to get mired down in controversy over possible tax reforms. But inasmuch as The Largest Corporations and their very functioning in the economy are especially affected by present taxes, at least a few matters can be pointed out.

Caprice in the corporate net income tax

First, it can be mentioned that liabilities for corporate *net income* taxes, such as they are now, fall very unevenly upon corporations. These differences arise from many sources. Some reflect specific Congressional intent; others reflect general policy, such as deductibility of interest expense, which, quite incidentally, tends to encourage debt financing, which is more appropriate for some industries than for others. Other differences reflect differences in the natures of assets, some industries employing relatively greater proportions of depreciable assets than others; certain industries have been selected by Congress for more favorable treatments by this device or that.

Altogether, the impacts of the corporate net income tax, with their consequences for profitability, capital formation and allocation, and industry structures are capricious.

Second, liabilities of individual firms and industries for corporate net income tax bear no rational relationships either to benefits derived from "externalities" provided by government (such as use of the transportation network) nor to charges the community is put to because of different impacts that various industries and companies have on various parts of the System as a whole. The overhead social costs of public services are not allocated in any way in accord with use, but on the arbitrary basis of dollar net profits. In consequence, again, some firms and some industries, through no explicit intent of Congress, are subsidized by others, and by individual taxpayers and partnerships.

The data in Exhibit 79 illustrate these points.

EXHIBIT 79
Unequal impacts of the federal tax on corporate net income; *Manufacturing* corporations, 1971 (values in $ billions except as noted)

	Corporations with assets of $250 million or more		Corporations with net income and with assets reported at less than $10 million
	With net income	Without net income	
Numbers of firms	286	49	121,988
Assets	$383.0	$54.3	$39.4
Receipts	381.7	53.6	142.7
Income subject to tax, after deductions, etc.	26.3	–	6.7
Income tax, after credits, etc.	10.6	–	1.7
Net income (deficit) after tax	15.7	(1.6)	4.9
Income subject to tax, etc., as percent of receipts	6.9%	–	4.7%
Income tax as percent of income subject to tax	40.3%	–	25.4%
Income tax as percent of receipts . . .	2.8%	–	1.2%
Income tax as percent of assets	2.8%	–	4.3%
Income tax as percent of net worth	5.3%	–	4.7%
Percent of all federal income taxes after credits, etc; nonfinancial corporations	45.9%	–	7.4%
Average assets per firm	$1.3	$1.1	$1,169.8 thousands

Source: Exhibit 78.

Taxes and manufacturing corporations; example of unevennesses

Large manufacturing corporations *without* net income were just about as large, measured either by assets or receipts, as large manufacturing firms that did report a profit. And yet they paid no federal income tax. Firm for firm, profitable or not, all these large manufacturing companies benefited in varying ways and degrees from the various services and contributions to the System as a whole made by the federal government, and, also in varying degrees, had impacts upon the System. But the unprofitable bore none of the costs thereof.

On the average, each of the 49 largest unprofitable manufacturing firms was about 1,000 times as large as the average of the smaller profitable manufacturing firms, those with assets of less than $10 million. Whereas these 122,000 smaller, profitable manufacturing firms did pay federal income tax, the largest unprofitable did not, even though, firm for firm, they almost surely, in dollar terms, benefited directly and indirectly far more from services provided by the federal government and, again, had greater impacts on the encompassing System.

Although Congress can scarcely have had the explicit intent, the profitable largest manufacturing firms were taxed relatively more heavily than the smaller profitable manufacturing firms. Most notably, the income tax (net after credits) paid by the largest firms represented 40.3 percent of their income subject to tax (net after deductions), but only 25.4 percent of the income subject to tax of the smaller profitable corporations. In relation to receipts, the income tax paid by the largest profitable firms represented 2.8 percent; the income tax paid by the smaller firms represented 1.2 percent of receipts. On the other hand, although the largest profitable manufacturing firms held almost ten times the total value of the assets of the smaller firms, they paid only six times as much in federal income tax. This is a consequence of the more rapid capital turnover and associated lesser capital-intensivity of the smaller corporations.

If there were any *intended* differential impacts on relative abilities to generate and/or retain capital, and hence on dynamics of industry structures, as between the largest and the smallest profitable manufacturing companies, the rationale does not leap quickly to mind. Nor does any clear rationale appear as regards the distribution of the costs of providing services by the federal government.

Effective tax rates also vary widely among industries in mystifying ways. But that is another whole story.

*   *   *   *   *

So much for impacts of government tax policy on the corporate community, especially upon the growth of companies, large and small. Although providing specific incentives for corporations to grow larger, and more conglomerate, has been no explicit intent of national policy, such have, indeed, been important consequences of the ways we levy taxes on individuals and corporations. Although there may be interesting reasons for distributing the burdens of the costs of services supplied by the federal government in very different ways among large and small firms, among profitable and unprofitable firms, and among different industries, these scarcely account for the great differences that do, in fact, exist. In a word, the differences in impacts are largely unintended and capricious.

Again, it is well to recall that a majority of the odd consequences of the corporate net income tax work out into the economy at large through the nexus of large corporations.

A short digression on the value-added tax

This is also no place to enter the debate about substitutes for the capricious corporate net income tax and for the double taxation of corporate earnings, once in the hands of the corporations, and again in the hands of shareholders, if and when these earnings are distributed as dividends. There *are* ways of dealing with these matters, which have so seriously to do with the formation of capital and the structures of industry.

Details aside, the intent and the effect of a value-added tax is to distribute the costs of services provided by government among all corporations, large and small, profitable and unprofitable, and in whatever industries, roughly in proportion to all the other resources and inputs, aside from goods and services purchased from other corporations, they draw from the ambient System, and thereby add to the stream of national product as it flows through their conversion processes. If elements of subsidy and arbitrariness remain (and, depending on the politics and particulars of the specific tax, there would probably be some), they would be far less than now. The workings of free markets would have far greater impacts on the economy than they can now.

Double taxation of corporate earnings eats up a large share of the ability of the economy to create capital. It also results in allocations of capital that are only partly justified by prospective rates of return. It is possible to ameliorate both of these situations by eliminating the corporate income tax (having substituted a value-added tax) and levying upon corporations withholding taxes, at a flat and uniform rate, to correspond to some stipulated average fraction of the tax liability of shareholders for their equity in those earnings. In effect, these withholdings are not a tax on the corporation, as such, but upon the stockholders. These withholdings would be collected *whether or not* dividends were distributed. The individual shareholder, whether he received dividends or not, would receive tax credits on his individual return equal to his share in the withholdings. This would not necessarily affect the progressive taxation of individual incomes. Stockholders in higher tax brackets would pay taxes beyond their credits. Shareholders in lower brackets would also receive tax credits and, if these were greater than the taxes due from the individuals, they would receive refunds.

The value-added tax, together with withholding of, and credits for, taxes on stockholders' equity in corporate earnings, has several points in its favor. Such taxation could be a much more rational way of distributing the total tax burden and assessing the costs of government among all corporations. It would eliminate the double taxation of corporate earnings and, accordingly, promote some of the capital formation we badly need. It would reduce present artificial forces that have major impacts on capital allocation and corporate and industry structures.

The interest in, and the literature about, the impacts of taxation on the structure of industry, the composition of the Gross National Product, the formation and allocation of capital, and such matters, seem to be mounting in quantity and increasing in sophistication. With greater specific recognition of the centrality of very large corporations in the structure of industry and in the generation of production and income, their place and roles in the System will surely come in for much more, and more penetrating, explicit attention.[9]

LARGE CORPORATIONS AND ANTITRUST POLICY

As stated earlier, we have no national policy as to *large* corporations *as such*. Section 1 of the Sherman Act forbids "every contract or combination in the form of trust or otherwise, or conspiracy in restraint of trade or commerce among the several states, or with foreign nations. . . ." In principle, most Americans surely endorse this policy easily enough, and with little enough thought, even though each and every contract of every sort, ipso facto, limits the freedom of action of the contracting parties to deal with others. The section's categorical language would appear to close the door upon any pragmatic showing that *some* particular contracts or combinations *might* be socially desirable and in the public interest. But courts foresaw the possibility, and held that only *unreasonable* restraints were illegal. In any event, Section 1, it is clear, does not exempt *small* corporations from its effects. Subject to the escape hatch of "reasonableness," Section 1 outlaws conspiracies, large *or* small, that would affect interstate commerce. Europeans and Japanese, and their governments, on occasion find concerted corporate action to be in what those countries believe to be their national interest. In particular circumstances, they are quite prepared to find that cartels and other forms of mutual support enhance their national abilities to compete with firms of other nations and for business in foreign markets. Those businessmen and their governments find our very different policy strange and, happily for them, to their profit.

The Clayton Act as amended outlaws the acquisition by one corporation of the assets or the equity of another where such acquisition would substantially lessen competition in any line of commerce in any section of the country. On its face, this act would appear to relate to a *method* of growth—acquisitions and mergers—rather than to growth or to size, as such. Conceivably, the act impartially outlaws both the merger of the two blacksmiths of a village and the two largest automobile companies.

As matters presently stand, it is conceivable, under the Clayton Act, that *some* acquisitions or mergers may be found actually to *strengthen* competition, as when a corporation—especially one that is smaller than the largest in a given line of commerce—acquires and merges with one still smaller that is in danger of failing. But suits actually brought and cases decided do not hold out much hope for such findings; still less do they for mergers that would strengthen the ability of American firms to compete with foreign companies, either at home or abroad, or both.

As a matter of "pure logic," this portion of the Clayton Act does not seem necessarily to be concerned with size as such; but practically, the powers of the federal government are not *likely* to be turned upon small firms engaged in small lines of commerce and that, accordingly, are small relative to, say, the Largest 559, The 1,000, or, even the largest 2,000.

Section 2 of the Sherman Act, which is concerned with monopolizing or attempting to monopolize, is a different matter. A "monopoly," by its very nature and concept, is large *relative* to *something*— relative at least to that which is, or may be, monopolized. Accordingly, Section 2 does go to *size,* not necessarily to *absolute* size, but in any event to *relative* size. That size is relative to "any part of the trade or commerce among the several States or with foreign nations . . ." which any "person" (and that, of course, includes any corporation) may "monopolize" or "attempt to monopolize." The "any part of the trade or commerce" could be something very small, say the commerce in sauces made of a species of Capsicum pepper, or something sizable, like the trade or commerce in virgin aluminum ingot, computers, photographic equipment, soup or, say, automobiles or even ready-to-eat breakfast cereals.

It is in this very area that the ambiguity, the ambivalence, the irresolution of enunciated policy that reflects the uncertain will of the people as expressed through the authority of Congress stands out most clearly.

Presumably, but it is not all that sure, if a monopoly (which can be far less than 100 percent of a line of commerce or of a relevant market—say, 64 percent) has been achieved by dint of hard work, diligence, superior skill in research, design, fabrication, and in marketing, and not by brutality, artifice, unfair competition, predation, conspiracy or other deplorable behavior, it is not to be struck down. The law, *maybe,* will not be turned against the competitor who, having been encouraged, *as a matter of public policy,* to compete, and to compete energetically, not just casually, succeeds in gaining a preeminent position in the esteem and custom of buyers. But this is not certain.

After all, the basic rationale, the philosophical underpinning of a free and competitive society is that the individual consumer, the society at large, and even posterity will best be served by energetic competitive behavior of competitors. Nowhere is a word to be heard or found that all or any competitors are guaranteed success or even survival. Competition, according to this bracing, astringent philosophy, is not an Alice-in-Wonderland caucus race in which everyone at least gets a prize, if not a tie for first. No one has ever promised any competitor a rose garden. But, hold! There *are* concerns lest *competitors* be injured. Antitrust legislation runs to preserving *com-*

petition, a noun that bespeaks a *process* rather than structure; a process that is prized for the socially desirable benefits it brings about. But, query: "Can you have competition, a process, without competitors, a structure?" And should not the most energetic, diligent, skillful of competitors be restrained from competing *too well,* lest he "hurt" or even drive out competitors? Should the largest, or even a "large" competitor be required to compete gently? For, if *competitors* are hurt or driven out, or even unequally and seriously constrained, what will become of "competition"? Visible, clearly identifiable competitors, it is often assumed and supposed, are required for there to be competition. Are competitors to be protected in the interests of consumers?

Even that is not all. We are, we suppose, committed to a pluralistic, decentralized power structure. We want numbers of competitors to serve as checks and balances on each other, to assure diffusion of power throughout the society and economy. We are chary of power—especially of size combined with power. And there is more than a little standing to the thought expressed by judges that, even though Congress has never said so, We the People would rather have and preserve that pluralism, even though that might mean preserving competitors who are not the most efficient, not the most innovative, or responsive to the needs and desires of consumers, and whose continuation in business is really an economic drag.

One application of Section 2 of the Sherman Act does come very close, in effect, to striking at bigness as such and, accordingly, poses problems for large corporations and for the community as a whole. If a corporation has a "large" share (whatever that may be held to be) of a "relevant market" (however that may be defined by the individual judge—or jury—in a particular suit) could it stand in grave jeopardy of being found guilty of efforts to "monopolize" if it *behaves* as a *competitor?* If the company which has a "large," or "dominant," or two-thirds majority or greater share of a "relevant market" builds new, lower-cost plants; improves manufacturing methods; engages in research and development and introduces new products; develops new ways of making its products more useful, convenient or appealing or more readily available to consumers; reduces its prices—could it find these actions alleged and presented, and *accepted*—as evidence of *intent to monopolize?* The Aluminum Corporation of America, Kodak, and Xerox have found that the answer is Maybe or Yes. (Others, such as Clorox in its litigation with Purex, and I.B.M. in its case with Memorex, seem to have fared better.)[10]

The point, here, is that large companies that work hard to improve their products and services to customers; to better their terms of sale; to cut costs by installing new productive apparatus and better methods of production; to keep their prices down; to advertise to introduce new products that will create new demand—all such things that sound like *competition*—may find those actions categorized and castigated, to their astonishment and great cost, as *efforts to monopolize.*

Presumably, if a corporation in the considered opinion of a judge or a jury, gets to be "too big" in some particular context, as perceived and defined by him or them, it will find itself enjoined from behaving *as a competitor* lest it be found guilty of attempting to *monopolize.* Presumably, if it is to avoid being found guilty of attempts to monopolize, the firm will have to behave as a monopolist, instead, refraining from efforts to cut costs and prices and to give better terms and services to customers; refraining from improving their products and introducing new ones; from improving production technology and cutting costs; even if smaller competitors are doing such things and profiting thereby. Not only must the unhappy firm not take the initiative in such matters; it must not, it would appear, react as a competitor even when its smaller competitors are trying effectively to take business away from it.

The logic, here, is not at all that consumers are benefited by all this, but that *competitors* are! The ground for this seemingly non-Euclidean line of reasoning runs to the effect that Congress—so Judge Learned Hand inferred in the Alcoa case—was quite prepared to accept economic inefficiency and corporate irrationality in order to maintain larger numbers of relatively small, more or less evenly matched, even if inefficient, producers. A number of judges and juries have followed that line of reasoning—but not all.[11]

In courts, the issue is up in the air.

There, again, is the apparent dialectic: efficiency, in its broad sense, seemingly posed against pluralism and diffusion of power; economic values *versus* political values.

Taxes and antitrust

As has been pointed out, side effects of tax laws have been sources of major pressures on corporate growth. Double taxation of corporate earnings has been the source of major pressure toward "internal" growth through retention and reinvestment of corporate earnings. Internal growth has far overshadowed growth through mergers and acquisitions. The reorganization provisions of the Tax Code, which provide for tax-free treatment of gains from exchange of corporate equities, have certainly done as much, and probably more, to foster mergers and acquisitions as any other factor. Elimination of either or both of these tax provisions would do more to remove pressures toward corporate growth than any and all antitrust actions that might be taken to affect industry structures by the Department of Justice and Federal Trade Commission under present statutes and case law.

Accordingly, pursuit of antitrust objectives of slowing down corporate growth, whether internal or external, through amendment of tax law, might seem desirable from the point of view of committed "structuralists." As regards capital formation and conservation, however, those very results would be dreadful setbacks.

There is that wistful puzzler again: Is it possible for America to get the material necessities and benefits of modernity from an industry and economy based on small firms? Can't we have both? Is there no way to avoid a trade-off? The answers must be No.

There does promise to be a way out of this seeming dilemma. The economic horn may be seen to be blunted, if not clipped, once recognition is given to the realities of economies of scale, vertical integration and multiplant operations, systemwide competition among all sorts of substitute, alternative products of vying industries; and to the pervasiveness of longitudinal, dynamic facts that technological and economic progress and creative destruction of old ways, structures, and positions are more likely to come, as J. A. Schumpeter said almost 40 years ago, from large corporations than from the "ideal" shops of economically negligible little firms—the "pure" or "perfect" competitors.

The political horn of the dilemma may seem to be equally blunted when recognition is given to the reality that the large corporation is likely to be a particularly welcome and reliable ally of the individual as they both confront the enormous and almost ungovernable power of Big Government.

More of this in a moment.

Break-up

The idea of breaking up individual large corporations into numbers of smaller ones often appeals to people with misgivings about bigness. But there are problems. Legal problems presently standing in the way of wholesale dissolution suits by government or even private parties conceivably could be overcome by legislation. Technical problems are tougher. Many large production units simply cannot be divided up: they are integrated, almost organic systems of which individual elements can have no separate existence.

An ultimate problem is even tougher. For instance: the Standard Oil Company (New Jersey), now Exxon, in 1971 had assets of $20.3 billion. If broken up into as many as 80 units—let us forget any technical problems about breaking up large refinery complexes into separately owned and operated units—each and every new company could have been big enough to be on the 1971 list of The Largest Corporations, that is, of companies with assets at more than $250 million.

According to similar "meat-ax" arithmetic, United States Steel Corporation could have been broken up into 25 companies, each of which, in terms of simple dollar numbers, would still have been on the list. General Motors, arithmetically speaking, was the equal of 70 companies that could have made the list; Boeing, a mere 10 companies. American Telephone & Telegraph was the equivalent of *200* corporations that, individually, could make the list.

Blithely and simplistically assuming that, in any real sense, the 30 largest petroleum companies of 1971 could be broken up even into as many as 420 companies, *each of which,* hypothetically, could still make the list of The Largest, practical questions cannot be avoided as to whether, and in what sense, their behavior would be more competitive. And whether this more competitive behavior would result in more optimum investment, capacity utilization, more and/or better research and development, lower costs and prices, and all the rest. It is not easy to see that the answer would be Yes.

The same conceptual and practical difficulties arise in the case of every one of the major industries characterized by the occurrence and presence of very large companies.

As a developing nation, to repeat, we have moved through history into a new and different era. The ideological and hypothetical models of the past are dead of meaning. Memories of them haunt us.

No doubt, without going so far, it would be *possible,* through a policy of break-up, to create *more* companies. It is not in the cards in any practical sense that dissolution could lead to *small* companies.

Technical questions aside, as to simple physical feasibility of breaking up complex production systems, latter-day Trust Busters stand before profound policy questions as to whether and how much the American people are prepared to forego economies of scale, of integration, of capital-intensivity, of multiplant and multiproduct systems, of technology-intensivity. As was pointed out earlier in great detail, through *large* companies, *very* large companies—large organizations, in any case—is the *only* way many modern goods and services can be produced and made available *at all.*

THE LARGE CORPORATION, A MODERN INSTITUTION OF THE MODERN ORDER

Legal theories aside, the large corporation in America has become, in fact, an institution "affected," or "clothed," however lightly, with the public interest.

Early on, the business corporation was conceived to be a creature of the sovereign or of a legislature (as a successor to sovereign power), brought into being and existing at its pleasure. By mid-19th century, however, following the landmark case of *Dartmouth College* v. *Woodward* (1819), and in the course of enactment of "free incorporation" statutes by the states, the corporation had come to be an entity endowed with an existence of its own and well-nigh indefeasible, substantially beyond the reach of government. But concepts as to the independence of the corporation became too absolute; pressures developed for constraining their freedom of action. Court opinions and decisions since *Munn* v. *Illinois* (1877), including Supreme Court decisions in *Stone* v. *Farmer's Loan and Trust Co.* (1886) and in *Charles Wolff Packing Co.* v. *Court of Industrial Relations of the State of Kansas* (1923), have sought to describe, often with confusing language and results, the responsibilities and obligations, as well as the privileges and immunities, of corporations.

Under law, it is now clear that business corporations are, at least, not the free-wheeling, socially irresponsible entities they once seemed to be, or threatened to become. Now, at law and in fact, more than mere private enterprises, they are *institutions* with lives of their own and with rights and privileges, and immunities, but restrained by obligations and responsibilities, much like unto natural persons. But they *are* institutions, not "persons"; "private," they are, but not quite private; "public" in a sense, but not public. In any event, because large corporations and their workings *are* central to the wellbeing, to the very survival of the entire community, they are, inevitably, "affected with" and "affected by," and they most manifestly do affect the public interest.

Many implications flow from that set of facts.

Corporate morality

The concept of the modern business corporation continues to evolve—through greater vision and sensitivity on the part of some leaders in the business community, through statutes, administrative regulations, and litigation, both public and private. The responsibilities of corporations, and of their directors and managers, have increased and are increasing; their freedom of action has been curtailed. Whether these changes have affected just the right spheres of action, and no others, in just the right way and, whether, in a welter of specifics, emergent standards are now too high or not yet high enough, need not detain us here. They have happened. They are happening.

In a generalizing shorthand, one can say that the social expectations as to corporate behavior are now closely analogous to those prevailing as to other important private institutions—for instance, universities, hospitals, and foundations: the expectations are that in ideal, if not practical, terms, they will be managed with competence; with honesty, responsibility, and prudence; with adherence to law; with circumspection, dignity, and propriety; and with a decent respect for the welfare, as well as the opinions of mankind—all to a level short of infallibility.

The paradigm of acceptable behavior by large corporations and their directors and managers is no longer the freebooting, self-seeking, rugged individualists of two or three generations ago.

Corporations that do not learn this lesson willingly and on their own are likely to learn it unwillingly at the behest of some outside agency, as through stockholder derivative suits and class actions, for example, or through government action.

Corporate values

Corporations and their leaders are not likely to gain great credibility, nor open-minded interest on the part of the community in their problems if they appear insensitive to humane values and purposes. William Blake, at the beginning of the 19th century, wrote of the "dark Satanic mills" of industry, and millions still sing of the "New Jerusalem" that is to be built *despite* the business community. The no-doubt humane and sensitive management of a well-known and well-run company, in 1978, still proclaims that the corporate purpose is "to provide a good return to its stockholders." Period. No other purpose; no larger framework of decision-making. Such talk of a self-denigrating, simplistic, unitary sense of identity, let alone corporate action based on such a simplistic lodestone of policy will not do.

In all truth, some corporations have been, and some still are, run with no great regard for the shared, upward-looking values of the American community—with no great concern, that is, for the physical environment, for the dignity of employees, for candor in discourse, for example. In fact, corporations, no less than individuals, are multifaceted. They have little reason to place themselves in an undeserved poor light: they do have reason to *be* and to let their actions say that they are "good societies" in a benevolent nation.[12]

The little foxes

Besides getting into difficulties because of indiscreet and unlawful actions of top-level executives, major corporations have found themselves in trouble, sometimes grave, because of doings of middle- and even lower-level managers. Their transgressions have involved bribery of officials at home and abroad; bribery of employees, of customers, and suppliers; conspiracy among salespeople of competitors to rig prices and bidding procedures; negligence in following and supervising safety and environmental-protection practices. People down in the organization who get involved in such matters, are modern-day little foxes that spoil the vines and their tender grapes.

Often, such actions have been in direct contravention of explicit policies laid down by boards and chief executives. In large organizations where thousands of labor-days of human behavior take place every day, usually in many different locations, it is clearly not possible to monitor every action, every movement, of every person. Management can work to eliminate internal pressures that make undesired behaviors seem relevant to people down in the organization; enunciate clearly and repeatedly what corporate policies are in such matters; monitor as best as may be (which may not be a great deal) activities susceptible of monitoring and auditing; administer appropriate and prompt discipline, including discharge, in instances of violation.

Even after all such things are done, deplorable incidents may still happen. Lapses from grace and acts of the Old Adam are about as likely to occur within the corporation as elsewhere in the human condition.

Some corporations have learned to their sorrow how much trouble they can get into through individual, ill-advised actions far down in the organization.

The governance of corporations

Until recently, what went on inside corporations and how they were run—as contrasted to what they did—were not widely thought of as matters of community concern. But that is history. In implicit recognition of the important institutional nature, role, and consequence of the corporation, various legal and communal sanctions are now in place that constrain the *governance,* beyond the behavior, of the corporation.

For instance, the Financial Accounting Standards Board, the American Institute of Public Accountants, and the New York Stock Exchange have joined with the Securities Exchange Commission to prescribe the contents of financial disclosures by corporations and acceptable means of valuing revenue, cost, and balance-sheet items. Pressures are developing to constrain corporations in the design of their management information and control systems, even the organization for designing and operating those systems.

Numerous official and unofficial pressures are operating on boards of directors and managements to nominate and select directors who are utterly independent of the management of the corporation and of each other, and with no actual, and presumably, no potential conflict of interest with the corporation. This sort of pressure is making for committees composed exclusively of "outside" members for dealing with compensation; with nomination of directors and key executives; with supervision of the auditing and publication of the corporation's financial and other material information. More subtle pressures are urging corporations in the direction of obtaining demographically representative boards.

Stockholders' derivative suits and class actions by parties and groups allegedly affected by corporate actions seek, in effect, to impose standards of responsibility upon directors and managers that would go far beyond the traditional norms of what was to be expected of prudent men and women.

Equal-opportunity legislation and administration of such statutes stemming from evolving community sentiments as to individual rights, and very real possibilities of injunctive and punitive litigation, now constrain the freedom of managers to hire, fire, retire, assign, promote, and pay whom they choose and how. Civil rights now follow the individual through the doors, right on to the factory floor and into the offices.

All this is to be expected. More is surely yet to come. And it all follows on from the fact that the corporation has left behind in history its status of *private* enterprise and now has become an institution. The "letter" of many of these growing constraints is truly suffocating, often offends common sense, and is sometimes scarcely more than hostile and punitive. But their "spirit" can be basically in harmony with the corporation's own interest: if the corporation is to be a moral, democratic force in the political system, of course it will have to operate with due regard for communal values and aspirations. Some corporations, it does seem, need a bit of encouragement of a "stick behind" to help them line themselves up on the side of the angels.

It really is too bad, just the same, that Congress, the President, the courts do not give to bureaucrats and other public custodians and censors the admonition that the old Bishop gave to the newly ordained young priests: "Above all, not too much zeal!"

Corporations, no doubt, are flattered by all the attention; but they will be understood if, like the man in Lincoln's story who was being ridden out of town on a rail, they feel, "If it wasn't for the honor, I'd just as soon walk."

Separation of state and corporation

Unforeseen by the Founding Fathers was the possibility that, as freestanding independent institutions, business corporations, labor unions, and other private corporate entities might emerge as additional Estates, along with Church and Press, counterpoised across from the power of government in our constitutional system of checks and balances. The potential beneficent effect of such a development in our system of checks and balances is contingent upon steadfastly guarded independence and separation between government and independent institutions in a fashion analogous to the independence and separation of church and state, of press and state. In our time, separation of state and corporation, of state and labor union, of state and university, of state and hospital, of state and party, have become as important as the separation between church and state, and press and state, laid down by the Founding Fathers and the legislatures of the original 13 states, when they adopted the First Amendment to our Constitution.

If one or the other of these independent institutions loses credibility and public support or becomes moribund; if formerly counterpoised institutions fuse, or when one captures another, the system of checks and balances is seriously impaired, institutions become politicized and even weapons of special interests; the integrity of the individual and the family and of other institutions come under peril; democracy, itself, is in danger of extinction. We have seen this in our own time, in Spain, Germany, Iran, Italy, Russia, China, Libya, and in—how many?—Latin American and African countries.

The individual and the community at large, as well as business corporations, themselves, have a great stake in the enhancement and preservation of the independence, credibility, and acceptability of the corporation as an institution. Government, history shows too clearly and painfully, is not necessarily and inherently benign. On the contrary, as with other forms of power, unchecked political power, whether exercised by tyrant, dictatorship, or vast bureaucracy with a life of its own, inevitably devolves into oppression. With strong credibility and a high level of acceptability in the community, the corporation, along with other independent institutions, can stand at very least as a moral counterpoise to the growing mass and powers of government. In the absence of such standing and repute, not only does the corporation, itself, become vulnerable to thrusting political power, the individual and the community as a whole, including other institutions, are deprived of a potential champion against ever-present threats of obtrusion by government into their lives and actions.[13]

Much has been written, and properly so, about the dangers of actual or threatened capture by the corporation of the state or components thereof, such as legislatures, courts, or executive agencies. Such capture, of course, violates the treasured separation and leaves the community open to corporate predation.

Less has been said of the dangers of capture of the corporation by the state. We see consequences of such enthrallment, however, in the decay and degeneration of the railroads, for example, and in widespread consumption and dissipation of capital and sapping of managerial energy and imagination among our public utilities. One of our presidents, a military man himself, warned us of dangers of the mutual confusion, if not simple and sophisticated corruption, inherent in the fusion of state and corporation manifested by mutual dependency in the military-industrial complex.

For many reasons, expediency of one kind or another often seems to suggest the desirability of using resources and authority of government to bail out, or to give special advantage to, this or that company or even whole industry, or simply to take over and "nationalize."[14] Whatever the specifics, when this happens, a corporation or cluster of corporations that was independent becomes beholden; beholden for its very life on instruments of government directed by, and in the interests of political power. Private power withers; political power waxes. Without a need to point fingers at woeful recent examples in the United States or at state-run enterprises abroad, it is clear that this collapsing and fusing of powers and interests inherently carries potentials for all manner of hard-to-discover, and even harder-to-correct abuses.

We have seen what happens when the state captures the church, the university, the union, the hospital. The prospect of gaining access to public monies and/or public power is an ever-present temptation to those who might better be zealous to maintain the integrity of their institutions. The possibility of getting access to the public purse without paying a price in terms of dependency always seems great, at first. When independence is lost, the priceless quality of separation and of checks and balances of powers stands out all too clearly.

The same is true of corporations and industries. The price of accepting special treatment or acquiring the status of "chosen instrument" is likely to prove a Faustian bargain, resulting in a figurative and maybe a literal "loss of soul." The point of this is to illustrate the importance of the corporation, not just as an economic institution, but as a part of our underlying political system.

Disenchantment with consequences of failure to preserve separation of state and corporation seems to have led to a surge of interest and support for deregulation and to frequently expressed desire for more reliance on competition, free of government meddling, for protection of the public interest. Our very tentative effort to depoliticize the Post Office seems to be in line with the development.

Two conditions have to be met if the corporation, again like any other institution, is to fulfill its potential as a promising component of our political system. Its legitimacy has to be credible. It has to be vital.

If the corporation is to enhance its status as a legitimate and respected institution, it must, like any other institution, appear with clean hands in the court of public regard and trust. Fortunately, most do, most of the time. Unfortunately, we have seen exceptions. If corporations are to be regarded as worthy institutions, companies that have engaged in questionable and illegal practices will have to repudiate and have done with secret accounts, political slush-funds, covert operations, and domestic and worldwide bribery and corruption. Those businessmen who, for dark purposes, skulk around the world with satchels of currency, and who pass out large undocumented sums to grafters gravely harm the respect and credibility an institution must have if it is to be effective in the complex political system of our democracy.

VIABILITY OF CORPORATIONS

To be operative in our system of checked and balanced powers, any institution has to *be*. It has to be viable. Vital. And so it is with corporations.

At every step of the way, from initiation through years of operation, evolution, and transformation, the corporation is affected with, and affects interests of the community: *Economically,* through payroll and purchases; through property, social security and other taxes; through interest payments and dividends. *Politically,* through power to allocate resources in response to market realities and pressures rather than in accord with ideology and demagoguery. With "voice" with which to express views, independent, and perhaps momentarily unpopular, as to public policy. With resources and well-wishers to defend its own against other interests. A population of viable, vital corporations, as is true of other institutions, is a more reliable and effective counterpoise to other powers and in dynamic tension with them, than one with a shaky grasp on its own existence.

The basic *raison d'être* of the corporation is to *produce,* to serve needs for goods and services, at the moment and into the future. To do this, to survive, every corporation has to compete for resources in input markets with all others, and with public sector and nonprofit entities, as well: for labor, for capital, for materials, for space, for management, for services, for knowledge. It has to compete for customers and revenues, not only with other corporations of its own species, but with others outside its own genus. And in market places, as in environments of nature, competition among different species or even different forms of life is far more lethal and far more decisive as regards survival than competition within species; it is literally a matter of life and death, not of mere differences in profitability.

At the same time, a corporation must design a human and mechanical apparatus that will gather in and convert inputs into desired outputs and distribute them; all this effectively and efficiently.

As a living entity existing in a complex community, a corporation has to relate itself effectively to many other and very different kinds of entities also present: labor unions, suppliers, distributors, bankers, trade associations, stock exchanges, regulatory agencies, and individuals presenting themselves in the market for human services.

A corporation has to do all this successfully, not only every moment, but over time, over spans of time at least long enough to amortize tangible and intangible investments.

466

In an era of change of every sort, a corporation has, further, to evolve, to adapt, to engage in a continuous process of transformation in every component, in every element of its very being: its hardware, its software, its management, its many arrangements with other entities—its very nature and identity.

To do all this and to survive over time, a corporation has to defray all of its costs, recoup all of its investments, and have enough left over to amount to a competitively satisfactory return on risk equity.

Making all this come to pass is the responsibility of the corporation's directors and management. In all truth, not all corporations do so with any great success. Some, far from being overaggressive, have been far too content with things as they are and with mediocre returns.

At the same time, the political atmosphere for many years has not been greatly concerned with the health of the corporate community. To some extent, this has been out of benign neglect; to some extent, out of failure to understand the workings of the corporation and the sanctions to which it is exposed in its daily life; to some extent, perhaps, this has stemmed from innate hostility of political institutions to other institutions in the system of checks and balances.

For all such and whatever reasons, the corporate community as a whole, far from moribund, has nevertheless been less flourishing than it might well have been as a major source of impetus in the economy. This is an enormous topic in its own right, and contentious; but a few life-signs serve to raise significant questions.

Corporate vitality

Early in 1964, the Dow-Jones Index of 30 Industrial stock prices, a widely used measure, stood at about 800. At the close of 1977, 14 years later, the index stood at about 840. (At the end of 1978, it stood at about 805.) Between 1964 and 1977, the earnings on this Dow-Jones "portfolio" of stocks of the 30 largest corporations increased at a compound average annual growth rate of about 5 percent—in current, inflated dollars! The dividends from this sample "portfolio" increased at a compound average annual growth rate of about 2.6 percent.[15]

Over those same years, the all-items Consumer Price Index, the all-commodities Wholesale Price Index, and the Gross National Product price deflator, all three, about doubled, or a trifle less, rising at an average annual compound rate of about 5.48 percent.

Had the Dow gone up in the same proportions, it would have stood at something around 1,680 at the end of 1977.

The Gross National Product (in current dollars) from 1964 to

1977 increased from $635.7 billion to $1,887.2 billion, rising at a compound average growth rate of 8.73 percent. The real rate of growth in constant dollars was 3.08 percent; the rest of the apparent growth was due to inflation. Over these same years, corporate profits (also in current dollars), as estimated by the Department of Commerce, grew from $67.0 billion to $144.2 billion, increasing at a compound average growth rate of 6.07 percent.

If, over those years, corporate profits had increased at just the same rate as the GNP (8.73 percent), they would have amounted to almost $200 billion in 1977; the shortfall in failing to keep up with the GNP amounted in that one year to about $60 billion. Over the 13 years 1964-77, corporate profits, expressed in 1977 dollars, totalled about $1,750 billion. If, over those years, profits had merely kept up with GNP, they would have come, instead, to a total of about $2,300 billion of 1977 dollars. That shortfall of about $550 billion in 1977 dollars came to over 30 percent of profits acually realized; no mean figure![16]

In such terms as these, corporate returns on equity not only did not participate fully in the real growth of the economy; they did not even keep up with inflation. And yet, the president of the United States and other well-intentioned people decry, in abrasive strictures, what are only mythical exorbitant, "obscene," "immoral" profits. They should look at the record!

Managers of pension and trust funds, individual investors, and financial commentators are all too well acquainted with the mournful numbers; they know that capital gains and dividends that even keep up with inflation, let alone the growth of the GNP, occur most often in dreams.

The time has come, some time since, for a lull in the demogogic beating of old Populist tom-toms. What we greatly need, instead, is objective examination of the functioning of our economy; factors affecting the generation of income and wherewithal with which to implement national objectives; the formation of capital; the allocation of our resources; implementable national priorities; and concern with the relationship between the health of the economy and the health of our democratic political and social system.

RESULTS—THE PRAGMATIC SANCTION OF MANAGEMENT

The sanction of law and usage under which managers of small and family businesses run things is still the authority that goes with ownership. Directors and executives of The Largest Corporations, even collectively, rarely own more than a very small fraction of the equity of the entity for which they are responsible. The sanction under which they get position, operate, and stay in office is increasingly a very practical one: ability to produce *results*.

That sounds simple. But getting results, maintaining corporate vitality, and retaining the sanction to continue in managerial authority has become for directors and executives a far more complicated matter than it used to be, and more burdensome. To do that, and beyond that, the managers of our large companies now must deal with new issues scarcely imagined by their predecessors in office. Now, for most large corporations, the major preoccupation is the management of continuous adaptation to an environment characterized by surging technological, economic, political, and social changes, pressures, and altogether new opportunities. Especially are directors and executives finding themselves cast in the role of *magistrates* of institutions of public moment, judged according to new and evolving societal expectations, having little enough to do with ability to produce goods and services, wages and salaries, and profits.

To get results for a large corporation in such circumstances is sufficiently difficult that it must be a source of wonder that managements do as well as they do. Even the definition of results has undergone a sea-change that would astound the managers of an earlier generation.

New issues

New issues emerge on every hand. They relate to the relationships of corporations to employees; to stockholders; to managers and directors, themselves; to the financial community; to the physical environment; to customers; to concerned citizen groups of all sorts; to politics and the political process—just for example. The list could run on. Relationships with employees have changed and are changing dramatically. The civil rights movement, as mentioned earlier, has come *into* the corporation: equal opportunity in getting jobs; in assignments and transfers; in pay; in promotion; in retirement; in safety. Rights to information about job hazards, conditions of employment, compensation and benefit plans, retirement plans. Rights to being dealt with according to company *policy*—akin to "due process" and "equal protection"—rather than according to judgment and individual circumstances. Rights to safety. Increasing rights to job and wage security. Perhaps soon, *rights* to job-enrichment.

At every turn and every day, new issues arise in these connections as to how, specifically, matters and persons are to be dealt with: should women be denied assignment to higher-paid jobs that entail sex-specific hazards? Should seniority give way to affirmative action?

Stockholders were once quiet and quiescent. A few well-known gadflies showed up at annual meetings. Now, new issues are arising in consequence of government rulings, litigation, and community pressure as to proper subject matters for stockholder concern; as to methods of representation of minority views; as to stockholder participation in policy-making. For instance, cases have arisen where groups of stockholders have sought to persuade managements to withdraw from South Africa; perhaps we shall see moral concern as regards doing business in iron curtain countries, The People's Republic of China, and dozens of other nations notorious for suppression of human rights. Individual and groups of stockholders are seeking to place a variety of policy questions on annual proxies, and to influence in specific ways the selection of directors. Again, all this raises new issues of substantive policy and as to corporate governance.

New issues are arising as to disclosure—what is to be disclosed, in what form, and how the information is to be arrived at. One currently controversial issue along these lines relates to whether and how corporations should estimate profits, taking into account replacement costs of depreciable assets. Another relates to whether and how corporations should disclose forecasted operating and financial data.

Another couple of examples.

Boards and managers face a growing cluster of issues connected with risk management: Considering possible risks, should certain products be introduced or withdrawn? Apart from dollars-and-cents issues, assuming risk insurability (which is often uncertain), questions arise as to whether the game is worth the candle in such terms as possible treatment in the press, if all does not go well, and distractions of inquiry and potential litigation.

Legal means exist whereby a corporation can make known the opinions of the board and management on existing and proposed legislation and regulation and as to candidates for elected office. Knotty issues of principle and practice arise as to whether and how these means should be used.

The list of new issues confronting directors and managers could go on and on. The point is that management, now, is far, far more than merely the applied technology of running a business for tangible and economic results.

Managing transformation in a world of change

It seems the world used to stay in place longer than it does now. It now seems that, in simpler times, once an enterprise was set up and going, the firm could be operated for years on end with only occasional adjustments. Managing, it now seems, was all but synonymous with running ongoing operations; results were defined largely in terms of the technical and economic efficiency with which the assets and resources in place were used. For many years, now, and indefinitely into the future, the environment has changed and will be changing so greatly and so rapidly that the management of *change*—transformation—rather than of operations, is coming to be the major preoccupation of directors and top managers.[17]

Even elements of the physical component of the environment of the corporation change. Some of our basic, bellwether industries, like steel and nonferrous metals, historically were based upon some of the world's richest mineral deposits. The comparative advantage this gave was enormous; but, now, other nations have at least as good, if not better, more extensive, and better located, resources than we. With our great rivers, it never occurred to an earlier generation that lack of water could be a constraint to industry; but that is now the case in certain regions of the country. On the other hand, improved transport and communications have shrunk the physical dimensions of the business environment, in terms of cost, and have opened up access and opportunities at home and abroad, previously beyond economic reach.

Up until World War I, one of our great comparative advantages was a rapidly increasing labor force of poorly educated but relatively low-cost and willing immigrants. Now, our labor-cost per hour is one of the world's highest. But, no country has a better-educated, more responsible, and responsive population, ready and eager to cope with advanced technologies of every sort, and ever reaching out for new services, new products. The rapidly changing attitudes, values, wants, occupational preferences, and locations of this now urban and industrial population pose new problems for corporations, both on the production and marketing sides of their business. But in those changes are implicit new worlds of opportunity.

The culture of America not so long ago was agrarian in its coloration and was rural in its outlook. Now, it is industrial and urban, with a strong and growing strain of advancing technology. The economic, social, and political expectations and *demands* of men and women and ethnic minorities are rising and becoming homogeneous. These are sources of constraints upon business; but they are also sources of great new opportunities in what can be produced, and how, and what can be sold.

Every business is surrounded not only with competitors for inputs and for sales but with eager suppliers of a growing and amazing array of services, parts, components, and equipment. All of these make possible the performance of tasks and the production and sale of an expanding universe of outputs that, not long ago, were scarcely imaginable.

The systemic evolution of the environment of the corporation renders obsolescent every single aspect of its workings, its inputs, and their sources; its productive facilities and production processes; its technologies; its organization; its perspectives and ways of thinking; its products and services; its marketing. The only question is how rapid is the obsolescence in each particular. On the other hand, more new opportunities are opening up in every aspect of the business for economies and profits. If one corporation does not respond to these negative and positive stimuli, plenty of others may, or will.

Altogether, these changes place corporations under continuing and gathering pressures to engage in constant quest for successful adaptations in everything they do and how they do it. And that is why it is that management of *transformation,* not mere management of operation, now has to be the focal concern of directors and top managers.[18]

It is painfully clear from various sorts of indicia that many major corporations seem to be headed by people who are not greatly responsive to this new imperative.

The new magistrates[19]

Webster's defines "magistrate," in part, as "a person clothed with power, as a public civil officer; a public civil officer invested with executive or judicial powers...." Except for the word "public," the term magistrate applies easily enough to the heads of corporate governments. And even the word public is not really astray. Noted earlier was the fact that, in an operational sense, our large corporations *are* "public"; not, indeed, in the legal sense of being *owned* by the state, but in the operational sense of being institutionalized instrumentalities of production that greatly affect the public interest and weal. Commentators, especially dedicated critics of business, point out that a number of our *very* large corporations have more employees and stockholders—direct "constituents," so to say—than some of our less populated states, and more assets than the total assessed value of real property in those states; in such terms, some corporations are larger than many members of the United Nations. Although the intention of these critics is not altogether friendly in making these observations, they are not entirely wrong.

In all truth, the directors and executives of our large corporations do have authority and do exercise great powers. Their decisions affect directly, well or ill, large numbers of employees and their families; only somewhat less directly, the communities where those families live; indirectly, the entire economy.

The pragmatic sanction upon which that authority and those powers rest depends, in turn, upon the ability of these leaders of the corporation to produce *results:* to maintain the viability of the corporation, its healthy functioning; to cope with all sorts of new issues in precedent-setting ways; to set new kinds of goals and objectives and to oversee continuous processes of transformation that will direct the evolution of the corporation in successful adaptation to its changing environment.

The results demanded are manifold, for many purposes must be served, many constraints observed, many expectations fulfilled.

Directors and managers will be greatly helped, in seeking such results, to the extent that they remain aware of the public nature of their role and to the extent that they remain aware of the deeply rooted ambivalent and ambiguous feelings Americans have about bigness and power. People who are sanctioned leaders of large corporations need also to bear in mind that these large organizations *are* institutions; that, although they are indeed essential engines of plenty, engines of growth, engines of change, they are also powerful and fearsome. This awareness should work as a useful constraint, discipline, and inspiration.

NOTES

1. *United States* v. *United States Steel Corporation,* 251 U.S. 417 (1920).

2. See, e.g., *The Energy Antimonopoly Act of 1979* (S.1246) and *The Small and Independent Business Protection Act* (S.600).

   Some of the bills, as mentioned, reflect particular concerns related to corporate size in energy, as in coal and oil and gas, and in other natural resources. Running throughout are detectable populist yearnings for a never-never, "good" industrial structure composed of myriads of *small* entities.

3. Italics added; op. cit., p. vii.

   Of course, it's desirable, at any given time, to maintain full employment of the American people, and full utilization of its productive apparatus—if those goals can be achieved without harmful side-effects such as surging inflation and suppression of saving and investment. More important, is maintaining *growth* of production *over time* to provide for a growing population and growing workforce with rising individual and collective needs, and maintaining industrial *development* and *technological change* in the interest of increasing productivity and economic and commercial strength in international competition. But on such matters, Keynes' *General Theory* . . . was silent, nor have they been of great interest to his followers.

4. Conceiving of the world in a static, "cross-section" mode leads even intelligent, well-meaning people into foolishness that flies in the face of histories and facts of *system development* of nations around the world for over these past hundred years. See, Lester C. Thurow; *The Zero-Sum Society* (New York: Basic Books, 1980); e.g., "Only seldom is economic growth a process without losers"; or, again, "To increase investment, someone's share of the national product must decline." (Op. cit., pp. 22 and 77.)

5. Federal Trade Commission, Bureau of Economics, *Statistical Report on Mergers and Acquisitions,* November 1977, Tables 14 and 26, et passim.

6. The "go-go," euphoric enthusiasm in the 1960s, even on the part of supposedly sophisticated investors, for the stocks of actively acquiring "conglomerates" had roots in the simple arithmetic fact that the reported *earnings* per share of an acquiring company will increase if its price-earnings ratio is greater than that of an acquired company. Expansive, aggressive conglomerates of those years could, and did, sustain a pattern of increasing reported earnings per share, quarter by quarter, year by year, for considerable periods of time largely through the fact of a continuing flow of appropriately designed acquisitions.

   These apparently increasing earnings were enough to cause many investors to bid up the prices of the stocks of these conglomerates. The rising prices often resulted in still higher price-earnings ratios that made it even easier to engineer further acquisitions. And so it went—for a while.

   The end of the line was reached. Companies could not go on acquiring others forever. Investors came to see through the financial legerdemain. The price-earnings ratios of the stocks of many conglomerates collapsed; market prices of their shares fell by as much as 90 percent, or even more.

   Another lesson had been taught—at least to many of that generation—that there is no such thing as a free lunch.

7. Although written a decade ago, an outstanding study of conglomerates remains that of Harry J. Lynch: *Financial Performance of Conglomerates* (Boston: Harvard Graduate School of Business Administration, 1971). This study did concentrate on some of the

more notably successful, and "aggressive" and "acquisitive" of the conglomerates. Another work of lasting value is that of Jesse W. Markham, *Conglomerate Enterprise and Public Policy,* also published by the Division of Research of the Harvard Business School (1973). Professor Markham demonstrated that the rise of conglomerates conspicuous in the Sixties had little effect on the structures of industries. See pp. 167-71.

8 Mergers and acquisitions are delicate enough simply because of human problems of executives and boards, the complexity of financial bargaining and arrangements, problems of publicity and disclosure, and the need for speed in consummation of transactions. Companies that have gotten into antitrust problems, as well, have found themselves in very difficult and embarrassing circumstances. Unless the stakes are very high, indeed, and the probabilities great that possible litigation can be won within a reasonable time, companies are careful to give potential Section 7 and Section 2 problems a wide berth.

9. A few items of the literature are listed below, in chronological order:

Tax Institute Symposium, 1950, *Taxation and Business Concentration* (Princeton: Tax Institute, Inc., 1952).

Clara K. Sullivan, *The Tax on Value Added* (New York: Columbia University Press, 1965).

Joseph A. Pechman, *Federal Tax Policy,* rev. ed. (Washington, D.C.: The Brookings Institute, 1971).

Dan T. Smith et al., *What You Should Know about the Value Added Tax* (Homewood, Illinois: Dow Jones-Irwin, Inc., 1973).

Richard W. Lindholm, *Value-Added Tax and Other Tax Reforms* (Chicago: Nelson-Hall, Inc., 1976).

Price Waterhouse, *Value Added Tax* (New York: Price Waterhouse, 1979).

10. See, for instance, *United States* v. *Aluminum Co. of America,* 148 F. 2d 416 (2d Cir. 1945); *Berkey Photo Inc.* v. *Eastman Kodak Company,* 457 F. Supp. 404 (S.D.N.Y. 1978); *SCM Corp.* v. *Xerox Corp.* (1978-2) 5 Trade Reg. Rep. (CCH) 62, 392 (D. Conn. 1978); *Purex Corp., Ltd.* v. *Proctor and Gamble Co.,* 419 F. Supp. 931 (C.D. Cal. 1976) appeal to the 9th circuit. *However,* since this was written, the U.S. Court of Appeals for the Ninth Circuit in the month of May 1979 has remanded the Clorox-Purex case back to the District Court to consider the possibility raised in *Greyhound Computer Corp.* v. *International Business Machines Corp.,* 559 F. 2d 488 (9th Circuit, 1977), "that 'otherwise lawful practices that unnecessarily excluded competition' could be actionable under (Section 2 of the Sherman Act) when used by the dominant firm in an industry." The District Court had found that Clorox had done nothing after being acquired by Proctor & Gamble that it had not done before. But the Circuit Court held that: "Clorox's position was significantly different before and after the acquisition. After the merger, even *relatively innocuous competitive acts could become actionable* if the impact of those acts reduced competition by raising entry barriers and by dissuading smaller firms from aggressive competition." (Italics added.)

No matter how you slice that, what the Circuit Court is saying, in effect, is that there *are* different standards of lawful behavior for small and large firms: large firms may not respond *even innocuously* even if *small* firms compete aggressively, lest the smaller firms be injured. In other words, large companies should stand impassive and unresponsive, like entrenched monopolists, while small competitors take their business away from them.

If this is what Congress intends Section 2 of the Sherman Act to mean, it could now affirm that the policy of the American people is that *large* corporations should compete no more than innocuously, if at all! If that is not the intent, now is a good time for our Representatives and Senators to speak up!

I.L.C. Peripherals Leasing Corp. v. *IBM,* 458 F. Supp. 423 (N.D. Cal. 1978) (known as *"Memorex* v. *IBM";* two cases joined together); *United States* v. *E. I. Du Pont de Nemours & Co.* (Cellophane) 351 U.S. 377 (1956); *United States* v. *Grinnell Corporation,* 384 U.S. 463 (1966). In contrast to the Ninth Circuit Court, as cited above, and illustrating the present disarray of antitrust policy, stands the recent finding of Administrative Law Judge Miles Brown in an action brought by the Federal Trade Commission against *E. I. Du Pont de Nemours & Co.* This action charged that the company had attempted to *monopolize* the market for titanium dioxide, a widely used white pigment. In some ways, this was a re-run of the Alcoa case.

Du Pont, among other things, it was said, had developed plans for vigorous growth through large-scale expansion of plant capacity; the company had followed an aggressive, but not specifically "predatory," low-price policy. The defendant had developed its own production technology, which, as it was perfected, gave it a significant, even decisive, advantage cost over rivals.

Generally such a corporate strategy would be regarded as desirably *competitive. Competition,* it would seem, is supposed to work like that. But if a company is *big,* as is Du Pont, then successful efforts to achieve superiority and advantage over competitors may be regarded, apparently as by the Federal Trade Commission in this case, as attempts to "monopolize." Developing a *major* cost advantage over rivals is far from "innocuous!" Who knows but what it may result in "monopolization!"

According to such a point of view, higher-cost producers should be protected from expansion by the low-cost producer. But on this specific point, Judge Brown held that: "Any theory that higher cost producers must be protected against the effects of expansion by their lower cost competitors is not sound economic theory." (Docket No. 9108; *Initial Decision;* September 4, 1979; p. 46.)

What will come of this confused and confusing jurisprudence remains to be seen.

One promising indication of the advent of more rational and pragmatic approaches to descriptions, measurement, and explanation of industry structures and, especially, of dynamic developmental processes is found in the emergence of a new breed of economists apparently more interested in exploration than in the documentation of foregone conclusions and efforts to shore up traditional orthodox, hypothetical doctrine. These would include, for example, Donald J. Dewey; Yale Brozen; John S. McGee; Harold Demsetz; Jesse W. Markham; J. Fred Weston, among others. See their papers prepared for the Columbia Law School Conference on Industrial Concentration, reported in the proceedings of that conference, *Industrial Concentration: The New Learning,* Harvey J. Goldschmid, H. Michael Mann, and J. Fred Weston, eds. (Boston: Little, Brown and Company, 1974).

11. Professor Robert H. Bork has explored this puzzling anomaly in *The Anti-trust Paradox; A Policy at War with Itself* (New York: Basic Books, Inc., 1978), Chap. 2, et passim.

12. See John D. Glover, *The Attack on Big Business,* pp. 328-32.

13. There are those this very day, who, in various ways, would replace *State* by *Federal* chartering of corporations. Their purpose: to give the Federal government even greater control than it now has over these important institutions. In effect, these advocates would repeal the free incorporation statutes won, State by State, so slowly and with such difficulty in the first half of the 19th century. These new statutes recognized that individuals, groups and corporations have a constitutional right to associate themselves, and to form corporate entities, for constructive, innocent, and lawful purposes. Although, in legal theory, corporations are still "creatures" of the several States—despite massive Federal regulation—charters may not unreasonably be withheld by the State.

Prior to the passage of these free-incorporation statutes, each of the State legislatures, as successors to the sovereign Crown of England, granted or denied individual corporate charters, one by one. This power to grant or deny, to this or that approved or unfavored group, authority to form a corporation gave the legislatures a potential hammer-lock on the economic life of the community. The legislatures were quite willing to use this leverage. Granting and withholding of corporate charters were matters of partisanship, favoritism, extortion and bribery, conflicting private interests and doctrines.

Placing the life and death of our corporations at the mercy and pleasure of Congress, or, worse, of a Federal bureaucracy, is not an appealing prospect for those who are concerned with the everlasting need for clear and sustained separation and counterpoising of powers in our political, economic, and social system.

14. As the author was re-reading a draft of this chapter, on August 4, 1979, he recalled that during the preceding few days (*a*) Wheeling-Pittsburgh Steel Corp. expected to obtain $150 million of loan guarantees from the Economic Development Administration of the Farmers Home Administration to build a rail mill and install pollution control equipment on existing facilities; that opposition was reported from CF&I Steel Corp., a subsidiary of Crane Corp., and from United States Steel Corp., and Bethlehem

Steel Corp., on grounds that the loan guarantee would create additional rail-making capacity where sufficient capacity already exists (*The Wall Street Journal,* August 2, 1979, p. 17); (*b*) that Chrysler Corporation reported a loss of $207.1 million for the second quarter and announced that it wanted the federal government to give it $1 billion of cash advances against proposed special tax credits (*The Wall Street Journal,* August 1, 1979, p. 3); (*c*) that Thomas A. Murphy, chairman of General Motors Corporation, said he was firmly opposed to the government's providing special financial aid to its ailing competitor; he was quoted as saying that Chrysler's request for up to $1 billion in federal aid presents a basic challenge to the philosophy of America, the free enterprise system (*The New York Times,* August 3, 1979, p. 1).

The loan to Wheeling-Pittsburgh was made.

The "bailout" of Chrysler was effected. Or is it going down the drain, anyway?

The consequences—political as well as economic—will emerge over time.

Now in January of 1980, there is talk, perhaps idle, about public "assistance" for Ford.

15. Michael L. Farrell, *The Dow Jones Investor's Handbook, 1978* (Princeton: Dow Jones Books, 1978), pp. 16-17; et passim.

16. *Economic Report of the President . . . 1979,* Tables B-1, B-3, and B-81.

17. See John D. Glover and Richard F. Vancil, *Management of Transformation* (New York: International Business Machines Corporation, 1968).

18. See John D. Glover and Gerald A. Simon, eds., *Chief Executives Handbook* (Homewood, Ill.: Dow Jones-Irwin, Inc., 1976), Part III, "Corporate Strategy"; et passim.

19. See, Glover and Simon, *Handbook,* the article "The Many Roles of the Chief Executive," pp. 14-16.

APPENDIX A
Notes to Exhibit 1

1. Company size is measured by value of assets. See Chapter 1, Note 3.

2. Sources of data for 1929 are: Adolf A. Berle, Jr., and Gardiner C. Means, *The Modern Corporation and Private Property;* and Gardiner C. Means; *The Structure of the American Economy, Part I* (Natural Resources Committee; Washington, D.C., June 1939).

3. Data reported in each instance, as relating to 1971, were for the calendar year ending December 31, 1971, or for the fiscal year which included that date. Sources consulted for 1971 data were several: the *Fortune* list of "500 Largest Industrial" corporations for 1971; *Value Line* reports for that year; the *Compustat* data bank; and *30,000 Leading U.S. Corporations* (New York: Year, Inc., 1973). In most cases, annual reports, "10-K" reports to the Securities Exchange Commission, proxy statements, prospectuses, and the like, were also consulted. It was from these latter sources that efforts were made to determine exact corporate names. This detail was harder to accomplish than might be supposed. In some instances, even in the "10-K" reports to the Securities Exchange Commission, which call for *exact* corporate names, companies referred to themselves by a number of different names. Companies are listed by their 1971 names; in a number of instances, where applicable, their 1929 names are given in company footnotes.

4. The category "nonfinancial corporations" means just that. It does not correspond to the *Fortune* concept of "industrial corporations," which, in turn, is not quite synonymous with "manufacturing." The category "nonfinancial" as used here means simply *everything* other than "financial." "Nonfinancial" includes, for instance, manufacturing of all kinds; services; trade and distribution; transportation; broadcasting. The corporations covered by Berle and Means would be called "nonfinancial" as that term is used here.

5. The corporations listed here are "public" corporations, in that their common stock, and often other securities, are traded on major or regional exchanges or on over-the-counter markets. They do not, consequently, include "private" corporations, some of which are of a size to be included here.

6. The minimum assets value for inclusion on the list of larger nonfinancial corporations of 1971 was $250.0 million. This was the lower limit of the largest size category used by the Internal Revenue Service in its tabulation *Corporation Income Tax Returns, Source Book, Statistics of Income, 1971* for classifying reporting corporations by size. This figure corresponds reasonably closely to the asset size of the smallest company on the 1929 list—$81.5 million, as expressed in something like 1929 dollars. (See Note 7, below.)

7. For various purposes of analysis and comparison, an effort has been made to convert reported 1929 asset values into something like "1971 dollars" in order to allow for inflation. This was done by multiplying 1929 values by 3.0675. This factor converted the assets, for instance, of the smallest company on the Berle-Means list—the then United States Smelting, Refining & Mining Company—from $81.5 million, as reported for 1929, to almost exactly $250.0 million. This latter figure, by way of example, is taken as the approximate 1971 equivalent of 1929 assets reported as $81.5 million. See Chapter 1, Note 4.

8. The corporations listed here are, in principle, American corporations. Excluded from the list, even though their presence in American industries and markets is important, are such prominent non-American corporations as International Nickel, Alcan Aluminum, Ltd., and Lever Brothers. Berle and Means excluded from their list American corporations, a majority of whose assets were located outside the United States.

9. The "Industry Categories" as conceived and defined here represent an effort to accomplish two objectives: first, to establish a system for classifying corporations according to "industries" as major industries are principally structured in the "real world"; second, to establish a classificatory system for categorizing and assembling corporate data, by industries, that could be related as closely as possible to major data banks relating to the American economy, especially those compiled by federal government agencies, such as the Internal Revenue Service, the Bureau of Economic Analysis, and the Bureau of Labor Statistics. These statistical sources are now pretty much—but not yet entirely—based on the "Standard Industrial Classification" of the Office of Budget and Management, as established in 1963 and modified in 1967 and 1972.

In fact, the "SIC" categories relate to *"establishments"*—that is, to *individual* places of employment: plants, offices, and other places of employment—*not to "corporations."* But, an integrated petroleum company, for instance, may have a number of "establishments—places of employment—that, for certain government data gathering purposes, are categorized in all of the following SIC "industries":

Oil and gas exploration services.
Oil and gas field services.
Crude petroleum and natural gas extraction.
Pipe lines, except natural gas.
Natural gas transmission.
Transportation on rivers and canals.
Coastwise transportation.
Deep sea transportation (both domestic and foreign).
Petroleum refining.
Wholesale trade in petroleum and petroleum products.
Gasoline service stations.

Some companies, of course, are more integrated than others, reaching over more or less of the entire process from discovering oil and gas reserves all the way to retailing. Moreover, companies not presently active in certain parts of that system for finding, producing, and distributing petroleum products, often—if not always—have the option of developing such activities, and in the past, many petroleum companies have followed a strategy of becoming more integrated, either by moving upstream from distribution to refining, or from refining to production, or downstream from production to refining, from refining to distribution. See John G. McLean and Robert W. Haigh, *The Growth of Integrated Oil Companies* (Boston: Harvard Graduate School of Business Administration, 1954).

Similar situations are found in other industries in which integrated companies figure importantly, such as Lumber, wood products and paper; Iron and steel; Nonferrous metals; and, Motor vehicles and equipment.

Accordingly, the Industry Categories used here are defined in terms of specific SIC "industries" that have been rearranged and assembled, sometimes a little arbitrarily, into clusters that correspond as closely as possible to industrial structures as they exist. Details as to the composition of these Industry Categories are given in Appendix B, "Industry Categories."

10. Individual corporations are categorized by industry, in principle, according to that Industry Category in which they had the largest fraction of their *sales*. This is the same procedure as is used by the Internal Revenue Service and the Securities Exchange

Commission in compiling industry data based on returns and reports of corporations. In the main, this poses no great problems: there can be little question, for instance, that General Motors Corporation is properly categorized under Motor Vehicles and Equipment, and Whirlpool Corporation under Household Appliances. But, when it comes to "conglomerates" such as International Telephone and Telegraph Corporation, Greyhound Corporation, and Ling-Temco-Vought, Incorporated, for instance, any categorization may be highly arbitrary, their activities being as varied as they are. To compound matters, public reports of a number of such companies, including, even, their annual "10-K" reports to the Securities Exchange Commission, do not disclose their activities in any meaningful or useful fashion. They may break down their total sales figure into such broad or even meaningless categories as "industrial and consumer products," "leisure goods and services," "electronics," and so on.

In a handful of instances, for such reasons, categorization has been not only a bit arbitrary, but, even, speculative. If, in some instances, the reader is surprised by the categorizations here of certain firms, it is quite possible that their "10-K" disclosures, such as they are, describe companies that differ substantially from the "images" these companies have been at some pains to concoct and project. For example, one conglomerate, which seemed to have tried to emit a "high-technology" image was not classified as "nonfinancial" because of the fact that the largest individual fraction of its revenues came from operations of financial subsidiaries, including personal loan operations; its other operations were quite diverse, but not necessarily of a "high-technology" nature.

II. COMPANY NOTES*

1. Youngstown Sheet & Tube Co., a company on the 1929 list of The 200 Largest Nonfinancial Corporations, merged in 1969 with Lykes Corp., to form Lykes-Youngstown Corp.

2. Jones & Laughlin Steel was merged into Ling-Temco-Vought, which is classified, here, under Meat and meat products because sales of such products accounted for the largest particular fraction of that company's sales in 1971. See Note 29, below.

3. Wheeling-Pittsburgh Steel represents a merger, in 1968, of Wheeling Steel, which was on the list of 1929, with Pittsburgh Steel. The merged company was among the Next 359 Largest Companies in 1971.

4. Crucible Steel, on the list of 200 in 1929, was merged into Colt Industries in 1968. Colt was among The Next 359 in 1971. The largest individual fraction of Colt's sales in 1971 were such as to classify the company in this industry.

5. Armco Steel was adopted in 1948 as the name of what had been American Rolling Mill Company in 1929.

6. Cliffs Corporation, which was included in the list of 200 Largest Nonfinancial Corporations in 1929, merged into Cleveland-Cliffs Iron Company, 1947. In 1971, the latter company was not large enough to be included among the 559 largest.

7. Name changed, 1971, from National Lead Co. NL Industries was among The Next 359 in 1971.

8. American Metal Company, Limited, changed its name to American Metal Climax, Incorporated, in 1957, following merger with Climax Molybdenum Company. (The company is now known by the name Amax, Inc.)

9. Name changed to UV Industries, Incorporated, in calendar year 1972. Included in Electrical machinery, equipment in 1971.

10. A controlling interest in Glen Alden Coal was acquired by Rapid American in 1969, and the company was merged into the latter in 1972. (See Note 93.)

11. Pittsburgh Coal merged into Consolidation Coal in 1945; Consolidation Coal merged into Continental Oil Company in 1966.

*The sources used for most of these footnotes were Moody's *Manuals* for 1930, 1968, and 1972; company annual reports and other sources were also consulted.

12. A successor company, Philadelphia & Reading Corp., merged into Northwest Industries, 1968, the successor to Chicago & North Western Railway Co. In 1929, the Chicago & Northwestern was included among The 200 Largest Corporations. In 1971, Northwest Industries was included among The Next 359 Largest.

13. Standard Oil Company of New York changed its name to Socony-Vacuum Company, Incorporated, in 1934; to Socony Mobil Oil Company, Incorporated, in 1955; and to Mobil Oil Corporation, 1966.

14. When The Texas Corporation acquired the assets and assumed the liabilities of the Texas Company (Delaware) and the Texas Company (California) in November 1941, The Texas Corporation changed its name to the Texas Company. In May, 1959 the company adopted the name of Texaco Incorporated.

15. Shell Union Oil Corporation adopted the name of Shell Oil Company in 1949.

16. Name was changed from Sinclair Consolidated Oil Corporation to Consolidated Oil Corporation in 1932, and to Sinclair Oil Corporation in May, 1943. This latter was acquired by Atlantic Richfield in 1969.

17. Consolidated Oil Corporation (formerly Sinclair Oil Corporation, see Note 16, above) purchased The Prairie Pipe Line Company and the Prairie Oil and Gas Company in 1932.

18. Union Oil Associates, Incorporated, was merged into Union Oil Company of California in 1932. Union Oil Associates, Incorporated, was purely a holding company for 57 percent of the capital stock of the Union Oil Company of California in 1929. The Pure Oil Company was merged into Union Oil Company of California in 1965.

19. Vacuum Oil Company was acquired by Standard Oil Company of New York [Mobil Oil Corporation] in 1931.

20. The Richfield Oil Corporation was merged with the Atlantic Refining Company in January, 1966. The name of the Atlantic Oil Corporation subsequently (May 3, 1966) changed to Atlantic Richfield Company. Atlantic Refining and Richfield were both on the list of "200" in 1929.

21. Stock interests in Tidewater Associated Oil Company were acquired by Getty Oil Company in 1933, and Tidewater was merged into Getty Oil Company in September, 1967.

22. Name changed from Ohio Oil Company in 1962.

23. Cities Service Company was included among public utilities in 1929 because utilities accounted for the greatest proportion of the company's then business. Subsequently, the company divested itself of its utility properties; accordingly, it is shown among petroleum companies in 1971.

24. United Fruit Company, included among the 200 largest firms in 1929, was merged into AMK Corporation in 1970 to form United Brands Company. AMK had acquired the meat-packing company John Morrell & Co., in 1969. United Brands, in 1971, was categorized in the Meat industry on the grounds that the sales of its meat-packing subsidiary, John Morrell & Co., contributed sales of $847 million out of a total $1,449 million. The sales of bananas and related products of its United Fruit subsidiary accounted for sales of $397.6 million.

25. American Sugar Refining Company changed its name to Amstar Corporation in 1971.

26. Name changed in 1971 from National Biscuit Company.

27. Name changed from Corn Products Refining Company to Corn Products Company in May 1959 after merger with Best Foods, Incorporated; subsequently, the company assumed its present name.

28. The meat packer of 1929, Armour and Company, merged with Baldwin-Lima-Hamilton in 1965. Baldwin, considerably earlier, had been a producer of steam locomotives; Lima had been a producer of steam shovels and other heavy equipment; "B-L-H" had made certain acquisitions, including in fields of electronics. Greyhound acquired 100 percent of the stock of the surviving Baldwin-Lima-Hamilton Corporation in 1970.

29. Wilson and Company, Incorporated was merged into Ling-Temco-Vought, Incorporated, in June, 1967. Meat and meat products accounted for the largest proportion of

Ling-Temco-Vought's sales in 1971, larger, even than the sales of Jones & Laughlin Steel. See, also, Note 2, above.

The 1929 assets of Jones & Laughlin Steel and of Wilson and Company, which in 1971 were important components of Ling-Temco-Vought, were as follows:

	1929 assets as reported ($ millions)	*1929 assets in 1971 dollars ($ millions)*
Jones & Laughlin	$222.0	$681.0
Wilson & Company	98.0	300.6
Total	$320.0	$981.6

30. National Dairy Products Corp. changed its name to Kraftco Company in 1969.

31. Name changed from American Tobacco Company in 1969.

32. Name changed from R. J. Reynolds Tobacco Company in 1970.

33. Name changed from Liggett & Myers Tobacco Co., in 1968; Liggett & Myers, among The 200 Largest in 1929, was among The Next 359 in 1971.

34. Lorillard Co. was acquired by Loew's Theaters in 1968. A predecessor corporation of the latter, Loew's Incorporated, was included in the motion picture industry in 1929. In 1971, the largest fraction of the sales of the surviving company, Loews Corporation, came from tobacco products.

35. American Woolen Company was merged, in 1955, into Textron, Inc., then a textile company. In 1971, Textron, by then a conglomerate, was classed under Aircraft because sales of its aircraft subsidiaries accounted for the largest individual fraction of its total sales. (The term "conglomerate" is here used to denote a company of heterogeneous component subsidiaries put together through mergers and acquisitions.)

36. The name of International Paper & Power Co., was changed to International Paper Co., in 1941.

37. Long-Bell Lumber Corp. was merged into International Paper in 1956.

38. Minnesota & Ontario Paper Co. was acquired by Boise Cascade Corp., in 1965.

39. Company was known as Allied Chemical and Dye Corporation until 1958, when the present name was adopted.

40. Koppers is listed among The 200 Largest in 1929 and among The Next 359 in 1971.

41. United States Rubber Company changed its name to Uniroyal, Incorporated, in 1967.

42. The name of International Shoe Company, among the 200 largest of 1929, was changed to Interco Inc., in 1966; the latter was among The Next 359 in 1971.

43. In 1929, Pittsburgh Plate Glass Co., by name.

44. Name changed, in 1967, from American Radiator and Standard Sanitary Corporation to American Standard, Incorporated.

45. Crane was listed among The 200 Largest in 1929 and among The Next 359 in 1971.

46. Walter Kidde & Co., in 1969, acquired United States Lines, which was a successor company to International Mercantile Marine, one of The 200 Largest Corporations of 1929, which was classified under Water transportation.

47. The Singer Manufacturing Company changed its name to The Singer Company in May, 1963. For 1929 it was listed in Machinery; for 1971, it was listed under Home Appliances.

48. Formerly United Shoe Machinery Co. In 1929, company was listed among The 200 Largest; in 1971, it was listed among The Next 359 Largest. Name was changed to USM Corporation in 1968.

49. The Studebaker Corporation, an automobile manufacturer in 1929, was merged with Packard Motor Car, another automobile company, in 1954, to form Studebaker-Packard Corp. This latter was merged with Worthington Corporation, in 1967, to form the successor company, Studebaker-Worthington. For 1971, this successor company was listed under Machinery.

50. International Harvester Company was listed in 1929 in the Farm, construction and mining machinery category because that was its principal business in that year. The company was included in the Motor vehicle category for 1971 because motor trucks and service parts accounted for the largest fraction (about 44 percent) of company sales in that year.

51. Westinghouse Electric and Manufacturing Company changed its name to Westinghouse Electric Corporation in 1945.

52. International Telephone and Telegraph Corporation was listed under Telephone, telegraph, and other communications services in 1929, and under Radio, TV, and communication equipment in 1971.

    It is extremely difficult, on the basis of information disclosed to the public, to determine the facts necessary to classify a number of conglomerates. (The term "conglomerate" is here used to denote a company of heterogeneous component subsidiaries put together through mergers and acquisitions.) This is true of International Telephone and Telegraph.

    In 1929, ITT was engaged primarily in communications; but after World War II, the company sold its investments in two large telephone operating subsidiaries.

    The classification of ITT under Radio, TV, and communication equipment industry in 1971 is somewhat conjectural, and more than a bit arbitrary. The company did not consolidate its wholly-owned Hartford Fire Insurance Company and the consolidated subsidiaries of that holding. Nor did the company consolidate other "ITT Finance Subsidiaries." Premiums earned of the Hartford company and its subsidiaries came to $1,335 million; income of other finance subsidiaries came to $130 million. If these companies had been consolidated into ITT, it is possible—even likely—that ITT would have been properly classified as a "financial" corporation and, accordingly, not listed here among "nonfinancial corporations."

    The biggest single category of the company's reported sales was described as $2,037 million of "Industrial and Consumer Products"—scarcely revelatory information. Among such products, the company reported, were such products as mufflers and hub caps, pipe fittings, and cassette recorders.

    Other than that, the company reported $1,588 million of sales—22 percent of the reported total, excluding revenues from insurance and financial operations—of "Telecommunication Equipment," without further breakdown. This datum was the somewhat arbitrary and perhaps inexact basis for the classification of the company.

    Beyond these matters, it is possible—one cannot infer surely—that more than 50 percent of the company's sales and/or assets may have been located outside of the United States; in that case, the company would not have been listed here at all.

53. Western Electric Company, Incorporated is a wholly-owned, but, in public reports, *unconsolidated* subsidiary of American Telephone and Telegraph Company. It is listed separately here primarily because it was an important element of the communications equipment industry in 1971. Western Electric's assets are not included in those given in this exhibit for AT&T, but it is not counted as a separate company in determining the roster of The 200 Largest Nonfinancial Corporations in 1971.

54. Sylvania Electric Products, Incorporated; GTE Automatic Electric Company; and other manufacturing subsidiaries of General Telephone and Electronics Corporation were wholly-owned *consolidated* subsidiaries of GT&E. The *estimated* assets of these manufacturing subsidiaries, $1,100.0 million, are shown separately under this industry, Radio, TV, and communication equipment, in the interest of comparability between American Telephone and Telegraph Company and General Telephone and Electronics Corporation, and because these manufacturing subsidiaries were significant elements in the communications equipment industry. The assets of GTE Automatic Electric, Sylvania and other manufacturing companies in 1971 were estimated from various prospectuses and other sources. These assets have been deducted from the reported assets of General Telephone, $8,619.9 million, to avoid double counting. The manufacturing subsidiaries of General Telephone are not counted separately in determining the rosters of The 200 Largest, and The Next 359 Largest Nonfinancial Corporations of 1971.

55. Name changed from American Car & Foundry Co. The company was among The 200 Largest Nonfinancial Corporations in 1929 and among The Next 359 Largest in 1971.

56. In 1964, American Locomotive Company merged into Citadel Industries, which was later in the same year acquired by Worthington Corporation. Worthington subsequently was merged with Studebaker. See Note 49.

57. Pullman, Incorporated, was formerly named Pullman Railroad Compnay. In 1929, the company was listed under Railroad transportation and was included among The 200 Largest Corporations.

58. In the years of the Great Depression, and since, even up to the time of this writing, in 1978, railroad corporations have undergone tremendous reorganization. In the notes that follow, certain major mergers and acquisitions are traced. Some railroad companies, such as the "New Haven," disappeared into the upbuilding of larger systems; others are still extant, but not large enough to be listed among The 559 Largest Nonfinancial Corporations, for example, the St. Louis-San Francisco Railway Company. The contraction of the railroads, both relatively and absolutely, in concrete terms and in dollar terms, is one of the most notable features of the changing industrial structure of the United States over the past four decades.

It was not practical—and not to the central points of this work, in any event—to try to trace the intricacies of the many bankruptcies, regulatory proceedings before the Interstate Commerce Commission, and other tribulations whereby the railroads of America have devolved to their present state.

59. Penn Central Company represented a merger, in 1968, of the Pennsylvania Railroad Company with the New York Central Railroad Company, and included the New York, New Haven, and Hartford Railroad.

60. In 1929, according to Berle and Means, Alleghany Corporation, a holding company complex, controlled the following railroads through large, but not necessarily majority stock ownership:

Companies	Assets 1929 ($ millions)
Chesapeake & Ohio Railway Company	$549.9
Missouri Pacific Railroad Company	630.6
Pere Marquette Railway Company	177.2

Berle and Means included the above assets in the Alleghany Corporation estimated total of $1,600 million.

According to Berle and Means, Alleghany also controlled the following railroads through minority, sometimes small, stock interest:

Erie Railroad Company	$560.9
Kansas City Southern Railway Co.	146.1
New York, Chicago & St. Louis Railroad Co.	350.0 (est., Berle and Means)
Wheeling and Lake Erie Railway Co.	104.1

61. Santa Fe Industries owns about 96 percent of Atchison, Topeka, and Sante Fe Railway Co.

62. Union Pacific Corporation is an "upstream" holding company, organized in 1971, which owns the Union Pacific Railroad.

63. Atlantic Coast Line Railroad Company and Seaboard Air Line Railway Company were merged. The resultant company was named the Seaboard Coast Line Railroad Company; subsequently the company was named Seaboard Coastline Industries, Inc.

64. The Burlington Northern represented a merger, in 1970, of the Northern Pacific; the Great Northern; the Chicago, Burlington & Quincy; and the Spokane, Portland, and Seattle.

65. The "Chicago and St. Paul" was among The 200 Largest Nonfinancial Corporations in 1929 and among The Next 359 in 1971.

66. Name changed from Illinois Central Railroad.

67. Consolidated financial statements of Southern Railway Company included accounts of the company and subsidiary companies in which the company directly or indirectly held 80 percent or more of the voting stock.

68. The Reading, one of the anthracite carriers, was among The 200 Largest Nonfinancial Corporations in 1929 and among The Next 359 in 1971.

69. Assets of Norfolk and Western were those reported in the "System Consolidated Balance Sheet," which consolidated the assets of company and its subsidiary operating and lessee-controlled railroad companies, including the following:

New York, Chicago and St. Louis Railroad Company (merged into Norfolk and Western Railway Company in 1964).

The Delaware and Hudson Company, a wholly-owned subsidiary of Dereco, Incorporated, whose assets were included in the Norfolk and Western System.

Wabash Railway Company, leased in October 1964, for eight years by Norfolk and Western Railway Company.

The Erie Railroad, which was merged into Erie Lackawanna Railway Co., which was acquired in 1968 by Dereco, a subsidiary of Norfolk & Western Railway Co.

The Delaware, Lackawanna and Western Railroad Company, which was merged with the Erie Railroad Company in October, 1960. The new company which resulted from the merger was named the Erie Lackawanna Railway Company. This was acquired, in 1968, by Dereco, a subsidiary of Norfolk and Western.

70. The Chesapeake and Ohio Railway Company controlled the Baltimore and Ohio Railroad Company through a 92 percent stock interest. The C & O/B & O also had 72.3 percent voting control of Western Maryland Railway Company's assets, carried here at book value less the stated book value of the C & O/B & O investment therein.

71. Chicago, Rock Island & Pacific Railway Co. was among The 200 Largest Nonfinancial Corporations in 1929 and among The Next 359 Largest in 1971. For many years, pursuit of ownership of the "Rock Island" by other railroads was the object of continual litigation before the Interstate Commerce Commission and elsewhere.

72. The St. Louis—San Francisco Railway Company was among The 200 Largest in 1929 and among The Next 359 Largest in 1971.

73. Missouri-Kansas-Texas Railroad Company was controlled by Katy Industries, Incorporated. Katy Industries, Incorporated, was organized to acquire stock of the railroad company.

74. Acquired, 1968, by an "upstream" holding company, Boston & Maine Industries, Inc.

75. Among The 200 Largest Nonfinancial Corporations in 1929, the company was acquired by Alton Railroad, 1931; this latter was acquired, in 1947, by Gulf, Mobile & Ohio Railroad Company; this company was among The Next 359 Largest in 1971.

76. The Western Pacific Railroad Company, in 1970, became a subsidiary of an upstream holding company, Western Pacific Industries, Inc.

77. Chicago Great Western Railroad Co. was merged with Chicago Northwestern in 1964.

78. An upstream holding company formed to hold the Kansas City Southern Railway.

79. Lehigh Valley Railroad Co. merged into Pennsylvania Railroad, 1963.

80. A successor company to Denver & Rio Grande Western Railroad Co. The company was among The 200 Largest Nonfinancial Corporations in 1929 and among The 359 Next Largest in 1971.

81. The Virginian Railway Co., was merged into the Norfolk & Western in 1959.

82. The properties of Interborough Rapid Transit Company were acquired by the City of New York in 1940.

83. Brooklyn-Manhattan Transit Corporation acquired by City of New York in 1940.

84. The name of Hudson & Manhattan Railroad Company, a surviving corporate shell, the transit properties having been acquired by the City of New York, was changed to Hudson & Manhattan Corp., in 1962.

85. Assets of Third Avenue Railway Company were sold to New York City; the property was later dismantled.

86. Boston Elevated Railway Company was purchased by the Massachusetts Transit Authority in 1947.

87. Chicago Railways Company was acquired by Chicago Transit Authority, 1947.

88. Assets of The United Railways and Electric Company of Baltimore were sold to Baltimore Metropolitan Transit Authority. The corporate remains were liquidated, 1968.

89. Transit properties of Philadelphia Rapid Transit Company were acquired by Philadelphia Transportation Co., 1940; the corporation was liquidated, 1968.

90. The listings of companies in the electric, gas, and sanitary services category are given quite separately for the years 1929 and 1967. No effort is made to relate 1971 utilities to their corporate antecedents of 1929.

   The order shown for 1929 is that of Berle and Means. Their ordering, reproduced here, was based upon intercorporate holdings of securities and other arrangements indicative or suggestive of corporate control. The ordering for 1971 was based on descending values of reported assets of that year.

   In consequence of the Public Utility Holding Company Act of 1935, the electric and gas utilities industry was utterly reorganized. Noncontiguous, noninterconnected subsidiaries of holding companies were, alternatively, reorganized into contiguous, interconnected systems, "spun off," or otherwise disposed of. It is scarcely possible to trace the unscrambling that took place, nor, for our purposes, is there any point to trying to do so. Only a few of the major individual companies—say four or five—came through the process of reorganization relatively unscathed. But, overall and for practical purposes, there was little significant continuity among the major corporations of this industry. Even when *names* of surviving corporations are similar to those of corporations in existence in 1929, the physical *properties* owned by them in 1971 were often greatly different from those held by "ancestor" corporations. Accordingly, no effort was made to show relationships among the corporations in existence in 1929 and those of 1971.

91. In the 1929 list of Berle and Means, a holding company, Electric Bond & Share Company, was shown as controlling, in various fashions, American Gas and Light Company and the three following listed companies and, in addition, American and Foreign Power Co., a subsidiary not shown separately. Gardiner Means later dropped Electric Bond & Share on the grounds that a major fraction of its assets, held by American and Foreign Power, were located outside of the United States.

92. Company became a component of General Telephone and, later, of General Telephone & Electronics Corporation.

93. United Cigar Stores Company of America entered into reorganization proceedings in July, 1937, and the company was merged into United Cigar-Whelan Stores Corporation. The company name was changed to United Whelan Corporation in July, 1957. A majority ownership in a successor company, McCrory Corp., was acquired by Rapid American Corporation in 1972.

94. Marcor, Inc., represents a merger, in 1968, of Montgomery Ward & Co., which was on the 1929 list of 200 Largest Nonfinancial Corporations and Container Corporation of America, which was not. Marcor was later acquired by Mobil Oil.

95. Marshall Field & Co. was among The 200 Largest in 1929 and among The Next 359 in 1971.

96. R. H. Macy & Co., was among The 200 Largest in 1929 and among The Next 359 in 1971.

97. In 1966, Paramount Pictures Corporation, which was a successor corporation to Paramount Publix—after many ordeals and adventures—was merged into Gulf and Western Industries, Inc. Gulf and Western Industries, a conglomerate, was classified, for 1971, as a financial corporation, inasmuch as financial operations accounted for the largest individual fraction of its business.

98. Kinney Services, Inc., includes Warner Brothers Pictures, Inc., which was on the list of 200 Largest Nonfinancial Corporations of 1929.

APPENDIX B

Industry Categories and their composition

The concept of Industry Category or Industry System is discussed in Chapter 6. The concept is derived, of course, from that of "community," which is of central significance in the science of ecology.* A "community" is any identifiable collectivity of living things that are closely interrelated, possibly in many different ways, and whose "welfare," numbers, and behaviors are to an important degree mutually determining. The community is a *system*. Any change that affects any part of that system will activate other, subsequent effects that will fan out and spread through the system along the network of relationships that links each entity with others and, through them, with all.

The overall structure of American industry is, so to speak, a *super*-"community," or super-"system," made up of many component "communities" and "subcommunities" of incorporated and unincorporated business units. Individually, each of these communities is an evolving organic entity; collectively, they constitute an organic, evolving whole. Aside from the individual fortunes of particular businesses, these several "tiers" of communities, through and because of many complex networks of all kinds of relationships (such as input-output relationships), "oscillate" cyclically and grow or decline and evolve secularly in collective, systemic fashion.

---

*See, e.g., Macfadyen, *Animal Ecology,* 2d ed. (London: Sir Isaac Pitman & Sons, Ltd., 1963), especially Chap. 12; or Edward J. Kormondy, *Concepts of Ecology* (Englewood Cliffs, N.J.: Prentice Hall, 1969), especially Chap. 1; or Eugene P. Odum, *Ecology* (New York: Holt, Rinehart and Winston, 1963), especially Chaps. 1 and 2. Also John D. Glover, *Environment: "Community," "Culture," "Habitat" and "Product";* a chapter in a work in progress, *Strategic Guidance of Corporations—A System of Concepts and Analysis;* prepared for use as a teaching note at the Harvard Business School: Boston, Mass. (file 4-367-018).

Communities of businesses can be perceived, defined, and measured (and studied), in many dimensions: geographically (the entities in a particular region); "vertically" (input-output relationships); "horizontally" (interesting groups of "like" entities, say airlines and electric and gas utilities); or in terms of complex Industry Categories: composed of entities that interact among themselves either or both "vertically" *and* "horizontally." Examples would be Petroleum, Chemicals and allied products, and Lumber . . . wood products . . . paper and allied products, as defined here.

None of these "communities," none of the Industry Categories described and used here are *closed systems;* they are all *open.* None of them is really *bounded.* In this, they are like communities in ecological systems. At least around the "edges," there are always interactions and mutual interpenetrations between "adjacent" communities and with other Industry Categories. "Boundaries" for various purposes and convenience, can be drawn around "communities" and Industry Categories and Systems in the mind, but never *in fact.* Any defined boundaries will necessarily be somewhat arbitrary as to where lines are drawn. Recourse must ultimately be had to empirical data, influenced no doubt, by appeal to "reason."

Businesses, individually and collectively, in varying ways and to varying degrees, interact with many different kinds of businesses that are component parts of other "communities," "industries," or Industry Categories.

Because of this inherent openness, each and every business is linked more or less directly, more or less importantly, with each and every other one, close at hand or at a distance. No business is an "island."

The whole of American industry, the American economy, is an *open* system linked to other economies by imports and exports; flows of capital and persons; by multinational enterprises, ventures, and transactions.

Such, indeed, are the realities of the "anatomy" and "physiology" of American industry, in total, and of its component industrial "communities." The Industry Categories described here represent an effort to perceive, describe, and explain American industry in such terms and to place our very large corporations in contexts where they have their existence and where they function. The construction and structures of these Industry Categories reflect a conviction that organic entities cannot only, indeed, cannot be best studied *in vitro* or *in museo.*

The compositions of the Industry Categories are as set forth in Exhibit 80 in terms of the Standard Enterprise Classification (1963) and Standard Industry Codes (1972).

EXHIBIT 80

Composition of Industry Categories by Standard Enterprise Classification (1963) and Standard Industry Codes (1972)

Industry Categories‡		Composition: a. "Standard Enterprise Classification," "Minor Industry Codes," 1963* b. Standard Industry Classification, 1972 "Major Groups" and "Groups"†
1. Agriculture, forestry and fisheries	a. b.	Farms; Agricultural services, forestry, and fisheries (0110; 0200); Major Groups 01, 02, 07, 08, 09.
2. Iron and steel	a. b.	Iron ores; ferrous metal processing and basic products, and primary metal products not elsewhere classified (1010; 3310); Groups 101, 331, 332.
3. Nonferrous metals	a. b.	Copper, lead and zinc, gold and silver ores; Miscellaneous metal mining; Nonferrous metal processing and basic products (1020; 1098; 3330); Groups 102, 103, 104, 105, 106, 108, 109, 333, 334, 335, 336, 339.
4. Coal	a. b.	Coal mining (1100); Major Groups 11, 12.
5. Petroleum	a. b.	Crude petroleum, natural gas, and natural gas liquids; Oil and gas field services; Petroleum refining; Miscellaneous petroleum and coal products; Pipe line transportation; (1310, 1380, 2910, 2998, 4060); Major Groups 13, 29, 56.
6. Construction	a. b.	Building construction; General contractors, except building construction; Special trade contractors (1510; 1520; 1700); Major Groups 15, 16, 17.
7. Food and kindred products, except: Meat; Dairy; Alcoholic beverages; Bottled and canned soft drinks and flavorings	a. b.	Canned and frozen foods; Grain mill products; Bakery products; Sugar; Other food and kindred products (2030, 2040, 2050, 2060; 2090) Major Group 20, except Groups 201, 202, 208
8. Meat and meat products	a. b.	Meat products (2010); Group 201.
9. Dairy and dairy products	a. b.	Dairy products (2020); Group 202.
10. Alcoholic beverages	a. b.	Malt liquors and malt; Alcoholic beverages, except malt liquors and malt (2082; 2084); Group 208 except Industries 2086 and 2087.
11. Bottled and canned soft drinks and flavorings	a. b.	Bottled soft drinks and flavorings (2086); Industry 2086, 2087.
12. Tobacco manufacturing	a. b.	Tobacco manufactures (2100); Major Group 21
13. Textile mill products	a. b.	Weaving mills and textile finishing; Knitting mills; Other textile mill products (2228; 2250; 2298); Major Group 22.
14. Apparel and other finished fabric products	a. b.	Men's and boys' clothing; Women's, children's, and infants' clothing; Miscellaneous apparel and accessories; Miscellaneous fabricated textile products (2310; 2330; 2380; 2398); Major Group 23.
15. Lumber and wood products and paper and allied products, except: furniture	a. b.	Logging, lumber, and wood basic products; Millwork, plywood, and prefabricated structural products; Other wood products, except furniture; Pulp, paper, and board; Other paper and allied products (2410; 2430; 2498; 2620; 2698); Major Groups 24, 26.
16. Furniture and fixtures	a. b.	Household furniture; Furniture and fixtures, except household furniture (2510; 2590); Major Group 25.
17. Printing and publishing and allied industries	a. b.	Newspapers; Periodicals; Books, greeting cards, and miscellaneous publishing; Other printing and publishing (2711; 2712; 2715; 2798); Major Group 27.

EXHIBIT 80 *(continued)*

Industry Categories‡	*Composition:* *a.* "Standard Enterprise Classification," "Minor Industry Codes," 1963* *b.* Standard Industry Classification, 1972 "Major Groups" and "Groups"†
18. Chemicals and allied products, except: pharmaceuticals; soaps, cleaners, and toiletries	*a.* Basic chemicals, plastics, and synthetics; Paints and allied products; Chemical products not elsewhere classified; Chemicals and allied products not allocable (2810; 2850; 2898; 2899); *b.* Major Group 28, except Groups 283, 284.
19. Pharmaceuticals and medical equipment and supplies	*a.* Drugs; Optical, medical, and ophthalmic goods (2830; 3830); *b.* Groups 283, 384
20. Soaps, cleaners, and toiletries	*a.* Soap, cleaners, and toilet goods (2840); *b.* Group 284.
21. Rubber and tires	*a.* Rubber products; Miscellaneous plastics products (3010; 3098); *b.* Major Group 30.
22. Leather and leather products	*a.* Footwear, except rubber; Leather, and leather products not elsewhere classified (3140; 3198); *b.* Major Group 31.
23. Nonmetallic mineral mining; stone, clay, concrete, and their products	*a.* Crushed, broken, and dimension stone; sand and gravel; Other nonmetallic minerals, except fuels; Cement, hydraulic; Concrete, gypsum, and plaster products; Other nonmetallic mineral products (1410; 1498; 3240; 3270; 3298); *b.* Major Groups 14 and 32, except Groups 321, 322, 323.
24. Glass and glass products	*a.* Glass products (3210); *b.* Groups 321, 322, 323.
25. Fabricated metal products, except: machinery, transportation equipment, metal cans	*a.* Cutlery, hand tools, and hardware; Plumbing and heating apparatus, except electric; Fabricated structural metal products; Screw machine products, bolts, and similar products; Metal stampings; Other fabricated metal products (3420; 3430; 3440; 3450; 3461; 3498); *b.* Major Group 34, except Group 341.
26. Metal cans	*a.* Metal cans (3410); *b.* Group 341.
27. Machinery, except: electrical; farm, construction, and mining; office, computing, and accounting	*a.* Metalworking machinery; Special industry machinery; General industrial machinery; Service industry machines; Other machinery, except electrical (3540; 3550; 3560; 3580; 3598); *b.* Major Group 35, except Groups 352, 353, 357.
28. Farm, construction, and mining machinery	*a.* Farm machinery; Construction, mining, and materials handling machinery and equipment (3520; 3530); *b.* Groups 352, 353.
29. Office, computing, and accounting machines	*a.* Office and computing machines (3570); *b.* Group 357.
30. Electrical machinery, equipment, and supplies, except: Radio, TV, and communication equipment; electrical components and accessories; household appliances	*a.* Other electrical equipment and supplies (3698); *b.* Major Group 36, except Groups 363, 365, 366, 367
31. Household appliances	*a.* Household appliances (3630); *b.* Group 363.
32. Radio, TV, and communication equipment; electronic components and accessories	*a.* Radio, television, and communication equipment; Electronic components and accessories (3660; 3662); *b.* Groups 365, 366, 367, 483.
33. Scientific, measuring, and control devices; watches and clocks	*a.* Scientific and mechanical measuring instruments; Watches and clocks (3810; 3870); *b.* Groups 381, 382, 387.
34. Photographic equipment and supplies	*a.* Photographic equipment and supplies (3860); *b.* Group 386.
35. Motor vehicles and equipment	*a.* Motor vehicles and equipment (3710); *b.* Group 371

EXHIBIT 80 *(continued)*

	Industry Categories‡		Composition: a. "Standard Enterprise Classification," "Minor Industry Codes," 1963* b. Standard Industry Classification, 1972 "Major Groups" and "Groups"†
36.	Aircraft, guided missiles, and parts	a. b.	Aircraft, guided missiles, and parts (3720); Groups 372, 376.
37.	Ship and boat building and repair	a. b.	Ship and boat building and repair (3730); Group 373.
38.	Railroad equipment and streetcars, and other transportation equipment	a. b.	Transportation equipment not elsewhere classified (3798); Group 374.
39.	Other miscellaneous manufacturing	a. b.	Ordnance, except guided missiles; Miscellaneous manufactured products, except ordnance, and manufacturing not allocable (3930; 3990), etc.; Major Group 39 and Groups 375, 379, 383, 384, 385.
40.	Rail transportation, terminals, and related services	a. b.	Rail transportation; Transportation services not elsewhere classified; Lessors of railroad property, and of real property not elsewhere classified (4011; 4098; 6528); Major Groups 40, 47.
41.	Transit	a. b.	Local and interurban passenger transit (4020); Major Group 41.
42.	Motor transportation	a. b.	Trucking and warehousing (4030); Major Group 42.
43.	Water transportation	a. b.	Water transportation (4040); Major Group 44.
44.	Air transportation	a. b.	Air transportation (4050); Major Group 45.
45.	Electric, gas, and sanitary services	a. b.	Electric companies and systems; Gas companies and systems; Combination companies and systems; Water supply and other sanitary services (4910; 4920; 4930; 4940); Major Group 49.
46.	Telephone, telegraph, and other communication services, except: radio and TV broadcasting	a. b.	Telephone, telegraph, and other communication services (4808); Groups 481, 482, 489.
47.	Radio and TV broadcasting	a. b.	Radio and television broadcasting (4830); Group 483.
48.	Wholesale trade	a. b.	Groceries and related products; Machinery, equipment, and supplies; Motor vehicles and automotive equipment; Drugs, chemicals, and allied products; Dry goods and apparel; Farm products—raw materials; Electrical goods; Hardware, and plumbing and heating equipment; Metals and minerals, except petroleum and scrap; Alcoholic beverages; Paper and its products; Lumber and construction materials; Petroleum and petroleum products; Other wholesale trade (5004; 5008; 5010; 5020; 5030; 5050; 5060; 5070; 5091; 5092; 5095; 5096; 5097; 5108); Major Groups 50, 51.
49.	Retail trade, except: general merchandise; food stores	a. b.	Building materials, hardware, and farm equipment; Automobile and truck dealers; Other automotive dealers; Apparel and accessory stores; Furniture, home furnishings, and equipment stores; Eating and drinking places; Drug stores and proprietary stores; Gasoline service stations; Liquor stores; Other retail stores; Wholesale and retail trade not allocable (5210; 5241; 5243; 5248; 5250; 5260; 5270; 5291; 5292; 5298; 5409); Major Groups 52, 55, 56, 57, 58, 59, less Industry No. 5961.
50.	General merchandise and mail order	a. b.	General merchandise stores (5220); Major Group 53 and Industry 5961.
51.	Food stores	a. b.	Food stores (5230); Major Group 54.
52.	Motion pictures	a. b.	Motion pictures (7800); Major Group 78.

EXHIBIT 80 *(concluded)*

Industry Categories‡	Composition:
	a. "Standard Enterprise Classification," "Minor Industry Codes," 1963*
	b. Standard Industry Classification, 1972 "Major Groups" and "Groups"†
53. Services, except: motion pictures	*a.* Hotels and other lodging places; Personal services; Advertising; Business services, except advertising; Automobile services and miscellaneous repair services; Other amusement and recreation services; Offices of physicians and surgeons; Other medical services; Educational services; Services not elsewhere classified; Nature of business not allocable (7000; 7200; 7310; 7398; 7500; 7900; 8011; 8019; 8020; 8098);
	b. Major Groups 70, 72, 73, 75, 76, 79, 80, 81, 82, 83, 89.
54. Real estate	*a.* Real estate operators (except developers) and lessors of buildings; Lessors of mining, oil, and similar property; Subdividers, developers, and operative builders; Other real estate and combinations of real estate, insurance, loan, and law offices (6510; 6521; 6550; 6598);
	b. Major Groups 65, 66.
55. Nature of business not allocable	*a.* Nature of business not allocable (9000).

* As used by IRS *Source Book,* 1971.

† Approximate equivalents, 2-digit, 3-digit, and 4-digit codes.

‡ Use of the asset data given by the IRS for the several enterprise and industry "codes" in calculating aggregate assets of Industry Categories and Presence-indexes therein of Largest Corporations surely results in certain over- and under-statements.

The presence of American multinational corporations in American industry is *over-*stated to the extent they hold *and* operate assets located in other countries. This upward bias is probably fairly important in the case of, for example, Petroleum; close to zero among the Electric and gas utilities.

On the other hand, to the extent that the presence of foreign corporations is ignored or understated, *total* assets in Industry Categories is understated and the presence of American corporations is correspondingly *over-*stated. This particular distortion may be significant in Chemicals, Pharmaceuticals, and Motor vehicles.

There is no help for it that is worth pursuing. Adjustments, if they could be made, to correct for these nitty but snaggy problems would surely not change the message of the data nor conclusions drawn from them.

Similar problems of overstatement and understatement arise in consequence of attribution of *all* of the assets of large diversified or conglomerate firms to a single Industry Category. Correction was attempted in the case of the manufacturing subsidiaries of American Telephone and Telegraph and General Telephone and Electronics. In other instances, such as estimating and allowing for the presences of General Motors and General Electric in Home Appliances, such correction was either not possible or, for present purposes, not really significant, or both.